20th CENTURY WORLD HISTORY

COURSE COMPANION

Martin Cannon

Richard Jones-Nerzic

David Keys

Alexis Mamaux

Michael Miller

Giles Pope

David Smith

Aidan Williams

OXFORD
UNIVERSITY PRESS

OXFORD
UNIVERSITY PRESS

Great Clarendon Street, Oxford OX2 6DP

Oxford University Press is a department of the University of Oxford.
It furthers the University's objective of excellence in research,
scholarship, and education by publishing worldwide in

Oxford   New York

Auckland Cape Town Dar es Salaam Hong Kong Karachi
Kuala Lumpur Madrid Melbourne Mexico City Nairobi
New Delhi Shanghai Taipei Toronto

With offices in

Argentina Austria Brazil Chile Czech Republic France Greece
Guatemala Hungary Italy Japan Poland Portugal Singapore
South Korea Switzerland Thailand Turkey Ukraine Vietnam

Oxford is a registered trade mark of Oxford University Press
in the UK and in certain other countries

© Oxford University Press 2012

British Library Cataloguing in Publication Data

Data available

ISBN: 978-0-19-838998-9
10 9 8 7 6 5 4 3 2 1

Printed in Great Britain by Bell & Bain Ltd, Glasgow

MIX
Paper from
responsible sources
FSC® C007785
www.fsc.org

Acknowledgments

p18 David Low/Solo Syndication, p20 Bettmann/Corbis UK Ltd., p21 Mansell/Time Life Pictures/Getty Images, p51t David Low/Solo Syndication, p51b David Low/Solo Syndication, p58 Punch Limited/TopFoto, p63 Bettmann/Corbis UK Ltd., p64 Hulton Archive/Getty Images, p65 David Low/Solo Syndication, p74 David Low/British Cartoon Archive/Solo Syndication, p76 Bettmann/Corbis UK Ltd., p80 Bettmann/Corbis UK Ltd., p81 Bob Thomas/Popperfoto/Getty Images, p82 Columbia/Kobal Collection, p85 David Low/Solo Syndication, p91 Leslie Gilbert Illingworth/Solo Syndication, p94 Frank Shershel/GPO/Getty Images, p96 Leslie Gilbert Illingworth/Solo Syndication, p97 TopFoto, p100 John Phillips/Time Life Pictures/Getty Images, p103 Leslie Gilbert Illingworth/Solo Syndication, p105 United Nations Relief and Works Agency, p108 Hrant Nakasian/United Nations Relief and Works Agency, p110 Hulton-Deutsch Collection/Corbis UK Ltd., p111 TopFoto, p112 Leslie Gilbert Illingworth/Solo Syndication, p113 Rolls Press/Popperfoto/Getty Images, p118 Ephraim Mose Lillien/Imagno/Getty Images, p121t Bettmann/Corbis UK Ltd., p121b Michael Cummings/Solo Syndication, p122 Hector Mata/AFP/Getty Images, p123 Bettmann/Corbis UK Ltd., p124 Nicholas Garland/Daily Telegraph, p127 TopFoto, p129 Hulton Archive/Getty Images, p130 Al Anwar, p133 Alain Denize/Kipa/Corbis, UK Ltd. p134 Nicholas Garland/Daily Telegraph, p135 The Print Collector/Alamy, p136 TopFoto, p137 Leslie Gilbert Illingworth/Solo Syndication, p147 Keystone/Getty Images, p149 Revolutionary Committee of the Sichuan Art Academy/International Institute of Social History (IISG), p152 Keystone/Getty Images, p157l International Institute of Social History (IISG), p157r Yaakov Kirschen/Dry Bones, p170 Toshio Sakai/AFP/Getty Images, p174 Bettmann/Corbis UK Ltd., p180 Associated Press/PA Photos, p185 Vitaly Armand/AFP/Getty Images, p188 Sipa Press/Rex Features, p191l Edmund Valtman/Prints & Photographs Division/Library of Congress, p191r David Horsey, p199 Associated Press/PA Photos, p206 Lordprice Collection/Alamy, p212 Hulton-Deutsch Collection/Corbis UK Ltd., p213t Henry Guttmann/Getty Images, p213 Hulton Archive/Getty Images, p218 AP/TopFoto, p220 Bettmann/Corbis UK Ltd., p221 akg-images, p225 Illustrated London News Ltd/Mary Evans Picture Library, p226t Time & Life Pictures/Getty Images, p226b Rue des Archives/Tallandier/Mary Evans Picture Library, p227bl Swim Ink 2, Llc/Corbis UK Ltd., p227bc Mary Evans Picture Library, p227br Mary Evans Picture Library, p227t Illustrated London News Ltd/Mary Evans Picture Library, p228 Keystone/Getty Images, p232t Hulton-Deutsch Collection/Corbis UK Ltd., p232b Pictorial Parade/Getty Images, p234 Central Press/Getty Images, p236t Keystone/Getty, Images 236b Bettmann/Corbis UK Ltd., p237t Apis/Sygma/Corbis UK Ltd., p237b Apis/Sygma/Corbis UK Ltd., p238t INTERFOTO Pressebildagentur/Alamy, p239b UPPA/Photoshot, p244 Ullstein Bild/akg-images, p245 Bettmann/Corbis UK Ltd., p246t Central Press/Getty Images, p246b Associated Press/PA Photos, p247t Dinodia Images/Alamy, p247b akg-images, p250 Bettmann/Corbis UK Ltd., p251 Ullstein Bild/akg-images, p252 Martin Cleaver/PA Photos, p254 Bettmann/Corbis UK Ltd., p270 © David Manning/Library of Congress, p273 Bettmann/Corbis UK Ltd., p274 Bettmann/Corbis UK Ltd., p276 Associated Press/PA Photos, p281 Associated Press/PA Photos, p282 Associated Press/PA Photos, p301 Mayibuye/Link Picture Library, p308 Greg English/Link Picture Library, p309t A. Benny Gool/PictureNET Africa/Link Picture, p309bl Roger Bosch/I-Africa/Link Picture Library, p309br Louise Gubb/I-Afrika/Link Picture Library, p311 Kevin Kallaugher, p323 Daniel A. Guggisberg, p334 Vladimir Mayakovsky/David King Collection, p357 akg-images, p358 The Granger Collection/TopFoto, p363 David King Collection, p372 PA McCann/The Print Collector/Alamy, p375 Ullstein Bild/akg-images, p379l Mark Kauffman/Time Life Pictures/Getty Images, p379r Harry Dempster/Express/Getty Images, p381 Terry

Fincher.Photo Int/Alamy, p383 Associated Press/PA Photos, p392 Bettmann/Corbis UK Ltd., p396 Bettmann/Corbis UK Ltd., p397t Bettmann/Corbis UK Ltd., p397b Keystone/Getty Images, p400 Remi Benali/Corbis UK Ltd., p401t Bettmann/Corbis UK Ltd., p401b The Dmitri Baltermants Collection/Corbis UK Ltd., p402 Bettmann/Corbis UK Ltd., p403 Karen Kasmauski/Corbis UK Ltd., p404 Central Press/Getty Images, p419 Ullstein Bild/akg-images, p420 Bettmann/Corbis UK Ltd., p423 Ullstein Bild/akg-images, p425 Ladislav Bielik/©Peter Bielik, p427 Ingrid Kruse/Ullstein Bild/akg-images, p430t Dominique Faget/AFP/Getty Images, p430b akg-images, p431 Leszek Wdowinski/Reuters/Corbis UK Ltd., p434 Chris Niedenthal/Time Life Pictures/Getty Images, p457 Paul Carmack/©1945 Christian Science Monitor, p462 Peter Arnett/Associated Press/PA Photos, p465 UPPA/Photoshot, p469 Associated Press/PA Photos, p472 Bettmann/Corbis UK Ltd., p473 Gert Schuetz/akg-images, p474 Bettmann/Corbis UK Ltd., p476 Ullstein Bild/akg-images, p492 Mary Evans Picture Library, p496 AFP/Getty Images.

Cover image: Leemage/Getty Images

The authors and publisher are grateful for permission to reprint the following copyright material:

Account of gas attack 1916 from www.eyewitnesstohistory.com, reprinted by permission of Ibis Communications, Inc.
Timothy Garton Ash: extracts from The Magic Lantern: The Revolution of 1989 Witnessed in Warsaw, Budapest, Berlin and Prague (Random House, 1990), copyright © Timothy Garton Ash 1990, reprinted by permission of Random House, Inc. and the author c/o Rogers, Coleridge & White Ltd, London.
Associated Press article 'Kurds recount gas attack horror at Saddam trial', 23.8.2006 reprinted by permission of The YGS Group.
N Baynes (ed): extracts from The Speeches of Adolf Hitler April 1922 – August 1939 (OUP, 1942), reprinted by permission of the Royal Institute of International Affairs.
Ahron Bregman and Jihan El-Tahri: extracts from The Fifty Years War: Israel and the Arabs (BBC/Penguin Books, 1998), copyright © Ahron Bergman, Jihan El-Tahri 1998, reprinted by permission of Penguin Books Ltd.
Wilfred Deac: extract from article on Suez Crisis, Military History, April 2001, reprinted by permission of the Weider History Group.
Jonathan Fenby: extract from The Penguin History of Modern China (Penguin, 2008), reprinted by permission of David Higham Associates.
TG Fraser: extract from The Arab-Israeli Conflict (Palgrave, 2004), reprinted by permission of Palgrave Macmillan.
CJ Friedrich & ZK Brzezinski: extracts from Totalitarian Dictatorship and Autocracy (Harvard University Press, 1956/2e 1965), reprinted by permission of the publishers.
Vaclav Havel: extracts from The Power of the Powerless: Citizens against the state in central-eastern Europe edited by John Keane (ME Sharpe, 1985), reprinted by permission of the publishers.
T Haworth: extracts from Twentieth Century World History: The World since 1900 (Longman, 1993), reprinted by permission of Pearson Education Ltd.
Paul Johnson: extract from A History of the Modern World (Weidenfeld & Nicolson, 1983), reprinted by permission of the publisher, an imprint of The Orion Publishing Group, London
J Joll: extract from Britain and Europe (A & C Black, 1961), reprinted by permission of the publishers.
Henry Kissinger: extracts from Diplomacy (Touchstone, 1995), reprinted by permission of the publishers, Simon & Schuster, Inc.
Nicholas Kristof: extract from 'Beijing Death Toll at least 300: Army tightens control of city but angry resistance goes on', New York Times, 5.6.1989, copyright © 1989 The New York Times. All rights reserved. Reprinted by permission of PARS International Corporation and protected by the Copyright Laws of the United States.
John Laver: extracts from Nazi Germany 1933-45 (Hodder & Stoughton, 1991), and Russia 1914–1941 (Hodder & Stoughton, 1991), reprinted by permission of Hodder & Stoughton Ltd.
Thomas M Leonard: extracts from Castro & the Cuban Revolution (Greenwood Press, 1999), reprinted by permission of ABC-Clio Inc/Greenwood Publishing Group.
Major James T McGhee: extract from 'The Soviet Experience in Afghanistan: Lessons Learned', Military History, 14.6.2008, reprinted by permission of the Weider History Group.
Nelson Mandela: extracts from Long Walk to Freedom (Abacus, 1994), reprinted by permission of Little, Brown Book Group Ltd.
Rita Markel: extracts from Fidel Castro's Cuba (Twenty First Century Books, 2008), reprinted by permission of the publishers.
Newsweek: 'Crucial features of South Africa's interim rule are still not clear', Newsweek, 8.3.1993, reprinted by permission of Newsweek.
AK Ocran: extract from A Myth is Broken: an account of the Ghana coup d'etat of 24th February 1966 (Longman, 1968), reprinted by permission of the author.
George Orwell: extracts from Nineteen Eighty Four (Penguin, 1949), reprinted by permission of AM Heath & Co Ltd.
J Patterson: extract from Grand Expectations: The United States 1945-1974 (OUP, 1996), reprinted by permission of Oxford University Press.
M Ravallion and S Chen: extract from 'Fighting Poverty: Lessons from China's Success', copyright © The World Bank, reprinted by permission of The World Bank
Mark Robson: extracts from Italy: Liberalism and Fascism 1870-1945 (Hodder & Stoughton, 1992), reprinted by permission of Hodder & Stoughton Ltd.
Arthur M Schlesinger, Jr: extract from A Thousand Days: John F Kennedy in the White House (Houghton Mifflin, 2002), copyright © 1965, and renewed 1993 by Arthur M Schlesinger, Jr, reprinted by permission of Houghton Mifflin Harcourt Publishing Company. All rights reserved.
Charles D Smith: extract from Palestine and the Arab-Israeli Conflict (St Martin's Press, 1988), reprinted by permission of Palgrave Macmillan.
Margaret Thatcher: extract from The Path of Power (HarperCollins, 1995), reprinted by permission of the publishers.
JF Traynor: extract from Challenging History: Europe 1890 – 1990 (Nelson, 1991) reprinted by permission of the author.
D Williamson: extracts from War and Peace-: International Relations 1919–1939 (Hodder Murray, 2003), reprinted by permission of John Murray (Publishers) Ltd.
Jan Wong: extract and figure from Red China Blues (Anchor Books, 1997), reprinted by permission of the publishers, Random House, Inc.

We have tried to trace and contact all copyright holders before publication. If notified, the publishers will be pleased to rectify any errors or omissions at the earliest opportunity.

Course Companion definition

The IB Diploma Programme Course Companions are resource materials designed to provide students with extra support through their two-year course of study. These books will help students gain an understanding of what is expected from the study of an IB Diploma Programme subject.

The Course Companions reflect the philosophy and approach of the IB Diploma Programme and present content in a way that illustrates the purpose and aims of the IB. They encourage a deep understanding of each subject by making connections to wider issues and providing opportunities for critical thinking.

These Course Companions, therefore, may or may not contain all of the curriculum content required in each IB Diploma Programme subject, and so are not designed to be complete and prescriptive textbooks. Each book will try to ensure that areas of curriculum that are unique to the IB or to a new course revision are thoroughly covered. These books mirror the IB philosophy of viewing the curriculum in terms of a whole-course approach; the use of a wide range of resources; international-mindedness; the IB learner profile and the IB Diploma Programme core requirements; theory of knowledge; the extended essay; and creativity, action, service (CAS).

In addition, the Course Companions provide advice and guidance on the specific course assessment requirements and also on academic honesty protocol.

The Course Companions are not designed to be:

- study/revision guides or a one-stop solution for students to pass the subjects
- prescriptive or essential subject textbooks.

IB mission statement

The International Baccalaureate aims to develop inquiring, knowledgable and caring young people who help to create a better and more peaceful world through intercultural understanding and respect.

To this end the IB works with schools, governments and international organizations to develop challenging programmes of international education and rigorous assessment.

These programmes encourage students across the world to become active, compassionate, and lifelong learners who understand that other people, with their differences, can also be right.

The IB learner profile

The aim of all IB programmes is to develop internationally minded people who, recognizing their common humanity and shared guardianship of the planet, help to create a better and more peaceful world. IB learners strive to be:

Inquirers They develop their natural curiosity. They acquire the skills necessary to conduct inquiry and research and show independence in learning. They actively enjoy learning and this love of learning will be sustained throughout their lives.

Knowledgable They explore concepts, ideas, and issues that have local and global significance. In so doing, they acquire in-depth knowledge and develop understanding across a broad and balanced range of disciplines.

Thinkers They exercise initiative in applying thinking skills critically and creatively to recognize and approach complex problems, and make reasoned, ethical decisions.

Communicators They understand and express ideas and information confidently and creatively in more than one language and in a variety of modes of communication. They work effectively and willingly in collaboration with others.

Principled They act with integrity and honesty, with a strong sense of fairness, justice, and respect for the dignity of the individual, groups, and communities. They take responsibility for their own actions and the consequences that accompany them.

Open-minded They understand and appreciate their own cultures and personal histories, and are open to the perspectives, values, and traditions of other individuals and communities. They are accustomed to seeking and evaluating a range of points of view, and are willing to grow from the experience.

Caring They show empathy, compassion, and respect towards the needs and feelings of others. They have a personal commitment to service, and act to make a positive difference to the lives of others and to the environment.

Risk-takers They approach unfamiliar situations and uncertainty with courage and forethought, and have the independence of spirit to explore new roles, ideas, and strategies. They are brave and articulate in defending their beliefs.

Balanced They understand the importance of intellectual, physical, and emotional balance to achieve personal well-being for themselves and others.

Reflective They give thoughtful consideration to their own learning and experience. They are able to assess and understand their strengths and limitations in order to support their learning and personal development.

A note on academic honesty

It is of vital importance to acknowledge and appropriately credit the owners of information when that information is used in your work. After all, owners of ideas (intellectual property) have property rights. To have an authentic piece of work, it must be based on your individual and original ideas with the work of others fully acknowledged. Therefore, all assignments, written or oral, completed for assessment must use your own language and expression. Where sources are used or referred to, whether in the form of direct quotation or paraphrase, such sources must be appropriately acknowledged.

How do I acknowledge the work of others?

The way that you acknowledge that you have used the ideas of other people is through the use of footnotes and bibliographies.

Footnotes (placed at the bottom of a page) or endnotes (placed at the end of a document) are to be provided when you quote or paraphrase from another document, or closely summarize the information provided in another document. You do not need to provide a footnote for information that is part of a "body of knowledge". That is, definitions do not need to be footnoted as they are part of the assumed knowledge.

Bibliographies should include a formal list of the resources that you used in your work. "Formal" means that you should use one of the several accepted forms of presentation. This usually involves separating the resources that you use into different categories (e.g. books, magazines, newspaper articles, Internet-based resources, CDs and works of art) and providing full information as to how a reader or viewer of your work can find the same information. A bibliography is compulsory in the extended essay.

What constitutes malpractice?

Malpractice is behaviour that results in, or may result in, you or any student gaining an unfair advantage in one or more assessment component. Malpractice includes plagiarism and collusion.

Plagiarism is defined as the representation of the ideas or work of another person as your own. The following are some of the ways to avoid plagiarism:

- Words and ideas of another person used to support one's arguments must be acknowledged.
- Passages that are quoted verbatim must be enclosed within quotation marks and acknowledged.
- CD-ROMs, email messages, web sites on the Internet, and any other electronic media must be treated in the same way as books and journals.
- The sources of all photographs, maps, illustrations, computer programs, data, graphs, audio-visual, and similar material must be acknowledged if they are not your own work.
- Works of art, whether music, film, dance, theatre arts, or visual arts, and where the creative use of a part of a work takes place, must be acknowledged.

Collusion is defined as supporting malpractice by another student. This includes:

- allowing your work to be copied or submitted for assessment by another student
- duplicating work for different assessment components and/or diploma requirements.

Other forms of malpractice include any action that gives you an unfair advantage or affects the results of another student. Examples include, taking unauthorized material into an examination room, misconduct during an examination, and falsifying a CAS record.

Introduction

This book is designed to be a companion to the study of 20th-century world history. It follows the International Baccalaureate Diploma Programme history course for first teaching in September 2008 and first examinations in 2010. This volume covers the Route 2, 20th-century world history higher and standard level core syllabus. Written by experienced IB history teachers and examiners, it contains a wealth of teaching and learning ideas, as well as providing historical background and analysis of the syllabus content.

History is an exploratory subject that encompasses many academic and social disciplines. It encourages an understanding of the present through critical reflection upon the past. The IB Diploma Programme 20th-century world history course provides both structure and flexibility, fostering an understanding of major historical events in a global context. It requires you to make comparisons between similar and dissimilar solutions to common human situations, based on political, economic and social circumstances and the interpretation of events as they unfold. Through the study of history you can develop a strong international mindedness recognizing common humanities and you will have a better understanding of the world, and of our responsibilities to society.

As a study of the human condition, history explores how we came to be what we are today. It can be a contentious subject; it led Soviet leader Nikita Khrushchev to comment, "Historians are dangerous people. They are capable of upsetting everything." The authors of this book hope that it will assist you in becoming effective historians and critical thinkers.

This 20th-century world history course companion has a number of special features:

IB Learner Profile links The attributes of the IB learner profile fit closely with the aims of the IB history curriculum and are illustrated in the book with specific activities and questions.

TOK links History is an area of knowledge that is an integral part of the IB Diploma Programme theory of knowledge (TOK) course. Different areas of knowledge—including the human and natural sciences, ethics and the arts—as well as each of the ways of knowing have been included, to offer practical application of real-life issues that can be explored collectively or individually.

Definitions Alongside the text there are definitions of historical concepts and terms which will deepen an understanding of the historical topics being covered.

Biographies The study of history focuses on people and their interaction with each other and their environment. Some short biographies of important people linked to the main text give more background and context to the topics covered.

Activities and discussion points All chapters contain a wide range of classroom and individual activities to encourage active learning and participation. These activities are designed to deepen understanding of the historical debates and issues under discussion in the text.

Source analysis There is a strong accent on the critical analysis of source material particularly in the chapters on the three prescribed subjects. This underlines the principle that history is not only a study of the past but also the process of interpreting, recording and understanding a topic through analyzing its sources to validate knowledge claims.

Exam practice Each chapter contains sample examination questions that are all modeled on the type of questions written for the external examinations.

Recommended further reading Each chapter concludes with suggestions for further reading. This is to encourage a richer and deeper understanding of all the topics covered in the book and to underline that history should be studied through reading a range of primary and secondary sources not a single book.

Guidelines for study

Source evaluation and analysis

As an IB Diploma Programme history student, you will need to understand source evaluation. It is tested in paper 1, and through extended essays and internal assessment. No one can be a genuine historian without being able to test sources for their usefulness and reliability. You may be surprised at the variety of sources that are used by historians. These include: official documents, diaries, memoirs, speeches, books, journals, letters, newspapers, films, photographs, cartoons, paintings, artefacts, buildings, maps and charts. All sources are the product of human labour—through writing, speaking, compiling, drawing, photographing, building and other forms of production. However it was made, you can learn about it by asking the following simple questions:

- **Who** produced it? (i.e.—wrote, said, drew it etc.) This will lead you to think about the person who created it, and if he/she is known to you, or what you can find out about him/her.

- **Where** was it produced? The place should give you more clues about how and why it was produced. What was happening there at the time?

- **When** was it produced? The date is very important in source evaluation. Is the source contemporary with the event referred to? Or, was it written or produced in hindsight? Perhaps it is a fake?

- **Why** was it written, presented, told etc.? The person producing it must have had a reason. And, whether it was important or trivial, it could reveal certain truths or emphasize certain things, perhaps functioning as a form of propaganda.

- **To whom** was it directed? To a particular person or intended audience? This could tell us a lot; it might be official, public or private. It could also be what the recipient wanted to hear or see, or what the producer wanted us to be made aware of.

You have probably received similar advice about questioning sources before—below is an example of how this advice can be applied to IB history paper 1.

The wording for question 3 is as follows: "With reference to their origin and purpose, assess the value and limitations of Source X and Source Y for historians studying …"

For "origin" you can name the person responsible for it, the date and place it came from, and the person or audience it was intended for. The source details provided will help you.

For "purpose" you must explain the aims, give the reasons for why it was produced. What was the person who said, wrote or produced it trying to do?

For "value", you can go back to the origin and purpose; it could be valuable because it is about an event that the author saw. Or, you know the position held by the author, and can then judge if his/her purpose was to convince or deceive. Note that a source that is not reliable, that is, does not mean what it says, can still be of value providing you recognize that it is propaganda, clouding the facts, covering up the mistakes made, or intended to support personal gain.

Likewise, with "limitations", use your knowledge of the source's origin and context to help you in your assessment of its limitations.

Far too many students judge a source to be of little value because the writer was not an eyewitness to the events, or is biased because it is, for example, about the Soviet Union and written by an American. Students often describe content, rather than evaluating the context, and confine the description of its origin to the title of a book and the name of its author. In desperation, a limitation is suggested based on the fact that the source is a translation from the original language. Be careful in using the terms "primary", "secondary" and "bias" to evaluate sources. Do use the introductions to the sources, which can often aid you. And finally, always assume that the sources used in an IB examination are genuine, and not there to trick you!

History Paper 1

For the IB history course for first teaching in 2008 and first examinations in 2010, you must study in depth, one prescribed subject for paper 1. The choice of prescribed subject will have been based on several factors, including student interest, available resources and the selected paper 2 topics and higher level option. Some schools may base their choice on the need to complement other papers, while others may choose the subject to extend student knowledge. The study of history does not fit neatly into watertight compartments, and the three IB external components will all help to produce a wider and deeper historical understanding, and international outlook.

The IB history paper 1 in Route 2, 20th-century history helps to develop two important skills in historical analysis: the ability to evaluate and use sources, and to study a topic in depth. The three chapters on the prescribed subjects are designed to help students to develop these skills, so that they can approach the examination with confidence.

Before you sit the examination, familiarize yourself with the wording and mark value of the questions. You are given five minutes reading time. Use it wisely to read through the sources and the questions. You will only receive the prescribed subject for which you have been entered. You are given one hour to answer the four questions on the paper. The first question addresses comprehension/understanding. Do not write too much. Usually a 2-mark question requires only two relevant points, and a 3-mark question three points.

The second question will require you to compare and contrast two sources on an aspect common to both. A running comparison will score better than sequential accounts of the two sources. Do not worry if there is more to compare than contrast, or vice versa. If only one source is tackled, 2 out of the 6 marks available is the maximum you can score. The third question asks you to evaluate two sources according to their origin, purpose, value and limitation. Evaluate each source separately, and address all the points for each one.

The fourth question is a mini essay based on an aspect explored in the sources. It is often based on a quotation from one of the sources. This requires you to evaluate the sources based on the information provided and your own historical knowledge. Material from the sources and your own background research is demanded. Ensure that you draw on both the sources and relevant background information. There is usually, but not always, a valid point that can be drawn on from each of the five sources, so do not spend too much time trying to discover just one. Plan your time around this mini essay. Some students, especially those for whom English is a second language, find themselves rushed to complete this paper. If necessary finish the mini essay in note form.

History paper 2

The history paper 2 component consists of five sections, and you are required to study two of them. However when it comes to the exam, you may find another question in another section that you can tackle because it links with work you have done in your prescribed subject or for your higher level work.

Paper 2 is the most international component of the history course, therefore some questions will name two countries from different regions, or state that two countries, each chosen from a different region must be used. There is a map on the front of the question paper that shows the IB regions: Europe, Africa and the Middle East; North America and the Carribean; Latin America; and the Asia Pacific. You will notice that the chapters in this book on the 20th-century world topics all contain material from different regions. These chapters adopt a range of approaches to the topics. Some concentrate more on the depth and detail focusing on a limited range of examples; others deal with the material thematically.

Before the examination study the command terms, and the markbands in the *IB History Guide* that will indicate what you have to do to obtain a high grade. Use your reading time to decide which questions to answer, then narrow them down to your final choice, ensuring that you have sufficient knowledge to answer them, and that you understand all the demands of the questions. If possible, write a short rough plan in your answer booklet, and hand it in with the completed questions. It gives the appearance of being well-organized.

Focus on the question; do not include unnecessary information. Too many students see the name of a person or event they have studied, and pour out all they know on the subject. A description of the context is necessary, but avoid irrelevant or excessive background material. Many of the exam questions lend themselves to a thematic approach. It is often better to adopt this approach rather than writing a chronological narrative. But do not ignore chronology. Dates are important, especially to show that you understand the relationship to the events as they unfold and their effects upon the lives of the individuals and nations concerned. Many questions have two demands (for example, to account for the reasons and the results), or require evidence from two different countries or sets of circumstances (as in a comparative analysis of two rulers, wars or states).

Most students are able to write satisfactory essays in the allocated time, but as a last resort, if you find that time is running out, and you still have more relevant material to give as important evidence, put it in note form and add a conclusion. It is not length but the degree of analysis and appropriate detail that will help you to achieve high grades.

Authors

Martin Cannon teaches at the Western Academy of Beijing, China. He is chief examiner and a team leader for the extended essays. He has taught in Mexico, Peru, Sri Lanka, Yemen, France, Malaysia and China.

Richard Jones-Nerzic teaches history, TOK and film at the British International School, Bratislava. He received an IB diploma from Whitchurch High School in Cardiff, UK. He is co-ordinator of the European History e-Learning Project.

David Keys teaches at the British International School, Bratislava, Slovakia, where he has helped to establish the IB History Programme. He has taught History and English in Turkey, Saudi Arabia and the UK and is a translator and writer.

Alexis Mamaux is currently teaching at the United World College of the American West in New Mexico, USA. She is an assistant examiner and team leader for history and the extended essay.

Michael Miller is a teacher at Upper Canada College and has taught IB history since 1996. He is currently a deputy chief examiner in history, a workshop leader and a principal examiner. He is a team leader for the marking of history and extended essays.

Giles Pope currently works at the International University in Vienna. He taught IB history at the International School of Kenya, was a teacher and administrator at the Danube International School, Vienna, and is a history examiner and workshop leader.

David Smith teaches at Ecole Lindsay Thurber Comprehensive High School in Alberta, Canada. He is a workshop leader for IB Americas, an assistant examiner, an application reader, and a faculty member for the Online Curriculum Centre.

Aidan Williams teaches at Braeburn College in Nairobi. He has led workshops for IB and has been an examiner for eighteen years. He has been a senior examiner for ten years.

Contents

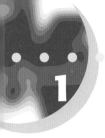

1 Peacemaking, peacekeeping— international relations, 1918–36

The issues, conflicts, disputes and attitudes that arose during the period from 1918 to 1936 cannot be understood or appreciated without a sound knowledge of the experience of the First World War. This involves not simply an understanding of the causes, events and statistical cost of the war but something much more profound. The First World War was for many a **total war** with all the characteristics attached to that term. The war was a cataclysmic event for Western society, a descent into a brutal and largely futile struggle that undermined or destroyed much of the pre-war world. What was lost was confidence, optimism, stability and faith in the future. Massive political, social and economic upheavals occurred, which influenced events up to the outbreak of the Second World War and even until today.

> **Total war** A war in which opponents mobilize all available societal resources—economic, industrial, military, human, political/ideological—in the war effort.

This chapter is designed to assist in the study of the post-war peacemaking and peacekeeping efforts, which form the basis of prescribed subject 1. It addresses the issues relating to creating a settlement at the end of the First World War and the challenges of promoting and maintaining peace in the period from 1918 to 1936. The difficulties in arriving at a peace settlement that reflected both the idealism of US president Woodrow Wilson and the security and territorial concerns of the other powers were particularly complex. Continuing challenges to the Versailles settlement from Germany and Italy created the need to revise and re-examine the Treaty of Versailles on a number of occasions. The period is also concerned with the problems of implementing new ways to preserve peace, such as the League of Nations. Finally, the threats to a peaceful world order presented by revolutionary political movements such as Bolshevism and fascism, as well as the Great Depression, are examined.

Sources that could be used in questions are included throughout the chapter and focus on the following areas:

- the aims of the participants and peacemakers: Woodrow Wilson and the Fourteen Points
- the terms of the Paris peace settlements 1919–20: Versailles, St Germain, Trianon, Neuilly, Sèvres/Lausanne (1923)
- the geo-political and economic impact of the treaties on Europe; the establishment and impact of the mandate system
- enforcement of the provisions of the treaties: US isolationism— the retreat from the Anglo-American Guarantee; disarmament— Washington, London, Geneva conferences
- the League of Nations: effects of the absence of the major powers; the principle of collective security and early attempts at peacekeeping (1920–5)
- the Ruhr Crisis (1923); Locarno and the "Locarno Spring" (1925)
- the Great Depression and threats to international peace and collective security: Manchuria (1931–3) and Abyssinia (1935–6).

By the end of the chapter, you should be able to:

- understand the conflicting aims of the countries involved in the Versailles settlement
- be aware of the terms of the Versailles settlement
- appreciate how these terms may have led to disagreement and conflict
- understand the concepts behind the League of Nations and why these proved difficult to carry out
- be aware of the problems of disarmament
- understand the impact of new political philosophies and economic upheaval
- know and understand the significance of major conferences and agreements reached during this period
- compare and contrast the reaction of major countries to the events of the period
- use the documents to form your own understanding and opinions on the issues presented
- form your own opinions and viewpoints on the controversies in this period.

Background to the period 1918–36

The period under discussion breaks into two parts. These are separated by the onset of the Great Depression in 1929. In the 1920s there appeared to be little threat to international peace. The powers were exhausted from the war, the defeated nations were too weak to try and reverse the verdict and there was a general revulsion at the thought of another conflict. The foundation of the League of Nations and the idealism of the **Fourteen Points** encouraged many people to believe that a new era of peace would emerge. This was illusory but was supported by the absence of immediate threats to peace and because the League experienced a few successes in dispute resolution. Nevertheless, there were many potential threats and the only nations interested or able to maintain the status quo were Britain and France.

The Great Depression exposed the weakness of the post-Versailles settlements and is regarded by some as the greatest cause of the Second World War. It encouraged Japanese aggression and the rise of Hitler and exposed the inability of the League to maintain the peace. The revisionist powers who had recovered their strength saw an opportunity to pursue their agendas for territory and economic strength.

Fourteen Points A series of principles written by Woodrow Wilson as a basis for ending the First World War and creating a more peaceful and progressive world.

Integrating the theory of knowledge (TOK)

This prescribed subject provides many opportunities for the student to explore the nature of historical knowledge and how historians evaluate and analyse information of various types. This chapter will both increase your understanding of the methodology used by historians and the discipline of history itself.

Through the various questions and exercises you will be able to develop your critical thinking skills in support of the integrated theory of knowledge. There is ample room for debate both on specific issues and about broader philosophical themes. This chapter deals with fundamental aspects of human nature in the relationship between peace and war, and self-interest versus altruism.

An analysis of whether human nature tends to certain fixed patterns of behaviour or might evolve and develop is also worth pursuing. There are a variety of questions and activities in this chapter to initiate discussion.

Approaching this subject

Prescribed subject 1 covers the period from the end of the First World War to 1936, by which time the prospects of another war were increasing. This is a very important subject as it not only links two of the most influential events of the 20th century—the two world wars—but it examines efforts at peacekeeping and why they failed. This should allow for further discussion about the ways that we might develop strategies to prevent war in the present. Students who are doing this topic are also likely to choose topic 1 in 20th-century history, on the causes, practices and effects of war, and topic 3 on single-party states. For example, knowledge of the First World War will provide valuable background to assist in understanding the work of the Paris Peace Conference in 1919. The material in this unit provides excellent supporting material for these topics and will help explain and interpret the significance of the events in this prescribed subject.

Not all the events that impact on the peace process are included in this prescribed subject and students are encouraged to locate other examples that relate to or help explain the topics. An example would be the Russo-Polish war of 1920–1 as a route to exploring the geo-political impact of the Paris peace settlements or the role of the League of Nations. In addition, some examples of successful efforts by the League to prevent conflict are not described. Students might wish to examine these and deepen their understanding of the strengths and weaknesses of the League.

Students will also be required to focus on the understanding and critical evaluation of source material. These sources are numerous and exist in both written and visual forms. The written forms include books, newspapers, articles, letters, speeches, memoirs and government documents. Visual documents include maps, political cartoons, graphs, statistics and photographs. These sources of information will present many different viewpoints.

Activity:

The First World War in visual art, film and literature

Literature	Art	Film
Siegfried Sassoon, *Memoirs of an Infantry Officer*, 1930	Cubism: camouflage patterns and Cubist space.	*All Quiet on the Western Front*: novel by Erich Maria Remarque, 1929; film Dir. Lewis Milestone, 1930
Robert Graves, *Goodbye to All That*, 1929, also his poetry.	Dadaism: anti-art and anti-war. Hugo Ball, Tristran Tzara, Cabaret Voltaire	*Gallipoli*, 1981, Dir. Peter Weir
Ernest Hemingway, *A Farewell to Arms*, 1929	Otto Dix, his paintings, drawings and print cycle, *The War*, 1923–4	
The escapist novels of F. Scott Fitzgerald	Franz Marc, *The Fate of the Animals*, 1913	

Visual art, film and literature are valuable resources through which to judge attitudes, emotions, and reactions to historical events or ideas. Add further examples and details to this chart.

- What does art, film and literature tell you about how the First World War affected people—not only physically, but in terms of their view of the world, their optimism, their faith in the future etc.?

- Consider the views of people from all sectors of society—in terms of their gender, age, occupation and ethnic background.

The Paris Peace Conference

The aims of the participants in the peace process were the goals that each nation hoped to achieve. In essence, each country wished to gain some advantage from their victory. The losers were not present, so their concerns were not raised. This is a fairly traditional view of peace conferences in that the winners expect to extract some territory or other concessions from the losers.

Versailles was complicated, however, by the presence of Woodrow Wilson and his Fourteen Points, which completely altered the traditional approach to peace conferences. Wilson's ideal was not to create a winner's peace treaty but rather create an environment of generosity in which permanent peace might be assured. This was an entirely new concept and made the work of the conference much more difficult. Some countries, such as Italy, were expecting significant rewards but were left disappointed and embittered. Those countries on the losing side were also disappointed as Wilson was forced to compromise and allow some of the victors to impose harsh conditions on the losers. This is the genesis for the argument that the Treaty of Versailles satisfied neither winners nor losers.

Aims and goals—some background issues

The aims and goals of the nations that met in Versailles were framed not only by their war experiences but by hopes and aspirations that had existed prior to the war. These encompassed such things as national liberation or independence from an imperial power. These desires were present not only in European states such as the Balkans but in the Middle East and Asia as well. Powerful movements for political and social reform had existed prior to the war and would have to be addressed. The Bolshevik Revolution in Russia and revolutionary pressures in other countries, often brought to a head by the war, would similarly need to be confronted.

Before examining the specific aims or goals of these nations, however, certain background factors which influenced the participants should be appreciated. These were events or ideas that the participants could not control but which they had to be aware of in their decision making.

The Bolshevik Revolution had introduced a new political philosophy to Europe—one that challenged virtually every aspect of Western liberal civilization. There was real fear that **Bolshevism** was a "virus" that would spread and engulf much of Europe and perhaps beyond— fears were expressed in the Unites States and Canada about its presence there. The peacemakers would not only have to work to restore peace but would also have to try and address some of the grievances that might attract populations to the communist ideology.

Bolshevism A radical, revolutionary movement under the leadership of Lenin which seized power in Russia in 1917. It promoted an anti-capitalist philosophy and supported world revolution and class warfare.

Even before the Versailles conference, the geo-political situation had changed dramatically. No fewer than three of the Great Powers who had been present in 1914 had collapsed and, in two cases, had dissolved into their constituent parts. In addition, the Ottoman Empire had dissolved and created a power vacuum in the Middle East. This was unprecedented and the assumption that the Great Powers who had begun the war would be present at the conclusion was unfounded. The nations making the decisions at Versailles were Britain, France and the United States.

The war itself was different from others, not only in size and destruction on many levels, but in its introduction of grandiose objectives. Terms like the "war to end all wars" and a war "to make the world safe for democracy" were new concepts. They may have been introduced to give some meaning to the catastrophic and often senseless slaughter on all fronts or to encourage the combatants to fight to the end. In any event, they introduced an idealistic tone and raised expectations about the peace that would be hard to satisfy.

The states that made the decisions at Versailles were all democratic nations, something not seen at previous conferences. It would mean that the leaders of these countries would be influenced in their actions by popular opinion at home or the need to fulfil political promises made during the war. Political leaders had engaged in extravagant rhetoric or promises to their populations to maintain support for a war that had seemed futile to many and for which enthusiasm was declining. The development of the mass media had allowed governments to produce extensive propaganda during the war, which often used inflammatory images and accounts of the enemy. These were designed to excite, enrage or encourage the population to maintain their dedication to the war effort. When the nations came to Versailles, the emotions that they had released among their populations would have to be satisfied in some way. This may well have played a role in the demands or positions that their leaders took. Modern technology made the reporting of the details of the conference to the national populations easy and immediate, adding another aspect to the work of the delegates—daily scrutiny and a relentless demand for information from reporters.

The other powerful influence on the aims and goals of the conference was the idealism of President Wilson and the Fourteen Points. This was an entirely new phenomenon in international conferences which, in the past, had dealt with pragmatic, concrete questions. Delegates were used to making changes to boundaries, levying indemnities and adjusting the balance of power in some way— exercises in **Realpolitik**. Wilson called for the creation of an entirely new system based on a new set of assumptions about how relations between nations were to be carried out. It assumed that war could be prevented entirely if people would just make the effort.

Discussion point: Bolshevism

What aspects of the Bolshevik Revolution caused it to be feared by Western countries?

Describe the conditions of the working classes that prompted political leaders to fear that the revolution might spread.

A clear understanding of how Bolshevik philosophy and values clashed with traditional liberal Western values is important.

Bolshevism was described as a virus because it was seen to deny or destroy many aspects of contemporary Western institutions—social, economic, cultural and political.

Realpolitik An approach to international relations based on practical self-interest rather than moral or ideological considerations.

Source analysis

A cartoon entitled "Peace, perfect peace" by David Low, first published in *The Bulletin* (Sydney) on 15 May 1919. The caption reads 'Signor Orlando has returned to Paris, and the Big Four are in harmony again.'—Cable."

Questions

1 What message about the Paris Peace Conference is prompted by the cartoon?

2 What does it suggest about the ability of the conference to solve the world's problems?

Activity:

The speeches and promises of the Allied leaders

Examine the political platforms or speeches of the Allied leaders prior to the Paris Peace Conference. An example would be British prime minister Lloyd George's platform during the election of December 1918.

- What promises did the leaders make to their populations or what expectations did they create through these speeches?

- Compare these promises with the positions that they took at Versailles.

- What evidence can be found of differences between the leaders' promises and their positions during the conference?

- What are some reasons for these differences?

- Were the public aware and how did they react? Discuss the impact of the development of the mass media—the instant reporting of events and decisions—and how this influenced public opinion.

TOK link

Integrating ways of knowing—emotion and reason

TOK is ideally placed to encourage internationalism and aims to embody many of the attributes in the learner profile that promote self-awareness, reflection, critical thinking, empathy, and a sense of responsibility. Emotions play a powerful role in determining thoughts and actions, and in shaping the pursuit of knowledge. Reason is the way in which people construct meaning and justify knowledge claims. How far do these qualities inform the actions of the peacemakers who created the treaties after the First World War?

 Why were President Wilson's Fourteen Points and other foreign policy ideas regarded as idealistic? What aspects of human nature did they seek to change?

1 Explain what you understand by the term "idealism":

- Is idealism mainly to do with emotion, or is it connected with our capacity for reason too?
- Can we ever know anything purely through our emotions?
- How do emotions interact with other ways of knowing such as reason, sense perception and language?
- In what way can it be argued that idealism is both a positive and negative quality?

2 Examine Wilson's Fourteen Points and identify which specific points most reflect idealism, rather than reason? How and why?

3 Consider each of these linking questions to TOK in relation to the actions of Wilson and the other peacemakers in the post-war period:

- What part does emotion play in the acquisition of knowledge?
- Should emotion play a role in the evaluation of knowledge claims?
- Does all knowledge require some kind of rational basis?

Discussion point:

 What was different about the Paris Peace Conference compared to other peace conferences.

Explain this in terms of the outcomes.

What similarities and differences can be seen between the aims, goals and methods of Versailles and those of the Congress of Vienna in 1815?

Activity:

Make a chart

On 8 January 1918, President Woodrow Wilson addressed the United States Congress outlining the Fourteen Points as the American terms for peace. Read through the points, and make a summary in chart form, as started below.

Divide the points up —individually or in groups—to report on compliance with the objectives stated and the proposed border agreements and principles of self-determination specified.

The 14 Points
1 Commitment to public diplomacy and declaration of agreements.
2 Freedom of navigation on open seas (outside territorial borders).
3 Free trade. Removal of trade barriers.
4 Arms reduction.

The aims of the participants

The aims of the Paris Peace Conference represented two fundamental and perhaps irreconcilable approaches. On the one hand, there was clearly a wish to develop a new order of international relations that would secure a permanent peace based on a genuine spirit of reconciliation and compromise. The goal in the words of one British diplomat was not merely to liquidate the war but to found a new order in Europe. We were preparing not only peace but permanent peace. Contradicting this idealism and generosity of spirit was a strong desire to punish those who had caused the conflict and to extract maximum compensation for their victims. Ultimately, the settlements were an awkward compromise between these conflicting emotions. Idealism and revenge were somehow to be reconciled in the same documents.

The United States—Woodrow Wilson and the Fourteen Points

American goals were not expressed in traditional terms such as territorial acquisitions, indemnities (compensation payments) or restoring the balance of power. They were broadly expressed in the Fourteen Points, which were designed to create a peaceful world by removing what Wilson believed to be the reasons for war. President Wilson's goal was to establish democracy and **self-determination** and so eliminate many of the causes of war. This was an idealistic approach which often lacked specifics but which assumed the inherently peaceful and rational nature of human society. This was reflected in one of Wilson's most important goals: the **League of Nations**, which would be a forum for the reasonable and rational settlement of disputes.

Wilson's specific aims involved some punishment of Germany as the cause of the war and the establishment of a period of probation, after which Germany could be admitted to the League of Nations. Otherwise the Fourteen Points were the basis for negotiation with the other powers and for Wilson's goal of incorporating the establishment of the League in the Paris settlements. He did not worry about details which might cause difficulty, as he felt that these could be ironed out later through the spirit of co-operation which the League would create.

The United Kingdom

British aims fell into two categories. The first could be described as limited and representing traditional British foreign policy:

- the elimination of the German fleet as a threat to Great Britain and her empire
- the end of the German Empire as a potential source of conflict
- the defeat of German plans to establish control of Europe
- a return to normal European relations and trade that would restore the British economy and act as a bulwark against Bolshevism.

> **Self-determination** The principle that countries should be established according to the wishes of the people concerned.

> **League of Nations** An international organization created in 1919. It was designed to provide a method of resolving international tensions in a peaceful manner through the concept of collective security.

Woodrow Wilson (1856–1924)

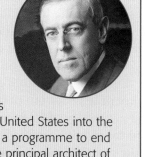

A distinguished academic, Woodrow Wilson became president of Princeton University in 1902. He was subsequently elected governor of New Jersey and then president of the United States in 1912. As president he oversaw the passage of many significant pieces of reform legislation which were in line with his progressive principles. He was re-elected for the presidency in 1916 and led the United States into the First World War. He drafted the Fourteen Points as a programme to end the war and design a better post-war world. As the principal architect of the Versailles settlements, he promoted the idea of the League of Nations. He was awarded the Nobel Peace prize in 1919. His efforts to involve the United States in the League of Nations failed to pass the US Senate and Wilson suffered a stroke which prevented him from contributing to further debate into post-war US policy.

In addition, the United Kingdom did not wish to get involved in any alliance or guarantee in Europe on behalf of any specific country. This was a traditional British policy, valuing freedom of action. British interest did not favour French territorial ambitions in Europe beyond the recovery of Alsace-Lorraine which might create a French threat to the balance of power. Great Britain and France had been rivals for centuries and only a common adversary had brought them together. The UK saw no need to support France in an attempt to dominate or control Europe; British interest lay in maintaining the balance of power and intervening only when this was threatened.

> ### Georges Clemenceau (1841–1929)
>
> Georges Clemenceau was premier of France at the time of the Versailles peace negotiations. A strong right-wing nationalist, he served as a cabinet minister in the French government from 1902 until his appointment as premier in 1917. He opposed any talk of a peace settlement short of absolute victory and arrested politicians who wanted to negotiate peace in 1917. At Versailles he insisted on a harsh treaty of peace that would permanently cripple German power through territorial losses and economic penalties. He was unsuccessful as he clashed with Wilson and Lloyd-George, who wished to be more conciliatory. France did recover Alsace-Lorraine but failed in her attempts to seriously weaken Germany. Clemenceau's failures led to his loss of the 1920 election, after which he retired from politics.

The second set of British aims were non-traditional and involved seeking a declaration of German war guilt and the requirement for Germany to pay extensive **reparations** far beyond the mere physical damage caused by the war. These goals were a response to popular emotions which had built up during the war about Germany as an aggressor and destroyer. They also reflect campaign promises made by Lloyd George in the December 1918 election.

> **Reparations** Payments made by a defeated country to the victorious countries as compensation for war damages and punishment for aggression.

France

French aims must be understood in the light of fears about future security against Germany. Germany had been growing more powerful than France since the mid-19th century and the gap was getting wider as Germany possessed a larger population and greater industrial potential. France was convinced that it would not be able to defend itself if Germany returned to its pre-war strength. France had suffered over two million dead and wounded during the war. Northern France had been a major battle zone and had suffered enormous devastation of land, industry and housing. French goals were therefore to place as many restrictions on Germany as possible in order to reduce her power in the long term. The French sought to weaken Germany through clauses in the treaties which would require:

● extensive disarmament
● territorial reduction
● heavy reparations to weaken the German economy.

The French premier Georges Clemenceau wanted a partial dismemberment of Germany in order to remove any threat to France. In addition to recovering Alsace-Lorraine, he had ambitions to control Luxembourg and Belgium; he also wanted to make the area west of the Rhine a French puppet state. This would be a buffer against future German attacks. Finally, he wished to acquire the Saar region in western Germany as financial compensation for German destruction. Above all, France wanted to have a firm alliance with the United Kingdom and the United States written into the peace settlements as a guarantee against further German aggression. France wanted concrete measures and was not interested in the vague guarantees offered by the League of Nations.

Italy

Italy's aims were simply to achieve the territorial gains that had been promised in the Treaty of London. These included annexation of the Dalmatian coast, Trieste and South Tyrol. These regions were not necessarily populated by Italians but Italy had been promised them in return for entry into the First World War and expected the deal to be honoured. Broader concepts such as self-determination were not looked on favourably if these interfered with Italy's own territorial or economic goals. Italy was insistent on these aims and walked out of the conference when its rights to the Dalmatian Coast territories were denied.

Japan

Japan wanted recognition for its dominant position in China as well as possession of the former German territories in China and the Pacific. The Japanese were not in sympathy with self-determination but wished to acquire a larger empire for reasons of security and economic strength. Japan felt entitled to the former German possessions as it had captured them and saw them as a reward for contributing to the war effort. Another consideration was that Japan wished to take its place among the major powers. Acquiring an empire seemed to be a prerequisite to being respected as a major power in the world. In addition, Japan sought recognition through a statement recognizing racial equality in the peace settlements.

Source analysis

The following documents relate to the aims of the participants in the Paris Peace Conference.

Source A

Woodrow Wilson had already revealed, in the Fourteen Points, what he wanted to see emerge out of the war—a Europe whose nationalities would rule themselves as open, democratic societies. Before the end of the war he had declared that the peace should show "no discrimination between those to whom we wish to be just and those to whom we do not wish to be just. It must be justice that plays no favourites …" But any Germans who thought that Wilson's "justice" meant that they would be treated generously were in for a shock. In the President's eyes Germany had been wicked, and "justice" demanded that Germany be punished.

Source: Howarth, T. 1993. *Twentieth Century World History: The world since 1900*. London, UK. Longman. p. 39.

Question

Woodrow Wilson had often spoken about "peace without victory". Is this reflected in the document? What may have caused him to change his mind?

Source B
British aims

Great Britain: a satisfied power?

In contrast to France, Britain, even before the great powers met in Paris, had already achieved many of its aims: the German fleet had surrendered, German trade rivalry was no longer a threat and Germany's colonial empire was liquidated, while the German armies in Western Europe had been driven back into the Reich. Britain's territorial ambitions lay in the Middle East, not Europe. In January

1919 Lloyd George envisaged the preservation of a peaceful united Germany as a barrier against Bolshevism. Above all he wanted to avoid long-term British commitments on the continent of Europe and prevent the annexations of German minorities by the Poles or the French creating fresh areas of bitterness, which would sow the seeds of a new war. Inevitably, then, these objectives were fundamentally opposed to the French policy of securing definite guarantees against the German military revival either by negotiating a long-term Anglo-American military alliance or by a partial dismemberment of the German empire.

The logic of British policy pointed in the direction of a peace of reconciliation rather than revenge, but in two key areas, reparations and the question of German war guilt, Britain adopted a more intransigent line. Lloyd George and Clemenceau agreed in December 1918 that the Kaiser should be tried by an international tribunal for war crimes. Under pressure from the Dominions, who also wanted a share of reparations, the British Delegation at Paris was authorized to endeavour to secure from Germany the greatest possible indemnity she can pay consistently with the well being of the British Empire and the peace of the world without involving an army of occupation in Germany for its collection.

Source: Williamson, D. 2003. *War and Peace: International relations 1919–39*. 2nd edn. Tunbridge Wells, UK. Hodder Murray. p. 24.

Question

Why could British aims be seen as moderate?

Source C
French aims

Although the leaders of the three great Allied powers believed Germany was to blame for the war, they disagreed about what to do with her in defeat. The French Prime Minister, Georges Clemenceau, and the French people knew what they wanted to write into the treaty of peace—revenge, compensation for all they had suffered, and guarantees that a similar war would never happen again. For four years they had believed that the only good German was a dead German. Now they felt that the only safe Germany would be a crippled Germany, stripped of her wealth and most of her armed forces, and separated from France either by the creation of a new state between them or making sure that what remained of the German army stayed well away from the French border. In the east, a line of new states able to defend themselves would take care of any future German ambitions in that direction.

Source: Williamson, D. 2003. *War and Peace: International relations 1919–39*. 2nd edn. Tunbridge Wells, UK. Hodder Murray. p. 23.

Questions

1 Identify French aims at the Versailles Conference.
2 How are these to be accomplished?

Source D
Italian and Japanese aims

The aims of both Japan and Italy were concentrated on maximizing their war-time gains. Vittorio Orlando, the Italian Prime Minister, was anxious to convince the voters that Italy had done well out of the war, and concentrated initially on attempting to hold the Entente to their promises made in the Treaty of London, as well as demanding the port of Fiume in the Adriatic. Japan wanted recognition of its territorial gains. The Japanese Government also pushed hard, but ultimately unsuccessfully, to have a racial equality clause included in the Covenant of the League of Nations. It hoped that this would protect Japanese immigrants in America.

Japan's gains in the war

The war has presented Japan with opportunities to increase its power in China and the Pacific region at a time when the energies of the European Powers were absorbed in Europe. The Japanese declared war on Germany on 23 August. The British had originally intended that the Japanese navy should merely help with convoy duties in the Pacific, but the Japanese refused to be relegated to a minor role and, much to the alarm of Britain, Australia and the USA, proceeded to seize German territory in the Chinese province of Shantung as well as the German Pacific islands. In January 1915 the Japanese pushed their luck further and presented China with the Twenty-One Demands, which not only included the recognition of the Japanese claims to Shantung and southern Manchuria but also proposed that the Chinese government should appoint Japanese advisers. This last demand would have turned China into a Japanese protectorate and was only dropped after strong British and American objections. However, the rest of the demands were accepted by China in May 1915.

Source: Williamson, D. 2003. *War and Peace: International relations 1919–39*. 2nd edn. Tunbridge Wells, UK. Hodder Murray. p. 25.

Questions

1 Identify the aims of Japan and Italy.
2 Who would oppose these claims?

General issues for consideration

On top of their specific aims, all the powers represented at the Versailles Conference were expected to deal with a number of general questions.

The treatment of Germany

This included issues involving Germany's colonies, her borders, disarmament, reparations and war guilt and the prosecution of individuals for war crimes.

The Austro-Hungarian Empire

This had collapsed and a new political map was emerging in Eastern and Central Europe. How should the boundaries of these states be determined? How could provision be made for self-determination?

The Ottoman Empire

What to do with the Middle East? How would the territory be divided up? How to resolve the conflict between Arabs and Jews?

Russia

How could the dangers posed by the spread of Bolshevism be addressed and prevented?

Non-European states

Representatives from various non-European states—including Vietnam, China and Japan—made representations for an end to colonialism and/or recognition of racial equality. These were largely ignored but the issues had to be addressed at some time in the conference.

General ideas for change

The Fourteen Points had suggested that the Versailles Conference should champion a higher level of conduct that applied not only to international relations but also to politics, economics and social issues. The sacrifices made during the war had led many individuals to expect something better to emerge. Overall, it could be seen that Woodrow Wilson presented aims of an idealistic, long-term nature. These relied on the idea of human beings as being inherently peaceful, rational individuals who would work towards a peaceful world if given the opportunity.

This was in sharp contrast to the traditional attitudes of European diplomacy, which stated that peace was an unlikely occurrence and that one should always be prepared for the possibility of conflict. Rather than vague new ideas like **collective security** and the League of Nations, Europeans wanted specific alliances and agreements that would address the real issues that would undoubtedly arise in the future. This might be seen as a more cynical or pragmatic view, based on historical experience.

Wilson and others, however, condemned the old diplomatic practices as having been responsible for war and asked the world to strive for a

Activity:

1 The aims of the European powers and Woodrow Wilson —as reflected in the Fourteen Points—were in sharp philosophical contrast. What were the most important differences between them?

2 Add a column to the chart created for the activity on p. 19 and head it "Aims of the European Powers". Identify the aims of the major powers when they arrived in Paris. Use the chart to identify potential points of friction or conflict.

new level of understanding and co-operation. Could humans embrace more altruistic principles or would they continue to rely on traditional power relationships and force? Should one trust the goodwill of others or buy a secure set of locks?

German aims

Germany asked for an armistice in October 1918, based on the terms of Wilson's Fourteen Points and his speech of January 1917, the theme of which was "peace without victory". In this speech, Wilson expressed the view that reconciliation of the opposing sides would be necessary to prevent the outbreak of further wars.

Germany had not been defeated or invaded at the time that the armistice was requested and therefore could have expected some form of compromise peace under which neither side dominated. Germany would have expected to attend the peace negotiations as had happened at Vienna in 1815, following the Napoleonic wars. While some form of sanctions or territorial concessions might be expected, Germany would not have expected to be humiliated and severely punished. Kaiser Wilhelm II had abdicated and Germany had established a democratic republic. The Germans felt that this would help them gain sympathy especially from Wilson, who favoured democracy as a guarantee of peace.

? **How does the experience of war affect a nation's approach to the peace process?**
What did Germany hope would be the outcome of the peace settlement?

The terms of the Paris peace treaties, 1919–23

The terms of the Paris peace treaties are extensive and very detailed. The most important of the treaties is the one with Germany, which contained a number of controversial terms such as the war guilt clause, the territorial changes and the disarmament clauses. The other treaties dealt with the Austro-Hungarian and Ottoman empires—breaking them up into new states and territories. The Sèvres treaty, which dealt with the Ottoman Empire, had its terms changed at Lausanne in 1923. It is important to note this and the reasons why.

The terms of the Paris peace treaties are subject to enormous debate. They are condemned as being either too harsh or too lenient, for hypocrisy in making deals which violated Wilsonian principles, for being naïve and unrealistic and for being the cause of the Second World War. A sound knowledge of the most important terms is crucial if one is to be able to participate effectively in the various controversies about the individual terms or the nature and impact of the peace settlements as a whole. Furthermore, comparing the terms to the aims of the participants will also give some insight into how the treaties were received in both the victorious and defeated countries.

The five treaties

There are five treaties which make up the Paris peace settlements. The most well known is the Treaty of Versailles, which was the treaty that dealt with Germany specifically. There are four others—St Germain, Trianon, Neuilly, and Sèvres/Lausanne—which must also be studied as their terms have importance for the geo-political and economic future of Europe. Apart from the clauses that dealt with specific issues, each of the treaties of the Paris Peace Settlement incorporated the **Covenant of the League of Nations**.

The Treaty of Versailles, which was between Germany and the Allied and Associated Powers, was the focal point of the conference. It contained 440 clauses including the Covenant of the League of Nations. The terms are divided into a number of major categories: economic, military and territorial. The terms of the treaty were based on the acceptance by Germany and her allies of the **war guilt clause** (number 231 in the Treaty). This stated:

> The Allied and Associated Governments affirm and Germany accepts the responsibility of Germany and her allies for causing all the loss and damage to which the Allied and Associated governments and their nationals have been subjected as a consequence of the war imposed upon them by the aggression of Germany and her Allies.

This statement justified all of the economic, territorial and military concessions, limitations and restrictions that Germany was forced to make and/or accept as stated in the Treaty.

Covenant of the League The agreement, containing the principles on which the League was to operate that all nations signed when they joined the League of Nations.

War guilt clause This is article 231 of the Treaty of Versailles in which Germany agreed to accept full responsibility for the outbreak of the First World War.

The issues arising from the terms of the Paris peace settlements

A number of points about the terms of the treaties should be noted:

- None of the defeated countries or Russia attended the Versailles Conference or took part in the discussions. All the major decisions were made by the United States, France, United Kingdom and Italy, who were known as the Council of Four.
- The treaties were the result of compromises in the aims of the major powers; these aims were often very contradictory and hostile, which led to difficult decisions and an imperfect document.
- The often stated view of the terms of the Treaty of Versailles was that they were not soft enough to allow for reconciliation with Germany but not harsh enough to cripple German power. This meant that when Germany recovered its strength, it would use this power to revise the Treaty, perhaps through another major conflict.

Germany's reaction

The Germans' reaction to the terms was based on their hopes and expectations, perhaps too optimistic, that the treaty would incorporate the spirit of the Fourteen Points and Germany would not suffer excessive punishment. They were very bitter when the Treaty was presented, as they resented the war guilt clause as well as the

Summary of the peace settlements, 1919–23

The main issues	The Versailles Settlement, June 1919	The Eastern European, Balkan and Near East peace settlements
Problems Revolutionary condition of Europe Russian civil war Diverging Allied aims Competing nationalism Desire for revenge Hunger, disease, economic chaos Allied lack of military strength as a result of demobilization **Principles** Independence for subject nations International rule of law through the League of Nations Disarmament and reparation from defeated powers Determination to prove German war guilt Selective application of the 14 points	**Territorial changes** Independent Poland Plebiscites in Upper Silesia, Schleswig and West Prussia Alsace-Lorraine to France Saar administered by League of Nations Germany loses colonies and foreign investments **Reparations** Reparation Commission fixes amount of 132 milliard gold marks in May 1921 Prolonged struggle to force Germany to pay, 1921–3 France occupies Ruhr in Jan 1923 Dawes Commission Jan 1924 **Disarmament** Abolition of conscription Regular German army of 100,000 Very small fleet Allied Control Commissions in Germany until 1927 Rhineland occupied for 15 years **League of Nations** Collective security New principle of mandates Weakened by absence of USA Germany and defeated powers initially excluded	**St Germain** Czechoslovakia set up Slovenia, Bosnia, Dalmatia to Yugoslavia Istria, Trieste and S. Tyrol to Italy Galicia to Poland Austria not to integrate with Germany **Trianon** Hungary loses 2/3 of its pre-war territory to Austria, Czechoslovakia and Romania **Neuilly** Bulgaria loses territory to Greece, Romania and Yugoslavia **Sèvres** Turks cede Middle East empire; Greeks gain Thrace; Straits controlled by Allies Revised at Lausanne, 1923: Greeks expelled, Constantinople back to Turkey **Riga** Russia defeated by Poland, August 1920 Poland's eastern frontiers fixed by Treaty of Riga, March 1921

Source: Williamson, D. 2003. *War and Peace: International relations 1919–39*. 2nd edn. Tunbridge Wells, UK. Hodder Murray. p. 41.

fact that they had been given no real opportunity for discussion and were forced to sign it without any negotiation of the terms. This was a source of humiliation to Germany, who, as a Great Power, felt that it should have been treated with more consideration and not as a common criminal. The Germans could not accept what was seen as a **Diktat** and not as a genuine agreement.

The manner in which the treaty was presented and the statement of responsibility for the war were particularly resented. The reparations payments were objectionable, but perhaps more so were the territorial losses which saw the country divided into two parts. The denial of the principle of self-determination meant that ethnic Germans in Austria and Czechoslovakia could not become part of a greater German nation. Germany was excluded from the principle of self-determination, even though this was a pillar of Wilson's Fourteen Points, and had been applied to create other nations on the basis of their ethnic identities.

> **Diktat** The German term for the Treaty of Versailles which they were forced to sign without being allowed to negotiate any of the details. This was an important factor in the anti-Versailles resentment of later years.

This German embitterment is compounded by the fact that Germany did not see herself as a defeated nation in November 1918. She had defeated Russia and her territory had not been invaded or conquered by Allied troops. In fact, the German army was occupying land in France and Belgium when the war ended—not the normal situation for a defeated power. Germany's banishment from the League of Nations was seen in Germany as a further insult to her status as a Great Power and contrasted poorly with the treatment given to Napoleonic France at the Congress of Vienna in 1815.

The terms were so objectionable that no future German government could accept them, and how to react to the Treaty became a matter of prolonged and bitter dispute. The Treaty of Versailles was rejected by the German population who wanted to see it revoked or revised. The argument in Germany was not whether the treaty should be revised but exactly how to do this. The extremists such as Adolf Hitler took one approach while moderate nationalists such as Gustav Stresemann took another. Nevertheless, the objective of all groups was the same—to find ways for Germany to escape the burdens and restrictions imposed by the Treaty.

Debate and criticism among the Allies

In the Allied countries, a vigorous debate arose over the terms of the Treaty and to what extent they were too harsh, too lenient or had failed to bring about the peaceful world envisaged by those who had embraced the Fourteen Points so enthusiastically. The importance of this debate is reflected in how willing the Allies would be to enforce the Treaty in the years to come. It would have to be enforced, as the Germans refused to accept it as a legitimate agreement and would therefore be trying to escape its limits at every opportunity. If all of the Allies could not agree, then the future international co-operation needed to enforce the Treaty and operate the League of Nations would be in doubt.

The Allied criticism of the terms was first expressed by **John Maynard Keynes**, who wrote an attack on the Treaty as a **Carthaginian peace** based on a spirit of revenge, totally ignoring the economic consequences for Germany and Europe if the German economy were to be weakened by the Treaty. His view was that Europe would be poorer and more prone to another war as a result of the economic and territorial burdens placed on Germany. The Keynesian view has been disputed in recent years but at the time it helped form the basis of revisionist sentiment. As a result of his attack, people in Britain began to see the Treaty as unjust and were prepared to recognize the need for adjustments to the terms which were unfair to Germany. This view was reflected as early as March 1919 by the prime minister, David Lloyd George, in his Fontainebleau memorandum on the terms of the Treaty of Versailles.

JM Keynes A prominent British economist who wrote a book condemning the Versailles settlement as excessively punitive towards Germany and damaging to the recovery of European prosperity.

Carthaginian peace The extremely harsh treatment of a defeated power designed to permanently eliminate them as a future threat.

Reaction of the United States

The most important reaction to the terms of the Treaty may be that of the United States. The US senate refused to ratify it, based on their opposition to **Article X** of the League of Nations Covenant. This meant that the United States did not sign the Treaty of Versailles and therefore its role in the supervision and enforcement of the Treaty evaporated. This had enormous implications for the enforcement of the treaty and the success of the League of Nations.

Article X An article from the Covenant of the League under which members of the League agreed to use their power to resist aggression wherever it might occur. This is also known as the collective security clause.

The effect of the terms on Germany

Another significant aspect of the terms to consider is their actual effect on Germany. The short-term consequences may seem very severe, although there is historical debate on this point, and there is scope for further exploration as to how much Germany lost and to what extent her economy was damaged. It is important to understand the difference between the impacts of the First World War on the European economy and the impact of the Treaty of Versailles itself. Many of the problems would have occurred as a result of the collapse of empires, for example, regardless of the treaty.

In examining the treaties of St Germain, Trianon and the others, students may come to realize what many historians have noted: Germany was actually stronger after the war than before it. This somewhat surprising outcome is based on the realization that the disappearance of Austria–Hungary and the temporary collapse of Russia had altered the balance of power in the east. The new, small, weak states that had emerged on Germany's eastern border would not be able to restrain her if she chose to expand in that direction. The war and the Treaty had created a power vacuum that a revisionist Germany might be tempted to fill. These new states also contained unhappy minority groups, who would prove to be a source of internal dissension.

The Treaty of Rapallo

Another consequence of the terms of the Treaty of Versailles which saw Germany excluded from the League of Nations was the **Treaty of Rapallo** of 1922 between Germany and Soviet Russia. This allowed Germany to escape the disarmament clauses of the Treaty of Versailles and was a direct result not only of her resentment of the treaty but her exclusion, along with the Soviets, from the League. Her status as an outlaw further encouraged her to seek any means possible to evade the restrictions that had been placed on her.

Treaty of Rapallo A treaty signed in 1922 between Germany and the USSR. This was a treaty of mutual assistance that allowed the Germans to develop weapons in violation of the Versailles Treaty.

Source analysis

The following documents relate to the terms of the Paris settlements.

Source A

Comments on the terms of the Paris settlements

The year 1919 was the high watermark of democracy in world history … Still … "the war to end war" turned out to be the harbinger of even greater disaster. World War I had shown that the balance of power did not exist any longer … The failure to integrate Russia in some fashion into a European system created serious uncertainties … that the Paris settlement did not become a world settlement was also owing to the withdrawal of the United States from Woodrow Wilson's great design.

HAJO HOLBORN

The historian, with every justification, will come to the conclusion that we were very stupid men … We arrived determined that a Peace of justice and wisdom should be negotiated: we left it conscious that the Treaties imposed upon our enemies were neither just nor wise … the sanctimonious pharisaism [hypocritical self-righteousness of the authors] of the Treaties is their gravest fault.

HAROLD NICOLSON

The territorial settlement in Europe was by no means the wholesale, iniquitous, and cynical perversion of Wilson's principles of self-determination which has been pictured.

PAUL BIRDSALL

… this treaty ignores the economic solidarity of Europe, and by aiming at the economic life of Germany it threatens the health and prosperity of the Allies themselves … by making demands the execution of which is in the literal sense impossible, it stultifies itself and leaves Europe more unsettled than it found it.

JOHN MAYNARD KEYNES

Mr. Keynes … predicted that in the next thirty years, Germany could not possibly be expected to pay more than two milliard marks a year in reparation. In the six years preceding September 1939, Germany, by Hitler's showing, had spent each year on rearmament alone about seven times as much … Now … while the economic defects of that settlement were, for the most part, illusory or exaggerated, the present writer shares the opinion of those who have maintained that the political defects were the really decisive ones … to put it shortly, in the failure, and one might also say, in the deliberate failure, to establish a true balance of power.

ETIENNE MANTOUX

… it is by the territorial settlements in Europe that the Treaties of 1919 and 1920 will finally be judged … a fair judgment upon settlement, a simple explanation of how it arose, cannot leave the authors of the new map of Europe under serious reproach. To an overwhelming extent the wishes of the various populations prevailed.

WINSTON CHURCHILL

… the Peace Treaties have created juster conditions throughout Europe, and we are entitled to expect that the tension between States and races will decrease.

THOMAS MASARYK

The Peace Conference, representing the democracies, reflected the mind of the age; it could not rise measurably above its source. That mind was dominated by a reactionary nostalgia and a traditional nationalism … It was not so much the absence of justice from the Paris Peace Conference that caused the ultimate debacle; it was the failure to make the most of what justice there was.

CHARLES SEYMOUR

Source: Lederer, I. 1960. *The Versailles Settlement.* Boston, USA. Heath and Co. p. xi.

Source-based exercise

Take as your starting point any one of these statements, and provide an analysis of the point of view, and to what extent you agree with it. Refer to the terms of the treaties, along with the maps and statistics included in this chapter to support your argument.

Source B

German reactions to the Treaty of Versailles

"Bloodshed and tears".

Berlin, May 10

At the sitting of the Prussian Diet held on Thursday the Prime Minister, Herr Hirsch, in a speech on the Peace conditions, declared: In these conditions there is no trace of a peace of understanding and justice. It is purely a peace of violence which for our Fatherland is thinly-veiled slavery, and out of which will result not peace for the whole of Europe, but merely further bloodshed and tears.

Source: *The Times*, May 12, 1919, p. 14

Fritz Ernst recalls, in 1966, how he felt about the Treaty of Versailles in 1918:

In our high school in Stuttgart, as indeed in most of the secondary schools in Germany after 1918, there was a noticeable rightist trend, which most of the teachers followed … We believed it was a stab in the back that alone had prevented a German victory … We did not know what the actual situation of the war had been in 1918; we were taught to hate the French and British and to despise the Americans.

Erich Ludendorff's evidence to a Reichstag committee after the war:

> The war was now lost … After the way our troops on the Western Front had been used up, we had to count on being beaten back again and again. Our situation could only get worse, never better.

The reaction of a German newspaper, *Deutsche Zeitung*, in June 1919:

> Vengeance! German nation! Today in the Hall of Mirrors [in the Palace of Versailles] the disgraceful Treaty is being signed. Do not forget it. The German people will, with unceasing work, press forward to reconquer the place among nations to which it is entitled. Then will come vengeance for the shame of 1919.

Source: Radway, R. 2002. *Germany 1918–45.* London, UK. Hodder and Stoughton. p. 7.

Source C

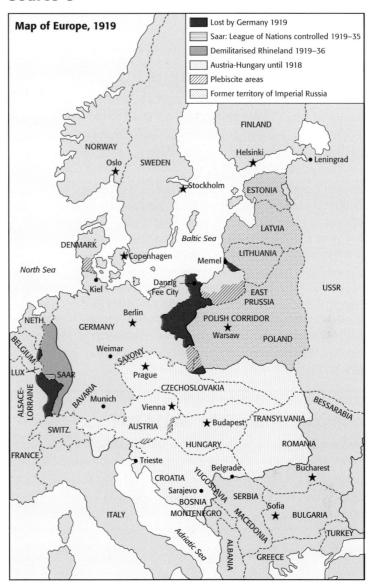

Map of Europe, 1919

Source: Darby, G. 2007. *Hitler, appeasement and the road to War.* 2nd edn. London, UK. Hodder Murray. p. 12.

Source-based questions

1 Identify the general German reaction to the Treaty, through analysis of sources B and C.

2 What evidence supports or refutes their attitudes?

TOK link

Do you agree with the statement of Kaiser Wilhelm II, that the "The war to end war has ended in a peace to end peace"?

Do the terms of the treaties reflect idealism or practical goals?

Self-determination and nationalism were supposed to encourage future peace. To what extent did this happen?

Discussion point:

Opinions of the Versailles settlement

Select three different historians' views on the Versailles settlement. Explain their position and provide evidence to support it.

With reference to the origin and purpose of each of these sources, discuss its value and limitations.

The impact of the treaties: Europe and the mandate system

The Paris settlements had a distinct impact on the geo-political and economic situation of Europe after the First World War. The geo-political impacts were the creation of a number of new states in Central and Eastern Europe and the redrawing of the frontiers of Germany and France. The economic impacts were the weakening of the German economy through territorial loss and reparations and the destruction of the free trade zone in Eastern and Central Europe which had existed before 1914.

Beyond Europe, in the colonies of the defeated powers, the main impact of Versailles was the establishment of the mandate system. This was an attempt to make imperialism more progressive. The system did not in fact work and it ended up being a thinly disguised way to add territory to the empires of the victorious powers.

It is crucial to understand what geo-political changes the treaties did not make. The Bolshevik Revolution, the political weakening of Britain and France, the power of the United States, war debts and general economic weakness, among other problems, were caused by the First World War, not by the treaties. It is easy to become confused as to what changes resulted from the war and which were created by the actions of the peacemakers at the Paris Peace Conference.

The impact of the First World War

The issues, attitudes and policies that developed during the period 1918–36 cannot be understood or appreciated without a sound knowledge of the experience and impact of the First World War on all those who participated in it. These experiences and impacts are often described as cataclysmic. To fully understand what that term means and the dimensions of those impacts on Western society, one must examine the experience of the war from a number of vantage points.

The war caused the deaths of millions of people—mostly in Europe and the Middle East. The dead were composed of soldiers and civilians who died from battle wounds, disease, starvation and ethnic conflict. What is most significant about these deaths is not only the sheer number but the manner in which they occurred. Soldiers on the Western Front died in millions in what can only be described as a strategic stalemate. After four years of war the battle lines had not shifted appreciably from the opening days of the war—the whole experience seemed to have been a futile orgy of mud and blood which had resolved nothing. This was a far cry from the romantic, chivalrous ideas of war that had existed in 1914 and that had seen huge crowds welcoming the onset of war as an opportunity for glory and adventure.

The collapse of these images had left a deep scar on the European psyche—optimism replaced by a deep pessimism reflected in a loss of faith in the values of the pre-war world, in the institutions and philosophies that had dominated the world before 1914. The number and manner of the deaths had left a huge scar. The introduction of new and terrible weapons of mass destruction such as poison gas, air bombardment of civilians and ever more powerful armaments had created a vision of even more destructive wars in the future. The prospect of another Armageddon-like experience terrified Europeans and caused them to search desperately for alternatives to war—any alternative no matter how unlikely in practice.

This fear of war was not only based on physical destruction. The war had destroyed so much else that was familiar. The confidence and optimism of Europeans about their levels of education, progress and an ever-improving world had been shattered. How could a society at the peak of human development have allowed itself to engage in so mindless and brutal a conflict? Everywhere one looked in 1918—one could see evidence of a shattered world.

The political landscape had altered spectacularly with the collapse of the Austro-Hungarian, Russian, German and Ottoman empires. A look at the map of Europe in 1914 and in 1919 gives some idea of the enormous political changes that had occurred. There were not only a myriad of new countries but they had new political systems. The monarchy was out; republicanism was in. Even more disturbing to some Europeans was the fact that they had lost the leadership of the world to the United States whose troops had rescued the exhausted European armies in 1918 and whose economy was now the largest in the world. Added to this was the fact that the hopes for a better world were centred on the person of US President Woodrow Wilson.

Revolutionary political ideology had burst onto the scene through the Bolshevik revolution in Russia. This was an event that would not have transpired without the pressures created by the First World War. This was not merely a political revolution but a philosophical one as well. Bolshevism challenged the very pillars of Western society: religion, property, family, democracy and individualism. What was worse— it was threatening to spread and engulf Europe in a tide of revolutionary violence and anarchy. The war had unleashed this monster and another war might see further destructive ideas emerge.

Other major changes had taken place due to the war. The social structure of Western society had been transformed. Women in Western countries had received the vote and their role in the war had guaranteed that they would continue to demand changes to social and economic structures that would satisfy their demands for equal treatment. The war had been a "total war" that had not only called for intense physical effort from all sectors of society but had placed great emotional demands on it as well. This was the first mass media war in which governments unleashed masses of propaganda to raise the emotional commitment to the war—anger, revenge, vilification of the enemy were all widely expressed sentiments used to maintain the flow of recruits to the killing fields and to sustain the sacrifices demanded of the civilian populations. This near-hysterical campaign to support the war had considerable consequences. The harsh aspects of the Versailles Treaty can be traced back in part to the promises of revenge on the enemy made by politicians during the war. The moderation and consideration shown at the Congress of Vienna in 1815 could not be replicated at Versailles when so much emotion and expectation had been created.

It is easy to be cynical about the chances of success for the League of Nations and to mock those who believed in them. But the experience of the First World War convinced Europeans that another war would see the end of civilization and that any chance to avoid it should be embraced uncritically.

It is understandable therefore to comprehend why people felt that entirely new ideas and methods to resolve conflicts would have to be found and that humanity should rely on reason rather than strength to resolve disputes and maintain peace. A sense of interdependence and mutual support rather than rivalry and conflict was the only way forward that offered a chance to avoid another war. This helps to explain the over-optimism of the 1920s and the reluctance to confront the dictators in the 1930s: compromise was better than the alternative.

Geo-political impacts of the treaties on Europe

The collapse of the Romanov, Hohenzollern and Hapsburg empires had allowed the creation of no fewer than ten successor states in Central and Eastern Europe and the Balkans. The Paris Peace Conference took on the task of defining the frontiers of these new states, ostensibly in accordance with the principle of self-determination—that countries should be established according to the wishes of the people concerned. This was a difficult problem as various nationalities did not always live in well-defined geographic areas but were scattered over a wide range of territories and/or intermingled with other racial or linguistic groups. This was the result of having lived in multinational empires in which people had some freedom to move around.

The most complex part of the problem was to create viable states in terms of economics, communications and security. It seemed logical that these states should be designed to be able to survive in the new world and this meant access to natural resources, trade routes, rivers and oceans. It is easy to see how this might complicate matters. Extending a country's borders to give it access to a trade route might mean incorporating some people from another ethnic group. This is clearly a violation of self-determination, but was judged necessary if the state were to be a viable economic entity.

There was no easy solution to this problem. Populations could have been relocated, but on humanitarian grounds as well as for more practical reasons this option was not taken up. The Allies asked the new nations to pledge to protect the rights of any minorities that remained within their borders. In addition to requiring a promise to protect minority rights, the peace conference provided a mechanism by which minorities could appeal to an international body for protection or redress. Minority groups could appeal to the League of Nations, which maintained a Minorities Commission—adjudication would be provided by the International Court of Justice. The effectiveness of these treaties varied greatly, but they were a step forward in emphasizing human rights.

The creation of these new states did not add to European stability but instead produced a number of small, vulnerable countries which often lacked political or economic stability. The manner in which they were constructed gave rise to internal tensions as well as

Activity:

The geo-political/ economic impact of the peace treaties

1 Wilson believed that self-determination would lessen the chance of war. To what extent do you agree with this statement?

2 Take the role of an official given the task of drawing the boundaries of the new states. Explain what considerations you used when drawing the boundaries of Poland, Hungary and Czechoslovakia.

ongoing disputes with neighbouring states. The factors that led to the design of these states were numerous and complicated: ethnic, linguistic, cultural, strategic and historical factors all played a role. In addition, the aims and expectations of the Allies influenced the decisions on the frontiers of the new states.

Self-determination meant that a common language and ethnic background should decide the nature of the state. In practice, this principle was violated in a number of cases, such as the South Tyrol, the **Polish Corridor** and the Sudetenland. There were also many cases where ethnic groups were so intermingled that it was impossible to separate them effectively. In practice this meant that about 30 million people ended up as minorities in other countries.

> **Polish Corridor** A strip of territory forming part of the new Polish state created in the Versailles settlements. This territory divided Germany into two parts and fuelled German hatred of Versailles and Poland.

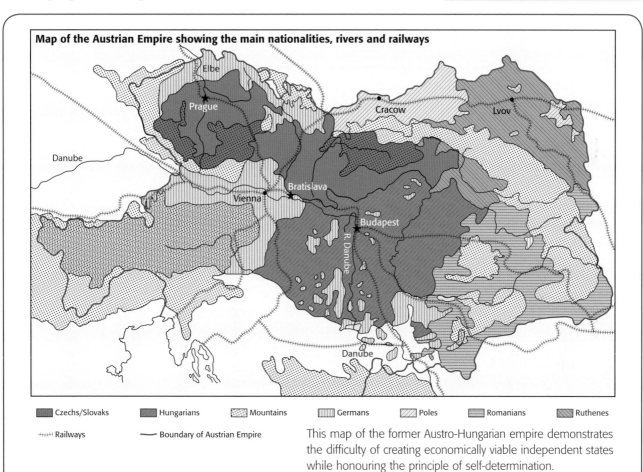

Map of the Austrian Empire showing the main nationalities, rivers and railways

Legend: Czechs/Slovaks | Hungarians | Mountains | Germans | Poles | Romanians | Ruthenes | Railways | Boundary of Austrian Empire

This map of the former Austro-Hungarian empire demonstrates the difficulty of creating economically viable independent states while honouring the principle of self-determination.

In place of Empires

When their arms were not being twisted by Italians, Poles, Czechs and Greeks, the Big Three tried to deal sensibly with the rest of Europe. The trouble was that the continent's problems were too knotty to be unravelled quickly and to every one's satisfaction.

The principle of national self-determination meant that new frontiers should be drawn according to the wishes of the peoples concerned. But the people of Central and Eastern Europe did not all live in tight compartments labelled "Polish", or "Czech" or "Hungarian" or "Italian". There were places in which a few people of one nationality (for example, Hungarians) dominated a majority of, say, Romanians. One man's idea of a part of Poland could very

well be another man's idea of a part of Czechoslovakia. There was also the question of whether the frontiers proposed for a new state made military and economic sense. Surely, whereever possible, a country should have access to the sea or to a major navigable river? Surely it made military sense to draw lines on the map along "natural" boundaries such as rivers and mountain ranges? But what if, for example, by granting Czechs or Slovaks access to the River Danube, you included in their new state lands where most of the people were Hungarian? What kind of self-determination would that be?

Source: Howarth, T. 1993. *Twentieth Century World History: The World since 1900*. London, UK. Longman. pp. 41–2.

The Allies had to make an assessment as to whether self-determination or economic/strategic viability should be the deciding factor in the design of the new states. There was little point to a nation being ethnically homogeneous if it could not survive. It was hoped that stable, democratic governments would be developed in these countries and it was realized that economic prosperity would be a key to this. It was this thinking that led to the creation of the Polish Corridor to give Poland access to the Baltic and the decision to make Danzig a free city to maximize opportunities for trade.

The problems for these new states began immediately. Their economic situation was particularly challenging. Before the First World War, the Austro-Hungarian Empire had been one economic unit. After the war this was destroyed and replaced by a group of small, fragile economic units scrambling to survive, erecting trade barriers and interrupting the normal flow of commerce that had existed for centuries. This is a problem that might have been addressed by the peace conference, as it was clearly not in keeping with the spirit of the third of the Fourteen Points which supported the removal of trade barriers.

Serious disputes broke out between those states which had lost key industries or access to resources. An example would be the dispute between Poland and Czechoslovakia over the Teschen area, which had large coal reserves and strategic rail connections.

The lack of economic and diplomatic co-operation among the new states not only made them prone to hostilities with each other but also rendered them weak and vulnerable to the territorial ambitions of either Germany or Russia in the future. Both of these were determined to revise the verdict of the First World War and the new small states would prove tempting targets. Their inability to work together to prevent the danger posed by Russia and Germany made their survival doubtful in the face of a strengthened USSR and Germany.

German empowerment

The Treaty of Versailles—with all of the provisions designed to blame Germany for the war, to reduce her territory, to confiscate her colonies, to limit her military and to collect reparations—was deeply resented in all parts of German society. The humiliation of having to sign the treaty without benefit of any negotiation only heightened the sense of anger and humiliation felt by the vast majority of the German population.

The territorial terms meant that Germany lost 12 per cent of her population and 13 per cent of her pre-war territory. The most significant losses were Alsace-Lorraine, which was returned to France, and the territory taken to create the Polish Corridor, which divided Germany in two. A further humiliation was that Germans were not permitted to participate in the process of self-determination as the Allies forbade the incorporation of Germans outside Germany, in Austria and Czechoslovakia, into the Weimar Republic.

These losses and the sense of injustice felt by many Germans meant that they were determined to seek a revision of the treaty at the earliest opportunity. The fact that the countries on her eastern border were weak and, in fact, represented a power vacuum would prove a powerful temptation for Germany when she had recovered her strength. The irony of the First World War was that although Germany had been defeated, she was actually in a stronger position than she had been before the war, particularly in the east. The Great Powers that might have restrained her were gone, replaced by a power vacuum.

Soviet revisionism

A significant development at this time, not created by the Treaty of Versailles, was the emergence of the Bolshevik regime in Russia. Immediately after the war, Russia was weakened by the effects of political revolution and civil war. As such, she did not pose an immediate threat to the new states of Eastern Europe which might be seen as a buffer against the spread of Bolshevism virus. In fact, Russia had been defeated in a war with Poland and had lost considerable territory as a result. When Russia recovered her strength, however, she, like Germany, would very likely seek a revision of the verdict of the First World War and her target would be the newly created states. Their weakness and inability to co-operate with each other would make them a target for Soviet revisionism.

The new states and their relationship with Germany and Russia was a little like the old saying "while the cat's away, the mice will play". When the cats returned, however, the mice would be in dire straits. Any doubt about the hostility of Germany and Russia to the new states was erased by their co-operation in the Treaty of Rapallo in 1922. This treaty, which would serve to undermine the restrictions of Versailles and restore the strength of these two nations, made it clear that they were determined to revise the territorial arrangements of Versailles.

The Little Entente, 1921

A number of the new states, Czechoslovakia, Yugoslavia and Romania, were aware of their vulnerability and formed the **Little Entente** in 1921. Its original intention was to protect them from the **irredentist** claims of Hungary, which was angry about the territorial losses that she had suffered through the treaties. The Little Entente was a model of co-operation, particularly military and economic, among its members. If it had expanded, it might well have strengthened the whole region and made it less vulnerable to the revisionist ambitions of Germany and Russia. However, as will be seen, rivalry and hostility among other new states prevented this development.

The alliance was supported by France, which was seeking a counterweight to the possibility of a German resurgence. The loss of Russia as an ally had forced the French to seek another way to balance German power and discourage their aggression by creating the prospect of a two-front war. In line with this policy, France made an alliance with Poland in 1921.

Poland was the most powerful of the new states and would have been an important addition to the Little Entente, but her ongoing hostility towards Czechoslovakia over **Teschen** made this impossible. This was an example of how the disputes which occurred when the new states were formed made it difficult for them to co-operate for their mutual benefit or protection.

Little Entente An alliance of Czechoslovakia, Yugoslavia and Romania in 1921 to safeguard their new independence from other central European states such as Bulgaria and Poland. France tried to develop this into a counter-balance to German power.

Irredentism A desire to recover former territory.

Teschen was an area of rich mineral resources claimed by both Poland and Czechoslovakia. They had engaged in hostilities over it in 1918. This dispute poisoned the relationship between the two countries throughout the inter-war period.

Source analysis

The following documents relate to Russia and Germany and the Treaty of Rapallo.

Source A
Weimar attitudes towards Soviet Russia

Dr Walter Simon, Foreign Minister of the Weimar Republic, in a speech to the Reichstag, 26 July 1920.

I am not as worried about Eastern developments as perhaps many of you are. I came to know Chicherin at Brest-Litovsk and I regard him as an unusually clever man. I do not believe it is in the interest of the Soviet Republic to overrun Germany with murdering and burning hordes. What the Soviet Republic needs is economic aid. It has robbed itself of a large part of its economic strength by an excessive emphasis on the Soviet idea which would have made the reconstruction of the ruined economic system possible. I do not belong among those who see nothing but chaos in Russia. I know from reports of independent and knowledgeable men that a truly enormous creative work has been accomplished, a work which in many respects we could do well to take as an example. I am prepared and willing to give you the evidence.

Source B
Treaty of Rapallo

Extract from the Treaty of Rapallo, 16 April 1922.

Article 1

(a) The German Reich and the Russian Socialist Federal Republic mutually agree to waive their claims for compensation for expenditure incurred on account of the war, and also for war damages, that is to say, any damages … on account of military measures, including all reparations in enemy country. Both parties likewise agree to forgo compensation for any civilian damages. …

b) The public and private legal relations between the two states … will be settled on the basis of reciprocity.

Article 3 Diplomatic and consular relations will immediately be resumed. …

Article 4 Both Governments have furthermore agreed that … the general regulations of mutual, commercial and economic relations shall be effected on the principle of the most favoured nations. …

Article 5 The two Governments shall co-operate in a spirit of mutual goodwill in meeting the economic needs of both countries. … The German Government, having lately been informed of the proposed agreements of private firms, declares its readiness to give all possible support to these arrangements.

Source C
Soviet reassurance to France over the Treaty of Rapallo

Extract from a letter from Chicherin to the French foreign minister on the Treaty of Rapallo, 29 April 1922.

In the statements of French Government leaders, the treaty between Germany and Russia … signed at Rapallo is regarded as an act directed against French interests. The assumption has frequently been made that secret clauses of a military and political character … are attached to the treaty of Rapallo.

The Russian Delegation declare in the most categorical terms that the Treaty of Rapallo does not contain a single secret clause, military or political, and that the Russian Government is not a party to any act the operation of which is directed against the interests of France or of any other nation.

The Treaty of Rapallo has no other object than the settlement of questions which have accumulated between two States which were at war with one another and which feel the mutual necessity of re-establishing peaceful relations …

In this respect, Russia's policy remains unchanged, notwithstanding the hostility which France has thought it necessary to show in regard to Russia in the last four years.

Source D
German proposals to partition Poland after Rapallo

General von Seeckt, in proposals to Reichswehr leaders, 11 September 1922.

Poland's existence is intolerable, incompatible with the survival of Germany. It must disappear, and it will disappear through its own internal weakness and through Russia—with our assistance. For Russia, Poland is even more intolerable than for us; no Russian can allow Poland to exist … Poland can never offer any advantages to Germany, either economically, because it is incapable of any development, or politically, because it is France's vassal. The re-establishment of the broad common frontier between Russia and Germany is the precondition for the regaining of strength of both countries …

We aim at two things: first, a strengthening of Russia in the economic and political, thus also in the military field, and so indirectly a strengthening of ourselves, by strengthening a possible ally of the future … and by helping to create in Russia an armaments industry which in case of need will serve us.

Source E

The shape of the future in the Treaty of Rapallo

The revisionist powers were not only deficient in force, but separated by differences of policy, interest and outlook too wide to permit of the formation of an opposing group. But there were dangerous possibilities for the future. The normal tendency towards a reversal of combinations after a great war in itself suggested an ultimate rapprochement between Russia, Germany and Italy: the first two had fluttered the dovecotes of Europe as early as 1922 by the conclusion of the Treaty of Rapallo, whilst the opposition between France and Italy was becoming increasingly acute, and the dissatisfaction of the latter at her treatment during the Peace Conference tended inevitably to bring her into the revisionist camp. With each reconciliation of existing differences between these three Powers, and with the ultimately inevitable recovery of Germany, a situation could therefore be seen approaching in which the worst features of the pre-war system might easily be reproduced.

Source: Rayner, EG. 1992. *The Great Dictators*. London, UK. Hodder and Stoughton Murray, pp. 12–15.

Source-based questions

1 a Identify the reasons given in Source A why the USSR is not a danger to Germany.

   b What is the author's purpose?

2 Compare and contrast the reasons for signing the Treaty given in Sources A, B and D.

3 With reference to their origin and purpose, evaluate the value and limitation of Sources C and D for a historian studying the Rapallo treaty.

4 Using these documents and your own knowledge, explain the impact of Rapallo on the geo-political settlement created at Versailles.

Economic impacts

In economic terms, the Treaty of Versailles affected the European economic situation more by what it did not do than by what it did. It did not deal with any economic question directly except that of reparations. Most critically, it failed to deal with the issue of Allied war debts. This created bad relations among the debtor nations and the United States for many years and contributed to general economic instability as nations struggled to pay off their loans. The debt issue created pressures which contributed to the **Ruhr** Crisis in Germany and the poisoning of relations between France and Britain. A number of international conferences tried to resolve the debt issue as a means of alleviating tensions over reparations and assisting in economic recovery. They were all unsuccessful, as the United States refused to cancel the debts of its Allies, thus weakening their recovery and forcing them to continue to demand reparations from Germany. The irony is that the United States was compelled to offer financial aid to Germany through the **Dawes Plan** in the aftermath of the Ruhr Crisis. This might have been averted to some extent if they had addressed the Allied debt issue earlier.

The economic terms of the Treaty were condemned by JM Keynes, who argued that demanding high reparations from Germany, along with the loss of territory and resources, was a foolish decision. It would hurt all of Europe as it would prevent the recovery of Germany, which was the economic engine of Europe. The Allies, in punishing Germany, were only punishing themselves. The Keynes view has been challenged by other historians but it had considerable support in the post-war period and contributed to the call for the revision of the Treaty. Considerable sympathy developed in Britain and the United States for German requests to revise the

> **Ruhr** The centre of German heavy industry. It was occupied by France and Belgium in 1923 to force Germany to pay reparations.

> **Dawes Plan** This was created by the United States in order to restore economic and political stability to Germany. America would lend money to Germany to rebuild industry and pay her reparations to Britain and France.

treaty and the reparations payments. This led to a serious rift between the UK and France over the treatment of Germany.

The Treaty also failed to develop any effective organization to promote and ensure international trade, particularly among the newly created European states. This failure to develop stronger trading links would add to the catastrophic impact of the Great Depression of 1929.

The establishment and impact of the mandate system

Many people believed that colonial disputes had been a major cause of the First World War. Woodrow Wilson addressed this concern in the fifth of the Fourteen Points, which proposed:

> a free, open-minded and absolutely impartial adjustment of all colonial claims, based upon a strict observance of the principle that in determining all such questions of sovereignty the interests of the populations concerned must have equal weight with the equitable claims of the government whose title is to be determined.

Liberal opinion in Europe and America as personified by Wilson would not permit the victors simply to annex the colonies of Germany and the Ottoman Empire.

This meant that instead of merely distributing the colonies of the defeated powers as spoils of war, the decision was to create the mandatory system to administer them. The administration of these territories would be supervised by the League of Nations. The mandates were given to the countries which had conquered them from the Germans and Ottomans in accordance with Article 22 of the League Covenant. This states that the purpose of the mandate system was the well-being and development of the people in these territories. The League was also charged with ensuring that slavery did not occur in these territories and that an open door for trade would be maintained. The proponents of this system saw it as a vehicle to educate and improve colonial populations, with the intention of the territories becoming independent democratic states.

The territories were divided into three classes of mandate, depending on their degree of development and how soon they would be ready for independent status:

- The "A mandates" were those countries which would be ready for independence in the very near future. These comprised the former Ottoman states in the Middle East: Lebanon, Syria, Palestine, Transjordan and Iraq
- The "B mandates" were less advanced and had no immediate prospects for independence. These comprised the German colonies in Africa, which were divided between France, Britain and Belgium
- The "C mandates" were thinly populated and economically underdeveloped. They were handed over directly to the nations that had conquered them. This meant that German possessions in the Pacific were distributed between Japan, Australia and New Zealand. Southwest Africa was given to South Africa.

The mandate system was devised in Paris but the actual decisions on how to divide German territory had been made prior to the conference. Documents such as the Sykes–Picot Agreement between the United Kingdom and France in 1916 had divided the Ottoman possessions between these two powers.

The mandate system seems like a thinly disguised form of territorial annexation. The Japanese in particular annexed and fortified their Pacific island mandates, in clear violation of the terms of the mandate agreement. The impact on the people in the territories was minimal and they were treated in the same way as other colonial populations. Racial equality and progress toward independence were discussed, but little or no real effect was given to these concepts. However, it should be noted that, for the first time, a system of accountability was introduced. This created the idea that colonial powers had specific responsibilities to their subject peoples and that their actions could be scrutinized by an international body.

The allocation of mandates gave rise to a number of controversies. The majority of the mandates went to the UK and France, victors in the war and already in possession of the world's largest empires. This was particularly galling to the Germans, who lost everything, and the Italians, who received nothing despite being on the winning side. This lent support to the nationalist movements led by Mussolini and contributed to Italy's determination to acquire territory outside Europe.

Another major area of controversy caused by the mandate system was the Middle East. The Arabs in the Middle East who had helped the UK defeat the Ottoman Empire had hoped for land and independent status. The British and French, however, had already decided to divide the area between them according to the Sykes–Picot Agreement. Their use of the mandate system gave them control of the Middle East after the war—control that was sanctioned through the League of Nations. This infuriated the Arab population and led to a number of uprisings in the post-war period against both the British and the French.

A further controversy was created by the British decision to proceed with the Balfour Declaration of 1917, which had given British support for a national homeland for the Jews in Palestine.

 What was different about the mandate system in comparison to previous wars, following which the victors simply annexed the territory of the losers?

Source: Catchpole, B. 1983. *A Map History of the Modern World*. Toronto, Canada. Irwin. p. 33.

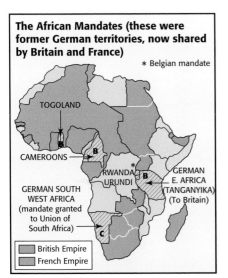

The African Mandates (these were former German territories, now shared by Britain and France)

The Middle East Mandates (These were former possessions of the Ottoman Empire of Turkey shared by Britain and France)

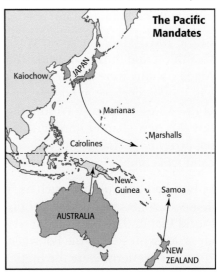

The Pacific Mandates

Enforcement of the terms of the treaties

The lack of enforcement of the Treaty of Versailles raised as many questions as the terms themselves. The United Kingdom and the United States showed little enthusiasm for the Treaty after it was signed and consequently had little desire to enforce its provisions. They were influenced by their traditional isolationism and the fact that revisionist views of the Treaty's harshness were already circulating. Consequently, the French lost the much desired Anglo-American Guarantee and were left to try and enforce the Treaty alone—beyond their ability. The failure of enforcement allowed Germany to begin to evade the Treaty and plan its overthrow at the earliest possible moment.

The disarmament conferences that were organized after the war in the spirit of the Fourteen Points were largely unsuccessful due to a lack of co-operation and a failure to resolve the issues that supported expanded arms programs, particularly in the 1930s.

US isolationism

The roots of US isolationism run very deeply in the American tradition. They go back to the time of George Washington's presidency, when he counselled the nations to avoid foreign entanglements, and to the advice of Thomas Paine who wrote that Europe was too thickly planted with kingdoms to be long at peace. Over the years many people had come to the United States of America to escape Europe and its conflicts. The physical separation of North America from Europe had created an enormous psychological barrier as well. Part of the American ideology was that it was a better society than the European states, and should remain aloof and uncorrupted. The United States had a hemispheric mentality, as demonstrated by the **Monroe Doctrine** and her ideas of Manifest Destiny. The purpose of these was to give control of the western hemisphere to the United States but to exclude all foreign influences as far as possible. In addition, the United States did not maintain large armed forces in peacetime and showed little inclination to intervene outside its own areas of interest.

At the end of the First World War, the United States was the wealthiest and most powerful economic entity in the world. All Allied nations were in debt to her financially and her armed forces had proven decisive in ending the war on the western front in favour of the Allies. Woodrow Wilson, the president of the United States, saw this new chapter in American intervention as providing an opportunity to change the way in which international relations were conducted and to prevent further wars.

Wilson had used phrases such as "making the world safe for democracy" as rallying cries for his country's involvement in the First World War and he now sought to make such sentiments a reality. His ideas, as expressed in the Fourteen Points and in the concept of a League of Nations, were the methods that he thought would inspire

The Monroe Doctrine was an attempt to prevent any foreign presence in the western hemisphere beyond that already established by 1823 when the doctrine was announced. In later years it was extended to give the United States the right to interfere in the internal affairs of nations in the Western hemisphere.

and create a new international order. American involvement would be critical and would allow the United States to become the leader in the creation of a new, more peaceful and progressive system of international relations. This would be very much in line with American views of themselves as a utopian society acting as an inspiration to the rest of the world.

However, in spite of a massive effort to promote the League of Nations and the Treaty of Versailles, the United States did not ratify (formally accept) the Treaty and, therefore, did not join the League. The effort at ratification, and the stress and fatigue involved in the campaign, cost Wilson his life. The reasons for the failure of his efforts are reflected in the comments of Margaret MacMillan:

> The Americans had a complicated attitude towards the Europeans: a mixture of admiration for their past accomplishments, a conviction that the allies would have been lost without the United States and a suspicion that, if the Americans were not careful, the wily Europeans would pull them into their toils again.
>
> Macmillan, M. 2001. *Paris 1919*. London, UK. Murray. p. 14.

The US Congress could not reach agreement on the Treaty and the Covenant of the League. The Treaty would have required that the US Senate vote in favour by a two-thirds majority and this proved impossible to achieve. There was no consensus on America's role in the world. Some individuals wanted the United States to return to a traditional policy of isolation and do no more than act as beacon of liberty and progress. Others believed that the United States had a responsibility to participate in world affairs and help to influence their direction in the future. But they could not accept the Covenant of the League of Nations and, specifically, Article X, which would have compelled the United States to take part in matters in which she had no interest.

The other aspect is that the ratification of the treaty became a matter of political partisanship within the United States between Democrats and Republicans, with Wilson being opposed by the Republican leader of the Senate, Henry Cabot Lodge. The Republicans had not been included in the Versailles delegation and this partisan behaviour by Wilson may have doomed his efforts, as he remained adamant and unwilling to compromise with his political rivals on the terms of the Treaty. The result of the failure to ratify was that the United States did not become a member of the League of Nations. In addition, the United States did not ratify the **Anglo-American Guarantee**, made to ensure French security in case of a German attack. These decisions, along with the election of a Republican, Warren Harding, as president in 1921, whose slogan was a "return to normalcy", signalled that the United States was returning to its traditional policy of isolationism.

Anglo-American Guarantee
A treaty proposed after the First World War in which the United States and Britain would guarantee to defend France against German aggression. It was not ratified by the United States Senate and thus never came into force.

The Anglo-American Guarantee
The Versailles Conference had encountered several roadblocks in reaching a settlement with respect to Germany because of the rigid views of France. The French were obsessed with their future security against another German attack and were proposing a partial dismemberment of Germany in order to achieve this. Specifically, the

French wished to detach the Rhineland area from Germany and create an independent state that would be neutral and/or under French influence.

Wilson could not support the French position and neither could Lloyd George, but they realized that the French would stand firm unless they received a firm guarantee of military support from the USA and the UK in the event of German attack. On 28 June 1919, the Anglo-French agreement was signed. Both countries pledged to come to the aid of France if she were attacked by Germany. This agreement was not in sympathy with Wilson's views that such guarantees would be unnecessary as a result of the creation of the League, but he had no choice as the French would have created great difficulties in other areas if the issue had not been resolved. Unfortunately for France, the Anglo-American Guarantee that they had sought was never ratified by the US Senate and thus never came into force. As a result of the US failure to ratify, the British also withdrew from any military commitment to France.

British isolationism

This British action should be understood in light of traditional British foreign policy. The British through their history were also isolationists, who avoided firm commitments to other nations, particularly in peacetime. This was not the same type of isolationism as practised by the United States but rather was an active isolationism. The British were ready to intervene in European affairs but wanted to retain their freedom of action to intervene elsewhere when and where they felt best suited their needs. British policy was always to intervene against any power seeking the hegemony (dominance) of Europe and as such they refused to tie themselves to any one country or group of countries.

There was a fear in the UK after the war that France might try to achieve dominance in Europe. There was also a reluctance to support France as she might become embroiled in a war with Germany. The likeliness of this was due to French support of Poland and the countries of the Little Entente, who might find themselves in conflict with a revisionist Germany. The sense that Germany had been too harshly treated at Versailles was growing and the British were not prepared to go to war to defend an unfair settlement or place herself in a position where she might have to defend an unpopular treaty.

Furthermore, the United Kingdom—similar to many other countries after the First World War—wanted to limit the chance that she would be involved in any kind of conflict. The prospect was simply unacceptable to the population after the horrors of the war.

 What are the implications of the cancellation of the Anglo-American Guarantee to the enforcement of the Treaty of Versailles?

Discussion point:

Could the Anglo-American Guarantee have prevented another war?

Explain the most important historical reasons for US isolationism.

Activity:

Debate on the Treaty of Versailles

1   Conduct a debate on the Treaty of Versailles that pits the position of Wilson against his opponents.

2   Conduct a debate on the resolution that "A peaceful post-war world depended entirely on the continued involvement of the USA in world affairs and organizations."

IB Learner Profile link

Principled

There are differences in the way nations and individuals see their role and responsibility in the world. What encourages us to intervene in international crises?

 What are the motives that encourage either individuals or nations to make sacrifices in defence of a principle or to correct a wrong?

Consider the following questions:

● Why was it possible for American idealists to reject the Paris settlements?

● What human motives might be involved in the decisions to support or reject the Treaty of Versailles?

● Do nations always base their actions on self-interest? Do individuals?

Disarmament

The Washington Naval Conference and the Far East

The arms race had been identified as one of the major contributors to the outbreak of the First World War and as such was targeted by Wilson in the Fourteen Points. It was a goal of the Paris settlements and the League of Nations that progress be made towards reducing armaments to limit the threat of war. Ironically it was the United States who did not sign the Versailles treaty and who did not join the League that organized the most successful disarmament conference of the post-war period.

After the First World War, the arms race continued in the naval arena, as the United States, United Kingdom and Japan were investing large sums of money to expand their fleets. This naval race had been caused by a combination of the American desire to have a "fleet second to none", the British tradition of having the world's largest fleet as a matter of security and the Japanese desire to defend herself and her new empire and to increase her international stature and prestige.

The decision to call a conference to address the naval arms race was based on two major issues: the cost of the arms race which neither the UK nor Japan could afford and an American desire to spend less on arms according to her traditional policy. The other major factor for the conference to address was the need to defuse the increasing tension between Japan and the USA in Asia and the prospect that this might become a major conflict involving other countries.

Japan and the United States had been suspicious of each other's intentions in China and the Far East for a number of years and the situation had become more difficult after the war, as the Japanese had expanded their territory and sought to further dominate China, to the possible exclusion of other countries and their trade relations. The loss of trade and the possible threat to US possessions in the Philippines were issues that were increasing tensions and the talk of war between the two was becoming more common. Japan felt threatened by the US naval build-up and the reluctance of the United States to recognize her position in Asia.

This was of particular concern to the UK, who had had a defensive alliance with Japan since 1902 and who might find herself dragged into a USA–Japan war on the side of Japan. Such a prospect, while seeming remote, was enough to encourage the UK to support the naval disarmament conference and a resolution of tensions in the Far East. In addition, the UK was under pressure from Canada and Australia to end the Anglo-Japanese Alliance in order to avoid a confrontation with America.

The Washington Conference (1921–2) was the most successful of the post-war disarmament conferences, though its successes were limited and not permanent. That is typical of all post-war disarmament conferences, which produced very limited and usually short-term results. The most critical point to make about disarmament conferences is that they cannot succeed in a vacuum. The reasons for arms races have to be addressed before disarmament can take place. In a world where many nations had grievances or territorial ambitions and distrusted their neighbours, disarmament would have little chance of making progress. Many nations—for example, Germany, Russia, Japan, Italy—would see rearmament as the only way to redress their grievances. Believing that disarmament could take place under such circumstances was probably foolish and may have encouraged aggression rather than prevented it.

 What issues would have had to be resolved in order to make disarmament a possibility?

The Washington agreements

The most important agreement was the decision to limit the size and number of the battleships in their fleets as well as limiting the size of cruisers and aircraft carriers. Of particular importance was the fact that they agreed to maintain a constant ratio of naval armament for the USA, UK and Japan of 5:5:3. All nations were to destroy battleships until the maximum fleet size permitted was reached. In addition, no new battleships were to be constructed for ten years. The agreement also limited the construction of bases in the Pacific, which succeeded in reducing the possibility of conflict and gave Japan dominant influence in the eastern Pacific as neither the USA nor the UK could establish new bases there.

The success of the conference was that it did result in the destruction of weapons and place limits on future armament. It was a beginning to the process of further disarmament negotiations which would cover other types of weapons.

The weapons reduction took place because the underlying political issues that had spurred the arms race were also settled. Two agreements were signed—the Four Power Agreement and the Nine Power Agreement—which were designed to reduce tensions in the Far East and limit the possibility of conflict.

- The Four Power Agreement involved the USA, Japan, the United Kingdom and France. This agreement replaced the Anglo-Japanese Alliance and guaranteed the rights of all the signatories to their possessions in Asia. They agreed to defend each other in the event of external attack.
- The Nine Power Agreement confirmed the Open Door for trade in China and guaranteed its territorial integrity. This agreement collapsed with the Japanese invasion of Manchuria in 1931.

The conference was not perfect but was embraced by the public as an example of progress towards peace and by the nations concerned as they all achieved some benefit, strategic and/or financial.

The United Kingdom avoided a ruinous naval race that it could not afford after the First World War but which the British had felt compelled to enter, with serious implications for her domestic economy. The UK also dissolved the Anglo-Japanese Alliance, thus removing a source of friction with the United States. This was done without giving offence to Japan, who had been very attached to the alliance and might have reacted badly to a British desire to end it.

Japan, although seemingly irritated by the fact that she had a smaller fleet than the USA or the UK, actually benefited the most from the conference. The Japanese avoided an expensive naval race but gained tremendous security as no new American or British bases could be established within 3000 miles (4800 km) of Japan's borders. This gave her complete control of the eastern Pacific and China in the event of any future disputes.

The United States was able to reduce armaments spending, in line with the decision to retreat into isolation, and was able to reduce the possibilities of friction in the Pacific at least for the immediate future.

These agreements depended entirely on the co-operation of the parties involved, as they lacked any enforcement provisions. They were successful because the nations involved all felt that they had achieved a positive result and because the small number of participants made it easier to reach agreement. The timing was also beneficial as there was great public interest and support for the cause of disarmament in the years immediately following the First World War. The agreements were very vaguely worded and might easily be ignored if one or more nations found themselves in changed circumstances where the agreements no longer served their best interests. This situation would occur in the case of Japan's invasion of Manchuria in 1931.

An important point to note is that the agreements failed to include two major powers: Germany and Russia. Both these nations would be interested in increasing their armaments and military strength in the future, which would prove a challenge to the entire concept of disarmament.

The London Naval Conference

The London Naval Conference of 1930 was the third in a series of meetings whose purpose was to reduce the naval armaments of the major powers. The first meeting had been the Washington Conference in 1921, which had limited the number and size of capital ships. Another conference in Geneva in 1927 had proved unable to reach an agreement. In 1930 the five major naval powers—the USA, the UK, Japan, Italy and France—met in London to revise and extend the agreement reached in 1922 in Washington.

This treaty made minor revisions to the ratio of capital ships established at Washington, moving from 5:5:3 for the USA, the UK and Japan to 10:10:7. France and Italy refused to take part in this new agreement; however, they agreed to continue the ban on building capital ships for five years. Other agreements were reached on the size and number of cruisers, destroyers and submarines that each nation could possess. In addition, the rules regarding submarine warfare were tightened and required that submarines could not sink ships unless the crew and passengers had been removed to a place of safety. The treaty was to remain in effect until 1936.

The success of the London treaty must be seen against the backdrop of the Great Depression, when governments were looking for ways to cut expenditures in the face of falling tax revenues. There was little enthusiasm for spending money on armaments in a time of domestic economic hardship. This was especially true in the democracies, where defence spending was unpopular compared to domestic relief programmes. Therefore it was easy to agree to limit armaments despite the strategic objections of the professional naval officers.

The London Naval Treaty, 1936

In 1935 the major powers met to renegotiate the London treaty of 1930, which was due to expire in 1936. The conference was a failure—the Japanese walked out, as did the Italians. Japan did not wish to submit to limits on her naval construction and demanded equal tonnage with the United Kingdom and the United States. The UK, France and the USA signed a treaty in 1936 with respect to cruiser tonnage but all agreements on limiting the number and size of warships collapsed after 1936 in view of the Japanese and German rearmament programs and the increasing number of crises and conflicts in the world.

The Geneva Disarmament Conference, 1932–4

The Paris Peace Settlement had limited armaments for Germany and her allies during the First World War. Wilson's Fourteen Points had supported a move to general disarmament as a goal for the post-war world. Public support for disarmament was encouraged by a number of factors:

- the idea of collective security and the League of Nations that would ensure a more peaceful world and reduce the need for extensive armaments
- a belief that arms races in various forms had been a major cause of the war and that reducing arms would reduce the chance of another war

 Were there any threats to peace that might have disrupted the possibility of disarmament discussions being successful?

 Why was there continued support for disarmament in the democracies?

- the sheer cost of arms at a time when nations were struggling to recover from the economic dislocation of the war. This made arms reduction programs attractive, economically and politically, especially in the democracies, and was particularly true after the onset of the Great Depression in 1929
- the impression after the relatively peaceful 1920s that the risk of war had been greatly reduced and that large military establishments were no longer necessary. The optimism of the Locarno Pact and the Kellogg–Briand Agreement served to support this general viewpoint.
- The League of Nations was to promote the cause of world disarmament as part of its mandate to maintain peace. The League began to prepare for a world disarmament conference, which was convened in Geneva in 1932. Thirty-one nations attended, including the USA and the USSR, who were not members of the League.

Problems for the Geneva conference

By 1932 a number of crises had occurred, as well as increasing demands to revise the Paris peace settlements. The onset of the Depression had reduced the atmosphere of optimism and international co-operation that had existed in the 1920s and replaced it with narrower, nationalistic attitudes. Nations which were fearful of their own security or who were under pressure to revise treaties would be less likely to subscribe enthusiastically to a program of general disarmament.

Another big issue was the problem of distinguishing between offensive and defensive weapons. The United States had called for the elimination of offensive weapons as a way to make all nations feel secure. The disagreement over what constituted an offensive as opposed to a defensive weapon led to many frustrating and inconclusive debates, which helped to undermine the conference. In addition, whatever decisions it made, the conference had no enforcement mechanism and no organization to oversee compliance. The difficulties of enforcing disarmament should be obvious when one considers that, as early as 1922, Germany was evading the disarmament provisions of the Treaty of Versailles through the Rapallo Treaty with Russia.

Another problem for the conference resulted from a simple but often overlooked political fact: disarmament would not proceed unless all nations felt secure in reducing their armaments. In this case, France was unwilling to reduce her military spending without a firm guarantee of support and protection from the other major powers. The United Kingdom and others were unwilling to give such a guarantee and therefore the French refused to consider arms reductions, particularly in the face of a resurgent Germany.

Germany used the conference as an opportunity to expose the hypocrisy of the other countries. Either the other countries should disarm to the German level, as outlined in the Treaty of Versailles, or Germany should be allowed to expand her forces to match theirs. Germany, in the absence of any support for these proposals, withdrew from the Geneva conference in July 1932.

After a strenuous diplomatic effort, Germany rejoined the conference in 1933, but Adolf Hitler was now chancellor of Germany. He repeated Germany's demand for equal treatment and, when this was not forthcoming, he withdrew from the conference and then from the League itself. Hitler had no interest in disarmament, but the unwillingness of the powers to give Germany equal treatment gave him an excuse to embark on his own rearmament scheme. This made the French look unco-operative, as they had proven unwilling to consider arms reduction though in fact they had little choice in the absence of any support from Britain and the United States.

Italy was also not interested in reducing its armed force in light of its imperial ambitions. Benito Mussolini, the Italian dictator, tried to divert the work of the conference to a Four Power Agreement involving the UK, Italy, France and Germany. This group would carry out peaceful revisions of the treaties, would make Germany an equal partner and would resemble Locarno as a means of negotiating between France and Germany. The pact was never ratified because of French objections but it showed a move away from the League to a Concert of Europe model.

The disarmament conference broke up without reaching any agreement. It was clear that Europe was entering a period of increased tension and that nations were going to have to consider what would be the best course of action to protect themselves and their vital interests. There were two fundamental approaches:

1   Increase arms spending to defend oneself, as in the case of the Maginot Line in France, or force concessions from other nations, following Hitler's model.

2   Attempt to negotiate a settlement of the outstanding issues and problems with other nations as a way to avoid the escalation of tensions and the need to rearm. This was the case with the Anglo-German Naval Agreement, as well as Mussolini's abortive Four Power pact, which sought to produce negotiated settlements and to recapture the spirit of Locarno.

What was once again clear was that disarmament could not be discussed unless the resolution of fundamental sources of conflict was reached. As long as Germany, Russia, Italy and Japan were determined to revise the Paris settlements and recover lost territory, there was little hope of arms reduction in the long term.

Activity:
Debate
Organize a debate on the resolution that the reduction of arms is the best guarantee of peace.

Activity:

By 1932, the chances for a successful disarmament conference were rapidly disappearing. Summarize why disarmament failed. Use the questions below to help you.

1   What possible strategies could have been suggested to revive the disarmament process?

2   Which nations had little real interest in disarmament and why?

3   What are the conditions necessary for a successful disarmament agreement?

4   What does Rapallo show about the possibilities of disarmament and its enforcement?

"BETTER MAKE IT WIDE ENOUGH TO HOLD YOURSELF TOO, BIG BOY." *(Copyright in all countries.)*

THE CONFERENCE EXCUSES ITSELF. *(Copyright in all countries.)*

These cartoons by David Low, satirizing the failure of the disarmament talks, were originally published in London's *Evening Standard*: "Better make it wide enough to hold yourself too, Big Boy" on 1 July 1932; and "The Conference Excuses Itself", on 23 May 1934.

TOK link

Disarmament

After the First World War nations wanted to reduce arms for economic reasons and to promote peace. They were not successful in their quest for arms reduction, despite popular support and various international conferences.

More general issues that can be addressed here are:
- Why do nations have arms?
- What would motivate them to reduce or eliminate military stockpiles?
- How realistic is disarmament as a strategic objective?

- What are the possibilities for the elimination or reduction of weapons?
- What policies might help to limit the spread of weapons?
- How do the broader issues of global disarmament relate to the possession of arms by individuals?
- To what extent can or should the personal possession of arms be regulated?

Think in terms of human psychology:
- Does the history of disarmament test our understanding of human nature?
- Are humans inherently violent, or fearful?
- Will there always be reasons to have weapons?

The League of Nations

The League of Nations was the most ambitious and idealistic outcome of the peace treaties. It set forth a new vision of international co-operation and collective security to ensure the peaceful settlement of disputes. It had little chance of success, as many of the major powers were not members and the concept of collective security was too abstract and idealistic for countries raised in a tradition of self-interest and traditional diplomacy. It did have a few successes in resolving disputes involving small powers but at no time did it intervene successfully in a dispute involving a major country—it did not have any power of its own or the support of the international community in such circumstances.

The idea for the creation of an international organization to prevent the outbreak of war was inspired by the catastrophic events of the First World War. There had been proposals prior to the war to create organizations to prevent or limit wars and to resolve disputes. The Hague conferences in 1899 and 1907 had proposed various forms of disarmament and had established the concept of an international court to resolve disputes.

The United Kingdom and France had put forward ideas for an international peace organization during the war but it was the influence and power of Woodrow Wilson and the United Sates that brought the League into being. A plan for a League of Nations was incorporated into Wilson's Fourteen Points, which were the basis of the Paris peace discussions. Wilson's desire to see the League formed became his first priority at the Paris negotiations. There was considerable support for an international peacekeeping organization in light of the devastating experience of the war. Many countries and individuals were convinced that a new approach in international relations was necessary if the world were to avoid total destruction in the future.

Wilson was so determined to persevere with the creation of the League that he was even prepared to compromise some of his principles expressed in the Fourteen Points. His general view was that any problems—errors or injustices which occurred in the Paris settlements— could be resolved later through the League, but first the League had to exist. The League was to be a permanent international body in which all nations would meet, discuss and settle disputes in a peaceful manner. The Covenant of the League was written into the Versailles settlement with Germany in order that all signing nations would become members. There were 26 articles in the League Covenant. The key was Article X, which stated that "all members undertake to respect and preserve as against external aggression the territorial integrity and political independence of all members of the League."

This was the basis of the concept of collective security. This is a revolutionary concept as it calls upon all League members to assist in resistance to aggression without reference to whether the incident was vital to their interests or not. This reverses centuries of tradition in international diplomacy. Countries would have to answer the call regardless of their level of interest in the crisis or its outcome. Money and manpower would have to be sacrificed in defence of a principle and not of vital interests as had been the case in the past.

Apart from the prevention of international conflict, the League would undertake activities that would deal with a range of economic and humanitarian issues affecting the daily life of ordinary people in all countries. The League would have a permanent headquarters, a secretariat and a group of civil servants who would administer the special departments of the League. These would include the mandates commission, the drugs department to end the drug trade, the slavery commission, and a refugee department. In addition, the International Court of Justice was established in The Hague to deal with legal matters between members and the International Labour Organization was created to improve working conditions and workers' rights in the member states.

The absence of three major powers

A major impact on the effectiveness and function of the League was the absence of a number of major powers, who were defeated states from the First World War, and therefore not invited to be members. This meant that from the outset a group of states had been labelled as criminal or outlaw states. This could not be reconciled with the ideas of reconciliation that Wilson had proposed and the idea of an international community. Furthermore, these outlaw states had no interest in supporting the League or its principles and had no desire to support the Paris settlements. The League became a guardian of the status quo, not an impartial arbiter of disputes. The lessons of 1815 had been forgotten.

A banned major power was the Soviet Union, which Wilson had insisted be excluded. The USSR was a major power, or would be when it recovered its strength. It had no desire to accept the status quo as decided at Versailles or the verdict of the First World War and would present a serious challenge in the years to come as it sought to recover lost territory. Excluding the USSR from the League only increased the Soviet Union's hostility towards other countries and confirmed their suspicion that there was a conspiracy to destroy them.

The greatest of the absent powers was the United States. Their absence was catastrophic, both diplomatically and psychologically. The United States was the wealthiest nation in the world and had the greatest potential to intervene in the interest of maintaining peace. They were the only nation to have emerged from the war in a stronger position than when the war began. The other victors, the United Kingdom and France, were exhausted and had limited ability to enforce the decisions of Versailles or the League. The absence of the USA meant that challenges to the status quo established at Versailles, particularly from major powers, would meet limited resistance from a collection of small or exhausted states. In addition, the League had been the special project of the president of the United States, who had pressed for its creation and inserted its Covenant into the peace treaties with the defeated countries of the First World War. US rejection of the League and its principle of collective security undermined the credibility of the organization and its fundamental principles. It gave support to those countries who did not wish to fulfil their pledges under the Covenant although they were prepared to give support to the concept of peace.

The absence of three Great Powers had a number of serious consequences for the League. The League and the concept of collective security depended on collective action. The absence of the force that these three powers could bring to a crisis would limit the effectiveness of the League's reaction in a crisis. The fact that these three were outside the League meant that they had no stake in supporting its actions or decisions. In the case of Germany and Russia, both countries had much to gain by overturning the existing geo-political settlements. Their exclusion removed any chance for negotiated settlements of their grievances. The ability of the League to use some of its methods to discourage aggression, such as economic sanctions, would prove hollow if these three countries did not abide by League policies with respect to an aggressor.

The real impact of the exclusion of Russia and Germany occurred in 1922 when they signed the Treaty of Rapallo. They agreed to extend diplomatic recognition to each other and both denounced reparations. They agreed to economic and military co-operation. The significance of this development cannot be underestimated. Germany was able to develop weapons forbidden by the Versailles treaty, build factories to produce weapons which could not be seen by the League inspectors and train large numbers of personnel. In effect the disarmament provisions of the Treaty of Versailles were dead and the League had no recourse.

In addition, the co-operation of Russia and Germany did not bode well for the survival of the new states of Eastern and Central Europe. The mice could play while the cats were away but by 1922, the cats were serving notice that they would return. The folly of the policy of exclusion was evident to all.

The absence of certain Great Powers significantly diminished the prestige of the League. The League was supposed to be the agency to arrange peaceful reconciliations and support disarmament. After the war the first successful disarmament conference at Washington was organized and led by the United States (not a League member). The Locarno Treaty which resolved Franco-German relations in 1925 and provided great hope for lasting peace was negotiated without reference to the League as Germany was not even a member.

The other absence issue with respect to the great powers can be seen in the limited enthusiasm for enforcing the provision of the Treaty of Versailles in any way that might create conflict. This was particularly the case with the United Kingdom. British attitudes were affected by the American withdrawal. The immediate effect was the cancellation of the Anglo-American guarantee to support France in the event of a

German attack. This began a British return to her traditional policy of isolationism in order to preserve her freedom of action. The UK would not commit to intervention in Europe without American support and was suspicious of French ambitions.

The difference in attitude towards the treaty between the UK and France was a major problem for the League. The French wanted the League to police the Versailles settlement in order to suppress any German aggression or attempt to revise the treaty by force. The British wanted a more conciliatory approach, to rebuild the German economy in order to improve British trade. The UK wanted Germany as a counterweight to French ambitions and did not wish to engage in any major confrontation without American support. British attitudes were reflected in other countries including Canada and the other Dominions who were not prepared to support League sanctions if they interfered with their interests. Clearly Canada would not support any League action which targeted the United States for example.

Lastly the absence of the defeated countries or those that had been banned like Russia meant that the League was a league of victors whose goal seemed to be to enforce the status quo as determined at Versailles. This situation could not be successful in the long term as the defeated and revisionist powers would continue to launch challenges to the status quo which might lead to conflict. The fact that two of these revisionist powers, Russia and Germany, were potentially powerful meant that serious problems would be encountered in the future if changes to the Paris settlements were not made.

The other serious problem with respect to the absence of countries is that a number of important ones dropped out between 1919 and 1939. This further weakened the League through their absence and by the fact that there was no penalty for quitting.

Collective security

Collective security was the cornerstone of the League of Nations and the basis of a new theory for international relations. It is stated in Article X of the Covenant in which all the members undertook to protect all other members against aggression. This was new departure in diplomacy whereby the old alliance systems and the balance of power would be scrapped in favour of collective security. This is a very different system from traditional alliance and the difference must be made clear if one is to understand the problems of collective security.

Traditional alliances were made between nations with mutual interests and were designed to protect or defend against specific threats or specific nations. The treaty, like a contract, contained clear terms under which it was to operate and what the obligations of all the parties were. Nations enter into treaties or alliance with a clear idea of what their obligations are and because they perceive it to be in their national interest to do so. This is the basis of the traditional diplomacy: nations take action to defend or advance their own vital interests. Theses vital interests are well established and understood by all components of the country to be the reasons on which foreign policy decisions, including war, will be based.

Collective security is a more abstract concept. It does not specify where threats may come from or what the response should be under certain circumstances. It assumes that all nations are equally prepared to act in defence of the principle that aggression is wrong and must be resisted. It assumes that all nations will see each challenge to peace in exactly the same light and will be willing, regardless of the cost or how their own interests will be affected, to defend the principle. The fact is that not all nations see every crisis in the same way and are able or willing to make the kind of sacrifices—either monetary or human— to intervene. South American nations, for example, would see little reason to take part in a dispute in central Europe—certainly they would have trouble convincing their populations that they should do so.

Collective security failed as a concept because it ignored reality and required a level of altruism that humans have not yet been capable of. It failed because it asked nations to surrender their freedom of action, their sovereignty and enforce policies with which they disagreed or to intervene against countries with whom they were friends or had profitable relationships or who might do them harm. Collective security, the force of world opinion and the threat of world action to deter aggression was a wonderful abstract concept. It bore no relationship to the world of the 1920s. The evidence that collective security would not work was the fact that it was not very collective if three of the largest nations were not even members of the League. Even the United Kingdom and France, who were the foundation of the League, had grown further apart in their attitude towards enforcement of the treaty and the status of Germany. In the event of a dispute involving Germany there was a real possibility that they would not agree on how to react.

The lack of enforcement

The weakness of collective security as a deterrent to aggression is demonstrated by the fact that it was felt necessary to reinforce the obligations of League members to resist aggression. This occurred in 1923 with the Draft Treaty of Mutual Assistance which was presented to the Council in 1923. This agreement would have required all members to come to the aid of a victim of aggression to an extent determined by the League Council. The proposal was supported by France which continued to be fearful of German aggression but rejected out of hand by the United Kingdom and the Dominions who wished to retain their freedom of action.

The same fate was suffered by the Geneva Protocol for the Pacific settlement of International Disputes. This attempted to enforce compulsory arbitration in all disputes and would have labelled as an aggressor anyone who did not submit. This proposal was rejected by the British and the Dominions.

It was clear that few members of the League were willing to take on the open-ended commitments that collective security entailed.The reasons for this are not mere selfishness or an unwillingness to advance the cause of peace. The fact is that in the aftermath of the First World War the prospect of armed intervention would not have gained support from the population in any nation. The armed forces in most nations had been sharply reduced and, following the First World War, there was widespread opposition towards the use of military force to resolve other countries' disputes. This was particularly true if the aggressor was a large country where considerable risk or sacrifice would be required. This was the lesson of the Corfu dispute in 1923, led by Mussolini, in which members of the League took no action. In addition, the uncertain economic situation at the end of the war discouraged nations from actions which would have cost money, incurred debt or undermined trading relationships.

Collective security was a concept that attracted great popular emotional support but nothing of a concrete nature. It was an illusion, a mirage in which desperate populations wanted to believe. As with all mirages, the closer one got to it, the more it faded. If there is to be collective security then the collective has to agree the world in 1920 was far from agreement on many fronts.

Early attempts at peacekeeping 1920–5

The League had a mandate to resolve disputes between nations in order to preserve peace and prevent a resort to war between nations. In the early years of the League it was called on to intervene in a number of disputes, some violent, between nations. Its record of success in these disputes is mixed but allows us to understand the strengths and weaknesses of the League and collective security.

The success that the League enjoyed in this period include: the Aaland Islands, Upper Silesia, the Greco-Bulgarian War of 1925, There were also a number of incidents where the League failed to resolve or play any role in the dispute. These would include: the seizure of Fiume, Vilna, the Russo-Polish War, the Corfu incident and the Ruhr invasion.

There seem to be some common factors which explain why the League was successful in resolving some disputes and unsuccessful in others. In all of the successful cases, the antagonists were small or medium powers who were unwilling to resort to violence. This allowed the League to negotiate and enforce a settlement to these disputes which both parties would accept. Where the League was unsuccessful the dispute involved a major power that refused to submit to the League, or countries determined to resort to violence who were not willing to seek peaceful solutions.

The Corfu incident in 1923 was an ominous warning of the potential weakness of the League and the enforcement of collective security. Italy was a major participant and when she resorted to violence the League did not have the power to compel her to stop or submit to arbitration. This was the case on every occasion when a major power decided to pursue a policy in contravention of the League. Peacekeeping would succeed in the disputes of small countries, provided that the stronger members (i.e. the UK and France) could agree on a course of action. This was often not the case.

Source analysis

The following documents relate to the problems of collective security.

Source A

In the end, collective security fell prey to the weakness of its central premise— that all nations have the same interest in resisting a particular act of aggression and are prepared to run identical risks in opposing it. Experience has shown these assumptions to be false. No act of aggression involving a major power has ever been defeated by applying the principle of collective security. Either the world community has refused to assess the act as one which constituted aggression, or it has disagreed over the appropriate sanctions. And when sanctions were applied, they inevitably reflected the lowest common denominator, often proving so ineffectual.

Source: Kissinger, H. 1995. *Diplomacy*, New York, USA. Touchstone. p. 249.

Source B

THE GAP IN THE BRIDGE.

This cartoon was originally published in *Punch*, London, 10 December 1919.

Question

Refer to sources A and B, and further discussion in this chapter, to explain why the League was unable to enforce its policies or maintain peace.

Early problems for the League

The power of the League of Nations to resolve these disputes was not always apparent. In the absence of the United States—whose Senate finally rejected the Versailles Treaty in March 1920—it was essential that the remaining powers were in agreement on major issues. This was by no means the case. The repudiation by the United States of the entire peace settlement increased the reluctance of successive British governments in the 1920s to underwrite in any tangible way the European territorial settlement. In the dispute between Turkey and Greece of 1920–23, Britain and France took opposite sides. While France endorsed Poland's aims in Russia and Silesia, Britain pointedly did not. In addition, the distractions caused by major problems in Ireland and the Empire made it impossible for Britain to concentrate

> **Activity:**
>
> ### The League of Nations: Successes and Failures
>
> Choose one intervention by the League in a peacekeeping role that achieved its goals and one that did not. Put forward ideas as to why one succeeded and the other failed. Use these ideas to examine other cases to determine if some general principles can be determined.

on upholding the interests of the League before national concerns. While France fretted about Germany, the United Kingdom sought to redevelop trade links with her former enemy. The historian Sally Marks points out that the powers had assumed that the treaties would be honoured although this was emphatically not the case:

> The Dutch refused to relinquish the Kaiser, and Germany did not surrender alleged war criminals. Nor did she disarm on schedule or meet reparations quotas. Austria could not and did not pay reparations. Poland did not accept her frontiers; Italian troops did not evacuate Fiume; and Turkey did not accept the Treaty of Sèvres. Nothing much happened. The will to enforce the treaties was lacking or at best divided.
>
> Traynor, J. 1991. *Challenging History: Europe 1890–1990*,
> London, UK. Nelson. p. 123.

TOK link

Does the study of history widen our knowledge of human nature?

Case study: The League of Nations

The League of Nations put forward a new idea of collective security in international relations. From this point forward, all members of the League were required to take part in opposing aggression of any type, anywhere it occurred. Prior to this, nations had only opposed aggression when it affected their own interests.

● What human or humanitarian values are encouraged by the concept of collective security?

● Which human tendencies make this difficult to implement?

● Are democracies more likely to implement collective security?

● Are there any effective ways to deter aggression without resorting to force?

● Can or should one differentiate between different types of aggression?

● Why was there a difference between the public's in-principle support of collective security and the actual, physical support (i.e. military) in times of crisis?

IB Learner Profile link

Caring, principled, risk-takers

Caring Collective security, which is the basis of the League of Nations method to resolve conflicts and preserve peace, requires that all member nations come to the aid of any member who is threatened by or in conflict with another nation.

How is this different to the rationale for intervention or active involvement in conflicts in the past? How does this show a more empathetic approach?

Principled The countries that joined the League signed a Covenant—an agreement or contract—to behave in a certain way with respect to preventing or resisting aggression.

 Did the members of the League act with integrity and honesty in fulfilling the terms of the Covenant that they signed?

(In particular, consider the relationship to Article X.)

Did their actions demonstrate support for the principles of fairness, justice and respect when they were called upon to protect fellow members from aggression?

Risk-takers The League of Nations and the concept of collective security were new and unproven territory for the nations of the world. To fulfill the goals of the League, nations would have to risk lives, money and perhaps the support of their own populations if the Covenant were to be enforced.

Did the members of the League take risks to support the principles of the League? If they did not do so, why not?

The Ruhr Crisis

The Ruhr Crisis and the Locarno treaties represent the lowest and highest points of international relations in the 1920s. The French invasion of the Ruhr plunged Germany into political and economic chaos with a real threat of anarchy or revolution. The French were portrayed as bullies and lost considerable international support. The crisis did however have a positive outcome as it caused the United States to become involved in the financial rebuilding of Germany through the Dawes Plan. The Locarno Treaties which emerged partially from the Ruhr Crisis promised permanent solution to Franco-German tensions and as such set the tone for a general wave of optimism in the 1920s. This was echoed subsequently in the Kellogg–Briand Pact.

The Ruhr Crisis, a result of the Franco-Belgian invasion and occupation of the Ruhr area of Germany in 1923 has its roots in French fears about security. France had been increasingly concerned about security since the collapse of the Anglo-American guarantee that would have given the French support in the event of a German attack. In addition, France had been unsuccessful in her attempts to partially dismember Germany. By 1921 the United States and the United Kingdom were retreating into isolation and removing themselves from affairs on the Continent. In the UK there was growing sympathy for the idea that Germany had been treated too harshly and that she should be allowed to recover economically as a means to promote general European recovery. The British prime minister Lloyd George made a number of attempts to persuade the French to ease the German burden in the interests of peace and economic progress. He attempted to organize a review of German obligations at the Genoa Conference in 1922 but this failed when the Germans made a treaty (Rapallo) with the USSR.

The reparations commission had determined in 1921 that Germany should pay 132 billion gold marks to the allied powers. The French were anxious to enforce the reparations settlement in full for two reasons. They owed money to the United States and were hoping to use reparations payments to pay their debts. More importantly they could continue to weaken Germany by collecting the reparations and thus limiting the speed and extent of German economic recovery which could pose a serious threat to them in the future. The British attitude towards reparations was ambivalent. They needed money to pay the United States but were also aware that continued German economic weakness would limit the recovery of British trade.

The German signing of the Rapallo Treaty further convinced the British that if Germany were not conciliated she would slip into the Soviet orbit which would prove disastrous. The French were convinced that Germany was trying to avoid her obligations and should be made to pay. French premier Raymond Poincaré took a hard-line approach to Germany and her treaty obligations: only force would convince the Germans to fulfil their obligations. The opportunity arose when Germany missed a delivery of timber as part of her payments. The French had Germany declared in default despite British objections and on 11 January 1923 French and Belgian troops invaded the Ruhr.

The French object was to collect reparations through seizing the output of the mines and factories of the Ruhr and shipping them to France. The German workers refused to co-operate and went on strike and engaged in acts of sabotage to prevent the French from obtaining any materials. These acts included the flooding of mines, burning of factories and destruction of railroads and ships. This led to violence and the imprisonment of leaders of the resistance movements as well as the death of a number of protestors.

The greatest crisis however was the catastrophic inflation that resulted from the French invasion and the response of the Weimar government. The Weimar government which was already struggling with a serious inflation problem brought on by the war and its own policies now compounded the problem exponentially. In order to support the workers in the Ruhr in their strike actions, the government simply printed more money to the point that paper money became worthless. Prices for goods rose to hundreds of billions of marks.

The collapse of the Weimar government

Inside Germany, the principal victim was the middle class who had saved their money and planned for the future. Their savings were entirely wiped out and they were left demoralized and cynical about their future. They had lost faith in the system and would be vulnerable to the appeal of extremists in politics who promised to restore pride, faith and hope. It is not surprising that Hitler made his first attempt to seize power at this time.

This was a clear signal to the Allies that Germany was in danger of complete collapse and that a state of anarchy might well develop. This would open the door to revolutionary activity which might see Germany embrace communism. This was an anathema to the West and they realized that they would have to find some solution to the problem. The collapse of the German economy also meant that the Allies were not receiving reparations payments but their hopes for European economic recovery were in serious jeopardy. The question for both the German government and the Allies was how to resolve the crisis that had developed.

The breakthrough came with the appointment of Gustav Stresemann as chancellor of Germany. Stresemann called off the passive resistance in the Ruhr and announced that Germany would comply with her obligations under the treaty of Versailles. The French were willing to come to an agreement as the Ruhr occupation had been an economic failure and had damaged French relations with her former allies (the UK and the USA).

The key player in the solution of the Ruhr Crisis and the reparation issue which had triggered it was the United States. The USA was the wealthiest power in the world and power to whom the British, French etc. owed huge war debts. The Americans demanded payment from the United Kingdom and France but they could not pay if Germany did not pay them. The impasse was resolved by the intervention of the United States under the leadership of Charles Dawes. His plan allowed Germany to reschedule her reparations payments so that the total amount was reduced and the deadlines were extended. In order for the German economy to recover extensive foreign loans, largely from the United States, were arranged, In addition much private American capital flowed into German businesses and German government bonds.

The resolution of the economic crisis and Germany's willingness to co-operate with the Allies was part of an important policy decision that had been made in Germany prior to the Ruhr Crisis. This was the **Policy of Fulfilment** by which the Weimar government had decided that it would be useless to continue to defy the Treaty of Versailles in the hopes of having it modified. Instead they decided to comply as far as possible with the treaty and in so doing create an environment that would convince the allies that Germany was worthy of some revision of its terms based on her good citizenship and co-operation. The Policy of Fulfillment was adopted by Stresemann and his successors until the rise of Hitler. It proved successful in gaining a number of concessions for Germany and rehabilitating her international reputation.

> **Policy of Fulfilment** A policy introduced in Weimar Germany in support of German co-operation with the terms of the Treaty of Versailles in order to gain concessions in the future from the Allied powers.

The spirit of Locarno

After the resolution of the Ruhr Crisis, Stresemann proposed to the Allies that Germany would be prepared to accept its current boundaries with France and Belgium and have their obligation enforced by international treaty. This proposal for détente was welcomed by the British and supported by the new French premier Aristide Briand. The result was the **Locarno Treaty** signed in October 1925. The most important part of the Locarno Treaty was that Germany accepted its borders with France and Belgium as permanent and these borders were guaranteed by the UK and Italy. Germany would also join the League of Nations.

> **Locarno treaty** An agreement signed in 1925 by the UK, France, Germany and Belgium in which Germany agreed to accept her western borders as determined at the Versailles settlement. This was seen as a great step towards permanent peace in Europe.

This seemed to be a genuine breakthrough in Franco-German relations and addressed the security concerns that had driven French policy at Versailles and in the years after. It would allow Germany to be rehabilitated without posing a threat to Western Europe. The French and the British might also repair their relationship which had been damaged by French insistence on a hard approach to Germany.

Germany agreed to seek changes in her eastern borders by means of discussion, agreement and arbitration with Poland and Czechoslovakia. It should be noted that while the Western borders of Germany had been fixed by international guarantee, this did not occur in the east. Britain refused to guarantee the countries to the east of Germany. This allowed Germany to assume that her Eastern borders could be changed and with little objection from the Allies.

The results of the Locarno treaties were that Germany accepted the results of the First World War on her western borders but not in the east. The overall result of the Treaty was a sense of euphoria, the "spirit of Locarno" the order of the day. The general mood was of great optimism: tensions had been reduced as Germany had accepted it borders and renounced violence, prosperity was returning to Europe, democracy was flourishing in Germany and a general sense of optimism prevailed.

The sense of progress towards peace and a new relationship between the Allies and Germany was evident in the next few years. Germany joined the League of Nations and obtained a permanent seat on the League council. The Allies removed their troops from the left bank of the Rhine and the Allied commission to supervise German disarmament departed in 1927. By 1930 the Allied occupation armies had left Germany and she became an independent state once again. The spirit of Locarno was perhaps best exemplified in 1928 when the Kellogg–Briand pact was signed by 65 countries. They agreed by this action to renounce war as an instrument of national policy. The work of Stresemann and Briand in arranging the Locarno agreement was recognized when they were awarded the Nobel Peace Prize in 1926.

Locarno seemed to be proof that the First World War and its tensions had finally been resolved. The economic prosperity of the 1920s, the failure of communism to spread beyond the USSR and the willingness of Germany to accept the decision of Versailles were strong indications that a new era might well be at hand. But how much Locarno really accomplished towards a permanent peace must be looked at more critically, in view of the fact that the League was not strengthened and the principle of collective security remained uncertain in its practical application to meeting Europe's long-term security needs. Germany did not agree to accept her eastern border which is of great significance because this is where her worst grievances against the territorial settlement of Versailles were found. Her continued co-operation with the USSR in the Treaty of Rapallo meant that she was continuing to evade the disarmament clauses of the treaty and also working with a country that wanted to redraw the map of Eastern Europe.

It must also be remembered that the Locarno spirit was closely tied to the economic health of Europe that prevailed in the 1920s which allowed reparations to be paid, political extremism to disappear and a sense of international co-operation to flourish. If Europe were to continue towards a peaceful future, the optimism of this period would have to be maintained and this was largely based on economic health—specifically the support of the United States.

Charles Dawes (1865–1951)

Charles Dawes was a prominent US businessman and public servant who gained a reputation for reforming the budget process in the United States. In 1923 Dawes was asked by the League of Nations to chair a committee on German reparations. The Dawes report was a very detailed analysis of the problem and contained a recommendation for the stabilization of the German economy and a more reasonable schedule for reparations payments. Dawes was awarded the Nobel peace Prize for his work and his work laid the basis for American investment in the German economy which produced the Golden Age of Weimar from 1925–29. Dawes later served as vice-president of the United States and as a delegate to the Geneva Disarmament Conference in1932.

Gustav Stresemann (1878–1929)

Gustav Stresemann was a successful German businessman who first entered politics in 1907. A dedicated German nationalist, he had opposed the Treaty of Versailles. Realizing that Germany could not gain her goals by force, he set out to improve her position after Versailles through diplomacy. He was appointed chancellor in 1923 and brought an end to the economic crisis caused by the Ruhr occupation. As Foreign Minister he accepted the Dawes plan to reduce reparations, negotiated the Locarno Agreement and oversaw Germany's entry in the League of Nations. He was awarded the Nobel Peace Prize for his role in the Locarno negotiations. His determination to restore German power and pride was uppermost in his policies at all times. He believed, however, that co-operation and negotiation with the Allied powers would be the most effective way to realize his goals. He died suddenly in 1929, just before Germany was decimated by the Great Depression.

Source analysis

These documents relate to the Locarno Treaty.

Source A

Stresemann skillfully proposed international arbitration for a new schedule of reparations, expecting an international forum to prove less exacting than France alone was likely to be. In November 1923, France accepted the appointment of an American banker, Charles G. Dawes, as "impartial arbiter" to reduce France's reparation claim—a galling symbol of the disintegration the wartime alliance. The Dawes Committee's recommendations establishing a reduced schedule of payments for five years were accepted in April 1924.

Over the next five years, Germany paid out about $1 billion in reparations and received loans of about $2 billion, much of it from the United States. In effect, America was paying Germany's reparations, while Germany used the surplus from American loans to modernize its industry. Forced to choose between a weak Germany and a Germany capable of paying reparations, France had opted for the latter, but then had to stand by as reparations helped to rebuild Germany's economic and, ultimately, its military power. By the end of 1923, Stresemann was in a position to claim some success.

Source: Kissinger, H. 1995. *Diplomacy*. New York, USA. Touchstone. p. 272.

Source B

The Locarno Pact was greeted with exuberant relief as the dawning of a new world order. The three foreign ministers—Aristide Briand of France, Austen Chamberlain of Great Britain, and Gustav Stresemann of Germany—received the Nobel Peace Prize. But amidst all the jubilation, no one noticed that the statesmen had sidestepped the real issues; Locarno had not so much pacified Europe as it had defined the next battlefield.

The reassurance felt by the democracies at Germany's formal recognition of its Western frontier showed the extent of the demoralization and the confusion that had been caused by the mélange of old and new views on international affairs. For in that recognition was implicit that the Treaty of Versailles, which had ended a victorious war, had been unable to command compliance with the victors' peace terms, and that Germany had acquired the option of observing only those provisions which it chose to reaffirm. In this sense, Stresemann's unwillingness to recognize Germany's Eastern frontiers was ominous; while Great Britain's refusal to guarantee even the arbitration treaties gave international sanction to two classes of frontier in Europe–those accepted by Germany and guaranteed by other powers, and those neither accepted by Germany nor guaranteed by the other powers.

Source: Kissinger, H. 1995. *Diplomacy*. New York, USA. Touchstone. p. 274.

Source C

Cartoon by David Low, published in *The Star* on 1 December 1925.

Source D

Austen Chamberlain on the Locarno Treaties 1925

(b) I believe that a great work of peace has been done. I believe it above all because of the spirit in which it was done and the spirit which it has engendered. It would not have been done unless all the governments, and I will add all the nations, had felt the need to start a new and better chapter of international relations; but it would not have been done unless this country was prepared to take her share in guaranteeing the settlements so come to …

We who live close to the Continent, we, who cannot disassociate ourselves from what passes there, whose safety, whose peace and the security of whose shores are manifestly bound up with the peace and security of the Continent, and, above all, of the Western nations, must make our decision; and we ask the House to approve the ratification of the Treaty of Locarno in the belief that by that treaty we are averting danger from our own country and from Europe, that we are safeguarding peace, and that we are laying the foundations of reconciliation and friendship with the enemies of a few years ago.

Source: Joll, J. 1961. *Britain and Europe*. London, UK. Adam and Charles Black. p. 284

Question

What different attitudes towards the outcome of Locarno do Sources A–D demonstrate?

Depression and threats to international peace and collective security: Manchuria 1931–3 and Abyssinia 1935–6

> The Great Depression is the single greatest reason for the collapse of international peace. It led to aggression and the collapse of international co-operation in the Manchurian crisis where both the League of Nations and collective security were exposed as hollow concepts. It brought Hitler to power, undermined the Geneva disarmament talks and weakened the United Kingdom and France—the guardians of the status quo. This in turn made it possible for Mussolini to engage in aggression in Africa and bring about the final collapse of any hope for preserving peace, by ending the Stresa Front agreement and providing a useful ally for Hitler.

The impact of the Great Depression

The causes of the Great Depression are not the focus of this prescribed subject. Rather it is how that event influenced the development of international relations in the years after 1929. This should be appreciated not only with reference to the two specific topics, Manchuria and Abyssinia, that are included in the prescribed subject but also in how it had an impact on the ability of the world to continue its search for peace and harmony.

The Depression was not caused by the Wall Street crash of 1929. This was merely the signal that it had arrived. The roots of the Depression can be found in the weakened state of many nations after the First World War, particularly Germany and the United Kingdom which had been economic powerhouses prior to 1914. In addition, the turmoil in Russia and Eastern Europe had further weakened trade and world markets. The burden of war-debts, government deficits, and the political and social turmoil as a result of the First World War had all played a role.

The Depression not only altered the world in a tangible economic form but also devastated its spirit. It resulted in a terrible struggle to survive by any means—nations were no longer willing to co-operate through trade and exchange but adopted an exclusionary, bomb-shelter mentality, where they cut off contact with their neighbours, raised tariffs and ceased to care much about the world beyond their own borders. This narrow attitude was probably worst in the democratic states where citizens demanded that their governments devote their money and resources to domestic problems and ignore the wider problems of the world. No energy was to be wasted on international agreements or the means to enforce them—domestic hardship was to be the focus not armaments to control aggressive foreign states.

Depression did produce aggressive states—those who were driven to extremes of hardship saw war and conquest as a solution to their problems as shown in Japan's attack on Manchuria. The Japanese, terribly afflicted by the decline of world trade, argued that without Manchuria they would starve. The world economic system was broken—it was every nation for itself.

The Great Depression, more than any other reason, brought Hitler to power in Germany, seriously endangering efforts to maintain peace. Hitler had as his primary goal the destruction of the Versailles settlement by whatever means. His solutions to Germany's economic weakness was to advocate territorial expansion—Lebensraum—to seize much-needed resources. This was a clear challenge to those hoping to avoid another war.

A clear understanding of the impact of the Great Depression on the efforts to maintain world peace is therefore crucial. It should be seen as the single greatest reason for the collapse of all previous efforts to develop international understanding and co-operation. The Depression destroyed not only the economic welfare of the world but also its optimistic spirit represented by the spirit of Locarno, Kellogg–Briand, the League of Nations and other attempts at international co-operation. These progressive, idealistic agreements that had encouraged people to imagine a new form of international diplomacy were forgotten or ignored in the selfish, cynical world of the 1930s where the survival of the fittest was becoming the order of the day.

The Depression created the reasons for aggression in the Manchurian crisis and robbed nations of the physical ability and motivation to co-operate to preserve peace. The result was that the League and its founding principle of collective security were exposed as hollow, impotent ideas unable to guarantee or even hold out hope for a peaceful future. The simple fact was that the powers who had pledged support for collective security were now even less able to stand behind it, assuming that they had any desire to still do so.

The Depression seriously weakened Britain and France who had tried to defend the Versailles agreement and the precepts of the League. Their weakness was exposed by the Manchurian crisis which served to encourage further aggression in the form of Mussolini's attack on Abyssinia, ending the Stresa Front agreement and providing Hitler with an ally in his desire for conquest.

Discussion point:
Japan's invasion of Manchuria

- Why did they embark on this course of action?

- What response did the international community make to this flagrant act of aggression?

Discuss the impact their action or inaction had on international relations in subsequent years?

TOK link
Integrating areas of knowledge–human sciences and ethics

It is often said that human behaviour is unpredictable, and that it is impossible to study human actions in a scientific manner. Observing human activities involves ways of knowing that include perception, emotion, value judgments and self-knowledge.

Students should consider the relationship between the subject matter and the methods employed by the human sciences—including observation, value judgments, principles of motivation, language usage, statistical evidence, quantitative instruments for gathering information etc.—that may influence the conclusions reached.

Ethics involve a discussion of the way in which we live our lives and justify moral actions. An examination of the past can be problematic as we may make judgments about historical events and personalities from a quite altered contemporary perspective. Conversely, it is also necessary to take into account the legacy of past decisions and attitudes that have a bearing on the present day political and historical context of nation states and the identity and beliefs of peoples living throughout the world today.

Manchuria 1931–3

Comprehension of the reasons for the Japanese takeover of Manchuria must take into consideration a wide range of issues. The first aspect that warrants consideration is the Japanese economy. Japan had undergone an industrial revolution from the late 19th century and had become the largest industrial power in Asia. This growth and development was based, like that of the UK, on the success of her exports to the rest of the world. Japan has few natural resources and, exacerbated by the growth of the population through economic development, could not feed herself. She depended on the export of manufactured goods principally to the United States to maintain her prosperity. The collapse of the American markets and higher US tariffs created enormous hardship in Japan with massive unemployment and reports of starvation in rural areas.

The disastrous economic situation led to a decline in the prestige of the liberal democratic government and demands for action by radical nationalist groups often composed of army officers. They demanded that the government take action to protect the population and insulate Japan from the failures of the liberal capitalist economic system. Their specific objective was to take over the Chinese province of Manchuria which held a vast wealth of natural resources of all kinds.

The decision to go to Manchuria was made easier because Japan had made significant economic investments in the region since the Russo-Japanese war, and had maintained troops in the city of Port Arthur to protect her interests. Furthermore, as a result of civil war in China Manchuria had become an autonomous province under its own warlord. Japan had been pushing to expand her control of China throughout the 20th century and had increased her presence there as a result of the Treaty of Versailles and the concessions forced from a weak Chinese government during the First World War.

Militarily, the Japanese decision to invade Manchuria made good sense and posed few risks. Manchuria lies in close proximity to Japan and its colony Korea (Japanese since 1910). China was dissolved in civil war and could offer no resistance. Since the Washington conference of 1922, Japan had military supremacy in East Asia and none of the Great Powers had the forces or bases in the region to oppose her. Lastly the depression had caused further cuts in armaments spending in the West and the UK, France and the USA were in no position to intervene.

Japan invaded Manchuria on the pretext that her property and citizens had been attacked by Chinese troops. The incident was manufactured by the radical nationalists to force the civilian government to support military action. The Chinese were rapidly defeated and in 1932, Japan established the puppet state of Manchukuo. This was a clear challenge to the principle of collective security and the League. China was a member and appealed for support against Japan. What would or could be done about this flagrant violation of the Covenant and international peace agreements? The short answer is that nothing would or could be done. We need to understand why that was the case.

Legacy for the League

Did the Japanese withdrawal signal the end of the League? The point is debatable but it may not have had as much influence as some authors suggest. Japan and Manchuria were not central concerns to European powers, and the issue may well have been treated as a local one. No vital European interest had been at stake in Manchuria, so it did not necessarily threaten the viability of the principal of collective security in application to a crisis that was more central to Europe.

The USA and the UK were not able to co-operate on a policy with respect to Manchuria. Neither country wanted to be responsible for taking the lead. This made it even less likely that any effective response could be mounted against the Japanese violation of the Covenant. Collective security in the Far East was dead as of this moment. The UK and the USA had entered into a policy of **appeasement** to be able to accommodate the demands of the revisionist powers in the hopes that they would become less aggressive and not create conditions for another world conflict.

Appeasement A policy practiced by the UK and France in the late 1930s that sought to avoid war with Germany by revising the treaty of Versailles to eliminate the clauses considered unfair by Germany. The policy held that reasonable revisions and negotiations would be the best way to avoid war.

Failure of collective security, Manchuria 1931

The only members of the League with substantial military force were the United Kingdom and France. Neither power had the bases in the Far East to support an effective challenge. Only the UK had a large navy, but, being 5000 miles away, was not in a good position to engage its warships in the Far East. Furthermore, the British Navy was itself in a state of crisis, having recently experienced a mutiny over proposed pay cuts. There was also a crucial absence of motivation to undertake a military mission. Nations normally engage in hostilities when something of vital interest to their security or welfare is at stake. This clearly was not the case with Manchuria and it would not have been possible to convince the British public that such an expedition with the resulting cost in lives and resources was to their advantage. Democracies cannot make major foreign policy decisions that the public will not support—especially wars.

The mood of the 1930s made it even less likely that the United Kingdom would intervene. The public attention was on the internal economic problems of the depression. No one would support money for war when many were hungry and unemployed. Furthermore the anti-war pacifist movements were very strong especially in the UK and people preferred to put their faith in the League or to believe that war should occur only in self-defence.

The United States might have been expected to take a stronger position on the Japanese actions. It was the Americans who had claimed to be a friend of China and who had supported the **Open Door Policy** to prevent China from coming under the influence of a single power. The United States had been suspicious of Japan and her rival for power in the Pacific for many years and might have interpreted their Manchurian action as a serious challenge to American interests. Nevertheless the USA took no action over Manchuria.

Open Door American policy which supported equal access for all countries to trade and economic opportunities. It opposed colonial and other political restrictions to trade and investment.

The precise reasons for this failure to respond, included the lack of armed forces or bases necessary to support any military expedition. The US policy of isolationism which had grown stronger after the

First World War would have made it difficult to develop any enthusiasm for an initiative in Asia—not a vital interest to most Americans. The United States was also severely affected by the Depression and the population was focused on the internal domestic crisis, with little interest in foreign affairs and a marked unwillingness to devote any further resources to them.

A strategic consideration also influenced British and US policy. The United Kingdom and the United States had extensive property, trading networks and investments in China and the Far East. Neither power was in a position to defend these in the face of Japanese hostility. Any serious attempt to oppose the Japanese action might result in retaliation against these interests.

The League of Nations was supposed to maintain peace and resist aggression against any of its members. Yet the League was largely ineffective as it had no armed forces of its own. Moral condemnation and disapproval by the world community was one way that an aggressive nation might be deterred. But Japan could hardly be expected to worry about moral condemnation when its very survival was at stake and the nations condemning her were the products of a failed international economic system.

Japan withdraws from the League

The League's response to the crisis was to send out a fact-finding mission under Lord Lytton. By the time the report was produced, the entire matter was likely to have been forgotten. The Lytton Commission Report, which was issued in 1932, recognized that Japan had some justifiable grievances about the situation in Manchuria but should have tried other solutions before resorting to force. It suggested that China grant independence to Manchuria and that Japan withdraw its forces. This did not represent a strong condemnation but Japan refused to accept the criticism and withdrew from the League of Nations. Manchuria became part of the Japanese Empire as the puppet state of Manchukuo.

Discussion point:
Economic sanctions

Economic sanctions depended on the willingness of nations to undertake a boycott or other economic action against the aggressor. It also meant that all nations would have to participate.

 Why wasn't this a realistic option? Discuss in relation to the vested interests of the League and non-League members.

Activity:

Did Manchuria encourage the aggressive action of neighbouring states?

Debate the resolution that "self-defence is the only justification for war".

Trial by Geneva by cartoonist David Low published by the *Evening Standard* on 24 November 1932.

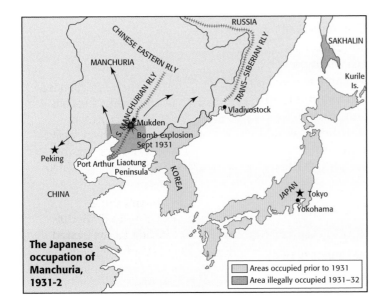

The Japanese occupation of Manchuria, 1931-2

Areas occupied prior to 1931
Area illegally occupied 1931–32

Source: Catchpole, B. 1983. *A Map History of the Modern World*. Toronto, Canada. Irwin, p. 53.

Abyssinia 1935–6

The Abyssinian crisis is widely regarded as the ultimate example of the failure of the collective security principle. It sent a clear and perhaps final signal that the League of Nations no longer played an important role in world affairs.

Background to the crisis

The crisis and its impact however cannot be understood without sound knowledge of the significant events in this period, since 1933. The single most important threat to world peace was the rise to power of Adolf Hitler and the return to the international scene of Germany, now bent on reasserting her position in the world. The rise of Hitler precipitated a series of events that served to heighten the sense of crisis in the world and to demonstrate the resurgence of German power and ambition. These included the collapse of the Geneva disarmament talks due, in part, to the German position, Germany's withdrawal from the League of Nations and Hitler's announcement of rearmament policies in flagrant violation of the Treaty of Versailles.

All European nations were likely to be affected by this new aggressive German posture and Italy was no exception. Until the rise of Hitler, Italy had played a significant role in Europe as a signatory of the Locarno agreement and as a member of the League. She had also been a defender of the Versailles Treaty when, in 1934, she took steps to discourage the German annexation of Austria in defiance of the Treaty. Nevertheless it was clear to Mussolini that his position in central Europe was going to be weakened by the German resurgence and that he might be faced with a confrontation with Hitler if Germany demanded the return of the South Tyrol area that was entirely German speaking. Italy had acquired South Tyrol from Austria as a result of the Treaty of Versailles despite the fact that it was a clear violation of the concept of self-determination.

Mussolini met with the other countries who could be targets of German revisionism—most notably the UK and France—in an attempt to reach an agreement to counterbalance German power. The three countries met in the Italian town of Stresa and reached an agreement in which they pledged to resist any German attempt to modify the Versailles Treaty by force. This agreement, had it continued, might have been effective in restraining Hitler. It would certainly have removed a potential enemy and secured the Mediterranean lifeline to the Suez Canal and India that the UK so valued.

Why Abyssinia?

Why did Mussolini set out on a campaign to conquer Abyssinia? The resurgence of Hitler and the fact that Italy could no longer play a significant role in Western or Central Europe encouraged Mussolini to look elsewhere for territory, empire and a sense of importance. Mussolini had always wanted Italy to play a bigger role in world affairs. This was part of the national strength and pride of the Fascist ideology. One of his ambitions was to expand Italy's colonial holding in Africa in emulation of the French and British and to satisfy his dreams of a "new Roman Empire" in Africa and the eastern Mediterranean. Abyssinia was a logical choice for Mussolini as it was the only African territory available. (All the rest were already claimed.) It was also conveniently located next to two existing Italian colonies and was the location of a humiliating event in Italian history. In 1896, Italy had tried to conquer Abyssinia but failed—the only European nation to be defeated in its attempt to subdue a native African state. Revenge for the defeat at Adowa was a factor in the Italian decision.

There were also economic factors as Mussolini believed that there were oil deposits in the region and that it might be developed as an outlet for the surplus Italian population, destined to migrate to the Americas, in a newly reconstituted Italian Empire. These Italian populations would not only help provide resources and markets for Italian industry but also a pool of army recruits in future years. The native population could bolster the Italian forces much as the French had done with their African recruits.

A final important factor in Mussolini's decision to attack may have come from his relationship with the UK and France forged by the **Stresa Front**. Both of them had already conceded that Abyssinia lay within the Italian sphere of interest. He also assumed that their friendship would allow him to pursue his colonial ambitions in return for his allegiance as part of the anti-Hitler coalition. It was not an entirely unreasonable assumption and certainly fitted in well with his support for Realpolitik.

The lack of opposition to Italy

The conflict began in a small way in 1934 with a border skirmish between Abyssinia and Italian Somaliland. This was an excuse for Mussolini to move large numbers of troops into the region in preparation for a full-scale invasion. The dispute had been referred to the League for arbitration in September 1935.

Stresa Front An agreement signed in 1935 by Britain, France and Italy to maintain the Locarno agreement and support the independence of Austria. It might have deterred Hitler but if collapsed as a result of Abyssinia.

Activity:

What was the purpose of the Hoare-Laval pact? Why is it referred to as an example of Realpolitik?

Conduct a debate on the resolution that "sacrificing Abyssinia was less important than maintaining the Stresa Front".

The invasion began in October 1935. On 7 October Italy was declared the aggressor and on 18 November 51 states voted to impose economic sanctions against Italy. The sanctions did not include oil and steel and the UK did not close the Suez Canal to Italian shipping. Even apart from the fact that the sanctions excluded strategic material like oil, they were ineffective as so many large nations (such as Germany and the United States) were not bound by them. These sanctions were little more than an irritant. The UK and France found themselves in a difficult situation. They had either to make the sanctions work, so that the League was seen as a genuine force for peace, or they would have to placate Italy in order to maintain the Stresa front against the real threat: Hitler. In the end they accomplished neither.

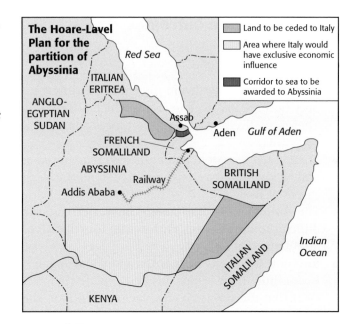

Their solution was a compromise known as the **Hoare-Laval Pact** named after the French prime minister and the British foreign secretary. The proposal was to give Mussolini two-thirds of Abyssinia including the most fertile regions and leave the rest as an independent state. The compromise never took effect as the plan was leaked to the press and caused an enormous negative reaction among the public, especially in Britain. The compromise was abandoned: Hoare resigned and the Italian invasion continued.

> **Hoare-Laval Pact** A plan devised by the French and British foreign ministers to settle the Abyssinian crisis and avoid losing Italy as an ally against Hitler. It failed due to the lack of public support and Mussolini's refusal to accept only part of Abyssinia.

There was no way to stop the Italian invasion without force and neither the UK or France was prepared to go to that extreme. By May 1936 the war was over and the whole of Abyssinia was in Italian hands. The damage caused by this event was monumental both to the League and to the concept of collective security, in its impact on the viability of Locarno and Stresa as barriers to German aggression. Hitler exposed the complete collapse of these agreements through his reoccupation of the Rhineland in March 1936.

The significance of the crisis

The significance of Abyssinia should not be underestimated. The League and its concept of collective security were exposed as entirely hollow, the more so because the leading powers in the League were unwilling and unable to apply it. The UK and France could not apply any sanction or take any action that risked a war—their populations would not support it. The result was that while they denounced the aggressors, they did not prevent their actions or protect the victims, only serving to annoy those responsible and reveal the weakness of the powers defending Versailles and the League.

In addition it was clear to Mussolini that the United Kingdom and France were unwilling to support his goals in Africa and the Balkans. If he wanted to fulfil his territorial ambitions, his only option was to associate himself with a more powerful nation: Germany. Hitler also saw that UK and France were not willing to resort to force even when their opponent was as weak as Italy and this strengthened his determination to press forward with Germany's territorial demands and revision of the Versailles settlement.

Summary of the outcomes

Collective security and the League of Nations were exposed as entirely hollow concepts.

- Diplomacy still worked in the era of self-interest. Nations would only become involved in issues which affected their vital interests. Therefore, there was no support for a campaign against Italy over Abyssinia.
- The United Kingdom and France were exposed as militarily weak and lacking in any motivation to defend the Versailles Treaty at threat of war.
- The strong pacifist movements in Western countries made it very difficult to develop any enthusiasm for collective security beyond an intellectual interest.
- Revisionist nations such as Germany and Japan were encouraged to continue their campaigns and expand their territory as it was clear that there was no effective opposition to their plans.
- Mussolini allied with Hitler—partly due to the failure of the UK and France to support him and partly out of the recognition that they were unlikely to win a major conflict in the event of a European war.
- This created a serious strategic problem for the British in the Mediterranean, and the potential for disaster in the event of a European war.

Recommended further reading

Blinkhorn, Martin. 2000. *Fascism and the Right in Europe* 1919–1945. London, UK. Pearson Education.

Brown, Richard and Daniels, Christopher. 1991. *Twentieth Century Europe: Documents and Debates*. London, UK. Macmillan.

Catchpole, Brian. 1983. *A Map History of the Modern World*. Toronto, Canada. Irwin.

Goldstein, Erik. 2002. *The First World War Peace Settlements 1919–1925*. Harlow, UK. Pearson Education.

Howarth, Tony. 1987. *Twentieth Century History*. London, UK. Longman.

Joll, James. 1961. *Britain and Europe*. London, UK. Adam and Charles Black.

Laver, John. 1992. *Imperial and Weimar Germany 1890–1933*. Sevenoaks, UK. Hodder and Stoughton.

Lederer, Ivo. 1960. *The Versailles Settlement*. Boston, USA. Heath and Company.

Overy, Richard. 1994. *The Inter-War Crisis*. London, UK. Pearson Education.

Radway, R. 2002. *Germany 1918–45*. London, UK. Hodder and Stoughton.

Traynor, J. 1991. *Challenging History Europe 1890–1990*. London. Nelson.

Wolfson, Robert and Laver, John. 2007. *Years of Change: European History 1890–1990*. 3rd edn. Tunbridge Wells, UK. Hodder and Stoughton.

Robson, Mark. 2002. *The Rise of Fascism 1915–45*, 3rd edn. Tunbridge Wells, UK. Hodder and Stoughton.

Exam practice

Source analysis

These documents refer to the Abyssinian Crisis, 1935–6, and the League of Nations.

Source A

Extract from the Conservative Election manifesto, 1935.

The League of Nations will remain, as heretofore, the keystone of British foreign policy … We shall therefore continue to do all in our power to uphold the Covenant and maintain and increase the efficiency of the League … We shall take no action in isolation, but shall be prepared faithfully to take our part in any collective action decided upon by the League. We shall endeavour to further any discussions which may offer the hope of a just and fair settlement, provided that it be within the framework of the League and acceptable to the three parties to the dispute— Italy, Abyssinia and the League itself.

From the Conservative Election Manifesto, *The Times*, 28 October 1935

Source B

Extract from a speech by Pierre Laval at Geneva, 2 November 1935.

Now that the Co-ordination Committee has fixed the date for the entry into force of certain economic measures, I should like to remind you that … my country is loyally applying the Covenant … We have all … another duty to fulfil, one that is dictated by the spirit of the Covenant. We must endeavour to seek, as speedily as possible, an amicable settlement for the dispute. The French Government and the United Kingdom Government are agreed to co-operate in this sphere.

This duty is particularly imperative for France, which on 7 January last signed a treaty of friendship with Italy. I shall therefore stubbornly pursue my attempt … to find elements that might serve as a basis for negotiations. It is thus that I have initiated conversations, though I have never had the slightest intention of putting the results into final shape outside the League. It is only within the framework of the League that proposals can be examined and decisions reached.

Source C

Extract from a speech by Neville Chamberlain to the 1900 Club, reported in *The Times*, 11 June 1936.

The aggression [in Abyssinia] was patent and flagrant, and there was hardly any country to which it appeared that a policy of sanctions could be exercized with a greater chance of success than against Italy. There is no use for us to shut our eyes to realities. The fact remains that the policy of collective security based on sanctions has been tried out … The policy has been tried out and has failed to prevent war, failed to stop war, failed to save the victim of aggression. I am not blaming anyone for the failure … I want to put forward one or two conclusions which, it seems to me, may fairly be drawn … I see, for instance, the other day that the President of the League of Nations Union issued a circular in which he said that the issue hung in the balance and urged a campaign of pressure on members of Parliament with the idea that if we were to pursue the policy of sanctions and even intensify it, it was still possible to preserve the independence of Abyssinia

That seems to me the very midsummer of madness. If we were to pursue it it would only lead to further misfortunes which would divert our minds as practical men from seeking other and better solutions. … If we have retained any vestige of common sense, surely we must admit that we have tried to impose upon the League a task which it was beyond its powers to fulfil.

Source D

Extract from a speech by Emperor Haile Selassie to the League of Nations Assembly, 30 June 1936.

I assert that the issue before the Assembly today is not merely the question of a settlement in the matter of Italian aggression. It is a question of collective security; of the very existence of the League; of the trust placed by States in international treaties; of the value of promises made to small States that their integrity and independence shall be respected and assured. It is a choice between the principle of the equality of States and the imposition upon small Powers of the bonds of vassalage. In a word, it is international morality which is at stake…

On behalf of the Ethiopian people, a Member of the League of Nations, I … renew my protest against the violations of treaties of which the Ethiopian people have been the victim. I declare before the whole world that the Emperor, the Government and the people of Ethiopia will not bow before force, that they uphold their claims, that they will use all means in their power to ensure the triumph of right and respect for the Covenant.

Source E

A photograph of Emperor Haile Selassie addressing the League of Nations on 30 June 1936, and accusing Italy of being an aggressor and using poison gas in the invasion of Ethiopia, which began on 3 October 1935.

Source-based questions

1 **a** According to Source D, what were the issues before the League of Nations Assembly?   *[3 marks]*

    b What message is conveyed by Source E?   *[2 marks]*

2 Compare and contrast the views expressed in Sources A and B about the relations of their countries with the League of Nations.   *[6 marks]*

3 With reference to their origin and purpose, assess the value and limitations of Sources C and D for historians studying the treatment of the Abyssinian crisis by the League of Nations.   *[6 marks]*

4 Using the sources and your own knowledge analyse the statement made in Source C that the Abyssinian crisis was a task imposed upon the League of Nations "that it was impossible to fulfil".   *[8 marks]*

2 The Arab-Israeli conflict, 1945–79

The roots of the Arab–Israeli dispute of the 20th century are sunk deep into the soil of the Middle East and are a complex network of geo-political, religious, ethnic and personal relationships. Observers may not even agree on the precise geographical location of the Middle East, let alone who or what constitutes an Arab and an Israeli. The region has been the heart of many great empires in the past and the birthplace of three of the world's major religions. These statements are an indication of why people have fought for control and influence in the region.

This chapter focuses on prescribed subject 2 and addresses the development of the Arab–Israeli conflict from 1945 to 1979. It also requires consideration of the role of outside powers in the conflict either as promoters of tension or as mediators in attempts to lessen hostilities in the region. The prescribed subject requires study of the political, economic and social issues behind the dispute and the specific causes and consequences of the military clashes between 1948–9 and 1973. The nature and extent of social and economic developments within the disputed territory of Palestine/Israel during this period and their impact on the populations should also be studied. The end date for the prescribed subject is 1979 with the signing of the Egyptian–Israeli peace agreement.

Source-based exercises are included throughout the chapter and focus on the following areas:

- the last years of the British Mandate, the UNSCOP partition plan and the outbreak of civil war
- British withdrawal, the establishment of Israel, the Arab response and the 1948–9 war
- demographic shifts: the Palestinian diaspora 1947 onwards, Jewish immigration and the economic development of the Israeli state
- the Suez Crisis of 1956: the role of the United Kingdom, France, the United States, the Soviet Union, Israel and the UN
- Arabism and Zionism, and the emergence of the PLO
- the Six Day War of 1967 and the October War of 1973: causes, course and consequences
- the role of the United States, the Soviet Union and the UN
- Camp David and the Egyptian–Israeli peace agreement.

By the end of the chapter, you should be able to:

- understand the origins of the disputes in the Middle East and in particular their affect upon relations between the Arabs and the Jews
- identify the points of conflict which have happened since the establishment of the state of Israel in 1948
- understand the economic and social situations in parts of the Middle East and the impact of demographic shifts in the area
- evaluate the role of the major powers and the impact of the Cold War in the Arab–Israeli conflict
- compare and contrast the different viewpoints that key protagonists and historians hold about the events in the Middle East
- evaluate and use documents from diverse sources to assess the events between 1945 and 1979
- recognize the subjective nature of historical evidence
- organize and express historical ideas and information.

Approaching this subject

Prescribed subject 2 follows the development of the Arab–Israeli conflict from the middle of the 20th century immediately prior to the establishment of the state of Israel and the bloody struggle in the 30 years that followed. It is, by its very nature, a contentious subject for schools to implement. However, that may be one of the best reasons for adopting it. If you have chosen this subject it is likely that you will be focusing on the 20th-century history topic 1 "Causes, practices and effects of wars", and perhaps topic 3 "Origins and development of authoritarian and single-party states" or topic 5 "The Cold War".

The skills to concentrate on are those of source evaluation. Written sources include textbooks, speeches, newspaper articles, biographies, telegrams, private correspondence, official communiqués and secret memos. In addition, there is an abundance of visual sources to look at, including photographs, graphs, statistical data and political cartoons. Material is available showing different perspectives, and many websites from governments and vested interest groups, all of which you will need to evaluate critically.

Integrating the theory of knowledge (TOK)

With each of the prescribed subjects there is more than enough opportunity to explore the nature of historical knowledge, and how historians validate knowledge claims. You will be encouraged to increase your understanding of the methodology and practice of the discipline of history through the material in the chapter and in developing your critical thinking skills through the TOK programme. The truths revealed through analysing the circumstances and events remain highly contentious. Since this subject deals with religion, politics, ideology, the Cold War and the human condition, the approach adopted by TOK becomes even more valuable. You will be required to evaluate knowledge claims by exploring knowledge issues such as validity, reliability, credibility, certainty, and individual, as well as cultural, perspectives.

The roots of the Arab-Israeli dispute, 1900–45

This first section provides the necessary background to the emphasis in this chapter on Arab–Israeli hostilities post 1945. A series of promises and agreements, made early in the 20th century in the Middle East and Ottoman Empire both during and after the First World War, contributed to a situation which developed deep suspicions and would soon produce conflict. The role of the major powers, particularly the UK and France, coupled with a rising nationalist sentiment in the area, helped to establish the conditions which were to prevail well into the 20th century.

The period between the two world wars saw the development in importance of the region in world affairs due to its strategic position and the rising demand for oil. During the British Mandate in Palestine, from 1922 to 1945, political institutions were introduced. However, Arab–Jewish conflict developed under British rule and British attempts to govern the territory increased the divide between all parties. The terrible effects of the Holocaust on the Jewish people in the Second World War in turn helped to create international sympathy for their cause after 1945.

The break-up of the Ottoman Empire

The Ottoman Empire in 1900

At the turn of the 20th century most of the Middle East was still, nominally at least, under the rule of the **Ottoman Empire**. From the late 19th century, some European powers, notably Britain, Russia and France, had interfered in Turkey, the "Sick Man of Europe", in an attempt to secure trade routes, concessions and influence in the crumbling empire. The Ottoman Empire was itself imploding, and experiencing disruption throughout its territory. The Young Turk movement, formed within the heart of the realm, carried out a revolution in 1908 against the old Sultan Abdul Hamid II. The Arabs of the Ottoman Empire too were increasingly restive, anticipating a growing Arab consciousness, which was to become a feature of the Arab–Israeli conflict later in the century.

> **Ottoman Empire** The land controlled by the Ottoman Turks from the late 14th century until the end of the First World War.

The impact of nationalism

Growing nationalism was also linked with other minorities in the Ottoman Empire. In the late 19th century, Jewish nationalism became equated with the movement known as **Zionism**. Zionism was the movement which had as its goal the creation of a Jewish state in **Palestine**: the ancient homeland of the Jews. The bigger picture of the Middle East was one of Great Power rivalry, in which these local aspirations were seen as relatively insignificant. Just as other areas of the world (most recently, Africa and Asia) had become part of the struggle for supremacy and influence among the major powers, so too was the Middle East about to become a victim of the stresses and strains of imperialism.

> **Zionism** The movement to create a national home for the Jews in Palestine. The organization was founded by Theodore Herzl in the late 19th century.

> **Palestine** Derived from Philistia, the land of the Philistines, an area bordering the Dead Sea and the Mediterranean, now usually associated with modern day Israel.

The Middle East in the Great War

The First World War saw the sun set on the Ottoman Empire. Its disintegration had gathered pace in the previous decade when Germany added her predatory instinct to that of the French and the British in the Middle East. The Kaiser's influence in Constantinople appeared to threaten Britain's position in the Persian Gulf and potentially, therefore, her access to India. So when war broke out in August 1914 and Ottoman Turkey joined the Central Powers two months later, the United Kingdom and France began to plot the division of the Middle East.

With neither ally trusting the other, policy came to be made by a handful of individuals, many of them acting on their own whims, friendships and rivalries against a backdrop of intrigue and military activity, in which the Middle East was essentially a sideshow to the more significant events that took place on the battlegrounds of Europe. The destiny of the Arabs and the Zionists at that time was subservient to greater causes—at least in the eyes of the British and French governments. They looked at progress (or the lack of it) on the battlefields, the collapse of tsarist Russia, their ally, the increasingly important role of the United States and their own strategic interests. From 1915 onwards, when the Allied attack on Gallipoli failed to dislodge Turkey from the war, a series of meetings, and verbal and written pledges, began to formulate policy. These discussions would sew the seeds of the Arab–Israeli dispute that would continue for the rest of the century and beyond. Less than a year later, Georges Picot, First Secretary of the French embassy in London, started negotiations with Henry Sykes, a young Englishman serving on one of the government committees looking into the future of the region for the British. The eventual Sykes–Picot agreement, which evolved in the autumn of 1916, came after the Arabs themselves had risen in revolt under the leadership of Sharif Hussain, the Hashemite ruler of Mecca, in June 1916.

Also at that time, one of the best-known personalities in the region stepped onto the Middle Eastern stage. Thomas Edward Lawrence (TE Lawrence), the traveller, scholar, linguist, author and proponent of the Arab cause, better known as Lawrence of Arabia, was arguably the best known Englishman of the 20th century. The roles that Lawrence played in the Arab Revolt were those of spokesman for the Arabs and guerrilla leader for the British against the Turkish forces in Arabia. However, decisions which were being taken behind the backs of the Arabs and the Jews in the melting pot of the First World War would profoundly affect the Middle East and set the stage for future conflict.

In 1917 there were a number of successes for the Arab cause in the region, including the takeover by the British General

TE Lawrence (1888–1935)

Better known as Lawrence of Arabia, he was one of the most colourful personalities of the early 20th century. Author, scholar, military strategist and an inspiration in the Arab uprising against the Ottoman Turks during the First World War, Lawrence became an international celebrity, but chose to retire from the limelight after the war when he wrote his great work, *Seven Pillars of Wisdom*, about the Arab Revolt. He was disappointed by his country's policies towards the Arabs between the wars and died in a motorcycle accident in 1935.

Allenby of the city of Jerusalem in December. The entry of the United States into the war earlier in the year, and the Bolshevik takeover of Russia in November, meant that attention turned to the Western Front once more. At the same time, a decision—unknown to the Arabs—was made by the British government. Britain's Foreign Secretary (minister), Arthur Balfour, had prepared a letter to Lord Rothschild, chairman of the British Zionists, in which he envisaged the recognition of Palestine as a national homeland for the Jewish people. The so-called **Balfour Declaration** of November 1917 had come about partly from a desire to encourage Jewish businessmen in America to support President Wilson's call for war loans, and partly from fears that Russia would withdraw from the war. It was also an indication of the growing influence of the Zionists, particularly among members of the British community. When the news reached the Arabs in 1918, it was a political bombshell.

> **Balfour Declaration** A resolution named after the British Foreign Secretary in 1917 calling for the establishment of a Jewish homeland in Palestine.

Changes in the Middle East, 1918–21

The last year of the First World War saw, in October, the collapse of Turkey, following the capture of Baghdad, Damascus, Beirut and Aleppo, and the subsequent surrender of the other Central Powers. Unintentionally, perhaps, Britain found herself the heir of a new empire. With the defeat of Germany, the collapse of Ottoman Turkey and tsarist Russia, and 1 000 000 troops stationed in the area of the Middle East, Britain was now the dominant military power in the region. At the beginning of 1919, as the leaders began to meet in Paris, anticipation ran high among the Arabs. But there was unease in Palestine following the publication of the Balfour Declaration and, as far as Arab and Zionist feelings were concerned, the lines were already drawn. There followed a complex series of meetings over the future of the Middle East, which was influenced by Anglo-French imperial interests, Wilson's ideas of self-determination and the manoeuvrings of individuals representing their own interest groups.

As the peacemakers were meeting in Paris to deal with the more major issues, two American commissioners Henry King and Charles Crane went to the Middle East. The King–Crane Commission interviewed representatives from the Arabs and the Jews in Palestine and returned with a recommendation that the Zionist programme should be dropped and that there should be a limited expansion of the Jewish community within the Arab state. Their findings were not published and other proposals were worked out.

Factors influencing the decisions which were eventually made regarding the status of the Arabs and the Jews in the Middle East included Anglo-French relations (which were becoming increasingly important to the United Kingdom, conscious of the possible withdrawal of the United States from European affairs); the fear of Bolshevism;

AJ Balfour (1848–1930)

Arthur Balfour was a British prime minister and, for three years, Foreign Secretary in the UK's war-time government. In 1917 he wrote a letter, known as the Balfour Declaration, stating the Government's view to "favour the establishment in Palestine of a national home for the Jewish people on the understanding that nothing shall be done which may prejudice the civil and religious rights of existing non-Jewish communities in Palestine". He later said, "I am more or less happy when being praised, not very comfortable when being abused, but I have moments of uneasiness when being explained."

and a resurgent Germany. Another major consideration was that of oil, now being seen as a vital commodity and a future source of energy. The oilfields then under British control lay in Iraq and Mesopotamia, and it was already becoming clear that it would not be in the UK's best interests to allow these areas to come under Arab rule. A way around this was found through the **mandate** system.

> **Mandate** An authorization granted by the League of Nations to a member nation to govern the former German or Turkish colonies, such as the British Mandate in Palestine in 1920.

At San Remo in April 1920, the League of Nations gave France mandatory rights in Syria and Lebanon, and the UK in Iraq and Palestine, with the boundaries of the territories determined as those that had been drawn up in the 1880s. The Balfour Declaration was included in the obligations for the governance of Palestine, thus binding Britain to Jewish interests. Lord Curzon, the Foreign Secretary at that time, commented that "it was clear that this mandate has been drawn up by someone under the fumes of Zionism". The mandates were ratified by the League of Nations and Britain found herself tied to a much greater degree than she had anticipated in the Middle East. It is justifiable to see the seeds of the Arab–Israeli conflict growing from the decisions reached at San Remo. The mandate system was imposed on an unwilling Arab population, who from the start resented the treachery of promises made and a betrayal of their justifiable rights of self-determination.

In 1921, Palestine and Mesopotamia became the concern of the Colonial Office under Winston Churchill, who sought the advice of TE Lawrence. The latter was instrumental in helping establish the rulers of the Arab states, albeit under the mandate system. Later that

TOK link

Hollywood and history

Lawrence of Arabia, directed by David Lean, tells the story of the Arab Revolt in the First World War and the life of TE Lawrence. Released in 1963, the film was the winner of seven Academy awards, including Best Picture. It portrays the background and many of the personalities associated with the division of the Middle East during the Great War. As you watch it, consider the way the director has treated Lawrence through the eyes of the major figures, including Sharif Hussain, Prince Abdullah, Prince Feisal, General Allenby and Sharif Ali.

After the war, TE Lawrence wrote *Seven Pillars of Wisdom*, describing his version of the Arab Revolt. Lawrence states:

> *In these pages the history is not of the Arab movement, but of me in it. It is a narrative of daily life, mean happenings, little people. Here are no lessons for the world, no disclosures to shock peoples. It is filled with trivial things, partly that no one mistake for history the bones from which some day a man may make history, and partly for the pleasure it gave me to recall the fellowship of the revolt. … All men dream: but not equally. Those who dream by night in the dusty recesses of their minds wake in the day to find that it was vanity: but the dreamers of the day are dangerous men, for they may act their dream with open eyes, to make it possible.*

As a student of history, what do you understand by Lawrence's comment that "no one mistake for history the bones from which some day a man may make history"?

How is history made? Who determines what is to become historical fact and what isn't?

Does this indicate to you why there may be problems with the nature of history as a discipline?

year, Feisal, Sharif Hussain's eldest son, accepted the throne of Iraq, while a year later Abdullah, Hussain's third son, took control of Transjordan. Two years after that, in 1924, Ibn Saud, leader of the ultra-orthodox Wahhabi movement, defeated Hussain and proclaimed himself king of Hejaz; in 1932 he took the title of King of Saudi Arabia.

In a flurry of action spanning less than a decade, the map of the Middle East had been redrawn, and relations between the Arabs and the Jews were to move into a new phase. It is important to recognize that few decisions were reached with a view to the interests or the wishes of the inhabitants of the region; promises made to individuals were often the product of war-time expediency with a wider view of their European and world impact. For the Palestinian Arabs and the Jews, the struggle was just beginning. The former believed that they had a right to the land from historical precedent—even Wilsonian ideals of self-determination. Likewise the latter believed in their claim because of their past history. It would be difficult for either side to accept the legitimacy of the other.

Changes in the Middle East, 1917–21

Former Turkish areas set up as British Mandates in 1921, and subsequently independent (Iraq in 1932, Transjordan in 1946)

Arab states helped by Britain in their war against Turky, 1915–1918 and receiving British financial subsidies

Arab areas under British rule or control in 1914; all of them were independent by 1971

Former Turkish areas coming under French control in 1920, but subsequently independent (Syria in 1943, Lebanon in 1944)

Palestine in 1922

Discussion point: questions to consider on Hollywood and history

How does the director David Lean portray the character of TE Lawrence? Is he sympathetic or critical?

Explain and justify your reasoning with evidence from the film.

The American journalist Jackson Bentley comments at Lawrence's funeral, "he was a poet, a scholar, and a mighty warrior. He was also the most shameless exhibitionist since Barnum and Bailey [creators of the first circus in the USA known as 'The Greatest Show on Earth']."

What do you think he meant by these comments and how are they supported by Lawrence's actions in the film?

You may be interested in David Lean's other historical films, *Bridge on the River Kwai*, released in 1957, and *Dr Zhivago*, released in 1965. Both of them are historical epics, based on major works of literature.

How useful are films as historical evidence?

What do you think the drawbacks and benefits might be of learning history from Hollywood?

Activity:

Historical films

List six films from the last three years, which are based on either historical characters or historical events and give a brief synopsis of the plot or life of the main character(s). Do any of these films contain controversial material or interpretations of events?

The British Mandate in Palestine, 1922–45

British rule, 1922–39

The British rule in Palestine between the wars was characterized by hostility, suspicion and shifts in policy, all of which contributed to create a more complex situation in the region on the eve of the Second World War. The decade after the San Remo conference in 1922 saw continued Jewish immigration and the doubling of their population by 1930. It appeared to the Arabs that the United Kingdom was following a more lenient policy towards the Jews. Although relations were, on the whole, conciliatory, there were some flashpoints which served to illustrate that tensions were never far from the surface. The promises given to the Zionists by the British in 1917 reflected the real sense of betrayal felt by the Arabs. The rejection of Arab demands for independence, British support for the Zionist position, increased Jewish immigration and the uncertainty of the political situation were all met with resentment and led to several bloody clashes, which left hundreds dead and bitterness on all sides.

Major developments in the period between the wars

Disturbances broke out in May 1921 in Jaffa, just prior to the signing of the San Remo agreement, and minor disturbances occurred throughout the decade—but, in August 1929, the biggest riots occurred near the **Wailing Wall** in Jerusalem. Orthodox Jews attempted to attach a curtain to the Wall to separate men from women at prayer, but the Arabs saw this as a step to claiming control

> **Wailing Wall** A part of the outer wall of the sacred Jewish temple in Jerusalem, destroyed by the Romans in AD 70. It also forms the base of the Dome of the Rock. For the Jews, the Wall represents the only remaining part of Solomon's Temple, a relic of the ancient kingdom of Israel. For the Muslims, too, the area is a holy site; the Dome of the Rock is the third most sacred spot in Islam, the place from where the Prophet Mohammed was taken into heaven.

Activity:

The Ottoman Empire: "the Sick Man of Europe"?

1 Investigate the impact and influences which the Ottomans had on a particular region or modern country in the Middle East. Look at aspects such as the culture, religion, architecture, food and customs.

2 Choose any one of the following personalities involved in the historical development so far and see what further information you can find on him.
   - Theodore Herzl
   - Arthur Balfour
   - Sherif Husain
   - King Feisal
   - TE Lawrence
   - Lord Curzon
   - Ibn Saud

3 After you have investigated the impact and influences the Ottomans had on a region or country of the Middle East, discuss how this might have influenced events later in the period.

Essay writing

Draft an outline for the following essay:

- "Both the Zionists and the Arab nationalists believed Palestine had been promised to them." How did this happen and to what extent were the Western powers responsible for this situation?

Written commentaries

Write 300+ word commentaries on each of the following:

1 The impact of the Ottoman Empire's break-up for the Middle East.

2 The role of the Great Powers and their interests in the Middle East.

3 The impact and significance for the region of the peace settlements made at the end of the First World War.

Test your knowledge

Write a brief statement on, or orally explain the significance of, each of the following:

- the Balfour Declaration
- the Sykes–Picot agreement
- the San Remo conference
- Theodore Herzl and Zionism
- the significance of TE Lawrence
- the mandate system and the League of Nations.

of the temple area and they reacted with violence. In the disturbances, the old Jewish community at Hebron was wiped out. Altogether, over 250 people were killed, roughly an equal number of Arabs and Jews, and hopes of a peaceful Palestine were shattered.

In the 1930s the Arabs grew more radical as their demands for independence were not met. In 1935 a Muslim leader, Izz al-Din al Qassam, preached resistance and urged Arabs to prepare for revolution. He was shot and killed by British soldiers in November of that year and became a martyr to the cause of Arab nationalism. In 1936, an Arab uprising followed a general strike which had been declared in April. The revolt was caused by fears over increasing Jewish immigration and what the Arabs saw as the pro-Zionist policy of the British government. The mufti of Jerusalem, Al-Husseini, called for resistance to the British and violence followed against both the colonial government and the Jews. The latter fought back through groups such as **Haganah** and the more radical **Irgun**. The revolt continued on and off for the next four years.

In response to the disturbances, the British government appointed a Royal Commission to investigate and, in July 1937, the **Peel Report** published its findings, concluding that partition into separate Arab and Jewish states was the best solution to the problem. The report also recommended that an Arab state be merged with Transjordan and a restriction placed on Jewish immigration. It was a significant departure from traditional British policy in the region. Arab opposition to partition was strong, adding more fuel to the revolt and, by 1939, the uprising had cost the lives of over 500 Jews and 3000 Arabs—with no solution in sight.

In May 1939 the British government issued a White Paper (government report) proposing the creation of a single state in Palestine within ten years. Both Arabs and Jews rejected the White Paper; the former wanting immediate independence and a restriction to Jewish immigration, while the latter felt that the promises made in the Balfour Declaration had been violated. The White Paper represented an act of political expediency for the British, and exhibited little concern for either the Arabs or the Jews in Palestine. This was the price they were prepared to pay at that time to pursue their own interests.

A strange brew of tensions had emerged in the time between the wars. A number of British officials on the ground in Palestine were clearly sensitive to the Arab cause and saw Zionist demands as a threat to British interests in the region. Yet the officials were at odds with the politicians of their own government back in London, many of whom were sympathetic to the Zionists. Adolf Hitler's rise to power in Germany in January 1933 resulted in an increase in the number of Jewish immigrants from

Haganah An underground Jewish group created in 1920, Haganah became a countrywide organization that involved young adults. The name means "defence" in Hebrew.

Irgun An extreme Jewish organization founded in 1931 after a split within Haganah. Irgun advocated armed Jewish insurrection against British rule and war against Palestinian Arabs. The name means 'national military organization'.

Peel Report Named after the leader of the British Commission which met in 1937 and whose report recommended partition in Palestine.

Activity:

Test your knowledge

Write a brief description to explain the significance of each of the following:

- the Wailing Wall
- immigration issues.

This cartoon by David Low was published in the *Evening Standard* on 30 July 1937. Ormsby-Gore (British diplomat) is saying, "After all, it does give you a national standing." How did the cartoonist see British policy in Palestine following the Peel Report?

Germany into Palestine. But the period had also served to widen the gap between the two sides. In 1919 Jews made up only 10 per cent of the population; but by 1940 they had grown to around 460 000—that is, nearly 30 per cent of the total population of 1.5 million. Such an environment, with increased immigration, conflicting policies by the British, the radicalization of both Jewish and Arab extremists and the coming impact of the **Holocaust** and war, created a situation in which a British withdrawal was almost inevitable, and a conflict between the two sides, Arab and Jew, was probably unavoidable.

The impact of the Second World War on the British Mandate in Palestine

The Second World War had a profound influence on events in the region and around the world. At the outbreak of war, the Jewish leader David Ben Gurion commented, "We shall fight for Britain as if there is no White Paper. We shall fight the White Paper as if there is no war." Many Jews fought on the side of the United Kingdom and the Allies and, when the United States joined to fight, many Americans took up the cause, hoping for the creation of a Zionist homeland after the war. In May 1942, a number of American Zionist supporters met at the Biltmore Hotel in New York and drew up what became known as the **Biltmore Programme**. Meanwhile the Arab cause had not been helped by their own leaders, many of whom had fled the country after the failed Arab uprising in 1939. The mufti of Jerusalem, Al-Husseini, who had left Palestine in 1937, allied himself with Iraqi rebels against British rule and then went to Germany to support Hitler's campaign against the Jews.

By 1945, the Holocaust had led to the deaths of an estimated six million Jews in the death camps of Europe. The horror of this campaign prompted considerable sympathy for the Jewish people at the end of the war, especially in the United States. In addition, Europe was faced with a massive refugee problem and this in turn created pressure to allow increased numbers of Jewish immigrants into Palestine. Maintaining the Palestine mandate had already caused major difficulties for the British and after the Second World War they had other priorities closer to home. Despite the UK winning the war, the empire was in decline, and it was looking for an honourable way out of the situation in Palestine.

> **Holocaust** The term given to the killing of almost six million Jews by the Nazis in the Second World War.

> **Biltmore Programme** The result of a meeting of American Jews in a hotel of the same name, this called for the immediate creation of a Jewish state in Palestine and an end to the restrictions on immigration.

Activity:

Essay writing

Write 300–400 words to address each of the following:

1 Research the importance of the religious sites on Mount Zion in Jerusalem to each of the three major religions: Judaism, Christianity and Islam.

2 What were the main issues that divided the Arabs, the Jews and the British in the inter-war period?

3 To what extent were the British responsible for the situation that existed in the Palestinian mandate by 1939?

Activity:

Palestine between the wars

You will already have been considering which were the factors that led to the worsening situation in Palestine in the period between the wars. You may have formed opinions about why the situation didn't improve under the British Mandate.

Use the columns of the table below to make your own summary notes from the information you have so far. If you feel that you need to make additional columns, go ahead!

Jewish immigration into the mandate territories	The rise of Arab nationalism	The effect of the world economic crisis after 1929	Lack of consistency in British policy decisions	The strategic importance of the region in the world	The rise to power of Adolf Hitler in Germany	The radicalization of both Jewish and Arab policies in the region

Source analysis

The following documents relate to the British Mandate in Palestine, 1922–45. The prescribed subject starts in 1945, but the issues raised will provide a useful background to the conflict.

Source A

The Report of the Palestine Royal Commission (Peel Report), July 1937.

Considering the attitude which both the Arab and the Jewish representatives adopted in giving evidence, the Commission think it improbable that either party will be satisfied at first sight with the proposals submitted for the adjustment of their rival claims. For Partition means that neither will get all it wants. It means that the Arabs must acquiesce in the exclusion from their sovereignty of a piece of territory, long occupied and once ruled by them. It means that the Jews must be content with less than the Land of Israel they once ruled and have hoped to rule again. But it seems possible that on reflection both parties will come to realize that the drawbacks of Partition are outweighed by its advantages. For, if it offers neither party all it wants, it offers each what it wants most, namely freedom and security. …

To both Arabs and Jews Partition offers a prospect—and there is none in any other policy—of obtaining the inestimable boon of peace. It is surely worth some sacrifice on both sides if the quarrel which the Mandate started could be ended with its termination.

Source: Laqueur, W and Rubin, B. (eds). 1991. *The Arab–Israeli Reader: Documentary History*. 5th edn. New York, USA. Penguin. pp. 48–9.

Source B

British White Paper—Statement of Policy, May 1939.

The Royal Commission and previous Commissions of Enquiry have drawn attention to the ambiguity of certain expressions in the Mandate, such as the expression "national home for the Jewish people" and they have found in this ambiguity and the resulting uncertainty as to the objectives of policy a fundamental cause of unrest and hostility between Arabs and Jews. His Majesty's Government are convinced that in the interests of the peace and well-being of the whole people of Palestine a clear definition of policy and objectives is essential.

1   *The objective of His Majesty's Government is the establishment within ten years of an independent Palestine State in such treaty relations with the United Kingdom as will provide satisfactorily for the commercial and strategic requirements of both countries in the future. …*

2   *Jewish immigration during the next five years will be at a rate, which, if economic absorptive capacity permits, will bring the Jewish population up to approximately one-third of the total population of the country … of some 75,000 immigrants over the next five years.*

After the period of five years no further Jewish immigration will be permitted unless the Arabs of Palestine are prepared to acquiesce in it.

Source: Laqueur, W and Rubin, B. (eds). 1991. *The Arab–Israeli Reader: Documentary History*. 5th edn. New York, USA. pp. 54–64.

Source-based questions

1   In Source A, the Peel Report comments, "Partition means that neither will get all it wants." How and why does the report argue that partition would be in each side's interests?

2   What excuses does the Peel Report offer as to why the British government has been unable to keep all parties happy in the mandate?

3   Do you think the Peel Report upheld the spirit of the Balfour Declaration of 1917? Explain your answer.

4   In Source B, what are the main reasons why the White Paper indicated that the British government could no longer support the idea of two independent states in Palestine?

5   Do you think that the White Paper would have been more acceptable to the Arabs or to the Jews? Explain your reasoning.

6   Compare the Peel Report (1937) and the White Paper (1939) on the future status of Palestine as an independent state.

The last years of the British Mandate, UNSCOP and war, 1945–8

In the period following the defeat of Nazi Germany in 1945 the situation in the Middle East had partially reverted to that which had existed prior to the outbreak of war. Other circumstances were now to create a situation where the UK was to be eclipsed as the dominant power. The USA now came to play a more significant role, both directly and indirectly, in the events which were to see the creation of a new state in the region and the outbreak of a bloody and long-running conflict.

Britain and the post-war Middle East, 1945–6

At the end of the Second World War, the United Kingdom remained the paramount power in the Middle East with its holdings nominally intact. The web of British possessions included the island of Cyprus, substantial oil interests in the Persian Gulf, the Anglo-Iranian Oil Company, holdings in Iraq, treaties with former British Mandate territories of Iraq, Jordan and Palestine and the strategic jewel of the Suez Canal in Egypt. Yet this impressive list of territories was to some extent a chimera, a figment of imagination, in the British Empire. The UK had emerged from the war a winner; but the country had been shattered by the war against the Axis powers and faced major financial difficulty after six years of hardship. The UK would have to cut her losses and readjust to a new reality regarding her position in world affairs.

The Cold War was a major dilemma confronting the UK in the post-war period. This was by no means the only difficulty. The intervention of the United States in the war was to bring its own problems and benefits to the British position in the Middle East. The other force, which the UK had to face, was the growing tide of nationalism within its empire. The decision to grant India and Pakistan independence was to shift the centre of gravity away from the Far East and towards the Middle East and make the region of even greater importance for Britain's strategic control. Thus the newly elected British Labour government was to face a multitude of problems in the immediate post-war world, of which Palestine and the aggravated Arab–Israeli issue was only one item on the agenda. In Palestine, the British faced the problem of what to do with the mandate and, since the Second World War, the issues had become even more complex. Among these were:

- whether to implement the policies made by previous British governments, including the White Paper recommendations of 1939
- the growing involvement of the United States in Palestine
- the development of the Cold War and Soviet interests in the region
- the actions of the Arab leadership during the war itself
- how to handle the activities of the Hebrew resistance movements, particularly in the winter of 1945–6
- the general outpouring of pro-Jewish feeling in the post-war world
- the large number of displaced persons (DPs), and a significant percentage of Jews that had to be dealt with as soon as possible.

Developments in Palestine, 1945–6

Events in Palestine were soon to spiral out of British control, with the result that—less than two years after the end of the war—the UK was prepared to surrender its mandate to the United Nations. As indicated above, there were myriad concerns for British foreign policy under the new Labour government and the new Foreign Secretary, Ernest Bevin, the man entrusted with the task of handling these affairs. A hard pragmatist, Bevin was not particularly sympathetic to the Zionist cause and, together with prime minister Clement Attlee, moved in the direction of a solution, hand in hand with the Americans.

Meanwhile, within the mandated territories, the Arabs and the Jews were unhappy to see the British return. The former had always suffered from the lack of political structure, and leadership too, following Mufti Al-Husseini's contacts with Hitler and the Nazis. The Arabs in general were thus in poor condition to conduct a vigorous and determined campaign to represent their own interests in the post-war world. Despite what had happened to their numbers in the rest of Europe during the war years, the Jews, on the other hand, were in a stronger position in Palestine. The **Jewish Agency**, which continued to represent Jewish interests to the British, was led by David Ben Gurion as its key figure.

Meanwhile, Zionist underground activity had begun to increase and in 1945 the three main Jewish groups, Haganah, Irgun and **Lehi**, formed what was known as the "United Resistance" with the aim of creating an independent homeland as soon as possible. Between October 1945 and July 1946, when the most infamous act of violence took place, the Jewish underground succeeded in killing or wounding a number of British soldiers and tying up 100 000 personnel in the territories.

Diplomacy and the role of the United States

As British security forces were under pressure in Palestine, the politicians were trying to find a solution. The Anglo-American Committee of Enquiry was set up in November 1945 to examine "the political, economic and social conditions in Palestine as they bear upon the problem of Jewish immigration and settlement therein". The members listened to representatives from all sides and met with refugees over the following few months before coming to their conclusions. Of the six American members of the committee, at least three were certainly sympathetic towards the Zionist cause but, when the committee made its final recommendations in April 1946, partition was rejected as unworkable and not in the best interests of the population of the mandate. They had struck a compromise which in reality pleased no one, stating ambiguously: "any attempt to establish an ... independent Palestinian state would result in civil strife that might threaten the peace of the world".

Meanwhile, President Truman was moving more towards the Zionist camp, appearing to succumb to Jewish pressure groups at home. American domestic politics was to become an important component of any solution to the Arab–Israeli situation. On the day that the committee released its findings, Truman made a speech declaring his support for the admission of another 100 000 Jews into Palestine,

Jewish Agency A political organization established after the First World War to aid Jewish immigration into Palestine.

Lehi Also known after its founder Abraham Stern as the Stern Gang, Lehi was a radical armed Zionist group dedicated to the creation of a Jewish state in Palestine. Lehi was responsible for the assassination of the UK's top official in Palestine, Lord Moyne. On 6 November 1944, members of Lehi shot Moyne three times. He was rushed to hospital but died of his wounds. As well as being the highest British official within Lehi's reach, Moyne was regarded as personally responsible for Britain's Palestine policy.

which angered the British government. With the mid-term elections coming up in the United States, "it seemed to the British that winning the election in New York was more important than dead bodies in Palestine". It was against this backdrop that the Jewish underground movement took matters into their own hands and attacked the King David Hotel in July 1946.

The King David Hotel in Jerusalem was a luxury hotel, opened to the public in 1931. Due to the location and comfort of the establishment, the British Mandate government requisitioned part of the hotel in 1938 and set up their military command centre in the hotel building.

Following the return of the British in numbers to Palestine after the war, they decided on tough measures to regain their authority. Facing a number of acts of sabotage against British installations and the killing of soldiers and policemen in Palestine, the British authorities launched a campaign in June 1946 to search for weapons, munitions and explosives. The authorities rounded up hundreds of Zionists and sealed off Tel Aviv, parts of Jerusalem and Haifa.

The attack on the King David Hotel

The attack on the King David Hotel was carried out in response to these pressure by the extremist group Irgun. Together with Haganah, the mainstream Jewish organization that had operated since the 1930s, Irgun was joined by the radical wing of the Zionists known as Lehi. Haganah had not, up until that time, pursued a campaign of assaulting and killing British servicemen or civilians, unlike the other two groups, but things were to change.

In July, despite its initial approval of the attack, Haganah requested repeated delays in response to the changing political situation, but the plan was finalized and the specific hour chosen to minimize civilian casualties. The attack would take place on 22 July at 11 a.m. The plan called for members of Irgun to be dressed as hotel employees and to carry the explosives (approximately 350 kg of explosives hidden in six milk churns) to the hotel wing below where the British offices were located. The operation was delayed, starting at 12 noon, but a skirmish followed between the infiltrators and two British soldiers who became suspicious and intervened. Irgun still succeeded in placing the bombs, escaped and, as a decoy, detonated a small explosive in the street outside. Arab workers in the kitchen were told to flee, which they did. Irgun have always maintained that they gave explicit precautions and telephoned the British authorities, so that the whole area would be evacuated. This is one of the contentious issues about what happened on that day.

A few minutes before 12.45 p.m. on 22 July 1946, the explosives detonated. The southern wing of the seven-storey hotel collapsed, killing 91 people (the figure was later adjusted to 92), including British, Jews and Arabs, and wounding dozens more. Many had been caught by the blast inside the building, apparently unable to escape in time. The official Israeli position has always maintained that Irgun did warn the British authorities and that the latter failed to evacuate the building, which, resulting in many unnecessary casualties.

Irgun claims that, after leaving the hotel and before the explosives went off, their leader, Yisrael Levi (Gidon), instructed two female members of the gang to telephone the message to the hotel, to the office of the *Palestine Post* and to the French Consulate (which lay next to the hotel) in order to give the authorities time to evacuate the building. The evacuation did not happen and so the question remains, why did the British not do this? Menachim Begin, the leader of Irgun on the day of the attack, later reported that he was saddened and upset that the British did not evacuate the hotel. He also reported that the British refused to evacuate the building because the officer in charge, Sir John Shaw, said, "We don't take orders from Jews".

The reactions to the attack

The success of the Jewish underground movement against a stronghold of British rule in Palestine sent shock waves around the world. Those who died in the blasts included 29 Britons, 41 Arabs, 17 Jews and 5 others. The British government reacted strongly against the outrage. Clement Attlee spoke in the Commons the next day of the "brutal and murderous crime committed yesterday in Jerusalem", calling it "an insane act of terrorism" and a "dastardly outrage". In a private letter to Truman, Attlee said, "I am sure you will agree that the inhuman crime committed in Jerusalem on July 22nd calls for the strongest action against terrorism".

The leadership of the Jewish Agency also condemned the attack, expressing "their feelings of horror at the base and unparalleled act perpetrated today by a gang of criminals". David Ben Gurion, at that time in Paris, condemned the action in an interview, calling Irgun "an enemy of the Jewish people".

Irgun issued an initial statement accepting responsibility for the attack but blamed the British for its failure to respond to the warning. A year later, Irgun said that they were acting on instructions from the "United Resistance" group to carry out the attack as soon as possible.

Source evaluation

A cartoon by Leslie Illingworth published in the British *Daily Mail*, 15 August 1946. A notice outside the entrance to a temporary shelter marked "Palestine" reads "No More Squatters allowed, by order HM Govt", while people labelled "illegal" and "immigrant" are waiting by the gate.

Questions

1 Identify the different sets of figures shown in the cartoon. What is the cartoonist's opinion (as far as you can make out) of the claims of the different groups?

2 How sympathetic is he to their plight? What helps you in forming an opinion?

Consequences of the attack

The immediate repercussions of the bombing were that the UK hardened its attitude to what it deemed were terrorist organizations and that it worsened relations between the British and the **Yishuv**. The UK recognized that its mandate to run Palestine was coming to an end. The troubles experienced by the British before the war in Palestine had now worsened and were unlikely to improve. The British commander in Palestine, General Sir Evelyn Barker, issued an order that all Jewish places of entertainment would be out of bounds to all ranks, with a concluding comment that these measures would "be punishing the Jews in the way the race dislikes as much as any by striking at their pockets and showing our contempt for them". The order was rescinded two weeks later, but the anti-Semitism in this statement had damaged Britain's image.

> **Yishuv** The Jewish community in the land of Israel.

As a result of the almost universal condemnation of the attack, the moderates in Palestine began to exercise control and, less than two weeks later, at a meeting in Paris, the Jewish Agency terminated the armed struggle against the British. This provoked resentment among some of the extremists, and both Irgun and Lehi continued to support violent action against the mandate power. A year later, having been condemned by many, Irgun released a statement saying that, "telephone warnings were given at 12.10 to 12.15. And if it is true, as the British liars have announced, that the explosion occurred at 12.37, they still had 22 minutes at their disposal in order to evacuate the building … Therefore responsibility for the loss of life amongst civilians rests solely with them."

The bombing arguably strengthened the hand of those who advocated a rapid settlement on the issue of Palestine. The British determined to hand over the mandate to the United Nations soon afterwards.

In July 2006, right-wing Israelis and former members of Irgun met to commemorate the bombing. A plaque was erected outside the restored building which presents the facts as Irgun claims, "For reasons known only to the British, the hotel was not evacuated." The British ambassador wrote a protest denying that the British had been warned, adding that, even if they had been, "this does not absolve those who planted the bomb from responsibility for the deaths". The controversy over the plaque and the celebration of the bombing went to the heart of the debate over the use of political violence in the Middle East. The Israeli prime minster, Benjamin Netanyahu, argued in a speech celebrating the attack that Irgun were governed by morals: "It's very important to

> ### Discussion point:
>
> #### A case study in violence
>
> The attack and subsequent destruction of part of the King David Hotel in Jerusalem and the deaths of 92 people may be relatively small by today's standards of brutality. Nevertheless, it represented the biggest and deadliest attack against the British in the history of the mandate. Even today, over 60 years on, the attack provokes controversy. (See source analysis documents, pages 96–7.)
>
> This case study asks you to look at a number of different viewpoints regarding the events and subsequent accounts of the episode as an example of historical interpretation. It can also be examined through the lens of theory of knowledge, and a discussion on the following questions:
>
> **What is history? How reliable is historical knowledge? Should history be used as a vehicle for nationalism?**

make the distinction between terror groups and freedom fighters, and between terror action and legitimate military action", he said. The writing on the two plaques on the hotel reads:

The original wording

The Hotel housed the Mandate Secretariat as well as the Army Headquarters. On July 1946 [sic] Irgun fighters at the order of the Hebrew Resistance Movement planted explosives in the basement. Warning phone calls had been made urging the hotel's occupants to leave immediately. For reasons known only to the British the hotel was not evacuated and after 25 minutes the bombs exploded, and to the Irgun's regret and dismay 91 persons were killed.

The amended version

Warning phone calls had been made to the hotel, the *Palestine Post* and the French Consulate, urging the hotel's occupants to leave immediately. The hotel was not evacuated, and after 25 minutes the bombs exploded. The entire western wing was destroyed, and to the Irgun's regret, 92 persons were killed.

The Times. 20 July 2006.
http://www.timesonline.co.uk/tol/news/world/middle_east/article690085.ece

Towards partition: UNSCOP and developments in Palestine in 1947

By the end of 1946 the situation in the mandate was becoming increasingly untenable for the British. With other issues pressing on their resources—including the Cold War, economic hardships at home, a hard, miserable winter and the decision to hand over India—sentiment was moving in the direction of submitting the problem of Palestine to the United Nations. A conference was scheduled in London in February 1947, during which time proposals were presented to the Arab and Jewish delegations. Ernest Bevin (British Foreign Secretary under Attlee's post-war Labour government) made an effort to strike a balance between the two sides, proposing a transition to independence over a five-year period, but neither side was willing to compromise. Frustrated, Bevin delivered a speech in which he "hurled Palestine into the arena of the United Nations".[8]

As a result of this decision, the UN established **UNSCOP** in May 1947. The neutral eleven-man committee toured the Palestinian mandate collecting evidence from both sides and prepared to report back to the UN at the beginning of September. The Arabs, however, believing that the commission was weighted against them, refused to co-operate fully with its members. It was to prove a disastrous choice of action, for the Jewish groups offered full co-operation and actively promoted their own interests.

UNSCOP United Nations Special Committee on Palestine.

During this time two events were to influence the decision of the neutral members of the committee regarding the future status of Palestine.

1   Early in July, two British soldiers were kidnapped by Irgun and held hostage. When the British executed three Jewish terrorists who had earlier been sentenced to death, Irgun hanged the kidnapped soldiers and booby-trapped their bodies. A wave of anti-Semitism swept across a number of British towns.

2   The other episode, also in July, was the propaganda gained for the Jews when Haganah publicized the arrival of a refugee ship to the port of Haifa. The British cargo ship had been renamed *Exodus* and was crammed with 4500 Jewish refugees, many of them former inmates of Nazi concentration camps seeking a home in Palestine. Sailing from the south of France (and filmed by American newsreel cameras), the Royal Navy intercepted the ship and its passengers, landed them in Haifa, but then, amid the glare of publicity, sent them back to Europe. Some of the passengers, including many orphaned children, declared a hunger strike. With the eyes of the world upon them, the British authorities forcibly removed some from the ship and transferred them to displaced persons camps in Germany. Protests erupted on both sides of the Atlantic. The ensuing public embarrassment over the *Exodus* affair undermined Britain's reputation in the eyes of the world and played a significant role in the diplomatic swing of sympathy toward the Jews and the eventual recognition of a Jewish state the following year.

The *Exodus*, with the banner saying, 'HAGANAH Ship EXODUS 1947'.

The UNSCOP Report, August 1947

When the committee presented its report at the end of August, it was unanimous in calling for an end to the British Mandate within two years and for a partition into an Arab state and a Jewish state, with the city of Jerusalem to be governed under international trusteeship. This was a recognition that the claims of the two sides were fundamentally irreconcilable and that partition was the most practicable solution. How the land was to be divided was not clarified but the two groups were expected to co-operate in an economic union and share a common currency. The Arabs refused to accept the settlement. According to the UNSCOP plan, the Jewish state would be larger than the Arab state even though Jewish land ownership was less than 10 per cent of the territory and the number of Jews represented about one third of the total population. The Jews, who had used their diplomacy, accepted the partition proposal.

The following two months saw intense lobbying of world opinion by both sides but particularly the Jewish representatives. Britain refused to wait for the debate in the UN General Assembly scheduled for November and, in late September, announced that they would withdraw from Palestine and hand over the mandate to the United Nations.

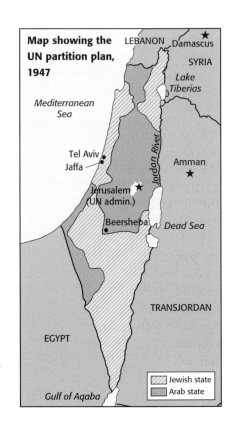

Map showing the UN partition plan, 1947

LEBANON
Damascus
SYRIA
Lake Tiberias
Mediterranean Sea
Tel Aviv
Jaffa
Jordan River
Amman
Jerusalem (UN admin.)
Beersheba
Dead Sea
TRANSJORDAN
EGYPT
Gulf of Aqaba

Jewish state
Arab state

The UN vote for partition, November 1947

In order for the resolution to be accepted, a two-thirds majority vote was needed in the General Assembly. Most observers assumed that the Assembly vote would deny the partition plan. The consensus was that the majority of states outside Europe would support the Arabs, and that the Soviets would oppose the United States and therefore reject the creation of an independent Jewish state in the Middle East. Even at that late stage, it was uncertain how President Truman and the USA would vote. There would be an election the following year, and many in the US government were conscious of the need to keep the Arab states and the oil lobby on their side. Truman commented in his memoirs that he had never "had as much pressure and propaganda aimed at the White House" as he had in this instance.

Attitudes towards the UN partition of Palestine, 1947	
Countries/lobby groups	**Position on partition and related issues**
United Kingdom	• Strongly opposed the partition plan • Refused to co-operate with the UN • Supported the restriction of Jewish immigration into Palestine
New Zealand	• Strongly supported partition and called for its enforcement • Favoured Jewish immigration into Palestine, especially refugees and displaced persons • Discouraged Jewish immigration to New Zealand, particularly from Central and Eastern Europe because of opposition from trade unions and pro-British political groups
United States	• Strongly favoured partition • Encouraged immigration of large numbers of Jews into Palestine • Permitted only limited Jewish immigration into the USA
Soviet Union	• Strongly favoured partition • Encouraged immigration of large numbers of Russian Jews into Palestine
Arab states	• Strongly opposed partition • Demanded a unitary state of Palestine • Called for an immediate suspension of all Jewish immigration
Jewish Agency	• Strongly favoured partition • Called for immigration of millions of Jews • Actively lobbied for international support for their position

Source: Macintyre, Ron. 1997. *Palestine–Israel: Conflict in the Holy Land*. Australia. Palgrave Macmillan.

On 10 October 1947, the USA announced a statement in favour of partition. Three days later, the Russians surprised the United Kingdom and the United States by announcing that it too supported partition in Palestine. Some in the West attributed ulterior motives to the Soviet action but this decision certainly helped the Jewish cause. The UK, on the other hand, announced that it would abstain in the vote. However, the day before the vote was scheduled, the resolution for partition was still short of the two-thirds majority vote needed to pass it, and further pressure was brought to bear on delegates from around the world, particularly by the USA and its supporters. The final General Assembly vote was taken on 29 November and the partition plan endorsed by the necessary two-thirds majority: 33 countries had supported the plan; 13 countries had voted against and ten had abstained.

Source analysis

Other opinions of the attack on the King David Hotel.

Source A

For decades the British denied they had been warned. In 1979, however, a member of the British Parliament introduced evidence that the Irgun had indeed issued the warning. He offered the testimony of a British officer who heard other officers in the King David Hotel bar joking about a Zionist threat to the headquarters. The officer who overheard the conversation immediately left the hotel and survived.

Source: "The Bombing of the King David Hotel", *Jewish Virtual Library*. http://www.jewishvirtuallibrary.org/jsource/History/King_David.html.

Source B

[The] *British position was made more resolute by the blowing up of the King David Hotel in Jerusalem, a wing of which was used as British army headquarters: ninety one were killed. This was perpetrated by Begin's Irgun working in an alliance with Haganah. Begin has claimed that the British were warned, but no satisfactory evidence has been produced.*

Source: Ovendale, Ritchie. 2004. *The Origins of the Arab–Israeli Wars*. Harlow, UK. Pearson Education. p. 108.

Source C

The Haganah radio later broadcast a report that on receiving the warning Sir John Shaw, the Chief Secretary of the British administration, had said:
"I give orders here. I don't take orders from Jews"
and insisted that nobody leave the building.

Source: Katz, Samuel. 1966. *Days of Fire*. Tel Aviv, Israel. Karni Press. (Hebrew).

Source D

At first, the Mandatory government denied having received a telephone warning, but testimony submitted to the interrogating judge made it clear beyond a doubt that such a warning had in fact been given. Moreover, the **Palestine Post** *telephone operator attested on oath to the police that, immediately after receiving the telephone message, she had telephoned the duty officer at the police station. The French Consulate staff opened their windows as they had been told to by the anonymous woman who telephoned them, and this was further evidence of the warning.*

Source: "The Bombing of the King David Hotel", Irgun website. http://www.etzel.org.il/english/ac10.htm

Source E

The Jewish Agency's motive was to destroy all evidence the British had gathered proving that the terrorist crime waves in Palestine were not merely the actions of "fringe" groups such as the Irgun and Stern Gang, but were committed in collusion with the Haganah and Palmach groups and under the direction of the highest political body of the Zionist establishment itself, namely the Jewish Agency. That so many innocent civilian lives were lost in the King David massacre is a normal part of the pattern of the history of Zionist outrages: a criminal act is committed, allegedly by an isolated group, but actually under the direct authorization of the highest Zionist authorities, whether of the Jewish Agency during the Palestine Mandate or of the Government of Israel thereafter.

Source: "The King David Massacre", *Israeli Crimes*. http://www.deathmasters.com.

Source F

The Irgun, under Menachim Begin, then decided to blow up the King David Hotel in Jerusalem. … Haganah assented initially, but they later withdrew support following an appeal by Weizmann. … Begin then undertook the operation on his own and scheduled it for the middle of the working day. The resulting explosion, on July 22nd, killed ninety-one British, Jewish and Arab personnel and wounded dozens more. … the logic of Zionist terrorism was bearing fruit. That is, the Lehi and Irgun preferred to kill British soldiers rather than officers in order to bring home to the British public at large the cost of maintaining a hold on Palestine.

Source: Smith, Charles D. 1988. *Palestine and the Arab–Israeli Conflict*. New York, USA. St Martin's Press. p. 188.

Source G

Political cartoon by Leslie Illingworth in the British newspaper the *Daily Mail*, 23 July 1946, entitled "Zionist terrorists attack the King David Hotel".

Source H

Photograph of the King David Hotel from the south, after the explosion on 22 July 1946.

Source-based questions

Examine Sources A–H and answer the following questions.

1 From the sources is it possible to determine:
   a Why the British chose the King David Hotel as their headquarters?
   b Why the planned attack was delayed by Haganah?

2 Compare and contrast the views expressed about why the hotel was not evacuated by the British in Sources B, C and D.

3 With reference to their origin and purpose, assess the value and limitations of Sources A, E and F for historians analysing why there were so many casualties in the King David Hotel bombing.

4 What is the attitude of the cartoonist to the bombing? How do you think Sources G and H might influence British policy in Palestine?

5 How can you explain the comments made by the Jewish Agency that the bombing was a "base and unparalleled act perpetrated today by a gang of criminals"?

6 How far do you see the bombing of the King David Hotel as "the straw that broke the camel's back" for the British with respect to their decision to hand over the mandate of Palestine to the United Nations in the following year?

Activity:
Research

1 Research the origins and activities of the three Hebrew resistance groups: Haganah, Irgun and Lehi.
   ● How and why were they formed and what were the essential differences between them?
   ● How did each contribute towards creating a Zionist state?

2 Find out about forces of occupation in other countries. Around the same time, the British were engaged in struggles with other nationalist groups in the British Empire who were calling for independence. These included Ireland, Kenya and India.
   ● Can you see any modern parallels with the later occupation of countries such as Afghanistan and Iraq?
   ● What are the particular problems facing occupying forces?

Was it rational for the British to make promises both to the Arabs and to the Jews about what they would do with the territory of the Ottoman Empire after the First World War?

- Reason is a way of extending our knowledge from known factual information. Can you list the reasons why the British acted the way they did in 1916–18?

- Both reason and emotion are ways of knowing which are often based on value judgments. What were some of the premises and conclusions involved in making apparently contradictory statements to the Arabs and the Jews?

The bombing of the King David Hotel in 1946 was the bloodiest attack against the British in Palestine.

- Is it possible to justify assassination and the murder of civilians as happened in the hotel bombing?

- Is it acceptable to call Irgun a terrorist organization or freedom-fighting heroes? How important is language in determining people's perceptions of an organization and/or event?

- Machiavelli wrote in *The Prince* that the leader must protect the state no matter the cost and no matter what rules he or she breaks in the process. Do the ends always justify the means?

- Is it possible to call **Fatah**, Hamas, Islamic Jihad and al-Qaeda freedom fighters?

- Can indiscriminate bombing ever be considered ethical? Is it possible to describe such behaviour as utilitarian (i.e. in that it brings benefit to the greater number of people)?

From partition to war, November 1947 – May 1948

In the ensuing six months, people had time to ponder the significance of the vote which had led to the partition of the mandate, and to reflect on the ramifications of what had taken place. The decision was greeted with outrage and riots in the Arab world. In securing the vote, there was no doubt that the Jewish cause had been amply served by its representatives and proponents in different countries around the world. In addition, they had been able to capitalize on sympathy for the victims of the Holocaust, as well as taking full advantage of incidents such as the publicity surrounding the Exodus incident. The role of President Truman and the United States had proved to be crucial in determining that vote and the establishment of the Jewish state. Meanwhile, the Cold War also contributed to the situation in the Middle East. Despite the fact that the USSR had voted for partition, its motives were looked upon with suspicion by the Western powers, who believed that the Russians were looking to seek a foothold in the region. By the time of the vote, the Berlin blockade was in full swing and in February 1948 a coup in Czechoslovakia established a pro-Soviet government in that country.

The Arab leaders had once again failed to deliver, and the rivalries that existed within their ranks diminished any chance of them acting in unison to back their cause. Despite the Arabs and Palestinians having considerable support from some governments around the world, and numerically and morally holding a strong position, their tactics failed to benefit them and they were reduced to bluster and threats. Just as before, in the period of the mandate, the divided leadership of the Arabs and lack of cohesion in their aims contributed to their failure to capitalize on their potential advantages. The Arab Higher Committee spokesman at the United Nations, Jamal Husseini,

> **Fatah** A radical Palestinian organization founded in the 1950s by members of the Palestinian intelligentsia, including Yasser Arafat, to liberate Palestine.

said that the partition line "would be nothing but a line of fire and blood". The Arabs would "fight for every inch of their country" and drench "the soil of our beloved country with the last drop of our blood".

As the New Year arrived, the two sides began to ready themselves for the conflict that seemed to be inevitable. Again the Arabs were less well co-ordinated, and had no clear political strategy to pursue. In addition, the ambitions of some Arab leaders were tied to self-interest. Transjordan's King Abdullah saw an opportunity to absorb Jerusalem and some parts of Palestine into his kingdom. Other Arabs remained deeply suspicious of each other and failed to co-operate when they appeared to have the upper hand. In comparison, the Jewish movement had superior leadership and organization, and had roughly equal numbers in terms of the irregular fighters they could put into the field. The thousands of Jews who had fought in the Second World War provided an experienced group of soldiers for the Jewish Agency. Furthermore, the Agency had a strategy known as "Plan D", which contributed to their success in the early months before the official declaration of war by the Arabs. The Plan, which had been drawn up by Haganah even before the partition plan had been approved saw the need to gain control of vital areas of the Hebrew state and defend its borders from attack. The ultimate measure of success for Plan D lay in paving the way for the successful declaration of statehood by the Israelis in May 1948.

At the same time the Arabs attacked Jewish settlements while the Zionist forces tried to maintain links between their centres of population. The Arab states and the **Arab League** proclaimed a jihad against the Jews and threatened to drive them all into the sea, but once again they succeeded in putting themselves in an unfavourable light in the opinion of much of the world.

> **Arab League** Organization started in 1945 to promote Arab affairs and co-operation.

Deir Yassin

A month before the declaration of the state of Israel and the outbreak of the first Arab–Israeli war, a number of Arabs were killed by Jewish paramilitaries in the village of Deir Yassin near Jerusalem. The death toll varies according to different accounts: lowest estimates put the deaths at around 100 people and the highest at 254. The importance of the incident lies in the myths and facts which have surrounded the events and the aftermath in the Arab–Israeli conflict. It encouraged Palestinian refugees to flee the territory and contributed to the final decision of the Arab states to intervene directly in Palestine in 1948, against the creation of the state of Israel.

This was by no means the only massacre to take place. Within a week, the Arabs attacked and killed 77 medical personnel in a convoy, which they stated was an act of revenge for Deir Yassin. In years to come, other atrocities were committed, illustrating the vicious nature of the conflict in Palestine in which neither side had a monopoly on truth.

The outbreak of the War of Independence, May 1948

On 14 May 1948 in Tel Aviv, the state of Israel was declared, with the position of president going to Chaim Weizmann and that of prime minister to David Ben Gurion. Eleven minutes later, the United States recognized the state of Israel. On the same day, forces from the neighbouring Arab countries invaded.

Two weeks before the creation of Israel, members of the Arab League met to make the decision to go to war. The official aim of their intervention was to liberate Palestine and "drive the Jews into the sea". But the divisions that had plagued Arab unity earlier in the century continued to play a part at this moment too and, far from being united, many of the parties who intervened had their own agendas to follow. Syria, Saudi Arabia, Iraq, Lebanon and Egypt each declared war against Israel. Despite the Arab states having a combined population of some 40 million, and the newly fledged Jewish state counting less than 750 000, the imbalance between the two sides was not so apparent. Estimates put the Arab forces in the field at fewer than 30 000 men, while, in May, Israeli numbers stood at 65 000. It was more than numbers, however, that indicated Israeli advantages. Although four of the six Arab countries bordering Israel in 1948 had threatened the Jewish state, they had done little to prepare for armed conflict. Each state pursued its own political and territorial objectives during the war and this lack of unity and the failure to integrate were to lead to disaster on the battlefield.

Despite its apparent vulnerability, Israel had strengths. Their command structure was unified and co-ordinated and, among their numbers, they could count on experienced Jewish soldiers who had seen action in the Second World War. Various extremist groups could contribute small but significant numbers of dedicated fighters to their cause and after the Holocaust they were fighting for their very survival as a people. Although still relatively weak in the beginning, the Israeli forces were able to import a significant amount of heavy weaponry such as tanks and aircraft to enable them to offset this disadvantage.

There were in fact two wars in this period; the first took place from mid-May until a truce was signed on 11 June with King Abdullah of Jordan's forces occupying parts of Jerusalem and, with the Egyptian army, halted in the Negev desert. The truce brought more time for both sides to address their relative weaknesses but neither intended to curb their ambitions at that stage. The UN Security Council sent Swedish representative Count Bernadotte to Palestine with a proposal to halt the fighting and call for more consultations between the two

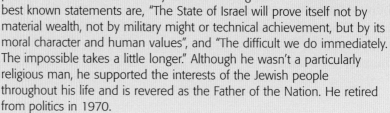

David Ben Gurion (1886–1973)

Ben Gurion was one of the giants of the Israeli state from its creation and became its first leader in 1948. He was a staunch Zionist and chairman of the Jewish Agency before he entered politics, serving two terms as prime minister in 1948–53 and 1955–63, thus making him the longest serving prime minister in Israel's history to date. Among his best known statements are, "The State of Israel will prove itself not by material wealth, not by military might or technical achievement, but by its moral character and human values", and "The difficult we do immediately. The impossible takes a little longer." Although he wasn't a particularly religious man, he supported the interests of the Jewish people throughout his life and is revered as the Father of the Nation. He retired from politics in 1970.

sides. Within a month fighting broke out again. Israel took over much of Galilee and seized Nazareth, as well as breaking the Egyptian blockade in the south. They drove Jordanian forces to the Gulf of Aqaba and crossed into southern Lebanon. Meanwhile Count Bernadotte pushed for compromise but was seen as pro-Arab by the Israelis; in September, members of Lehi assassinated him. Fighting continued until the end of 1948, by which time the Arabs had suffered a crushing defeat. Armistice negotiations began in January 1949 on the Greek island of Rhodes and an agreement was signed a month later. The 1948 war was the costliest for Israel—6000 Israelis were killed and 30 000 wounded out of a population of only 780 000.

The consequences of the first Arab–Israeli war

The shock of defeat was compounded by severe consequences for the Palestinian Arabs, who had been part of an exodus of people, and this has remained a problem until today. There is little doubt that the Israelis actively pursued a policy of expulsion from the territories and, during the first war, more than three quarters of a million Arabs fled or were expelled. Most have not been able to return and are scattered in neighbouring countries, becoming refugees and pawns in relations between Israel, her Arab neighbours and the international community. These events for the Palestinians have become known as **al-Nakba**. For Israel, by the end of the war the population had increased to a million as more Jews chose to return to **Eretz Israel**, the homeland. Militarily, Israel retained some of the areas occupied in the conflict which were originally awarded to the Arabs as part of the partition, such as Ramallah and Beersheba. In 1949 Israel occupied almost 80 per cent of the area of the original Palestinian mandate, and 20 per cent more than she had been promised in the partition plan. Importantly, Israel had more defensible borders and emerged as a coherent and stable state.

The impact of the war on the region was also felt domestically by many Arab states. Military defeat split the Arab League; Egypt quarrelled with both Syria and Iraq, each blaming the other for the setbacks. Meanwhile, Jordan gained territory and annexed the West Bank and East Jerusalem a year later. The Arab states demanded a return to the situation prior to the outbreak of hostilities but this was rejected by Israel, who was now in a state of siege with her neighbours. The UK, one of the last Western countries to recognize the state of Israel, had been shown to be indecisive and weak. Within a short time, British influence in the region was eclipsed by that of the United States and the balance of power had shifted. Zionism appeared to have won, but the twilight of the British Empire was to be overtaken by the dawn of the Cold War and, within a decade, another major war was to follow in the region.

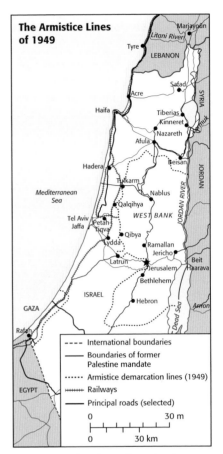

Source: United Nations Information System on the Question of Palestine (UNISPAL). http://domino.un.org/unispal/nsf.

Nakba (al-Nakba), meaning "day of the catastrophe" held on 15 May, the day of commemoration for the Palestinians of the beginning of the 1948 exodus.

Eretz Israel Hebrew term for the land of Israel.

Activity:

The Arab–Israeli war and its consequences, 1948–9

1 The Deir Yassin massacre was the most significant in the early dispute between Israel and the Arabs. Research other examples of massacres perpetrated against communities in the 20th century. You might consider some of the following:

- The Armenian genocide: Ottoman Turkey, 1915
- Oradour-sur-Glane: SS Nazi troops, June 1944
- The Qibya massacre: the Israelis against an Arab village, 1953
- My Lai, South Vietnam: US troops massacre of civilians, 1968
- Duc Duc village: North Vietnamese troops, 1971
- Cambodia after 1975: Pol Pot and the Khmer Rouge

- **Sabra** and Shatila massacres, Lebanon: Lebanese militia, September 1982
- Halabja, Iraq: Iraqui forces use chemical weapons on the Kurds, March 1988
- Srebrenica, Bosnia: the massacre of Muslims Serbian soldiers, July 1995.

2 The journalist Anne Karpf commented, "Deir Yassin is important not only because it launched a cycle of violence and counter violence." Israeli revisionist historian Benny Morris said, "It was the single event that did most to precipitate their flight." Research the Deir Yassin massacre and comment on the accuracy of these statements.

Source analysis

The following documents relate to the last year of the British Mandate, UNSCOP and the partition plan.

> **Sabra** A native-born Israeli Jew (from the Hebrew word for 'prickly cactus').

Key dates

15 May 1947	The UN Special Committee on Palestine (UNSCOP) formed
29 November 1947	The UN General Assembly approves the partition of Palestine

Source A

Statement by Britain's Foreign Secretary, Ernest Bevin, 14 February 1947.

> *His Majesty's government have of themselves no power to award the country* [Palestine, which had been administered by Britain since April 1920] *either to the Arabs or to the Jews, or even to partition it between them. We have, therefore, reached the conclusion that the only course open to us is to submit the problem to the judgment of the United Nations.*

Source B

UNSCOP, headed by Swedish judge Emil Sandstrom, went to the Middle East to start its survey. It solicited the help of both the Jewish Agency–which was formed in 1929 as the main body representing the Jews in Palestine–and the Arab Higher Committee–which was formed in 1936 to represent the Arabs. While the Jewish representatives gladly co-operated–hoping to illustrate the merits of Partition–the Arab representatives boycotted

[refused to deal with] the UN mission. They did this because they did not think the UN had the moral right to surrender any portion of Palestine to the Jews and because the Jewish community only constituted one third of the total population of Palestine and owned about eight percent of the land, yet would receive over half the land under Partition.

The task of UNSCOP seemed daunting: how to resolve the struggle of two peoples to control one land in a way that would avoid bloodshed? At an early meeting Emil Sandstrom polled the committee members as follows: "Does anyone favour an Arab state in all of Palestine?. No reply." Does anyone favour a Jewish state in all of Palestine? No reply. At a later date, however, eight members of the committee advocated Partition and three the Unified State.

Source: Bregman, A and El-Tahri, J. 1998. *The Fifty Years War: Israel and the Arabs*. Harmondsworth, UK. Penguin Books.

Source C

Political cartoon by Leslie Illingworth in the British newspaper the *Evening Standard*, 13 October 1947, entitled "British soldier in the stocks". Herschel Johnson (US ambassador to the UN) in the crowd is saying, "Carry on John", while Ben Hecht (Hollywood screenwriter and Zionist) shouts, "Scram tyrant!".

Source D

UNSCOP, Recommendations to the General Assembly, September 1947.

That the Mandate should be terminated and Palestine be granted independence at the earliest practicable date. The basic premise underlying the partition proposal is that claims to Palestine of the Arabs and Jews, both possessing validity, are irreconcilable, and that partition will provide the most realistic and practicable settlement. Only by means of partition can these conflicting national aspirations find substantial expression and qualify both peoples to take their places as independent nations in the international community and in the United Nations. In view of the limited area and resources of Palestine, it is essential that the economic unity of the country should be preserved.

Source E

Testimony on the Palestinian Arab reaction to the UNSCOP proposals, 29 September 1947.

The case of the Arabs of Palestine was based on the principles of international justice; it was that of a people which desired to live in undisturbed possession of the country where Providence and history had placed it. One thing was clear; it was the sacred duty of the Arabs of Palestine to defend their country against all aggression. The Zionists were conducting an aggressive campaign with the object of securing by force a country, which was not theirs by birthright. Thus there was self-defence on one side and on the other, aggression. The raison d'être of the United Nations was to assist self-defence against aggression.

The claim of the Zionists had no legal or moral basis. Their case was based on the association of the Jews with Palestine over two thousand years before. On that basis the Arabs would have better claim to those territories in other parts of the world such as Spain or parts of France, Turkey, Russia or Afghanistan, which they inhabited in the past. Once Palestine was found to be entitled to independence, the United Nations was not legally competent to decide or to impose the constitutional organization of Palestine, since such action would amount to interference with the internal matter of an independent nation.

Source-based questions

1 **a**   Explain what you understand by the term "Irgun" written on the bomb in Source C.

   b   Why, according to Source B, were the Jews willing to co-operate with the UNSCOP committee but the Arabs boycotted the UN mission?

2   How consistent are Sources B, D and E in arguing that the proposed plan for partition is the 'most realistic and practicable settlement' (Source D) for the Palestine problem?

3   With reference to their origin and purpose, assess the value and limitations of Sources A and C for historians studying why Britain decided to hand over responsibility for the mandate of Palestine.

4   How far do you agree with the statement made in Source E that, from the events of 1947, there was "self-defence on one side and on the other, aggression".

Demographic shifts: the Palestinian diaspora, Jewish immigration and the economic development of the Israeli state

In 1947, over one million Palestinians lived in the region that became the state of Israel. Less than two years later, over 75 per cent of them had left to become refugees and most of them have remained in camps ever since. The Palestinian diaspora has not only been a human tragedy but has helped fuel the flames of the Arab–Israeli conflict. The Palestinians have tried to return to their original homes through negotiation, but some turned to violence and the majority of people have become pawns in a political game of propaganda. In turn, the Israeli state has expanded by encouraging Jewish immigration and consolidated its control over the territory it claims as its own. Israel has developed to become an economic power and the only nuclear power in the Middle East; it is recognized as the region's only Western-style democracy.

The origins of the Palestinian diaspora, 1947

When war broke out between the Arabs and the Israelis in 1948 many of the victims were the civilian population who fled from their homes to escape violence. Some had gone in 1947 in fear of the escalating violence under the British Mandate. Episodes such as Deir Yassin only encouraged others to become refugees. Whether this was a deliberate policy of the Israelis is open to dispute, although within a short time it became official policy not to allow Palestinians to return to their homes. Both Palestinians and Israelis tell different stories about the events of 1947–8 and the resulting **diaspora**. Al-Nakba— the term given to the diaspora by the Palestinians indicates their point of view—originated in the last months of the British Mandate and gathered pace when the first shots were fired in the War of

Diaspora A term meaning dispersion, scattering or forced exile.

Historiography in the refugee crisis

Debates in historical interpretation are the food and drink of many historians and have to be addressed by students of history. The Arab–Israeli conflict has produced interpretations and disagreements on a number of aspects, but probably the most contentious of these is that regarding the refugee crisis. Was it a deliberate policy by the Israelis to force the Palestinians out of the territories or was it simply a product of the wars brought on, so the Israelis claim, by the intransigence and aggression of the Arabs?

In 1947, and again in 1967, the two peak years of the Palestinian diaspora, the reasons for Arabs to flee their homes included the violence of war, the actions of their neighbours, the collapse of economic life, forcible expulsion, the destruction of their homes and land, the propaganda of Arab governments and fear itself. There is no doubt that some forcible expulsions occurred, but the majority of refugees fled either because they thought they had to, believing that it would be a temporary measure, or because they

were actively encouraged by Arab leaders. It was advantageous in the early days for Arab leaders to encourage mass flight in order to vilify the Israelis and secure sympathy for their own cause. Deir Yassin is a classic case. In Haifa, as early as April 1948, over half the city's Arab population had fled before the battle was joined. One of the "New Historians" Benny Morris, claimed that Haganah deliberately broadcast warnings to the Arab population to evacuate women, children and the elderly, using tactics of psychological warfare to get the Arabs to leave. He concludes that Jewish attacks were the main cause of the Palestinian panic and that of a collective hysteria brought on by events and encouraged by Arab leaders. He blames both Jewish and Arab leaders for the crisis; others go further. Israeli historian Ilan Pappé claims the expulsions were a deliberate policy by the Israeli government and refers to it as ethnic cleansing. Arab sources, without exception, blame the expulsions and the ensuing crisis on the actions of the Israelis.

Independence. The Palestinians claim that the Israelis followed a conscious policy of expulsion, citing among other evidence Haganah's Plan D, which they allege was a plan to occupy as much of Palestine as possible and to expel the population in what would later be called "ethnic cleansing". On the other hand, most Israelis see Plan D as a defensive arrangement to be used only when Israel was attacked. In recent times, a wave of so-called "New Historians", most of them Israelis, have challenged the accepted view of Israeli history to admit some responsibility for the refugee crisis. But, for whatever reasons, the resulting displacement of hundreds of thousands of people was a catastrophe for the Palestinians and a tragedy that is still largely unresolved today.

Barefoot and pushing their belongings in carts, Arab families leave Jaffa in 1948.

The role of the UN in the refugee crisis

The majority of the Palestinians fled to neighbouring countries, where they were at first welcomed and then became a problem as their numbers increased. The largest number of Palestinians is in Jordan where almost two million are living (2005 figures). Gaza and the West Bank contain almost the same number between them. At the end of 1948, the UN passed a resolution calling for the return of Palestinians to their homes and for compensation to be paid to those who chose not to return. In the following year, at Lausanne, a proposal was presented to allow the return of refugees conditional on acceptance that Israel would keep the territory gained in 1948. This was rejected by the Arab states, although in retrospect it may have been the best chance for a negotiated peace in the Middle East and for some of the refugees, at least, to regain their lands.

By 1950, the United Nations Relief and Works Agency (UNRWA) had helped set up camps in neighbouring Arab states to cope with the refugees. Projects to irrigate and develop the land were established and, in later years, as the refugee problem looked as though it was becoming a permanent issue, education, health care and job opportunities were paid for under the UN budget. Today, the percentage of Palestinians in camps remains about the same as it was in the early 1950s, with about 35 per cent of the refugees under the responsibility of the UN. The remainder have become part of the population of Arab countries in Egypt, Syria, Lebanon, Jordan,

Estimated Palestinian population worldwide, mid-1996		
Area	**Population**	**Percentage of total Palestinian population**
West Bank	1 572 000	21.3%
Gaza	963 000	13.0%
Israel	1 095 000	14.8%
Jordan	2 272 000	30.7%
Lebanon	356 000	4.8%
Syria	325 000	4.3%
Egypt	54 000	0.7%
Iraq	33 000	0.4%
Libya	38 000	0.4%
Rest of Arab countries	319 000	4.3%
USA	159 000	2.2%
Other countries	209 000	2.8%
Total	**7 395 000**	**100%**

Source: Palestinian Central Bureau of Statistics for Palestinians in West Bank/Gaza.

Saudi Arabia and the Gulf states, or have sought refugee status elsewhere, including the United States and Europe. The failure of the Arab states to secure an independent Palestine was to have severe implications for some Arab regimes. In Egypt, it helped Nasser (president of Egypt and hero of the Arabs from 1954 until his death in 1970) and others overthrow the king, while later in the decade it contributed to the removal of the monarchy in Iraq. The issue of Palestine would also fundamentally determine alliances and politics in other Arab countries, as well as the fate of pan-Arabism as an ideology.

Jewish immigration and the economic development of the Israeli state

In Israel, the government, faced with the legal as well as the moral issue of what to do about the refugees, finally proposed laws forbidding the return of refugees to claim land and property. These were deemed necessary for Israel to move on as a viable state, with many of the new settlements built on land formerly belonging to Palestinian refugees, particularly in the West Bank. In the following years, the Israeli parliament, the Knesset, approved a series of laws which hindered the return of refugees. In 1950 the Knesset passed the Law of Return, which confirmed the right of every Jew (defined as a person with a Jewish parent or grandparent) to settle in Israel, followed in 1952 by the Citizenship Law, which granted immediate citizenship to immigrants. Where immigration to the former British Mandate of Palestine had been a problem for the Arabs prior to 1948, these new laws encouraged more Jews to seek a future in the modern state. This in turn had a profound effect upon the economic development of Israel which, within 30 years, became an industrial economic power in the region, providing its citizens with a standard of living largely unparalleled by its neighbours.

The face of Israel changed dramatically in the 40 years after its establishment. The Zionist dream espoused by Herzl and others was becoming reality. A refuge was available for all those Jews persecuted for their beliefs and for those who sought to rebuild the state which they believed was given to their ancestors long ago. Under the British Mandate the majority of immigrants had been of European descent, mostly from Central and Eastern Europe. Many were experienced farmers and, after Hitler came to power, a percentage were well-educated Jews. The Eastern European Jews, who formed the majority of the early settlers prior to independence, were known as **Ashkenazim**. Jewish immigration was known as **Aliyah**; and by the early 1950s, over half a million Jews had settled in Israel, many fleeing renewed persecution in Eastern Europe and within hostile Arab countries. The Jews from Spain or Portugal were known as **Sephardim**, while those who came from Arab states such as Yemen, Iran, Iraq and Morocco were known as **Oriental Jews**. This blend of cultures did not always integrate smoothly in the new Israel. There was often suspicion between the Ashkenazim and the Sephardim, but ultimately all contributed to the building of the new state of Israel.

Israel faced many economic, as well as political, problems in the early years. There were few natural resources and imported raw materials were needed in order to survive. There had been very little

Ashkenazim Jews from France, Germany and Eastern Europe.

Aliyah Hebrew for 'ascent', referring to Jewish immigration into Palestine.

Sephardim Originally the Jews who were exiled from Spain and Portugal.

development of light industry prior to 1948. Oil, and even the most basic necessity—water—was to become a contentious issue between the new state and its neighbours. Israel was reliant on outside help to develop, and to begin with this came from the Americans via loans, and later from the unlikely source of the West German government after 1952, eager to make amends for the appalling treatment of Jews during the Holocaust. Reparations, donations from Jewish businessmen in the USA and loans provided the much needed impetus to aid agricultural development, advance transport and build the housing and infrastructure needed to sustain the new state.

Developments after 1967

A significant number of Jews immigrated to Israel in the 1980s and, after the fall of the Iron Curtain, over a million Jews came from the former Soviet Union. For the Palestinians, however, the period was one of more expulsions and diaspora. The war of 1967 provided another flood of refugees from the Palestinian population after the capture of Jerusalem, the West Bank, Gaza and Sinai. Some were refugees for a second time as military occupation forced them to flee their subsequent homes. In addition, the Israeli policy of building settlements on occupied land has meant that many Palestinians could not return to their original property. Those who did remain have been used by Israel for cheap labour and have been granted minimal political rights; this later contributed to the **Intifada** in the 1980s. In neighbouring countries, such as Jordan and Lebanon, the Palestinians proved to be more of a problem for the existing regimes and, after their expulsion from Jordan following **Black September**, moved to Lebanon where they were both victims of, and contributors to, the violence which has dogged that country for decades. As Israel grew more prosperous, those whose land had been taken from them remained victims in a world which had grown hardened to their plight.

Intifada Arabic for "uprising", the name given to the period of Palestinian resistance to Israeli occupation from 1987.

Black September The confrontation in 1970 between Jordan and members of the PLO (see page 120), which led to the expulsion of that organization from the country.

Activity:
The Palestinian diaspora and the state of Israel, 1945–79

No one disputes the refugee crisis, which developed as a result of the wars between the Arabs and the Israelis, but the differences of opinion come about because of what may have caused the crisis.

- List the possible reasons why local inhabitants might leave their homes and land.

- Ehud Olmert, Israeli prime minister, said on 30 March 2008, "I will not agree to accept any kind of Israeli responsibility for the refugees. Full stop. … I don't think that we should accept any kind of responsibility for the creation of this problem." How convincing are the Israeli government's claim that the Arabs chose to flee and that their own leaders caused the crisis?

- Nasser, president of Egypt, told an interviewer on 1 September 1961: "If the refugees return to Israel, Israel will cease to exist." What did he mean by this statement and what are its implications?

Activity:
Refugees in the 20th century

Research the plight of refugees, otherwise known as displaced persons (DPs), folllowing the adoption of the term to describe the mass migration of refugees from Eastern Europe at the end of the Second World War. Consider the causes and consequences for those who were displaced as a result of the further humanitarian crises listed below:

1   The Armenian genocide and aftermath in Turkey during the First World War.

2   The Vietnamese "boat people" in the 1970s and 1980s.

3   The Hutu and Tutsi refugees from the Rwandan Civil War in the 1990s.

4   The Bosnians, Kosovars and the ethnic minorities of the former Yugoslavia, following the Balkan War in the 1990s.

5   The refugees from Darfur and the Sudan in the early years of the 21st century.

Source analysis

The following documents relate to the Palestinian diaspora after 1947.

Source A

Photograph showing Palestinians on fishing boats by Gaza beach in 1948, about to leave the country.

Source B

Diary extract of the founder of the Zionist movement, Theodore Herzl, written in 1896.

> *When we occupy the land, we shall bring immediate benefits to the state that receives us. We must expropriate gently [take away] the private property on the estates assigned to us. We shall try to spirit the penniless population across the border by procuring [obtaining] employment for it in transit countries, while denying it any employment in our own country.*

Source: Zohn, Harry. 1960. *The Complete Diaries of Theodore Herzl*. Vol. 1. trans. New York. USA. Herzl Press.

Source C

On June 16th 1948, thirteen ministers of Israel's provisional government met to decide what to do with the Arab population- those who had fled and those who remained … For Moshe Sharett there was no hesitation. The Arab exodus was, "A momentous event in world and Jewish history". He added rhetorically,

"They are not returning, and that is our policy". Sharett's words expressed the desire of most of the Israeli leadership. It was a simple and radical solution. But could Israel deny 700,000 Arab inhabitants the right to return to their homes? In the 16th June Cabinet meeting, Ben Gurion was clear enough: "They [the Palestinians] lost and fled. Their return must be prevented … and I will oppose their return also after the war". This decision was endorsed by all thirteen members of the provisional government. The meeting sealed the fate of 700,000 Arabs to become permanent refugees.

Source: Bregman, A and El-Tahri, J. 1998. *The Fifty Years War: Israel and the Arabs*. Harmondsworth, UK. Penguin Books.

Source D

Extract from UN Resolution 194, 11 December 1948.

Refugees wishing to return to their homes and live in peace with their neighbours should be permitted to do so at the earliest practicable date, and that compensation should be paid for the property of those choosing not to return

Source E

Extract from *The Economist*, 2 October 1948.

Of the 62,000 Arabs who formerly lived in Haifa not more than 5,000 or 6,000 remained. Various factors influenced their decision to seek safety in flight. There is little doubt that the most potent of the factors were the announcements made over the air by the Higher Arab Executive, urging the Arabs to quit. … It was clearly intimated that those Arabs who remained in Haifa and accepted Jewish protection would be regarded as renegades.

Source-based questions

1 **a** According to Source B, what do you understand Herzl's plans are for the poor people already living in the country the Jews would inhabit?

   b What message does Source A communicate about the situation for refugees in 1948? How useful a source is this photograph?

2 What does Source E suggest were the reasons that Arabs became refugees in 1948? Is this confirmed by the other source documents?

3 With reference to their origin and purpose, assess the value and limitations of Sources C and D for historians studying the reasons why there was a refugee crisis after 1948 in Palestine and how the world responded to it.

4 How far is it possible to argue that the refugee crisis after 1948 in Palestine was the deliberate policy of the Jewish leadership?

The Suez Crisis of 1956: the roles of the UK, France, the USA, the USSR, Israel and the UN

In the years between the end of the War of Independence in 1949 and the outbreak of further conflict between Israel and the Arabs, a state of armed tension existed where, potentially, fighting could break out at any moment. The lack of official recognition of Israel's existence by the Arab neighbours lay at the root of this state of affairs. Meanwhile, within the Arab states themselves, discontent with the regimes manifested itself in the form of domestic disturbance and even open revolt. The issue of the Palestinian refugees, as well as regional insecurities, further exacerbated tensions. In 1956, the situation in the Middle East grew even more complicated and at the end of that year a war broke out; this not only involved the Arabs and the Israelis, but clearly indicated how the region had now become inextricably involved in the broader context of the Cold War.

Historical developments, 1950–5

The defeat and humiliation of the Arab states in the war against Israel in 1948–9 had a profound impact on the Arabs and helped promote not only a criticism of the ruling elites in many countries but also the development of more radical ideological movements and Arab nationalism. The manifestations of such trends are illustrated in the series of upheavals which took place in the Arab world between 1950 and 1955. In 1951, King Abdullah of Jordan was assassinated and succeeded by his grandson Hussein. In the same year, in Lebanon, the prime minister was assassinated; in Syria, a series of coups occurred, led by the military, and, in Algeria, a revolt began against the French in 1954, which developed into a bloody colonial conflict. But probably the most significant change took place in Egypt, where the monarchy was overthrown in a military coup in 1952, leading to the emergence of a key figure in the politics of the period, a man who was to dominate the Arab–Israeli dispute for most of the next two decades, Gamal Abdul Nasser.

The Egyptian Revolution and the emergence of Nasser

The plot to overthrow the monarchy in Egypt was hatched by a number of Egyptian army officers during the War of Independence against Israel. One of their number, Zakharia Mohiendin, recalled, "The Palestine war was one of the reasons for our 23rd July 1952 revolution … we had to change the situation". Farouk, the king of Egypt, was a man leading the life of a dissolute playboy. In politics he was an inept, corrupt and incompetent ruler, for whom many Egyptians felt nothing but contempt. The regime's collaboration with the colonial regime of the UK was unpopular but it was the failure in the war against Israel which precipitated the discontent to the point of revolt. Egyptian army officers under the leadership of General Mohammed Naguib removed Farouk in a bloodless coup and the king was sent into exile. The Free Officers Movement, who initiated the coup, began a series of far-reaching reforms for Egypt. Initially, Israel was not even on their agenda nor was the Palestinian cause

President Nasser waves at the crowds.

high among their concerns. Naguib's deputy in the coup was Nasser. Handsome, charismatic and a fervent Egyptian nationalist, the young officer (he was only 32 at the time of the coup) replaced Naguib in October 1954, and took Egypt into the leadership of the Arab world and towards conflict both with the Western powers and with Israel.

Initially, neither the West nor Israel saw Nasser as a threat. He was seen as educated, modern and a moderate in his views, a man with whom both could do

Gamal Abdul Nasser (1918–70)

Nasser can be regarded as one of the most important Arab political figures of the 20th century. Born in 1918, he joined the army in 1937 and became politically active, founding the Free Officers Movement, which aimed to get rid of both the British and the king from Egypt. He gained prominence for his part in the Falouja pocket resistance to the Israelis in the first Arab–Israeli war and later helped lead the revolution which ousted King Farouk in 1952.

He promoted the theory of Arab Socialism, became a key figure in the Non-Aligned Movement. He led Egypt from 1954, as prime minister and president, until his early death from a heart attack in 1970. He is still regarded as a hero in the Arab world, for restoring Arab dignity and for his resistance to the West and Israel.

business. The Americans in particular saw Nasser in a positive light and, it was rumoured, had played a part in the coup which brought him to power. American aid was forthcoming and even the Israelis opened up clandestine back-door channels to negotiate with Nasser and the new Egyptian government. To begin with, Nasser did well at home. He got rid of the monarchy and began a programme of land distribution, which made him even more popular. Ambitious schemes to revitalize the economy and extend the amount of cultivatable land in the country were put forward, the most important of these being the construction of a dam at **Aswan** to control the flooding of the Nile, the great artery of Egypt. However, the money for such a scheme was initially to come largely from the British and the Americans, and this early honeymoon with Nasser was not to last for long.

Aswan Dam A dam project across Lake Nasser to control the Nile in Egypt, built from 1960 with Soviet economic assistance.

Relations between Israel and Egypt had not improved in public since the emergence of Nasser but the latter's preoccupation with domestic issues had meant that little attention had been paid to either the Palestinians or his Jewish neighbours. In October 1953, the Israelis had retaliated against a **Fedayeen** raid in which two Israelis had been killed, and attacked the village of Qibya in Jordan. Sixty-nine people died in this raid (which was led by the future Israeli prime minster, Ariel Sharon) and the disproportionate nature of the Israeli reaction prompted international condemnation.

Fedayeen Arab armed militia groups whose purpose was to engage in guerrilla activities against Israel. The name is from the Arabic term meaning "self sacrifice".

In October 1954, the UK agreed to withdraw its forces from the Suez Canal Zone within 20 months and, in February 1955, negotiated an agreement with the United States, Turkey and Iraq, known as the **Baghdad Pact** (Iran and Pakistan were to join later in the year). While the USA saw this as a means of keeping Russian influence out of the region, the British prime minister, Sir Anthony Eden, thought it would be a way of isolating Nasser. At the same time, a revolt had broken out in the French colony of Algeria, in which Nasser gave aid to the rebels. Meanwhile a cross-border retaliatory raid by Israel into Gaza resulted in the deaths of a number of Egyptian soldiers, which poisoned relations between Israel and Egypt and sent Nasser looking for more sophisticated weaponry with which to defend his country.

Baghdad Pact A defence treaty founded in 1955 containing a number of Middle Eastern states.

The Aswan Dam and the Cold War

In April 1955, Nasser attended the first meeting of the Non-Aligned states at Bandung in Indonesia. There he had been wooed by, among others, the Chinese, who had hinted at providing him with weaponry. The Russians too, eager for potential allies in the Middle East, offered military assistance. With Egypt's earlier request for arms from the United States put on hold, Nasser accepted Soviet weapons (through Czechoslovakia) in September 1955. Meanwhile, money for the Aswan High Dam scheme—the symbol of the new Egypt which Nasser wanted to create—was to come from the World Bank, but with strings attached. When the Soviets hinted at the possibility of lending money to Egypt for the dam, alarm bells began to ring in London and Washington. The Cold War game was being played in a new part of the world.

Meanwhile the Israelis, too, were eager to improve what they saw as their military weakness. They hoped for backing from the United States and other Western powers, but lines were not yet so clear-cut for the major powers to support either Israel or the Arab side. In the UK, Anthony Eden was becoming more and more convinced that Nasser was a threat, who needed to be removed. He saw in Nasser and the situation as a whole echoes of the late 1930s and the policy of appeasement to Hitler which he was determined should not be repeated. France, meanwhile, viewed the support given by Nasser to the Algerian rebels against French rule as a significant threat to their interests and moved closer to the Israelis. In Washington, the Americans' main preoccupation was to stop Russian influence from expanding into the area but as yet their interests did not coincide exactly with those of the other Western allies. It was actions taken by Nasser in 1956 that would cement that relationship and ultimately bring about another war in the Middle East.

In 1956, relations deteriorated badly. When Jordan's King Hussein dismissed the pro-British former head of his army, Glubb Pasha, Nasser gave public support for the action and, in May, he offered diplomatic recognition to Communist China. This action thoroughly alienated the United States. President Eisenhower and his Secretary of State, JF Dulles, were furious and agreed with the British and the French that Nasser should be removed. One way of achieving this was not to follow through with the loans for the dam project, which Congress were now very unlikely to do, given Egypt's recognition of Communist China. Meanwhile, the last British troops left the Canal Zone in June 1956. Nasser's failure to secure the money for the Aswan project led him to take a gamble which was

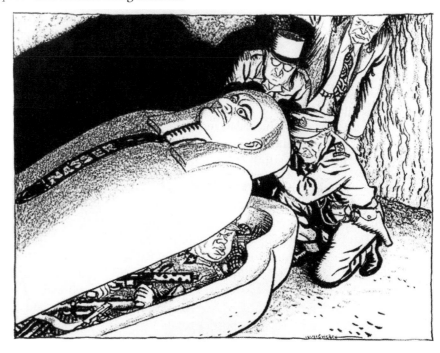

Cartoon by British cartoonist Leslie Illingworth in the *Daily Mail*, 12 November 1956. Eisenhower, Eden and Mollet uncover a sarcophagus labelled "Nasser" and discover Khrushchev within.

ultimately to result in war. On 26 July, he announced the nationalization of the Suez Canal to great popular support within Egypt and the Arab world. Challenging the Western powers, this action set in motion a series of events, which, once again, brought the focus of the world on the Middle East and Arab–Israeli issues.

The realignment of power in the region after 1948 had not only brought about changes in governments in the Arab states but had allowed a new form of Arab nationalism to take root and flourish. The decay of British influence in the region was part of the process, and that allowed and encouraged the Cold War players to become involved, making the Middle East a potential battleground. The impact on the Arab–Israeli dispute was to make the situation even more complicated and to entangle the two sides in the diplomacy of the Great Powers. It was not an auspicious development for the future of the region.

From crisis to war: July–October 1956

Nasser's nationalization of the canal came as a shock to the British, although, given the developments over the first part of the year, it should not have been a complete surprise. The question remained, what was going to be done about it? Prime Minister Eden and the British press made immediate comparisons between Hitler's annexation of the Rhinelands in 1936 and the threat to British prestige, arguing that this cut off the United Kingdom's sea links with the rest of her empire and that Britain's interests in the Middle East, and particularly oil, would suffer as a result. The military option was at first rejected and so it is worth looking at the diplomatic moves which were made in order to see how the Arab–Israeli conflict became intertwined with the Cold War.

The position of the United States was always going to be of great significance in this issue. The UK involved the Americans and the French in tripartite talks days after Nasser's nationalization of the canal. The UK was reluctant to use the United Nations at this stage because of Russia's seat and possible veto on the Security Council. What emerged from the talks with the Western allies was a decision to hold a conference in August over the future of the canal. At the same time, military preparations were started and, in secret, British and French military experts began work on what was to be known as Operation Musketeer, an invasion of the Canal Zone itself. At this stage, no Israeli role was considered and the crisis seemed to be one principally between Egypt and the Western allies. A meeting in late August of the stakeholder nations proposed the creation of the Suez Canal as an international waterway, whose board would report to the UN; Egypt was a notable absentee and rejected the proposal. A stalemate emerged, with Nasser seen as the major obstacle in the eyes of the Western media and a fear that behind Nasser's action lurked the greater menace of the Soviet threat.

In mid-October, top-secret meetings in Paris produced a plan for the Israeli army to invade Egypt and for the British and French to then intervene to stop the fighting, occupy the Canal Zone and remove

President Nasser is cheered in Cairo after announcing the Suez Canal Company, 1 August 1956.

Nasser. The date set for the operation was late October, only a week before the American presidential elections. Meanwhile, publically, negotiations carried on at the UN and through SCUA, the Suez Canal Users Association, which had come out of the earlier London Conference. Operation Musketeer, a clear example of power politics, was finally agreed to at Sèvres, outside Paris, on 25 October, with Eden giving orders that all copies of the agreement be destroyed—both the French and the Israelis kept their copies. On 29 October, Israeli forces attacked Egypt and the second Arab–Israeli war began.

The Suez War: October–November 1956

The war lasted less than a week and transformed the region. This was not because of military conquest but rather through the consequences that developed from the actions taken by some of the major powers. For the Arabs and the Israelis, the war only worsened the existing tensions between them.

Israel's attack across the Sinai resulted in their capture of most of the peninsula and Gaza and, within a day, their forces were close to the Canal Zone. What followed was the Anglo-French ultimatum to the two sides to withdraw. The Egyptians rejected this call and appealed to the UN. Twenty-four hours later, British and French aircraft attacked Egyptian airfields, destroying much of their air force, and dispatched their own invasion fleet from Malta. It was obvious that these plans had been prepared in advance and, in an election week in the United States, this angered their American allies. In Eastern Europe, troubles in the Hungarian capital Budapest had initially prompted the Soviets to withdraw their forces from the city but, on the same day that the Western allies attacked Egypt, the Soviets reversed their decision and began to put an end to the rebellion in the East European satellite state.

In Egypt itself, the canal was put out of commission and Anglo-French forces landed their troops in the Canal Zone. Militarily, Nasser's forces had been defeated and humiliated on their own turf but, diplomatically, it was a different story. Both the United Kingdom and France were condemned across the world for their actions. The two allies used their veto to reject a call for an end to hostilities in the Security Council but on 2 November the UN General Assembly met for the first time in emergency session and passed an American resolution calling for a ceasefire. The British prime minister, Anthony Eden, stalled, although by that time he was also being condemned by critics at home. Fighting in Egypt continued for another week, with Western forces capturing Port Said and most of the Canal Zone, until the British and French finally accepted a ceasefire on 6 November. The war came to a wretched end with Nasser still in power, the prestige of the UK and France in tatters and the Arab–Israeli conflict more complicated than ever.

Discussion point: the Suez Canal

Individually, or in pairs, find additional information on the background to the Suez Canal, which was built in the 19th century, including:

- the history of canal schemes linking the Gulf of Suez with the Red Sea

- the role of the British, French and the Ottomans in building the canal

- the takeover of the canal by Britain in 1875

- the strategic factors which resulted from the opening of the canal and the British involvement in Egypt and the Sudan.

 In the context of the information above, explain what you think Anthony Eden meant by calling the Suez Canal "the swing door of Empire"?

The results of the Suez War

For the Western powers of the United Kingdom and France

The war brought about the resignation of Eden and humiliation for the French Fourth Republic, which collapsed the following year. The failure of the British and French encouraged a wave of nationalism in their former colonies with a greater push for independence by some states. Some historians see the fiasco at Suez as having caused the UK to withdraw from her empire east of Suez and in Africa, as well as pushing her towards the newly forming European Community.

For the United States

The major reason why the Suez venture failed from the Western point of view was because of the role played by the USA. The Americans actively brought pressure to bear both at the UN and economically, selling sterling and holding up oil supplies to Europe. By default, it also brought the USA into the Middle East as British and French prestige suffered in the region.

For the Soviet Union

Indirectly, the USSR gained considerably from the Suez affair. Not only did it allow them to deal with the Hungarians (and set the tone for aggression in Eastern Europe for the next generation), as much of the world looked towards the Middle East, it also enabled them to portray themselves as defenders of the Arab cause against Western imperialists. Khrushchev rattling his rockets in the crisis certainly increased Russian influence in the region, helped break down the power of the West in the Middle East and allowed the Soviets to be seen as an alternative refuge in the Cold War.

For Israel

Once again Israel had beaten their Arab neighbour militarily and taken Gaza and most of Sinai, only to have to hand them back—a lesson which was not lost on its leaders in the future. Israel did retain a guarantee that the Straits of Tiran would remain open and, importantly, maintained the support of the United States.

For Egypt

Egypt and Nasser emerged from the Suez affair battered but triumphant; Egypt retained control of the Suez Canal. In the eyes of the Arabs, Nasser had stood up to "triple aggression" and had won; he was the undisputed champion of the Arab world: the Rais, the Leader.

Oil

Oil had been used as a weapon by the Arabs in 1956, but had not proved to be as effective a weapon as it would become later.

The main protagonists in the Arab–Israeli conflict had once again clashed, with Israel coming out on top—at least militarily; but the Suez affair also demonstrated how relations between the sides could no longer remain confined to the region. The Cold War had knocked on the door of the Middle East.

Arabism and Zionism: the emergence of the PLO

This section examines the evolution of two political ideologies and the development in the context of the region and the development of their beliefs. It can be noted that each ideology changed radically in response to the conditions and also because of certain individuals who shaped their development as a response to circumstances. In 1964 the PLO was formed and came to lead the struggle for the liberation of the occupied territories in Israel and the creation of an independent Palestinian state.

The development of Arabism and Zionism

The development of a national consciousness among both Arabs and Jews grew from the beginning of the 20th century. Pan-Arabism has become synonymous with Arab nationalism and, to a certain extent, with Arab socialism, particularly after the rise of Nasser. Zionism is a Jewish movement that arose in the late 19th century as a response to anti-Semitism, with the desire to establish a Jewish homeland in Palestine. Both ideologies have come to generate antagonism and bitterness right up to the modern day, each spawning more radical elements among their supporters.

Arabism became identified with Arab nationalism and an awakening of consciousness among the intellectuals in the Arab world. This had developed prior to the 20th century partially as a reaction to the Ottoman influence in the region but also because of contact with the development of European nationalism and the process of modernization. At the heart of an Arab consciousness was a desire for self-determination and independence although there was (and still remains) fundamental disagreements as to the form of government best suited for the Arab peoples. Aside from the political aspects, Arabism has also given rise to a development in Arab culture and a renaissance among the people of the Arab world. Several Arab movements—even football clubs—have been named "al-Nahda"(Arabic for "awakening"). Politically, however, the leadership had been taken over by a pan-Arab ideology, which has (unsuccessfully) tried to unite the Arabs in a union of nation states. The short-lived United Arab Republic of Egypt and Syria in the days of Nasser demonstrated the difficulties of any kind of political union, and the best that has emerged is the Arab League (formed in 1945 and now containing 22 member states), which does advance political, economic, cultural and social programmes designed to promote the interests of its member states.

Arabism in the period before 1948

The exchange of diplomacy between the British and the Arabs during the First World War encouraged the development of pan-Arabism and the hopes for a unified Arab state. The defeat of the Ottoman Empire gave further rise to those hopes, but the actions of the British and the establishment of the mandate system upset those Arabs who hoped for more out of the restructuring of the Middle East. The frustrations of the Arabs encouraged the development of Arabism in the 1930s into a more radical direction by intellectuals such as Constantin Zureiq and Michel Aflaq. Both were Syrians, the former promoting such terms as the "Arab mission" and "national mission" in respect to the Arabs. Michel Aflaq was the ideological founder of Ba'athism, a form of secular Arab nationalism, which attempted to combine socialism with the vision of a pan-Arab nation. (Aflaq later became the Syrian minister for education and influenced a young Saddam Hussein in Iraq). Arabism naturally became closely linked to the religion of Islam: to give their nationalism a historical dimension, they linked it with the history of Islam itself.

As long as the Middle East was under the control of foreign powers then this naturally helped Arab nationalism focus on the expulsion of the intruder; once this had happened, however, shortly after the Second World War, the disunity among the Arabs could be seen in the lack of progress towards political unification. What helped keep the Arab cause unified was their hostility to the Jews, but their lack of success in achieving Arab unity has been a major factor in the survival of the Jewish state in the Middle East.

In 1905 an Arab intellectual, Naguib Azoury warned of the impending conflict between the Arabs and the Jews:

> Two important phenomena, of the same nature but opposed, but which have still not drawn anyone's attention, are emerging at this moment in Asiatic Turkey. They are the awakening of the Arab nation and the latent effort of the Jews to reconstitute on a very large scale the ancient kingdom of Israel. Both these movements are destined to fight each other continually until one of them wins. The fate of the entire world will depend on the final result of this struggle between these two peoples representing two contrary principles.

Azoury, Naguib. 1905. "The Awakening of the Arab Nation". In Smith, Charles D. 2001. *Palestine and the Arab-Israeli Conflict.* 4th edn. Boston, USA. Bedford/St Martin's. pp. 55–6.

Zionism in the period before 1948

Zionism emerged at the turn of the 20th century as a direct response to the growth of anti-Semitism, as demonstrated by the 1894 **Dreyfus affair**. Over two thousand years of persecution and the Diaspora gave a focus to the international political movement towards a goal: the establishment of a Jewish state in the ancient homeland claimed by the Jews as a gift from God. Thus Zionism can be classed as a modern national liberation movement which achieved success with the establishment of the state of Israel in 1948. The origins of the movement have become inextricably linked with the name of Theodore Herzl, the father of political Zionism, who in 1896 wrote *Der Judenstaat* ("The Jewish State"), in which he called for a safe haven for the Jews. In 1897 he organized the first Zionist Congress held in Basel, Switzerland during which time a Declaration was adopted, stating: "The aim of Zionism is to create for the Jewish people a home in Palestine."

Dreyfus affair A political scandal in France, which followed the conviction for treason in November 1894 of Captain Dreyfus, a French officer, who was a Jew. He was later found innocent.

The first Zionist Congress

In 1897 Theodore Herzl outlined one of the most important goals for Zionism during the first Zionist Congress convention held in Basel (Basle), Switzerland:

We have an important task before us. We have met here to lay the foundation-stone of the house that will some day shelter the Jewish people. ... We have to aim at securing legal, international guarantees for our work.

And on 3 September 1897, he wrote:

Were I to sum up the Basle Congress in a word—which I shall guard against pronouncing publicly—it would be this: At Basle I founded the Jewish State. If I said this out loud today, I would be answered by universal laughter. Perhaps in five years, and certainly in fifty, everyone will know it.

Gilbert, Martin. 2008. *Israel: A History*. Santa Barbara, USA. McNally & Loftin Publishers. p. 15.

Theodore Herzl, founder of the Zionist movement

Like Arab nationalism, Zionism developed among the intellectuals. Following the death of Herzl in 1904, his mantle was picked up by Chaim Weizmann, who became the leader of the Zionist movement and the first president of Israel. The pledges made to Arabs and Jews during the First World War allowed the aspirations of both nationalist groups to develop, but these were fulfilled more for the latter than the former, and the resentment this caused helped to alienate each of them from the British and from each other. Zionism, like the cause of Arab nationalism, grew more radical as its demands were not met and the formation of Haganah and the more radical Lehi represents that shift to a more extreme position regarding the establishment of a national state. By time of the Second World War, and with it the Holocaust, the cause of Zionism had helped create an environment where the creation of a Jewish state was achievable.

Nasser and Arab socialism

The first Arab–Israeli war in 1948 did not help the cause of Arabism but it helped in the development of a more radical strain of nationalism, which in turn found a common focal point of hatred towards Israel and led to upheavals in Arab states in the region. Not only Ba'athism, but an Arab Nationalist Movement emerged properly in the 1950s, which was not only more radical, but hostile to the West and to Israel. It promoted a type of socialism, which was never really Marxist but instead focused on promoting social progress and developing Arab unity. A shared history, language and culture all helped foster an Arab nationalism but the ability to translate those factors into a political reality and even a common stance towards crisis was difficult to achieve in the period. The most notable attempt to put these ideals into practice came from Nasser in Egypt. Following the overthrow of the monarchy, the Egyptian revolution promoted social reforms which have become known as Arab socialism. Nasser became the leader of a pan-Arab ideological movement, which tried to unite the Arab cause, and which reached its height in the years after Nasser's success in the Suez War of 1956.

Because it was a vague concept, Nasser could define his own way for Arab socialism. He nationalized basic industries, promoted programmes of social welfare and attempted to improve the political representation of the poverty-stricken fellahin (peasants) in Egypt. "Social freedom is the only door to political freedom," declared Nasser.He stated that the three principles of Arab socialism were, "Socialism, Union and Freedom". It was to be a third way, an alternative to capitalism and communism, or a kind of co-operative socialism. Nasser's *Philosophy of Revolution*, published in 1955, promoted his interest in Arab unity as a common front to preserve Egypt and the Arabs against outside powers. He was the first statesman from the region to grasp the potential of a united Arab world.

Under Nasser's leadership in 1958, Egypt and Syria merged to become the United Arab Republic (UAR). Arab socialism appeared to be gaining credibility. But in using the state to achieve national liberation and economic development, both countries demonstrated the difficulty of carrying out a revolution without mass support. Nasser was the hero to many Arab nationalists, but some Muslim traditionalists opposed him, and the UAR collapsed in 1961. After defeat in the war of 1967, support for pan-Arabism declined, and Nasser concentrated on maintaining a united front against Israel to recover the occupied Arab territories. The Ba'ath party, active in many Arab states, and the rise of Islamic fundamentalism offered an alternative path to Arabism for many. The relative failure of Arabism encouraged one of the alternatives to come to the fore; in frustration with the lack of progress made for the poor and Arab national unity, some sought representation and action through such organizations as the **Palestine Liberation Organization (PLO)**.

> **The Palestine Liberation Organization** (PLO) was founded in 1964 to represent the Palestinians in their search for a return to their occupied lands in Israel.

The formation of the PLO

A decade after the creation of the state of Israel, it seemed to some in the Arab world that the international community and their own leaders had forgotten the Palestinian people expelled from their lands. Among these was a small group of Palestinians, soaked in the current development of Arab nationalism, who believed that the liberation of their homeland had to come in order for Arab unity to be achieved. In 1954 they took the name Fatah (Arabic for "conquest"). The organization, led by Yasser Arafat, Khali al-Wazir (Abu Jihad) and Salah Khalaf, had its headquarters in Damascus and adopted as its methodology a kind of low-level guerrilla warfare which would, they believed, attract others to their cause and gradually wear the Israelis down.

In 1964 at the Arab summit in Cairo, the Palestine Liberation Organization was established, forming an umbrella under which other resistance groups such as Fatah could operate. For statesmen like Nasser, who had

> **Articles from the original Charter of the PLO, 1964**
>
> **Article 16** *The liberation of Palestine, from an international viewpoint, is a defensive act necessitated by the demands of self-defence as stated in the Charter of the United Nations. For that, the people of Palestine, desiring to befriend all nations which love freedom, justice, and peace, look forward to their support in restoring the legitimate situation to Palestine, establishing peace and security in its territory, and enabling its people to exercise national sovereignty and freedom.*
>
> **Article 17** *The partitioning of Palestine, which took place in 1947, and the establishment of Israel are illegal and null and void, regardless of the loss of time, because they were contrary to the will of the Palestinian people and its natural right to its homeland, and were in violation of the basic principles embodied in the Charter of the United Nations, foremost among which is the right to self-determination.*
>
> **Source:** http://www.un.int/palestine/PLO/PNA2.html

encouraged its development, it was an opportunity to be seen as taking the initiative in the leadership of the Arab world, but it was also a way in which he might control the militants. A Covenant was drawn up later that year, in which the PLO laid claim to their Palestinian homeland and opted for armed conflict as a means to recover it. This was soon to be backed up with action. Before the end of the year, members of Fatah, Fedayeen fighters, attacked an installation in Israel, a foretaste of things to come. Growing activism among the Palestinians was to become more ambitious in scale and helped to promote two more violent wars within the next decade. In 1969, following a disastrous war for the Arabs, the leadership of the PLO was taken over by Yasser Arafat, a man who has done more than any other to bring the Palestinian cause to the eyes of the world.

Palestinian activism, 1967–79

In the next decade, the PLO and other organizations were to carry out a series of actions which would bring their cause to the attention of the world. Following the defeat of the Arabs in the 1967 war, a number of Palestinians and others took up alternative options to regain their territories from the enemy. More radical groups were formed, including the Popular Front for the Liberation of Palestine (PFLP), who believed that the leaders of the Arab governments were failing their cause, and that more extreme measures were needed.

Karemeh, March 1968

Early in 1968, an Israeli response to a series of raids across the borders into the West Bank of Jordan led to a significant clash. A small but powerful, armoured Israeli force attacked Fatah's headquarters, located in the Jordanian town of Karemeh. Refusing to retreat, Arafat's men fought back and, despite losing nearly six times as many men as the Israelis, the latter decided to retreat in the face of an attack by Jordanian soldiers who intervened. Hailed as a victory by the jubilant Arabs, the event not only restored a sense of pride to the Arab cause, but raised the profile of Fatah and particularly Yasser Arafat as a national hero who had defied the Israelis and triumphed. By the end of the year, Arafat's actions had brought him and the Palestinians to the attention of the world.

Black September, 1970

In the following 12 months, an average of one border incident a day occurred in the occupied territories between Israel and Jordan as the Fedayeen grew in confidence. The 1967 war had caused even more refugees to flood across the borders into the Hashemite Kingdom of Jordan, posing problems for the government of King Hussein. Fatah and other militant groups began to act with impunity within Jordan and it was there, in 1970, that one of the most outrageous acts occurred, which again brought the Arab–Israeli conflict to the attention of the world and resulted in the expulsion of the PLO from Jordan.

In early September, the PFLP, under the leadership of George Habash, hijacked five civilian airliners and landed three of them at Dawson's Field, west of the Jordanian capital Amman. With the world media's attention on them, the aircraft (once the passengers had embarked) were blown up. It was not the world's first hijacking (or "skyjacking" as it is sometimes known), but it was the first to receive major attention—which was precisely what the hijackers wanted. At the time a "poor man's weapon", with airport security checks so lax, hijacking was a relatively easy and a very effective way to gain the media spotlight.

British aircraft Flight BOAC 775 at Dawson's Field in September 1970

The PFLP demanded the release of political prisoners jailed in Israel and elsewhere, and some governments (including the UK) agreed. Arafat, under intense pressure, finally condemned the actions of the hijackers but his image had been tarnished; Jordan's King Hussein eventually decided to move against the PLO and declared martial law. In an episode known as "Black September", virtual civil war raged as Jordanian forces drove out the PLO. By the end of the month, Arafat and his followers were forced out of Jordan and had set up new bases in the south of Lebanon, where they were to remain for over a decade. At the end of the month, Nasser died. With the Arabs fighting each other, the conflict in the Middle East seemed as insoluble as ever. More acts of terrorism were to come.

Munich 1972

In 1972 Palestinian extremists grew even bolder in their actions. Three members of the Japanese Red Army, fellow Marxists who sympathized with the cause of the PFLP, shot dead 24 civilians at Lod airport in Israel. Then, in the summer of the same year, with the eyes of the world once again upon them, a faction of Fatah, who called themselves Black September, walked into the Olympic athletes' village in Munich and took 11 hostages from the Israeli weightlifting team. It was a story of high drama. The combination of Jews under attack again in Germany and the public profile that the ultimate tragedy received was just the kind of attention the extremists wanted. The hostages and the terrorists were taken to the airport where, in the abortive rescue attempt by the German authorities, all 11 hostages were

"We Arabs may be incapable of building a civilisation, but by Allah! we can blow up everybody else's ..."

How the Western press (UK) saw the events at Dawson's Field—cartoon published in the British newspaper the *Daily Express*, 14 September 1970

killed along with some of the Palestinians and a German civilian. The killings were widely condemned and in the following year the Black September group was abandoned. In 2005, film-maker Steven Spielberg made a powerful film called *Munich* on the events of 1972 and the revenge operation to assassinate the surviving members of Black September.

Palestinian recognition at the UN, 1974

In addition to media-grabbing activities such as skyjackings, the PFLP and other splinter groups continued their attacks on territories occupied by Israel. Boosted by the Arabs' relative success in the **Yom Kippur** war in 1973 (see page 125), the PFLP and Fatah attacked Israeli villages, some of these suicide missions, with the immediate aim of inflicting as much damage as possible. Arafat came under criticism from abroad as head of the PLO because he either condoned the violence or was unable to stop it. Despite that, the PLO was given a tremendous boost in 1974 when it was recognized "as the sole representative of the Palestinian people" by the Arab League. Later that year, Arafat himself stood at the podium of the UN in New York to address the General Assembly

Yasser Arafat (1929–2004)

Yasser Arafat, head of the PLO and holder of the Nobel Prize for peace in 1994, was the best-known face of the Palestinians during the second half of the 20th century. He spent much of his early life in Cairo and became one of the founders of Fatah, the radical group committed to armed struggle against Israel. In 1969 he became head of the PLO and, with his traditional chequered headdress, or keffiyeh, was "Mr Palestine" for millions around the world. He did more than anyone else to promote the interests of the Palestinian people and to adapt their cause to the changing needs of the Arabs.

In 1991 he persuaded the Palestinians to enter into negotiations with Israel and signed the Oslo peace accords in 1993. The Intifada (Palestinian uprisings) served his interests at first but then grew out of his control and, after 2002, Arafat was confined to the West Bank town of Ramallah where, regarded by many as the "father of his country", he died in 2004.

Yom Kippur Hebrew Day of Atonement, the day chosen for an attack by the Arabs in 1973.

Skyjackings

With the memories of 9/11 and the consequences of that day in 2001 evident in international travel from any airport today, air piracy is an ongoing concern. The first recorded skyjacking took place in 1930, when a group of Peruvian activists dropped propaganda leaflets in areas of their own country. But the high point of international skyjacking occurred mainly as a consequence of the frustrations of many supporting the Palestinians and the Arab cause in their war against Israel and Israel's supporters in the West.

There are many well-documented examples of terrorists taking over planes in the air. Some of these have been described in the text. Most skyjackings have a cause to publicize, although some use hostages as ransom for money or the release of prisoners held in jails or even to obtain political asylum, such as the case of some early skyjackings to Taiwan and from Cuba. It is in the context of the Middle East and the Arab–Israeli conflict, however, that the best-known incidents have taken place. These include:

- three aircraft taken to Dawson's Field, 1970
- Air France flight to Entebbe, Uganda, 1976
- Egypt Air flight to Malta, 1985
- Air China flight to Guangzhou, 1990
- Air France flight in Algeria, 1994
- Ethiopian Airlines flight crashed into the sea, 1996
- four US flights hijacked and crashed into the Pentagon and Twin Towers in New York, 11 September 2001

as the PLO were granted observer status by the United Nations Organization. With his gun holster empty, Arafat urged the UN to help the Palestinians regain their land, saying, "I have come bearing an olive branch and a freedom fighter's gun. Do not let the olive branch fall from my hand." The 1970s had seen a change in the fortunes of the PLO and Arafat had been the single most influential figure in bringing that about.

Arafat addresses the General Assembly, 13 November 1974.

The Entebbe raid, July 1976

In 1976, one of the most spectacular of all hijackings took place and, for one week, world attention was focused on the Ugandan airport of Entebbe. An Air France flight, hijacked from Athens by members of the PFLP, was flown to Entebbe where other terrorists, given refuge by the Ugandan leader Idi Amin, joined the hostage takers. They demanded the release of Palestinians held in Israeli jails and elsewhere in Europe and threatened to start killing the 105 Jews who had been singled out on the aircraft. The Israeli government was determined to resist the demands, and on 4 July secretly sent a rescue team of 100 commandoes by aircraft to land in Uganda and attack the hijackers. Within less than one hour, the commandoes had shot dead all seven hijackers and rescued the hostages. Only three hostages died in the attack, along with 45 Ugandan soldiers. It was a spectacular rescue mission and the Israelis lost only one man in the assault—their leader, Yonatan Netanyahu. The rescue was welcomed with admiration around the world and set the tone for actions by other governments in the face of air terrorism. The PLO and its factions continued to regard terrorism and hijacking as legitimate options for oppressed peoples, and still do so in the present day.

PLO timeline, 1964–82	
1964	Palestine Liberation Organization (PLO) is founded, with Ahmad Shuqeiri as its leader
February 1969	Yasser Arafat becomes leader of the PLO
September 1970	The PLO is expelled from Jordan
November 1974	The United Nations General Assembly grants the PLO observer status
January 1976	PLO militiamen massacre 500 Christian-Lebanese civilians in the Damour massacre
September 1976	The PLO is admitted as a member of the Arab League
August 1978	The PLO headquarters in Beirut is bombed, killing 150 people
Late 1982	Most of the PLO is relocated to Tunis after being driven out of Beirut during the Israeli invasion of Lebanon

TOK link

Language, perception, reason and emotion

An area of knowledge such as history is unique in that it is, more than any other discipline, a "service" subject. That means that every subject has a history.

? **Is that true for all other areas of knowledge?**

The study of history often makes use of all the ways of knowing. History needs language to communicate its findings and so language is vital to the historian. Historians must be careful in their choice of vocabulary and should try to be impartial in its terminology.

- Look up a current event from two or three different sources (such as newspapers and magazine articles) and decide which words are value-laden and which may be factual.

- Both reason and emotion may be employed in the selection of certain details in a story. Think of examples from your history course where evidence is selected and consider how that might be done and what criteria may be used.

- Historical accounts are partly descriptive and partly explanatory or analytical. Does the selection of material reveal value judgments have been made?

- Look at some of the Western political cartoons in this section. What is the cartoonist's perception of Arabs?

- To what extent does emotion play a role in a historian's analysis? Is (historical) objectivity possible?

Source analysis

The following documents relate to diplomacy and the PLO.

Source A

Political cartoon by Garland published in the British newspaper the *Daily Telegraph*, 15 November 1974. The cartoon shows Arafat holding an olive branch. The caption at the bottom reads: "Do not let the olive branch fall from my hand." (Yasser Arafat).

Source B

Arafat's speech to the UN, 13 November 1974.

The difference between the revolutionary and the terrorist lies in the reason for which each fights. Whoever stands by a just cause and fights for liberation from invaders and colonialists cannot be called terrorist. Those who wage war to occupy, colonize and oppress other people are the terrorists. ... The Palestinian people had to resort to armed struggle when they lost faith in the international community, which ignored their rights, and when it became clear that not one inch of Palestine could be regained through exclusively political means. ...

The PLO dreams and hopes for one democratic state where Christian, Jew and Muslim live in justice, equality, fraternity and progress. The chairman of the PLO and leader of the Palestinian revolution appeals to the General Assembly to accompany the Palestinian people in its struggle to attain its right of self-determination. ... I have come bearing an olive branch and a freedom fighter's gun. Do not let the olive branch fall from my hand.

Source: Washington Report on Middle East Affairs. http://www.wrmea.com/backissues/1194/9411070.htm.

Source C

United Nations General Assembly Resolution 3236, on 22 November 1974, recognizes the Palestinian people's right to self-determination.

> **QUESTION OF PALESTINE**
>
> *The General Assembly,*
>
> ***Having considered** the question of Palestine …*
>
> ***Reaffirms** the inalienable rights of the Palestinian people in Palestine, including:*
>
> ***a*** *The right to self-determination without external interference;*
>
> ***b*** *The right to national independence and sovereignty;…*
>
> ***Reaffirms** also the inalienable right of the Palestinians to return to their homes and property from which they have been displaced and uprooted, and calls for their return; …*
>
> ***Recognizes** that the Palestinian people is a principal party in the establishment of a just and lasting peace in the Middle East; …*
>
> ***Requests** the Secretary-General to establish contacts with the Palestine Liberation Organization on all matters concerning the question of Palestine;*
>
> ***Requests** the Secretary-General to report to the General Assembly at its thirtieth session on the implementation of the present resolution;*
>
> ***Decides** to include the item entitled "Question of Palestine" in the provisional agenda of its thirtieth session.*

Source: United Nations Information System on the Question of Palestine (UNISPAL) http://domino.un.org/UNISPAL.nsf.

Source D

Extract written by British historian Paul Johnson.

> *As a threat to the stability of all societies under the rule of law, international terrorism should have been the primary concern of the United Nations. But by the 1970s, the UN was a corrupt and demoralized body, and its ill-considered interventions were more inclined to promote violence that to prevent it. …*
>
> *As we have already noted, Idi Amin, a terrorist himself and a patron and beneficiary of terrorism, was given a standing ovation in 1975 when he advocated genocide. Yasser Arafat, head of the PLO, the world's largest terrorist organisation, was actually given a seat in the Assembly. The UN Secretariat had long since ceased to apply the principles of the charter.*

Source: Johnson, Paul. 1983. *A History of the Modern World*. London, UK. Weidenfeld & Nicholson.

Source E

Extract written by British historian TG Fraser.

> *Arafat's opportunity to underline that fact [Arab League recognition of the PLO as sole representatives of the Palestinians] came just two weeks later before the General Assembly of the United Nations in New York. In September, a number of states had proposed that 'The Question of Palestine' be debated by the Assembly and a subsequent vote invited the PLO to take part. The extent of that vote, 82 in favour, 4 against and 20 abstentions, showed how far the organisation had come in terms of international acceptance. Those who hoped he would use the occasion to signal the PLO's acquiescence [agreement] in a 'mini-state' solution were disappointed, but the reality of Arafat's position as head of a broad coalition made that impossible. Instead, he chose to set before the world body a full statement of Palestinian grievances and his dream of a future state in which Palestinians and Jews would live together. …*
>
> *Support for the Palestinians amongst the countries of Africa and Asia was high. In the summer of 1975 concerted effort to deprive Israel of her UN membership only just failed, but in November a resolution was passed in the General Assembly in which Zionism was identified as 'a form of racialism'. As the United Nations had ceased to be an actor of any consequence in the Arab–Israeli conflict, such things had little practical result, but they helped bring to the surface Israeli fears that the world's hand would always turn against the Jews and hence did nothing to encourage a spirit of compromise.*

Source: Fraser, TG. 2004. *The Arab–Israeli Conflict*. Basingstoke, UK. Palgrave.

Source-based questions

1. **a** What, according to Source E, was meant by a "mini-state'" solution?

   b What message concerning the role of the PLO in the Middle East is conveyed by the political cartoonist in Source A?

2. In what ways do Sources A and B support the opinions expressed in Source D?

3. With reference to their origin and purpose, assess the value and limitations of Sources C and E for historians studying the role of international organizations in the Middle East and beyond.

4. Explain how the recognition of the PLO by the Arab League and the UN might help to bring a possible solution to the situation in the Arab–Israeli dispute.

The Six Day War of 1967 and the October War of 1973: causes, course and consequences

Between 1967 and 1973 the Arab–Israeli conflict reached its lowest point. Two bitter wars were fought, which created thousands more refugees, brought the superpowers to the brink of conflict and allowed Israel to emerge as the dominant power in the region. The realignment of regional dynamics impacted upon domestic politics in the Arab states, saw the decline of pan-Arabism and the emergence of Palestinian nationalism. In 1973 the October War saw the Arabs emerge with a military victory for the first time and a claim to have won the conflict politically. Ominously, the world economy was affected by the use of oil as a weapon, which promoted a realignment of the superpowers in the conflict and the possibility of a resolution by the UN.

Causes of the Six Day War of June 1967

The war of 1967, like many aspects of the Arab–Israeli dispute, has been the subject of debate over responsibility for the conflict. The war was a tactical strike by a military machine in theory vastly outnumbered by its enemies but which achieved a stunning victory in less than a week and which decisively changed the face of the Middle East conflict. The immediate cause was the closure of the Straits of Tiran by Nasser in May and the withdrawal of the UN forces from the Sinai which, with the buffer removed, brought the two sides into direct contact. Israeli perceptions of their own vulnerability did the rest and they struck pre-emptively on 5 June to initiate the conflict that they saw as inevitable.

Israeli historiography blames the conflict on the actions of Nasser. However, the causes lie also in the situation left over from the earlier war of 1956: the power politics of the Arab states and the intrigues of the Cold War resulted in a classic example of **brinkmanship** which failed, precipitating a bloody clash. The residue of bitterness and mistrust left over from the Suez affair still simmered in the region. The neglect of the Palestinians was also a major factor in bringing about the war. The creation of the PLO in 1964 provided a stimulus for a possible resolution of Arab demands but was also seen as a struggle for control by the Arab–Palestinian cause. Throw into the mix the vanity of Nasser, pan-Arabism and Israel's fears, and you get a heady cocktail of volatility ready to explode.

> **Brinkmanship** A policy coined by US Secretary of State, JF Dulles, in 1956, meaning to push an opponent into a dangerous situation or confrontation to force a desired outcome.

Tensions existed between the Arabs themselves, particularly Egypt, Syria and Jordan, but in April 1967 Israel shot down Syrian MIG jets and a semblance of unity pulled the Arab states together. At the same time the Soviet Union provided false information to the Arabs about Israeli mobilization (probably the result of inaccurate information), demonstrating the Cold War facet of the regional conflict, precipitating Nasser to take action. Wanting to stand tall in the Arab world, Nasser demanded the withdrawal of UN forces from Egyptian land. Almost certainly Nasser did not intend war at this stage but, through brinkmanship, he lost control of events and, in secret, the Israeli cabinet approved a pre-emptive strike against their enemies, beginning with the destruction of the Egyptian air force.

The course and consequences of the Six Day War

Within 24 hours Israeli jets destroyed the air forces of four of their Arab neighbours—Egypt, Jordan, Iraq and Syria—and effectively assured themselves of victory in the war. It was one of the most decisive military strikes in any conflict and was the result of an Israeli military strategy planned years before by former chief of staff, Yitzhak Rabin. At the beginning of the war the balance of forces of the two sides was roughly the same: the IDF (Israeli Defence Forces) numbered just over 250 000 combat soldiers, with the number of tanks being evenly balanced. In air power, the Arab states had numerical superiority but their pilots lacked the training and skill of the Israelis. The actions taken by the latter early on 5 June meant that their ground forces could advance to Sinai and defeat the Egyptian army. Three days later, Egypt had suffered the loss of over 15 000 casualties, 800 tanks and over 300 aircraft and accepted a cease-fire.

Egyptian war wrecks lie scattered in Sinai in June 1967.

Meanwhile, Jordan had been attacked, with the IDF advancing to the Jordan River and into the West Bank and Jerusalem. King Hussein's well-trained army proved no match for the Israelis and, three days after the opening air campaign, the city of Jerusalem and all of the West Bank lay in Israeli hands. The seizure of Jerusalem, the capital of the ancient kingdom of Israel, was an emotional moment for many but represented a humiliation for the Arab cause. By this time, the outside world and in particular the Soviets and Americans were rapidly trying to bring about a ceasefire and prevent further damage. On 9 June, Israel struck Syria's Golan Heights and within 24 hours took the territory, by which time a UN-sponsored cease-fire came into effect. It had been a stunning victory for Israel and another major turning point in the Middle East conflict.

- After the fighting, with casualties of less than 1000 dead, the state of Israel had tripled in size and now found herself the strongest military power in the Middle East.
- For the Arabs, particularly Egypt, it had been another disaster; they had lost 15 000 dead and had once again been humiliated. In Egypt, Nasser resigned, but was swept back into office by popular demand; however, his leadership of the Arab cause had been severely damaged.
- The humiliation of 1967 provoked more domestic discontent at home for Arab regimes, with criticism of weak leaders, a decline in pan-Arabism and the rise of fundamentalist Palestinian and Islamic nationalism.
- The war created another mass of Palestinian refugees scattered across the region. The magnitude of their victory did not encourage concessions on the part of the Israelis and the weaknesses of the Arabs only fostered resentment, and promoted more fundamental solutions to the Arab–Israeli question.

- For the major powers, the prestige of the USSR came under attack, as their allies had been beaten; for the USA, Israel was confirmed as their major ally in the region.
- Diplomatically, the role of peace negotiatior fell to the United Nations. It came up with Resolution 242, in November 1967, a major landmark in the Arab–Israeli conflict that was not even partially achieved until 1992.

Developments between the wars: 1967–73

The situation between the wars was the result of the stunning victory in 1967 for Israel, but it was also indicative of the relationship which had existed for years between the two sides. Israel declared herself ready to hand back territories in return for a guarantee of full and lasting peace and the recognition of Israel's right to exist. The Palestinians would be dealt with separately and, in that, both sides seemed to be in agreement.

Meanwhile, a low-intensity conflict between Israel and Egypt, usually known as the War of Attrition, developed. Between 1967 and 1970, Israel lost more soldiers than they had in the 1967 war; the conflict was finally brought to a conclusion by the acceptance of a cease-fire in August 1970.

The Palestinians had taken matters into their own hands with the well-publicized hijackings of aircraft and, in Jordan, the events of Black September resulted in the expulsion of Fatah and the Palestinian leadership. This coincided with the sudden death of Nasser and the coming to power in Egypt of Anwar Sadat, a man whose policies were to change the stalemate of the Arab–Israeli situation in a radical manner.

Once Sadat had secured his power base at home, he began to take radical steps in Egyptian foreign policy. With Israel seemingly content to keep its newly gained territory, Sadat began to make clandestine overtures to the United States, which by now was looking to exit from Vietnam and was keen to rebuild bridges with the Arabs in the Middle East. The Soviet Union was unable to exert sufficient pressure on Israel, nor was it prepared to back the Arabs with sufficient force to regain land lost. Sadat made two radical decisions: the first of these was to go to war again with Israel—a limited one; the second was to remove all Russian advisors and begin to seeking a **détente** with the USA. In July 1972, 15 000 Russians left Egypt and later in the year Sadat secured an agreement with Syria that they would go to war with Israel in the near future.

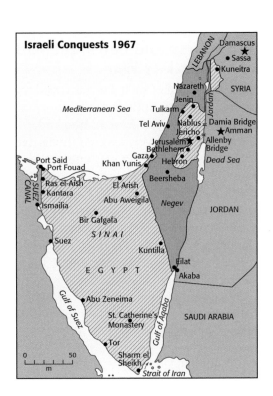

Détente The term given to a period of relaxation developed in the early 1970s in the Cold War, from the French word meaning "release of tensions".

The October War of 1973

Sadat's determination to force the issue of disputed territory with Israel was the cause of the fourth war in 1973. Sadat's aim was to break the stalemate and force the Israelis—and the world—to do something to resolve at least some of the issues in the Arab–Israeli conflict. "If you can get me ten centimetres of Sinai, I can solve the problem," Sadat is reported to have told his commanders. Taking the offensive for the first time was a gamble, but it paid off. The offensive called for a simultaneous air strike by Egypt and Syria on 6 October 1973, followed by a land offensive against the impressive Israeli defences across the Suez in Sinai and an attack on the Golan Heights by the Syrians.

The attack on the Jewish holy day of Yom Kippur caught the Israelis by surprise. Overconfidence, and the belief that the build-up was just another set of army manoeuvres by the Arabs, contributed to the unparalleled success of the initial Arab attacks and, within three days, the Israelis had to withdraw from key positions in the Golan and Sinai and sacrifice a large number of aircraft to stave off defeat. Initial counter-attacks failed but Egyptian forces, encouraged by their early success, pushed deeper into the Sinai only to be severely damaged by the Israeli forces under the command of Ariel Sharon. On 14 October, a major tank battle was fought in the Sinai and hundreds of Egyptian tanks were destroyed. Israeli troops crossed the Suez in the south and, in the Golan Heights, pushed the Syrians back. The tide of the battle had turned.

Moshe Dayan (1915–81)

Moshe Dayan served as minster of defence in various Israeli governments between 1950 and the 1970s. A colourful and charismatic personality, Dayan (who lost an eye during the Second World War) wore a black eye patch, which made him a recognizable figure in the diplomacy of the period. He served in the army and was both a warrior and, later in his life, a champion of peace, being a key representative for Begin's government in the **Camp David** agreements in 1978. He later disagreed with Begin over Israeli settlements in the occupied territories and resigned from the government. He was an author and a keen amateur archaeologist.

Camp David US presidential retreat in Maryland, the site of the accords made in 1978 in the Arab–Israeli conflict.

Meanwhile, on the diplomatic front, there had been a lot of activity by both superpowers as well as the international community. Fearful of the use of an oil embargo as an Arab weapon, as well as a return to the region of Soviet advisors, the Americans, through Henry Kissinger, tried to mediate. With Nixon embroiled in the Watergate scandal, Kissinger's role of shuttle diplomacy proved vital in resolving the conflict and achieving a ceasefire. Sadat, though, had played his hand deftly; gambling that initial Arab military successes would provide a springboard for negotiations and recognizing that neither superpower would be prepared to see their side defeated in a war, the Arabs accepted an armistice on 27 October.

Consequences

The consequences of the war were ones of mixed fortunes for the two sides. Israel claimed victory on the battlefield but the Israelis had been shown that they could be beaten and their appearance of invincibility was damaged. Politically, Sadat and the Arabs had won the war, with the Egyptian president emerging as a world figure and a hero to the Arabs. A year later, Golda Meir, the Israeli prime minister, and the defence minister Dayan, hero of the '67 war, both resigned. The UN passed Resolution 338 calling for a ceasefire as well as the implementation of earlier resolutions and, in the following year, the Egyptians, Syrians and Israelis agreed terms. The October War had once again turned world attention to the Middle East, promoted fears of an oil embargo and brought the superpowers close to confrontation. But President Sadat had another card to play—one which was to shock the Arab world, bring about a radical solution (at least in part) to the Arab–Israeli dispute and, ultimately, result in his death.

Source analysis

The following documents relate to the outbreak of the Six Day War of June 1967 between Israel and her Arab neighbours.

Key date

19 May 1967   United Nations Emergency Force (UNEF) withdrawn from Gaza and Sinai at Egypt's request

Source A

Statement to the Knesset by the Israeli prime minister, Levi Eshkol, 23 May 1967.

This morning a statement by the Egyptian President was published declaring his intention to block the international waterway which passes through the Straits of Tiran and joins the Gulf of Eilat with the Red Sea to the passage of Israeli ships. Any interference with freedom of passage in the Gulf and the Straits constitutes a gross violation of international law, a blow at the sovereign rights of other nations and an act of aggression against Israel. During the past few days, the Government of Israel has been in close touch with the Governments that have proclaimed and exercised the principle of free passage in these waters since 1957. After these exchanges, I can say that international support for these rights is serious and widespread.

Source B

Cartoon from a Lebanese newspaper dated 31 May 1967 showing Israel facing the guns of eight Arab states.

Source C

Excerpt from a statement by Soviet ambassador Nikolai Trofimovich Fedorenko to the UN, 24 May 1967.

Israel extremists apparently hoped to take Syria by surprise and deal a blow at Syria alone. But they miscalculated. Showing solidarity, Arab States—the United Arab Republic, Iraq, Algeria, Yemen, Lebanon, Kuwait, Sudan and Jordan—declared their determination to help Syria in the event of an attack by Israel. Considering that the presence of the United Nations troops in the Gaza area and Sinai Peninsula would give Israel advantages for staging a military provocation against Arab countries, the Government of the United Arab Republic asked the United Nations to pull its troops out of this area. Israel is once again to blame for a dangerous aggravation of tension in the Near East. But let no one have any doubts about the fact that, should anyone try to unleash aggression in the Near East, he would be met not only by the united strength of Arab countries but also by strong opposition to aggression from the Soviet Union and all peace-loving States.

Source D

Statement by President Nasser to Arab trade unionists, 26 May 1967.

We can achieve much by Arab action, which is a main part of our battle. We must develop and build our countries to face the challenge of our enemies. … What we see today in the masses of the Arab people everywhere is their desire to fight. The problem today is not just Israel, but also those behind it. If Israel embarks on an aggression against Syria or Egypt, the battle against Israel will not be confined to one spot on the Syrian or Egyptian borders. The battle will be a general one and our basic objective will be to destroy Israel. …

Today people must know the reality of the Arab world. What is Israel? Israel today is the United States. The United States is the chief defender of Israel. As for Britain, I consider it America's lackey [servant/slave]. Britain does not have an independent policy. Wilson always follows Johnson's steps and says what he wants him to say. All Western countries take Israel's view. The Soviet Union's attitude was great and splendid, it supported the Arabs and the Arab nation. It went to the extent of stating that, together with the Arabs and the Arab nation, it would resist any interference or aggression. …

The Gulf of Aqaba was a closed waterway prior to 1956. We used to search British, US, French and all other ships. … The Israelis say they opened the maritime route. I say they told lies and believed their own lies. We withdrew because the British and the French attacked us. This battle was never between us and Israel alone.

Source E

Recording of a telephone conversation between Nasser and King Hussein, monitored in Israel at 4.50 a.m. on 6 June 1967.

Nasser: *Do you know that the U.S. is participating alongside Israel in the war? Should we announce this? … Should we say that the U.S. and Britain (are participating) or only the U.S?*

Hussein: *The U.S. and England.*

Nasser: *Does Britain have aircraft carriers?*

Hussein: *[inaudible]*

Nasser: *Good. King Hussein will make an announcement and I will make an announcement … we will make sure that the Syrians (also) make an announcement that American and British aircraft are using their aircraft carriers against us.*

Source-based questions

1 **a** According to Source A, what were the consequences of the closure of the Straits of Tiran ?

   b What can be inferred from Source B about the situation facing Israel from her Arab neighbours? How accurate is this portrayal?

2 What evidence is there in Source C and Source D to support the claim that Israel was about to attack her neighbours? In what ways does Source B support this?

3 With reference to their origin and purpose, assess the value and limitations of Source D and Source E for historians studying the reasons for conflict between Israel and Egypt.

4 Was foreign influence in the Middle East the major reason for the outbreak of the Six Day War?

The roles of the USA, the USSR and the UN in international diplomacy, Camp David and the Egyptian–Israeli peace agreement

As a major player in the diplomacy surrounding the creation of Israel, the United States was drawn deeper into the Arab–Israeli conflict and, by 1967, was vital in sponsoring a settlement between the two major protagonists in the region. Emerging from four wars, Egypt and Israel forged a hard-fought compromise peace, which provided the basis for the establishment of regional security, at least for the two foremost players. It brought the USA more prominently into the picture but ultimately resulted in the assassination of one of the principal architects of the peace, Anwar Sadat, in 1981.

Developments and diplomacy, 1974–7

In the aftermath of the October War, the USA, itself partially paralysed by the events of Watergate and the traumas of withdrawal from Vietnam, saw Secretary of State Kissinger playing a significant role diplomatically in the Middle East through promoting talks at Geneva. When Gerald Ford replaced Nixon as US president in 1974, he brought pressure to bear on the Israelis to make some concessions in the interests of peace but was frustrated by their intransigence (unwillingness to compromise). He envisioned a comprehensive peace settlement which included not only the implementation of UN Resolutions 242 and 338 but also a part to be played by the Soviet Union and, perhaps, an opportunity to hear the voice of the Palestinians. In 1974 the PLO had been recognized as the sole representative of their people and Arafat himself had spoken to the General Assembly of the UN. The following year the UN adopted Resolution 3379, which described Zionism as "a form of racism and racial discrimination". The profile of the PLO had been raised during these years and the plight of the Palestinians was one which clamoured to be dealt with.

In 1976, civil war broke out again in Lebanon, the Israelis rescued their hostages from Entebbe in Uganda and, in the United States, a new president was voted into office. A Southern Baptist and a man of high moral principles, Democrat Jimmy Carter was to breathe new life into the Arab–Israeli situation and to be instrumental in bringing about the most significant peace development to date in the dispute. Carter and his Secretary of State, Cyrus Vance, both saw the way forward through reconvening the stalled Geneva conference which had been proposed by Kissinger, only this time to include representatives from the Palestinians themselves. The Geneva proposals hadn't borne fruit following the Yom Kippur war but, in essence, they had involved the Soviets as mediators, major territorial concessions by Israel, recognition by the Arabs of the Israeli state and a resolution of the growing Palestinian issue. However, Carter's desire to achieve a settlement was not enough and developments in Israel itself in June 1977 hardly made the prospects for peace any more likely. The **Likud** party, led by the arch-nationalist and former Irgun leader, Menachim Begin, defeated the Labour government for the first time. Begin's majority in the Israeli parliament, the Knesset, and

Likud A right-wing Israeli parliamentary party, which first formed a government under Menachim Begin in 1977.

his backing among the electorate had come about largely because of his hard-line approach to dealing with the Arabs, as well as support from the growing Sephardic Jewish community, based on his ideological belief in the Jewish claim to Eretz Israel. Given the dogmatic nature of Begin's character and his unswerving determination to hold lands such as the West Bank, it was difficult to see how any compromise would be possible, and many considered Begin's victory to be a setback for possible peace in the region.

The road to Jerusalem, 1977

Sadat, however, looked at the issues in a different way. His determination to achieve security for Egypt had led him to drop the Soviets as unreliable allies and to move in the direction of the United States and Europe. Economic decline and social upheavals at home convinced Sadat that a radical solution would be needed to break the deadlock. A visionary, and a man prepared to gamble, Sadat had taken Egypt to war in 1973 to claim a victory of sorts against Israel and he was now determined to take the lead with a dramatic gesture. He had tested the waters through intermediaries to see if Begin's government would be open to some kind of deal and then, on 9 November 1977, he invited the PLO leader Arafat to a meeting of the Egyptian parliament where he said, "I am ready to go to the end of the world, to their own homes, even to the Knesset in search of peace." This not only surprised his listeners but it stunned the world when, ten days later, Anwar Sadat descended the steps of the presidential aircraft in Tel Aviv to walk into history as the first Arab head of state ever to visit Israel and to take the first step on what was regarded as one of the most remarkable events in the latter half of the 20th century.

Sadat had been invited to the Knesset, where he delivered a speech to a full house explaining his decision to visit Jerusalem in order to break down the psychological barrier which, in his view, formed a large part of the bitter conflict between the two adversaries. He offered Israel recognition and a permanent peace based on agreements which would restore Arab lands, recognize the need for a Palestinian homeland and provide secure boundaries. Many Israelis considered his speech to be harsh; nevertheless, Begin's reply was hardly accommodating or open-minded to an opponent who had risked so much and had made the first dramatic move. Sadat's visit gripped the world, gained him the nomination as *Time* magazine's "Man of the Year" but earned him the hatred of most of the Arab states, who condemned him for grand treason against the Arab cause.

Anwar Sadat (1918–81)

Anwar Sadat, like his predecessor, was born in 1918 and served in the army and as a member of the Free Officer group. He was appointed vice-president by Nasser in 1964 but was considered by many to be a rather nondescript political figure when he suddenly became president on Nasser's death in 1970.

Soon after, he began to alter the course Nasser had taken and, in a bold move, expelled the Soviets from his country and declared war on Israel in 1973. At home he began a series of measures to liberalize the economy and initiated serious peace negotiations with Israel. In 1977 he became the first Arab head of state to visit Jerusalem, for which he was praised in the West but reviled by much of the Arab world. Sadat received the Nobel peace prize for his efforts, but was assassinated by disaffected Islamic military elements on the anniversary of the Yom Kippur war in Cairo in 1981.

Extracts from Anwar Sadat's speech to the Israeli Knesset in Jerusalem, 20 November 1977

I come to you today on solid ground to shape a new life and to establish peace. We all love this land, the land of God, we all, Moslems, Christians and Jews, all worship God. …

I have come to you so that together we should build a durable peace based on justice to avoid the shedding of one single drop of blood by both sides. It is for this reason that I have proclaimed my readiness to go to the farthest corner of the earth.

There was a huge wall between us that you tried to build up over a quarter of a century but it was destroyed in 1973. It was the wall of an implacable and escalating psychological warfare. … It was a wall of the fear of the force that could sweep the entire Arab nation. It was a wall of propaganda that we were a nation reduced to immobility. … Together we have to admit that that wall fell and collapsed in 1973. Yet, there remains another wall. This wall constitutes a psychological barrier between us, a barrier of suspicion, a barrier of rejection; a barrier of fear, or deception, a barrier

of hallucination without any action, deed or decision. A barrier of distorted and eroded interpretation of every event and statement. It is this psychological barrier that I described in official statements as constituting 70 percent of the whole problem.

Let me tell you without the slightest hesitation that I have not come to you under this roof to make a request that your troops evacuate the occupied territories. Complete withdrawal from the Arab territories occupied after 1967 is a logical and undisputed fact. Nobody should plead for that. Any talk about permanent peace based on justice and any move to ensure our coexistence in peace and security in this part of the world would become meaningless while you occupy Arab territories by force of arms.

As for the Palestine cause, nobody could deny that it is the crux of the entire problem … In all sincerity I tell you that there can be no peace without the Palestinians. It is a grave error of unpredictable consequences to overlook or brush aside this cause.

Source: http://www.jewishvirtuallibrary.org/jsource/Peace/sadat_speech.html

The following months saw not only Sadat's condemnation by the Arabs and the Palestinians but an intense series of meetings between the USA, Israel and Egypt to capitalize on the initiative of the trip to Jerusalem. Sadat hoped the move had been enough to transform the conflict but many long hours of negotiation and bitterness lay ahead before something was achieved. In July, to break the impasse which had developed and to bring a resolution to the conflict on which he seemed to have staked his presidency, President Carter invited both Begin and Sadat to the presidential retreat of Camp David.

The Camp David agreements, September 1978

On 5 September 1978, the main protagonists arrived at Camp David for a 12-day marathon session of negotiations. The issue of the West Bank and those of the Palestinian homeland and self-government were the main sticking points between the two sides. However, other issues were also of significance. The drive by the Israelis to build new settlements in occupied land angered many in the Arab world and in the United States too. Looking at the scenario objectively, it seemed as though Sadat had more to lose than the Israelis over negotiating a peace settlement. The Egyptians wanted a return of their occupied land and an Israeli withdrawal at least to the pre-1967 borders, as stipulated by UN Resolutions 242 and 336. Those demands were a minimum; provision for the Palestinians had acquired a much higher profile for all the Arab states and for the future stability of the region. For the Israeli government, an agreement with Egypt would remove the danger of their most powerful enemy and secure the southern borders of Israel. Surrendering the Sinai was worth the price, but to concede more than that was going to be difficult to justify.

The British cartoonist Nicholas Garland shows Sadat bearing a dove of peace as he approaches the black crows, which represent the other interested parties in the Middle East. The cartoon appeared in the *Daily Telegraph* on 18 November 1977.

Progress was slow and the personal animosity between Begin and Sadat blunted any clear initiatives. As political analyst and historian Stephen Shalom put it:

> On the Israeli side Begin was obstinate, while his delegation was flexible and even indulgent. The pattern of negotiations on the Egyptian side was the reverse: Sadat was flexible, while his delegation was rigid.

Shalom, R. May 2002. "Background to the Israel-Palestine Crisis". *Z magazine*. p. 373.
http://www.thirdworldtraveler.com/Israel/Background_I_P_Crisis.html

The planned five-day meeting turned into ten days, at which point, in utter frustration, Sadat and the Egyptian delegation packed their bags and requested a helicopter to take them back to Washington. The summit was resurrected by President Carter himself in a dramatic encounter with Sadat, which he described thus:

I explained [to Sadat] … that his action would harm the relationship between Egypt and the United States, he would be violating his personal promise to me … and damage one of my most precious possessions—his friendship and mutual trust. Approaching Begin, Carter presented him with photographs of the summit leaders with the names of each of the Israeli leader's grandchildren on them. Deeply moved, Begin commented, "We can't leave a war for these children to fight." Two days after that, Carter hammered out a deal which was announced to the world; the Camp David accords were signed in the White House on 17 September 1978.

The agreement was in two parts: the first—"A Framework for Peace in the Middle East"—dealt with the West Bank, Gaza, the implementation of the UN resolutions and a 'resolution of the Palestinian problem in all its aspects', but excluded Jerusalem, a major bone of contention. The second agreement—"A Framework for the Conclusion of a Peace Treaty between Israel and Egypt"—was more straightforward: Israel agreed to vacate the Sinai, restore diplomatic relations with Egypt and secure the southern borders with the country who had been her greatest threat in the 30 years of Israel's existence. This led to the signing of a formal treaty in March 1979. The agreement vindicated Carter's diplomacy and closed a chapter in the ongoing Arab–Israeli dispute.

Aftermath and summary

The nature of the settlement had left still-unresolved issues, notably that of the future of the Palestinians. The ambiguity of the wording was deliberate, in order to make the signing of the agreement possible. Semantics were used in the translations to justify action (or inaction) with regards to the implementation of the agreements relating to the Palestinians themselves. The agreements were regarded as a

Menachem Begin (1913–92)

Menachem Begin was a fervent Zionist, Irgun member and leader of the opposition Likud party for almost 30 years before he became Israel's prime minister in 1977. He negotiated the Camp David accords in the following year together with President Sadat of Egypt, for which they were both awarded the Nobel Prize for peace. Begin continued the building of Israeli settlements in occupied territory and was later responsible for the bombing of the Iraqi nuclear reactor in 1981 and the invasion of Lebanon in the following year. Criticism developed for Begin for the invasion and after the death of his wife, he resigned in 1983 and withdrew from political life. He died in 1992 and is buried in Jerusalem.

betrayal by the Arab world and Egypt was met with open hostility. Egypt was removed from the Arab League and, in October 1981, the architect of Egypt's diplomacy was assassinated by elements of his own army in Cairo. Three American Presidents—Richard Nixon, Gerald Ford and Jimmy Carter—attended his funeral. Israel continued to build settlements, refused to grant full autonomy to the Palestinians, formally annexed the Golan Heights and went to war with Lebanon in 1982. Relations between the two principal signatories could better be described as a cold peace.

Sadat, Carter and Begin clasp hands at the signing of the Egypt–Israel peace treaty on 26 March 1979.

Meanwhile the USA faced other threats in the region when, in 1979, the shah of Iran was overthrown, US hostages were taken by radical Islamic elements in Tehran and, at the end of the year, the USSR invaded Afghanistan. Carter lost the election that year to the Republican candidate, Ronald Reagan. US diplomacy meant that the US was at the forefront of the Middle East and both Egypt and Israel benefitted greatly from their friendship with the superpower. But the Arab–Israeli conflict was to continue through to the present day, with many of the issues which had divided the two sides still unresolved.

The Arab–Israeli conflict has been one of the major disputes of the 20th century. It combines elements of competing nationalisms, radical ideologies and bitter conflicts. The world has been drawn into the dispute both willingly and unwittingly through human rights issues, terrorism, oil and strategic imperatives. The search for peace in the region is a vital one for all concerned, but one which still eludes both the local and international community.

TOK link

History and science

> *History is as much art as science.* Ernest Renan

Is the main job of the historian to describe or explain the past? To what extent can the historian claim to be part artist and part scientist?

What do you understand by the scientific method? Is there a historical method?

History is part science in its approach to the collection and verification of evidence. As with other areas of knowledge, there is a variety of ways of gaining knowledge in group 3 subjects. These include archival evidence, data collection, experimentation and observation, inductive and deductive reasoning. All can be used to help explain patterns of behaviour and lead to knowledge claims in history. Students studying history are required to evaluate these knowledge claims by exploring knowledge issues such as validity, reliability, credibility, certainty and individual, as well as cultural, perspectives.

Having followed a course of study in group 3, you should be able to reflect critically on the various ways of knowing and on the methods used in human sciences and in so doing become an "inquiring, knowledgeable and caring" young person.

Discuss each of the following or write an essay on one of the titles below.

● Why do accounts of the same historical event differ?

● Whose history do we study?

● What determines how historians select evidence and describe/interpret or analyse events?

● "An historian must combine the rigour of the scientist with the imagination of the artist". To what extent then, can the historian be confident about his or her conclusions?

IB History Guide.

Exam practice

Source analysis
The following documents relate to the aftermath of the Suez War of 1956 and its consequences.

Source A
Political cartoon by Leslie Illingworth in the British newspaper the *Evening Standard*, 21 November 1956, entitled "Nasser in his Court", World leaders shown in the cartoon include Eisenhower, Nehru

Source B
The lessons of Suez, by British prime minister Margaret Thatcher.

The balance of interest and principle in the Suez affair is not a simple one. Over the summer [of 1956], however, we were outmanoeuvred by a clever dictator into a position where our interests could only be protected by bending our legal principles. At the same time, Suez was the last occasion when the European powers might have withstood and brought down a Third World dictator who had shown no interest in international agreements, except where he could profit from them. Nasser's victory at Suez had among its fruits the overthrow of the pro-Western regime in Iraq, the Egyptian occupation of the Yemen, and the encirclement of Israel, which led to the Six Day War—and the bills were still coming in when I left office.

As I came to know more about it, I drew four lessons from this sad episode. First, we should not get into a military operation unless we were determined and able to finish it. Second, we should never again find ourselves on the opposite side to the United States in a major international crisis affecting Britain's interests. Third, we should ensure that our actions were in accord with international law. And finally, he who hesitates is lost.

Source: Thatcher, M. 1995. *The Path of Power*. London, UK. HarperCollins.

Source C
Reflections on the political and economic impact of the Suez Crisis by a Belgian journalist.

What about the consequences of the Suez crisis for the Middle East itself and the oil-producing countries? In the longer term, the real threat is probably to them. The countries of the Middle East are undergoing rapid demographic expansion, which is causing serious problems. Most of them have been fortunate enough to benefit from rising oil production, which has been an unexpected bonus. But if, in the circumstances, Europe has less recourse to oil from the Middle East, the development of the region will be hampered and the existing difficulties will only be aggravated.

Egypt, which benefited indirectly from the oil boom, is in a similar position, made worse by the fact that the value of the Suez Canal appears to have been permanently diminished. Whatever solution is adopted, its direct and indirect benefits to Egypt have been reduced. In short, the Middle East is laying up economic and political difficulties for itself in the future.

Source: Baudhuin, Fernand. In *La Libre Belgique*, 13 January 1957.

Source D

Eisenhower's statement to Congress in January 1957 outlining US policy in the Middle East.

> *Thus we have the simple and indisputable facts:*
>
> *1 The Middle East, which has always been coveted by Russia, would today be prized more than ever by International Communism.*
>
> *2 The Soviet rulers continue to show that they do not scruple to use any means necessary to gain their ends.*
>
> *3 The free nations of the Mid-East need, and for the most part want, added strength to secure their continued independence …*
>
> *There is a general recognition in the Middle East, as elsewhere, that the United States does not seek either political or economic domination over any other people. Our desire is a world environment of freedom, not servitude … if the Middle East is to continue its geographic role of uniting rather than separating East and West.*

Source: Gorst, Anthony. 1997. *The Suez Crisis*. London, UK. Routledge.

Source E

Conclusions on Suez: extract from an article in an American military history magazine.

> *"Musketeer" proved to the world that the British and French were no longer superpowers. The result was a Middle Eastern power vacuum that could only be filled by the United States and the Soviet Union. Israel, besides demonstrating its growing military prowess, gained access to the Red Sea, Israel also won a respite from Egypt-based guerrilla raids. Nasser remained in power, and a crack appeared in NATO, accompanied by Anglo-French animosity and suspicion.*
>
> *The war's ultimate victors were Egypt and the Soviet Union. Nasser, who left to himself might never have gained the stature he did, emerged a hero of the Muslim world. The Soviet Union, after long peering through the keyhole of a closed door on what it considered a Western sphere of influence, now found itself invited over the threshold as a friend of the Arabs. The Soviets' influence in the Middle East, although it was not to last, included acquiring Mediterranean bases, supporting the budding Palestinian liberation movement and penetrating the Arab countries.*

Source: Deac, Wilfred. April 2001. *Military History* magazine. Washington, USA.

Source-based questions

1 a According to Source E, what did Nasser gain from the Suez crisis? *[3 marks]*

b What message is conveyed by Source A? *[2 marks]*

2 Compare and contrast the conclusions reached in Sources B and E about the Suez crisis. *[6 marks]*

3 With reference to their origin and purpose, assess the value and limitations of Sources C and D for historians studying the Suez crisis. *[6 marks]*

4 "The war's ultimate winners were Egypt and the Soviet Union." Source E. Using the sources and your own knowledge analyse this judgement and explain who were the losers. *[8 marks]*

Timeline 1917—79

1917		The Balfour Declaration. "His Majesty's Government view with favour the establishment in Palestine of a national home for the Jewish people."
1920		Britain is given the mandate to govern Palestine
1929		Arab riots in many areas; more than 130 Jews are killed
1936		A bloody Arab uprising, in which Palestinian and Jewish groups clash
1939		The White Paper of 1939 calls for the creation of a unified Palestinian state, in which power will be shared by Jews and Arabs
1946	22 July	King David Hotel bombing
1947	15 May	The UN General Assembly establishes a Special Committee on Palestine (UNSCOP)
	29 November	General Assembly votes to partition Palestine
1948	14 May	State of Israel proclaimed, as British mandate over Palestine ends at midnight US recognizes Israel
	15 May	Armies of Egypt, Iraq, Lebanon, Transjordan and Syria invade Israel

1949	24 February	Israel and Egypt sign armistice agreement
	11 May	Israel is admitted to UN membership
1950	24 April	Jordan annexes the West Bank, including East Jerusalem
1951	20 July	King Abdullah of Jordan is assassinated at the Al-Aqsa Mosque in Jerusalem
1952	23 July	Free Officers carry out *coup d'état* in Egypt, ousting King Farouk
	28 July	Egypt is proclaimed a republic
1953	14 October	Qibya massacre—over 60 Arabs are killed by Israelis
1954	17 April	Colonel Nasser becomes prime minister of Egypt
1955	27 September	Egyptian–Czechoslovak arms deal is announced
1956	24 June	Nasser elected President of Egypt
	26 July	Nasser announces the nationalization of the Suez Canal
	29 October	Israeli forces enter Sinai to attack the Egyptian army British and French forces invade the Suez Canal Zone
	7 November	General Assembly calls on the UK, France and Israel to withdraw
1957	6 January	President Eisenhower announces new US policy of "Eisenhower's Doctrine" in the Middle East
1958	1 February	Egypt and Syria merge and form the United Arab Republic
	14 July	Iraqi monarchy is overthrown; the King is killed Civil war in Lebanon
	15 July	US marines land in Beirut
1960	18 January	Egypt announces the USSR will finance the second stage of the Aswan High Dam
1961	29 September	Syria dissolves union with Egypt
1962	September	Civil war in Yemen. Egypt and Saudi Arabia intervene
1963	8 March	Officers group connected with Ba'ath party takes over power in Syria
	18 November	Military coup in Iraq; Arif becomes president
1964	3 February	The Palestine Liberation Organization is founded in Cairo
1967	19 May	UN Emergency Force is withdrawn at Egypt's request
	5 June	Israel air force strikes at Egypt and Syria—the Six Day War begins
	10 June	Israel occupies the Golan Heights. Syria accepts ceasefire
	22 November	Security Council adopts Resolution 242
1969	2 February	Yasser Arafat is appointed chairman of the PLO
	1 September	*Coup d' état* in Libya by Colonel Qaddafi overthrows the monarchy
1970	September	"Black September"—fighting between Jordanians and Palestinians
	28 September	President Nasser dies; succeeded by Anwar Sadat
1972	30 May	Lod airport massacre. Japanese Red Army members enter Lod airport in Tel Aviv, killing 24
	5 September	Eleven Israeli athletes are murdered by Black September in Munich's Olympic Village
1973	6 October	Yom Kippur War. Egyptian forces cross the Suez Canal, Syrian forces attack the Golan Heights
	15 October	Israeli forces cross Suez Canal
	17 October	Arab oil-producing states impose an embargo

1974	13 November	Arafat speaks at the UN General Assembly
	22 November	General Assembly votes in favour of granting observer status to the PLO
1975	1 September	Israel–Egypt Interim Agreement is signed in Jerusalem and Alexandria
	10 November	The UN General Assembly equates Zionism with racism
1976	27 June	Air France airliner is hijacked and flown to Entebbe
1977	9 March	President Carter announces new US policy for the Middle East
	9 November	Israeli jets attack PLO bases near Tyre
		President Sadat announces his readiness to come to Jerusalem to address the Knesset
	20 November	Sadat addresses the Israeli Knesset
1978	3 February	Carter and Sadat hold talks in Camp David
	6–17 September	The Camp David conference ends in the signing of two agreements at the White House
	20 October	President Sadat and Premier Begin win the Nobel Peace prize
1979	26 March	The Egypt–Israel peace treaty is signed at the White House

Recommended resources

Bregman, Ahron and El-Tahri, Jihan. 1998. *The Fifty Years War: Israel and the Arabs*. Penguin and BBC.

A collaboration between an Arab and an Israeli, a very readable account of the whole conflict since 1948 made to accompany the BBC TV three-part series.

Fraser, TG. 2004. *The Arab–Israeli Conflict*. Basingstoke, UK. Palgrave.

Laqueur, Walter and Rubin, Barry. (eds). 1991. *The Arab–Israeli Reader: Documentary History*. 5th edn. New York, USA. Penguin.

Ovendale, Ritchie. 2004. *The Origins of the Arab–Israeli Wars*. Harlow, UK. Pearson Education/Longman.

Schulze, Kirsten E. 1999. *The Arab–Israeli Conflict*. Harlow, UK. Pearson Education/Longman.

Smith, Charles D. 2004. *Palestine and the Arab–Israeli Conflict: A History in Documents*. Boston, USA; Bedford, UK. Palgrave Macmillan.

DVD *Six Days in June* by Eric Hammel. 1992. http://www.publicvideostore.org.

An account of the Six Day War, also a book of the same name.

DVD *Suez: A Very British Crisis*. 2006. BBC.

A three-part series on the Suez War of 1956.

3 Communism in crisis, 1976–89

The crises that the communist world faced in the 1970s and 1980s had their roots in the paradox of Marx's idea of the dictatorship of the proletariat. In both the People's Republic of China (PRC) and the Soviet Union—the Union of Soviet Socialist Republics (USSR)—the government claimed to represent the workers of the world, yet these were two of the most repressive regimes of their era: engaged in state-sponsored censorship, they functioned as police states, and were designed to prevent public expressions against government actions. In both countries, there had been attempts to modify the official positions of the Communist Party in order to address the ills that these countries faced, but reform was often followed by reaction. In the USSR, the de-Stalinization policies of Khruschev were followed by Brezhnev's return to strong central leadership; and in China, the brief attempts at reform such as the Hundred Flowers movement were followed by the Cultural Revolution. In the 1970s, there were further attempts to repair the ailing systems—with very different results for China and the Soviet Union.

This chapter focuses on prescribed subject 3; it addresses the major challenges—social, political and economic—facing the regimes in the leading socialist (Communist) states from 1976 to 1989 and the nature of the response of these regimes. In China, repressive measures managed to contain the challenges and the regime stayed in power. In the USSR and Communist Europe, challenges—whether internal or external in origin—produced responses that inaugurated reform processes that contributed significantly to the end of communism in Europe.

Sources for discussion and evaluation are included throughout the chapter and focus on the following areas:

- the struggle for power following the death of Mao Zedong (Mao Tse-tung); Hua Guofeng (Hua Kuo-feng); the re-emergence of Deng Xiaoping (Teng Hsiao-p'ing) and the defeat of the Gang of Four
- China under Deng Xiaoping: economic policies and the Four Modernizations
- China under Deng Xiaoping: political changes and their limits, culminating in the demonstrations in Tiananmen Square
- domestic and foreign problems of the Brezhnev era: economic and political stagnation; Afghanistan
- Gorbachev's aims and policies (glasnost and perestroika) and the consequences for the Soviet state to 1989
- the consequences of Gorbachev's policies for Eastern Europe to 1989; reform movements in Poland, Czechoslovakia and East Germany.

By the end of the chapter, you should be able to:

- understand the power structure in the People's Republic of China (PRC) and in the Union of Soviet Socialist Republics (USSR), 1976–89

- identify the political and party leadership in the PRC and the USSR

- explain the economic and political situations in the PRC and the USSR

- compare and contrast the viewpoints that different historians and countries have about events in the PRC and the USSR

- use documents from diverse sources to assess the events in the period 1976–89

- evaluate sources and formulate your own supported opinions regarding the nature of communism from 1976 to 1989.

Background to the subject

Although few outside the communist world realized it at the time, the choke hold that the Soviet Union had on Eastern Europe was being loosened, while the People's Republic of China was experiencing internal struggles. In both cases, the leaders of these countries were forced to question how they would achieve communism in this new, modern era, when confronted with a Western world that was still far ahead of them economically, especially in regard to the production of consumer goods.

In China, both Zhou Enlai and Mao Zedong died in 1976, leaving a power vacuum. The struggle for power that took place after Mao's death—between the radical Gang of Four and the more moderate elements of the Party—revealed a precarious Communist Party, in which future leadership seemed uncertain at best. After the struggle, a once-again rehabilitated Deng Xiaoping emerged as the dominant figure, and his policies prevailed. Included in these were a series of economic goals that were meant to help the country industrialize while continuing to support the agricultural sector. Additionally, Deng continued Mao's policies of opening up to the West, which simultaneously allowed for a dramatic increase in trade and improved foreign relations. The risk of this period of liberalization became apparent as the population grew increasingly outspoken against what it saw as repressive actions by the government and Party, which culminated in the events in Tiananmen Square in 1989.

In the same period, the Soviet Union saw the end of the old Communists such as Brezhnev, Andropov and Chernenko, all of whom came to power and met their demise at an advanced age. In 1985, the 54-year-old Mikhail Gorbachev came to power, ushering in what was hoped to be a new era in the communist Soviet Union. Make no mistake—Gorbachev was a Communist, but, like Deng Xiaoping before him, he recognized the need to adopt some more capitalist, open policies in an attempt to reinvigorate socialism and help the Soviet state retain its power and influence. Thus, a serious change in domestic and foreign policies was embarked upon, including a voluntary loosening of controls over the Soviet Union's Eastern European satellite states. Borrowing from his predecessors, Gorbachev seemed to prefer emancipation from above rather than revolution from below—à la Tsar Alexander II. Alternatively, he was seeking to improve the Soviet economy through cutting ties with the dependent satellite states.

Ultimately, Deng prevailed and Gorbachev failed. The PRC emerged from its crisis in a strong position; economically the state began to catch up with the West and was fast becoming an exporting nation, first to Japan and subsequently to the United States and other Western nations. At the same time, the grip of the government and the Chinese Communist Party over the population was confirmed in the Tiananmen Square massacre that ended this phase for China. Through his policies, Gorbachev began true economic reform in the Soviet Union and an improvement in the position of the government through a final withdrawal of Soviet troops from Afghanistan (in 1989); but the government and the Communist Party of the Soviet Union lost their hold not only over the satellite states, but also over the subject nations—especially in the western USSR—and ultimately over the population. By 1991, the USSR no longer existed, Gorbachev was ousted and the Communist Party was illegal.

Thus, the crises that communism faced in its two dominant countries were resolved in very different ways.

Approaching this subject

If you look at the curriculum objectives for prescribed subject 3 in the *History Guide*, you will see that the focus is on Communist China and the former Soviet Union. If you have chosen to do this subject, it is highly likely that you will also be focusing on the 20th-century history topic 5 "The Cold War" and perhaps topic 1 "Causes, practices and effects of wars", topic 3 "Origins and development of authoritarian and single-party states" or topic 4 "Nationalist and independence movements in Africa and Asia and post-1945 Central and Eastern European states". Topics 1, 3 and 5 can all provide valuable context for this subject, and provide the necessary background. Topic 4 can provide an interesting postscript to the era. These topics are covered in chapters 4, 6, 7, 8 and 9.

The main skills to focus on in this subject are source evaluation skills. In addition to knowing and understanding contemporary accounts, it is also critical to read a number of different sources offering different perspectives on these themes. Finding material with different perspectives on the Soviet Union and Eastern European states has become fairly easy since the demise of the USSR. Any student can do research on the Internet and within minutes find alternative interpretations of events; websites that belong to a variety of governments, educational institutions and ideological groups are readily accessible.

China, however, continues to be problematic, as information that is not from official sources is difficult to come by. There are a number of foreign correspondents, immigrants and children of immigrants, and academics who have spent considerable time in China and have attempted to provide alternative records, but this information is largely anecdotal and must be viewed as such. Additionally, there are

Chinese nationals who, writing under pseudonyms, contradict the government position or data on the interpretation of events. But these views must also be viewed cautiously, as it is difficult to assess the agenda of a writer, who chooses to remain anonymous.

Integrating the theory of knowledge (TOK)

With "Communism in crisis" there is ample opportunity to explore and question how historians know what they know. A number of the topics and issues presented in this chapter are extremely contentious. Since this subject covers the inner workings of totalitarian regimes, the official government view is of critical importance. At the end of each section of the chapter, there are a series of TOK questions and analyses that use these discrepancies in knowledge to address the relevant facts, and the manipulation of sources, in history.

China in crisis

> This section contextualizes the economic and political crises faced by the People's Republic of China after the deaths of Zhou Enlai and Mao Zedong in 1976. To this end, there are brief explanations of the political and economic repercussions of the Great Leap Forward, Mao's loss of power and the resulting Great Proletarian Cultural Revolution.

Background to the events, 1976–89

To understand how and why there was a power struggle in China after the death of Mao, the preceding decade must be summarized to some extent, starting with the removal of Mao as the head of government after the **Great Leap Forward** (GLF) and the Great Proletarian Cultural Revolution that followed it. Mao had been the undisputed leader of the People's Republic of China from its creation in 1949, but after the national economy plummeted in the Great Leap Forward other Chinese Communist Party (CCP) members began to question Mao's leadership. As a result, several new leaders emerged: Liu Shaoqi, who succeeded Mao in 1959 as the Chairman of the People's Republic of China and Deng Xiaoping as the Party's **General Secretary**.

The Chinese had been seriously destabilized by the GLF, particularly the peasants who found themselves in a state of famine as a result of government policies. Thus, the Party leadership looked for pragmatic (practical) solutions to the economic problems that China faced. This contradicted Mao, who was insisting on a continuation of revolutionary policies in an attempt to catch up with the West, while also competing with its rival for leadership in the communist world—the Soviet Union.

Great Leap Forward This policy was introduced by Mao in 1958 in an attempt to modernize the Chinese economy by mobilizing China's main resource: its population. The GLF had a long-term plan of eclipsing the productivity of Western powers by 1988. The majority of the population was placed on communes, where they were supposed to increase productivity and to assist in industrialization. The policy was quickly determined to be a failure as China lacked the necessary natural resources and was facing famine. In 1959 Mao announced the failure of the plan.

General Secretary The chief administrator and head of the Communist Party in any given country. This person is usually the de facto head of the country in addition to the actual head of the Party.

The role of Mao after the Great Leap Forward

Although Mao had been replaced by Liu as the head of government, he still retained the position of Chairman of the Communist Party and was the venerated elder in the government. Liu and Deng hoped to ease Mao out of power slowly, as he was so venerated by the Chinese population. Despite his role as the architect of the GLF, the population was unwilling to discredit him in any way and the politically astute Liu and Deng recognized this. Mao may have been fallible to the Party leadership, but the masses supported him unquestionably, especially the youth of China who had been raised on communist propaganda both in the school and in the teachings of their parents at home. Thus, the struggle for leadership of the Party and the country began as early as 1961. Perhaps even more than Lenin or Stalin, Mao had a strong **cult of personality** that made him seem omnipotent and all-knowing to the people of China. He used this to his advantage in the Cultural Revolution.

In 1962, Liu (after touring the countryside and seeing the results of the famines) convinced the Central Committee to allow peasants to grow on small, individual plots and make local crafts to sell at rural markets. He also began a program of incentives for those he felt were indispensible to the economic recovery of the nation. At the same time, the government allowed a bit more freedom of expression, leading to several satires of Mao.

Mao was alarmed by this return to capitalism, and felt that China was losing its revolutionary focus, especially among the Chinese youth. He also felt the bitter sting of the satires that criticized his leadership and revolutionary policies. Increasingly, he saw his wife as his primary confidante, and relied on her more and more for guidance and support. At the same time, high-ranking Party members no longer felt beholden (under obligation) to him as they followed what they saw as a necessary and pragmatic path toward recovery. While some Party leaders still gave Mao tremendous respect, others, such as Deng Xiaoping, openly challenged him in Party meetings. It is easy to dismiss the policies of the next few years as Mao's personal retaliation against those who undercut and opposed him, but this is too simplistic. Mao still believed fervently in revolutionary struggle and communism, and feared that his country and the Party were moving away from the ideals which had led them to establish the People's Republic of China in 1949. He feared that the new CCP leadership was **revisionist** or deviationist in its views, embracing capitalism and rejecting the ideology that had led to the establishment of the PRC.

Mao thus promulgated (promoted) the Socialist Education Movement. The idea behind this was that China needed to return to its rural roots, and even those in the cities needed to go to the countryside and assist in agricultural reforms. In the villages, these work teams would help the peasants to hold struggle meetings and identify the enemies of the people. Mao placed Liu in charge of the movement, as the one who had instituted agrarian reform. When those who supported Liu resisted this movement, Mao felt that his authority as leader of the Party and government were being challenged and sought a return to revolutionary ideals. This led to the Cultural Revolution.

Activity:

Contextualizing activity

What do you know about communism in the Republic of China before 1976? Put together two tables: one of the political leadership in the PRC in 1976 and one of the Party hierarchy. Where are the overlaps? What does this signify?

Cult of personality Although the dictionary definition refers to intense devotion to an individual, this is generally a statement about a government (usually authoritarian) that uses all means at its disposal to create a state where the commander in chief is raised to superhuman status. While not necessarily deified, the leader is seen to be above average people and has heroic status that demands unquestioning loyalty. The personality cult was most evident in the regimes of Stalin, Hitler, Mussolini, Mao and Kim Il-sung.

Revisionist In communist systems, reinterpreting Marxist ideas and values that retreat from the original revolutionary ideals that brought communism to power. The term is derisive and is meant to show the person accused of revisionism in a negative light.

In the summer of 1965, Mao went to Shanghai, where he began to prepare for his assault on the Party members who opposed him. Furthermore, Mao gained the support of Lin Biao—defence minister and the leader of the People's Liberation Army (PLA)—who was promoted to the number two position in the Party hierarchy. Mao called for the creation of Red Guards—revolutionary youth who would be the vanguard of a new struggle against elites. This meant the integration of the army into politics—something that China had studiously avoided up to this point. The PLA became a place where people could rise through the ranks and move away from their prior status as worker or peasant. As PLA members were readily accepted as Party members, positions in the army became highly competitive and millions were rejected each year. The PLA was also a place for indoctrination and, in 1964, Lin issued "Quotations from Chairman Mao" or the "Little Red Book" to all PLA members, increasing Mao's popularity and accessibility to the youth.

By 1965 the army was officially egalitarian; military ranks were abolished, with the idea that those who were most capable in any given situation would rise to leadership positions. But past success did not mean future guarantees of stability and rank. The PLA was made responsible not just for military operations, but for public security as well. It was enmeshed in all facets of public life, further increasing Lin's power. This would later be a great threat to both the Party and Mao.

The Great Proletarian Cultural Revolution

At this point Mao's wife, Jiang Qing, came to prominence in public affairs and emerged as a political figure. The Ministry of Culture began to form a series of committees to address the problems facing China, and Jiang was on the seemingly mild Committee for a Cultural Revolution. Under her direction, this former actress decided to launch an assault on the Beijing Opera, which she accused of being **bourgeois** and traditionalist. Her idea was to replace the traditional forms of operas with contemporary themes and totalitarian values. A number of opera were produced that tried to exemplify communist ideas. While her production of operas may seem innocuous (harmless) to outsiders, and Westerners in particular, many Chinese resented her using her influence to undermine the traditional operas that were beloved by so many.

It should not be surprising, then, that the true eruption of the Cultural Revolution came through a review of an opera. In the historical play *Hai Rui Dismissed From Office*, a loyal minister is imprisoned for criticizing a Ming dynasty emperor. In November 1965, the literary critic Yao Wenyuan wrote an article in which he attacked the play as a thinly veiled attack on Chairman Mao and his dismissal of defence minister Peng Dehuai for his criticism of the GLF. It is this theater review that provided the opening salvo for the Cultural Revolution. After this, numerous artists and writers were asked to explain their works, and were often forced to confess that their work had strayed from the Party line. This also led to the destruction of a number of antiquities, as they were seen as remnants of China's imperial and bourgeois past.

"There cannot be peaceful coexistence in the ideological realm. Peaceful coexistence corrupts."

Jiang Qing

Bourgeois A person whose opinions are based on capitalistic views or self-interest and that go against socialist doctrines.

Jiang Qing (1914–91)

Jiang Qing is one of the most colorful and contentious characters in the history of the Chinese Communist Party. Outside of China, she was known as the wife of Mao and lead member of the Gang of Four (see pages 150–5), but her career was vast and varied. At the age of 14 she became an actress and in the theater world was well known for her headstrong and dramatic antics off the stage; publicly she was best known for her portrayal of Nora in Ibsen's *A Doll's House* in 1935. Her life radically changed direction after she joined the CCP; she was arrested in 1933 for engaging in leftist activities and was briefly incarcerated. On her release she went to Shanghai to continue her career but upon the Japanese seizure in 1937 she joined communists in Yenan Province where she met Mao. They were married in 1939 and she became Mao's fourth wife. Although she was a dedicated communist, she spent the early years of their marriage in the background, entertaining politicians and foreign diplomats. The Great Proletarian Cultural Revolution marked her entrée into the political sphere. Using her influence and her former career, she spread the ideas of the Cultural Revolution via the media and arts, advocating a continuation of revolutionary principles and supporting the cult of personality of Mao. This put her at odds with a large number of Communist Party officials, whom she accused of being revisionist in their views of communism. After the Cultural Revolution officially ended, and Mao was increasingly ill and weak, she began to make a bid for power. With three colleagues from Shanghai, she formed the Gang of Four and they sought to undermine the potential leadership of Deng Xiaoping and, later, Hua Guofeng. After Mao died, and Hua was named as his successor, the Gang of Four were arrested and tried in 1981. To prevent her from becoming a martyr, Jiang was sentenced to life imprisonment and was incarcerated from 1976 until her suicide in 1991.

The Red Guard

Another component of the Cultural Revolution was the formation, militarization and radicalization of the Red Guards. What is often so stunning about the Red Guards is their youth: in 1966 there were roughly ten million Red Guards between the ages of nine and eighteen. At the same time that work teams were being sent to the countryside, the Red Guard went to the universities to root out those not sufficiently loyal to the Party. Schools and universities were closed for almost four years as the youth participated in these actions. Red Guards were given free railway passes so that they could travel throughout the country, criticizing those who did not follow the Party line. The chaos that ensued was encouraged by Mao and his followers, who felt that the resulting instability would strengthen allegiance to the Party.

Those who adhered to the ideas of the Cultural Revolution were termed Maoists and were seen as the true believers—those who sought communism in its unadulterated form. Those who did not embrace this view were suspect. Party members and government officials were removed from their positions and purged from the Party and/or placed under house arrest. Periodically, the Red Guard would make them engage in humiliating acts until they engaged in "self-criticism". Public figures such as Liu were purged and humiliated but not usually killed. However, those who were not in the public eye were often treated with brutality by the Red Guard.

The enthusiasm of the Red Guard took on an arbitrary nature, spinning out of control. Listening to Mao's admonishment to "learn revolution by making revolution", many of the youth confused revolution with violence and brutality. Sometimes this was against inanimate objects such as temples and historical texts; other times it was against individuals for the mildest of offences.

By the end of 1966, the Party leadership seemed to recognize that this Cultural Revolution was going beyond their control. While the Party concentrated on controlling the Red Guard, Mao enlisted others to his cause. Urban factory workers took up the torch in 1967, yet Mao soon regretted his decision to encourage them as their objectives tended to be materialistic rather than idealistic.

As one might expect, the army had to be called in to quell the violence. Mao had lost control of the campaign and disbanded the Red Guard, many of whom were sent to the countryside for rehabilitation. Millions from the towns and cities were also sent to the countryside for re-education, and the peasants were not entirely enthusiastic about having these untrained, unhealthy city people foisted upon them. People were hesitant to deviate in the slightest way from Party directives and thus any productivity that had been gained by the economic policies encouraged by Liu were reversed, as people feared producing anything more or different from what the government suggested.

The impact on education—the "Ten Lost Years"

The Cultural Revolution is often referred to as the "Ten Lost Years". Even though Mao encouraged schools and universities to reopen as early as 1968, this was impossible in many cases. The actions of the Red Guard had damaged both the infrastructure and faculty of so many institutions that they could not reopen. Even when they did reopen their doors, student's education standards were low as the entire educational system in China had been interrupted.

The Great Proletarian Cultural Revolution was declared over in April 1969 but there was no criticism, nor any repudiation of it. A new constitution was issued and Lin Biao was named as Mao's successor. The PLA and the Party **Congress**, two-thirds of which were military personnel, dominated the country. They were told very clearly that their role was temporary: once the country was stabilized and control re-established, they would revert to their previous position of answering to the Party, not directing it. But the problem remained: how to remove the military from their position of authority.

Renewed challenges to Mao's power

Mao was growing increasingly uncomfortable with Lin's following and the amount of power that was concentrated in the defence minister's hands. Mao wanted to remove him from power, but this was difficult to accomplish. According to the official Chinese record, Lin was preparing a coup against the government, and his son, Lin Liguo (an air force official) was assisting him. It is said that Lin Liguo was director of Project 5-7-1, a plot to assassinate Mao, that had the support of Moscow.

When their plan was exposed, it is said that Lin and his entire family fled the country. On 13 September 1971, they boarded a plane in Mongolia that crashed, leaving no survivors. According to the official report, the jet they commandeered lacked fuel, a navigator and a radio operator.

Congress A formal assembly of representatives gathered to discuss and resolve problems.

Activity:

Role play

Imagine that you are part of a group that has come together to criticize a teacher and decide if he/she should be punished for reactionary or counter-revolutionary teachings in the classroom. Assume a role appropriate to such an action.

Take it in turns, in character, to question the teacher and decide on the consequences for the teacher.

What sort of charges would be made against him/her? Would anyone defend him/her? Should the teacher engage in self-criticism?

With Lin gone, power reverted to Mao and Premier Zhou Enlai. Rather than ending the power struggle in China, this seemed to exacerbate it. Mao and Zhou were becoming increasingly frail, and while everyone close to them was expecting their demise, they continued to cling to life. Thus, the power struggle could not be an open one of succession but rather occurred behind the scenes until their deaths in 1976.

The number of candidates vying to succeed Mao and Zhou increased over time. Emerging as potential leaders were Jiang Qing and her followers, known as the Gang of Four; Deng Xiaoping, who had been rehabilitated in 1973; and Hua Guofeng, a relative newcomer to the Party, who became minister of public security in 1975.

TOK link

The arts, history, perception, emotion and language

All Communist governments exercised strict control over the media and the arts, using them in the service of the state. The arts encompass a broad field. It is one of the areas of TOK that concerns our comprehension of the world through the senses, and the role that different forms and genres play. What are the nature of knowledge claims made in the arts? If the arts and media have the power to influence and change the way people think, does that mean it should be controlled?

The Chinese Communists learned a lot about visual propaganda from other dictatorships such as Nazi Germany and Stalin's Soviet Union. In the period of the Cultural Revolution, the arts were used to great effect to influence public opinion.

*Educated youth must go to the countryside to receive re-education.*1969. Revolutionary Committee of the Sichuan Art Academy.

Source: The collection of Stefan R Landsberger and the International Institute of Social History, Amsterdam. http://chineseposters.net/about/index.php.

Chinese propaganda posters

- What does the poster illustrate? Is the work realistic? How much is it open to interpretation?
- What colours, shapes, designs, and symbols can you identify? (Refer to the original sources in colour at http://chineseposters.net)
- How would you describe the mood of the posters?
- What do you like or dislike about them? Analyse your reasons and emotions.
- Is this poster effective as propaganda?

Through perception and emotion, you have made knowledge claims. Another way of thinking about art is as a means of communication. Language can be considered to be a symbolic system which represents the world, communicating thoughts and experiences as well as value judgments.

What is the symbolic significance of the colours used in these images? According to the prevailing ideology, the color red symbolized everything revolutionary, everything good and moral; the color black, on the other hand, signified precisely the opposite.

TOK analysis

- What knowledge of art can be gained by focusing on its historical/social/cultural/political context?
- Do the arts offer an insight into the human condition and contribute to our knowledge of the world?
- How do the arts reinforce stereotypes?
- What is the role of sense perception in the arts? Compare this to its role in the sciences.
- To what extent is knowledge about the past different to other kinds of knowledge?

The struggle for power following the death of Mao Zedong

This section covers the emergence of the Gang of Four, Mao's apparent ambivalence regarding his potential successors and the emergence of Hua Guofeng following the death of Zhou Enlai. After the death of Mao in September 1976, the power struggle intensified and Hua, on the side of more moderate forces, defeated the radical faction of the Communist Party and the Gang of Four. However, Hua lacked the strong personality necessary to rule the PRC and, over a period of several years, a rehabilitated Deng Xiaoping eclipsed him and became the leader of Communist China.

The power struggle over who would succeed Mao is reminiscent of the power struggle that began after Lenin's stroke in 1921 and culminated in 1929 with Stalin as the uncontested leader of the Soviet Union. While it may not have been as brutal, it was certainly as complex. It began in 1971 with the death of Lin Biao and the emergence of the Gang of Four. Jiang Qing, as Mao's wife, was in a unique position of power and influence, especially as Mao grew weaker and appeared, increasingly, to rely on her.

There was a strong ideological current that guided the power struggle. On the one hand were the militant, revolutionary Gang of Four, who argued that communism had veered off course in the 1950s and that radicalism needed to be reintroduced into Chinese life; on the other were the **pragmatists** led by Deng Xiaoping, who argued that China needed to retrench and allow a bit of capitalist, Western programming to make China the world power that it deserved to be. This seemed to be the line that Zhou and Mao had been following after 1972, supported by Nixon's visit to China and the decision to trade with non-communist countries. In the middle was Hua Guofeng, relatively unknown prior to the Lin Biao affair, who found himself named as a potential successor.

> **Pragmatist** A practical person who endorses a straightforward manner of solving problems. For Deng and those who followed him, pragmatism meant a commitment to modernization even if this involved engaging in practices that could be seen as capitalistic, as the ultimate goal was still the achievement of communism.

Jiang Qing and the rise of the Gang of Four

Initially, Jiang Qing had very little involvement in government affairs, but in the 1950s she began to work with the Ministry of Culture, hoping to develop theater and opera by supporting works that were appropriate and consistent with the Communist Party line. Her work was increasingly political in nature, and in the 1960s she helped to develop and produce eight model operas that opened to mediocre reviews. She increasingly took control of the media in the hopes of controlling the national culture; she had immeasurable amounts of propaganda at her disposal that helped her further her personal power. A number of Party officials were becoming increasingly worried about the level of influence that she had over Mao, especially as the Cultural Revolution accelerated.

In November 1966, the 17-member Central Cultural Revolutionary Committee was formed, with Jiang as first vice-chairwoman and including her closest associates from Shanghai: Yao Wenyuan, Mao's chief propagandist; Zhang Chunqiao, deputy secretary of the Shanghai Municipal Committee; and Wang Hongwen, union leader and Jiang's protégé. Collectively, they would later be referred to as the Gang of Four. During the Cultural Revolution they stated that their mandate was to uphold the Thought of Mao, to eliminate bourgeois influences and revisionist tendencies and to eliminate the Four Olds: thought (or philosophy), culture, customs and habits. It was through the exhortations of this Committee that the Red Guards destroyed cultural icons and made public protests, usually by traveling to Beijing on the railway and participating in mass meetings. Although the Cultural Revolution was quelled by the PLA, beginning in 1969, Jiang retained her position of power and in 1969 became a member of the **politburo**, along with Zhang and Wan.

After the death of Lin, the Gang of Four began its bid for power in earnest. They announced that the Cultural Revolution should be ongoing, and continued criticisms of Lin and Liu on the one hand, and Confucius and Beethoven on the other. These seemingly random or arbitrary targets were calculated to help the Gang eliminate the potential threats to its power base. Zhou Enlai, who had been instrumental in the opening up of China, was the true object of criticism when Western cultural icons were criticized.

Meanwhile, Mao seemed to be increasingly reliant on his wife, nephew and bodyguard. It seems that he then began to lose confidence in Jiang Qing, and feared that she was controlling his access to knowledge and people. Thus, he separated from her, and would meet her only by scheduled appointment. He was extremely critical of the Gang of Four, but was not above using them against other members of the politburo to prevent any one faction from becoming too strong. His nephew, Mao Yuanxin, an ally of the Gang of Four, still had his confidence however. He was also Mao's liaison with the politburo after 1975, giving the Gang of Four an enormous advantage over their rivals. Mao's bodyguard, General Wang Dongxing, on the other hand, was incredibly suspicious of the Gang of Four and worked with others in the politburo against them.

Deng Xiaoping and the pragmatists

On the other side of the power struggle were more moderate or pragmatic members of the politburo. At the head of this group was Deng Xiaoping, a victim in the Cultural Revolution who had been rehabilitated in 1973 and was once again in power and actively seeking movement away from the revolutionary and chaotic tendencies of the Gang of Four. Deng had the support of Premier Zhou, who respected his pragmatic policies and sought a restoration of order. It was through Zhou that Deng was protected, even when there was yet another repudiation of him in 1975. In the midst of this power struggle, in early 1976, Premier Zhou died.

The Death of Zhou Enlai and the rise of Hua Guofeng

Many felt that the future path of China would be settled by the person Mao chose to succeed Zhou. The Gang of Four tried to have Zhang placed in the position of premier, and that would have signified a movement to the left and a more radical path for China.

> **Politburo** The political bureau of a given country was the executive organization of its Communist Party. In the Soviet Union, it was replaced by a larger Presidium in 1952 but was revitalized by Khrushchev in 1966.

Deng Xiaoping (1904–97)

Deng Xiaoping rose to power to become the head of the People's Republic of China in 1978 at the age of 74. By this time he had survived numerous purges of the Communist Party and had succeeded Hua Guofeng. The child of a wealthy landowner, Deng was sent to France to study where he became interested in the ideas of communism and how to apply them in his homeland. On his return, he joined Zhou Enlai and embarked on a revolutionary career that included participation in the Long March (1934–6), in which Chinese Communists escaped from Nationalists seeking to eliminate the threat that the Communists posed. As a member of the Red Army, he helped overthrow the Nationalist regime in the Chinese Civil War and was quickly promoted to the position of General Secretary in the CCP. Although Deng was a dedicated communist, he felt that China needed to pursue more liberal economic policies to industrialize and modernize, which put him in opposition to Mao. After the Great Leap Forward resulted in an estimated 30 million deaths, Deng proposed reforms that included incentives and free markets for farmers. As a result, he was declared a "capitalist roadster" and put under house arrest in 1966 and later exiled to southeastern China. Zhou rehabilitated Deng in 1973 and he was readmitted to the Party, though his status was still doubtful at the time of the deaths of Zhou and Mao in 1976. By 1978 he had been completely rehabilitated by the Party and, while he never held the position of Chairman, his appointment as head of the military, with control over the 1.2 billion-member People's Liberation Army, gave him the most power. He used this position to implement what he felt were overdue economic reforms, known as the Four Modernizations. Although he employed capitalistic economic policies, he remained a firm communist and was not interested in democratizing China. In 1989 it was his orders that led to the Tiananmen Square massacres. He retired shortly thereafter and maintained a presence in Chinese political life, but his power waned as he aged. He died in 1997, leaving a dual legacy of a greatly improved economy and a brutal, authoritarian regime.

Zhou's own choice for successor was the more moderate Deng, who had advocated programmes of economic development based on the injection of some degree of capitalism into China's planned economy. In the end, Mao chose the neutral and largely unknown Hua Guofeng as the new premier. He had been the top security official from Mao's home province of Hunan, and while the Party leadership was not particularly enthusiastic about the choice, no one truly objected to him either. Hua had some backing from those who supported Deng, but he cautiously enlisted the support of as many of the Party elders as he could. That Mao trusted his counsel and leadership was seen most clearly in the incident that took place in Tiananmen Square following the Qingming festival in 1976.

The Qingming festival, 1976

The population spoke out against the Gang of Four in the Qingming festival that took place in Beijing from 29 March to 4 April 1976. Immediately after the death of Zhou the period of mourning for their leader had been cut short, and they took advantage of this commemoration of the dead to publicly mourn Zhou and, by extension, support Deng while indirectly criticizing the Gang of Four and Mao. People took wreaths to Tiananmen Square and placed them at the Monument to the People's Heroes to honor Zhou and show their affection for him. They also wrote poetry on the ground around the memorial, both supporting Zhou and criticizing Mao and the Gang of Four, particularly Jiang. As the days passed, according to the account of the writer Jan Wong, the mounting number of wreaths and white paper chrysanthemums made it look as though an unseasonal snowfall had occurred in the square.

The authorities were stunned by the spontaneous outpouring of the people and were initially unsure how to react. Hua suggested that the government quietly and unceremoniously clear out the wreaths the day after the festival, and Mao agreed to this. The government hoped that this would end the criticisms and stem any confrontation between the government and the people. But they had sorely miscalculated the reactions of the people. As news of the clearing of the poems and wreaths spread through Beijing, rather than quell the population, it incited them. People from all sectors of society marched to the square, to protest against the government. They seemed emboldened by their actions and identified themselves by profession or inclination by standing under banners. More wreaths appeared in the square, with even stronger anti-Mao messages.

Hua sought Mao's guidance and dispatched his nephew to ask what he felt should be done about the demonstrations. Mao stated that they were in counter-revolution and should be treated as such. The politburo unanimously voted to support Mao's directive and the Mayor of Beijing dispatched trucks to the square to clear out the wreaths and violently subdue the remaining protestors. The trucks beat and arrested protestors, and it is said that a number of counter-revolutionaries were later beheaded in the square.

Thus the population was once again repressed, and Mao reasserted himself as leader. When Mao's nephew consulted with him about the demonstrations, he accused Deng of directing the protests, and so Deng was immediately removed from his positions and was supposed to be investigated for political mistakes. However, Deng fled from Beijing and sought refuge in Canton under the protection of General Ye Jianying (who would later be instrumental in the overthrow of the Gang of Four), where he remained until after the death of Mao.

The death of Mao

By now, Mao was so weak that he could no longer receive visitors and Hua took further control over affairs. It was fairly clear that Hua was Mao's choice to succeed him, but the others waited for the death of Mao for an opportunity to make yet another bid for power. Their chance came on 9 September 1976, when Mao died from Parkinson's disease. The Gang of Four planned to seize power using their influence over the media, urban militia and universities. What they did not take into account was the strength of Hua and the support that he would receive from politburo members and the military.

The defeat of the Gang of Four

Almost immediately after Mao's death, Jiang altered some of Mao's writings to make it appear as if he wished her to succeed him. To help her cause, she used her longstanding influence over the media to produce articles that showed successful leadership by women in China. It was later exposed that she had manipulated Chinese characters to change the intent of Mao's words to achieve her own ends, but she was not immediately discredited. She still had a strong following in the cultural realm and she had limited military support.

Thus, plans to take power continued, despite what should have been an irreversible setback.

Jiang had always seen Hua as weak and malleable and felt he would be easily defeated. Thus she was rather surprised by the eulogy that he delivered at Mao's memorial service. Quoting Mao himself, he issued a warning to the Gang of Four, using a speech in which Mao had criticized the Gang for factionalism. Most people saw this as a bold move to assert the power Mao had given him just before he died. This garnered him tremendous support, especially among those pragmatists and supporters of Deng.

In a politburo meeting, Jiang argued that Hua was incompetent and that she should be the Chair of the Central Committee. Hua argued that succession should be determined as it had been in the past—the vice-chairman should succeed the chairman until the next session of the Central Committee. When the Committee convened, they would then elect a new chairman. He gained important support when the defence minister (and protector of Deng) Ye Jianuang promised to support him as Mao's successor. Through notes that were published later it seems likely that Mao wanted Hua to succeed him—most famously, Mao wrote to Hua, "With you in charge I am at ease."

Realizing that their support base was quickly slipping away, the Gang planned to execute a coup on 6 October. Military support was to come from Mao Yuanxin, the chairman's nephew, and political commissar of the Shenyang Military Region. They were preparing for a march on Beijing to seize power from the government but they remained militarily weak. Their plans also included the assassination of a number of politburo members, including Hua and Ye. Despite the support of Mao Yuanxin, the Gang of Four lacked weapons, so Jiang tried to recruit members of the politburo to her cause. She approached Generals Chen Xilian and Su Zhenua to enlist their support, but both chose to inform Hua of Jiang's plans instead.

Once they knew of the Gang's plans, a meeting was held in the PLA command headquarters in which Hua, Ye, Chen and other allies of Deng agreed that they would launch a pre-emptive strike by safeguarding Beijing and arresting the Gang. On 5 October, Hua called an emergency meeting of the politburo for midnight. When Zhang and Wang arrived at the meeting, they were immediately surrounded, overpowered and arrested. Yao and Jiang were later arrested at their residences, as they chose not to appear at that particular politburo meeting. With these arrests, the Gang of Four saw almost all of their support slip away and their bid for power was undone. They were expelled from the Party and trials awaited them all.

Although the Gang of Four lasted a little longer in the public eye, they lacked credibility. Any notion that they acted for ideological reasons was gone; instead "Madame Mao" was portrayed simply as a power-hungry woman who had deceived her husband when he was weak and frail, and exploited his death to try to come to power. Mao's reputation remained untarnished but Jiang was vilified—if she appeared in a photo or poster with Mao, her image was blacked out, deliberately done in a manner so that people knew she had been officially removed. When knowledge of the defeat of the Gang became public, there were celebrations throughout China. The Gang's association with the Cultural Revolution made them enemies of a population that had suffered tremendously, and the people famously consumed copious quantities of alcohol to mark this change in the course of China's political leadership.

Jiang was detained for five years before the trials of the Gang of Four began in 1981. Most of the charges leveled at the Gang of Four related to the atrocities committed during the Cultural Revolution. The trials were highly publicized and televised, yet the records of the proceedings still remain largely unknown as the records of the trial have not been released. Only Jiang defended herself, steadfastly arguing that she simply carried out the orders of Mao. Her refusal to admit mistakes or confess made her even more unpopular among the masses. Jiang was found guilty and sentenced to death, but later the sentence was suspended and instead she faced life imprisonment. This avoided making her into a martyr. When she was diagnosed with throat cancer, they transferred her to a hospital where she took her own life in 1991, at the age of 77.

The other members of the Gang had similar fates. Wang Hongwen received life imprisonment and died in hospital in Beijing in 1992. Like Jiang, Zhang was initially sentenced to death but the sentence was commuted and instead he was imprisoned until he fell ill in 2002, at which point he returned to his family home in Shanghai where he died of cancer in 2005. Yao was sentenced to 20 years in prison; on his release in 1996 he returned to his home in Shanghai where he studied and wrote Chinese history. He died in 2005.

The re-emergence of Deng Xiaoping

Although the trials did not take place until 1981 and 1982, the Party was purged of the Gang and its followers by the end of 1976. The politburo took the position that this was a new era of change. There were some Party leaders that viewed Hua's succession as unconstitutional since he was chosen by Mao and not the Party, but, in the interests of unity, they appointed him. Chairman Hua was given three charges: to be Mao's successor, to rehabilitate Deng and to engage in modernization. Hua agreed to reinstate Deng and he was duly restored by the politburo. The army favored this measure; he had strong support in the Party, was cleared of responsibility in the Tiananmen Square incident and, after admitting to political mistakes (a common self-criticism for those who survived the Cultural Revolution and ensuing power struggle), he was restored to his previous positions. At the Tenth Central Committee meeting, three main decisions were made that were to shape the politburo:

- The actions of the Gang of Four were condemned.
- Hua was made chairman of the Party and Military Commission (in addition to being premier).
- Deng was restored to the politburo Standing Committee and to his position as vice-chairman of the Central Committee.

Hua made the important decision that China had once again to focus on industrialization, but that it had to do so in a different manner than had been previously attempted. Deng was put in charge of the Four Modernizations: agriculture, industry, science and technology and national defence. This helped to focus the economy and gave the country a clear direction to follow in terms of national development and objectives to achieve. It also gave Deng considerable economic and political power, which he managed well.

The politburo was reorganized and three power groups emerged. There were nine members who supported Hua, nine who supported Deng and three who supported Ye. If Ye had the fewest supporters, he also held the balance and this often made him the decision maker. Despite the tensions among these groups, the Congress called for "unity, stability and cooperation" in Party affairs.

The backdrop behind this was the fallout from the arrests of the Gang of Four, which Deng used to his strategic advantage. In response to Gang of Four edicts, Hua had adopted as policy what were called the Two Whatevers:

> We will resolutely uphold whatever policy decisions Chairman Mao made, and unswervingly follow whatever instructions Chairman Mao gave.

TOK link

History, perception and language

Those who cannot remember the past are condemned to repeat it.

George Santayana

History may be considered a human science among the areas of knowledge but, in contrast to the natural sciences, we cannot directly observe the past. Historiography, a study of the writings of history, is based upon evidence that has survived. What has survived as historical evidence can take many forms and the selectivity of the historian can be influenced by many factors such as ideology, perspective and purpose. You should be aware of how each of these factors, which can be reflected in the ways of knowing—through perception, emotion and reason—can also be transformed by the language used to record history.

Both the People's Republic of China and the USSR recognized the importance of history and controlling the past. Soviet leader Nikita Khrushchev said, "Historians are dangerous people. They are capable of upsetting everything."

TOK analysis

- How does "believing that" and "believing in" differ?
- What role does personal experience play in the formation of knowledge claims?
- What are the main difficulties for human scientists in trying to account for human behaviour?

Review the following statements and questions.

1 In the 1970s Lin Biao was vilified by the Communist party and seen as an object of criticism, yet he was later rehabilitated by the Chinese government. It was argued that he was trying to seize power and undermine the goals of communism.

2 Immediately after the death of Mao, both Jiang Qing and Hua Guofeng produced information that supported their rival claims as Mao's successor. Jiang Qing's information was discredited by the government and it claimed that she manipulated Chinese characters to change Mao's meaning.

- What were the charges levelled against Lin Biao and Jiang Qing?
- Where did the evidence supporting the accusations against them come from?
- Can you think of any reasons why the accusations against Lin Biao might have been false?
- Given that the Gang of Four lost the power struggle, can we be sure that Jiang Qing was the one who manipulated Mao's words?
- Is it possible that Hua did exactly what he accused Jiang of doing? How can we know the truth?
- Might your perceptions of what happened to Lin Biao and Jiang Qing be different if you were a young committed member of the Red Guard, an old Chinese farmer or a Western journalist unable to read or understand Chinese?
- How might these positions reflect on any knowledge claims made?

It was not a very popular policy with those who wanted to move away from the Maoist era and pursue new endeavors. As Hua had held the positions of head of security and premier during the times when some of the worst atrocities of the Gang were committed, he found himself implicated in their crimes as the evidence was gathered. In 1980 he resigned as premier and, in June 1981, he resigned as Party chairman and chair of the Military Commission. He was succeeded by Zhao Ziyang, Hu Yaobang—both protégés of Deng—and Deng, respectively.

For his part, Hua admitted that he had made mistakes, and was allowed to retain the position of vice-chairman until it was abolished in 1982. Unlike those previously defeated in power struggles, he was not harmed or imprisoned, signalling a change from the brutality of the previous power struggles of the 1960s. He remained a member of the Central Committee until 2002, when he was ten years beyond the retirement age of 70. In 2007, he was invited to attend the Party Congress as a special delegate and he died in August 2008.

Activity:

Assignment—you be the journalist

This is an activity in investigative reporting. Imagine that you are a member of the foreign press in China in 1981. Choose one of the members of the Gang of Four to profile for your newspaper or news agency.

Where will your information come from? What will the government tell you? Why do you need to find other sources? Who will you interview?

Try to be as objective as possible in compiling your biography.

Source analysis

The following documents relate to Hua Guofeng.

Source A

"With you in charge I'm at ease"—a propaganda poster presented to the heads of families of youth who had been sent down to the countryside, 1977.

Source-based question

Compare and contrast the perceptions of the Chinese leadership conveyed in Sources A and B.

Source B

This cartoon was created by the Israeli cartoonist Yaakov Kirschen and reflects his view of the succession of Hua Guofeng.

China under Deng Xiaoping

This section looks at Chinese policies after Deng consolidated his political control over the PRC. It focuses primarily on China's domestic policies, how China strove to overcome the devastation of the Great Leap Forward and the Cultural Revolution, and on attempts at retooling the economy to allow for improvement in four areas: agriculture, industry, science and technology and the military. These Four Modernizations, as they were called, were to be improved upon through pragmatism rather than ideology. To assist in the economic development of the country, there was also a change in the nature of foreign relations, and particularly the injection of foreign capital from countries outside of the Communist bloc.

The struggle for Party leadership between Hua and Deng was taking place while China was trying to change. The population had suffered ongoing hardships through the Great Leap Forward and the Cultural Revolution, and both Deng and Hua sought to improve the situation for the people of China. This led to a change in economic policies as early as 1977 that in turn led to a number of political changes.

By 1982 Deng had full control over the government and the Party, and he used his position to make changes that he felt were necessary to allow China to compete with the West on a number of levels. Although he is best known for his economic policies, his opening up to the West was of paramount importance. He also felt that it was time to separate the government from the Party in an attempt to implement policies that may have deviated from communist ideology. In the battle between **ideologues** and pragmatists, the latter clearly won, but this did not mean that Deng was not a communist. While he advocated adopting Western, industrial policies, he was very clear that the political system would remain firmly communist, and he never once hesitated to take actions against those who threatened the system. This was seen most concretely in the Tiananmen Square massacre of 1989 that ended this period in Chinese history.

Ideologue A person who advocates a particular ideology (system of ideas) and may even serve in an official capacity as the spokesperson for that ideology.

The third **plenum** of the 5th National People's Congress (NPC), held between 29 August and 10 September 1980, marked an approval of Party reorganization and there was a transfer of power. At this point the Party, and thus the government, committed itself officially to a policy of collective leadership that wanted to modernize China so that it could eventually surpass the West in industrial production and consumer goods. Deng outmaneuvered potential opponents in the government by resigning his position due to old age, thereby forcing his rivals to do the same. Thus, Deng and six vice-premiers resigned, paving the way for a younger leadership that supported the more pragmatic ideas that he espoused. It must be noted that these were not democrats; they were dedicated communists who were seeking to make corrections in the socialist system.

Plenum An assembly or meeting with all members present.

Economic policies and the Four Modernizations

Given the situation in which China found itself, it should not be surprising that Deng decided the guiding principle for the country would be "Economics in Command" as opposed to Mao's previous principle of "Politics in Command". Even before he managed to take control over the government and Party, China had adopted very pragmatic policies meant to modernize the country to make it both competitive and self-sufficient. Hua, like Deng, had advocated such policies and thus the change had begun with economic reforms under him. In 1978 a new Ten Year Plan was announced (see below) and the principles that it embraced were incorporated into the Party constitution that August.

Deng was put in charge of the reforms and quickly announced 100 000 construction projects that would cost approximately 54 billion yuan. While the projects were certainly necessary for China's development, there was a question as to how the government could pay for such projects. After such a grandiose beginning, the government did indeed moderate its outflow by a decision to approve only projects that could be completed quickly and that would earn foreign capital. In this spirit, 348 heavy industrial projects and 4800 smaller ones were stopped because they were either too costly or long-term. Zhou and Mao's opening up of China to the West proved most helpful to the economic reforms as it allowed for the export of Chinese goods to non-communist countries and allowed for a certain amount of foreign investment in China. This gave the government the capital necessary to make improvements, although transportation and energy remained a problem.

The Ten Year Plan

In February 1978, Hua Guofeng announced a new Ten Year Plan. This was an economic plan, meant to target specific sectors of the economy, with a focus on heavy industry. In the period 1978–85, the Chinese government set targets for development. In particular, the steel industry was a focus and it was hoped that steel production (that had fallen dramatically due to the Great Leap Forward) would increase from 21 million tons produced in 1973 to 60 million by 1985 and 180 million tons by 1999. Additionally, the government set targets for natural resource extraction in the fields of oil and petroleum, coal and non-ferrous metals. They also set goals for electricity, railroad and water transportation, which involved extensive public works projects and infrastructure development. To assist in industrial production, the Plan also focused on trying to improve agricultural output through providing new irrigation systems and mechanizing farming. The Plan proved to be too ambitious, however, and in 1979 the government readjusted their goals; nearly 350 projects were halted so that the Plan would not be so costly. Although some of the core ideas were lost, the Ten Year Plan was the method by which the Chinese set production goals in heavy industry and infrastructure development, while allowing a relaxation of socialist principles in smaller enterprises.

To achieve their objectives, the Chinese were adopting a number of polices that were reminiscent of Lenin's New Economic Policy (NEP) or, alternatively, Stalin's **Stakhanovite** movement. They included the use of incentives and bonuses to increase productivity and encourage individual initiatives and problem-solving in the industrial and scientific sectors and allowed for the production of diversified crops on small, tenured plots in which surplus produce could be sold at a profit to the agricultural sector.

Stakhanovism A system whereby workers voluntarily increase their levels of output in an attempt to gain incentives from the government for exceeding given quotas. Named after Alexei Stakhanov (1906–77), a Soviet coalminer, who in 1935 reportedly mined 14 times his quota in one day.

In June 1979 it was decided that there would be a three-year period in which the country would allow a certain amount of tweaking of the Ten Year Plan to improve the national economy. The cost of the Ten Year Plan in its first year had been approximately 37 per cent of GDP, and there was no way that the government could sustain this type of investment. The core of the economic reforms would remain the Four Modernizations: industry, agriculture, science and technology, and the military. These had originally been articulated by Zhou Enlai in 1975 and clarified by Deng in three documents. Although Deng had been labeled as deviationist by the Gang of Four, who named his articles the "Three Poisonous Weeds". Deng's revisions were resurrected once the Gang had been overthrown and the moderate, pragmatists had taken control of the politburo.

Agriculture

After years of focusing on industry to the detriment of the rural economy, it was decided that this was the most important sector for modernization. In 1977 the amount of grain per capita was still at 1955 levels. Now, the population had increased, so there was an increase in production, but not enough to meet consumption requirements. As 80 per cent of the population were still based in the country, this was seen as the cornerstone of the economy. The Ten Year Plan emphasized the need to move away from traditional, manual modes of farming and substitute it with mechanized farming that would increase yields. In addition, the ideas of personal incentives and diversification were approved of and supported.

In terms of central planning, the Ten Year Plan and the Four Modernizations for agriculture set quotas and had government directives on how increases in productivity would take place. The overall goal was to increase agricultural production by 4–5 per cent per year and increase food output to 400 million tons by 1985. Additionally, the Plan sought to mechanize 85 per cent of farming tasks, to promote the widespread use of chemical fertilizers and to expand water works so that the farmers had more and better access to water. To better distribute and regulate food production, 12 commodity and food base areas would be created throughout China.

However, what was more revolutionary in some respects was the implementation in 1979 of the Household Responsibility System. There had been attempts to put similar systems into place as early as the 1950s but they had been quashed by Mao. After his death (and the demise of the Gang of Four), the pragmatists' victory in the power struggle made it not only acceptable but desirable. According to this system, there was still no private land ownership but each farming household received a plot of land which they could use as they saw fit. They would contract with their local commune to provide a certain amount of work, plant a specified amount of crops, and a predetermined quota would go back to the commune in exchange for 15 years of land usage. The households had control of the labour within the household and could allocate it however they desired. Most importantly to the system, they could keep or sell all surplus produce. This method was so successful and desirable to the farmers that, by 1983, 90 per cent of households were participating.

This reform alone reportedly increased China's annual production by more than even the Ten Year Plan goals. It is estimated that productivity increased 15 per cent and that one third of the increase in agricultural production can be attributed to this system. According to Chinese government data, production increased an average of 6.7 per cent annually and grain output rose to 500 billion kilograms in 1996. This has made China the world's largest agricultural producer and given it the largest smallholder farming system.

The agricultural improvements allowed more farmers to leave their family plots but stay local, as increased productivity allowed for the development of local factories and the resurrection of local crafts. The success of the Household Responsibility System is reflected in its continued existence up to this day.

Industry

The Chinese leadership hoped that the Ten Year Plan would lead to improved infrastructure and industrialization that equalled or surpassed that which had taken place in the years since the creation of the People's Republic of China. Furthermore, they had a goal of creating an industrial infrastructure that would be equal to or better than developed capitalist countries. They no longer looked at the USSR as their chief competitor; instead it was the industrial West.

In particular, they focused on capital construction and improvements in heavy industries—iron, coal, steel and oil production were emphasized and the government willingly invested 54 billion yuan into these endeavors. The objectives were further clarified: 120 projects were to be completed, including 10 iron and steel complexes, 6 oil and gas fields, 30 power stations, 8 coal mines, 9 non-ferrous metal complexes, 7 trunk railways and 5 harbors. As stated above, early into the Plan it was realized that the targets were too ambitious and in 1979 objectives had to be scaled back in order to make them more reasonable and to provide less of a drain on the economy.

As part of the economic reform in industry, there were two phases to industrial reform.

- Phase 1, which took place from 1978 to 1984, was meant to improve the attitude of the industrial working class. There was a movement away from central planning to merely providing guidelines. Mirroring the Household Responsibility System, the Industrial Responsibility System was created, in which the supervisory body of a State-Owned Enterprise (SOE) would have a contractual agreement in which a percentage of the production and/or profits would go to the state and the SOE retained the surplus. This created incentives to improve levels of production, and later there was a focus on quality of production as well. Not wanting to replicate the reputation of other communist countries for producing poor quality products, contracts also included a section on the level of quality. By 1980 there were 6600 SOEs.
- Phase 2 was introduced in October 1984 with the "Resolution on the Reform of the Economic System". This further loosened government control over enterprises while retaining public ownership. This Resolution emphasized that ownership and management were distinct entities and that management should be given a certain amount of autonomy to improve production. This led to a situation in which private groups could lease small and medium state enterprises, while the largest ones remained directly under the control of the state.

Science and technology

The Cultural Revolution had profound effects on the scientific community, just as it had in all other academic areas. Due to the interruption of education (the "Ten Lost Years", see page 148), China was lacking in even the most basic technological expertise. They had shortages not only of scientists, but also of doctors, engineers and architects. Modernization sought to repair that damage and make China competitive with the advanced countries of the world; indeed, the goal for science and technology was to be only ten years behind developed countries by 1985.

In March 1978 the National Scientific Conference stated that there were four goals for China to achieve in the field of scientific and technological development: to reach 1970 levels of advanced nations; to increase the number of professional scientific researchers to 800 000; to develop the most current centres for experimentation; and to complete a nationwide system of science and technology research. They announced the initiation of 108 projects in 27 separate fields.

Military

Even before the death of Mao, military leadership recognized the need to make a series of changes to the People's Liberation Army. It was the PLA that took action in 1976 after the Tiananmen Square incident, and the loyalty of the majority of the military to Hua Guofeng had confirmed his leadership and assisted in the overthrow of the Gang of Four. Under defence minister Ye Jinuang, the PLA had become powerful, but it was recognized that this would be short-lived, unless the situation in China stabilized; indeed, the 1975 directive (issued when Zhou and Mao were both still alive) directed the military to withdraw from politics and concentrate on improving national defence and military training.

In 1979, a border war erupted between China and Vietnam that revealed a number of weaknesses in the Chinese army. Although the Chinese did indeed penetrate Vietnam and claimed victory, they had heavy casualties and suffered the effects of antiquated technology. Although ranked fourth in the Modernizations, Communist Party leadership recognized a need to update the Chinese army to become a global contender. Military leadership received the assistance of Deng who, in addition to advocating the Four Modernizations, assumed the position of chair of the Central Military Commission. This resulted in increased expenditure on the military.

At four million the Chinese army was the largest in the world but it lagged well behind other armies in advanced military technology. Mao had advocated a policy of "spirit over weapons" that had severely hindered the development of new technologies. Though they had successfully detonated a nuclear bomb in 1964 and had developed both ballistic missiles and hydrogen bombs, nuclear research had virtually halted. Even so, the Chinese were spending a tremendous amount of money on military expenditures: during the Plan, it is estimated that the government was spending up to ten per cent of GNP on improvements and purchasing new technology.

Not surprisingly, the science and military modernizations went hand in hand. One of the main reasons for the push for more centres of research was so that China could develop weapons that would put it on par with the more advanced military-industrial countries, yet they still lagged about 15 years behind. Even with the new technology, it took China years to integrate it into an antiquated infrastructure that had changed little since the Korean War.

Foreign capital—the Open Door Policy

The Ten Year Plan was ambitious, and needed huge amounts of capital to be successful. Therefore, the Open Door Policy seemed to come at the best time possible; when foreign investment was needed for advancement. After years of isolation, China was once again emerging. US president Nixon's famous visit to China and subsequent UN recognition of the People's Republic of China helped to pave the way for a further opening up of China to the outside world. In December 1978, the Party adopted the Open Door Policy. To realize the Four Modernizations, China needed to engage in trade with the West so that they could learn and/or import science, technology, capital and managerial skills.

To make trade with China more attractive than it had been, the government embarked on a policy to diversify exports, raise quality levels, devalue the yuan and build up currency reserves. Western nations quickly saw the value of China as a trading partner. Japan led the way, investing in China, and West Germany and the US soon followed. Hong Kong, with its special status and relations with both China and the West, was able to capitalize on the opening up of China and profited immensely from China's Open Door Policy. Through these policies, in 1981 China became a creditor nation.

However, more foreign capital was needed to modernize China. Chinese leadership sought to straddle the line between retaining state ownership of the main factors of production while allowing foreigners to come in and participate in the Chinese economy. The decision was made that all joint ventures with international partners needed to be at least 50 per cent Chinese so that China could maintain control over its own economy and economic development.

Naturally, this led to conflict within the Party as some leaders feared that China was heading towards capitalism. Also, some of the policies put into place seemed to echo the foreign domination that the **Qing dynasty** had been forced to endure, and the fear of humiliation at the hands of foreigners (especially the Japanese) was present in the minds of many Chinese. The establishment of **Special Economic Zones (SEZs)** seemed eerily reminiscent of the **treaty ports** that China had endured prior to Communist victory in the Civil War. This was an issue that China would struggle with into the 21st century.

*"Poverty is not socialism.
To be rich is glorious."*

Deng Xiaoping

Qing dynasty The royal family that governed China from 1644 until the collapse of the empire in 1911. The Qings were from Manchuria and established their dominance over the Ming dynasty that had previously ruled China. The Qing dynasty fell into decline in the 19th century and faced pressures from abroad as the Western powers exerted influence over their government. The end result was a revolution, in which the six-year-old Emperor Henry Pu-yi was forced to abdicate.

Special Economic Zone (SEZ) A region in a country where the economic policies are more liberal or lenient than they are in the rest of the country. In the PRC, the first of these SEZs was in Shenzhen.

Treaty ports Cities in China that were open to foreign commerce by unequal treaties. Under the terms of these treaties, foreigners were not subject to Chinese laws. The first treaty ports originated from the settlements after the Opium Wars in the 19th century.

Results of the Ten Year Plan

As with all projects of such magnitude, the results were mixed. According to official government accounts, the Plan was highly successful and characterized by great achievements, and to a large extent this is true. According to government statistics, the average annual growth rate was 11 per cent for agricultural and industrial production; and, in 1985, the GNP was 778 billion yuan. In certain areas, growth rates were much higher, especially in the production of steel, coal, oil and electricity, highlighting the emphasis on heavy industry in the Ten Year Plan. By 1985 investment in publicly owned enterprises had reached 530 billion yuan, showing success in the fields of infrastructure development and construction.

However, there were problems in this ten-year period, too. The workforce represented the struggle of the time—young specialists, often trained abroad using state-of the-art equipment, returned to China and had to integrate themselves into an outdated system. The older workers, who had been denied education due to the Cultural Revolution, often resented the younger workers who did not defer to them as elders. Understandably, they feared changes would make them irrelevant and unemployable.

And while growth meant increases in production, there was also inflation. Consumers had more products to choose from, and the quality was higher than it had been, but the improvements came at a cost and people were somewhat disgruntled by this change. Plus, the emphasis was on economic growth, modernization and the availability of consumer goods—other quality-of-life concerns were ignored. It was at this time that Beijing became incredibly polluted and deforestation took place throughout the country. There was also the implementation of the one-child policy, which placed severe penalties on women and families who had more than their quota. This policy was to have lasting social implications that are felt to this day; it also exposed the corruption in the Communist Party, as elites were often exempted from the policy. As the Party became entrenched and less revolutionary, there were more and more perquisites (perks) for Party members and their families. Children of the Party leadership led privileged lives, were automatically accepted into university and did not have to serve in the military.

Due to the Ten Year Plan and the Four Modernizations, China was certainly on its way to reaching its goal of being a leading modern state by 2040. The pragmatists in the Party took a long view and saw that national power would be measured by economic strength, and science and technology had done very well to reach their goals by the close of the Ten Year Plan. This was replaced by another Five Year Plan with slightly different goals.

Activity:

Assignment

Assess the Four Modernizations. What were the goals of the Modernizations? How far did they achieve these goals? Was this program successful? Why or why not?

TOK link

Human sciences, history and ethics

Political systems of autocracy, democracy and theocracy are allied with ideas of how people should live together in a society. Discussion of these principles of rule can generate precepts on the way we ought to live our lives, and the moral implications of our individual actions.

Knowledge issues can arise from an understanding of the world, our place within it, and how we validate our supporting knowledge claims.

The pragmatists in the Deng era advocated a loosening of central planning incentives for increased productivity and quality, and land tenure for small farmers.

> *Letting a hundred flowers blossom and a hundred schools of thought contend is the policy for promoting progress in the arts and the sciences and a flourishing socialist culture in our land.*

Mao Zedong, 1957

1   To what extent can the policies advocated in the Deng era be considered socialist? Explain your reasoning.

2   Can communism be democratic? What does that mean?

3   In 1957, Mao seemed to be supporting freedom of speech. Is freedom of speech possible under communism?

TOK analysis

● Do politics affect the ethics of a society?

● Are the following ideas political or ethical (or both):
   Justice, human rights, social responsibility, equality and freedom?

● Is the concept of private property ethical?

● Is the concept of society ethical?

● When confronted with an unjust situation, is a person obliged to act?

● Review the language of political debate, and judge its implications for yourself. (i.e. what does it mean to be a liberal? What is the difference between a socialist and a communist?)

From the work you've done you may be in a position to answer one of these former TOK prescribed essay questions.

1   It is often said that historical knowledge is somehow tainted by its selective nature and that the significance of "facts" is in the eye of the beholder. Could the same be said for all knowledge? Use at least two other areas of knowledge to illustrate your argument.

2   "History is part myth, part hope and part reality". Critically evaluate this claim and consider the extent to which it might be true of other disciplines.

3   "An historian must combine the rigor of the scientist with the imagination of the artist". To what extent, therefore, can the historian be confident about his or her conclusions?

Political changes and their limits

While the world applauded the PRC's economic development in the 1970s and 1980s, the government's harsh actions against dissenters apalled the world. This section explores the desire for political reform among the youth and intellectuals of China. In many respects, what happened in 1989 was a repeat and intensification of the events of 1976 after the death of Zhou Enlai. This time, the catalyst was the death of Hu Yaobang, leading first to memorials, then to protest and finally to armed repression of the young people who congregated in Tiananmen Square and refused to disperse. Deng ruthlessly ordered the suppression of the uprising and then denied the claims that many were killed or wounded when the army opened fire on the protestors.

It should not be surprising that economic development led to a desire for political change and, in particular, the rise of political dissent in Communist China. After the retributions that people had faced during the period of the Cultural Revolution and the Gang of Four, the climate was certainly more open in China; and opening up the country to the West made the proliferation of different ideas inevitable.

As stated above, the economic reforms led to conflict within the Communist Party leadership. Once again, there were three main power bases—those following Deng (the pragmatists), Hua and Ye (the balancer and military leader). Some of the more leftist members feared that the socialist goals of the state would be tarnished by both the economic reforms and the exchanges with the West. The leadership had to strike a delicate balance of adopting Western technology and managerial methods while keeping their own culture. Furthermore, pragmatic leaders such as Deng had to keep to the line that they were not adopting capitalism but were instead adopting Chinese-style socialism. To renounce socialism in any way would undermine the Party and thus the leadership and power structure in China.

It is true that China was undergoing a period of relative freedom. Many who had been imprisoned or sent down to the countryside during the Cultural Revolution were released and, just as Deng was rehabilitated, so were a number of other Party officials. In 1978 in Beijing, on Xidan Street near a bus station, posters and characters were put up on a brick wall. This came to be called Democracy Wall, a place where people, taking up the government's charge to "seek truth from facts" began to express their opinion on the way in which China had progressed over the past decade.

The participants in this action were former Red Guards and people who had missed out on formal education due to the Cultural Revolution. Their experience as militants in the 1960s, however, gave them skills of organization and collaboration which helped make this movement spread and gave voice to those who had been repressed in the Cultural Revolution. Just as they had criticized the establishment and traditional Chinese culture in the 1960s, they now criticized the Gang of Four and even Mao. But as people were emboldened, criticism widened to the Communist Party and the socialist system in place. Party leaders, most notably Deng, encouraged the criticisms as they were being articulated at a time when the Party was engaged in an internal struggle. Deng saw the dissenters as potential allies in his cause, and he could refer to them and their anti-Gang messages as support that came directly from the people themselves, and those who had previously supported the Maoists.

The Wall was not the only forum for dissent, however. In 1978 and 1979 a number of pro-democracy advocates published pamphlets and even established underground magazines in which they put forth a call for reform in China. Some of these, notably Beijing Spring, sold 100 000 copies to a public that was clamoring for different points of view regarding the system of government in China. Unlike other movements before and after, this one clearly stated a desire for freedom and political self-determination. The issue of human rights was also raised—a subject that had previously been taboo in China. The dissenters did not just address their own people and leadership—calls for criticism of their leadership were made to the United States, exhorting US president Jimmy Carter to condemn human rights abuses in China just as he had done in the Soviet Union.

In addition to the magazines, journals, big characters and poetry, people from rural China descended upon Beijing to petition the government to take action against those who had abused them. Those accused were largely local Party officials, and when their grievances were unanswered by the government, the masses began to protest. Once again Tiananmen Square was full of marchers demanding to be heard. The dissent was no longer simply against those who had committed past injustices, it was also against what was increasingly seen as a bureaucratic state, not one that represented the workers of China. The public's dissatisfaction manifested itself in the dissemination of even more anti-government statements.

The most famous of the pamphlets was Wei Jingsheng's Fifth Modernization, in which he stated that the most necessary condition for modernization was a fifth, unstated one—democracy. Wei openly criticized Deng and his policies in a series of articles, even suggesting that Deng was quickly becoming a fascist dictator and that his power needed to be curbed. Not surprisingly, Wei was arrested in March 1979 and the government held a show trial in October in which he was found guilty of treason and sentenced to 15 years imprisonment in solitary confinement, largely as a warning to other potential dissidents. The Wall itself was closed down in December; arrests were made and putting up posters was made illegal. Pro-democracy groups and reforming communists were pushed underground once again, but they kept the contacts they had made and would periodically resurface.

Activity:
A forum for dissent
Create Xidan Street for your class or study group. If there is space on the walls, or if you have a free bulletin board, you can use this as the place to gather the work. All students should generate a piece of work that they would like to place on the Wall. This wall can have manifestos, polemics, poetry, drawings, posters and any illustration or text that you feel will help to explain your opposition to the Chinese government.

Meantime, Deng was consolidating his power in the politburo and Central Committee. With Hua marginalized and now largely a ceremonial figure, Deng's focus was on economic vitalization and modernization. He spent a lot of time abroad, aligning China with developing countries and seeking new markets outside of the communist world. In the late 1980s, China's primary trading partner was Japan, and US investment was rapidly increasing. Foreign journalists were given more access to Chinese specialists. China seemed to be opening up once again.

Party and government policies were rather contradictory in the 1980s; on the one hand, intellectuals were encouraged to speak out and engage in what was termed political liberalization. On the other hand, warnings were made that modernization should not be an excuse to reintroduce bourgeois values. The government asserted less control over the news, allowing journalists to publish stories about negative aspects of Chinese life. A number of loyal, well-connected Party members openly criticized certain corruptions that they saw, while maintaining that they were loyal to the Party and to the ideology. Thus dissent, never far underground since the Democracy Wall, started a slow return to public life.

Beginning in 1986 there were demonstrations that were meant to encourage more students to become involved in local government. They also sought greater freedoms and improved living conditions. Initially, the government showed restraint in their actions against the students, seeking to disperse demonstrations, rather than arresting participants. In early 1987, Hu Yaobang, the General Secretary of the Party (who had been a proponent of political liberalization) resigned from office, stating that he had made uncorrectable mistakes. This signalled the government's attitude towards student demonstrations, but did not lead to their decline. Unlike previous student movements, they were not joined by workers or peasants, and the students' enthusiasm for protest declined as exams neared. The demonstrations dissipated for the time being.

Within the Party, Deng once again seemed to fear another power struggle. The resignation of Hu allayed his fears to some extent (as Hu had suggested in 1986 that Deng was getting too old and should consider retiring), but he also engaged in a bit of politicking and induced a number of retirements of communist hardliners, officially due to old age. But, at 83 himself, Deng had no intention of relinquishing his leadership of China.

Tiananmen Square, 1989

The calls for change were further encouraged by Gorbachev's policies of **glasnost** and **perestroika** and the weakening of communist hegemony in the Soviet satellites, but it was once again a death that would lead to massive demonstrations in Tiananmen Square. In April 1989, Hu died, and this in turn led to a number of rallies, in Beijing and Shanghai in particular, in favor of social change. This time it was not simply a student movement—all sorts of people defied a ban on public gatherings and this led to a demonstration in May in Tiananmen Square in front of the Communist Party headquarters.

Glasnost A political policy introduced by Mikhail Gorbachev in 1985 in the Soviet Union that allowed for criticism of past Soviet practices. It was created so that there would be more openness and government transparency, intended to reduce corruption.

Perestroika The economic policy introduced by Mikhail Gorbachev in the 1980s that called for a restructuring of the economy. This policy permitted wider economic freedoms, including entrepreneurship and private enterprise, while still retaining the framework of the Soviet planned economy.

Just as Deng had counselled restraint in 1976, Hu's successor, Zhao Ziyang, tried to work with the pro-democracy forces, hoping to prevent government actions from becoming violent. Instead, the students intensified things, engaging in a hunger strike and creating the Goddess of Democracy as a symbol of their commitment. The struggle wore on and the population increasingly sided with the protestors. Martial law was announced but not carried out. Instead, in Beijing, local residents disarmed the PLA as sympathetic soldiers were unwilling to take action against the population. Still, the government did not yet order a crackdown as it tried to wait out the demonstrators.

The actions in Beijing were made public to the world because thousands of journalists were on hand to cover Gorbachev's visit to China. Thus, as the world watched, Deng ordered the army to "take all necessary measures" to seize control of the square. On 3–4 June 1989, troops and tanks were sent in and ordered to clear the square, arrest protestors and end the demonstrations. Although some protestors tried to fight back, those who remained in the square were fired upon and hundreds were killed. Although there were reportedly riots in 80 cities around China, all the uprisings were quickly suppressed. The government denied that it had killed civilians.

Part of the problem was that the demonstrators' objectives were not clear—even to them. They knew they wanted more freedoms and they wanted the Party to reform, but they weren't sure what else they wanted. Also, they lacked clear leadership. This gave support to Deng's claims that the government was acting to prevent chaos descending on China once again. Zhao was removed and replaced by Jiang Zemin, a loyal Deng supporter. Although Deng resigned as chair of the Central Military Commission in 1989, he still remained the guiding figure in China's policies until his death in 1997 at the age of 92. There is some difference of opinion over whether his actions in Tiananmen Square consolidated his power or weakened it. Regardless, Deng still had tremendous power within the Party, and was able to use it to ensure that a loyal successor was appointed.

The outside world had applauded the demonstrators in Tiananmen Square but little about the repression. China was once again singled out as a human rights abuser by watch organizations like Amnesty International, but democratic states continued relations with China.

The country had begun this era with an uncertain future: it was questionable who would succeed Mao and what turn China would take. By 1989 it was clear that economic liberalization was encouraged and desirable, but the Communist Party remained firmly entrenched and there would be no political liberalization.

"The pressure against the system is building, and there comes a point beyond which one cannot turn back. However naive our faith may seem, we will continue the fight. Even if we are convinced the battle is lost from the beginning, at least for the time being we will have to answer the challenge."

Wuer Kaixi, a leader of the students' movement, now in self-imposed exile in the USA

Source analysis

The following sources relate to the democracy movements in China.

Source A

Let me respectfully remind these gentlemen: We want to be masters of our own destiny. We need no gods or emperors. We do not believe in the existence of any savior. We want to be masters of the world and not instruments used by autocrats to carry out their wild ambitions. We want a modern lifestyle and democracy for the people. Freedom and happiness are our sole objectives in accomplishing modernization. Without this fifth modernization all others are merely another promise.

Source: Wei Jingsheng. 5 December 1978. *The Fifth Modernization.*
http://www.rjgeib.com/thoughts/china/jingshen.htm.

Source B

Photograph entitled "Goddess of Democracy versus Chairman Mao", June 1989. The photo was found online but the author of the website and the photographer are anonymous.

Source C

Cable from the US embassy in Beijing to the Department of State, Washington DC, on the morning of June 4,1989.

The crackdown continued through the night, and by early morning June 4, as this cable reports, the PLA was in control of Tiananmen Square. Based on eyewitness accounts of the violence, this SITREP is the Embassy's initial effort to provide some detail on the final PLA assault on the approximately 3,000 demonstrators who had not yet left the square. "Some 10,000 troops," the document says, formed a ring around the square, and "a column of about 50 APC, tanks, and trucks entered Tiananmen from the east." Demonstrators shouted angrily, the cable states, and "PLA troops in Tiananmen opened a barrage of rifle and machine gun fire." Another column of military vehicles entered soon thereafter, and more gunfire ensued, "causing a large number of casualties." The document also describes violent PLA clashes with demonstrators on Changan Boulevard, the main thoroughfare in the Tiananmen area, and in other parts of Beijing. Embassy officials also report conversations with angry citizens, some "claiming that more than 10,000 people had been killed at Tiananmen." One woman claimed to have witnessed a tank running over 11 people. She also told Embassy officers that she had seen PLA troops "breaking the windows of shops, banks, and other buildings."

Source: *Tiananmen Square, 1989. The Declassified History.* A National Security Archive Electronic Briefing Book No. 16, George Washington University. http://www.gwu.edu/~nsarchiv/NSAEBB/NSAEBB16.

Source D

Breaking news in The New York Times.

Beijing death toll at least 300. Army tightens control of city but angry resistance goes on.

Army units tightened their hold on the center of the Chinese capital on Sunday, moving in large convoys on some of the main thoroughfares and firing indiscriminately at crowds as outraged citizens continued to attack and burn army vehicles. It was clear that at least 300 people had been killed since the troops first opened fire shortly after midnight on Sunday morning but the toll may be much higher. …

The area around central Tiananmen Square was completely sealed by troops who periodically responded with bursts of automatic-weapons fire whenever crowds drew close to the square. By ordering soldiers to fire on the unarmed crowds, the Chinese leadership has created an incident that almost surely will haunt the Government for years to come. It is believed here that after the bloodshed of this weekend, it will be incomparably more difficult to rule China.

… The number of casualties may never be known, because the Government has asked hospitals not to report any numbers on deaths or injuries. However, based on accounts pieced together from doctors at several hospitals, it seems that at least 200 died in the hospitals and that many other corpses were probably left in the hands of the military. "We had to concentrate on those who were still living," one doctor said today. "We had to leave behind most of those who already were dead."

When troops finally seized Tiananmen Square early Sunday morning, they allowed the student occupiers who held on to the center of the square for three weeks to leave and then sent tanks to run over the tents and makeshift encampment that demonstrators had set up. Unconfirmed reports rapidly spread that some students had remained in the tents and were crushed to death.

The troops sealed off Tiananmen Square and started a huge bonfire. Many Beijing residents drew the conclusion, again impossible to verify, that the soldiers cremated corpses to destroy the evidence.

The student organization that coordinated the long protests continued to function and announced today that 2,600 students were believed to have been killed. Several doctors said that, based on their discussions with ambulance drivers and colleagues who had been on Tiananmen Square, they estimated that at least 2,000 had died. But some of these estimates, based principally on antipathy for the Government, appeared to be high.

Source: Nicholas Kristof. 5 June 1989. *The New York Times*.

Source E

Extract from a book by Jan Wong. The author is a Chinese-Canadian, who wrote her memoirs as a student and later a journalist living and working in China. On the evening of 2–3 June 1989 she was staying in a hotel with a view of Tiananmen Square.

At 9:46 the crowd suddenly began stampeding away from the square. I couldn't figure out why. Then I saw that the soldiers had knelt into a shooting position and were taking aim. As the people ran, the soldiers fired into their backs. More than a dozen bodies lay on the ground. When the shooting stopped there was absolute silence. Some of the wounded began to crawl to the edge of the road. To my amazement, the crowd began to creep back toward the square. At 10:09 another murderous barrage sent them racing down the street toward the hotel. They crept back to the square again. At 10:22 there was another volley, lasting three minutes. I watched in horror as the soldiers advanced, shooting into the backs of fleeing civilians. The wounded lay, beyond the reach of rescuers, as the soldiers kept up their heavy fire.

Source: Wong, J. 1997. *Red China Blues*. New York, USA. Anchor Books.

Source-based questions

1 Wei Jingsheng was an electrician by profession who had been a member of the Red Guard in his youth. Assess how far Source A is consistent with his past as a revolutionary and his profession as a member of the proletariat.

2 In Source B, what is meant by "Goddess of Democracy versus Chairman Mao"?

3 With reference to origins and purpose, assess the values and limitations of Sources C, D and E for historians studying the democracy movement and Tiananmen Square, 1989.

4 Evaluate the sources above as if you were seeking to disprove the events of June 1989. How can the reports be discredited?

The USSR in crisis

Leonid Brezhnev came to power in 1964 after the fall of Nikita Khruschchev. This section provides the necessary background information to contextualize the problems of the Brezhnev era. It explains briefly how Brezhnev helped eject Nikita Khrushchev and consolidated control in the Soviet Union and over the satellite states.

Background to the Brezhnev era

Nikita Khrushchev was the undisputed leader of the Soviet Union but his power never came close to the absolutist heights of his predecessor, Josef Stalin. After Stalin died in 1953, the resultant power struggle between Lavrenti Beria, commissar for internal affairs and head of the Soviet intelligence agency, and the other potential successors was one of absolute rule (Beria) versus greater power sharing (Kruschev). The Khrushchev cohort prevailed and, although Khrushchev became the leader of the Soviet Union, final decisions rested with the politburo as a whole.

Khrushchev's policies dominated the period 1956–64. He faced constant pressures domestically and internationally. His regime was plagued with the domestic problems brought on by the **Virgin Lands and corn programmes** to increase agricultural production and the myriad struggles with the West and within the Eastern bloc itself. Khrushchev survived uprisings in Poland and Hungary; the Cuban Missile and Berlin Crises; and the Sino-Soviet split—but only just. In October 1964, the CPSU leadership censured him and he was removed from power. The official explanation was that he retired due to poor health and advanced age, but later the story changed. He was openly (if posthumously) accused of trying to revive the cult of personality and was criticized for his economic and foreign policies.

Khrushchev's removal from power was not marked by bloodshed, and this reflected a change in the Soviet attitude towards leaders who had outlived their utility. He lived for the rest of his life in relative peace in the Crimean peninsula, writing his memoirs; these were published posthumously by his son in 1971, providing history with his view of the events that he shaped.

After Khrushchev's removal, there was an attempt to broaden the power-sharing base within the CPSU leadership once again. In 1964, Leonid Brezhnev, as General Secretary, entered into a triumvirate with Alexsei Kosygin, the prime minister, and Nikolai Podgorny, who was named chairman of the **Presidium** in 1965. Initially Brezhnev felt he could work in

Presidium In communist countries, a permanent executive body that has the power to act for a larger governing body. Usually this body is led by the president of the Supreme Soviet. The Presidium was the executive body of the Communist Party of the Soviet Union from 1952 to 1966, replacing the politburo or Politbureau (which was renamed the Presidium during this period).

The Virgin Lands and corn programmes

These agricultural policies were intended to help produce more meat for the Soviet state. The government encouraged people to grow maize for feed in the hope of increasing yields of livestock, but they didn't want to lower the amount of other products grown. The Virgin and Waste Land programme was developed to increase arable land so that this would not happen. The scheme did increase production but not enough, and the Soviet Union lacked sufficient food for people in the cities. In the end, the USSR had to import grain, causing economic problems for those who succeeded Khrushchev.

the existing system but later decided that he wanted to combine the positions of General Secretary and Chair; Podgorny resigned in 1977, relinquishing his position to Brezhnev. Kosygin continued as prime minister and was especially effective in his work with Willy Brandt in the Federal Republic of Germany and the development of the policy of Ostpolitik, but he was careful not to eclipse Brezhnev and survived in office until his death in 1980.

IB Learner Profile link

Thinkers

What do you know about communism in the Union of Soviet Socialist Republics (USSR) before 1976?

Put together two tables: one for the political leadership in the USSR in 1976 and one for the Communist Party of the Soviet Union (CPSU) hierarchy.

Where are there overlaps? What does this signify?

? **How does this compare with the structures in Communist China? What are the similarities and differences?**

"Whatever else may divide us, Europe is our common home; a common fate has linked us through the centuries, and it continues to link us today."

Leonid Brezhnev, in a speech in Bonn, West Germany. 23 November 1981.

Leonid Brezhnev (1906–82)

Leonid Brezhnev was the leader of the USSR from 1964 until his death in 1982. Like many other members of the Communist Party leadership, he was affiliated with the Communist Party from his youth. Born in Ukraine in 1906 into a working-class family (his father was a steelworker), Brezhnev's childhood was interrupted first by the Russian Revolution and then by the Civil War. He joined the Communist Party as a member of the youth group (Komsomol) in 1923 and became a full Party member in 1931. Under Stalin, the Soviet Union was consolidating power in the Ukraine and Brezhnev assisted in this through Stalin's forced collectivization of agriculture and rapid industrialization in the form of the Five Year Plans. During the Second World War, Brezhnev continued serving the Party as an officer in the Red Army, achieving the rank of Major General. After the war, he was transferred to Moldavia and was elected secretary of the Central Committee for the Moldavian SSR in 1950. In 1952 he was transferred to Moscow, where he served in the Secretariat under Stalin. Although he was demoted after Stalin's death and sent to the Kazakh SSR as Party Secretary, he proved himself to be an effective administrator and thus was returned to Moscow in 1956, gaining the trust and respect of Soviet leader Nikita Khrushchev. In 1960, Brezhnev was named Chair of the Presidium of theSupreme Soviet—a position of high visibility but limited political power. As dissatisfaction with Khrushchev mounted, Brezhnev aligned himself with Khrushchev's rivals and they were successful in ousting him in October 1964. From that point forward, Brezhnev was viewed as first among equals, but was the public face of the Soviet Union and commanded the loyalty and support of the Party. Brezhnev's domestic policies reflected a desire to maintain the status quo, while his foreign policies showed a commitment to arms control and keeping socialist countries within the Soviet sphere. As he aged, he encouraged a cult of personality and favored his persona of military hero. Brezhnev was made a Hero of the Soviet Union, received the Order of Lenin and Order of Victory medals, as well as three Gold Stars, and was decorated with numerous other medals—114 in total. His death in 1982 was marked by great pomp and circumstance—four days of public mourning, including the closure of universities, public buildings and the roads to Moscow on the day of his funeral. Brezhnev led the Soviet Union for longer than all other Soviet leaders except Josef Stalin, and left a legacy of political and economic stagnation and hard-line tactics in relation to the satellite states and arms control.

Domestic and foreign policies and the problems faced by Brezhnev

When Leonid Brezhnev assumed power in the USSR in 1964, he was confronted by an ailing system. The planned economy had helped the Soviet Union industrialize, arm itself and develop technology to stay competitive with its political rivals, but it had failed to produce consumer goods or an agricultural surplus of agriculture. At the same time, a number of intellectuals and academics were openly challenging the regime and questioning the wisdom of the dictatorship of the proletariat. Internationally, Brezhnev pursued a somewhat contradictory policy of continued dominance over client states and détente that was epitomized in the SALT negotiations. The Brezhnev era culminated with the disastrous involvement in Afghanistan that, with economic decline, would provoke a desire for reform and the rise of Gorbachev.

Domestic problems

Economic stagnation

Brezhnev had to contend with the failed agricultural policies that plagued the USSR. From 1953 to 1970 the Soviet Union had seen an increased standard of living, but this began to reverse itself. In 1972 the USSR suffered a series of crop failures leading to food shortages. Furthermore, the USSR was spending tremendous sums of money on its military programme—after the Cuban Missile Crisis the Soviet navy was upgraded, and the space programme continued to use up substantial resources. Thus, approximately 25 per cent of Soviet GNP from 1964 to 1982 was spent on the Soviet military, in the hope of closing the gap between the USSR and the USA.

Brezhnev initially tried to introduce reforms that would promote the use of market forces to determine production, but these were blocked by hardliners who feared that the USSR could shift to capitalism. However, he was successful in reversing some of the effects of **collectivization** and allowed farmers to return to working on state-owned plots, giving them an incentive to keep or sell surplus product. This was the most successful part of the agricultural sector, thereby negating socialist, central planning.

Collectivization An agricultural policy in socialist or communist systems in which individual landholders give up their tenure (land ownership) and combine their plots with those of other landholders to create large farms.

Morale and productivity declined as living standards stagnated. Brezhnev tried to increase production of consumer goods to mollify the public in the Ninth and Tenth Five Year Plans (1971–5; 1976–80), but the availability of consumer goods remained limited, except on the black market. The USSR suffered yet another poor grain harvest in 1975, which exacerbated the economic distress that the country faced. To keep the citizens of the USSR and Eastern Europe fed, Brezhnev had to increase agricultural imports. While the rest of the world faced petroleum shortages in the 1970s, the USSR struggled to increase production to take advantage of the high demand for oil. This came at the expense of the expansion of the production of consumer goods and so criticism of the government became more and more open as people found ways to express their dissatisfaction.

Dissent

Soviet citizenry were increasingly emboldened to speak out against the government. Although repression and censorship were still in effect, it became clear that the brutality of the Stalinist regime was not going to return and intellectuals began to criticize the government openly. The first major example of this was the publication of Solzhenitsyn's *The Gulag Archipelago*, his autobiographical account of the treatment of Soviet citizens in the expanding network of camps. In 1974, Solzhenitsyn was exiled for the publication of this work.

Most dissidents used informal, unofficial publications—**samizdat** and **tamizdat**—to make their perspectives known. Some of these publications became journals, and gained a very strong following, distributing thousands of copies. Thus, opponents of the government found means by which to spread their ideas.

In addition to political dissenters, there were also national minorities who sought a voice in their own futures, and even agitated for some autonomy. The Jewish population in the USSR was receiving support from abroad, and, especially after the Helsinki Accords of 1975 committed the USSR to adhering to basic principles of human rights, international pressure was put on the Soviets to allow Soviet Jews to emigrate to Israel if they so desired.

In the Baltic countries of Estonia, Latvia and Lithuania, the situation was a little different. A number of countries, including the USA, had never recognized the incorporation of the Baltic States into the USSR as it had been done by force and through agreements with Nazi Germany. In the 1970s, nationalists in these Soviet Socialist Republics (SSRs) began to protest the influx of ethnic Russians into their areas, and agitated for rights granted to nationalities based on the initial principles espoused by Lenin before his death in 1924. Estonians, Latvians and Lithuanians would have to wait until the 1990s to gain independence, but the seeds were certainly sown in the Brezhnev era.

Samizdat Self-published pamphlets or articles that were illegally copied and distributed within the Soviet sphere to overcome censorship. Generally run on mimeograph machines, but often copied manually and passed on in very limited quantities.

Tamizdat Similar to the samizdat, but published abroad and smuggled back into the USSR.

Political stagnation

When Brezhnev came to power in 1964, he began his tenure in a position of collective leadership with Kosygin and Mikoyan but then emerged as the dominant figure in Soviet politics. By 1971 the politburo was controlled by his supporters, and he held a very conservative, even reactionary line with regard to Party politics. Under Brezhnev, there was some rehabilitation of Stalin, and he encouraged a cult of personality centered on his own person.

Brezhnev showed very little interest in reforming the government or Party structure within the Soviet Union. The need for reform was becoming increasingly critical as the Soviet hardliners and traditional bearers of power in the USSR were aging and dying. In 1974, he spoke of the "stability of cadres", a reference to assure the elderly, stagnant Party members that they and their positions were safe. This was mirrored in the economic sphere, where workers realized that they would not be dismissed from their positions for poor productivity. This may have improved people's sense of security but it had serious economic side effects.

Foreign policies and problems

While Khrushchev is generally remembered for his most spectacular foreign policy failure—the Cuban Missile Crisis—people tend to ignore one of his last actions as head of the Soviet State: the signing of the Test Ban Treaty in 1963. Perhaps in direct response to the sentiment that the superpowers had reached the brink of nuclear war, the three nuclear powers (the USSR, the UK and the USA) signed an agreement that they would no longer explode nuclear bombs in the atmosphere or underwater. In the coming year, both China and France became nuclear powers but neither signed this agreement. It was followed, in 1968, by the Nuclear Non-Proliferation Treaty, signed by the same three powers, with China and France again refusing to participate. (Both did eventually become signatories, but were initially reluctant to sign any treaty that committed their countries to limit any type of nuclear test or expansion.)

Upon his accession to power, Brezhnev was seen as the leader of a country that at the very least was committed to limiting warfare between the USA and the USSR. But by the end of the 1960s the USSR was pursuing a determinedly contradictory policy—on the one hand supporting and sustaining communist regimes and, on the other, trying to come to some sort of agreement with the USA on arms limitations. While many saw these policies as paradoxical, they are clarified in the Brezhnev Doctrine.

The Brezhnev Doctrine

The Prague Spring of 1968 marked a turning point in Brezhnev's foreign policy and made it clear to the world how the Soviets would react to any anti-communist activity within their sphere of influence. When economic stagnation and Slovak dissatisfaction led to increasing tensions within its borders, Czechoslovakia's Party leader (Novotny) was replaced by the Slovak Alexander Dubček. The Czechoslovak government put into place reforms unprecedented in the Soviet sphere. In August 1968, Soviet troops, with the assistance of other Warsaw Pact armies, invaded the country and reversed all the reforms. Dubček was removed from his position and eventually expelled from the Party; Soviet troops remained in Czechoslovakia until 1990.

The international significance of the Prague Spring and the resultant Soviet invasion was the articulation of the Brezhnev Doctrine in November 1968—interestingly, at a meeting of Polish workers. In his speech, Brezhnev made clear that the Soviet Union was determined to keep in place communist regimes that existed and would not allow for them to be overthrown internally or externally. Despite vocal criticism from the Western powers, no one came to the assistance of Czechoslovakia or any other socialist states in an open manner. (For further information on nationalist and independence movements in Czechoslovakia and Poland, see chapter 8).

"Our country, like every modern state, needs profound democratic reforms. It needs political and ideological pluralism, a mixed economy and protection of human rights and the opening up of society."

*Andrei Sakharov,
Soviet physicist and dissident*

Détente

Almost immediately thereafter, Brezhnev began a series of discussions with the United States to limit arms production. The Strategic Arms Limitations Talks (SALT) began in 1969 with US president Nixon. Given the economic stagnation that the USSR faced, limiting the development and production of weapons was desirable. Additionally, this served to show the USA that while they would support socialist regimes (in Czechoslovakia, North Vietnam and elsewhere), they wanted direct peace with the USA and avoidance of nuclear war. The desire for agreement with the United States may also have been the result of border clashes with China on the Ussuri River in 1969. This movement towards détente reached a conclusion in May 1972 when the USA and the USSR agreed to limit the number of anti-ballistic missiles they would produce in the future.

US–Soviet relations seemed on the road to further improvement in January 1973 as a result of the Paris Peace Accord, when the USA ended its involvement in Vietnam, and the Soviets entered into further discussions in Helsinki. These led to the Helsinki Final Act of 1975, in which the post-war frontiers of Eastern and Central Europe were finalized, and the Soviets agreed to adhere to international conventions on human rights.

Revolution and dissent

The USSR was taking an increasingly active role in Africa. After the Portuguese revolution in 1974, their African territories were decolonized and this almost immediately led to civil war in Angola and Mozambique. In both cases, there were Marxist groups that enlisted the assistance of first the Cubans and then the Soviets. In Angola, the **Popular Movement for the Liberation of Angola (MPLA)** received assistance from the Soviets, and in Mozambique it was **Frelimo** that had been receiving Soviet support since the colonial period and its founding in the 1960s. This seemed to confirm Soviet commitment to Marxist revolution. In Ethiopia, the Soviets helped overthrow the regime of Haile Selassie and put into place a communist revolutionary government that faced opposition from the Somali government. They in turn were driven out by Ethiopians who received armaments from the Soviet Union.

At the same time, the Soviets were increasingly confronted by dissent within the Soviet sphere. In the late 1970s there were political and labor movements rising in Eastern Europe. Most notably, the Solidarity movement began to take root in Poland, and the events there were troubling to the Soviet leadership that had suppressed movements in Hungary and Czechoslovakia. However, the Solidarity movement hit its peak just as the USSR was finding itself entrenched in Afghanistan and thus was hesitant to invoke the Brezhnev Doctrine yet again. (See pages 424–8 for more on Solidarity and Poland.)

Afghanistan

For the USSR, Afghanistan proved to be the most problematic foreign policy intervention of the era. In December 1979, Soviet troops invaded Afghanistan, ostensibly to give support to the beleaguered socialist government that had taken power in 1978. The Soviet

MPLA Popular Movement for the Liberation of Angola (Movimento Popular de Libertação de Angola in Portuguese)—the Marxist political party that has ruled Angola since its independence from Portugal in 1975.

Frelimo Liberation Front of Angola (Frente de Libertação de Moçambique in Portuguese)—the Marxist political party that fought the war of independence against Portugal and has ruled Mozambique since its independence in 1975.

government was continuing a long Russian tradition of intervention in the region which dated back to the late 19th century and its competition with the United Kingdom for domination of the region. Even during the early stages of the Soviet state, the Soviets sent military assistance to Afghanistan in an attempt to help them overthrow British control of their territory.

Soviet–Afghan military cooperation began in the Khrushchev era, when the Soviet military trained Afghan officers, making them sympathetic to the Marxist cause in their own country, and this continued in the Brezhnev era. In April 1978, the Afghan army seized power and executed the president and prime minister, Lieutenant General Sardar Muhammad Daud Khan. In place of the previous regime, the Marxist **People's Democratic Party of Afghanistan (PDPA)** was put in power under the governance of Nur Muhammad Taraki, who was named president of the Democratic Republic of Afganistan (DRA). The newly formed government faced factionalism within its own party ranks, as well as the problems of a poor country. It attempted to implement social and economic reforms in an attempt to secularize and modernize the country.

> **PDPA People's Democratic Party of Afghanistan**, the Marxist–Leninist political party that was founded in 1965 and later assumed control of Afghanistan after the monarchy was overthrown in 1978. The party split into two factions in 1967, which later vied for control of the Democratic Republic of Afghanistan.

In December 1978, the USSR and Afghanistan signed a bilateral agreement in which the Soviet Union agreed to assist the government in Kabul if they requested military assistance. The Afghan government was increasingly dependent on Soviet assistance for the maintenance of its power, and this in many respects weakened the moral authority of the government, with the result that anti-government attacks, especially by religious groups, increased.

Reforms imposed through violence led to increased civil strife in Afghanistan. Many religious and village leaders were arrested and imprisoned or executed for dissidence, and this further increased civilian hostility to the state. Those members of the traditional Afghan elite and intelligentsia who could, went into exile abroad, as the lower classes of Afghan society streamed into Pakistan, filling refugee camps. An estimated 27 000 political prisoners were executed by the PDPA government.

Rebel forces called the **Mujahideen** began to oppose the Marxist PDPA. Although the largest group consisted of pro-religious forces, in reality the Mujahideen was a loosely-organized coalition of people who opposed the restrictive, socialist nature of the regime. As in Iran, the religious bodies began to take a dominant role: religious leaders (mullahs) had a forum in which they could put forth their ideas and an organizational structure in place through the mosques and Islamic schools that existed in Afghanistan. They also relied on the backing of powerful local warlords. Over time, the amount of foreign aid, and the countries from which they received it, continued to increase.

> **Mujahideen** This was the name given to the loose alliance of rebels fighting against the Soviets and the DRA. The word comes from the singular *mujahid*, meaning a Muslim involved in *jihad*, that is, fighting in a war or other struggle. The Western press did not differentiate among the rebel forces and used the term when referring to all anti-Socialist forces.

The resistance to the PDPA began to target not just Afghan but Soviet leaders as well. In March 1979 alone, approximately 100 Soviet advisors were killed by members of the Afghan army that had mutinied in the city of Herat. The Marxists responded by attacking the city and killing approximately 24 000 inhabitants. Rather than suppress the opposition to the regime, this dramatic action fuelled opposition and, in an army of 90 000, half either deserted or joined the rebel cause. Further complicating the situation, in September 1979, Taraki was overthrown by his one-time collaborator Hafizullah Amin.

In December 1979, the USSR invaded Afghanistan and invoked the Brezhnev Doctrine to explain the invasion. The official rationale was that the PDPA had asked the USSR to intervene to prevent the Mujahideen from taking power. The problem that the USSR faced was that their objectives were unclear, to say the least. Within the Soviet government there were disagreements as to how and why to proceed: the KGB seemed to support a limited operation that would stabilize the situation and prevent it from spilling into neighbouring countries (including the SSRs of central Asia), while the defence ministry advocated the overthrow of the PDPA of Amin with the goal of protecting Afghanistan from invasion by Pakistan or Iran. The fear was that Amin (and Taraki before him) were engaged in pro-US activities and that his continued leadership could mean the end of socialism in Afghanistan.

By 27 December, there were 70 000 Soviet troops in Afghanistan, with no clear idea of how to fight in such a chaotic situation or what their desired outcomes were. The situation for the Soviets was tenuous at best, for while the Soviets controlled the cities and the highways, the guerrillas, aided by the United States, controlled the countryside.

Soviet forces killed Amin and all who witnessed the assassination, and replaced him with Babrak Karmal, another PDPA leader who had temporarily been deputy prime minister under Amin. This was the beginning of a ten-year intervention that cost the Soviet Union billions of dollars and tens of thousands of lives. The intervention was never very popular with the Soviet citizenry and led to international condemnation, including the decisions of the USA to limit grain sales to the USSR and boycott the 1980 summer Olympics that were being held in Moscow.

The rebel forces gained the support of the USA, largely because of their anti-socialist stance, and intelligence forces began to assist the rebels; President Carter signed the executive order allowing the CIA to conduct covert operations in Afghanistan. The precise point at which the USA actually began assisting the rebels is highly debated—official assistance began in 1980 after the Soviet

Nur Mohammed Taraki (1913–79)

Nur Mohammed Taraki was the first socialist leader of Afghanistan. Unlike other Marxist leaders, he came from a very modest background in rural Pashtun. He found employment in India, which later allowed him to study at Kabul University. Upon graduating, Taraki matriculated at Columbia University where he received a PhD in Economics. With his fluency in English and knowledge as an economist, he became attaché to the Afghan embassy in Washington DC in 1953, despite his affiliation with radical Marxist groups in Afghanistan. He was a founding member of the People's Democratic Party of Afghanistan (PDPA). In April 1978, after King Mohammed Daud called for the arrest and detention of PDPA leaders, the PDPA retaliated, killing most of the royal family and taking power themselves. On 1 May 1978, Taraki assumed the presidency of the newly-created Democratic Republic of Afghanistan. He served as President of Revolutionary Council, prime minister of Afghanistan and Secretary General of the PDPA. In September 1979, Taraki was ousted by his rival Hafizullah Amin and executed, although initial reports stated that he died of natural causes.

military presence was clearly established, but there is significant evidence to show that the United States had been assisting the military rebels for a considerable time before this.

By 1982 the Soviet politburo recognized that they had engaged in a war they could not win but they refused to admit defeat and withdraw forces. Since Afghanistan was in such a state of chaos, a diplomatic solution was impossible. Most of the founders and initial leaders of the PDPA had been killed in the power struggles of 1978–9 and thus Afghan leadership was weak. The Soviets continued to pursue a policy that lacked coherence, searching for a solution and continuing a highly unpopular and costly war but, having invoked the Brezhnev Doctrine, could not withdraw.

Entr'acte: Andropov and Chernenko

Brezhnev died in November 1982, leaving behind an aged, stagnant political leadership. The politburo was laden with his contemporaries and it was generally felt that the status quo would continue with the appointment of a new Soviet leader. People were somewhat surprised when 68-year-old Yuri Andropov, former KGB leader and Central Committee member, became the new head of the USSR. The final Brezhnev years had been marked by the frequent absences of its leader, who was ill and weakened and seemed increasingly to rely on his protégé Konstantin Chernenko; most insiders felt that Chernenko would be the successor to Brezhnev. However, Andropov somehow managed to outmanoeuver him.

Although those outside of the Soviet Union may have expected policies to remain much the same, Andropov did have some ideas for change. He charged many in the Brezhnev camp with corruption and attempted to negate the "stability of cadres" in favor of more accountability, in an attempt to improve productivity. He made public the facts of economic stagnation and proposed a solution: people needed to work harder and increase individual productivity. He tried to put into place policies according to which those "illegally absent" from work would be arrested, so that the Soviet citizenry would have a carrot and a stick to work harder. In 1983, he shut down much of the Soviet space program in an attempt to save money and slow the accelerating foreign debt.

Politically, Andropov tried to remove Brezhnev's followers (and Chernenko's supporters) and replace them with a new group of **nomenklatura** loyal to Andropov and more likely to promote changes needed in the stagnant Soviet system. In particular, he promoted younger Party members to the politburo, and with the help of the emerging Mikhail Gorbachev he tried to replace the elder Party members at the regional level, too. Gorbachev was strengthened by Andropov's tenure as head of the Soviet state, as he gained a loyal following in spite of Soviet agricultural failures.

Nomenklatura Political elites in Soviet society who held positions of power via the Communist Party.

To the outside world, the Andropov period was marked by a continuation of the foreign problems that had begun under Brezhnev. The situation in Afghanistan, which Andropov had instigated by insisting on a Soviet invasion in 1979, deteriorated and was the main source of discontent with the government at this time. Poland was under martial law in the Andropov period, and the Soviets unequivocally backed Wojciech Jaruzelski in his suppression of opposition movements and continued loyalty to the Warsaw Pact. The already poor relations with the United States were worsened in September 1983, when Soviets shot down a Korean Airlines flight that had strayed into Soviet airspace, killing all 269 people on board. The Soviets were the first on the crash scene and appropriated the black box, all the while maintaining that they had been provoked by the KAL plane.

In late 1983, Andropov stopped appearing in public due to poor health. In sources later released, it is clear that he intended for Gorbachev to be his successor. However, upon his death in 1984, Andropov was succeeded by Chernenko, who proved to be a very short-lived head of state. This was the Brezhnev generation's last assertion of their leadership over the state. Chernenko was largely a figurehead who was seen as holding the Soviet Union steady in preparation for a transition to a different level of leadership.

There were very few changes in the Chernenko period. Domestic and foreign policies remained the same, as the **gerontocracy** spent its last days in charge of the USSR. An increasingly frail Chernenko relied on his deputy, Gorbachev, to chair meetings and make his ideas known. It was his death in March 1985 that marked the real changes in the Soviet regime and signified the end of the Brezhnev era.

Gerontocracy A form of rule in which the leadership of a country is significantly older than the majority of the adult population and in which a small cadre governs the rest. This is not necessarily due to policy but because those who come from the ruling elite are of one generation.

Activity:

Stability

To give people in the USSR a sense of stability, Brezhnev introduced the concept of "stability of cadres". Apply this concept to another entity—be it political, economic or educational (you could use your school, for example). How could this help that entity? How could it harm that entity? Do you think this is a good policy?

Source analysis

The following sources relate to the Soviet intervention in Afghanistan in the Brezhnev era.

Source A

Extracts from a speech published in *Pravda* on 25 September 1968, popularly known as the Brezhnev Doctrine.

The peoples of the socialist countries and Communist parties certainly do have and should have freedom for determining the ways of advance of their respective countries.

However, none of their decisions should damage either socialism in their country or the fundamental interests of other socialist countries, and the whole working class movement, which is working for socialism.

This means that each Communist Party is responsible not only to its own people, but also to all the socialist countries, to the entire Communist movement. Whoever forgets this, in stressing only the independence of the Communist Party, becomes one-sided. He deviates from his international duty.

… The sovereignty of each socialist country cannot be opposed to the interests of the world of socialism, of the world revolutionary movement. …

It is from these same positions that they reject the leftist, adventurist conception of "exporting revolution", and of "bringing happiness" to other peoples. …

The weakening of any of the links in the world system of socialism directly affects all the socialist countries, which cannot look indifferently upon this.

Source B

Extract from Memorandum on protocol no. 149 of the meeting of the politburo (CC CPSU), on 12 April 1979. It concerns Soviet policy regarding Afghanistan prior to direct military intervention by the USSR.

Our future policy in connection with the situation in Afghanistan:

1 *To continue to support the leadership of the DRA [Democratic Republic of Afghanistan] in improving the combat efficiency and political awareness of the Afghan army, ensuring its loyalty and dedication to the revolutionary leadership, and in strengthening and improving the efficiency of the security organs, including the border patrol. …*

2 *As much as is possible, to examine and solve problems connected with provided economic assistance to Afghanistan, especially that which would accelerate and strengthen the political position of the revolutionary-democratic regime in the country. To*

advise the Afghan leadership on developing the principal sectors of the economy which would strengthen the productive capacity of the country, resolve social problems, and provide employment to the population.

3 *In contacts with the leadership of the DRA at all levels to always emphasize the importance of widening the political base which supports the party and the government. The importance of the consecutive implementation of the planned reforms, such as land reform, should be instilled in the leaders of the DRA. This has to be done carefully, devoting essential attention to the political and ideological side of reform. For example, the peasants should be convinced that they are getting the land only because of the revolution and will lose it if they will not protect the revolutionary authority. Similar explanations should be made in cases of other socio-economic reforms.*

To widen the political base of the PDPA, the Afghan leadership should be made to understand that it is essential to gradually create electoral organs, yet, of course, the leading role of the party should be maintained and strengthened in the state and political structure of the country. They should also understand that it is advisable to develop and enact a constitution which will secure the democratic rights of the people and regulate the activity of the state organs.

4 *It should be emphasized to the Afghan leadership that as the party ranks grow numerically, it is crucial to maintain the unity of the party leadership and membership. They should also be reminded about the advisability of collective decision-making on the most important issues along party and state lines. The People's Democratic Party of Afghanistan and the leadership of DRA should be given practical assistance in establishing the party organization, spreading mass information, and preparing party and state cadres.*

5 *To continue to draw the attention of the Afghan leadership to the necessity of carrying out appropriate work among the Muslim clergy of the country in order to fractionalize it and reduce the influence of reactionary Muslim leaders on the people. This influence could be diminished by encouraging religious freedom and demonstrating that the new power does not persecute the clergy as a class, but only punishes those who act against the revolutionary system.*

6 *The DRA leaders should be convinced of the necessity of the introduction and strict observance of law and order, based on revolutionary legality, as well as the*

→

necessity of a more reasonable approach to the use of repressive measures. This does not mean, however, that repressive measures should not be used against true infidels or those who engage in active counterrevolutionary activity. A person's fate should not be decided on the basis of circumstantial and unverifiable evidence, or verdict by two- and three-man commissions, without a true investigation and trial. This applies both to party and military cadres.

7 *Considering the importance of personal contacts in communicating our views and thoughts on the above questions to the DRA leadership, visits on various levels should be practiced on a more regular basis in order to normalize the situation in Afghanistan.*

9 *To help Afghan friends conduct political work among the people, including radio propaganda, which due to the high percentage of illiteracy plays a special role in Afghanistan. In our propaganda concerning Afghanistan, the traditional friendship and wide base of mutually beneficial cooperation between our two countries should be emphasized. This relationship not only exists today, but will continue to develop in the future. The achievements in socio-economic development of the Central Asian republics during the Soviet period should be described in a wide and clearly understandable manner; these republics should be used as an example to demonstrate the falsity of assertions concerning repression of religious expression, the Muslim faith included.*

Concrete proposals on the above positions, as well as any other measures, will be included as needed.

Please review these materials.

A. Gromyko. Y. Andropov. D. Ustinov. B.Ponomarev.

April 1, 1979

Source: Documents on the Soviet Invasion of Afghanistan. E-Dossier, no. 4. http://www.wilsoncenter.org/topics/pubs/e-dossier_4.pdf.

Source C

Extract from protocol no. 200 of the session of the politburo of the CC CPSU of 19 June 1980.

Measures on Afghanistan.

1 *To approve Comrade Brezhnev's proposals on the immediate measures on Afghanistan.*
   To proceed with the assumption that the Soviet Union will continue to provide political, military, and economic assistance to Afghanistan in order to help ensure the national independence and territorial integrity of Afghanistan, to strengthen the people's democratic regime and the leading role of the People's Democratic Party.

2 *To consider expedient to withdraw several military units whose presence in Afghanistan now is not necessary.*

To charge the Ministry of Defense of the USSR to make a decision on the number and composition of the troops to be withdrawn and on the time frame and the order of their withdrawal from Afghanistan.
To charge Comrade Andropov to coordinate the issues concerning the withdrawal of some Soviet military units from Afghanistan with B. Karmal.

3 *To use the withdrawal of some Soviet military units from Afghanistan as leverage for demanding that Pakistan and Iran cease their hostile actions against the DRA and to stop sending interventions from their territory into Afghanistan.*

Politburo CC CPSU

Source: Documents on the Soviet Invasion of Afghanistan. E-Dossier, no. 4. http://www.wilsoncenter.org/topics/pubs/e-dossier_4.pdf.

Source D

Extract from US president Jimmy Carter's address to the nation on the Soviet invasion of Afghanistan. It was delivered on 4 January 1980.

The Soviets must understand our deep concern. We will delay opening of any new American or Soviet consular facilities, and most of the cultural and economic exchanges currently under consideration will be deferred. Trade with the Soviet Union will be severely restricted.

I have decided to halt or to reduce exports to the Soviet Union in three areas that are particularly important to them. These new policies are being and will be coordinated with those of our allies.
I've directed that no high technology or other strategic items will be licensed for sale to the Soviet Union until further notice, while we revise our licensing policy.

Fishing privileges for the Soviet Union in United States waters will be severely curtailed.

The 17 million tons of grain ordered by the Soviet Union in excess of that amount which we are committed to sell will not be delivered. This grain was not intended for human consumption but was to be used for building up Soviet livestock herds. …

These actions will require some sacrifice on the part of all Americans, but there is absolutely no doubt that these actions are in the interest of world peace and in the interest of the security of our own Nation, and they are also compatible with actions being taken by our own major trading partners and others who share our deep concern about this new Soviet threat to world stability.

Although the United States would prefer not to withdraw from the Olympic games scheduled in Moscow this summer, the Soviet Union must realize that its continued aggressive actions will endanger both the participation of athletes and the travel to Moscow by spectators who would normally wish to attend the Olympic games.

Along with other countries, we will provide military equipment, food, and other assistance to help Pakistan defend its independence and its national security against the seriously increased threat it now faces from the north. The United States also stands ready to help other nations in the region in similar ways. …

The response of the international community to the Soviet attempt to crush Afghanistan must match the gravity of the Soviet action.

With the support of the American people and working with other nations, we will deter aggression, we will protect our Nation's security, and we will preserve the peace. The United States will meet its responsibilities.

Source: President Jimmy Carter, "Soviet Invasion of Afghanistan: Address to the Nation." Primary Documents at www.techtrain.org.

Source E

Extract from a scholarly journal that includes analyses of actions taken by military forces throughout the world. In this case, an officer in the US army is analyzing Soviet mistakes in their war against Afghanistan.

The Soviet leadership completely miscalculated the political and military situation in Afghanistan. They were unable to anticipate the anti-Soviet reaction that was generated in the United States and around the world. They failed to understand their enemy and the power Islamic Nationalism had on the will of the Afghani people to endure extreme hardships. They were unable or unwilling to prevent the Mujahideen from operating from sanctuaries in Pakistan.

Source: McGhee, Major James T. 14 June 2008. "The Soviet Experience in Afghanistan: Lessons Learned" in *Military History Online*. http://www.militaryhistoryonline.com/20thcentury/articles/sovietexperience.aspx.

Source F

Photograph showing Soviet forces leaving Afghanistan in 1989.

Source: *Timeline: Afghanistan.* http://news.bbc.co.uk/2/hi/south_asia/1162108.stm; accessed 5 December 2008.

Source-based questions

1 What is the message in Source F?

2 Is President Carter's statement of American actions in Source D consistent with the US policy of containment? Support your answer using your own knowledge.

3 How far do Sources B and C support the policy expressed in Source A?

4 With reference to origins and purpose, assess the value and limitations of Sources B and E.

5 Using these sources and your own knowledge, explain why and with what results the USSR became involved in Afghanistan.

TOK link

The USSR launched an invasion that led to a ten-year intervention in Afghanistan. The war was very unpopular, even though knowledge of casualties was limited in the Brezhnev era.

 How did the Soviet citizens know the war wasn't going well?

Gorbachev and his aims and policies

As the leader of the Soviet Union, Mikhail Gorbachev was hoping to revitalize the Communist Party and maintain a socialist system of governance through economic reform and political openness designed to modernize the state and mollify (satisfy) the population. Unfortunately for Gorbachev, his reforms were a Pandora's box for communism, and once these dual policies were implemented, the drive for democracy could not be contained, leading to the collapse of the regime.

When Mikhail Gorbachev came to power in 1985, he was the third successor in less than three years. The first four leaders of the USSR governed for over 60 years collectively; the final three would be in power for less than a decade. The Soviet state had been stagnant for too long and there was rising dissent. Gorbachev, himself a member of the Soviet nomenklatura, recognized that it was time for much needed reforms to try and bring the USSR back to a level competitive with the West and an emerging China.

Marking a trend in the new Soviet leadership, Gorbachev was relatively young and began his career outside of Moscow. Somewhat unusual for the time and place, he was trained as a lawyer and then was elected a Party member. He became a regional Party official in Stavropol (Caucasus) and in 1978 he was elected to the Central Committee and became the secretary responsible for agriculture. In 1980 Brezhnev made him a full politburo member at the age of 49, in an organization where the average age was over 70.

Gorbachev attracted the attention and support of Andropov, who had also felt the need for changes in Soviet society but knew that they would not be put into place during his tenure. Following Chernenko's death, Soviet Foreign Minister Andre Gromyko nominated Gorbachev for the position of General Secretary, and he was duly elected by the politburo, whose membership was in a period of transition.

Domestic policies—glasnost, perestroika and *demokratiztsiya*

Gorbachev had a different leadership style from his predecessors and it was under him that the USSR saw a wave of reforms that are often collectively referred to as perestroika, glasnost and *demokratiztsiya*. Although he faced ethnic unrest and political opposition, the main problem in Soviet society still seemed to be the economy and Gorbachev felt that there needed to be a full reorganization. This was not quite as new an idea as people generally thought; ideas for economic restructuring had been proposed as early as the 1960s but blocked by Party hardliners who feared any change away from central planning would mean a movement towards capitalism. When reviewing Gorbachev's policies it must be remembered that he was a

"I am a Communist, a convinced Communist! For some that may be a fantasy. But to me it is my main goal."

Mikhail Gorbachev

true Communist. Gorbachev was not a democrat or capitalist who wanted to end communism in the Soviet Union; he was seeking to repair an ailing system.

The first major reform of the Gorbachev era targeted alcohol. Like Andropov, Gorbachev was trying to target individual productivity and absenteeism, in addition to the tremendous social problem of alcoholism. With all this in mind, prices were raised on wine, beer and vodka, and the places and times for selling alcohol were restricted. There were arrests for public drunkenness and for being intoxicated at work. One clearly stated goal was to decrease vodka production by ten per cent in five years. This was achieved by 1986. In the end it did not have the desired effect and in fact cost the Soviet state almost 100 billion rubles in lost taxes lost due to a drop in official consumption. Many official vineyards and distilleries were forced to close. Unofficially, of course, alcohol remained readily available through the black market.

For a number of reasons, 1986 proved to be a watershed year in the Soviet Union. First, the policy of perestroika (economic restructuring) was announced. The government decided that it was time to decentralize planning and end price controls by the state. Many were very nervous about these changes on an ideological level as they seemed to put the Soviet state on the road to capitalism. More pragmatically, the removal of price controls would lead to an increase in prices. Soviet citizens benefited from a system that allowed them to purchase most goods at below the cost of production due to government subsidies. This was extremely costly to the Soviet state, since it was also subsidizing products that it supplied to other countries in its sphere of influence. Additionally, the state wanted to allow some degree of self-management but without losing ownership of the factories and other business enterprises.

In April the weaknesses of the system were further highlighted by the explosion of the nuclear facility in Chernobyl, Ukraine.

In December 1986, Gorbachev announced that the dissident Andrei Sakharov was to be released from his exile in Gorky. Sakharov, a physicist who became the most open opponent of the Soviet government, began to travel at home and abroad, presenting information on the repression of USSR citizens and explaining the conditions in Gulags. He did this until his death, and though his was the public face for Soviet dissent abroad, his appeal within the USSR was limited. Nonetheless, Sakharov's notoriety led to further stands against the government, and open criticism of the past.

The official recognition and acceptance of this came in 1988 when Gorbachev announced glasnost. This policy, translated as openness, led to a re-examination of Soviet history and an open debate on past government actions such as forced collectivization and Party purges. Former enemies of the state, especially those purged and executed by Stalin, were rehabilitated. Gorbachev's government was free to do this as most of the participants—and supporters—of such Stalinist policies were now dead, and the criticisms would not cause serious divisions within the CPSU.

The Chernobyl disaster

The Chernobyl nuclear plant, which had been opened in 1978 and had six reactors, was considered a model facility in the USSR. On April 26, a test on one of the reactors' cooling systems began at 1 a.m. Almost immediately, the emergency shutdown failed and the reactor exploded. Firefighters responded to the explosion, unaware that it had released toxic levels of radiation into the air. Although the inhabitants of the nearby town of Pripyat were aware of the fire, they had no idea of the danger it posed and continued about their daily activities. The Soviet government did not issue any warnings or notify the public of the disaster, although on 27 April Pripyat was evacuated.

It was only when Sweden made it known to the world community that high levels of radiation had reached its borders and pinpointed its source as the Ukraine that the Soviet government made the accident public knowledge. The Soviet news agency TASS reported that there had been an accident at the Chernobyl nuclear facility and that an investigation would be forthcoming. It was announced that there were casualties, but the numbers were not made public. Further evacuations were also announced, expanding the evacuation area to a 30-kilometer zone around the reactor.

The reactor continued to burn until 4 May and, in the meantime, helicopters dropped approximately 5000 tons of materials on the fire in an attempt to extinguish it. It was thought that the reactor had ceased emitting radiation on 6 May, but evidently the reactor had not been fully extinguished and new fires began on 15 and 16 May.

The investigation reported that the disaster was a result of human error and equipment failure. There were a number of inexperienced workers on staff that weekend and there was inattention to safety procedures. Additionally, the Soviet attitude of downplaying disasters for fear of repercussion certainly exacerbated the situation and slowed the rate of evacuation from the affected areas. The Soviet government refused assistance that was offered from foreign sources, perhaps in an attempt to avoid further international criticism.

In the official report, the death toll from the disaster never went above 31. The plant operators were found responsible for the explosion and were sentenced to hard labor. The reality was somewhat different and can be seen in Ukrainian attitudes and statements regarding the accident after the collapse of the USSR. The ability to keep information within the Soviet state was not possible in the face of an international incident and, with changing Soviet policies, criticism came from its citizenry, not just from the international community.

This led to a further questioning of socialist economic policies, and especially a criticism of central planning. In rejecting and criticizing forced collectivization, the government paved the way for agricultural reform and, eventually, wider economic changes. The Gorbachev era saw an end to collectivization and a transition to privatization, whereby farmers were granted long-term leases in an attempt to improve productivity. In a nod to Lenin's NEP, the state still remained the owner of the land, but farmers paid for their leases and were taxed on their product. It did not take much for nascent entrepreneurs to begin to make similar demands for change in the production of industrial and consumer goods.

Foreign policies

The costliness of Soviet subsidies to its satellite states (see above) in itself forced a re-examination of the role of the USSR in foreign affairs. Brezhnev had made relations with the satellite states in Eastern Europe a priority. Throughout the 1980s, Gorbachev sought to distance the USSR from these countries. In a series of speeches beginning in 1987 he encouraged the states to follow their own paths and be less reliant on the USSR. He made it very clear that the USSR would engage in a policy of non-intervention in the Warsaw Pact countries, a complete negation of the Brezhnev Doctrine. Henceforth, satellite states would pursue their own paths to achieving socialism and Gorbachev encouraged reform abroad.

Reactor 4 of the Chernobyl nuclear power plant, after the explosion on 26 April 1986.

The Soviets gained further credibility in their negation of the Brezhnev Doctrine with the decision to withdraw from Afghanistan. The war had been extremely costly, in terms of lives lost and public opinion, in addition to government coffers. At the height of their intervention, the Soviets had over 100 000 troops stationed in Afghanistan with no clear objective. The Soviets determined that it was necessary to withdraw; intervention was costly, made the USSR unpopular internationally and was extremely unpopular at home. Thus, as early as 1986, symbolic withdrawals began and, in a 1988 agreement in Geneva, the Soviets agreed to full withdrawal; by February 1989, all Soviet forces had left Afghanistan.

The United States certainly noticed this change in Soviet attitudes and this led to a series of meetings between Gorbachev and US president Ronald Reagan. These summits, notably in Geneva and Reykjavik, signaled an improvement in relations between the USA and the USSR, a remarkable reversal after the strain in their relations that had characterized the Brezhnev era. Reagan had tentatively resumed arms talks with the USSR in 1982 but these were abandoned until the Soviet leadership stabilized. With Gorbachev firmly in power, the talks on arms reductions began anew, with US determination to continue nuclear testing and to construct a defence shield (Strategic Defense Initiative or SDI) angering the Soviet leadership. After the Chernobyl disaster, limiting nuclear arms testing and development was a priority for the Soviet regime. The Reykjavik summit, held in October 1986, was seen as a failure, particularly in the USA, since it led to no agreement or framework for an agreement, yet the leaders began to develop a rapport and seemed willing and able to work together.

In December 1987, Gorbachev went to Washington and the result was the Intermediate-range Nuclear Forces (INF) treaty, which eliminated intermediate-range nuclear weapons in Europe. The summit meetings culminated in Reagan's visit to Moscow, where the leaders began the discussions for a new Strategic Arms Limitations Treaty (START) that would be finalized in 1991. With this treaty, both sides agreed to reduce their stockpile of nuclear arms—the Soviet Union by 25 per cent and the United States by 15 per cent.

When Gorbachev began his tenure as leader of the USSR, he was received enthusiastically at home and with cautious trepidation abroad. By the end of 1988 (and the end of the Reagan era in the USA), the situation was reversed. The Soviet economy was tanking and the Chernobyl accident highlighted all that was wrong in the authoritarian system, yet the decisions to free political dissidents, withdraw from Afghanistan and engage in arms limitations discussions created a paradoxical situation in which Gorbachev had become more popular in the United States than he was at home; an uncomfortable position that he would remain in until the collapse of the Soviet state in 1991.

"I believe, as Lenin said, that this revolutionary chaos may yet crystallize into new forms of life."
Mikhail Gorbachev

Activity:
Oral quiz in teams

Items needed: stopwatch or clock with second hand; a point-scoring system; any support materials that your teacher allows you to bring

The class is divided into four teams, who will score points for their answers to set questions relating to the situation in the Soviet Union after Gorbachev came to power. Each person on the team is the official spokesperson for one to three questions. In this way, information—and presentation—is shared. Teams are only given rough topics to start. These include:

1 Chain of command   2 Alcoholism
3 Glasnost   4 Perestroika
5 Afghanistan

Students/teams are given a question that correlates to one of the topics and have to answer on the spot. Each team has one minute to respond. The teams should answer in a different order each time so that it is not always the same team that answers first.

Questions:

1 Gorbachev became the third leader of the USSR in less than three years. Did the Soviet citizenry expect vast changes on his appointment?

2 Gorbachev's first major reform was limiting alcohol consumption for a number of socio-economic reasons. Did the alcohol reforms achieve what Gorbachev hoped they would?

3 Glasnost aimed to increase openness, especially with regard to public inquiries into Party affairs to limit or curtail the corruption of the entrenched nomenklatura? Did it succeed?

4 Perestroika was a policy of economic restructuring in order to allow the socialist system in the USSR to continue. Was perestroika a socialist policy?

5 Gorbachev's foreign policy marked a decided change from that of the previous regimes in that he was trying to limit Soviet intervention overseas. To what extent was the Soviet withdrawal from Afghanistan consistent with previous Soviet actions and policies?

As students answer the questions, they are awarded points by the moderator. The moderator can be a teacher or a student, and the awarding of points may very well seem arbitrary, but this is part of the exercise. The moderator can also deduct points for factual inaccuracies or generally annoying behavior (such as spouting off in Russian to a class full of people who do not understand the language).

After these questions are answered, two teams are eliminated and the two with the most points remaining go head-to-head on a final question. They are given two minutes to prepare and have up to 90 seconds to respond. Eliminated classmates get to be the judge of the most successful presentation.

Head-to-head question

Did Gorbachev's policies hasten or slow the demise of the Soviet Union?

TOK link

Psychology

The Chernobyl nuclear reactor explosion, 1986

The Chernobyl nuclear accident has had a profound impact on populations within the former USSR and in countries as far away as Sweden. The death toll continues to mount, as more people exposed to the radiation have developed cancer, with a high incidence of cancer in children born after the disaster. People who may (or may not) have been exposed to harmful levels of radiation live in fear of developing some sort of disease or genetic disorder as a result.

How much was the mismanagement of the Chernobyl nuclear disaster responsible for discrediting the Soviet regime, leading to its impending collapse in 1991?

Make an assessment of the long-term psychological impact on people living in the affected region, of exposure to nuclear contamination. What choices must be made by those who are physically healthy—or not?

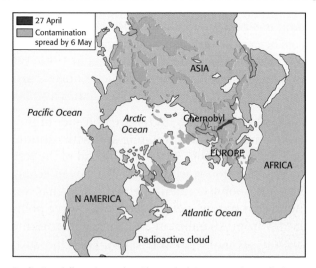

Radiation fallout from the Chernobyl Reactor. The radiation fallout exposed Eastern and Northern Europeans in particular to a high rate of exposure over a period of several weeks. The cloud can also be tracked across the northern latitudes, spreading much critical uncertainty about the long-term consequences for both human and animal populations and the environment.

Source analysis

The following documents relate to Gorbachev's reforms.

Source A

Extract from a speech that Mikhail Gorbachev delivered at Kansas State University in 2005 on the 20th anniversary of perestroika.

> For the USSR Perestroika meant overcoming totalitarianism and moving toward democracy, toward freedom. But this did not happen overnight. As we were moving forward, as we were taking steps in domestic policy, we saw increasing resistance, particularly among bureaucracy, the party bureaucracy, the state bureaucracy and the military bureaucracy. And among some people too, among part of our society Perestroika was seen as some kind of gift from heavens that something—that things will change for the better overnight. We were saying that change is something that everyone needs to do. All of us, from an ordinary worker to the general secretary of the Communist Party, needed to change. We had initial illusions, the illusion of being able to improve the old system, that we could give second wind to the old system without really changing it. But that failed and, therefore, toward the end of 1986 we began to contemplate political reforms. That was the first step along the path of reforming, replacing the system. We proposed a step-by-step approach to reforming Soviet society, moving gradually toward freedom and democracy and market economics. This ideology, this philosophy of Perestroika would result in bringing together the interests of individuals on the one hand and of the whole of society on the other hand. The most important thing, of course, was to place the individual, the human being at the center of this change.

Source: http://www.gfna.net/NEWSMSGinUSKSspeech.pdf

Source B

The cartoonist Edmun S Valtmann (1914–2005) was an Estonian-born American who lived through both the German and Soviet invasions of Estonia in 1940 and 1944 before emigrating to the USA in 1949. In the cartoon, Gorbachev leads a funeral procession burying Communism, as Lenin, Stalin and Marx look down from Communist Paradise.

'I CAN'T BELIEVE MY EYES!'

Source C

Cartoon by David Horsey, an American cartoonist, speculating on life in Russia after the socialist reforms of Gorbachev. The cartoon was published in 1996.

Source-based questions

1 With reference to their origins and purpose, assess the values and limitations of Sources A and B for historians studying the impact of Gorbachev's reforms.

2 What is the message intended in Source C?

The consequences of Gorbachev's policies for Eastern Europe

This section explores the impact of Gorbachev's reforms on the USSR's satellite states in Eastern Europe. Once Gorbachev announced that he would no longer pursue the objectives articulated in the Brezhnev Doctrine, countries began to challenge the dominance of the Communist Parties that had dominated Eastern Europe since the end of the Second World War. Gorbachev was unwilling to send troops in to preserve communist regimes and, by the end of 1989, multiparty states had replaced the single-party regime that the communists had enjoyed since 1945.

When reviewing the events of 1989 it often seems as if there were an overnight awareness of repression leading to a quick, spontaneous revolution across Eastern Europe, but this was not the case. The "revolutions of 1989", as they are collectively called, were the result of a long period of struggle against the domination of the Soviet Union and the Communist Parties in each individual country. The Eastern bloc was seen as critical to Soviet security, and indeed the Brezhnev Doctrine of 1968 was issued to justify action in Czechoslovakia and prevent its withdrawal from the Warsaw Pact.

The Brezhnev Doctrine endured well into the 1980s but when Gorbachev came to power in 1985, change was clearly afoot in Eastern Europe. Gorbachev was facing the same problems as his neighbors to the east—economic instability, lack of consumer goods —and was looking for ways to divest the Soviet Union of its responsibilities to other communist countries, which had cost the Soviets so much money over the years and resulted in the USSR becoming a debtor nation.

Gorbachev's promised reforms and his rejection of the Brezhnev Doctrine were not welcome news to the Party leaders in Eastern Europe. Although intervention from Moscow was always a concern, it also provided comfort, knowing that their regimes had the moral and military support of the USSR and other Warsaw Pact countries. The changes brought by Gorbachev threatened the stability of **apparatchiks** in Soviet satellite states in Eastern Europe. Whereas Brezhnev had seen Eastern Europe as critical to Soviet foreign policy, Gorbachev now sought to release the USSR from its role of patron.

Apparatchik A loyal and devoted member of the Communist Party establishment in a country where it is the only legal party; usually someone employed by the Party apparatus and thus entrenched in the system.

Seeing Soviet withdrawal from the internal affairs of Warsaw Pact countries as an invitation to act, dissenters in the Eastern bloc spoke out once again, and organized themselves. Witnessing Gorbachev's rehabilitation of dissidents and encouragement of glasnost, opposition in Eastern Europe grew. In some countries (such as Czechoslovakia), there had been an almost constant struggle against the communist regime; in others there was a radical change in a very short period. But 1989 signalled the end of communism in Eastern Europe: the collapse of the Stalinist regime in Romania was brutal for its totalitarian leaders, ending with the execution of Nicolae and Elena

Ceauşescu, but the other revolutions were notable for their opposition's passive resistance and the unwillingness of Communist Party leadership and the secret police to use the traditional techniques of terror and intimidation techniques. Unlike the Chinese communists in May 1989, the Eastern European communists surrendered to popular revolt, paving the way for integration with the rest of Europe.

Change had already begun in the Soviet satellites—the dominance of the Communist Party in Poland was called into question after the rise of the Solidarity movement, and in Czechoslovakia intellectuals had been in open defiance of the Soviets in their country.

Poland in the Gorbachev era

In 1985, Polish opposition was further encouraged when Gorbachev came to power in the USSR. Urged on by perestroika and glasnost, **Solidarity** reconstituted itself in October 1987, despite continued harassment by the government. Gorbachev had renounced the Brezhnev Doctrine, and the opposition was fairly certain that they would not face retribution (punishment) from the Soviet Union, even though they did face it from the Polish government. It is very telling (significant) that the situation in Poland was dictated by the Poles themselves, not by the Soviet Union or even by fear of Soviet reprisals in Poland. Nor was there fear of action coming from other Warsaw Pact countries. By the July 1989 elections, Poland was out of the grip of communism, even though it remained a member of the Warsaw Pact until its formal dissolution.

Poland's successful transition to democracy was soon mirrored by other satellite states in Europe. By the end of 1989, only Albania would remain as a communist country. (It is perhaps unrealistic even to refer to Albania as a satellite state. The regime of Enver Hoxha had been Stalinist, and after his death Albanians did not agree with many Soviet policies. The country then formed a tight alliance with China. Nonetheless, Albania was the one remaining communist country in Eastern Europe after 1989.)

East Germany's revolution and the fall of the Berlin Wall

The German revolution was the most televised and best known of the revolutions of 1989, due largely to the photo opportunities it provided. This revolution achieved with such apparent simplicity became a source of popular inspiration that went far beyond its borders: the masses brought about spontaneous change through their actions. This was not a revolt of the elites or simply a student movement that spread, but rather a change that the masses brought about through their actions.

The German Democratic Republic (GDR) was a paradox among the satellite states. On the one hand, it had a reputation for being the most loyal of all the satellite states, its leaders were communist hardliners and its secret police, the Stasi, were the most feared of all the Eastern European political police. The GDR received benefits

Solidarity The labor union founded at the Lenin Shipyard in Gdańsk in September 1980 in response to the economic crises facing Poland at that time. The leader of the union was Lech Wałęsa, an electrician who later became the president of Poland.

"As a nation we have the right to decide our own affairs, to mould our own future. This does not pose any danger to anybody. Our nation is fully aware of the responsibility for its own fate in the complicated situation of the contemporary world."

Lech Wałęsa

from the Federal Republic of Germany (FRG) through Willy Brandt's policy of *Ostpolitik*, which was meant to build a bridge between the democratic, capitalist West and its communist counterpart. While Berlin remained a sticking point for the East Germans, they received benefits from the city's location as Moscow saw it as a place to showcase communism to the outside world. In 1984, the two German states reached agreements for cultural exchange and the removal of mines on their borders, signalling an accord, or at least a commitment to the status quo for both states, rather than aggressive policies of containment.

This policy actually began during the Brezhnev era with the Helsinki Final Acts; in recognizing the post-war frontiers of Europe, the political decision to have two German states was not only acknowledged by the 33 signatories, it was legitimized. Thus, it seemed in 1998 that the GDR was an accepted, entrenched regime and no one foresaw the changes that would take place in the coming year; indeed East German leader Erich Honecker ignored the calls for reform embedded in perestroika and the dissent at home and in other Eastern European states. At 77, Honecker was the last of the communist leaders who had come of age at the same time as Brezhnev, Andropov and Chernenko. He remained firmly loyal to the Communist Party and was determined to keep the GDR a single-party state.

Events in the GDR, as was the case in Czechoslovakia, were precipitated by events outside of its own state. In Hungary, there had been tremendous pressure on the government to relax controls and, in particular, to stop limiting the travel of its citizenry, especially within the Warsaw Pact countries Thus, on 2 May 1989, the Hungarian government removed the fence on its border with the GDR and, while travel between the two countries remained legally unchanged, in practice, anyone dissatisfied with life in either country could cross the border. By September 1989 it is estimated that 60 000 East Germans had left for Hungary, making their way to Budapest (and others to Prague), seeking asylum in the West German embassies there. Budapest was suffering under the weight of all of these refugees; when the Hungarian foreign minister announced that East Germans would not be stopped if they sought to travel west to Austria, 22 000 East Germans crossed to the West.

The GDR was embarrassed by this action and tried to make some repairs to prevent the continued exodus. Responding to the actions of the Hungarian and Czechoslovak governments, the GDR promised East Germans safe passage to the FRG in a sealed train if they returned to the GDR. This served only to further exacerbate the situation; when one such train made a stop in Dresden, a number of locals tried to board and were beaten by the police.

In October, full-fledged dissent was in the streets of the GDR. Encouraged by the actions of opposition groups in other Eastern European countries, East Germans protested the lack of reforms in the Honecker government and the repressive regime that he embodied. Unlike his counterparts in the other countries, Honecker held firm and refused to grant any changes. He was even unmoved by Gorbachev's exhortations to reform when the Soviet leader came to Berlin to participate in the fortieth anniversary of the founding of the GDR. Gorbachev famously advised Honecker that "Life punishes those who wait too long." Honecker would not even allow the distribution of Soviet publications that he saw as too liberal and reformist; he had been more sympathetic to Deng Xiaoping and his treatment of dissenters at Tiananmen Square the previous May.

At this point, other members of the Party leadership felt that they needed to make changes or face revolution. The number of demonstrators agitating for change increased dramatically throughout October, nearing 100 000 in cities such as Leipzig. With such startling opposition to the regime, the politburo forced Honecker's resignation and fellow member Egon Krenz became the General Secretary of the Party and chairman of the Council of State on October 18. Krenz immediately announced that the GDR was going to implement democratic reforms and endorsed Gorbachev's ideas. Even so, demonstrations continued; on 4 November alone an estimated 300 000 congregated in Leipzig and 500 000 in Berlin, demanding immediate change. On that same day, Czechoslovakia opened its border and 30 000 East Germans left.

In response to the continued flow of its citizenry, the government proposed relaxing travel laws on 5 November but, rather than mollifying the population, it was criticized as too little, too late. The East Germans were making it abundantly clear to the government that change was not happening fast enough. The entire politburo resigned, leaving Krenz and his colleagues in government to respond to the population. On 9 November another travel law was proposed; a news conference was broadcast live on television announcing the authorization of foreign travel without advance notice and free transit through border crossings into West Germany. With this action, the Berlin Wall became an anachronism as East Germans poured into the streets, headed to Berlin and crossed into the West.

The GDR leadership had been hoping that this reform would increase its credibility and popularity as a People's Republic, but instead it hastened its demise. On 1 December, facing increased calls for further reforms, the government changed the constitution, eliminating the clause that gave the Communist Party a dominant role in the government. Two days later, Krenz and the Central Committee resigned. A coalition government was put in place but it became clear very quickly that this was a provisional government at best. Most Germans wanted the reunification of the country, and negotiations to that effect began almost immediately.

The revolution in the GDR was perhaps the most dramatic of the revolutions of 1989. Not only did communism collapse in East Germany but the map of Europe was redrawn as a result of the revolution. After 41 years as a separate state, the GDR ceased to exist and was incorporated into the FRG on 3 October 1990.

Czechoslovakia

In Czechoslovakia, the rise of Gorbachev and the resignation of the aging Gustáv Husák as General Secretary in 1987 opened up the country to further discussion and open opposition to the regime. Communists maintained control until the collapse at the very end of 1989, even going so far as to arrest demonstrators in Prague who came to commemorate the 20th anniversary of the Soviet invasion of Czechoslovakia. Soviet troops remained in the country, but Gorbachev made it abundantly clear that the USSR would pursue a policy of non-intervention in Warsaw Pact countries.

The entire year of 1989 was one of transformation for Czechoslovakia, as it made a peaceful transition from authoritarianism to democracy—a transition known as the Velvet Revolution (see also chapter 9). The announcement and the collapse of the Berlin Wall were further encouragement to students to speak out. As quickly as elsewhere, the Czechoslovak government lost its grip on power as the Soviets witnessed the dissolution of yet another Communist Party in Eastern Europe. The suggestion of a coalition government, that had been the impetus for intervention in Hungary in 1956 and in Czechoslovakia in 1968, was no longer seen as a critical issue. When elections were held, Gorbachev and his confederates watched with the rest of the world. On 28 December, Václav Havel was elected president and the political change was complete. A year that had begun with demonstrations and arrests of the opposition ended with the re-emergence of democratic, multi-party states in Central Europe.

"In everyone there is some longing for humanity's rightful dignity, for moral integrity, for free expression of being and a sense of transcendence over the world of existence."
Václav Havel

The revolutions of 1989 considered

In an attempt to correct the primarily economic problems of communism, reform had been the desire of Gorbachev and his colleagues in Eastern Europe; the result, instead, was revolution and the end of communism in Europe. There are a number of theories as to why these revolutionary attempts were successful when previous ones were not. Some will argue that this is a "domino theory" of sorts. When one country successful rejected communism, given the strictures of the regimes and their interrelatedness through the Warsaw Pact, it became inevitable that the other states would follow suit. For example, the removal of electric fences along the Hungarian border would have an impact on the neighboring countries. Another argument is the role of the international media; given the changes in communication, the totalitarian regimes were no longer able to staunch the flow of information, allowing people throughout Eastern Europe to see what was happening and, perhaps more importantly, to see the reactions of other peoples and governments.

Also of paramount importance, is the role of Gorbachev. His decision to reject the Brezhnev Doctrine for the impertinently named **"Sinatra Doctrine"** (that is, allowing the satellite states to "do it my way") showed individual populations that they no longer had to fear the influx of troops from Moscow or other Warsaw Pact countries if they rose up against their governments. Even in Czechoslovakia, where Soviet troops remained until 1990, the citizenry seemed not to fear external intervention.

Sinatra Doctrine The name given to Gorbachev's decision to allow Warsaw Pact countries to determine their own national affairs.

It was also a time for change, be it within the communist parties themselves or an entire regime change. The leadership of the communist parties was aging and dying; all the leaders of the satellite states were in their 70s. The new leaders—even within the communist party—came from younger generations who did not share the horrors of the Second World War but focused on their memories of repression by the Warsaw Pact governments. In addition, the students in all of these countries did not want to reform socialism, they wanted to overcome it. They saw the benefits of capitalism and democracy on their television sets and wanted similar advantages.

In all their actions the protestors consistently refused to engage in the use of force to bring about change. These were not violent revolutionaries, they were people who had learned the lessons of civil disobedience from Mahatma Gandhi and the Indian independence movement as well as the American civil rights movement. In their rejection of violence to oppose the regime, they exposed the secret police and government and party cadres as reliant on the use force to impose their will upon the people. Many people participated in the demonstrations of 1989 because they were willing to engage in passive resistance against governments they no longer had confidence in.

In 1985, Gorbachev came to power as a reforming communist, but it seemed fairly clear that he was determined to keep the socialist sphere intact. No one was aware that his calls for change within the Soviet Union, designed largely to reinvigorate a failing economy and make the USSR competitive with the West, would lead to the end of communism in Europe. Unlike the party leadership in China, the Europeans were either unable or unwilling to engage in economic reform while continuing as socialist states. Deng did not hesitate to use force against protestors; elsewhere this was not the case. In the end, China made economic reforms that allowed for material prosperity yet the regime continued; in Eastern Europe, economic reforms made the situation worse and communism ceased altogether.

Activity:

Short written response

In 1961 the GDR erected the Berlin Wall in the hope of stemming the flow of migrants who moved freely from east to west. Until November 1989, the Communists monitored the no man's land between East and West Berlin to prevent people from escaping to West Germany. This often led to families being split up as some individuals managed to leave. Imagine that you were one of the people who chose to go west.

Write a letter to your parents, inviting them to come and visit you now that there is freedom of travel. What will they see that they could not in East Germany? What did you miss about living in the East? How would your life be different? What would you want your parents to see?

TOK link

Discussion

Popular political change rarely comes from repression; it tends to come from economic distress and hardship that makes the population so uncomfortable that they are willing to take risks.

Source analysis

Below are five sources relating to the reform movements in Eastern Europe in the 1980s.

Source A

Extract from Václav Havel's 1978 essay, "The Power of the Powerless".

A SPECTER is haunting Eastern Europe: the specter of what in the West is called "dissent" This specter has not appeared out of thin air. … What is more, the system has become so ossified politically that there is practically no way for such nonconformity to be implemented within its official structures. …

Individuals need not believe all these mystifications, but they must behave as though they did, or they must at least tolerate them in silence, or get along well with those who work with them. For this reason, however, they must live within a lie. They need not accept the lie. It is enough for them to have accepted their life with it and in it. For by this very fact, individuals confirm the system, fulfill the system, make the system, are the system.

… if living within the truth is an elementary starting point for every attempt made by people to oppose the alienating pressure of the system … then it is difficult to imagine that even manifest "dissent" could have any other basis than the service of truth, the truthful life, and the attempt to make room for the genuine aims of life.

Source B

Extract from the list of 21 demands presented by the Inter-Factory Strike Committee to the Polish government in August 1980.

The Tasks of the Factories and Institutions on Strike, Represented by the Inter-Factory Strike Committee at the Gdánsk Shipyard

1. Acceptance of free trade unions independent of the Communist Party and of enterprises, in accordance with convention No. 87 of the International Labor Organization concerning the right to form free trade unions, which was ratified by the Communist Government of Poland.

2. A guarantee of the right to strike and of the security of strikers and those aiding them.

3. Compliance with the constitutional guarantee of freedom of speech, the press and publication, including freedom for independent publishers, and the availability of the mass media to representatives of all faiths.

5. Availability to the mass media of information about the formation of the Inter-factory Strike Committee and publication of its demands.

12. The selection of management personnel on the basis of qualifications, not party membership. Privileges of the secret police, regular police and party apparatus are to be eliminated by equalizing family subsidies, abolishing special stores, etc.

Source: *A force more powerful.* Website accompanying a documentary series. http://www.aforcemorepowerful.org/films/afmp/stories/poland.php#demands.

Source C

Excerpt of the minutes from the East German politburo concerning an easing of travel restrictions to West Germany.

Information by Comrade O. Fischer on the situation regarding GDR citizens departing via the −SSR.

Report compiled by:
O. Fischer

1. Comrade O. Fischer will make a suggestion, in agreement with Comrades F. Dickel and E. Mielke, for the SED Central Committee which allows for this part of the travel law that deals with permanent exit to be put into effect immediately through an executive order [Durchführungsbestimmung].

2. Comrade O. Fischer will inform the USSR's Ambassador to the GDR Extraordinary and Plenipotentiary, Comrade V[yacheslav I.] Kochemassov, and the Czechoslovaks about the proposal and the politburo's position. At the same time, consultations with the FRG are to be carried out.

3. The mass media should use their influence to help that GDR citizens do not leave their country. They should inform about people who have returned. Responsible: Comrade G. Schabowski.

4. Comrade G. Schabowski is assigned to discuss this problem with the representatives of the bloc parties [Christian Democrats, Liberal Democrats] in order to reach a joint position.

Source: SAPMO-BA, DY 30/J IV 2/2/2358. Translated for CWIHP by Howard Sargeant.

Source D

The fall of the Berlin Wall, 9 November 1989.

Source E

Extract from *Between Timisoara and Tirgu Mures* by Krzysztof Czyzewski from the Local Government and Public Service Reform Initiative website for transition countries of Eastern Europe and the former USSR.

In the time of the memorable autumn of nations in 1989 in a certain city in Banat that is called Timisoara by some people, and Temesvar by others, Romanians and Hungarians arm in arm stood up in protest against the regime of Ceausescu, which was the starting point of the upheaval in Romania. Nobody even mentioned ethnic minorities at that time. They talked about a democratic opposition, about the townspeople, about the citizens of Romania.

Source: http://lgi.osi.hu/ethnic/relations/1/czyewski.html.

Source-based questions

1 **a** Why are the revolutions of 1989 sometimes called "the autumn of nations" (Source E)?

   b What does Source C reveal about illegal migration from East Germany (GDR) in 1989?

2 With reference to their origins and purpose, assess the value and limitations of Sources C and E for historians studying the reform movements and revolutions of 1989.

3 Using these sources and your own knowledge, assess the accuracy of Havel's assertion that "the system has become so ossified politically that there is practically no way for such nonconformity to be implemented within its official structures"(Source A).

Exam practice

Source analysis

The following sources refer to the importance of Deng Xiaoping's Four Modernizations for agriculture.

Source A

Extract from *The People's Republic of China since 1949*, by Michael Lynch, London, 1998.

The Third Plenum of the 11th Central committee of the Chinese Communist Party, which met in December 1978, confirmed Deng's leadership of China. ... Its resolution on economic planning was essentially an acceptance of Deng's "four modernisations" programme.

This advocated rapid development of the national economy and the steady improvement of living standards of the people if the whole country which depended on the rigorous restoration and increase of farm production, and fully implementing the simultaneous development of farming, animal husbandry, forestry and fisheries. Also grain was to be the key product, and the policy of adapting to local conditions, with the appropriate concentration of certain crops in certain areas and the gradual modernisation of farm work introduced.

Source B

Extract from a conversation between Deng Xiaoping, leader of the PRC, and Paul TK Lin, director of the Institute of East Asia at McGill University of Canada.

Deng Xiaoping: What we want is socialism in which the productive forces are developed and the country is prosperous and powerful. We believe that socialism is superior to capitalism. This superiority should be demonstrated in that socialism provides more favouruable conditions for expanding the productive forces than capitalism does. ...

What is the most significant political task for China? It is the achievement of the four modernizations. During the drive for modernization we are bound to solve complicated problems and encounter difficulties.

Source: Deng Xiaoping. 26 November 1979. *We can develop a market economy under socialism.* http://english.people.com.cn/dengxp/vol2/text/b1370.html.

Source C

Extract from a report for the World Bank, written by Martin Ravallion and Shaohua Chen.

Consider the specific situation in China at the time reforms began: the Great Leap Forward and the Cultural Revolution had left a legacy of severe, pervasive rural poverty by the late 1970s. Arguably, there were some important but relatively easy gains to be had by simply undoing failed policies, notably by de-collectivizing agriculture. Much of the rural population that had been forced into collective farming with weak incentives for work could still remember how to farm individually. Returning the responsibility for farming to individual households brought huge gains to the country's poorest.

Source: *Fighting Poverty: Findings and Lessons from China's Success.* The World Bank. http://econ.worldbank.org.

Source D

Extract from *The Penguin History of Modern China*, by Joanthan Fenby, London, 2008.

To boost the rural revolution, state expenditure allocated to farming was increased to make it double the tax from the countryside. The concentration of rice and wheat was reduced where other crops were more suitable, including those that earned more cash rewards. Grassland was returned to pasturage. The state payment for grain was raised by 20%, and the official price for private sales went up by 50%. Prices for vegetable oil, meat and fish rose. This all fuelled inflation, but that was a cost the rulers were ready to pay to jump-start the heart of the nation. It was the greatest change since the early Communist Land reforms.

There was initial resistance in some places, and in Hebeia a reminder of how natural disasters could impede progress; drought between 1980 and 1982 brought huge losses, and 14 million people needed emergency rations as some ate treebark to survive. But by 1984, 98% of agricultural hosueholds had adopted the new system. Progress in the countryside brought new transport links; bus routes overcame the traditional village isolation, while railway platforms were piled with goods waiting to be taken to market. Doctors, teachers and lawyers set up rural practices.

Source E

A table showing the effects of Deng's reforms on the rural economy, from *China since 1919: Revolution and Reform*, by Alan Lawrance, London, 2004.

Grain output and gross agricultural production values, 1981–90				
	Grain output		**Gross agricultural production value**	
	Volume (million tons)	Annual growth rate (%)	Value (million yuan)	Annual growth rate (%)
1981	325.02	1.4	218.1	5.8
1982	354.50	9.1	248.3	11.3
1983	387.28	9.2	275.0	7.7
1984	407.31	5.2	321.0	12.3
1985	379.11	-6.9	361.9	3.4
1986	391.51	3.3	401.3	3.4
1987	402.98	2.9	467.6	5.8
1988	394.08	-2.2	586.5	4.0
1989	407.55	3.4	635.5	3.1
1990	435.00	6.7	738.2	6.9

Source: "Grain and Gross Agricultural Values Since 1981", *People's Daily*, 23 February 1991, p. 3, from *Zhongguo tongji nianjian [Statistical Year Book of China]*, 1990, pp. 335, 336.

Source-based questions

1 **a** According to Source A, why was the Third Plenum important?

[3 marks]

   b What message is conveyed by Source E? *[2 marks]*

2 Compare and contrast the views about Deng's agricultural reforms expressed in Sources A and D. *[6 marks]*

3 With reference to their origin and purpose assess the value and limitation of Source B and Source C for historians studying the importance of the Four Modernizations for agriculture. *[6 marks]*

4 Using the sources and your own knowledge analyse the successes and failures of Deng's agricultural reforms, as expressed in his Four Modernizations. *[8 marks]*

Recommended further reading

China Internet Information Center. http://www.china.org.cn.

The official website for the People's Republic of China, with official data and statistics.

Deng Xiaoping. 2001. *Deng Xiaoping: Selected Works 1975–1982*. Sacramento, California, USA. University Press of the Pacific.

Evans, Richard, 1997. *Deng Xiaoping and the Making of Modern China*. Revised edn. New York, USA. Penguin.

Garten Ash, Timothy. 1993. *The Magic Lantern: The Revolution of '89 Witnessed in Warsaw, Budapest, Berlin and Prague*. NY, USA. Vintage.

Gorbachev, Mikhail. 2000. *Gorbachev*. New York, USA. Columbia University Press.

Household Responsibility System. http://www.bookrags.com/research/household-responsibility-systemchin-ema-02/.

Hsu, Immanuel. 1990. *China without Mao: The Search for a New Order*. 2nd edn. Oxford, UK. Oxford University Press.

Judt, Tony. 2005. *Postwar: A History of Europe since 1945*. New York, USA. Penguin Books.

Lee, Edmund. "China's New Era: Beijing's Balancing Act". *Foreign Affairs*. vol. 51, no. 4. pp. 27–46. http://www.foreignpolicy.com/Ning/archive/archive/051/4.pdf.

Edmund Lee is a pseudonym used by a Chinese scholar from the People's Republic of China who specializes in eastern Asian politics. His articles in the 1980s provided a rare perspective: the unofficial Chinese point of view on government policies.

Marples, David. 2004. *The Collapse of the Soviet Union*. (Seminar Studies in History) London, UK. Longman.

Matlock, Jack. 2005. *Reagan and Gorbachev: How the Cold War ended*. New York, USA. Random House.

Meisner, Maurice. 1997. *Mao's China and After*. NY, USA. Free Press.

Remnick, David. 1994. *Lenin's Tomb: The last days of the Soviet Empire*. New York, USA. Vintage.

Stokes, Gale. 1993. *The Walls Came Tumbling Down: The Collapse of Communism in Eastern Europe*. New York, USA. Oxford University Press.

Tompson, William. 2003. *The Soviet Union under Brezhnev*. (Seminar Studies in History) London, UK. Longman.

Wong, Jan. 1997. *Red China Blues: My Long March from Mao to Now*. New York, USA. Anchor Books.

4 Causes, practices and effects of wars

This chapter looks at topic 1 "Causes, practices and effects of wars". The first part of the chapter consists of case studies selected from the *History Guide*'s material for detailed study, chosen to illustrate important aspects of 20th-century warfare. The thematic activities following the case studies are designed to help you explore some of the major themes identified in the *History Guide*. Topics in 20th-century world history are examined in paper 2. In order to help you prepare for this examination, a selection of sample exam questions is provided at the end of the chapter.

Throughout the chapter there are questions and activities designed to help you explore and analyse concepts that arise in more detail.

By the end of this chapter, you should be able to:

- analyse the relationship between causes, practices and effects of war in the 20th century
- demonstrate an understanding of the origins and causes of wars in the 20th century
- analyse the nature of 20th-century wars
- demonstrate an understanding of the different types of 20th-century war
- analyse the relationship of historical context to the causes, practices and effects of 20th-century wars
- demonstrate an understanding of the political, social and economic effects of war in the 20th century.

When asked the question "Why do wars begin?", the classicist Thomas Palaima replied that in fact they never end, highlighting that some form of warfare has been part of the human experience for as long as that experience has been recorded. Nevertheless, for as long as there have been wars, there have been attempts to stop them. This desire, if not inclination, towards peace took on even more significance in August 1945 when the atomic bomb put into human hands the power to end all life on earth.

Discussion point:

The desire for peace is embodied in the IB mission statement. How might the commitment to being international-minded help create a more peaceful world?

Return to this question again after you have worked through this chapter, and chapter 1 on "Peacemaking, peacekeeping—international relations, 1918–36".

The First World War: background causes, immediate causes and interpretation

This section examines the relationship between the long-term, short-term and immediate causes of war by examining the causes of the First World War. The long-term and short-term effects of militarism, industrialization, imperialism/nationalism and the alliance system are examined with a view to exploring how these developments worked in concert to make war more likely. Starting out with the July Crisis of 1914, as an immediate cause, this section examines the idea that it was not so much the crisis itself, but the management of that crisis that brought the European powers to war and posits the question of the inevitability of the war. It also looks at the importance of war plans both in precipitating the war and in determining, in part, the nature of the war, without focusing on the war itself. An important theme is the degree to which the causes—long-term, short-term and immediate—helped determine the size and scope of the war that followed.

Causes

It has become a cliché to speak of the causes of the First World War, the Great War, as a "powder keg" (background causes) ignited by a "spark" (immediate cause). While clichés can be trite and boring, they also encapsulate an essential truth. Whatever metaphor you choose, the causes of the First World War can be broken down into a number of trends that developed through the end of the 19th century and the beginning of the 20th century, leading up to the fateful events of July 1914, often called the July Crisis.

These causes did not work in isolation, however. They were interconnected. Militarism was dependent on industrial capacity. Colonial possessions required larger militaries. It is in this interconnectedness that we can begin to seek the causes of the war itself, as well as the scope of the war as it unfolded.

Background causes

It is important to think about what we mean when we say "cause". What we refer to as background causes are, in the strict sense, not causes—they did not make the First World War inevitable. Instead, in history, we must talk in terms of probabilities. What follows is a set of developments that made war more likely. These developments increased the suspicion, fear and tension between the European powers and therefore made war more likely. Further, they made a big war more likely. The trend towards larger militaries, industrial capacity and empires made the chances that a short, limited, regional war involving two, maybe three, countries would stay contained slim at best.

Militarism

Broadly speaking, we can talk about **militarism** as an overall societal emphasis on the military. The trend towards massive armies and navies at the end of the 19th century can be highlighted in two ways. On the one hand there are the precise, technical aspects that appeal to many military historians—warship tonnage, troop concentration, military expenditure. On the other hand, we should consider those aspects that appeal to the social historian—the relation of the military to the wider society. Both will be looked at.

It is certainly true that at the turn of the last century, the militaries of the major European powers were the largest in history. Paradoxically, most statesmen, if not generals, believed that this could help avoid a war. This early idea of **deterrence** held that the larger a country's military, the less likely other countries would be to attack. This might have been true if the size of militaries had remained static. The big problem was that they were growing. If a country was worried that a rival state's army was growing faster than its own, the temptation was to attack the rival preemptively before the differential was too great. In short, use your army before you lost it.

Regardless, the fact remains that the military forces that the European powers had at their disposal in 1914 were immense. There were approximately 200 army divisions in Europe in 1914 including reserves (part-time soldiers called up in the event of war). These massive armies were fed by varying degrees of conscription in all European powers with the exception of Great Britain. Men of military age were required to serve from two to six years. In fact, the terms of service were increasing. France passed the Three Year Law in 1913, increasing mandatory military service from two to three years. By all accounts, the Russian army was the largest in the world. The tsar's standing army numbered about 1.3 million and some claimed it could mobilize a further five million reservists. While these figures alone were enough to give pause to any would-be attackers, more alarming was the fact they were growing.

As impressive as the numbers may seem on paper, the reality reflected a dangerous contradiction. In the case of Russia, the likelihood that all of these conscripts would report for duty as required was wishful thinking and if they had it would have created an even bigger problem. The combination of poor infrastructure, massive distance between military depots and poor military organization meant that the most the Russian army could reliably call into service was about one-fifth of the able-bodied men of military age. This deceptive picture was a double-edged sword. To her rivals, inclined as they were to focus on the strength of other states, Russia was an imposing behemoth. To Russian military planners, aware of the deficiencies in their military apparatus, the theoretical or even actual size of the army meant that mobilization must be undertaken before any potential enemy could mobilize. This was to have ominous ramifications in July 1914.

Militarism was evident not only in the size of armies and navies, but also in the technology used by these forces. By 1914, modern industrial methods meant that the great armament foundries of

Militarism A political, diplomatic and social emphasis on military matters. Evidence of militarism often includes increased military spending, development of military technology, a general support for the goals and plans of a nation's military and the influence of military leaders on political decisions.

Deterrence Actions or policies designed to discourage an attack by making the consequences of the attack prohibitive.

Krupp and Skoda were producing artillery that could hurl a one-ton explosive projectile up to 10 miles (16 km). Machine guns could theoretically fire 400 to 600 rounds per minute. In practice, each machine gun was the equivalent of 80 rifles.

The HMS *Dreadnought* was revolutionary in all aspects: design, speed, armament, materials and production methods. How could one ship change the nature of naval warfare so completely? How might the production of HMS *Dreadnought* have affected the other background causes of the First World War?

The Anglo-German naval race was perhaps one of the starkest illustrations of militarism. When the British Royal Navy launched the revolutionary HMS *Dreadnought* in December 1906, it instantly made every battleship then afloat, including British ships, obsolete. If a country was to have a modern navy after 1906, it had to spend money on Dreadnoughts. When this was coupled with Germany's desire for a navy to rival the Royal Navy, as expressed in the Second Naval Law of 1900, it created an arms race that would see the size of these navies increase by a combined 197 per cent between 1900 and 1914.

Large or even growing militaries do not cause wars. They do, however engender suspicion and fear in rival states. When this suspicion is coupled with economic rivalry, imperialism and nationalism, it makes war more likely. Further, it makes a large, massively destructive war more likely.

Industrialization

Some historians have contended that by 1900 economic power equated to military power. Others contend that, while there is a strong relationship between these two concepts, the matter of what constituted a Great Power was more complex. What is not generally disputed is the massive increase in industrial output in the second half of the 19th century. The revolution in production that had taken root in England a century before had, by 1870, spread to the rest of Europe and across the Atlantic.

By all measures, Europe was far more industrialized in 1914 than it had been in 1880; this industrialization would help determine the nature of the war to come as the first total war of the 20th century.

Of course, increasing industrial output does not cause war any more than large armies do. There are, however, certain consequences of this increase in manufacturing that played a role

Chart 1: Military and naval personnel, 1880–1914					
	1880	**1890**	**1900**	**1910**	**1914**
Russia	791 000	677 000	1 162 000	1 285 000	1 352 000
France	543 000	542 000	715 000	769 000	910 000
Germany	426 000	504 000	524 000	694 000	891 000
Britain	367 000	420 000	624 000	571 000	532 000
Austria-Hungary	246 000	346 000	385 000	425 000	444 000
Italy	216 000	284 000	255 000	322 000	345 000
Japan	71 000	84 000	234 000	271 000	306 000
United States	34 000	39 000	96 000	127 000	164 000

Source: Kennedy, Paul. 1988. *Rise and Fall of the Great Powers: Economic and Military Conflict from 1500 to 2000*. London, UK. Fontana Press. p. 261

in making a general European war more likely. Among these consequences is the fact that the increase was not uniform among the powers. For example, while iron and steel production had increased in the United States by approximately 242 per cent between 1890 and 1913, it had actually decreased in the United Kingdom. More to the point for the British, Germany's steel production had increased by approximately 329 per cent in the same period. In absolute terms, in 1913, France was woefully behind all the powers except Austria–Hungary. These disparities helped create competitive economic tension between the powers, which in turn increased diplomatic and political tension.

In order to feed these massive industrial machines, the powers needed access to resources, which in turn created a **neo-mercantilist** mindset complemented by the drive for colonies in the second half of the 19th century. This thirst had been momentarily slaked by the "scramble for Africa" (see page 210), but by 1900 that well had gone dry. The European powers had claimed all of Africa, with a few small exceptions. Sources of raw materials, not to mention markets, had either to be wrung from existing holdings or wrestled, forcibly or diplomatically, from another power.

Not only had industrial output increased, so had trade. By 1913 the total of German exports was equal to that of the United Kingdom and in the lucrative American market the Germans significantly outsold the British. To protect and to increase this trade, the Germans needed a modern, powerful navy. It did not take long for the powers to harness their huge industrial potential once the war began. By 1914 France was producing 200 000 artillery shells a day. Even the backward Russian factory system was manufacturing 4.5 million artillery shells in 1916, a tenfold increase on the previous year. The connection between economic rivalry and military rivalry was evident.

The alliance system
If these great, interlocking alliances caused large-scale wars, the NATO and Warsaw Pact would have brought the Cold War to a disastrous end long before the communists states of Eastern Europe were dissolved at the end of the 1980s. Similar to the Cold War, Europe in 1914 was split into two rival, albeit smaller, alliances. These two alliances were connected by a secondary set of treaties, agreements and alliances to countries around the globe.

After Bismarck had finished forging the German Empire by means of "blood and iron" in 1871, he sought to preserve it by carefully shielding her from war. His method was to create an intricate set of alliances as part of a policy of deterrence. The Dual Alliance between Germany and Austria–Hungary, established in 1879, was a major part of that

> **Under what circumstances could a war be considered a total war by one of the combatants, but not other combatants in the same war? Can you give an example?**

> **Neo-mercantilism** An economic doctrine that emphasizes the need to decrease imports by moving towards self-sufficiency. This move to self-sufficiency often requires an increase in colonial holdings to supply raw materials and provide markets for finished goods.

Chart 2: Warship tonnage of the powers, 1880–1914					
	1880	**1890**	**1900**	**1910**	**1914**
Britain	650 000	679	1 065 000	2 174 000	2 714 000
France	271 000	319 000	499 000	725 000	900 000
Russia	200 000	180 000	383 000	401 000	679 000
United States	169 000	240 000	333 000	824 000	985 000
Italy	100 000	242 000	245 000	327 000	498 000
Germany	88 000	190 000	285 000	964 000	1 305 000
Austria-Hungary	60 000	66 000	87 000	210 000	372 000
Japan	15 000	41 000	187 000	496 000	700 000

Source: Kennedy, Paul. 1988. *Rise and Fall of the Great Powers: Economic and Military Conflict from 1500 to 2000*. London, UK. Fontana Press. p. 261.

shield. Within three years, the addition of Italy turned the Dual Alliance into the Triple Alliance, with each state pledging military support in the event that either of the other two became embroiled in a war against two or more opponents. To this Bismarck added the Reinsurance Treaty with Russia in 1887. The cumulative effect of these agreements was, as Bismarck had intended, to isolate France from the rest of Europe, something French diplomats were going to have to work hard to undo.

This work was made easier when Bismarck refused to approve German loans to Russia in 1887 and the post-Bismarckian foreign office elected not to renew the Reinsurance Treaty in 1890. Now

Activity:

Industry, war and power

Chart 3: Per capita levels of industrialization, 1880–1938 (Relative to GB in 1900)

	1880	1900	1913	1928	1938	
1 Great Britain	87	[100]	115	122	157	2
2 United States	38	69	126	182	167	1
3 France	28	39	59	82	73	4
4 Germany	25	52	85	128	144	3
5 Italy	12	17	26	44	61	5
6 Austria	15	23	32	-	-	
7 Russia	10	15	20	20	38	7
8 Japan	9	12	20	30	51	6

Chart 4: Iron and steel production of the powers, 1890–1938 (millions of tons; pig-iron production for 1890, steel thereafter)

	1890	1900	1910	1913	1920	1930	1938
United States	9.3	10.3	26.5	31.8	42.3	41.3	28.8
Great Britain	8.0	5.0	6.5	7.7	9.2	7.4	10.5
Germany	4.1	6.3	13.6	17.6	7.6	11.3	23.2
France	1.9	1.5	3.4	4.6	2.7	9.4	6.1
Austria-Hungary	0.97	1.1	2.1	2.6	-	-	-
Russia	0.95	2.2	3.5	4.8	0.06	5.7	18.0
Japan	0.02	-	0.16	0.25	0.84	2.3	7.0
Italy	0.01	0.00	0.73	0.93	0.73	1.7	2.3

Chart 5: Total industrial potential of the powers, 1880–1938 (Relative to GB in 1900)

	1880	1900	1913	1928	1938
Great Britain	73.3	[100]	127.2	135	181
United States	46.9	127.8	298.1	533	528
Germany	27.4	71.2	137.7	158	214
France	25.1	36.8	57.3	82	74
Russia	24.5	47.5	76.6	72	152
Austria-Hungary	14	25.6	40.7	-	-
Italy	8.1	13.6	22.5	37	46
Japan	7.6	13	25.1	45	88

Chart 6: Energy consumption of the powers, 1890–1938 (in millions of metric tons of coal equivalent)

	1890	1900	1910	1913	1920	1930	1938
United States	147	248	483	541	694	762	697
Great Britain	145	171	185	195	212	184	196
Germany	71	112	158	187	159	177	228
France	36	47.9	55	62.5	65	97.5	84
Austria-Hungary	19.7	29	40	49.4	-	-	-
Russia	10.9	30	41	54	14.3	65	177
Japan	4.6	4.6	15.4	23	34	55.8	96.5
Italy	4.5	5	9.6	11	14.3	24	27.8

Power ranking

1 Using the information in the above charts, rank the countries according to how powerful they were in 1914. What criteria are you using? What is your definition of power in this context? What happens to your ranking if you take into consideration the information in charts 1 and 2 on pp. 206–7?

2 What conclusions can you draw about the relationship between the information and a country's ability to conduct a war?

3 Compare and contrast each country's pre-war and post-war figures. What conclusions can we draw from the comparison? How did this affect your "power ranking?"

Source: Kennedy, Paul. 1988. *Rise and Fall of the Great Powers: Economic and Military Conflict from 1500 to 2000*. London, UK. Fontana Press.

Russia, too, was isolated. Between 1890 and 1894, France nurtured a closer relationship with tsarist Russia—offering loans totaling £400 million and coordinating military planning. This new friendship culminated in the Franco-Russian Alliance, formalized in 1894. The tsar pledged that Russia would attack Germany if Germany ever attacked France or aided Italy in attacking France. France agreed to do likewise if the Kaiser's forces ever attacked Russia or helped Austria–Hungary do the same. The German nightmare of a two-front war was now a distinct possibility.

While France and Russia saw isolation as a dangerous condition, Britain traditionally revelled in it. She emerged from her "splendid isolation" when it suited her and retreated behind her watery ramparts when it was prudent. British statesmen eschewed the rigidity of formal alliances. The diplomatic world, however, had changed by the turn of the century. Britain had been battered by her victory in the South African War. The naval race with Germany was pressuring her treasury. Tensions with France in Africa had nearly erupted into war. The time seemed right to begin a tentative emergence from isolation. First came an alliance with Japan and then a rapprochement with France. The Entente Cordiale of 1904 was the result. By this agreement, the United Kingdom and France agreed to settle differences in Africa as well as a number of smaller disputes around the world. Significantly, however, the Entente Cordiale contained no military commitments, preserving Britain's free hand, or so the British thought, in the affairs of continental Europe. By 1907 the British had settled old differences with the Russian Empire and the Entente Cordiale metamorphosed into the Triple Entente. It was a less rigid agreement than the Triple Alliance as the British refused to agree to any binding military action.

Each of these alliance systems was complicated by other agreements made by the powers, some of which were public and some secret. Two notable examples involved the United Kingdom and Russia. Britain's alliance with Japan has already been noted, but she was also linked to the largest empire on earth. Even the so-called independent "white dominions" of Canada, Australia and New Zealand were automatically committed to war should the UK declare war on another country. This almost guaranteed that were Britain to support one of her Entente partners militarily, the result would be a global war. On top of this, since 1839 the UK had guaranteed Belgium's perpetual neutrality. For her part, Russia had interests in the Balkans, which helped draw her into an alliance with Serbia, further complicating the web of treaties and agreements in the period 1900–14.

The net result of this interlocking, secretive and fairly rigid set of alliances was to increase the tension and suspicion of the great powers. While not causing the war, it made it more likely and ensured that it would be large in scope. The complex system was also arduous to maintain, requiring very subtle diplomacy, or what historians Robert Roswell Palmer and Joel Colton have called "the most Olympian of statesmanship". No such level of statesmanship was forthcoming in the summer of 1914.

Imperialism/nationalism

It is important to keep in mind that a nation is, at its heart, a group of people. In many ways, therefore, **imperialism** and **nationalism** are two sides of the same coin. The imperialism of one nation state will generally aggravate the nationalist feelings of those it dominates.

Imperial tensions between the European powers became dangerously high in the second half of the 19th century in large measure because of what has become known as the "scramble for Africa". Until 1850, the European exploration and subsequent exploitation of Africa had largely been limited to the coastal areas. By the 1870s, however, entrepreneurial explorers such as Henry Stanley had begun to awaken to the economic potential of the African interior, touching off a race by European states to claim their own colonies in Africa. The potential of this "scramble" to bring far-flung powers into conflict should be obvious. It certainly was to Bismarck. Despite his disdain for overseas colonies, Bismarck hosted a conference in Berlin in 1885 to hammer out the rules for claiming and exploiting Africa in hopes that these rules would stave off disagreements over ownership. Just

> A **nation** is group people who share a number of commonalities, generally including language, culture, historic development and territory.
>
> **Nationalism** is an emotional attachment to this people and a desire for its political independence.

> **Imperialism** A set of actions and policies by which one national group dominates another national group and its territory.

Activity:

The web of alliances, 1914

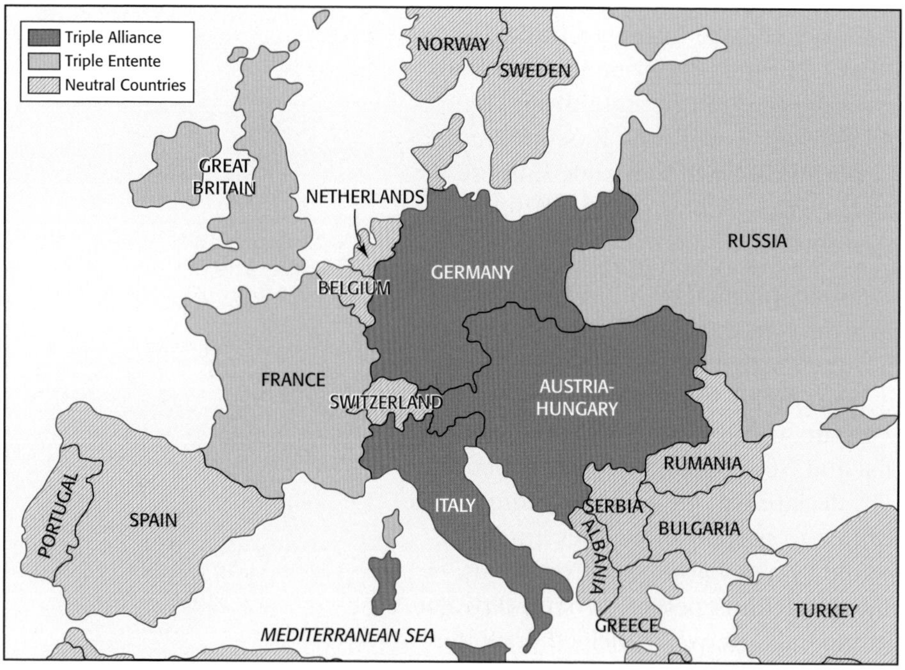

Map legend:
- Triple Alliance
- Triple Entente
- Neutral Countries

1 Using the above map, list the geographic advantages and disadvantages of
   ● the Triple Alliance
   ● the Triple Entente.

2 Using an outline map of the world in 1914,
   ● outline the two major alliance systems
   ● draw a red line between the alliances and any outside country with which there were military agreements

   ● draw a green line between the alliances and any outside country with which there were economic agreements
   ● draw a blue line between the alliances and any outside country with which there were cultural/national relationships.

3 What conclusions can you draw between alliances and the theory of deterrence?

as he had no interest in Germany acquiring her own colonies, he did not want disputes between other powers in some distant African land to jeopardize his new Germany by dragging her into a European war.

Despite his efforts, and in some ways because of his efforts, the European powers would come dangerously close to war over African questions after Bismarck's retirement in 1890. Part of the problem lay in Bismarck's desire to stay out of the colony game, the result of which was what the new Kaiser, Wilhelm II, thought was an insulting under-representation of Germany on the world stage. Young Wilhelm demanded that Germany get her "place in the sun" and developed a brash, provocative and ultimately dangerous **Weltpolitik** (world policy) to achieve it. The result of this ill-conceived policy became evident in 1905. During a state visit to French-controlled Morocco, Wilhelm boldly proclaimed that the status of Morocco should be re-evaluated at an international conference. Unfortunately for the Kaiser, this conference, held at Algeciras the following year, upheld French claimsto the territory. While the Kaiser had wished to assert German authority, and in the process drive a wedge between the Anglo-French entente, he served only to strengthen the entente and make the rest of Europe wary of German motives and methods on the world stage. When Germany sent the gunboat *Panther* to the Moroccan port of Agadir in 1911, to once again pressure France by calling into question her imperial claims, the UK unequivocally supported her ally. Wilhelm came away from Algeciras and the Agadir Crisis feeling that Germany was becoming dangerously isolated and victimized.

> **Weltpolitik** The foreign policy adopted by Germany at the end of the 19th century by which she sought to assert her influence around the globe.

The Balkans

The role that nationalism played in the growing international tensions at the turn of the century is best demonstrated in the Balkans. This region was populated by a number of ethnic groups broadly referred to as Slavs and centred in the small independent nation-state of Serbia. Political domination in the region had traditionally been split between two rival empires, the Austro-Hungarian and the Ottoman. By the end of the 19th century, the crumbling influence and power of the Ottoman Empire, coupled with Austria–Hungary's desire to retrench and expand her influence in the region, made this a very unstable part of the European political system. The flux in the region reawakened in Russia age-old Balkan aspirations. Growing numbers of radical pan-Slavic nationalists living under the Hapsburgs were convinced that their future lay not in a federated Austria–Hungary, but rather in a Greater Serbia or Yugoslavia. With Serbia's ambition to become the Piedmont of a pan-Slavic state added to this frightening situation, the

The Balkans, 1914

	Area of Turkey in Europe before Treaty of Berlin, 1878
	Area of Turkey in Europe before the Balkan Wars, 1912–13
	Area ceded by Bulgaria to Romania, 1913
-----·	Boundaries before the Balkan Wars
——	Boundaries after the Balkan Wars

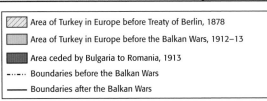

The Balkan region had many distinct national groups, most of whom had been part of the Ottoman Empire at one time. By 1914, the Balkan region was bordered by three of the major European powers and of strategic interest to all of them. Given this situation, explain what Otto von Bismarck meant when, in the 19th century, he said, "If there is ever another war in Europe, it will come out of some damned silly thing in the Balkans."

region was becoming dangerously volatile.

When Italy tried to wrest Tripoli from the Ottomans by force in 1911, Serbia saw an opportunity to profit from the sultan's divided attention and resources. Forming the Balkan League with Bulgaria, Montenegro and Greece, she went to war with Turkey. The profit was Albania and Macedonia, with the lion's share going to Bulgaria, a grievance Serbia quickly addressed by defeating Bulgaria in the second Balkan War in 1913. This time Serbian designs on Albania, and the consequent access to the sea, was thwarted by international intervention, spearheaded by Austria–Hungary. Russia, though a supporter of Serbian claims, backed down when faced with Austrian resolve, just as she had done when the Austrians annexed Bosnia, a Slavic territory, in 1908. The result was the creation of the Independent Kingdom of Albania. The sum total of this confusing ten months of war and negotiation was an Austro-Hungarian Empire determined to stop pan-Slavic nationalist claims, an emboldened Serbia determined to further pan-Slavic nationalist schemes and a twice-humiliated Russian Empire determined to reassert her authority.

It is important to read these background causes together. The massive size of European militaries was made possible by the prodigious increase in European industrial production, fed by raw materials garnered from global empires. The expansion of empires, partially necessitated by the hunger for resources, angered countries such as Germany and Austria–Hungary who wanted to expand their holdings, while simultaneously increasing the anxiety of those at whose expense this expansion would have to occur—countries such as the UK, France, Russia and Serbia, not to mention countless African and Asian peoples, who are often overlooked in this European drama—a drama that was shortly to become a global tragedy.

Immediate causes: the July Crisis

When asked what caused the First World War, people with even the most rudimentary of historical knowledge will likely reply that it had something to do with the shooting of a member of the Austrian royal family. As we have seen, however, this is woefully inadequate in explaining an event the scale and scope of the First World War. Indeed, when Archduke Franz Ferdinand, heir to the Hapsburg throne, and his wife Sophie were shot while visiting Sarajevo on 28 June 1914, they were not particularly unique in their fate. The archduke was but one of eight heads of state that were assassinated in the years 1881–1914, two of them being Hapsburgs. No, it was not the assassination itself that sparked the war. Rather, it was an inability to manage the ensuing crisis in the light of the background causes outlined above that tumbled the European powers into four years of disaster.

Kaiser Wilhelm II (1859–1941)

Kaiser Wilhelm II was the German emperor who led Germany throughout the First World War until his abdication in November 1918. He took a much more aggressive approach to foreign affairs than his father Frederick III. Wilhelm sought to enlarge Germany's imperial holdings outside of Europe and consequently increase Germany's influence and prestige on the world stage. He provoked international incidents over French holdings in Africa, while at the same time building a navy that he believed could rival the British Royal Navy. The Kaiser's unconditional support for Germany's Austrian ally during the July Crisis helped precipitate the First World War.

Political assassinations, 1881–1914

1881 Alexander II of Russia, Emperor of all the Russias

1894 Marie François Sadi Carnot, President of France

1895 Stefan Stambolov, Prime minister of Bulgaria

1897 Antonio Cánovas del Castillo, Prime minister of Spain

1898 Empress Elisabeth of Austria

1900 King Umberto I of Italy

1901 William McKinley, President of the United States

1903 King Aleksandar of Serbia

1904 Nikolai Bobrikov, Governor-general of Finland

1908 King Carlos I of Portugal

1908 Luiz Filipe, Crown prince of Portugal

1911 Peter Stolypin, Prime minister of Russia

1912 José Canalejas, Prime minister of Spain

1913 King George I of Greece

1914 Archduke Franz Ferdinand of Austria

Certain members of the Serbian military supported the Bosnian terrorist group "Union or Death", commonly known as the Black Hand, though it appears that this support did not extend throughout the Serbian government. Nevertheless, Austrian officials, specifically the chief of the general staff, Conrad Hotzendorff, and the chancellor, Leopold von Berchtold, wished to seize the opportunity afforded by the assassination to crush South Slav nationalism once and for all. This would mean war with Serbia. After a pledge of unlimited support from Germany, her only European ally, in the so-called **Blank Cheque**, the Austrians formulated their ultimatum to the Serbs. The exact nature and intent of the Blank Cheque has for years been debated, as has the authorship of the ultimatum itself (see the historiography chart in the activity on page 215). It would seem that the terms of the ultimatum were designed to be impossible to accept, offering as it did affront to many aspects of Serb sovereignty

Nevertheless, the Serbs capitulated to most of the demands, so much so that the Kaiser believed that with the Serb response "every reason for war drops away." Perhaps he was more surprised than many when Austria–Hungary went to war against Serbia within hours of this response on 28 July 1914.

The Russians viewed the size of the Austrian mobilization as a direct threat to their frontiers. To this was added the memory of the two previous Balkan humiliations. The tsar ordered partial mobilization against Austria on the night of 29 July. Understanding the alliance obligations that Germany owed to Austria, the Russian war minister, Sukhomlinov, persuaded Nicholas to change the order to full mobilization along the entire length of Russia's western frontier. As an increasing sense of panic gripped the Kaiser, he demanded that his cousin, the tsar, cease all military preparation. When this was not forthcoming, Wilhelm ordered the full mobilization of the German army, a mobilization that, as part of the Schlieffen Plan (see below), was directed against France, through neutral Belgium.

Some historians believed that the Germans were clinging to the hope that the United Kingdom would stay out of the looming conflict. Others thought that this was never a serious possibility. For his part, the British Foreign Secretary, Edward Grey, did nothing to dispel this notion, reserving the UK's freedom of action until the very last moment. When the German army crossed into Belgium on 3 August, the UK's treaty obligations brought her and her empire into what was now a world war.

Could this war have been avoided? It is easy to see where, during July 1914, different decisions, stronger leaders, better communication may have yielded a different outcome. This would have solved

> **Blank Cheque** A pledge of unconditional support given by Kaiser Wilhelm II of Germany to Franz Joseph of Austria in July 1914. The pledge was in reference to Austria–Hungary's dispute with Serbia and Russia.

Archduke Franz Ferdinand and his wife Sophie. Ferdinand was known to be a reformer when it came to the role of national groups within the Austro-Hungarian Empire, favouring some forms of semi-autonomy. Why might the fact that Ferdinand was a reformer in this regard make him dangerous to extremist groups like the Black Hand?

Archduke Franz Ferdinand of Austria (1863–1914)

Franz Ferdinand was the heir to the throne of Austria–Hungary; his assassination in June 1914 ignited the July Crisis that would lead to the outbreak of the First World War. After a standard military education and service in the Austrian army, Ferdinand found himself heir to the throne after the early death of his cousin, Emperor Franz Joseph's son. His promotion of greater autonomy for some of the nationalities within the Austrian army, specifically Czechs and national groups in the Balkans, alienated both the hard-core conservatives within the Austrian administration and hard-core nationalists within the empire. He and his wife were shot to death by a Bosnian nationalist named Gavrilo Princip while on a state visit to the Bosnian city of Sarajevo in June 1914. The ensuing crisis and the inability of the leaders of Europe to resolve it tumbled the world into war in August.

the crisis only. The underlying causes remained. The issue of what would become known at Versailles as "war guilt" is, therefore, far more complex than anyone at the Peace Conference, with the possible exception of Wilson, and indeed, many historians could simply state. The war was, in fact, the result of a complex set of long-term, short-term and immediate factors that stretched from the mid-19th century right up to the eve of the war.

War plans and opening moves

The opening days of the First World War have often been referred to as "war by timetable". Indeed, the act of mobilizing millions of soldiers required a level of co-ordination unprecedented in 1914. So vital was the railroad system to this endeavour that the German government had taken sole control of the entire German railroad system by the 1880s. The fact was that all the major European powers had to move millions of men to positions on their frontiers, so as to be able to carry out war plans of varying degrees of complexity.

The most famous of these plans was the Schlieffen Plan, named after its creator, Alfred von Schlieffen, chief of the German general staff from 1891 to 1905. In that time he conceived of a plan that was designed to deal with the Bismarckian nightmare of a two-front war, against France in the west and Russia in the east. The plan called for a massive concentration of German arms in the west against France. This force, composed of seven armies, would sweep through Luxembourg and Belgium into northern France in a great arc that would conquer Paris within 41 days of mobilization. Meanwhile, Russian forces would be held at bay by a combination of Austro-Hungarian armies and her own sluggish mobilization. The Schlieffen Plan was itself an immediate cause of the war, in that it depended upon Germany mobilizing first. In case of a threat by Russia, as in July 1914, Germany's entire grand strategy required the Kaiser to start a war with France.

At first glance it would seem that the German general staff also had a hand in the preparation of the French war plan. France's Plan XVII called for a massing of French armies on their eastern frontier, away from the main thrust of the German army. These troops would then rush gallantly eastwards, regaining at once the honour of the French army and the territories of Alsace and Lorraine. Whereas the Schlieffen Plan was built on meticulous timetabling and organization, Plan XVII rested on the ideas of *élan vitale* and the offensive spirit, prompt Russian mobilization and the coordinated assistance of the British army.

IB Learner Profile link

Choose any three of the characteristics in the IB learner profile and compare them to the characteristics displayed by one of the following leaders during the July Crisis of 1914:

- Kaiser William II— Emperor of Germany
- Lord Grey— British Foreign Secretary
- Tsar Nicholas II— Emperor of Russia
- Emperor Franz Joseph— Emperor of Austria

 If the alliance system was constructed in part as a deterrent to war, how did the Schlieffen Plan work at cross purposes to the alliance system?

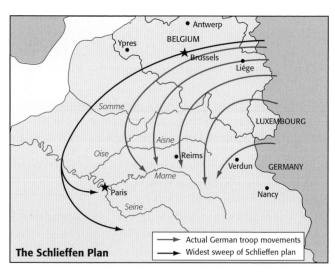

The Schlieffen Plan

→ Actual German troop movements
→ Widest sweep of Schlieffen plan

Schlieffen's original plan called for the capture of Paris within 41 days of mobilization. How did von Moltke's decision to wheel the first army in front of Paris, rather than around it, change the nature of the entire war?

In the context of French military doctrine in 1914, *élan vitale* was the preference of attack at the expense of prudent defense. Deficiencies in sound planning and tactical considerations could be overcome with sufficient enthusiasm and vigour.

Activity:

What caused the First World War?

Sydney Bradshaw Fay *The Origins of the World War*, 1929	Fay was writing in response to the finding of the Paris Peace Conference that Germany was solely responsible for the outbreak of the war. Fay maintained that it was a complex assortment of causes, notably imperialism, militarism and alliances, that pushed Europe into war. No one country plotted an aggressive war and many, including the UK and Germany, made genuine, though unskilled, efforts at mediating the July Crisis. In some ways, Fay and those who agreed with him are part of the larger movement to reintroduce Germany to the community of nations in the same way that the spirit of Locarno was (see pp. 62–3).
Fritz Fischer *Grasp for World Power*, 1961	In the wake of the Second World War, German historian Fritz Fischer re-evaluated his country's role in causing the First World War. In contrast to Fay, Fischer found that Germany sought an aggressive war of expansion in 1914. Germany was surrounded by hostile countries and her economy, culture and influence in decline. A successful war of expansion would solve these problems and was therefore plotted and encouraged in the years 1912–14. The July Crisis was deliberately managed to this end. Fischer maintained that these attitudes and desires were not held solely by a maleficent and deluded leadership. After examining a broad cross section of German society in 1914, Fischer concluded that these attitudes and aims had broad support from business interests, academics and all political parties in Germany. It is not difficult to understand why this was a contentious position in post-Second World War Germany.
Eric Hobsbawm *The Age of Empires*, 1987	Writing in the Marxist historical tradition, Eric Hobsbawm does not find the causes of the war in any one country or person, but rather in the system of industrial capitalism that dominated the economies of Western Europe. Hobsbawm argues that industrial capitalism's insatiable hunger for resources and markets fuelled the New Imperialism of the 19th century. While this need was temporarily slaked by the "scramble for Africa", it soon brought European countries into conflict. Further, within industrial powers, this competition required a close partnership between the government and arms producers, for whom peacetime profits had to be maintained. These profits were required so that the industry would be around for the next war, a war in which strength would be measured not in military strength alone, but also in industrial capacity. By arguing a systemic cause of the war, Hobsbawm and other Marxist historians bring a degree of inevitability to the war. Regardless of who led the countries, or which countries were involved, they believe the system would have caused a war eventually.
Niall Ferguson *The Pity of War: Explaining World War 1*, 1999	Niall Ferguson, like Fischer, blames one country in particular. For Ferguson, rather than Germany, responsibility rests with the actions, and in some cases inaction, of the UK. Ferguson believes that Fay was wrong, that anti-militarism was rising in Europe by 1914, secret diplomacy had solved many disputes, and that Germany and the UK were more than capable of settling their differences. Rather, he maintains that British political and military leaders had planned to intervene in a European conflict from 1905 and in fact would have violated Belgian neutrality themselves had Germany not done it first. Further, he maintains that the UK misinterpreted German intentions, seeing them as Napoleonic rather than as essentially defensive. These leaders misled the British parliament into a declaration of war.
John Stoessinger *Why Nations Go To War*, 1974	John Stoessinger finds liability for the war largely in the personal failings of those trying to manage the July Crisis. He believes that each of the leaders acted out of an over-inflated sense of both their own country's weakness and their enemy's strength. Further, the supreme leaders in Austria–Hungary and Germany failed to exercise sufficient control over their subordinates, who actively conspired to provoke at least a regional war if not a general European war. Once the "iron dice" were cast, none of the leaders had the nerve to order a halt to the mobilization, even though this was a completely viable option. Had different personalities been in positions of authority in July 1914, there may never have been a war.

1 Which historian has the most convincing thesis? Why?

2 Add your own row to the above chart. What do you believe caused the war? How might it have been avoided?

3 How might the era in which each of the above historians was writing have affected their views? Why is it important for students of history to understand the context in which historians write?

The Spanish Civil War: factions, fault lines and civil war

The Spanish Civil War, 1936–9, fought between forces loyal to the elected government (Loyalists) and those seeking to overthrow that government (Nationalists), is a prime example of how a deeply divided society can erupt in into civil war when there is no political mechanism to manage those divisions. This section looks at these divisions and how they helped bring about the war and determine the nature of the war once it had broken out. The Spanish Civil War is also important in the context of the 20th century because its nature reflects the ideological divisions that gripped the world in the immediate pre-Second World War period. Examining the context of this war exposes important strategic consideration of the European powers. As such, the nature and effects of foreign intervention, and in some cases non-intervention, are examined. The war has profound effects inasmuch as it involves, in one way or another, the major world powers on the eve of the Second World War.

Civil wars

Civil wars are armed disputes that erupt over often radically different ideas about the direction, governmental system or composition of a country. National fault lines along which these volatile differences develop can be ideological, regional, political, economic or religious. But differences do not in and of themselves cause civil wars. The other key ingredient is the lack of a political system with enough of a monopoly of force or perceived legitimacy to address the competing interests inherent in the divisions. Most established democracies, for example, have models of representation that provide a say in political decisions for differing political and ideological positions, or regional interests. Canada, for example, has a representative democracy that elects legislators from the entire country. This allows these members of parliament to represent the various regional interests in the country. Such democracies are able to maintain stability in large part because the citizens see the system as an effective and legitimate method to address competing interests or divisions within the country. When faith in the legitimacy of these democracies is insufficient to maintain stability, governments augment their legitimacy with a monopoly of force, generally military, police and security organizations. Other systems, notably, authoritarian forms of government, rely primarily on their monopoly of force to maintain unity amid societal divisions. In short, if a country has a political mechanism either to address the concerns of its factions or to force compliance, divisions will not become civil wars. Unfortunately for Spain, no such mechanism existed in the 1930s.

Civil war A war between rival factions within a country.

Background to the Spanish Civil War

Divisions cut across Spain in just about every conceivable direction. Regionalism and even localism fractured the country and often trumped loyalty to Spain as a whole. Basques, Catalans, Galicians and many other groups had cultural, linguistic, historic and economic differences that often precluded any form of national cooperation. While parts of Spain were economically strong and reasonably dynamic, other areas were backward in terms of industrial and agricultural production methods. In some regions, agriculture was dominated by small, peasant landholders, while others were dominated by vast estates.

These divisions were reflected in the myriad political organizations, parties and ideologies that took root across Spain throughout the 50 years prior to the Civil War. As in many countries, the traditional conservative triad of landowners, church and army anchored the political right in Spain. Land ownership across the country was concentrated in relatively few families. Half of the land in Spain was owned by a mere 50 000 individuals. The Catholic Church, though rocked by the forces of secularism in the 19th century, still had a great deal of influence in Spanish society, especially in education. At the other end of the political spectrum, regionalism again influenced the formation of political and ideological movements. In industrial areas, such as Barcelona and other parts of Catalonia, a form of anarchism that was based on trade union principles became popular. This **anarcho-syndicalism** advocated decentralized, worker control of factories, as well as the other stock and trade of unions—shorter working weeks, higher wages and better working conditions. If anarcho-syndicalism was largely an urban phenomenon, its country cousin was a more traditional anarchism. This movement, strong in poor, rural areas such as Andalusia, sought a revolution leading to a vague combination of land redistribution, decentralized authority and freedom from taxes. This revolution was to come about by an equally vague combination of spontaneous action and the creative potential of the masses. Anarchism was not the only left-wing ideology plying its trade in 1930s Spain. Variants of Marxism and socialism had been struggling for support from the late 19th century. But even the Marxists were fractured. Stalinists feuded with Trotskyites. Socialists argued with trade unionists. By the time of the Civil War, these different views had produced a dizzying array of organizations and political parties.

Anarcho-syndicalism A political doctrine that advocates replacing central government with decentralized worker control based on a trade union model. Found in numerous countries such as France and Italy, it achieved its greatest mainstream success in the Confederación Nacional del Trabajo (CNT) in Spain.

What makes a government legitimate?
How can a government enhance its legitimacy?

Spanish political parties, 1936–9					
Left		**Centre**		**Right**	
Confederación Nacional del Trabajo (CNT)	Anarcho-syndicalist union	**Partido Nacionalista Vasco (PNV)**	Basque Nationalist party	**Carlists**	King–church party
Federación Anarquista Ibérica (FAI)	Militant anarchists	**Unión Militar Republicana Antifascista (UMRA)**	Anti-fascist army officers' organization	**Confederación Española de Derechas Autónomas (CEDA)**	Right-wing coalition
Partido Comunista de España (PCE)	Spanish communist party	**Partido Sindicalista (PS)**	Syndicalist party	**Falange**	Spanish fascist party
Partido Obrero de Unificación Marxista (POUM)	Marxist–socialist workers' party	**Unión Republicana (UR)**	Moderate Republican party	**Bloque Nacional**	Anti-parliamentary party
Partido Socialista Obrero Español (PSOE)	Spanish socialist party	**Izquierda Republicana (IR)**	Moderate Republican party	**Renovacion Espanola**	Monarchist party
Unión General de Trabajadores (UGT)	Socialist trade union			**Unión Militar Española (UME)**	Fascist army officers' organization
Partit Socialista Unificat de Catalunya (PSUC)	Catalonian socialist party				

Immediate causes: the failure of the Second Republic and the Popular Front

By April 1931, popular support for the monarchy had been completely eroded. When the army withdrew its support for Alphonso XIII, he slunk into exile and general elections in June of that year brought a coalition of centre-left parties to power, led by Manuel Azaña. The new government wasted no time in enacting sweeping agricultural, labour and anti-clerical legislation. New laws protected tenants from eviction, encouraged collectives and co-operatives, and officially split church and state. The new government would recognize civil marriages and divorces. In order to reduce the influence of the army, the new government forcibly retired many officers, granting them full pensions. While such changes made some members of the political left happy, they did not go far enough for those on the extreme left. The conservative right was, of course, furious. Not only did the reforms succeed in alienating

Manuel Azaña (1880–1940)

Leader of the Accion Republicana, Manuel Azaña became prime minister in 1931 with a centre-left coalition. While prime minister, he introduced a number of far-reaching agrarian and anti-clerical reforms that were subsequently undone when his government fell and was replaced by a right-wing coalition in 1933. When the Popular Front formed the government in 1936, Azaña again became prime minister. He served as the president of the Republic throughout the Civil War, after which he lived in France until his death in November 1940.

the right, they left the majority of ordinary people dissatisfied as they made little more than a dent in the widespread poverty of rural Spain.

There was a great deal of opposition to Azaña's government. The Civil Guard, a form of national police force, rose in rebellion in August 1932 under General Sanjurjo. While the revolt was easily put down—in part with the cooperation of the CNT, the largest anarcho-syndicalist organization—it illustrated the degree of opposition that the government faced. Sanjurjo's rising also demonstrated the limits of the Republic's monopoly of force and legitimacy. While middle-class liberals supported the Republic, the radical left and the conservative right were not convinced. Strikes and disturbances continued through 1933. The elections of November 1933 reflected the unstable nature of Spanish politics, bringing a right-wing coalition to power. This new government was immediately denounced by the left, setting off a new wave of unrest. Neither the left nor the right seemed to have enough faith in the democratic decision-making process to trust it to their political rivals.

The suspicions of the left were, perhaps, well founded. The new government immediately began to reverse or ignore Azaña's reforms. The strikes and disturbances reached a crescendo with a short-lived declaration of autonomy by Catalonia and a far more serious revolt in the region of Asturias, crushed by hardened Spanish troops from Morocco. To some on the Spanish left, this revolt was an attempt to avoid the fate of the German left who had failed to resist the rise of the Nazis two years earlier and who were by the time of the Asturias revolt defunct. To others, it was confirmation that the radical left in Spain had abandoned the constitution and could not be trusted to govern. Both interpretations indicate a profound lack of faith in the democratic system upon which the Republic rested. Either interpretation seemed to point to political differences so entrenched that no democratic process could reconcile them.

The Popular Front and the generals' uprising

As was perhaps predictable, in 1936 the pendulum of Spanish electoral politics swung back to the left. The Spanish left had embraced an electoral strategy encouraged by the **Comintern** and practiced in France, known as the **Popular Front**. This strategy took the lesson of the Nazi rise in Germany, where infighting amongst left-wing parties had allowed the Nazis to elect candidates across the country, and aimed to prevent it from happening in other Western democracies. In the Spanish elections of 1936, in order to concentrate the moderate Republican and more radical left-wing vote, the left-wing parties co-operated organizationally and, for the most part, did not run candidates against each other. While this type of electoral co-operation was not new in Spain, the political developments both at home and in other parts of Europe gave it an urgency particular to the 1930s. It was essentially a defensive strategy, designed to stop the extreme right from taking power legitimately, as Hitler had done. The parties that participated still had deep political and ideological differences. They were able to agree on what they did not want, but seldom on policies that they did want. In that sense, the Popular

Popular Front A political strategy of electoral cooperation of left-wing parties designed to prevent vote-splitting and thus defeat right-wing parties. The strategy was especially popular in response to the rise of Fascist and other right-wing parties of the 1930s. Popular Front governments were formed in France and Spain in this period.

The **Comintern** or Communist International was an organization that originated with the Bolshevik seizure of power in Russia. Its mission was to coordinate and promote the spread of revolutionary Marxist–Leninism throughout the world. Although it contained representatives from many countries, it was largely directed from Moscow and eventually became little more than a tool of Soviet foreign policy.

Front was born out of a lack of faith in the democratic system, its members not trusting that democracy, traditionally practiced, could preserve freedom in Spain.

The lack of stability provided the pretext for an organized military insurrection, led by army generals Goded, Mola and Franco and dependent on the troops in Spanish Morocco. The rebellious core of the army was a cadre of junior officers, though many higher-ranking officers remained loyal to the Republican government. Logistical support for the uprising came from unlikely corners. The British Royal Navy at Gibraltar helped relay messages for the **rebels** and, when the Spanish naval ships that were to transport the troops from North Africa to the Spanish mainland refused to join the revolt, Hitler ordered German transport planes to take up the slack and transport the Moroccan regulars to the mainland, marking the beginning of increasing international intervention in Spain. These Moroccan troops were the most experienced in the Spanish army and would prove vital to the early survival and eventual success of the Nationalist cause.

The Republican government in Madrid, after ignoring warnings of a rebellion, did not act sufficiently fast to crush the revolt in its infancy. Once the scope of the crisis became clear, it also hesitated in arming the Unión General de Trabajadores (UGT), the Confederación Nacional del Trabajo (CNT) and other left-wing organizations who had sufficient manpower but insufficient fire power to resist the rebellious elements of the army. On the local level, quick action could determine whether the revolt was successful or not. If the local workers' organizations could obtain weapons and if they acted against the local garrison with confidence, most soldiers would submit to the authority of the Republic. If the rising, however, was allowed to gain momentum, army units would round up local political leaders, execute them and bring the town under the control of the Nationalists.

This pattern produced a patchwork of rebel and loyalist holdings early in the insurrection. The rebels held the Andalucian coast, including the city of Seville, and large swaths of north central Spain. In the capital, Madrid, the government maintained control, benefiting from the poor organization and hesitation of the rebels. The east of the country also remained loyal. In the anarcho-syndicalist stronghold of Barcelona,

Francisco Franco (1892–1975)

Francisco Franco was a competent officer who won fast promotion in the early part of his career, most of which was spent in Spanish Morocco. In 1925 he was appointed as the commander of the military academy at Saragossa. His conservative views made him a natural enemy of the Popular Front government elected in 1936. Along with generals Mola and Goded he led the Generals' Rising, which started the Civil War. He soon emerged as the leader of the Nationalist forces. During the Civil War he merged the major right-wing parties into the Falange Española Tradicionalista, with himself as leader. After the Nationalist victory, he became the dictator of Spain until his death in 1975.

In the context of the Spanish Civil War, the **rebels** were those members of the army and their supporters who attempted to overthrow the elected government in 1936.

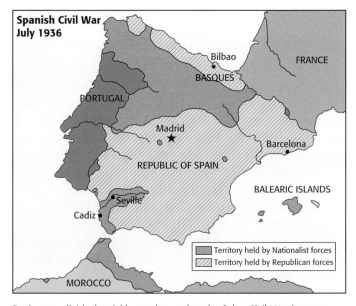

Spain was divided quickly on the outbreak of the Civil War between loyalist and nationalist forces. What factors might have affected which side would establish control of a region in July 1936 before any major engagements had been fought?

the CNT in conjunction with the Federación Anarquista Ibérica (FAI), with the help of loyal civil guards, fought a running battle through the streets against the 12 000 soldiers of the local garrison. As the tide turned in favour of the **loyalists**, General Goded himself, by then a prisoner of the government, urged the rebels to surrender. From that point, Barcelona would be the heart of loyalist Spain. The pattern, however, was clear; the government retained control only where it would accept the help of non-governmental organizations or in places where the army was too poorly organized to establish control. As a form of central control, even over its own forces, the government was weak.

> **Loyalists** Those who supported the elected government of Spain against the rebels during the Spanish Civil War.

The combatants and international reaction

The Republicans
The Republican forces comprised the elements of the military that remained loyal to the government, as well as various militias associated with working-class organizations such as Partido Obrero de Unificación Marxista (POUM) and CNT–FAI. These militias managed to arm themselves with weapons they had stockpiled over the turbulent years before the Civil War and with those they managed to seize from the army. The government was reluctant to arm them but, faced with the growing crisis, it eventually began to supply them with weapons. Although brave and enthusiastic, the volunteer members of the various militias lacked military training and leadership. Ideological, political and strategic differences made co-ordination between the militias very difficult, a fact that was exploited by the Nationalists.

The Nationalists
The Nationalists were made up of the military units that had rebelled in July 1936, augmented by volunteers from right-wing organizations such as the Falange and the Carlists. By introducing conscription in the areas they controlled, the Nationalists were able to increase their overall numbers, including Falange and Carlist militias, to approaching 300 000 men at any one time. By the end of the war, the Nationalists would have mobilized just over a million men. The Nationalists were supported by the Catholic Church in Spain and by other conservative elements such as landowners who were frightened by Republican land seizures and collectivization. These components coalesced under General Franco, who emerged as both the military and eventually the political leader of the Nationalist forces.

While Republican soldiers fought with bravery and enthusiasm, they often lacked reliable weapons, ammunition and military training. This situation was exacerbated by the fact that many elements of Spain's regular army joined the Nationalists. What steps could the Republican government have taken to address this situation?

The international brigades

The Western democracies, such as the United States and the United Kingdom, officially adopted policies of non-intervention and unofficially hoped for a Nationalist victory, frightened as they were of the spread of communism. Such policies were often at odds with popular opinion in these countries, which saw the war more in terms of the defense of democracy against authoritarian fascism. Non-intervention policies not only stopped official aid to the Republicans, but made it illegal for volunteers to travel to Spain and fight for the Republican cause. This prohibition, however, did not stop some 30 000 people, mostly workers and intellectuals, from smuggling themselves into Spain and enlisting in one of the numerous international brigades. The Brigades represented countries from all over the world, including the USA, UK, France, and Canada, but were generally organized by national communist organizations and coordinated by the Comintern, confirming for many Nationalist sympathizers that this was a battle against the spread of Soviet-dominated Communism to Western Europe, an interpretation that Franco publicly held until his death in 1975. Eventually, the Brigades were folded into the more regular Republican Army.

German support

Franco sought aid from Hitler as early as 25 July 1936, a request that the German leader was more than happy to grant. Twenty German transport planes were immediately dispatched to Franco, then still in North Africa, to carry troops to the mainland. Publicly, Hitler maintained that he too wanted to stop the spread of communism in Europe. It later became evident that German foreign policy could benefit from Spain's instability, situated as she was on France's southern border. Furthermore, a Nationalist victory could give Germany access to Spanish natural resources, especially those necessary for arms production. Throughout the course of the war, Germany supplied the Nationalists with artillery, small arms, tanks and vehicles. The most significant material contribution, however, was in aircraft. The German Luftwaffe (air force) formed the Condor Legion to fight in Spain. This consisted of fighter planes, transport planes and bombers, as well as the personnel to maintain and operate them. The Condor Legion provided the Nationalists with a distinct advantage, as the Republican forces had no air force to match it. The operations of the Condor Legion against Republican cities and towns, with the resultant civilian casualties, as in the Basque city of Guernica, presaged the widespread bombing of civilian targets during the Second World War. In all, around 12 000 German personnel served in Spain, fluctuating at any one time between 5000 and 10 000 men. This contribution was to prove vital to the Nationalists' victories, especially as the fighting wore on into 1937 and 1938.

Italian support

Mussolini had had his hand in Spanish politics from before the Civil War, financially supporting the monarchists. At the outbreak of the war, he pledged further aid, both material and personnel. By November 1936, Mussolini had reached a secret agreement with Franco, by which the Italian dictator would receive Spanish support in case of a war with France in return for a sizeable increase in aid to the Nationalist army. The Italian army in Spain, the Corpo Truppe Volontarie (CTV), would number close to 70 000 men and included militia volunteers as well as regular army units, 700 aircraft and 900 tanks. These Italian formations fought throughout the war, contributing in a number of important battles such as Guadalajara.

Soviet support

Stalin did not enjoy the geographic advantage that Hitler and Mussolini had in supplying their Spanish allies. He was also torn between a desire to lead the forces of world socialism and a distrust of the socialist and anarchist elements in Spain. Domestic concerns, Five Year Plans and the purges also occupied Stalin's energy. Nevertheless, by October 1936, Soviet material was arriving in Spain to bolster the Republican forces. Unlike the Germans and Italians, who allowed the Nationalists to purchase material on credit, the Republicans had to pay for Soviet aid with Spain's gold reserves. Most of the Republican's tanks and planes came from the USSR. The Soviets also played an important organizational role. Much of the recruiting and control of the International Brigades, including political commissars responsible for the ideological development of the Brigades, was handled by Soviet personnel. This influence combined with the broader ideological divisions within the Republican forces to create tension and outright conflict between militias ostensibly on the same side, and this at times hindered the war effort.

The Western democracies and non-intervention

In evaluating the response of the Western democracies to the Spanish Civil War it is important to remember that it was governed by their own domestic and foreign policy goals more than any altruistic support for either side in the war. Although the Popular Front government in France might be thought to be a natural ally of their counterpart in Spain, it proceeded very cautiously in offering any support largely because of the desire of its ally, the UK, to avoid confrontation with Italy and its own fear of provoking a resurgent Germany. In a misguided attempt to limit German and Italian aid to the Nationalists, the French Popular Front prime minister, Leon Blum, suggested a binding agreement between nations to remain out of Spanish affairs. The result was the creation of the Non-Intervention Committee, which effectively barred the sale of arms to either side in the Civil War, a stipulation that was upheld by the UK and France and ignored by Germany, Italy and the Soviet Union. The result was to force the Republic to rely even more heavily on the support of the Russians, exactly what the British wanted to avoid. The United States also refused to sell arms to the Republicans, Roosevelt's hands being tied by the **Neutrality Acts**. This, however, did not stop American oil companies selling oil on long-term credit to the Nationalists, as oil was not included in the Neutrality Acts. In the final analysis, non-intervention severely damaged the Republican war effort but had no real effect on the Nationalist forces.

Neutrality Acts A number of laws passed by the US Congress which sought to establish the United States as a formally neutral country. The first Neutrality Act of 1935 was intended to expire in six months, and prohibited America citizens from trading war materials with warring parties. Subsequent Neutrality Acts of 1936, 1937 and 1939 extended and expanded the 1935 Act to include credit and loans to warring parties. The Acts, however, did not include the trading of oil.

Foreign intervention in the Spanish Civil War					
Country	**Association**	**Personnel**	**Aircraft**	**Artillery**	**Armour**
Germany	Nationalists	17 000	600	1 000	200
Italy	Nationalists	75 000	660	1 000	150
USSR	Republicans	3 000	1 000	1 550	900
International Brigades					
United Kingdom	Republicans	2 000			
France	Republicans	10 000	300**		
USA	Republicans	2 800			
Canada	Republicans	1 000			
Czechoslovakia	Republicans	1 000			
Poland	Republicans	5 000			
Hungary	Republicans	1 000			
Yugoslavia	Republicans	1 500			
Germany/Austria*	Republicans	5 000			
Italy*	Republicans	3 350			

* International Brigade volunteers

** Purchased from French government before non-intervention agreement

Progress of the war

After the initial uprising of the generals, it became evident that there would be no quick end to the rebellion. Citizens on both sides took the opportunity afforded by the control of their respective sides to settle old scores with any number of political or even personal enemies. This led to a pattern of violent retribution whenever one side conquered new territory, further increasing the suffering of non-combatants. Republican targets were generally Falange members and Catholic clergy, while the Nationalists sought out anarchists, communists and trade union members. Both sides eventually used sham legality in the form of tribunals to lend an air of legitimacy to the violence. Fame was no protection from the vigilante violence—Nationalist militia in Grenada executed the poet Frederico Garcia Lorca early in the war.

Throughout most of the war, the Republican forces were generally on the defensive. They managed to stop a Nationalist offensive towards Bilbao, the Basque capital, in September 1936 and repulse the first of several attacks on Madrid in November of that year. After failing to conquer the capital city, Franco's forces laid siege to it. The resistance of Madrid would continue for three years and became the emotive rallying point for the Republic, immortalized in the words of Delores Ibárruri, known as La Pasionaria, *"No Passaran!"* (They shall not pass!).

Franco's army was bolstered in 1937 by the arrival of more Italian and German troops and material. He used this increase to launch two more attacks on Madrid, both of which failed. The isolated Basque region was also a target of the Nationalists early in the year, leading to one of the most notorious atrocities of the war. On 26 April, the German Condor Legion launched an air attack on the Basque city of Guernica. The planes flew side by side, carpet-bombing the city for two and a half hours. Civilians fleeing into the fields beyond the city were machine-gunned from above. This was a deliberate targeting of civilians in order to create terror and break their will to resist, a tactic the German air force would continue to use in Spain and later rely on in the Second World War. The horror of that day has been immortalized in Picasso's massive painting *Guernica*, a work the artist would not allow to be hung in Spain until it was again a democratic republic. The Basque region would hold out against Nationalist offensives until June

> **Dolores Ibárruri** (1895–1989)
>
> Known by the pseudonym "La Pasionaria", Dolores Ibárruri was a communist leader and member of the Spanish Communist Party (PCE). She was an elected member of the Spanish parliament, where she championed better working and living conditions for Spain's working class. During the Civil War, she was sent to Western democracies to try to gain support for the Republic. Her gift for public speaking made her one of the chief propagandists of the Republican government. After the Civil War she fled to the Soviet Union, where she lived until the death of Franco in 1975. She then returned to Spain and was once again elected to parliament.

1937, when its capital, Bilbao, fell. As the year progressed, the Republican forces gained more battle experience, fighting more effectively and launching offensives of their own, but these improvements were undermined by tension between the various left-wing parties of the Republic. In Barcelona, in May 1937, tension broke into open warfare pitting communists against anarchists. Clearly a concentrated and organized military effort against the Nationalists could not be pursued while the Republicans were shooting at each other.

Why the Republicans lost

As the war progressed, the Republicans saw a constant erosion of the territory they controlled. By October 1937, they had been reduced to a large territory to the south and east of Madrid and a much smaller piece of land surrounding Barcelona. The Republicans tried to reconnect these two areas of control with the Ebro offensive from July to November 1938, but were unsuccessful. Early in 1939, the last of the Republican strongholds fell, save for Madrid and Valencia, which continued to resist. Despite Republican control of the capital, in February 1939 France and the UK officially recognized the Franco regime as the legitimate government of Spain. The last of the Republican defenders surrendered on 2 April 1939. The Spanish Civil War was over.

The Republicans lost for several reasons. Lack of effective central command and control, political infighting, and insufficient arms and material all played a role in their downfall. Anarchists fought with communists and Marxist/Trotskyists fought with Stalinists. The weaknesses inherent in their military capability forced the Republicans into a predominantly defensive posture from which victory was impossible. Although they did attempt offensives, primarily in 1937, these were often costly and ineffective. For their part, the Nationalists were able to make effective use of the foreign aid they received, most notably the air power of the German Condor Legion. The use of Moroccan regular soldiers gave the Nationalists efficient fighting capability from the beginning of the war, whereas the Republican militias and other forces had to gain valuable experience at the expense of territory.

Aftermath and significance of the war

The immediate cost of the war was devastating. An estimated 500 000 people died between July 1936 and April 1939. Of these deaths, the vast majority were of non-combatants. The physical destruction would take decades to recover from, a fact exacerbated by the pre-war lack of development.

In terms of its broader impact, the Spanish Civil War has been described as a "dress rehearsal" for the Second World War. It is true that the images of this war would become commonplace half a decade later. Carpet-bombing of civilians, violent ideological reprisals linked to military operations, and the integrated use of airpower, armour and infantry made their debut in Spain. Symbolically, the war was a clarion call for the international left to confront the threat posed by expansionary fascism, a fact realized by Spain three years before the democracies of the West.

The war was cast in different roles depending on one's own political beliefs. To the intelligentsia of the West, the war was often characterized as a struggle between the forces of repression on the one side and freedom on the other. For the working classes of the world, it was about landed/industrial interests versus workers and unions. Industrialists, the Texas Oil Company, for example, saw the war as a struggle against expansionary communism and the particular brand of economic and proprietary authoritarianism that comes with it. In this way, the views and interpretations of the war reflected the internal divisions within both the Republican and Nationalist sides and help explain how the war captivated the imagination of the world in the late 1930s. The war figures prominently in the works of writers and artists such as André Malraux, Ernest Hemingway, George Orwell, Dorothy Parker, Paul Robeson and Woody Guthrie.

Strategically, the war brought fascism to both of France's major borders and gave the fascists direct access to the Atlantic, so vital to Britain's interests. In the event, Franco's reluctance to wholeheartedly throw his lot in with Hitler and Mussolini spared the Grand Alliance of the Second World War the reality of dealing with Spain as a declared enemy. This can be attributed to some key differences in fascism as practiced by Franco, Mussolini and Hitler. For his part, Franco's regime was able to survive into the 1970s by a mixture of broad right-wing support and repressive authoritarian tactics.

The American folk singer Woody Guthrie. The inscription on Guthrie's guitar reads "This machine kills fascists". What did he mean by this? What role can the arts play in times of war?

Art and literature inspired by the Spanish Civil War

- WH Auden,
  Spain 1937 (poem)
- Ernest Hemingway,
  For Whom the Bell Tolls (book)
- George Orwell,
  Homage to Catalonia (book)
- Pablo Picasso,
  Guernica (painting)
- Woody Guthrie,
  "*Jarama Valley*" (song)
- Ken Loach,
  Land and Freedom (film)
- Guillermo del Toro,
  Pan's Labyrinth (film)
- The Clash,
  "*Spanish Bombs*" (song)
- Herbert Read, "*Bombing Casualties: Spain*" (poem)
- The Lowest of the Low,
  "*Letter from Bilbao*" (song)
- Manic Street Preachers,
  "*If you tolerate this, your children will be next*" (song)
- Randy, "*Proletarian Hop*" (song)

Buenaventura Durruti (1896–1936)

Buenaventura Durruti was an anarchist leader during the Civil War. He led a number of strikes and uprisings in the turbulent years before the war. Once the war broke out, he urged co-operation amongst left-wing organizations in Barcelona. He led anarchist forces at Saragosa and later at Madrid, where he was killed in combat.

Francisco Largo Caballero (1869–1946)

Francisco Largo Caballero was the leader of both the Spanish Socialist Party (PSOE) and the Unión General de Trabajadores (UGT). He became prime minister of the Republic in September 1936 and brought together a broad left-wing coalition of communists, anarchists, anarcho-syndicalists, socialists and Marxists to lead the Republic during the Civil War. He took steps, much to the consternation of the anarchists, to centralize both military and social control and was dismissed in May 1937. He fled to France after the Civil War and was interned by the Nazis in Dachau concentration camp, where he died in 1946.

Activity:
What is evidence?

The Spanish Civil War was characterized by a bewildering range of propaganda produced by all sides. One of the most distinctive genres of this propaganda was the use of artistic posters to convey political messages. Look at the following posters from the Spanish Civil War and answer the questions that follow.

  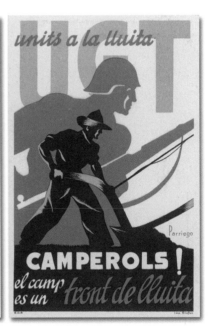

(From left to right) (1) L'industria Textil de Cara a la Guerra Poster, 1937. A pro-union poster for the UGT (Union General de Trabajadores). (2) "And you what have you done for victory?" Poster issued by the UGT and the PSOE (Spanish Socialist Party). (3) Spanish Civil War poster, c. 1937. "The farmer, too, is contributing to the war effort ... ". Poster issued by the UGT and CNT (The Anarcho-syndicalist Union).

1 What messages are conveyed by these posters?

2 Does the use of highly emotional language and expressive effects reinforce the propaganda value of these posters?

3 Of what significance are these posters to historians studying the Spanish Civil War?

4 Choose an organization involved in the Spanish Civil War and create a poster to support their cause.

Juan Negrin (1892–1956)

Negrin was a Spanish socialist. He became prime minister after Largo Cabellero's dismissal. He favoured the communists in his government, appointing them to important positions.

Battle	Opposing sides	Objective	Result	Casualties
Jarama, January 1937	Nationalists—attacking International Brigades—defending	To force a route to Madrid through the Jarama Valley	The Nationalists were able to cross the Jarama River, but the road between Valencia and Madrid remained in Republican hands.	Nationalists: 6000–20 000 Republicans: 6000–20 000
Madrid, November 1936 – March 1939	Nationalists—attacking International Brigades—defending Republicans—defending	To capture the besieged city of Madrid	The Nationalists tried on several occasions to capture the city, but were repulsed. The relief or capture of Madrid influenced strategic decisions on other fronts, such as Brunete. Some of the worst infighting among Republican factions took place in Madrid.	Nationalists: 5000 (1936) Republicans: 5000 (1936) Unknown for the entire siege
Brunete, July 1937	Republicans—attacking International Brigades—attacking Nationalists—defending	To relieve pressure on the encircled city of Madrid	Initially the Republicans made some gains. These were mostly reversed when Franco reinforced his troops. The siege of Madrid remained. Both sides committed retaliatory executions. The Republican setback and high casualties caused dissatisfaction and even mutiny in some Republican and International units.	Republicans: 25 000 Nationalists: 17 000
Aragon, June 1937	Republicans—attacking International Brigades—attacking Nationalists— defending	To relieve pressure on the Basque city of Bilbao	The Republican forces failed to draw Nationalist troops away from their offensive on Bilbao, which fell on 19 June.	Republicans: 1000
Malaga, February 1937	Nationalists—attacking Italian CTV—attacking Republicans (mostly CNT militia)—defending	To capture the city of Malaga in south-western Spain, an anarchist stronghold	Malaga fell within a few days after heavy bombardment and a concentrated attack. After the fall of the city, Nationalist troops executed thousands of Republican sympathizers.	Republicans: unknown Nationalist: unknown Italian: 300
Ebro, July–November 1938	Republicans—attacking International Brigades—attacking Nationalists— defending	To slow or halt the Nationalist movement towards Valencia	Although inflicting heavy casualties on the Nationalists, the Republicans suffered even greater losses that essentially destroyed it as a fighting force.	Republicans: 50 000 Nationalists: 35 000
Guadalajara	Nationalists—attacking Italian CTV—attacking Republicans—defending International Brigades—defending	To capture the city of Guadalajara in an attempt to further encircle Madrid	The Italian CTV were decisively repulsed, in part by Italian Internationals fighting for the Republic.	Nationalists and Italian CTV: 6500 Republicans and International Brigades: 6000

The Algerian War of Independence: guerrilla war and decolonization

The Algerian War, 1954–62, as an example of a 20th-century guerrilla war, highlights many significant historic developments. First, the war is partially a response to the colonial policies of France and as such helps illustrate the relationship between nationalism, imperialism, decolonization and warfare in the 20th century with its profound effects on both Algeria and France. In this section we also examine the strategy and tactics involved in fighting guerrilla wars for both the guerrilla and regular forces, and in so doing explore the brutal nature of this type of warfare for all those involved, including non-combatants.

Guerrilla war

Guerrilla comes from the Spanish word for "little war" and was originally applied to the Spanish resistance to Napoleon's occupation of that country in the early 19th century. It generally involves irregular forces involved in an ongoing struggle with an established regular army. Tactical, strategic and political goals are all closely related in most guerrilla movements.

> **Guerrilla war** A war between irregular forces and established armies.

"Irregular" refers to forces that are not widely recognized as belonging to official, full-time, professional armies. Guerrilla soldiers can be farmers or workers one moment and fighters the next. They seldom wear uniforms, nor are they concentrated in any identifiable base. Guerrilla units are generally small and restrict themselves to "hit and run" engagements. As it achieves success, a guerrilla movement may grow in both strength and organization and by the end of the struggle may appear very similar to a regular army. Such was the case in China and Vietnam. Mao Zedong wrote of guerrilla war as a process or continuum, which starts small and in its later phases grows in size and sophistication.

Guerrilla strategy varies depending on the movement's political goals. Many of the late 20th-century guerrilla movements have concentrated on national independence or liberation, generally from European colonial control. In these cases, the overall strategy is one of endurance and nuisance. Guerrilla forces will not engage in the kind of decisive battle that will bring about its demise, but instead harass the enemy until the cost of pursuing the war is no longer worth the benefits and the occupying power withdraws. Relying as they do on the support, coerced or voluntary, of local populations and not depending on a formal military training, guerrilla armies enjoy a seemingly limitless supply of potential soldiers. This advantage can be pushed to a logical though awful extreme with the conscription of child soldiers. Chief among the weaknesses inherent in guerrilla movements is a difficulty in obtaining an adequate supply of modern weapons. This was often overcome in the second half of the 20th century with the sponsorship of guerrilla movements by larger, wealthier states—rather ironic for those guerrilla forces bent on national liberation.

Guerrilla tactics rely on mobility and stealth. Attacks are generally designed to strike and withdraw before the strength of the conventional forces of the enemy can be brought to bear on the fewer and more lightly armed guerrillas. Because guerrilla forces are often indistinguishable from the general population, the psychological strain on enemy forces can be overwhelming. This, in fact, is one of the key strengths of guerrilla tactics, but can also lead to horrific atrocities on the part of the regular force against civilians suspected of guerrilla activity. Supply and logistics for guerrilla forces are simplified by the small size of the units involved. Many guerrilla units live off what they can take from or are given by the general population. Recognizing this fact, many anti-guerrilla tactics involve restricting access to such support, which again can lead to added hardship on non-combatants.

Though forms of guerrilla war have been practiced since the 19th century, it seemed to reach a zenith with the victory of Mao's people's army over the Chinese Nationalists in 1949. Ever since Mao so ably mobilized his meager resources to conquer and rule the third largest country in the world, using a well-honed guerrilla doctrine, independence movements have been trying to emulate his example. This approach enjoyed a period of concentrated success in the period of mid-20th century decolonization—a success that has been difficult to duplicate since. A fine example of the success of guerrilla movements against European colonizers can be found in the Algerian War of Independence, often referred to simply as the Algerian War.

Twentieth-century guerrilla wars			
War	Guerrillas	Opponents	Result
Chinese Civil War, 1922–49	Communists	Nationalists	Communists gained more and more support, transforming the war into more of a conventional war. The communists won in 1949.
French Indochina War, 1945–54	Viet Minh	France	The Viet Minh forced the French colonial administration to quit the country in 1954.
Vietnam War, 1965–73	Viet Cong	USA, South Vietnamese army	With the help of regular soldiers from North Vietnam, the Viet Cong were able to force the USA from the country in 1973 and then defeated the South Vietnamese army in 1975.
Algerian War, 1954–62	FLN	France	After a bloody war, Algeria declared independence in 1962 with the FLN forming the new government.
Afghan Resistance, 1979–89	Mujahadeen	USSR	With American aid and after ten years of guerrilla fighting, the Mujahadeen forced the Soviets from Afghanistan. This led to a civil war between Mujahadeen factions.
Indonesian War of Independence, 1945–9	Republicans	The Netherlands	After four years of negotiation and fighting, the Netherlands recognized the independence of Indonesia
Mau Mau Uprising (Kenya), 1952–60	Mau Maus (KCA)	UK	Although intensely violent, the revolt collapsed. Eventually the British administration would recognize an independent Kenya.
Malaysian Insurgency, 1948–57	MNLA	UK	The guerrilla campaign was not widely supported and was defeated by the British army. The UK recognized an independent Malaysia of its own accord in 1957.
Cuban Revolution, 1957–9	26th of July Movement	Cuban national army	After a progressively more successful military campaign, Castro's guerrillas were able to force the surrender of the government forces

Causes of the Algerian War

Algeria had become a French colonial possession through a series of military campaigns during the 1830s and 1840s. As France exerted more and more control over the territory, floods of European settlers came to take advantage of cheap land and job opportunities. Successive French governments aimed to assimilate Algeria both administratively and culturally, attempting to make it an integral part of France. As the process of assimilation brought more European technology and investment, it also attracted more settlers throughout the late 19th century. Some natives resisted the assimilation with guerrilla-style attacks on French troops and European settlers. The combination of the military campaigns and the European settlement with its accompanying European illnesses meant that, by the 1870s, the native population of Algeria was declining while the settler population was increasing. Economic inequalities aggravated Muslim discontent with the colonial regime. By the time the war broke out, 75 per cent of the Muslim population was illiterate in Arabic. Unemployment among Algerian Muslims ran to over a million, with twice that number underemployed. In many ways, this pattern of colonization and resistance can be seen as both a long-term cause of the Algerian War and the rationale for the guerilla tactics employed.

The first half of the 20th century would expose French society to both a disastrous victory and a humiliating defeat and occupation in the two world wars. The social consequences of these wars is reflected in the contradictory impulses of the French government and French society at large. On the one hand, there was a desire to break with the past and reject the values and systems that had brought France to the brink of destruction. But there was also a desire to recapture the glory, influence and power of France in the 19th century. These contradictory impulses were evident in French colonial policy in the post-Second World War era. The desire to reject the past was manifest in the granting of independence to Tunisia and Morocco with relatively little friction in the mid-1950s. A longing for the past was seen in the ferocity with which the French tried to maintain control of their Indo-Chinese holdings and Algeria.

The end of the Second World War can be seen as providing a more immediate cause of the Algerian War, although it preceded the outbreak by nine years. Celebrations marking the surrender of Nazi Germany in May 1945 turned violent when Algerian nationalists staged demonstrations and were in turn confronted by European settlers, generally referred to as *pieds-noirs*. When the violence subsided some weeks later, 6000 people—Muslim, *pieds-noirs* and French soldiers—were dead.

This event revealed the three sides that would become involved in the Algerian War nine years later, the French government, the *pieds-noirs* and Algerian nationalists, of which there were a number of organizations. Although for the most part the French army would be the strong arm of the French government, there were times when it acted as a fourth side, protecting its own interests at the expense of the government's orders. The brutality and violence of the 1945 riots anticipated the viciousness of the war to come.

Pieds-noirs (literally "black feet") were French settlers and descendents of French settlers in Algeria. A well-known pied-noir is the writer Albert Camus.

231

The Algerian nationalist movement was, as many such nationalist movements, fractured by method and goal. The Union Démocratique du Manifeste Algérien (UDMA) sought negotiated equality and autonomy within a French state. The older strand of nationalism, the Ulema, favoured statehood based on traditional Islamic law. A hybrid of these two visions found expression in the Movement for the Triumph of Democratic Liberties (MTLD) after 1945, which combined a reverence for traditional Islam, a left-wing social agenda and complete independence from France. It was from the MTLD that the Front de Libération Nationale (FLN), led by Ahmed Ben Bella, would emerge, eventually encompassing most Algerian nationalist aspirations. These aspirations were fuelled by poor economic conditions for Algerian Arabs, income differentials and the accompanying inaccessibility of landownership.

Ahmed Ben Bella (1916–)

Ahmed Ben Bella was one of the founders of the Front de Libération Nationale (FLN). In 1956 he was captured while traveling to Tunis. He spent most of the war in a French prison. He later became Algeria's first president until he was deposed in a coup by forces led by Houari Boumedienne in 1965.

Houari Boumedienne (1932–78)

Boumedienne was the commander of the FLN's military wing, the ALN, stationed in Tunisia. He later took control of the independent Algeria in a coup and ruled as president from 1965 to 1978.

Outside influences also played a role in the timing of the outbreak of hostilities in 1954. Mao's example only grew in luster, having taken control of China in 1949 and, three years later, fighting the United States to a standstill in Korea. It seemed as though anything might be possible. The French defeat at **Dien Bien Phu** and their subsequent withdrawal from Indochina also seemed to present a historic opportunity for Algerian nationalists. Although there had been guerrilla-style attacks throughout the French occupation of Algeria, the FLN began to plan a marked increase in co-ordinated attacks shortly after the French military disaster at Dien Bien Phu, even though there were very few similarities between the two causes or situations.

 Why do nationalist movements tend to be fractured? How does this affect the post-colonial administration of successor states?

Dien Bien Phu A battle between the Viet Minh and the French army between March and May of 1954. This Viet Minh victory drove the French from Indochina and led to the partition of the country into North and South Vietnam.

- Unlike the Viet Minh, the FLN did not have any particular ideological orientation.
- While the Viet Minh enjoyed the sponsorship of a major power, China, the FLN had no such aid.
- While Indochina was geographically remote from France and thus more difficult to support, Algeria was close.
- French law prohibited the use of conscripts in Indochina, but there were no such restrictions on the use of French conscripts in Algeria.

Nevertheless, the FLN judged the time to be right and on 1 November 1954 it conducted a number of co-ordinated bomb attacks across Algeria. This marks the start of the Algerian War.

Advantages and disadvantages of conscription	
Advantages	**Disadvantages**
Increases the pool from which to draw soldiers	Soldiers may lack motivation
Makes the size of the army predictable	Subjects the military to all the social factions in a country
Can spread the burden of military service across social classes and groups	Can breed resentment in the population as a whole as a form of governmental control and interference
Can integrate the military into society more thoroughly	Military losses are felt throughout the population
Increases civil participation and sense of civic responsibility	Constant turnover of troops can make training expensive
	Requires close cooperation between military and civilian authorities

Practices

Lacking a major sponsor state and the weapons that such a state could supply, the FLN was limited to small actions, bombings of infrastructure mostly, throughout 1954 and into 1955. The French had no such limitations. The government in Paris made it clear that Algeria was part of France and would remain so. To that end, the French bolstered its military presence in Algeria, sending paratroopers and **Legionnaires** who then conducted a campaign of assassination and retaliation against suspected FLN supporters. This campaign bit deep into the FLN leadership. As in most guerrilla wars, a brutal pattern emerged in Algeria during 1955. FLN attacks would provoke retaliatory attacks by the French army, who would use vicious tactics both to discourage civilian support for the FLN and to obtain information about their activities. In an effort to coerce such support, the FLN would put often brutal pressure on Algerian civilians and terrorize the *pieds-noirs*. It was on non-combatants that much of the hardship of this and other guerrilla wars fell.

Legionnaires Soldiers in the French Foreign Legion, an elite formation within the French army. The Legion, created in the 1830s, accepts volunteers from foreign states, but also contains substantial numbers of French citizens.

This was made evident in August 1955 when a unit of FLN guerrillas descended on the city of Philippeville. By the time the guerrillas had left, 123 civilians, Muslim and *pieds-noirs*, had been murdered. The retaliation of the French military claimed 1200 victims by its own estimates, 12 000 by outside estimates. This type of retaliation was an example of the principle of **collective responsibility** adopted by both French and FLN forces throughout the war and designed to discourage support for the enemy. Again, it was the civilians that bore the brunt of it. Because the violence was meted out by both sides and fell on both European and Algerian populations, the Philippeville massacres and aftermath radicalized the moderates on both sides. *Pied-noir* gangs conducted their own terror campaigns against Algerians, who in turn joined the FLN in greater numbers.

Collective responsibility The practice of holding all members of a population responsible for the actions of a few of its members.

The French administration intensified its efforts throughout Algeria during 1956. It moved those suspected of actively supporting the FLN, sometimes whole villages, and imprisoned leaders, while at the same time implementing limited economic reforms to alleviate some grievances. This approach was supplemented by an aggressive military campaign in which Foreign Legionnaires and paratroops used helicopter transport to move into remote areas and root out FLN fighters, a tactic that the United States would adopt in Vietnam ten years later. Helicopters, it seemed, allowed anti-guerrilla forces to rely

IB Learner Profile link
Reflective

Under what circumstances would you support your country's decision to go to war?

Do you support conscription?

less on infrastructure such as roads and thereby removed a major guerrilla target. In some ways, their use gave to the regular force the mobility previously enjoyed only by the guerrillas.

The FLN continued to be plagued by supply issues, despite receiving some support from Nasser's government in Egypt. By the end of 1956, however, French military strength in Algeria reached 500 000. This coordinated approach dealt a significant blow to the FLN, which lost over half its fighting strength during that year. France was using half a million soldiers to conduct operations against a force of about 30 000 irregular, guerilla fighters. The question became, as in all occupations, which side could last longer, in terms both of sustaining adequate material support and the will to continue the war.

In 1957, the FLN moved the war to the cities, most notably to the capital, Algiers. The "Battle of Algiers" was more a series of terror attacks by FLN guerrillas, including women, and reprisals by the French military. By moving the war to the cities, the FLN leadership hoped to gain more international attention and support. The danger in such a move is that it is harder to hide in a city because you need the support of more people. The possibility of betrayal is far greater in the city. The French used this fact against the FLN by terrorizing the population and using torture to extract information, eventually rooting out most FLN fighters in Algiers. As the French military began to rely more on torture, and as this fact became known in France, French public opinion began to turn against the war.

When France granted independence to Morocco and Tunisia in 1956 and 1957, it inadvertently supplied the FLN with a valuable resource—a place to hide. To neutralize this resource, the French military constructed a barrier between Tunisia and Algeria. The **Morice Line**, as it became known, consisted of an electrified fence, reinforced with anti-personnel mines, artillery and 80 000 soldiers patrolling its length. A similar line attempted to insulate Algeria from Morocco. Despite the complexity of the line, the FLN would launch attacks from the Tunisian and Moroccan side of the lines. One such attack led to a French air strike on the Tunisian town of Sakiet. The FLN continued to build up a significant conventional military

French president Charles de Gaulle greets Algerians. Despite repeated threats and attempts on his life, de Gaulle insisted on remaining very much in the public eye. Why would he take such risks? What are the advantages and disadvantages of such an attitude for a government leader? "Demoralize the enemy from within by surprise, terror, sabotage, assassination. This is the war of the future." In light of 20th-century wars, to what extent do you agree with Adolf Hitler in this regard?

> The **Morice Line** was a fortified barrier between Algeria and Tunisia designed to keep FLN fighters and supplies in Tunisia from getting to Algeria.

Activity:

Attrition and guerrilla wars

Ho Chi Minh, leader of the Viet Minh forces and later North Vietnam in its struggle against France and the United States, once said:

You can kill ten of my men for every one of yours I kill, but even at those odds, you will lose and I will win.

1 Explain why Ho thought this to be true.

2 What disadvantages for the guerrilla forces are involved in pursuing a strategy of **attrition**?

3 Is Ho's statement valid for all guerrilla wars? Why or why not?

4 Research two other guerrilla wars, each taken from a different region. Does Ho's claim apply to these conflicts?

> **Attrition** In military terms, the doctrine that seeks to weaken the enemy by depleting and destroying their resources, human and material, to the point that they surrender or otherwise abandon the fight.

force behind the Morice Line and, although it never played a significant role in the war itself, it posed the question of whether the Morice Line and the accompanying French military force would need to be permanent. Again, France was faced with the question of whether or not Algeria was worth such an ongoing effort.

The presence of sympathetic border countries is a dilemma faced by many counter-insurgency efforts. The Ho-Chi-Minh trail in Vietnam that ran from North Vietnam to South Vietnam through neighbouring Laos and Cambodia would frustrate the American effort throughout the war and lead to the disastrous invasion of Cambodia in 1971. Even in the early 21st century, such refuge has played a significant role in the conflicts in both Iraq and Afghanistan. Efforts to deal with such support always carry with them the danger of widening the war.

Discussion point: torture in a democracy

Alan Dershowitz, a high-profile legal scholar, has made the argument that the limited use of torture can be necessary in democratic states.

If torture is going to be administered as a last resort in the ticking-bomb case, to save enormous numbers of lives, it ought to be done openly, with accountability, with approval by the president of the United States or by a Supreme Court justice.

Source: Interview with Wolf Blitzer. CNN, 4 March 2003. http://edition.cnn.com/2003/LAW/03/03/cnna.Dershowitz.

1 What does Dershowitz mean by a "ticking-bomb case"?
2 Do you agree with Dershowitz? Why or why not?
3 Would Dershowitz advocate a similar use of torture by authoritarian regimes? Why or why not?
4 Does his justification for torture apply to the French in Algeria?

Foreign support for guerrillas		
War	**Guerrillas**	**Supporter(s)**
Algeria	FLN	Egypt
Vietnam	Viet Minh and Viet Cong	USSR; China
Afghanistan	Mujahadeen	USA
Angola	MPLA	Cuba
Nicaragua, 1974–9	Sandinistas	Cuba
Nicaragua, 1981–7	Contras	USA
Pakistan	Mukti Bahni	India

Guerrilla campaigns traditionally wed military and political goals. The degree to which the political fate of France was tied to the insurgency in Algeria was clearly illustrated in May 1958. After the fall of the government in Paris and before a new one could be formed, the pieds-noirs and leading military commanders in Algiers conspired to take control of the civil administration of Algeria. The conspiracy was not restricted to Algeria. An important component of the rebel generals' plan, and what they said would stave off further action on their part, was the political resurrection of Charles de Gaulle. De Gaulle was seen by many as a force of political stability. The army trusted him as a former military man. At that point, the *pieds-noirs* trusted him as a leader who believed that Algeria should remain under French control. In France the left and right trusted him as someone who would put the best interests of France ahead of political squabbling. De Gaulle, however, was himself circumspect about what he believed those interests to be. A new constitution brought about the birth of the French Fifth Republic and with it de Gaulle as president.

A new French military commander, Maurice Challe, and renewed efforts brought FLN forces in Algeria to the brink of destruction throughout 1959. Despite its weakness in Algeria,

Jacques Massu (1908–2002)

Massu was the commander of the elite 10th Parachute Division stationed in Algeria. Massu had a reputation for ferocity and determination, especially after the Battle of Algiers, where he authorized and encouraged the use of torture and other coercive tactics. He was later dismissed after publicly criticizing government policy in 1961.

the FLN continued to launch terrorist attacks in France, making the cost of the war more evident to French civilians. Throughout the war there were some 42 000 terrorist attacks in France, claiming 2800 civilian lives. Such attacks affected de Gaulle, who appears to have seen Challe's victory over the FLN in the field as a temporary success in an endless conflict. De Gaulle was also acutely aware that since 1945 the process of **decolonization** was accelerating around the world and that, as a result, the age of European colonialism was waning. He decided to put the issue of Algerian independence or self-determination to a referendum, in both France and Algeria. Believing de Gaulle had betrayed them, *pieds-noirs* set up barricades in the streets and Challe refused to take action against them. The *pieds-noirs* took them down of their own accord a week later. The referendum passed and, to the horror of the French military commanders in Algeria and the *pieds-noirs*, de Gaulle set about negotiating the future of an Algerian state. This development illustrates an important point about guerrilla war in the cause of national independence. Even though the insurgency seemed near defeat, it was the prospect of it flaring up after a period of dormancy that frightened de Gaulle and the rest of France. This was especially threatening given the military presence of the FLN in Tunisia. As Henry Kissinger would later say, "A conventional army loses if it does not win. A guerrilla army wins if it does not lose." De Gaulle understood this and determined that Algeria was not worth the cost. For de Gaulle that cost appeared to be a never-ending guerrilla war.

> **Decolonization** The global movement in the second half of the 20th century toward independence for territories that had been ruled as colonies of European states. The movement was especially prevalent in South Asia and Africa during this period. Decolonization could be accomplished by either peaceful or violent means.

There were still difficult negotiations ahead. Complicating matters was the fact that the FLN did not, in the end, speak for all Algerian nationalists, a fact further complicated by the hundreds of thousands of Algerian Muslims who remained, in varying degrees, loyal to France, including some 60 000 who served in the French military. With the support of the *pieds-noirs*, the military staged a short-lived coup in Algiers in 1961, though not it seems with the support of much of the conscripted rank and file of the army. Finally, in 1961, desperate *pieds-noirs* and some military officers formed a deadly terrorist organization known as the Organisation de l'armée secrète (OAS). The OAS conducted bomb attacks and shootings throughout Algeria and France until 1962, with both Algerian Muslims and the French army as their targets.

French paratroopers clear houses during the Battle of Algiers. Fighting a guerrilla war in an urban setting is different to fighting in the field. What comparative advantages and disadvantages does fighting in an urban setting have for both sides in a guerrilla war?

Effects

As in all wars, the most immediate effect was in the form of casualties. Counting the dead is a difficult and political task in all wars and becomes especially difficult in a guerrilla war. Guerrilla armies seldom keep accurate records of troop strength for security reasons, which makes counting the dead far from easy. It is in the interests of both sides to under-report their own casualties and over-report those of the enemy for morale and propaganda purposes. There can also be propaganda value in over-reporting the civilian casualties caused by the enemy. Counting civilian deaths is likewise a challenge and even more so in a guerrilla conflict when the line between civilian and soldier is, by definition, blurred. Accurate census data is necessary and this not always available.

Charles de Gaulle (1890–1970)

Charles de Gaulle was a soldier, politician and statesman in France. When successive governments of the Fourth Republic could not manage the Algerian War, he came back to French politics after a 12-year hiatus and founded the Fifth Republic, in which he served as president. Both *pieds-noirs* and the army saw him as a man of honesty and integrity and supportive of their position. Once in power, however, de Gaulle soon came to believe that a stable France that included Algeria was not viable. He began talks, first secret and later public, with the FLN and negotiated the cease-fire agreement and later the final agreement setting out Algerian independence. For his troubles, de Gaulle survived a number of assassination attempts.

Maurice Challe (1905–79)

Maurice Challe took command of all French forces in Algeria in 1959. He organized a successful campaign against the FLN, virtually driving them from Algeria by the end of the year. Challe sided with the *pieds-noirs* when it looked as though de Gaulle would favour Algerian independence, eventually taking part in the revolt of the generals in 1961, for which he served five years in prison. He was pardoned by de Gaulle in 1968.

Algeria, by all accounts, was a brutal and costly conflict. Estimates range from 500 000 to one million deaths. According to their records, the French military lost 18 000 dead and 53 000 wounded in the years 1954–62. When the FLN came to power in 1962, it conducted a campaign of retribution against those Muslims who it suspected had remained loyal to the French regime during and after the war. Estimates put the fatalities of this campaign at 150 000.

After the **Evian Accords** ended the fighting in 1962, there was a mass migration of *pieds-noirs* and loyal Algerians (*harkis*). Fear of FLN reprisals forced many to choose "the suitcase or the coffin", as many put it at the time. Close to a million *pieds-noirs* fled to France in the wake of the FLN victory, putting a significant strain on French society in terms of housing and social programs. Some 90 000 *harkis* also fled to France.

The legacy of the Algerian War is ambiguous. For some, it stands as an example of the power of guerrilla war in the cause of national liberation. For others, it stands for the brutality that guerrilla war can engender in both sides.

Evian Accords An agreement, signed on 18 March 1962 between the French government and the FLN. The agreement established a permanent ceasefire in the Algerian War and the removal of French forces. It guaranteed the religious and property rights of French citizens who remained in an independent Algeria. The Evian Accords were approved by an overwhelming percentage of French citizens in a referendum held in April 1962.

Harkis Algerian Muslims who fought for the French during the Algerian War.

Indo-Pakistan wars, 1947–9, 1965, 1971: religion, decolonization and war

While the Algerian War helped precipitate the decolonization of Algeria in the post-Second World war period, the series of wars that gripped the Indian subcontinent in the same period can be seen as a result of decolonization rather than a cause. The nature of British rule in India and then the manner in which it relinquished its control helped set the stage for three major wars between India and Pakistan in 1947–9, 1965 and 1971. Complicating and exacerbating these wars were the deep religious divisions within the region and the Cold War context within which they were fought. This Cold War context illustrates the challenges in maintaining a sovereign foreign policy in a region of strategic importance to the superpowers. Among other things, the results of this series of wars include the creation of the country of Bangladesh, the proliferation of nuclear weapons, and ongoing tension and conflict over regions such as Kashmir.

Background causes

Great Britain had established colonial control over the Indian subcontinent from the mid-15th century until the late-19th century. The British ruled with a combination of indirect and direct rule, depending on which better served its economic and strategic interests. Taken as a whole, this approach to imperialism can be seen as one of divide and conquer, the British having realized the simple fact that the Indian subcontinent was not a single entity but rather a geographic region split by religion, ethnicity, language, economics and, eventually, politics and even ideology. Seen this way, India was a British invention. The two major religious groups were the Hindus and the Muslims, but even these major groups were divided by geography, language, culture and religious interpretation.

Throughout the late 19th and early 20th century, India developed a distinct nationalism that sought independence from the British Empire. Central to this nationalism was an organization called the Indian National Congress, founded in 1885. Officially, the Congress was a secular and inclusive organization seeking to unite all Indians in the cause of national independence. In practice, the Congress was seen by some as an elitist, urban organization that did not speak for India in all its diversity. The strong personality of Mohandas Gandhi, with his strict egalitarian beliefs and extreme emphasis on non-violence, attempted to unite the varied and often competing interests that emerged in the nationalist movement. Many of these diverse currents have been explored in recent historiography. The Muslim League was founded in 1906, as a Muslim counterweight to the Hindu-dominated Congress. Mohammad Ali Jinnah, once a member of the Congress, joined the Muslim League and later emerged as its leader. As time passed, Jinnah became more and more convinced that the Congress's emphasis on democracy and majority rule would reduce the Muslim population of India to a secondary role in the political, economic and social life of an independent India.

While Gandhi was trying to unite Indian nationalists, Great Britain was trying to maintain its control of the subcontinent. This became increasingly difficult in the wake of Britain's pyrrhic victory in the First World War and impossible after the defeat of the Axis powers in the Second World War. Understanding this, the UK's Labour government dispatched Lord Louis Mountbatten to India as the viceroy, with a mandate to negotiate independence. It was immediately evident to Mountbatten that, despite Gandhi's optimism, if India was allowed to secede as a whole, a civil war was inevitable. It was to avoid such a catastrophe that Mountbatten imposed **partition** on India, creating a predominantly Hindu state, India, and a predominantly Muslim state, Pakistan.

> **Partition** The division of a territory into two or more smaller, independent territories.

Regardless of how carefully they are drawn, lines on a map seldom correspond to populations on the ground or to economic realities. The partition of India was no exception, setting off a human tragedy of enormous proportions. Huge numbers of Hindus who found themselves inside the borders of Pakistan abandoned their homes and fled to India. Likewise, Muslims in India escaped into Pakistan. As many as 14 million Muslims and Hindus fled. Integrating these refugees into Pakistani and Indian society proved nearly impossible. The savage and horrific violence that accompanied this massive migration claimed between 500 000 and one million victims. Memories of the violence have coloured relations ever since.

Where the Algerian War was a definite catalyst to decolonization of that country, the Indo-Pakistan wars of 1947–9, 1965 and 1971 can be seen partially as a consequence of a poorly planned decolonization process. The background causes of the conflicts that followed therefore lie in part with the way in which the British imposed partition on their Indian colonial holdings. In this way the British played a role in setting the stage for the future wars. Mountbatten's decisions may have prevented a civil war in the short term, but were certainly a factor in causing the wars that followed. The partition, hastily put together, ignored many ethnic and religious complexities in India. The result was a confused military and political situation as well as the chaotic human tragedy mentioned above. Well into independence, the British continued to play a role in the military in both countries, creating an awkward situation when the first of the three wars broke out.

Mohandas Gandhi (1869–1948)

Trained as a lawyer, Gandhi became a spiritual and eventually a political leader in the Indian subcontinent. He advocated the use of non-violent civil disobedience as a mass movement to persuade the British to quit India. He worked with the Indian National Congress as well as the Muslim League to negotiate independence in 1947. Although himself a Hindu, Gandhi had a vision of an undivided India where Muslim and Hindus lived together, a vision that was dashed by the eventual partition of India. He was assassinated in January 1948.

Mohammad Ali Jinnah (1876–1948)

Mohammad Ali Jinnah was a Muslim leader in the Indian subcontinent. Although once a member of the Indian National Congress, he joined the Muslim League in 1916 and quickly rose as one of its most influential members. Jinnah came to believe that despite being officially secular, the new independent India state would be dominated by the Hindu majority. He therefore favoured a separate independent Muslim state. Ironically, he saw this Muslim state as secular, even though the division would be based on religious populations. This state became Pakistan and Jinnah became its first Governor General.

The 1947–9 war

Immediate causes

Partition created a curious political geography in the subcontinent. While India remained a geographic whole, Pakistan had two distinct parts, the physically larger but more sparsely populated West Pakistan and the more populous but smaller East Pakistan. Deep ethnic, religious and economic differences also separated the two Pakistans. These differences would simmer for over 20 years until they boiled over in 1971.

Issues associated with partition were exacerbated by the diverse nature of British rule in India. While the British had ruled much of India directly, there were many so-called princely states in which the British ruled through local princes, potentates and maharajas. Under Mountbatten's partition plan, these states could choose to join either Pakistan or India or become independent. By the time independence was granted at midnight on 14 August 1947, only three of these states chose independence. The largest of the three was Kashmir and it would prove to be complicated. A Hindu maharaja ruled the state, but the majority of the population was Muslim. Kashmir was strategically important to both India and Pakistan.

In the tumultuous period immediately before and after partition, Kashmir was not spared the ethnic strife that engulfed the rest of the subcontinent. Muslims rose up against the Hindu administration and Hindu minority throughout the territory. Hoping to capitalize on this discord and the basic demographic reality of Kashmir, the Pakistani government sent Muslim tribesmen into Kashmir in an effort to overthrow the government in August 1947, less than a month after independence.

Progress of the war

The tribesmen proved too much for the Kashmiri defenders. In desperation, the maharaja appealed to India for military aid in October 1947. Delhi set the condition for this aid, accession of Kashmir to India. The maharaja's acceptance of the conditions invited a more formal intervention on the part of the Pakistani army in May 1948, thereby igniting the first Indo-Pakistan War. As the war came so close on the heels of independence, the chiefs of staff of both armies were serving British generals who had served together in the British army before independence. While making for a strange situation, it probably helped in the brokering of the eventual **ceasefire**.

The Indian army used aircraft to transport troops quickly to Srinagar, the Kashmiri capital, where they were able to use numbers, discipline and a few armoured cars to push the Pakistani irregular forces well back. When the Indian forces encountered regular Pakistani units after May 1948, the fighting was less one sided, developing into something of a stalemate through the rest of 1948. The Indian army enjoyed initial success throughout the country, with one exception. In the high mountains the Pakistani army, with the help of local

Discussion point: Partition

Partition has long been a solution to the internal division that often accompanies decolonization. Ireland, the former Yugoslavia, Vietnam, Korea and other states have faced partition as a way of accommodating conflicting interests during transfers of powers.

What can affect where partition boundaries are drawn?

What are the potential problems?

Are there alternatives to partition?

Ceasefire An agreement to stop military operations; not necessarily a final end to hostilities.

irregular forces, were moderately successful. The fledgling United Nations, after studying the conflict, brokered a ceasefire that came into effect on 1 January 1949.

Effects

As in all wars, the most immediate effects are on those who suffer through the conflict. Each side lost about 1500 regular soldiers and the civilian casualties ran into the tens of thousands. Politically, the most significant result of the war was that Kashmir formally became part of India, despite the majority of its citizens being Muslim. This was also despite the fact that the Pakistani army occupied some northern sections of Kashmir at the time of the ceasefire. The Pakistani government attempted to recognize this territory as "Free Kashmir"—a move not taken up by the international community. Pakistan never recognized Kashmir as part of India, giving rise to repeated border clashes well into the 21st century. These border disputes would spark another border war over Kashmir in 1965.

The 1965 Kashmir War

Immediate causes

Border clashes between India and Pakistan were not limited to the Kashmir region. All along the border, army patrols routinely fought small skirmishes. Nevertheless, it was inevitable that should major hostilities break out elsewhere on the border it would spread to Kashmir. Such was the case in 1965.

Much had happened in the time since the first war over Kashmir. India was developing into a democracy, albeit with one dominant party, while Pakistan was far more authoritarian with the military playing a very influential political role. By 1958, the military seized control of Pakistan in a coup, putting General Ayub Khan in control. Both countries sought allies among the developed states of the world. Pakistan became a member of two Western alliance systems, SEATO and CENTO. India's policy of **non-alignment** became very difficult when faced with the growing prospect of a border war against China. As a result of deteriorating Sino-Soviet relations, the Kremlin tried to establish ties with India. The United States also supplied arms to both India and Pakistan as a bulwark against the expansion of communism in any form. India's poor showing in the war with China in 1962 led her to seek even greater support from abroad, and this was eagerly provided by the Soviet Union. Pakistan, in turn, saw an opportunity in India's weakness and

Non-alignment A political doctrine pioneered by Jawaharlal Nehru, prime minister of India, whereby a state does not associate itself with the ideology or political goals of any other states. Generally this means that the states eschew formal alliances.

Government and war			
Authoritarian		**Democratic**	
Advantages	Disadvantages	Advantages	Disadvantages
Efficient decision making	Lack of accountability protects military incompetence	Genuine mass mobilization	Must maintain public support
Easy to maintain secrecy	Lack of institutionalized accountability means regimes rarely survive defeat	Participatory leadership	Friction between public disclosure and secrecy
		Accountability promotes military competence	
		Institutionalized accountability protects system in defeat	
		Flexible response to challenges	
		Ensures consensus going to war	

tried to draw closer to China, a diplomatic feat made more difficult by her close relationship with the United States. This complex diplomatic web was not the cause of the 1965 war. It does, however, illustrate the degree to which these regional and limited wars, as most conflicts of the time, were affected by broader Cold War developments. In so far as foreign aid made both the Indian and Pakistani armies more effective, this involvement can be seen as exacerbating the tensions and thereby intensifying the wars.

Military Aid								
Power	Clients*	Nature	Power	Clients*	Nature	Power	Clients*	Nature
USA	Nicaragua, 1990–2000	Material Financial	USSR	Afghanistan, 1978–89	Material Financial Advisors Personnel	China	North Vietnam, 1954–79	Material Financial
	Cuba, 1902–59	Material Financial Advisors		Cuba, 1961–90	Material Financial Advisors Personnel (1962)		North Korea	Material Financial Advisors Personnel (1950–3)
	Pakistan	Material Alliance (CENTO, SEATO) Financial		China, 1949–62	Material Financial Advisors Personnel		Pakistan	Material Financial Technological
	Israel	Material Financial		North Korea	Material Financial Advisors			
	El Salvador	Material Financial Advisors Alliance (Rio Pact)		Egypt	Material Financial Advisors			
	Panama	Material Financial Advisors Personnel Alliance (Rio Pact)		India, 1962–74	Financial Material			
	South Vietnam, 1954–73	Material Financial Advisors Personnel Alliance (SEATO)						

<f/n>*   The use of the term "client" does not indicate complete subservience; these are not satellite states. Rather, it indicates which state is receiving the aid.

The 1965 Kashmir War started far from Kashmir, in a marshy flood plain in the west of the subcontinent called the Rann of Kutch. A diplomatic dispute about the negligible resources of the area resulted in a border clash in 1965.

Progress of the war

Military engagements in the Rann of Kutch were fairly limited. A major battle was fought in April 1965, in which the Pakistani army scored a decisive victory over the Indian army before a ceasefire was negotiated by the British government. Flush with this victory and with exaggerated beliefs about the ability of the Pakistani soldier vis-à-vis the Indian soldier and the receptiveness of the Kashmiri population to Pakistani rule, hawks in the Pakistani parliament thought the time ripe for an aggressive move against Kashmir. The move came initially in the form of "guerrilla" attacks across the border in August 1965, designed to provoke a general uprising against Indian rule. These "guerrillas", some 30 000 in number, were for the most part regular Pakistani soldiers dressed as Kashmiri civilians. The ruse was quickly exposed, paving the way for units of both regular armies to engage each other. Initially, these engagements were fought within Kashmir using infantry as well as tanks and air power, as supplied by both countries' newfound patrons.

By early September, the Indian army took the fight to Pakistan, crossing the border in the Punjab region. This led to a major, though indecisive, engagement around Sialkot that involved large numbers of tanks. By mid-September, the pattern of stalemate returned to the front, enticing both sides to accept the UN's ceasefire proposal. Soviet prime minister Alexsei Kosygin invited both sides to a conference in Tashkent in January 1966, where they eventually agreed on a permanent ceasefire in Kashmir.

Effects

The Pakistani army lost about 3800 soldiers, and the Indian army some 1000 fewer, numbers dwarfed by the 13 000 civilians killed during the fighting. Diplomatically, the war produced some interesting revelations to the two sides. Pakistan discovered the limits to its friendship with the United States, who suspended arms shipments to both sides during the war, judging it to be largely Pakistan's fault. The US build-up in Vietnam may have played some role in this decision as well. Economically, Pakistan's expanding economy was significantly damaged as a result of the war, delaying further progress that had relied on American aid and advice.

For her part, India lost the unconditional support of the Soviets, who adopted a more balanced approach to the two countries, as witnessed at Tashkent. Given the recent Sino-Soviet split, the Soviets did not want to drive the Pakistanis even further into the arms of the Chinese. Nevertheless, India continued to rely on Soviet arms in the post-1965 period, increasing the size of its military and improving its operational capabilities, a fact that would become evident in six years when yet another Indo-Pakistani war erupted.

Ayub Khan (1907–74)

Ayub Khan trained as an officer in the British army, eventually rising to the post of chief of staff in independent Pakistan, the first native-born Pakistani to hold this post. Setting the precedent for military control, Ayub Khan led a bloodless coup in 1958. Perhaps anticipating détente by ten years, he maintained close ties with both China and the United States. He led Pakistan into the 1965 war against India with high hopes. After initial success, he felt betrayed when the United States embargoed arms against both Pakistan and India and took much of the blame for not achieving Pakistan's war aims.

The Indo-Pakistan war of 1971

Immediate causes

As we have seen, the partition of British India not only split India and Pakistan but divided Pakistan itself within the now divided subcontinent. East Pakistan, in Bengal, was separated from West Pakistan by 1000 miles (1600 km) and vast linguistic, economic and cultural differences. While East Pakistan produced the lion's share of Pakistani revenue, it received only a quarter of the national income. The overwhelming majority of political positions were held by Westerners though they made up a minority of the country's population. As the disparity grew, so too did East Pakistani dissatisfaction.

This dissatisfaction was registered at the ballot box in the elections of December 1970, elections that followed close on a horrific cyclone a month earlier that claimed 300 000 lives across the region. For the first time, the election brought the Awami Party, based in East Pakistan, to power at the expense of the Pakistan People's Party and its leader Zulfikar Ali Bhutto. The Awami Party put forward policies that essentially amounted to autonomy for East Pakistan within the Pakistan state, a prospect that was unacceptable to the president, Yahya Khan, to Bhutto and to the military. As a result, on 25 March 1971, the Awami Party was outlawed, its leaders arrested and massive numbers of troops were airlifted to East Pakistan until total troop strength reached approximately 75 000.

The Pakistani military then began ruthlessly to suppress what it saw as an uprising in East Pakistan. As many as 300 000 citizens of East Pakistan were killed in the resulting violence. It was the escalation of this essentially internal conflict that would compel India to intervene.

When the violence erupted in March 1971, close to six million refugees began streaming across the border into India, seeking a sanctuary from the Pakistani army, a number that would reach ten million by the end of the war. At the same time, an East Pakistani guerrilla movement developed, called the **Mukti Bahni**. Now India had a client to support in a conflict that was rapidly beginning to have grave consequences on her own domestic situation. The refugees were quickly outstripping India's ability to care for them. As the guerrilla force grew to over 100 000, the Indian army began to

Mukti Bahni The guerrilla army raised in East Pakistan to fight for independence from Pakistan. The Mukti Bahni grew to 100 000 fighters at one point and received material support from India.

mass troops on the border with East Pakistan. While India's high command made military preparations for war, India's prime minister, Indira Gandhi, set about preparing the diplomatic field. In August, India signed a 20-year Treaty of Peace, Friendship and Cooperation with the Soviet Union. In an effort to get a diplomatic solution or at the very least to explain the plight of India in this situation, Gandhi visited the United States, the United Kingdom and the Soviet Union. The intention was in part to shore up support in the event that Indian intervention became necessary to stop China from becoming involved. In any case, as November approached, the high mountain passes between China and India would be impassable by the Chinese army, a fact that no doubt influenced the timing of India's invasion. The entire situation was aggravated by another cyclone that hit the region in November 1971, creating for India an urgent refugee crisis of her own and prompting many to demand that these Indian refugees be given priority of aid. In all, the combined refugee problem threatened to undo the economic and agricultural progress that India had been experiencing. Gandhi had economic studies indicating that caring for these multitudes would be far more expensive than a projected war against Pakistan.

In many ways, this war was significantly different from the previous two Pakistani wars. Most obviously, but for strategic engagements, this dispute did not involve the Kashmir region, although there was always a very real danger that it could escalate to involve the still disputed Kashmir. Explaining the reluctance of the United States to aid India, Secretary of State Henry Kissinger maintained that India intended to use the dispute in East Pakistan to make a move on Kashmir. Another key difference is that this war started out as a civil conflict within Pakistan, a conflict between Muslims, equally as vicious as any between Hindu and Muslim. Further, India had little interest in controlling East Pakistan, advocating instead an independent Muslim state. Further, East Pakistan had not been attacked by India in the 1965 war. This would all seem to cast some doubt on those who would characterize all the conflicts of the region as primarily religious in nature.

Yahya Khan (1917–80)

After commanding an infantry division in the 1965 war with India, Yahya Khan took the post of army chief of staff in 1966 and, within the context of that position, became the president of Pakistan in 1969. He soon made preparations for democratic elections, which, when held, brought the East Pakistani dominated Awami Party to power. When this party set out a policy that would lead to virtual autonomy for East Pakistan, Yahya Khan postponed calling the national assembly and embarked upon a brutal repression of the Awami Party specifically and East Pakistan in general. The end result of this repression was the Indo-Pakistan War of 1971 and the eventual independence of Bangladesh. In the wake of the defeat in 1971, Yahya Khan relinquished power to the Pakistan People's Party (PPP) and its leader ZA Bhutto. Yahya Khan died in 1980.

Progress of the war

That exact start of this war is hard to pinpoint. There is evidence that India supplied artillery support to the rebels as early as 22 November, distinguishing it from largely retaliatory artillery strikes that had been going on since summer. India maintains that it attacked only after air strikes by the Pakistani air force on 3 December. The air strikes seem to have been in emulation of the Israeli air strikes at the start of the Six Day War in 1967. While the Israeli strikes were a complete success, destroying Egypt's air force while it was still on the ground, the Pakistani attempt was a dismal failure. The Pakistanis targeted the wrong air bases, allocating too few aircraft to each target. In any event, unlike the Egyptian jets, much of the Indian aircraft were protected in strong bunkers.

The next day, the Indian army attacked across the border into East Pakistan en masse. In all, the Indians enjoyed a numerical superiority in the east of 160 000 to 90 000. Rather than large, cautious advances that had been its hallmark in the previous two wars against Pakistan, the Indian army opted for a more mobile and rapid assault. The nature of the war was partially dictated by geography. Unlike in West Pakistan, East Pakistan was surrounded on three sides by India. India therefore adopted a three-pronged attack that quickly pushed the Pakistani forces back. The arms embargo that the United States had imposed during the 1965 war was still in effect, limiting the arms that Pakistan had at its disposal. This disadvantage was compounded by physical distance between East and West Pakistan, making re-supply very difficult. As India's goal was to foster an independent East Pakistan—one that was reasonably viable or that could at the very least receive back the 10 million refugees currently hiding in India,—destruction to infrastructure, cities and towns was kept to a minimum.

Predictably, the war could not be contained to East Pakistan. Early in the war, engagements were fought along the border between West Pakistan and India. These were mostly strategic as the major war aims for both sides were focused in East Pakistan.

Zulfikar Ali Bhutto (1928–79)

Bhutto rose to prominence in the cabinet of Ayub Khan and was very influential in directing Pakistan's foreign policy in the years 1963–6. He was integral in drawing Pakistan and China into closer diplomatic ties. After falling out with Ayub Khan over the 1965 Kashmir War, he founded the Pakistan People's Party. He helped administer martial law in the period immediately preceding the Indo-Pakistan War of 1971, and came to power as Pakistan's prime minister in 1973. Bhutto's government was ousted by a military coup in 1977. The new military government tried Bhutto for complicity in the murder of a political opponent and found him guilty. He was executed in April 1979.

Indian prime minister, Indira Gandhi, and Pakistani president, Zulfikar Ali Bhutto, signing the Simla Agreement, ending the 1971 War. Both leaders were members of political dynasties within their countries. Gandhi was the daughter of Jawaharlal Nehru, the first prime minister of independent India, and the mother of Rajiv Gandhi, who succeeded her as prime minister after her assassination. Bhutto's daughter would later become prime minister of Pakistan before she was assassinated in 2007.

The war in the west did involve one of the only naval engagements in this series of wars. On 4 December, an Indian naval task force launched a missile attack on the Pakistani port city of Karachi. The Pakistani navy lost two vessels and the port was heavily damaged, while the Indian navy suffered no substantial losses. By 17 December, India had declared a unilateral ceasefire.

Jawaharlal Nehru (1889–1964)

Nehru was a follower of Mohandas Gandhi and an active leader in the Indian National Congress, eventually becoming the first prime minister of independent India. In international affairs he pioneered the non-aligned bloc, which sought to break away from the strictures of the Cold War power blocs, a notion that never really came to fruition. After defeat at the hands of the Chinese in 1962, Nehru drew closer to the Soviets, with the predictable alienation from the United States.

Effects

In terms of political and military goals, the war of 1971 was an unmitigated Indian success. The Indian army suffered 1700 dead in the two weeks of war. Although Pakistani casualties are unknown, India managed to capture approximately 90 000 Pakistani prisoners. India acquired some territory in West Pakistan. India had demonstrable evidence of the strength of each of the three branches of its military against its chief regional rival. Diplomatic efforts—and the weather—had managed to keep China from intervening and at the same time provided the Indian army with Soviet arms. Although India's actions were condemned by the United Nations, predictably this had little meaning. East Pakistan became the independent nation state of Bangladesh. As a result of this war, India established itself as the dominant power in the region.

There were, however, broader consequences of this war. Although it would not supply either side with weapons, the United States sent an aircraft carrier into the Bay of Bengal during the conflict. India interpreted this correctly as a not so subtle threat in support of Pakistan. The prospect that such regional conflicts could potentially draw in nuclear powers, such as the United States or China, prompted India to accelerate her own nuclear program, exploding her first nuclear weapon in 1974. This, of course, necessitated the development of a Pakistani nuclear program that admittedly would not bear its deadly fruit until 1998.

Indira Gandhi (1917–84)

The daughter of Nehru, Indira Gandhi became the heir to this political legacy when she became the prime minister of India in 1966 and leader of the Congress Party's left wing. She initiated India's nuclear program in the wake of the Chinese victory in the Indo-Chinese War of 1962 and the Indo-Pakistani War of 1965. When the flood of Pakistani refugees poured over the border into Bengal, her military and diplomatic preparations paved the way for the Indo-Pakistani War of 1971 and the eventual independence of Bangladesh.

The Falklands (Malvinas) War

The war that erupted in 1982 between Argentina and the UK over the disputed Falkland Islands (Malvinas) in the South Atlantic illustrates what can happen when countries fail to resolve disputes diplomatically. The abortive attempt of the USA to mediate the crisis further highlights the challenges that interconnected alliances face in international diplomacy. This section also examines the difficulties of fighting in such a remote area and how military technology can provide new solutions.

Background causes

Located in the South Atlantic Ocean some 300 miles (480 km) off the coast of South America, the Falkland Islands are a rocky group of islands, home to about 2000 people mostly involved in sheep farming. Historically, France, Spain and Great Britain had occupied the islands, but without a great deal of enthusiasm, even leaving them unoccupied for a 50-year stretch in the 18th century. When Argentina won her independence from Spain, she laid claim to the islands, calling them the Malvinas. While the British were not necessarily committed to the occupation of the islands, and they were of negligible strategic or economic value, the British government was not about to have its foreign policy dictated by a fledgling South American republic. A small British force reasserted control over the islands in 1833, from which time they have been continuously occupied by the British, though the Argentines have never relinquished their claims to the territory. It is these events, predating the war by some 150 years, upon which both the Argentines and the British would base their case for war in 1982. There were, however, some more important and immediate background factors that need to be considered.

By 1981, Argentina had been ruled by an increasingly unpopular military **junta** for five years. The junta took power in a coup designed to restore order during a time of deep political instability. Ideologically, the junta was on the far right and as such used its extensive authoritarian power to repress all elements of the left—unions, political parties, intellectuals and eventually anyone who was suspected of criticizing the regime. Some estimates put the victims of this "dirty war" as high as 30 000, collectively known as The Disappeared. This extreme social pressure within Argentina was compounded by a severe economic crisis, stemming from crippling foreign debt. The junta calculated that a quick patriotic war would help galvanize public opinion behind the government.

In terms of broader foreign policy aims, the junta, and many previous regimes in Argentina, considered that the position of Argentina as a power was dependent on control of the South Atlantic. Geographically, the most important position upon which such control depended was Antarctica. The 1959 **Antarctic Treaty**, which essentially internationalized and demilitarized the Antarctic, meant that Argentina

Junta A committee or council that rules a country. The term often applies to military rulers of Latin American countries.

Antarctic Treaty A treaty by which the signatories pledge to keep the Antarctic a demilitarized and nuclear weapons free zone, and to cooperate in the promotion of scientific enquiry in the Antarctic.

would have to look elsewhere for an anchor in the South Atlantic. As Chile asserted more authority over Tierra del Fuego (a group of islands off the southern tip of South America separated from the mainland by the Straits of Magellan), the Falklands (Malvinas) became vital to Argentina's position in the South Atlantic. In 1980, with improving relations with both its northern neighbours and the USA, with its new anti-communist president, Ronald Reagan, the time seemed right for a settling of accounts with the UK over the Falklands (Malvinas).

Economic instability also played a role in the British decision to go to war. Prime Minister Margaret Thatcher's economic policies, designed to fight inflation through austerity measures that involved widespread **privatization**, anti-union legislation and higher taxation, caused deep divisions in the country. These policies led to a sharp rise in unemployment in the UK in the years leading up to the Falklands War. The austerity measures meant a certain downsizing of the military, which, in turn, necessitated a re-evaluation of what the British could realistically assert military authority over. Such a re-evaluation determined that a permanent diplomatic solution to the Falklands question needed to be found. The most workable solution appeared to be some form of leaseback, in which the islands would belong to Argentina, but would be administered by the United Kingdom. While such a solution seemed to make practical sense, it was unacceptable to some hardliners in the British government and became untenable once representatives of the islands' British citizens were included in the negotiations with the Argentine government.

> **Privatization** The economic practice of selling government assets to private owners.

Britain did not initiate the conflict and, therefore, we cannot say that Thatcher planned to use the war to bolster public support, but domestic concerns did indeed help to dictate Thatcher's response to the crisis. The personality of Margaret Thatcher must also be considered. As the first woman to lead a large, industrialized Western state, she had forged a reputation for an uncompromising and unyielding approach to governance, as was evident in the British coal strikes after the Falklands conflict. Nothing in her past suggested that Thatcher would back down from a challenge to British **sovereignty** in the Falklands or anywhere else.

> **Sovereignty** The ability of a country to act independently of any outside authority.

Immediate causes

Although negotiations on a Falklands (Malvinas) settlement had been attempted at various points in the 20th century, they broke down once again in early 1982. With a deteriorating domestic situation and pressure from hardline members of the junta, General Galtieri, the leader of the junta, decided to force the situation. Military preparations began in early 1982 amid a great deal of secrecy, suggesting that what Galtieri wanted was not just any solution to the dispute, but a military one. Had he wanted to use the military to pressure the British into a diplomatic solution, it made no sense to hide the preparations. It seems that by 1982, the junta had decided to force the question by means of military action.

A small dispute involving Argentine scrap metal merchants on another disputed island, South Georgia, gave the junta the opportunity to go ahead. The Argentine navy seemed deliberately to provoke the British when, in March 1982, they transported the merchants to the island for a second time, traveling in silence and not notifying the British government, planting as they did the flag of Argentina, and refusing to leave when asked to do so. The British response was to dispatch the soon to be recalled ice patrol vessel HMS *Endurance* from Stanley, the capital of the Falklands, to evict the Argentines from South Georgia. Instead of confronting a small party, the *Endurance* and the Royal Marines aboard, however, were greeted by a full Argentine occupation force. The British, for their part, made little genuine effort to defuse the South Georgia incident. This, combined with faulty Argentine military intelligence suggesting to the Argentineans that the UK was already preparing to take substantial aggressive action in the South Atlantic, indicated that neither side was acting with anything like a complete picture of the situation or clear plan of action. Believing, as they did, that a British task force was on its way to the South Atlantic, most in the junta concluded, therefore, that time was of the essence and on 26 March ordered a full invasion of the Falklands to be carried out on 2 April.

It would seem, then, that this conflict was caused by a lack of clarity on both sides. Argentinean goals were unclear from the start. Did they want to occupy and exercise sovereignty over the Malvinas? Did they want to pressure the British government into negotiating an arrangement by which the British government would lease the islands from Argentina? Or did they simply want to inject a sense of urgency into the negotiations? As the planning and operation proceeded, the junta meandered its way to a goal of further negotiations, but this was done with little consistency. It was also unclear on the relationship between military posturing and diplomacy in resolving the situation. Were the military actions designed to bring the United Kingdom to the table in order to negotiate a solution, or were these preparations the solution? When this lack of clarity was combined with faulty military intelligence, war became hard to avoid. The British were likewise unclear in what they wanted from the Falkland Islands. Their response to this uncertainty was to stall for time by not taking the negotiations as seriously as the Argentines did, leaving the impression that they wanted the status quo. When it opted for an ambiguous, though nonetheless military, response to the South Georgia incident in spite of other indications that it was abandoning the South Atlantic militarily, the British government bolstered the Argentine misconception of the situation.

Margaret Thatcher (1925–)

Margaret Thatcher was the prime minister of the UK from 1979 to 1990. During her tenure she moved the British economy decidedly to the right in an effort to fight inflation. These moves included privatization, increased indirect taxation and higher interest rates. Such moves brought her government into conflict with the Labour Party and a number of trade unions. In terms of foreign policy, Thatcher was a fervent anti-communist and staunch supporter of Ronald Reagan and the United States' approach to the Cold War. While she took a hard line against the USSR, Argentina in the Falklands conflict, and Irish Republican Army prisoners, she did not support economic sanctions against the apartheid regime in South Africa.

IB Learner Profile link
Communicators

 Write and deliver a speech presenting the case for war from the point of view of general Galtieri addressing the Argentine public.

Practices

Operation Rosario and its aftermath

The Argentine plan for invasion called for amphibious landing with tracked landing vehicles. This force was to take the airport and the capital. Commandos were to land at a separate location to seek out the small force of Royal Marines that defended the island and capture the British Governor. In all, some 500 Argentines were to attack the islands. Not wanting to give the impression that they intended a long occupation, much of the invasion force was to be withdrawn, thus paving the way for negotiations. The islands were defended by about 60 Royal Marines, who were able to improvise a defence once intelligence indicated that a landing was imminent. Fortunately for the Argentines, the Royal Marine commander believed the landing would happen at a different location on the island and so the invasion force landed largely unopposed. Once they realized that the British were responding in force, the evacuation order was reversed and the Argentines began reinforcing their positions on the islands.

In fact, though they had helped precipitate it, the invasion caught the British largely by surprise and came at a time when, in accordance with Thatcher's downsizing efforts, the Royal Navy was reducing its size, including decommissioning its aircraft carriers and the aforementioned ice breakers in the South Atlantic. Nevertheless, within five days of the Argentine invasion, the British military had put together a naval task force and had set sail for the South Atlantic. This task force was a substantial response, consisting of destroyers, frigates, merchant ships, and two aircraft carriers, HMS *Invincible* and HMS *Hermes*, and included civilian passenger liners *Canberra*, *Uganda* and the *Queen Elizabeth II*, that were pressed into service. In all some 65 ships carried a landing force of 7000 troops. The 13 000-km voyage would be split in two, with the task force making a supply stop at Ascension Island, an island owned by the United Kingdom on which there was an airstrip administered by the United States military. The USA would continue to give practical support to the British throughout the conflict while still trying to find diplomatic solutions, an ambiguous position that confused many and angered the Argentines.

As soon as the crisis looked like it could easily escalate into a shooting war, diplomatic efforts to stop it erupted with a fury. These efforts centred on three main forums, the United Nations, the Organization of American States (OAS) and a well-meaning but ineffectual mediation effort by the US Secretary of State Alexander Haig. Strangely, it was Argentina that brought the matter before the UN Security Council. Faulty Argentine intelligence believed that a military task force had left for the South Atlantic even before the invasion of the islands as a show of force. Argentina brought this

General Leopoldo Galtieri (1926–2003)

Leopoldo Galtieri was a member of Argentina's ruling military junta from 1976 to 1982, leading the junta from 1981 to 1982 during the Falklands (Malvinas) War. Galtieri was a fervent anti-leftist and directed the "dirty war" against left-wing critics of his government. This political stance endeared him to the US administration until the USA was forced to support its British ally in the Falklands (Malvinas) War. Galtieri's regime did not survive Argentina's defeat in the war. He stood trial for his participation in the "dirty war" and the mismanagement of the Falklands (Malvinas) War. He was acquitted of the former, convicted of the latter and sentenced to 12 years in prison. He was pardoned in 1990.

before the Security Council as an act of aggression, seeking a denunciation and the associated justification for her own military plans. The Argentines did not want to tip their hand regarding the actual invasion and therefore any approaches to members of the Security Council for support were tentative and ineffectual. The British had no such issues of secrecy and took the initiative, bringing a resolution to the Council on 3 April. Resolution 502/1982, drafted by the British, called for a cessation of hostilities, a withdrawal of Argentine military forces, and a diplomatic solution to be found that respected principles of the charter of the UN. This last demand, with its emphasis on the principles of the UN, was no diplomatic pandering. The charter emphasizes the principle of self-determination and the British knew that, if left up to the islanders, the Falklands would be forever British. The resolution passed. The British had won the first diplomatic round.

The Latin American states of the OAS generally supported the Argentinian cause. The OAS proved a troublesome forum for the USA during the crisis, as she was both a member of NATO with the UK and a member of the OAS with Argentina. This apparent conflict of interests was compounded by the Rio Pact of 1947, the terms of which bound the signatories—most Latin America countries and the United States—to regard an attack on one as an attack on all. By the end of April, Argentina had won a resolution under the Rio Pact, denouncing the UK and calling for a cessation of hostilities. The United States abstained from the vote and, considering the Argentines as the aggressors, ignored the resolution.

Alexander Haig's diplomatic mission was in many ways doomed from the start. The position of the United States was not ideal for that of a mediator as it was more closely connected to the British than the Argentines. The consequences of an Argentine failure, in terms of American foreign policy, paled in comparison with the implications for the UK. Dealing with the junta also proved difficult for Haig. There appeared no clear decision-making process between the three generals. As Haig's mission came to an unsuccessful end, the USA lined up more clearly with the UK, providing material, logistical and intelligence support.

Faithful to British strategy of the past 400 years, Thatcher's government set up a blockade of the area surrounding the Falkland Islands on 12 April, calling it a Maritime Exclusion Zone (MEZ) to avoid the semantics of the word "blockade", suggesting as it did an act of war. The MEZ stated that the British would consider any Argentine military vessel within the zone a legitimate target. As the task force approached the islands, the MEZ was changed to a Total

Activity:
Disputed territory

As we have seen, the Falklands (Malvinas) are not the only disputed territories in the world. Choose one of the territories from the list below and answer the following questions.

1 What are the arguments for each side's claim of ownership?

2 What steps have been taken to solve the problem—war, negotiation, third-party arbitration?

3 What is the probability that the situation will escalate into a war? Justify your answer.

● Arunachal Pradesh—India and China

● Cyprus—Greece and Turkey

● Kuril Islands—Japan and Russia

● Ogaden—Somalia and Ethiopia

● Hans Island—Denmark and Canada

HMS *Antelope* is hit by an Argentinean air strike. The British Royal Navy dominated the Argentinean navy from the start of the conflict, but British ships continued to be vulnerable to attack from the air. How has air power changed the nature of naval warfare since the Second World War?

Exclusion Zone (TEZ), in which any vessel, military or civilian, found in the 200-mile (320 km) zone without British permission was a legitimate target. The notice also indicated the same for any aircraft, preventing the Argentines from reinforcing from the air.

The Falklands (Malvinas) dispute, 1982		
	Diplomatic	**Military**
9 January	UK protests unauthorized landing on South Georgia	
12 January	Junta begins preparation for invasion	
8 March	British prepare plan in case Argentina invades the islands	
19 March	Argentine scrap metal merchants arrive on South Georgia without permission and plant Argentine flag	
24 March		HMS *Endurance* arrives at South Georgia with 24 Royal Marines
28 March		Argentinean military cancels all leave for personnel and begins flying military aircraft over the islands
29 March		UK sends three nuclear submarines to South Atlantic
31 March	UK asks USA to mediate with Argentina	
2 April		Argentine forces invade Falklands (Malvinas)
3 April	UN Security Council passes Resolution 502 demanding Argentine withdrawal	
5-9 April		British task force sets sail for South Atlantic
8 April	US Secretary of State Haig begins mediation mission in London	
10 April	Haig arrives in Argentina EEC (European Economic Union) imposes economic sanctions on Argentina	
12 April		UK proclaims Maritime Exclusion Zone
19-22 April	UK and Argentina respond negatively to Haig's plan	
22 April		British task force arrives in South Atlantic
25 April		British recapture South Georgia Argentine submarine *Santa Fé* successfully attacked by Royal Navy
27 April	Haig presents last plan to Argentina and UK. It is rejected	
28 April	Organization of American States (OAS) supports Argentina in dispute	
30 April	USA formally supports UK in dispute	UK proclaims Total Exclusion Zone (TEZ)
1 May		Air war begins over Falklands (Malvinas)
2 May	Peru proposes peace plan—rejected by Argentina	British Royal Navy sinks the *Belgrano*
4 May		Argentine air force sinks HMS *Sheffield*
7 May	UN Secretary General attempts to mediate dispute	
21 May		British forces land at San Carlos. Argentine air force sinks HMS *Ardent*
21–29 May	OAS condemns British actions	Battle of Goose Green
8 June		Battle of Fitzroy
11–14 June		Battle of Stanley
14 June	Argentina surrenders	

After easily retaking South Georgia on 25 April, and in the process disabling the Argentine submarine *Santa Fé*, the British force proceeded on to the Falkland Islands. When the task force arrived on 1 May, it wasted no time in launching air attacks on the Argentine defenders, who lost several aircraft. The next day, a Royal Navy submarine torpedoed the Argentine cruiser *Belgrano*, which sank taking 321 sailors with her. Whether or not this action conformed to the British rules of engagement became a source of controversy after the war. For the most part, Argentine naval forces stayed clear of the Royal Navy from that point. The Argentine air force fared better, sinking the destroyer *Sheffield* with a French-made Exocet missile fired from a French-made Etenarde jet. The Argentine air force would continue to have success against the Royal Navy ships throughout the war, especially when they moved into the close quarters around the islands to support land operations. By 20 May, last attempts at mediation by Peru and the United Nations failed and the effort to retake the Falklands was about to begin.

> ### Alexander Haig (1924–)
>
> Alexander Haig was the US Secretary of State in Ronald Reagan's first administration. An army general who had served in Vietnam, Haig held posts in the Nixon and Ford administration and as commander of NATO forces. As Secretary of State, he attempted to mediate a settlement of the Falklands (Malvinas) crisis in 1982 without success.

Sheltering their invasion fleet between the two main islands, the British landed at San Carlos, across the island from the capital, establishing three separate beachheads on 21 May and putting 4000 men ashore, meeting little resistance. The British achieved surprise through a combination of Argentinean missteps and diversionary attacks. Argentine air attacks were repulsed through the day, though at the cost of one British ship sunk and two damaged. Air attacks on the invasion fleet continued for several days, with one long-range, though unsuccessful, attack on the more distant British aircraft carriers. As the British forces began to move inland, the Argentine air force continued to harass the staging area. Nevertheless, move inland the British did.

The first objective, however, was not Stanley—the British command instead opting for a more limited attack on the Argentine garrison at Goose Green and Darwin to further secure the beachhead. The attack began on 27 May and, after two days of fighting, the 500 attackers forced the surrender of the approximately 700 Argentine defenders. After an abortive and costly blunder at Fitzroy, the British forces moved on to surround the capital and in a series of smaller engagements captured high ground surrounding the capital. From this position of strength, the British forces moved on to Stanley and compelled the eventual surrender of the Argentine garrison and its 12 000 survivors on 14 June 1982.

Effects of the war

Capturing and holding the islands from 2 April until 14 June had cost Argentina 746 dead and 1200 wounded. Almost half of the Argentine dead were lost at sea when the *Belgrano* sank. Recapturing the islands cost Britain 250 dead and 770 casualties, and US$1.19 billion, although this figure does not include the replacement of lost equipment and ships. In many ways, this war had ramifications that reached far beyond these sterile numbers.

Unable to sustain their position in the face of public outrage against both the war and the "dirty war" that it had conducted against its own citizens, the military junta resigned, paving the way for free elections, which would bring Raul Alfonsin to power. The war only exacerbated the dismal financial situation in Argentina, a situation that would plague it well into the 21st century.

While failure meant political defeat for the junta in Argentina, it meant political advantage for the government of Margaret Thatcher. She capitalized on the wave of patriotic sentiment that accompanied the recapture of the islands and parlayed it into an election victory the following year, despite deep divisions within British society and enduring economic woes. Having gone to such great lengths and expense to preserve its position in the South Atlantic, the UK had little choice but to reassert her presence there. A new air base was built, garrisoned with some 1500 troops who were still there on the 25th anniversary of the conflict. With the growing prospect of large offshore oil deposits in the South Atlantic, the British stance in 1982 almost seems prescient.

Thematic Activities

Use the material from this chapter, as well as information from outside sources, to complete the following activities.

Types of 20th-century war

Activity:

Complete the chart and then answer the questions that follow:

Type	Definition	Examples	Elements	Analysis as a means of dispute resolution
Civil war				
Total war				
Guerrilla war				
Limited war				

1 How might a war fit into more than one category? Give an example.
2 What factors might lead an army to choose guerrilla tactics rather than conventional war? What are the disadvantages of using guerrilla methods?
3 How might perspective affect which category a war might fit into? In other words, how might a war be a total war for some people and not for others? Give an example.
4 How might the concept of nuclear war fit into the above chart?

Origins and causes of wars

Activity:

You are an official with the German Foreign Ministry in July 1914.

You have been given a 15-minute audience with the Kaiser and von Moltke.

Prepare a presentation to persuade them of one of the following:

● that war is necessary

● that they should avoid a war at all costs.

Activity:

What is more likely to cause a war—ideological differences or religious differences?

Use examples from the 20th century to support your answer.

IB Learner Profile link

Choose three of the elements of the IB learner profile.
Choose a 20th-century war.

Analyse the extent to which the leaders of the warring sides reflect these elements.

Reflect on how the learner profile and the IB mission statement might lead to a more peaceful world.

Nature of 20th-century wars

Activity:

Women and war

Use information from this chapter and supplementary research to complete the following chart regarding the impact of war on women.

War	Total casualties	Women casualties	Military role/ changes	Civilian role/ changes	Political role/ changes
First World War					
Arab–Israeli conflict					
Falklands (Malvinas) War					
Spanish Civil War					

Activity:

Defence budgets

Objective:

Appreciate the relative importance of air, land and sea forces to various 20th-century military scenarios.

Most modern militaries are divided into three main branches (two if the country is land locked): army, navy and air force. Each of these branches must compete for its share of the country's annual defence budget. The ultimate decision is then generally made by the political leadership of the country. In some countries, there is no difference between the military and political leadership.

Activity:

Choose one of the following country scenarios:

● India 1974

● Pakistan 1974

● Argentina 1981

● United Kingdom 1981

Divide up into four groups:

● Army chiefs of staff

● Navy chiefs of staff

● Air force chiefs of staff

● Political decision makers

Each group of chiefs prepares a brief, outlining what percentage (0%–100%) of the defence budget their branch should receive. The political decision makers will outline the defence goals of the country, including likely threats and geographic areas of concern.

Each group of chiefs presents their brief to the political decision makers, who will adjudicate the requests and make a final judgment, justifying its decision.

Factors that each group should consider:

● Likely enemies

● Likely fronts

● Past military experience

● Potential allies

● Available technology

Activity:

Resistance to occupation

Use the information in this chapter and outside research to complete the following chart on resistance movements.

War	Occupier	Resistance movement	Resistance methods	Result
First World War — Belgium				
Second World War— France				
Second World War —Phillipines				
Falklands (Malvinas) War				
Arab–Israeli conflict				

Gas warfare

Read the following two accounts of the use of gas in warfare and answer the questions that follow

Kurds recall gas attack horror at Saddam trial

BAGHDAD, Iraq. A survivor testified Wednesday at the genocide trial of Saddam Hussein that Iraqi warplanes bombarded a Kurdish village with chemical weapons in 1987 and helicopters pursued those who fled into the hills and bombed them.

For a second day, survivors took the stand in the trial, in which Saddam and six co-defendants are charged over the 1987–8 Anfal campaign, a military sweep against the Kurds of northern Iraq in which tens of thousands of people were killed.

After hearing from four survivors, chief judge Abdullah al-Amiri adjourned the trial until Sept. 11, to give time to consider an appeal from defense lawyers about the court's legitimacy.

Earlier, Adiba Oula Bayez described the Aug. 16, 1987 bombardment of her village of Balisan, saying warplanes dropped bombs that spread a smoke that smelled "like rotten apples."

"Then my daughter Narjis came to me, complaining about pain in her eyes, chest and stomach. When I got close to see what's wrong with her, she threw up all over me," Bayez, a mother of five, said. "When I took her in to wash her face ... all my other children were throwing up."

"Then my condition got bad, too. And that's when we realized that the weapon was poisonous and chemical," she said.

Bayez said the villagers fled to nearby caves on mules, "but the helicopters came and bombed the mountains to prevent the villagers from taking refuge anywhere."

Like many villagers, she was blinded by the gas, she said. In the caves, people were vomiting blood, many had burns. "All I knew was that I was holding tight my five children," she said. "I couldn't see, I couldn't do anything, the only thing I did was scream, 'Don't take my kids away from me.'"

The villagers were taken by the military to a prison camp, and Bayez said four people kept in the same room with her died. On the fifth day in jail, she pried open her swollen eyes with her fingers to see, and "I saw my children's eyes swollen, their skin blackened," she said.

Another Balisan resident, Badriya Said Khider, said nine of her relatives were killed in the bombing and the military sweep afterwards, including her parents, two brothers, husband and son.

A man claiming to be a former Kurdish guerrilla, or peshmerga, also took the stand, accounting several attacks he witnessed in 1987 and 1988, including an August 1988 chemical weapons attack on the village of Ikmala in which his brother's family was killed.

"On the ground outside their house, my brother Saleh and his son Shaaban were on the ground dead, hugging each other, and a few meters (yards) away was my brother's wife," said Moussa Abdullah Moussa. "I can't tell the feeling I had. Only the eye and heart that saw that can describe it."

The accounts resembled those of two other survivors of the attack on Balisan and the neighboring village of Sheik Wasan who testified Tuesday in the trial. Bayez's husband, Ali Mostafa Hama, testified on Tuesday. The survivors are testifying as plaintiffs in the case. Asked by the judges whom she wished to file her complaint against, Bayez exclaimed, "I complain against Saddam Hussein, Ali Hassan al-Majid and everyone in the [defendants'] box. May God blind them all."

Source: www.msnbc.msn.com/id/14475531/#storyContinued

Account of gas attack, 1916

Arthur Empey was living in New Jersey when war broke out in Europe in 1914. He was enraged by the sinking of the *Lusitania* and loss of the lives of American passengers. When the USA did not immediately declare war, Empey boarded a ship to England, enlisted in the British Army and was soon manning a trench on the front lines.

We join his story as she sits in a trench peering towards German lines. Conditions are perfect for a gas attack—a slight breeze blowing from the enemy's direction. The warning has been passed along to be on the lookout:

We had a new man at the periscope, on this afternoon in question; I was sitting on the fire step, cleaning my rifle, when he called out to me: "There's a sort of greenish, yellow cloud rolling along the ground out in front, it's coming–" But I waited for no more, grabbing my bayonet, which was detached from the rifle, I gave the alarm by banging an empty shell case, which was hanging near the periscope. At the same instant, gongs started ringing down the trench, the signal for Tommy to don his respirator, or smoke helmet, as we call it. Gas travels quietly, so you must not lose any time; you generally have about eighteen or twenty seconds in which to adjust your gas helmet.

A gas helmet is made of cloth, treated with chemicals. There are two windows, or glass eyes, in it. Inside there is a rubber-covered tube, which goes in the mouth.

You breathe through your nose; the gas, passing through the cloth helmet, is neutralized by the action of the chemicals. The foul air is exhaled through the tube in the mouth, so constructed that it prevents the inhaling of the outside air or gas. One helmet is good for five hours of the strongest gas. Each Tommy carries two of them slung around his shoulder in a waterproof canvas bag. He must wear this bag at all times, even while sleeping. To change a defective helmet, you take out the new one, hold your breath, pull the old one off, placing the new one over your head, tucking in the loose ends under the collar of your tunic.

For a minute, pandemonium reigned in our trench, Tommies adjusting their helmets, bombers running here and there, and men turning out of the dugouts with fixed bayonets, to man the fire step. Reinforcements were pouring out of the communication trenches. Our gun's crew was busy mounting the machine gun on the parapet and bringing up extra ammunition from the dugout.

German gas is heavier than air and soon fills the trenches and dugouts ... We had to work quickly, as Fritz generally follows the gas with an infantry attack. A company man on our right was too slow in getting on his helmet; he sank to the ground, clutching at his throat, and after a few spasmodic twistings, went West [died]. It was horrible to see him die, but we were powerless to help him. In the corner of a traverse, a little, muddy cur dog, one of the company's pets, was lying dead, with his two paws over his nose. It's the animals that suffer the most, the horses, mules, cattle, dogs, cats, and rats, having no helmets to save them.

A gas, or smoke helmet, as it is called, at the best is a vile-smelling thing, and it is not long before one gets a violent headache from wearing it.

Our eighteen-pounders were bursting in No Man's Land, in an effort, by the artillery, to disperse the gas clouds. The fire step was lined with crouching men, bayonets fixed, and bombs near at hand to repel the expected attack. Our artillery had put a barrage of curtain fire on the German lines, to try and break up their attack and keep back reinforcements.

I trained my machine gun on their trench and its bullets were raking the parapet. Then over they came, bayonets glistening. In their respirators, which have a large snout in front, they looked like some horrible nightmare. All along our trench, rifles and machine guns spoke, our shrapnel was bursting over their heads. They went down in heaps, but new ones took the place of the fallen. Nothing could stop that mad rush. The Germans reached our barbed wire ...

Suddenly, my head seemed to burst from a loud "crack" in my ear. Then my head began to swim, throat got dry, and a heavy pressure on the lungs warned me that my helmet was leaking. Turning my gun over to No. 2, I changed helmets. The trench started to wind like a snake, and sandbags appeared to be floating in the air. The noise was horrible; I sank onto the fire step, needles seemed to be pricking my flesh, then blackness.

I was awakened by one of my mates removing my smoke helmet. How delicious that cool, fresh air felt in my lungs. A strong wind had arisen and dispersed the gas. They told me that I had been "out" for three hours; they thought I was dead.

I examined my first smoke helmet, a bullet had gone through it on the left side, just grazing my ear, the gas had penetrated through the hole in the cloth.

Out of our crew of six, we lost two killed and two wounded. That night we buried all of the dead, excepting those in No Man's Land. In death there is not much distinction, friend and foe are treated alike.

Source: *Eyewitness to History,*
www.eyewitnesshistory.com/gas.htm

1   Compare and contrast the two accounts of being attacked by gas. How might you account for the differences?

2   What can you surmise about the goals of the Iraqi forces? What were the goals of the German army?

3   Gas was not used extensively in 20th-century wars after 1918. Why might this be?

4   Construct a chart comparing the advantages and disadvantages of gas as a weapon. Is gas any more or less "humane" than other weapons? Explain your answer.

Effects and results of war

Activity:
Economic impact

Complete the following chart regarding the economic impact of war.

	Pre-War			Post-War		
	Inflation	**Unemployment**	**GNP**	**Inflation**	**Unemployment**	**GNP**
First World War — Britain						
Algerian War— France						
Falklands (Malvinas) War —Argentine						
1971 Bangladesh War—India						

Activity:
Ending wars

The wars in column A below ended with written agreements. Those in column B ended without formal treaties (although they may have ended with ceasefire agreements).

Choose one war from column A and one war from column B.

Compare and contrast the end of each war.

Analyse the impact of ending a war without a treaty as opposed to ending a war with a treaty.

A	B
First World War	Second World War
Algerian War	Spanish Civil War
	Kashmir War 1965

Activity:
Territorial changes

On an outline map of 1914 Europe, draw in the borders of following successor states:

- Estonia
- Latvia
- Lithuania
- Czechoslovakia
- Yugoslavia
- Austria
- Hungary
- Poland
- Finland

1 On what basis did the diplomats in Paris draw these borders? Did these same principles apply to territories outside of Europe? Why or why not? Give an example.

2 Which 1914 countries would have objected to these boundaries? Why?

3 Identify points of potential conflict based on the 1919 map.

Activity:

1 Divide up into two groups:
  ▶ Leaders (see below)
  ▶ Reporters

2 Leaders prepare a brief on the results of the war for their country:
  ▶ Economic impacts of the war
  ▶ Social impacts of the war
  ▶ Political impacts of the war
  ▶ Post-war relations between the combatants

3 Reporters prepare questions to ask the leaders on each of the following areas:
  ▶ Economic impacts of the war
  ▶ Social impacts of the war
  ▶ Political impacts of the war
  ▶ Post-war relations between the combatants

4 Each leader makes a 3–5 minute presentation explaining the impact of the war on their country. After each leader has finished the presentation, it is the reporters' turn to ask questions, to which the leaders will respond.

Debrief questions

1 Compare the relative impacts of each war on the combatant sides.

2 To what extent does the nature/type of the war (civil, total, limited, guerrilla) affect the impacts of the war?

3 To what degree can statistics describe the impacts of war?
  What aspects of war do statistics fail to capture?

Leaders

Spanish Civil War—Francisco Franco, Dolores Ibárruri

Algerian War—Charles de Gaulle, Ahmed Ben Bella

1971 Indo-Pakistan war—Yahya Khan, Indira Ghandi

Falklands (Malvinas) War—Margaret Thatcher, General Leopoldo Galtieri

Exam questions

1 Analyse the causes of **either** the Malvinas/Falklands War (1982) **or** the Iran–Iraq War (1980–8).

2 Discuss the economic causes of **one** 20th-century war.

3 "A European War rather than a World War". To what extent do you agree with this judgement of the First World War?

4 For what reasons, and with what results, were "limited" wars a factor in the second half of the 20th century?

5 Compare and contrast the use of naval warfare in **two** wars each chosen from a different region.

6 Assess the importance of war at sea, **and** war in the air, in one 20th-century war.

7 Examine the impact of resistance movements in **two** wars each chosen from a different region.

8 Assess the social results of **two** wars, each chosen from a different region.

9 Analyse the political results of **either** the Algerian War (1954–62) **or** the Chinese Civil War (1946–9).

10 Assess the impact of technological developments in **two** wars, each chosen from a different region.

Further reading

Kennedy, Paul. 1988. *Rise and Fall of the Great Powers: Economic and Military Conflict from 1500 to 2000*. London, UK. Fontana Press.

Keegan, John. 1993. *A History of Warfare*. New York. USA. Alfred A Knopf.

Causes of the First World War

Keegan, John. 1998. *The First World War*. Toronto, Canada. Key Porter Books.

Mombauer, Annika. 2002. *The Origins of the First World War: Controversies and Consensus*. New York, USA. Longman.

Ferguson, Niall. 1999. *The Pity of War: Explaining World War I*. New York, USA. Basic Books.

Fromkin, David. 2004. *Europe's Last Summer: Who Started the Great War in 1914?* New York, USA. Alfred Knopf.

Stoessinger, John. 2008. *Why Nations Go To War*. 10th edn. Belmont, CA, USA. Wadsworth.

The Spanish Civil War

Beevor, Antony. 2006. *The Battle for Spain: The Spanish Civil War, 1936-1939*. New York, USA. Penguin Books.

Thomas, Hugh. 2003. *The Spanish Civil War*. London, UK. Penguin Books.

The Algerian War

Horne, Alistair. 1978. *A Savage War of Peace: Algeria, 1954-1962*. New York, USA. Viking Press.

Talbot, John. 1980. *The War Without a Name: France in Algeria, 1954-1962*. New York, USA. Alfred Knopf.

Alexander, Martin and Keiger, J.F.V. 2002. *France and the Algerian War, 1954–1962: Strategy, Operations and Diplomacy*. New York, USA. Routledge.

Indo-Pakistan wars

Stoessinger, John. 2008. *Why Nations Go To War*. 10th edn. Belmont, CA, USA. Wadsworth/Cengage Learning.

Schofield, Victoria. 2000. *Kashmir in Conflict: India, Pakistan and the Unfinished War*. New York, USA. IB Tauris

Falklands (Malvinas) War

Boyce, David George. 2005. *The Falklands War*. New York, USA. Palgrave Macmillan.

Freedman, Lawrence and Gamba-Stonehouse, Virginia. 1991. *Signals of War: the Falklands Conflict of 1982*. Princeton, USA. Princeton University Press.

Freedman, Lawrence. 2007. *The Official History of the Falklands Campaign*. New York, USA. Routledge, Taylor & Francis Group.

5 Democratic states: challenges and responses

This chapter looks at topic 2 "Democratic states: challenges and responses". Two distinct periods in the history of two nation states, selected from the *History Guide*, are the focus for detailed study here— the United States of America 1953–1973 and South Africa 1991–2000. The two examples illustrate widely different experiences with democratic systems of government in the second half of the 20th century. In the period in question, for the USA, democracy had moved far beyond the right to vote for the majority of its citizens (with the notable exception of African-Americans and Native Americans), while in South Africa, voting rights for the large proportion of its citizenry —the black majority—was the main focus of the reform movement.

The USA, as the world's oldest democracy, serves as a model for constitutional reform. Since achieving independence, the constitutional practices of the United States have been exported throughout the world—with varying degrees of success. The period 1953–73 saw huge changes in American society and politics. In covering these changes, this chapter explains the concepts behind the sometimes complicated processes of the American political system. The reader will encounter many of these concepts again in the section on South Africa: federalism, electoral systems, presidential powers and political parties in a parliamentary system, the role of an independent judiciary. These are constitutional issues which affect the functioning of democracies all over the world.

Beyond constitutional issues, this topic deals with the economic and social problems which are the real substance of politics in a democracy. Not surprisingly, these take on very different forms in different countries. The United States, as the world's leading, advanced industrial economy, was in quite a different position to South Africa, during this period, which was in many ways still a developing nation. Nevertheless, there are similarities: economic policies focused on improving economic growth and providing more jobs; the advancement of rights for racial and ethnic minorities, and the demand for equality in improving the status of women, were major areas of focus for political and social reform.

The challenges to democracy were different: political extremism caused by an unpopular war (Vietnam) and a constitutional crisis (Watergate) caused a period of uncertainty in the USA; while South Africa saw the growing force of the anti-apartheid movement. For both countries, the struggle against racial segregation and ethnic-racial discrimination was an increasingly volatile issue. In the responses to these challenges, we see political parties and activists using legal, parliamentary methods to force governments to recognize the rights of disadvantaged sections of society and ensure equal opportunities for all. The fact that peaceful processes of change proved more effective in the end than extremism and violence clearly shows the strength of democratic processes.

After reading this chapter, you should have a deeper understanding of the major themes of topic 2. The focus is on analysing complex political processes and comparing and contrasting trends in different countries. The major themes are as follows:

- The nature and structure of democratic (multi-party) states
  - ▸ constitutions (written and unwritten)
  - ▸ electoral systems, proportional representation, coalition governments
  - ▸ the role of political parties; the role of an opposition
  - ▸ the role of pressure (interest/lobby) groups
- Economic and social policies
  - ▸ employment
  - ▸ gender
  - ▸ health, education
  - ▸ social welfare
- Political, social and economic challenges
  - ▸ political extremism
  - ▸ ethnicity, religion, gender
  - ▸ movements for the attainment of civil rights
  - ▸ inequitable distribution of wealth/resources

The United States, 1953–73

This section on the United States begins by providing some background to Dwight D Eisenhower's presidency, which ran from 1953 to 1960. An economic boom led to a huge rise in most people's standard of living. Following 20 years of Democratic rule, Eisenhower's presidency is remembered as a conservative period dominated by the Cold War and anti-communism.

John F Kennedy's election to the presidency in 1960 introduced a new era. He promised to "get the nation moving". How far he really succeeded in this in his short term in office is questionable. The issue of civil rights for African-Americans came to the forefront of domestic politics.

Lyndon B Johnson's presidency continued the liberal start made by Kennedy. His social reforms did much to change American society. African-Americans, led by Martin Luther King, succeeded in getting Congress to pass a civil rights bill (law) but race riots broke out in the late 1960s. The women's movement campaigned to improve women's rights. There was also a growing awareness of the need to improve entitlements for Native Americans. The later part of Johnson's presidency was dominated by the Vietnam War, which increasingly divided the nation.

Richard Nixon succeeded Johnson as president in 1969. A Republican, Nixon was less interested in social reform than in foreign policy. He succeeded in ending American involvement in the Vietnam War and introduced détente with China and the USSR. Nixon was re-elected in 1972 but became virtually powerless due to the Watergate scandal and was forced to resign in 1974.

Background

Because the United States is such a large country it has great regional variations which play an important part in American political life. In the 1950s the South was still more rural and traditional than the industrial, urbanized Northeast. Politically, Southerners tended to vote Democrat, but that was changing. In contrast to other Democrats, Southerners were more conservative, especially on the issue of civil rights. California, a favoured destination for Americans, who have always been a geographically mobile people, was growing fast economically and, by the 1960s, had the biggest population of any state in the Union. It is no accident that two presidents in recent times—Richard Nixon and Ronald Reagan—came from California. By the 1970s, Florida, Texas, Arizona and California were known collectively as the "Sunbelt" and had overtaken the old industrial Northeast and the Midwest as desirable destinations for internal migration and centres of dynamic economic growth.

The population in 1950 was 151.7 million and growing fast. A "baby boom" generation grew up during the 1960s and had very different attitudes to the older generation. In the middle of the 20th century, Americans were still predominantly of European origin. But immigration from Latin American coutries, in particular, in the late 1960s, saw an increase in the ethnic (cultural and linguistic) mix, of the American population, marked by a rise in the proportion of the population who are Hispanic. African-Americans accounted for around 10–11 per cent of the population in the period we are studying. They were the descendants of African slaves, who had been transported to America by Europeans in colonial times. Still mostly concentrated in the South, where the slave plantations had been, they were in the process of migrating to northern cities to escape unemployment and **racial segregation**. Although equal to whites under the Constitution, a range of state laws in the South prevented African-Americans from exercising their rights. Beyond that, they suffered from racial discrimination in many parts of the country. One of the biggest social and political movements for change was initiated during this period—the civil rights movement—in a campaign to end segregation and improve the situation for African-Americans. The Native American population was much smaller—less than half a million according to official figures in 1950. Those who still lived on reservations lacked the opportunities enjoyed by whites. Due to their low life expectancy and even smaller numbers, as a proportion of the population, Native Americans found it even more difficult than African-Americans to draw attention to their lack of civil rights.

> **Racial segregation** means the separation of races in society. Segregation in the southern states of the USA was in the form of separate public and private facilities in transportation, hotels, restaurants and movie theatres.

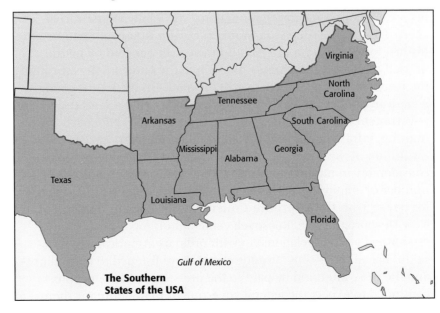

The Southern States of the USA

A booming economy

In the quarter century after the Second World War, the American economy boomed as never before. The United States was by far the richest country in the world. Gross national product (GNP, the total value of all goods and services produced nationally in one year) grew by more than five times, rising from $200 billion in 1945 to 1.1 trillion in 1970. Per capita GNP (GNP divided by the number of the population) rose from $1450 in 1949 to $4022 in 1974. This post-war boom, more than anything else, determined Americans' attitudes and expectations.

After the hard years of the war, demand for consumer goods expanded rapidly. Automobile sales rocketed. In the 1950s it was televisions. New technologies revolutionized daily life: nylon clothes, plastic toys, frozen food, to mention a few examples. Driving the technological revolution forward were the research departments of great corporations such as IBM and General Motors. The United States went from being the world's first consumer society in the 1920s to being the first "affluent (prosperous) society" in the 1950s. Nevertheless, prosperity passed millions by—notably African-Americans, Mexican-Americans and Native Americans.

The economic boom helped bring about enormous social changes. More Americans than ever could afford to go to college or university. Small-hold farmers escaped from rural poverty by finding jobs in the booming factories of the cities. The rural farm sector declined in importance. The number of women in employment continued to increase. But in the 1950s women were still confined to certain "female" jobs, such as nursing or teaching, and earned much less money than men. Many professional training institutions, such as law and medical schools, still refused to take women. Women's efforts to improve their status resulted in the rise of a women's liberation movement in the 1960s.

Political life

By the end of 1952 when Harry S Truman was coming to the end of his presidency, Democrats had occupied the White House for 20 years. Truman's predecessor, Franklin Delano Roosevelt, had begun his first four-year term in 1933. Roosevelt set a record by getting himself re-elected three times. He steered the United States through the troubled waters of the Great Depression. His New Deal changed American politics for good by vastly expanding the role of the federal government in the economy and all aspects of social life such as housing, infrastructure and the alleviation of poverty. As an institution in the American political system, the presidency gained considerably in importance during Roosevelt's time in office. The number of employees in the federal government grew. In a struggle for power with the **Supreme Court** over the constitutionality of his New Deal programme, Roosevelt came out on top. Roosevelt had established a direct relationship with ordinary Americans by his skilful use of radio—his "fireside chats" were listened to by millions—and the close attention he paid to the press. As a result, people continued to expect the federal government to do more for them—in managing the economy and providing **social security**, for example.

The **Supreme Court** heads the judicial branch of government (the law courts). Its job is to determine the constitutionality of laws. In the American system of government, the judiciary is entirely separate from the executive branch, which is headed by the president. Although Supreme Court judges are appointed by the president, they are appointed for life, so cannot be removed. An independent judiciary is an essential feature of truly democratic states. It is only possible to have a genuine opposition to the government if people are not afraid to speak up. This will not be possible if judges can be influenced by the government.

Social security is a feature of most advanced industrial societies and involves insurance against sickness, accidents, unemployment and old age. The cost of social insurance is usually borne by compulsory payments made by employers and employees. In the 1950s and 60s the range of social security benefits available was enhanced by social welfare policies to help disadvantaged social groups.

To finance this, federal government spending increased steadily in the post-war period. Income tax, which financed much of that spending, increased too.

Roosevelt did much to fundamentally alter America's relationship with the rest of the world. He led an isolationist nation into the Second World War and left it as the "world policeman" in 1945. This was the situation which Vice-President Truman inherited in April of that year, when Roosevelt died. The United Nations, which Roosevelt had done so much to found, was soon paralysed by the onset of the Cold War. The growing menace of world communism and Western Europe's weakness left the United States as the sole defender of the "free world".

Much of Truman's presidency was dominated by the Cold War. By 1947 it was clear to Truman that the USA had to commit itself to containing Soviet expansion. In that year he made the announcement, known since as the Truman Doctrine, that the USA would step in wherever needed to help resist takeovers by "armed minorities" (communists). The Marshall Plan, named after Truman's Secretary of State (foreign minister), George Marshall, followed soon after. Both committed the United States to spending vast sums of money to reconstruct Europe and save countries all over the world from communist takeovers. The Cold War spread from Europe to Asia in 1949 when China went communist. The United States now found itself committed to defending the anti-communist Chinese regime in Taiwan as well as Japan, which was still under American occupation. The US armed forces, which had been rapidly demobilized after the Second World War, had to be expanded again to meet the new threats. A nuclear arms race began when the Soviet Union succeeded in exploding an atomic bomb in 1949. Truman reluctantly approved plans to build the "Super", a thermonuclear device hundreds of times more powerful than the atomic bombs which had destroyed Hiroshima and Nagasaki. The first hydrogen bomb was exploded in 1952, the Soviets following with theirs in 1953. Conducting the Cold War diverted funds from reform programmes and forced Truman to concentrate increasingly on security and defence issues.

At home, Truman's presidency was in many ways a continuation of Roosevelt's policies. The broad range of **liberal** economic and social reforms known under Roosevelt as the "New Deal" became "Fair Deal" under Truman. But Truman slowed down the pace of reform. With the economy booming, economic and social problems were in any case less pressing. Americans, Truman felt, had had enough of rapid change after Roosevelt's reforms and the war. Besides, the Cold War was diverting attention to America's defence needs. Congress was no longer in a mood to approve major spending increases on social security.

The Korean War
Although topic 2 is not specifically concerned with war or foreign policy, the Korean War (which you will be able to read about in chapter 9) had a significant impact on the domestic policies of the USA. Korea was a former Japanese colony that had been divided into

The political term **liberal** is associated in the USA with the Democrats, although not all Democrats were liberal. (Southern Democrats were conservative on many issues.) In particular, liberalism is associated with Roosevelt's New Deal reforms and their continuation after the Second World War. Liberal political programmes aimed to give rights and equal opportunities to disadvantaged groups. President Johnson's Great Society reforms of the 1960s are seen as a continuation of this liberal tradition.

a communist North and a pro-Western South after Allied occupation forces withdrew. In 1950 the North invaded the South. Truman immediately decided to commit American armed forces to defending the South and got the UN Security Council to approve it. The Korean War was a big war, even by 20th-century standards. Although Americans did not watch the war every day on television, as they did later on with the Vietnam War, it nevertheless had a great impact. By the end of the war, nearly 1800 000 American servicemen had been sent to Korea and over 130 000 of these were either dead or wounded. Casualties among Koreans and Chinese were much higher. Relying on air power, the United States dropped massive amounts of bombs on North Korea. US defence spending increased from $13.1 billion in 1950 to $50.4 billion in 1953. This forced the Truman administration to cut down on civilian spending. By 1952 Americans were weary of fighting a war which had settled down into a stalemate, with no end in sight.

Red Scare

A Red Scare had swept the country in 1919 after the Bolshevik Revolution brought communists to power in Russia. A second, bigger scare occurred after the Second World War. Although the Soviet Union became an ally against Hitler's Germany during the war, the spirit of the wartime alliance soon disappeared after 1945. With the fall of an "iron curtain" across the continent of Europe, Americans of Eastern European descent had every reason to feel actively anti-communist. Communism's atheist ideology offended many Americans. Its rejection of private property appalled a post-war generation which was busily trying to get ahead, buy homes and accumulate consumer goods.

In 1949 the Soviet Union exploded an atomic bomb and China went communist. People were reluctant to accept that Soviet science was sufficiently advanced to produce the bomb and suspected that spies had handed over atomic secrets. The Truman administration was blamed for having not done enough to "save" China. In 1950 two spy cases caught the public's attention. Alger Hiss, a State Department (US ministry for foreign affairs) official accused of spying for the Soviets, was sent to prison for five years. Klaus Fuchs, a German-born scientist from England who had worked on the atomic bomb, was convicted of handing over secrets to the Soviets. As a result of the Fuchs investigation, Julius and Ethel Rosenberg, two members of the American Communist Party, were arrested for being part of a ring of spies associated with Fuchs. The Rosenbergs had played a relatively minor role in spying for the Soviet Union but in the tensely anti-communist atmosphere of the early 1950s they were condemned to death and died on the electric chair.

Leading the anti-communist crusade were the Federal Bureau of Investigation (FBI) and its powerful director J Edgar Hoover, and the House (of Representatives) Committee on Un-American Activities (HUAC). Hoover became director of the FBI in 1924 and retained the position until his death in 1972. Effective as a crime-fighter, he had also been accumulating evidence on political radicals since the 1920s. By the early fifties, he controlled a vast network of informers and undercover agents. Hoover was considered politically untouchable. He was a well-known figure nationally, who had skilfully built up his public image as a patriotic, incorruptible champion of law and order. He was known to have accumulated a large amount of potentially damaging information—often of a sexual nature—on people in high places in Washington. The Red Scare made him more powerful than ever. Much of the information which Congressional committees of investigation used against people accused of having communist sympathies came from the FBI.

In the HUAC, politicians—including the later president Richard Nixon—found they could boost their careers by accusing others of being "red" or "pink". Among others, Hollywood stars were forced to testify before the Committee. Many actors with **left-wing** sympathies ended up being blacklisted (categorized as unemployable) by the major movie studios. Refusing to testify on the grounds of the **fifth amendment**—according to which no US citizen can be forced to testify against him- or herself—did not help. It merely raised suspicions that people had something to hide. Teachers in public (state) schools and colleges were frequently required to take oaths denying that they were communists. Some 600 of them are estimated to have lost their jobs as a result.

President Truman did little to protect innocent people from the witch-hunt. In 1947, as the Cold War intensified, he had ordered "loyalty boards" to be established to check the political reliability of employees in all government departments. As the Red Scare intensified, the loyalty boards were abused, enabling thousands of innocent government employees to be intimidated. People being investigated were not entitled to see the evidence brought against them. By 1952, 1200 government employees had been dismissed and another 6000 had resigned. No one among them was proved to have been a spy. Ironically, this did nothing to stop accusers, notably Republican Senator Joseph McCarthy, from accusing the Truman administration of being soft on communism.

McCarthyism was the peak of the Red Scare. Senator McCarthy quickly came to public attention in 1950 by claiming that there were over 200 communists working in the State Department (foreign ministry). McCarthy may have been basing his claims on FBI information but he seldom produced any hard evidence to back up his claims, maintaining that this information was classified as secret. McCarthy was a demagogue who skilfully played on people's fears. He also appealed to many ordinary Americans' resentment of the liberal "eastern Establishment", personified by Secretary of State Dean Acheson. The press carried stories on McCarthy but did little to investigate the truth of his accusations. With the Red Scare at its height and the Alger Hiss spy case fresh in people's minds, public opinion seemed to favour McCarthy. Riding the anti-communist wave, Republicans supported him. Based on his power in various Senate committees, McCarthy continued for four years to intimidate people inside and outside the government with unfounded accusations concerning their communist sympathies. In the end he over-reached himself by investigating the army in 1954. His

Left-wing and **right-wing** are terms for describing political tendencies in the 20th century. They still have some relevance today. Left-wingers or leftists were and are identified with socialists and communists (liberals in the USA) and are usually associated with programmes of social reform. Right-wingers or rightists are associated with extreme conservatism. Right-wingers are usually resistant to change by social reform, often idealize the past and are nationalistic and, in the case of extreme rightists, sometimes even racist in their views. One should be careful to distinguish between conservatives and right-wingers. Most conservatives are moderates.

The **fifth amendment** is one of the first ten constitutional amendments, known collectively as the **Bill of Rights**, which protect US citizens' rights. Amendments to the Constitution, of which there were a total of 27 by 2008, need a special two-thirds majority in both houses of Congress and ratification (confirmation) by three-quarters of the States' legislatures, in order to become law.

committee's sessions were televised. Viewers were disgusted by the bullying, abusive style of his cross-questioning. Later in the year the Senate voted by a convincing majority (including half the Republican senators) to condemn McCarthy's behaviour. The era of McCarthyism was at an end.

The 1950s—the Eisenhower era

Following Roosevelt's lengthy domination of the presidency, Congress in 1951 passed the 22nd amendment preventing any president being elected for more than two terms of office. The idea behind the amendment was that it was unhealthy for a democracy to be dominated by any one person for too long. Roosevelt's prestige among Americans had been so great that he appeared unbeatable. As a consequence, he died in office. The temptations for a president to misuse his power in such a situation were undeniable. When Roosevelt died in April 1945, Truman was left to serve almost the whole of the 1945–8 term of office. Nevertheless, as the vice-president succeeding a dead president, Truman had not been elected. Thus, by the 1952 presidential election year, Truman had only been elected once (in 1948). The 22nd amendment would not have stopped him running for the presidency again, had he wanted to. As a candidate, Truman would have had the advantage of being the incumbent (someone who already occupied the president's office). Nevertheless, he decided not to offer himself as a candidate.

By the early 1950s, Truman had become unpopular. There were a number of reasons for this. First, there was the war in Korea, which was dragging on. In 1951 Truman had been forced to dismiss General MacArthur, the legendary commander of UN forces (mostly American) in Korea. MacArthur had disobeyed orders by advocating an all-out war against North Korea and China, using nuclear weapons if necessary. But MacArthur was a national hero after the Second World War and Truman's popularity declined as a result. In the same year, two corruption scandals involving tax and revenue funds made Truman's administration an easy target for Republicans. **Inflation** had set in as a result of the Korean War and there was criticism of Truman's handling of the economy. With the Red Scare in full swing and Eastern Europe under Soviet domination, Republican criticism that Truman was too soft on communism looked justified.

The Democratic Party chose Governor Adlai Stevenson of Illinois as its presidential candidate. Stevenson, sophisticated and eloquent, was popular in the liberal wing of the party. But Stevenson's liberalism was out of step with Congress and the nation. Republicans, such as Richard Nixon and Senator McCarthy, sarcastically mocked Stevenson's intellectual speeches and liberal approach to foreign affairs. Republicans coined the slogan "Korea, Communism and Corruption" to associate Stevenson with the failures of the Truman administration. But the Republicans' biggest asset in the 1952 election was General Eisenhower, popularly known simply as "Ike".

The cartoon shows Eisenhower's Secretary of State (foreign minister) JF Dulles and Senator "Joe" McCarthy. The words on the desk read "State Department". What message did the cartoonist want to express?

High government spending can increase **inflation** by increasing the amount of paper money in circulation. As well as increasing government spending, the Korean War caused a boom in the economy by stimulating demand for steel and other defence-related goods. Booms can also be inflationary. Because labour is in strong demand, workers can demand higher wages, triggering wage increases in all sectors of the economy, thus causing all goods and services to rise in price. Price rises then trigger the next round of wage increases and so on.

Eisenhower was a hugely popular war hero who had been supreme commander of Allied forces during the D-Day invasion of France. Ike projected a homely image, played golf and had a photogenic smile. People stuck "I like Ike" stickers on their car bumpers. Eisenhower presented himself as a figure who could appeal to all Americans. He was not a professional politician and appeared to be above everyday party politics. He avoided the temptation to gain popularity by joining with McCarthy and other Republicans in attacking "reds". Eisenhower had much to offer the presidency. He had organized military actions involving millions of men during the Second World War. Then and later on, as NATO's first military commander, he was personally acquainted with many other world leaders, including Soviet ones. At a time of great international tension, his expertise on defence issues and foreign affairs was reassuring for Americans.

Eisenhower's vice-presidential running mate was Richard Nixon, who went on to become president himself in 1969. Nixon complemented Eisenhower. He was young (38 years old in 1952), whereas Eisenhower (aged 61) was old for a presidential candidate. Nixon was a Californian, while Ike came from the Midwest. While Ike's image was non-partisan (not strongly linked to any political party), Nixon had proved himself a leading organizer among Republicans and had made national headlines as an anti-communist. He effectively attacked the Truman administration by telling Americans that he and Ike would "clean up the mess in Washington".

But Nixon briefly found himself to be the centre of a corruption scandal in the election year. There were suspicions in the press about a private election fund. Nixon successfully talked his way out of the scandal by skilfully using television. In a televised speech, known as the "Checkers speech" (Checkers was the name of his daughter's dog), Nixon convinced millions of Americans that he was a hard-working, honest family man with nothing to hide.

Eisenhower also used television to great advantage during the 1952 campaign. With the help of an advertising studio, he made a series of short question-and-answer "spots". Eisenhower's answers contained little factual information but were designed to project his winning smile and trustworthy manner. The TV spots were very effective. Through television, politicians

Discussion point: role of the media in a democracy

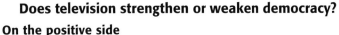

Does television strengthen or weaken democracy?

On the positive side

Television brings politicians into our living rooms on a daily basis. During elections we have a chance to hear and see politicians engaging in televised debates and answering tough questions from interviewers. During the lead-up to an election, this helps voters to form an opinion on presidential candidates and other party leaders.

On the negative side

- Politicians prepare their public statements carefully. They avoid saying things which could lose them votes among certain groups of voters (ethnic minorities, old people, poor people, etc.). Often what they say in private is very different to their public statements.

- A large proportion of the population do not know the details of the complex issues which politicians are talking about.

- Politicians in opposing parties often contradict or ridicule each other concerning what is the best thing to do for the economy, the environment, crime, etc., making it difficult for voters to decide.

- Politicians make promises before elections that they do not always keep once they have been elected.

- People sometimes vote for a politician because of his/her looks and charisma—in the case of Kennedy, for example—rather than what he/she stands for.

were now able to reach millions of people directly. Elections were becoming more about the personalities of individuals than party programmes. As the role of television grew, the importance of political parties and their organizations decreased.

In 1952 Eisenhower and the Republicans stood for limiting federal government spending, which had significantly increased under the Democrats. Since Roosevelt, Republicans had opposed "Big Government". However, Eisenhower did not commit himself to cutting any particular government programme—support for farmers or veterans' pensions, for example—which would have been unpopular with millions of voters. Similarly vague was Eisenhower's promise to "go to Korea" and bring the war to an honourable end. He did not say how he intended to finish the war. But, as Eisenhower well knew, his great military reputation would persuade people to see in him the most likely person who could successfully bring the conflict to an end.

Not surprisingly, Eisenhower won a landslide victory. His personal popularity caused people who traditionally voted Democrat, as in the South, to vote for him. He "carried" (won) four Southern states. In contrast to the 1948 election, voters turned out in large numbers. Americans agreed with Eisenhower that it was "time for a change", as the Republican slogan went. In the **Congressional election**, the swing to the Republicans was not quite so clear, although they won a small majority in the **House of Representatives** and a majority of one in the **Senate**. A new era had begun. The Republicans had not been in control of both the presidency and the Congress since 1930.

As he had promised, Eisenhower moved quickly to end the war in Korea. A ceasefire was signed in July 1953. Eisenhower benefited from the fact that the Chinese had by this time grown weary of fighting and Stalin's death (in 1953) removed an obstacle to negotiations. The ceasefire was not a victory over the communists. The North–South dividing line remained roughly where it had been before the war. Nevertheless, the South had been saved and most Americans were satisfied with Eisenhower's handling of the war.

Eisenhower also made sure that his administration could not be accused of being "soft on communism" by making it easier to dismiss government employees suspected of disloyalty and giving the FBI a free hand. Senator McCarthy posed less of a threat to Eisenhower, a Republican president, than he had to Truman. Nevertheless, when McCarthy began investigating the army in 1954, he demanded the right to cross-question leading figures in the administration. Eisenhower resisted but refused to confront McCarthy head-on.

Eisenhower's refusal to confront McCarthy was typical of his approach to the presidency. He aimed to stay out of controversial issues, keeping the presidency above partisan (party) politics and preserving his own popularity. His main concern was to keep federal spending down and control inflation, which had increased during the Korean War. Although in principle opposed to Big Government, Eisenhower nevertheless made no attempt to dismantle the **welfare programmes** inherited from the Democrats. That would have been unpopular. In fact, welfare spending increased slowly but steadily

Congressional elections take place at the same time as presidential ones. Election Day is early in November.

The principle of the **separation of powers** (between the legislative, the executive and the judicial branches of the government) in the Constitution ensures that the election and powers of the president remain quite separate from those of Congress (the legislative branch). Although it does not seem logical, it is perfectly possible for voters to return a Democratic majority to Congress while voting in a Republican president. This kind of split vote happened quite often and gives the American political system its unique complexity. A successful president has to be skilful in managing Congress.

The situation contrasts with most parliamentary systems in the world, where the party with the biggest vote in a parliamentary election automatically gets to nominate the head of government (usually the leader of that party). In this case, there is no separate election for the head of government, who is a member of parliament and can rely on a majority there.

Welfare programmes in the United States in the 1950s originated from the social security programmes of the New Deal era. Welfare programmes aimed at eliminating poverty among disadvantaged social groups increased under President Johnson. In Europe after the Second World War, the state administered most welfare programmes directly. But in the USA social welfare placed more emphasis on private or quasi-governmental agencies and private finance through contributions by employers.

during Eisenhower's presidency—from 7.6 per cent of GNP in 1952 to 11.5 per cent in 1961. Eisenhower's moderate conservatism suited the mood of Americans in the 1950s.

Another issue over which Eisenhower moved very cautiously was civil rights. The political issue of racial discrimination against African-Americans was building up in the 1950s, despite Eisenhower's determination to keep the federal government out of it. In the South, "Jim Crow" laws kept public facilities such as transportation and schools, as well as bars, restaurants, hotels and movie theatres, legally segregated. African-Americans were prevented from voting through intimidation and so-called literacy and other tests.

Congress (the House of Representatives) and the Senate—the US political system

To legislate is to make laws. The legislative branch of the US federal government is Congress. (This is not to be confused with the legislatures of the individual States, which are the representative assemblies of the states.)

Congress is divided into the Senate, in which the states are represented, and the House of Representatives, in which the people are represented. The states are represented equally (regardless of their size or population), each state sending two senators. Senators are elected for six years, with one third being elected every two years. By contrast, members of congress are elected to the House of Representatives for only two years. Thus senators are less sensitive to the ups and downs of public opinion than House Representatives, who continuously have to worry about getting re-elected. Senators are seen as senior statesmen who advise the president. Their approval is needed when the president makes important appointments, such as secretaries of state (ministers who head government departments or ministries), federal judges and ambassadors. In keeping with the constitutional principle of "checks and balances", the Senate's ratification (approval) is also needed before treaties signed by the president can come into effect.

All legislation (laws in-the-making, referred to as "bills") requires the approval—usually by a simple 50 per cent majority—of both the House and the Senate. Finally, the president's signature is required before a bill can become law.

In the rest of the country blacks were discriminated against in housing, education and at work. Knowing how explosive the issue was, Eisenhower refused to respond to calls for reform made by the National Association for the Advancement of Coloured People (NAACP) and the Congress for Racial Equality (CORE).

Although Eisenhower kept the executive out of the race issue, he could not stop the Supreme Court, led by Chief Justice Earl Warren, from forcing change upon the South. In 1954 the Supreme Court ruled that public schools had to be desegregated. In 1956 it ruled the same for buses. The school ruling took many years to put into practice fully but everyone could see that it would have huge consequences and it encouraged activists to carry out other protest actions. The Supreme Court's bus ruling came after the famous bus boycott (refusal to ride the buses) led by the Reverend Dr Martin Luther King and his followers in Montgomery, Alabama. Rosa Parks had sparked the boycott by courageously refusing to give up her seat to a white person.

Eisenhower ran for re-election in 1956 and beat Adlai Stevenson, again the Democratic candidate, even more convincingly than in 1952. Despite Eisenhower's continuing personal popularity, people increasingly voted Democrat in Congressional elections during the course of the1950s. The Republicans' ideas on reducing Big Government and cutting taxes appealed to business people and the rich but did not attract the majority of Americans, who still preferred the Democrats' ideas on welfare spending and federal assistance for disadvantaged groups.

Kennedy and Eisenhower meeting to discuss the handover of the presidency after Kennedy had won the election in 1960. The difference in their ages is obvious. Voters were ready for a young, fresh face after eight years of Eisenhower.

Democracy and elections in the USA

The USA is the world's oldest democracy. It has the world's oldest written constitution. (Britain's is older but is not all in writing.) As a republic (only the Swiss republic is of longer standing)– its head of government was always elected by the people. By the 1820s, property qualifications for voting had been dropped in all states and the principle of "one man, one vote" for white men had been accepted. That included presidential elections, despite the electoral college system (see page 272). (African-Americans, most of whom were still slaves, did not have the vote and neither did Native Americans. American women–as in most European countries–had to wait until the early 20th century.) By contrast, the French and British had to wait until the 1870s and 1880s until they got the right of "one man, one vote" in genuinely multi-party parliamentary elections.

Because of its federal constitution, the USA has an extraordinary number of elections. Americans get to vote for representatives at the federal, state and local government levels. If you were of voting age and lived in Los Angeles, here are the people you could vote for:

- the governor of California
- a member of the city council
- a member of the House of Representatives
- the county commissioner
- a member of the Californian legislative assembly
- a senator
- the president of the USA
- a member of the Californian Senate.

By the end of the Eisenhower era, the mood was shifting again. American society had changed. People were more urban, more middle class, better educated. Many had grown impatient with the cautiousness and lack of activity shown by the Eisenhower administration. That applied particularly to African-Americans. But the whole nation had also been shocked in 1957 by the Soviet Union's success in putting the first man-made satellite, the "sputnik" into space. People asked themselves if American science and technology, and the whole education system, had fallen behind their counterparts in the communist world.

 Which of the people listed above would be local, state or federal government officials?

Although Eisenhower was generally credited with handling foreign policy well, he looked clumsy in 1960 when the Soviet leader, Nikita Khrushchev, confronted him with evidence of having permitted high altitude flights in Soviet air space for spying purposes—the U2 flights. The U2 incident ensured that the Paris summit conference would be a failure. With tension building up over the divided city of Berlin, East–West relations were getting worse.

Eisenhower left two other difficult foreign policy problems to his successors. When the young radical Fidel Castro came to power in Cuba in 1959, Eisenhower publicly took a strong stand against him, while secretly authorizing the CIA in 1960 to build up a force to

Johnson and Kennedy during the Democratic convention at which Kennedy was nominated as the party's presidential candidate. Prior to the nomination, Johnson was competing with Kennedy for the candidacy. Consider their body language and facial expressions in this photo. What impression are the two politicians giving to fellow Democrats, the press and the public at the convention?

invade Cuba. In Vietnam, where the communist North was destabilizing the pro-Western South, he avoided direct US military action. Nevertheless, Eisenhower committed the United States to supporting a corrupt, unpopular regime in the South.

Eisenhower surprised many in his farewell speech. Despite being a leading Cold War warrior and a top general, he warned the nation prophetically about the political dangers of building up a vast, permanent peacetime defence establishment. This was a new feature of national life, Eisenhower pointed out. As an employer for millions and a powerful **lobby**, the "military-industrial complex" was a danger to people's liberties, to democratic processes and to a peaceful foreign policy and had to be vigilantly controlled.

The 1960s—civil rights movement and Vietnam

President Kennedy and the new frontier
Eisenhower was prevented by the 22nd amendment from standing in the 1960 presidential election. Instead, Richard Nixon won the Republican nomination by skilfully using his position of public prominence as vice-president. The Democratic nomination was more hotly contested. John ("Jack") F Kennedy beat the other contenders, including Senator Lyndon B Johnson of Texas and Senator Hubert Humphrey of Minnesota.

Kennedy (43 years old) was one of the youngest presidential candidates in US history. He was cultured, handsome and charismatic. He also came from a very rich family. Humphrey complained that Kennedy had used his wealth to influence people unfairly in the important West Virginia **primary election**, which Kennedy won. Although Kennedy had not shown himself to be particularly liberal in the Senate, he convinced many Americans, especially young people, that he stood for change. He promised a "New Frontier" for the United States. In a clever choice, he picked the influential Lyndon Johnson to be his vice-presidential running mate. Kennedy correctly calculated that Johnson, a Texan, could help win over voters in the South.

The contest between Nixon and Kennedy was more one of style than substance. The domestic policies which they argued for did not show any great differences. Both candidates spent record sums of money on TV ads. Kennedy promised federal aid for education, a higher minimum wage and medical insurance for the elderly. Nixon advocated a more significant role for government in promoting economic growth, assuring voters that he would be an active president, unlike Eisenhower. In foreign policy, Nixon was a well-known anti-communist who, as vice-president, had been closely associated with Eisenhower's policy of containment. But Kennedy appeared to be just as tough on world communism. He argued that there was a "missile gap" which favoured the Soviet Union and he seemed to favour an invasion of Cuba. To make up for the fact that he was a Catholic in a predominantly Protestant country, Kennedy skilfully appealed to the American tradition of **secularism**. Kennedy reminded voters that the separation of church and state was absolute

Literally a large public room, a **lobby** is a political pressure group (a group with the same economic interests or an ethnic group) which lobbies politicians to act on its behalf. Lobbying is an important part of the political process in Washington.

Primary elections or simply "primaries" are elections inside political parties to elect the candidates who the parties will put forward for voters to choose at national elections.

Secularism The United States was the first country to adopt a thoroughly secular form of government by separating all ties between religion and government. Shortly after independence, measures were taken in several States to "disestablish" the British national church, known as Episcopalian in the USA and Anglican in Britain. Because their ancestors emigrated from various countries, Americans have always belonged to a variety of churches. Thus secularism has been an important part of the American political tradition almost from the start.

in the United States. "I am not the Catholic candidate for President", he reassured voters. "I do not speak for my church on public matters and the church does not speak for me."

The election produced the closest result of the century. Kennedy received 49.7 per cent of the popular vote to Nixon's 49.6, although the **electoral college** vote gave Kennedy a bigger lead (because he carried some big states). Nixon's advisors urged him to demand a recount but he considered that it would be divisive and conceded defeat. The Democrats' victory in the 1960 elections was clearer in Congress, where Democrats won convincing majorities in both the Senate and the House of Representatives.

Why did Kennedy win? Although he had not promised to take action on civil rights, Kennedy benefited from receiving approximately 70 per cent of the black vote, considerably more than Adlai Stevenson had received in 1956. The press loved Kennedy's charm, intelligence and warmth and was equally enthusiastic about his sophisticated, beautiful wife, Jackie. Johnson helped win over undecided voters in the South, especially in Texas. Eisenhower, who never liked Nixon personally, did little to help his Republican successor.

Once again, television played a decisive role. For the first time in a presidential election, there was a series of televised debates between the contestants. In the first debate, Kennedy looked tanned, handsome and relaxed, whereas Nixon, who had a cold, appeared pale. Unfortunate lighting and make-up made him look unshaven on people's TV screens. Although Nixon spoke well, viewers favoured Kennedy. The televised debates gave Kennedy, until then unknown to the mass of Americans (in contrast to Nixon who was already vice-president), the chance to become nationally known.

At 43 years of age in 1961, Kennedy was the youngest American president ever. His youth, energy and charisma inspired many Americans to hope for a better future. Young people—the baby-boomers were beginning to come of age—

The president of the United States is not elected directly but by an **electoral college**. Each state has a number of electors. In practice, each political party offers a list of electors. These party-selected electors are all pledged to vote for the party's presidential candidate. The voters in the states then vote for this list and the party which gets the biggest vote wins all the electors' votes for that state. Because some States are bigger than others, they have more electors. Presidential elections are therefore more about winning key states than getting the biggest vote nationwide. In a closely run election, it is possible for one candidate to get more votes than another nationwide but still to lose the election (because the other got more votes in the electoral college).

The electoral college system is complicated and not fully democratic. It originated more than 200 years ago, like the rest of the Constitution (apart from the Amendments). At that time (1787), America was not yet a fully democratic society. That Americans have kept the electoral college system shows how traditional they are when it comes to the Constitution.

Nixon (left) and Kennedy (right) in one of their televised debates in 1960. Kennedy "won" the first debate because he looked relaxed and suntanned. But as you can see, a television studio in the 1960s was a difficult place to appear relaxed and informal. What does this say about Kennedy's approach to working with the medium of television?

African-Americans, other ethnic minorities and women's rights activists all fastened their hopes for change on Kennedy. Whereas Eisenhower had often appointed business leaders to head government departments, Kennedy appointed academics and intellectuals to these and other important advisory positions. A passionate liberal reformer was Robert (Bobby) Kennedy, the president's brother, who Kennedy appointed to the position of **attorney general**.

Kennedy received very high approval ratings (in public opinion surveys) among Americans by his skilful use of television. He was the first president to allow presidential press conferences to be televised. People appreciated his knowledgeable self-confidence when dealing with journalists' questions.

Kennedy was assassinated after less than three years in office. This fact has helped promote a "Kennedy myth" among later generations. Kennedy's untimely death meant that he never had a chance to fulfil the hopes that had been placed upon him. But neither did he have a chance to disappoint them. Consequently, many Americans continue to rate Kennedy above even Washington, Lincoln or Roosevelt. Widely held conspiracy theories concerning Kennedy's assassination—some arguing that he was killed by a deadly alliance of right-wing reactionaries—have added to the Kennedy myth. That Kennedy showed greatness in his short presidency cannot be denied. But contrary to the myth, his greatest achievements lay in his conduct of foreign, not domestic (home) affairs.

In the United States, the **attorney general** is the head of the Justice Department, and is the most senior legal advisor to the president.

President Kennedy's domestic reforms

On the positive side	On the negative side
He set up a presidential commission to examine the status of women. Among other things, the commission recommended equal pay for equal work and helped inspire feminist activists to unite in their struggle for equality.	Kennedy failed to get Congress to act on the issues of health insurance (for the elderly) and urban planning.
The Peace Corps was launched in Kennedy's presidency. Young volunteers were trained to give educational and technical assistance to developing countries.	He did not strongly support a bill for federal aid for schools when it encountered resistance in Congress.
Kennedy's administration succeeded in getting moderate reform laws through Congress aimed at ● improving mental health services ● providing federal aid for house-building ● vocational (job) training.	
He initiated a bill (law), that Congress passed after he died, which introduced a series of tax cuts. The idea was a highly original strategy to promote economic growth by allowing individual people and companies to keep more of their income. Much of this increased income, it was argued, would then be invested, leading to greater economic growth. The strategy was used again by later presidents but economists were divided about how much the tax cuts contributed to the economic boom of the 1960s.	

Both positive and negative

Kennedy initiated a civil rights bill in 1963 aimed at ending segregation in the South. But the bill ran into opposition in Congress, particularly from Southern Democrats. Kennedy was not able to overcome this resistance and it took his death and President Johnson's skill in handling Congress to get the bill passed in 1964.

Kennedy backed the Apollo space programme. This eventually succeeded in putting a man on the Moon in 1969. But critics said that the programme cost billions of dollars that would have been better spent elsewhere. The programme did not bring any significant scientific results.

On the whole, Kennedy was a moderate reformer. Elected by such a slim majority, he felt that he did not have the voters' backing to embark on a major reform programme. Although the Democrats were in the majority in Congress, conservative Southern Democrats opposed some of Kennedy's reform ideas, making it difficult for Kennedy to push them through. Due to his early, tragic death, we do not know if Kennedy would have succeeded in translating the hopes for change that he symbolized into effective reforms.

Kennedy's inspiring inaugural speech (formally beginning his term as president) in January 1961 is often quoted. "Ask not what your country can do for you—ask what you can do for your country," he told his fellow Americans. But he went on to say to his worldwide audience, "Ask not what America will do for you, but what together we can do for the freedom of man." In fact most of the speech was about the current world situation, then dominated by the Cold War. In the short time during which he was president, Kennedy devoted most of his time to America's foreign relations.

In foreign policy, Kennedy launched an Alliance for Progress with Latin American countries, designed to help economic and social reform in those countries by providing US funds. In the Berlin Crisis (see Chapter 9), Kennedy took a tough stand, refusing to give way to Khrushchev's pressure to give up West Berlin. In 1961 the Soviet leader was forced to approve the building of a wall to keep West

Activity:
Points of view

Historians advance particular points of view. Practise evaluating the interpretations of historians by summarizing and commenting on the differences in these two interpretations of Kennedy's presidency.

1 President Kennedy's achievements were looked on favourably in the emotional time just after he died. The first source is from a historian, Arthur Schlesinger, who was a White House aide in the Kennedy administration.

   He had had so little time, yet he had accomplished so much: the new hope for peace on earth, the elimination of nuclear testing in the atmosphere, and the abolition of nuclear diplomacy, the new policies towards Latin America and the third world, the reordering of American defense, the emancipation of the American Negro, the revolution in national economic policy, the concern for poverty, the stimulus to the arts, the fight for reason against extremism and mythology. Lifting us beyond our capacities, he gave his country back to its best self, wiping away the impression of an old nation of old men, weary, played out, fearful of ideas, change and the future; he taught mankind that the process of rediscovering America was not over.

   Source: Schlesinger, A. 1965, *A Thousand Days. John F Kennedy in the White House*. New York, USA. p. 362.

2 "Revisionist" historians of a later generation criticized Kennedy for being more concerned with image and style than real issues. Kennedy's extra-marital love affairs also became public knowledge. In foreign policy he was criticized for taking unnecessary risks in Vietnam and the Cuban Missile Crisis. Here, James Patterson, writing in 1990, evaluates Kennedy's record in domestic policy.

   The deadlock delaying the [civil rights] bill served as an apt [appropriate] symbol of Kennedy's larger record in the field of domestic policy between 1961 and 1963. Indeed, his prospects in Congress … seemed no better in 1963 than they had been earlier. On November 12, 1963, the New York Times noted, "Rarely has there been such a pervasive attitude of discouragement around Capitol Hill and such a feeling of helplessness to deal with it. This has been one of the least productive sessions of Congress within the memory of most of its members." This was a glum but accurate description of the prospects for domestic change at the time. Kennedy had aroused liberal expectations but he had failed to overcome the long-entrenched power of the conservative coalition in Congress. New frontiers still stood in the distance.

   Source: Patterson, J. 1996. *Grand Expectations. The United States 1945–1974*. Oxford, UK. Oxford University Press. p. 485.

Berlin separated from communist East Germany. Kennedy visited West Berlin in 1963 and made his famous "Ich bin ein Berliner" ("I am a Berliner") speech, to the delight of West Germans.

In Vietnam, Kennedy continued Eisenhower's policy of supporting the government of President Diem, which was becoming increasingly unpopular. There was a military coup in 1963 shortly before Kennedy's assassination. Diem was assassinated but his successors were no more effective. Kennedy increased American commitment to South Vietnam by sending several thousand military advisors. He hoped—against the advice of some of his advisors—that this kind of support would prove sufficient help for South Vietnam to be able to defend itself successfully against the North. When he died, Kennedy left behind him an unsolved and rapidly growing problem for the USA in Vietnam.

Kennedy is best remembered for his handling of the Cuban Missile Crisis. On becoming president in 1961, he approved plans left by the Eisenhower administration for CIA backing for an invasion of Cuba by a force of exiled Cubans. The Bay of Pigs invasion in that year was a complete failure. Nevertheless, Kennedy approved further invasion plans, as well as plans to assassinate Cuban leader Fidel Castro. Castro, fearing invasion, turned to the Soviet Union for help. In stationing nuclear missiles on Cuba, Khrushchev saw an opportunity to restore Soviet credibility abroad after the defeat of Berlin. Cuba would be protected from invasion and the Soviet Union would gain a major strategic advantage.

The Cuban Missile Crisis occurred in October 1962 as Kennedy received photographic evidence of the Soviet missile sites. Kennedy immediately formed an Executive Committee of the National Security Council and met secretly for a week with the Council to work out a response to the Soviet threat. All the military options were weighed up. A naval blockade—a "quarantine", as Kennedy called it—of Cuba was decided upon. Then, on 22 October, Kennedy announced the details of the crisis to the nation and the tough position which he was taking with regard to the missiles. Kennedy's firm but reasonable approach to dealing with Khrushchev helped make a solution possible. Khrushchev agreed to withdraw the missiles but claimed a Soviet victory. The United States agreed informally not to invade Cuba and to withdraw its missiles from Turkey. Whoever had "won", Americans felt that Kennedy's handling of the crisis had succeeded in steering the United States and the world through the most dangerous crisis yet.

The civil rights movement

The civil rights movement of the 1960s grew out of the courageous actions of individual activists in the 1950s, backed up by the epoch-making decisions of the Supreme Court. The Supreme Court's famous rulings on desegregating schools and buses have already been mentioned. Groups of black activists sprang up all over the South in the early 1960s. Among them were many church ministers. They were increasingly joined by idealistic young people—among them some whites—from the North. But black activists were divided

TOK link

Ways of knowing—language, emotion, reason and perception

You will have read or listened to a number of speeches and seen major developments on television. You are encouraged to visit the website *The Living Room Candidate* (http://www.livingroomcandidate.org) that features over 300 commercials, from every American presidential election since 1952. It provides an excellent forum for the role of media in a democracy and addresses the TOK concepts of ways of knowing as well as some areas of knowledge.

Seeing, reading and hearing about events provides us with a window to the world, but we need to be able to assess the reliability of what we are seeing and develop skills that will guide us in making knowledge claims.

TOK questions

- To what extent do our senses tell us about the world as it really is?

- How does technological change affect the way language is used and communication takes place?

- If knowledge claims cannot be rationally defended, should they be renounced?

- Are patriotism and racism examples of collective emotions? Is faith an emotion, a feeling or neither?

1 Select any two speeches on a common theme from the period of Eisenhower's presidency to the present administration of President Barack Obama. Listen to the speech and identify any obvious appeals to emotion and how that appeal is achieved. Is your perception affected by knowing who made the speech? Dissect each speech and identify the following elements:

- any appeals to reason or logic

- the use of emotive language, vocabulary and body language

- any knowledge claims made

2 Look at the activity on page 274 "Points of view" and apply the same analysis to the assessment of:

- President Kennedy's achievements in the two extracts provided

- the speeches provided below by two key figures from the civil rights movement in the United States in the 1960s.

Extract from a speech by Malcolm X, on his return from Mecca, in which he explains his views on racism and violence (March 1964).

I don't speak against the sincere, well-meaning, good white people. I have learned that there are some. I have learned that not all white people are racists. I am speaking against and my fight is against the white racists. I believe that Negroes have the right to fight against these racists, by any means that are necessary. I am for violence if non-violence means we continue postponing a solution to the American black man's problem—just to avoid violence. I don't go for non-violence if it also means a delayed solution. To me a delayed solution is a non-solution. Or I'll say it another way. If it must take violence to get the black man his human rights in this country, I'm for violence exactly as you know the Irish, the Poles or Jews would be if they were flagrantly discriminated against."

Source: Spartacus Educational. http://www.spartacus.schoolnet.co.uk/USAmalcolmX.htm

Extract from a speech by Dr Martin Luther King Jnr at the march on Washington, 28 August, 1963.

I am happy to join with you today in what will go down in history as the greatest demonstration for freedom in the history of our nation. Five score years ago, a great American, in whose symbolic shadow we stand today, signed the Emancipation Proclamation … But one hundred years later, the Negro still is not free. One hundred years later, the life of the Negro is still sadly crippled by the manacles of segregation and the chains of discrimination. One hundred years later, the Negro lives on a lonely island of poverty in the midst of a vast ocean of material prosperity. One hundred years later, the Negro is still languished in the corners of American society and finds himself an exile in his own land. And so we've come here today to dramatize a shameful condition …

But there is something that I must say to my people, who stand on the warm threshold which leads into the palace of justice: in the process of gaining our rightful place, we must not be guilty of wrongful deeds. Let us not seek to satisfy our thirst for freedom by drinking from the cup of bitterness and hatred. [Applause] We must forever conduct our struggle on the high plane of dignity and discipline. We must not allow our creative protest to degenerate into physical violence. Again and again, we must rise to the majestic heights of meeting physical force with soul force.

Source: Spartacus Educational. http://www.spartacus.schoolnet.co.uk/USAdream.htm

among a number of movements—the NAACP, CORE and Martin Luther King's Southern Christian Leadership Conference (SCLC). The NAACP had grown in earlier years and had many older activists who were not prepared for the more radical actions which younger blacks demanded. The Student Non-Violent Coordinating Committee (SNCC), established in the late 1950s, attracted younger activists with its willingness to engage in militant actions and its inspiring song "We Shall Overcome". The SNCC attracted well-educated young activists, who contrasted with working-class and older blacks who resented being drawn into conflicts by radical outsiders.

Martin Luther King (second row on the left) taking the first desegregated ride on a bus in Montgomery after the Supreme Court ruling in his favour. This photo appeared nationwide in newspapers. How did people (white and black Southerners, people in other regions, politicians, newspaper editors) react when they saw it?

Martin Luther King became the leading figure in the civil rights movement after rising to national prominence during the Montgomery bus boycott. After that King campaigned for the civil rights cause all over the South. He was a powerful public speaker. King shaped the civil rights movement by persistently applying a strategy of non-violent protest. His refusal to show anger in the face of racial discrimination that was sometimes violent sprang from his Christian faith. He was a Baptist church minister. As a political strategy, King's adoption of non-violent protest owed much to the example of Mohandas Gandhi's struggle for Indians' civil and political rights. King's success in getting his followers to renounce violence in the pursuit of their aims persuaded millions of Christian Americans that his cause was just.

Despite the divisions among African-Americans, the civil rights movement gathered strength in the early 1960s. A decisive event was the election of President Kennedy. Activists sensed that Kennedy's election symbolized a change of mood in the nation. By carrying out protest actions which deliberately broke unjust segregation laws, they aimed to provoke violent white reactions, thereby forcing the whole nation to recognize the evils of racism. By bringing things to a head, they hoped that President Kennedy would take the decision to act on the race issue.

Civil rights activists developed new methods of non-violent protest. In "sit-ins", young blacks would remain sitting for hours at lunch counters, while nervous white restaurant owners refused to serve them. In "freedom rides", groups of activists would ride interstate buses through the South and use whites-only facilities in the bus terminals. They were successful in provoking white violence, from both the police and racists like members of the Ku Klux Klan. Thousands of civil rights demonstrators were beaten and some were killed. Hoover's FBI provided little protection and sometimes collaborated with Klansmen.

Hoover even had King's telephone wire-tapped, wrongly suspecting that he was under communist influence.

Things came to a head in 1962 as an activist called James Meredith attempted to enrol in the University of Mississippi as its first African-American student. The US marshals sent to protect Meredith were overwhelmed by a hostile crowd, so Robert Kennedy had to authorize the use of federal troops to control the crowd. Until then, John and Robert Kennedy had attempted to prevent the federal government from being dragged into the race issue. They did not want to antagonize conservative Southerners in the Democratic Party and feared that introducing federal troops into the South could simply escalate the violence.

Malcolm X was a brilliant public speaker. He led the black Muslim movement and became known nationally through the media. However, he did not campaign in the South or elsewhere or organize protest actions like King. Does that mean that his impact on African-Americans was less significant than King's?

In 1963 King decided to make Birmingham, Alabama the centre of the civil rights struggle. Birmingham was one of the most thoroughly segregated cities in the South. King's demonstrators, many of them schoolchildren, were treated with savage violence by Birmingham police. For the first time, the demonstrations were shown nationwide on television. People throughout the country, including moderate whites in Birmingham, were shocked by the police brutality.

Sensing that he now had the majority of Americans behind him, President Kennedy decided to act. Two months after the Birmingham violence, Kennedy went on television to inform the nation that he was going to present a civil rights bill to Congress. Putting the presidency squarely behind equal rights, Kennedy said even after the abolition of slavery a hundred years earlier, African-Americans were still not free.

> … This nation … will not be free until all its citizens are free. We preach freedom around the world, and we mean it. And we cherish our freedom here at home. But are we to say to the world—and much more importantly to each other—that this is the land of the free, except for Negroes; that we have no second-class citizens, except Negroes; that we have no class or caste system, no ghettos, no master race, except with respect to Negroes?
>
> Hefner, RD. 1991. *A Documentary History of the United States*. New York, USA. p. 331.

A few months later a quarter of a million demonstrators, 50 000 of them white, marched through Washington to the Lincoln Memorial. There Martin Luther King gave his memorable speech, closing with the words:

> I have a dream … [of] that day when all God's children, black men and white men, Jews and Gentiles, Protestants and Catholics, will be able to join hands and sing in the words of that old Negro spiritual, "Free at last! Free at last! Thanks God almighty, we are free at last!"

Kennedy's civil rights bill passed into law in 1964, the year after he died. It was a great step forward. It strengthened the law courts' ability to put an end to segregation. But the violence was far from over. Moreover, most Southern African-Americans were still prevented from voting.

To focus on voting rights, King planned a series of demonstrations and marches in Selma, Alabama in 1965. Police violence was again shocking and Klansmen were murdering activists. In a televised speech to Congress, President Johnson put himself firmly behind the civil rights cause, closing with the emotional words, "we shall overcome". Public opinion was outraged by the Alabama violence. This helped President Johnson get a bill on voting rights through Congress despite the resistance of Southern Congressmen.

Over the next few years, African-Americans were able to use their newly-won voting rights to send black Congressmen to Washington and to get blacks elected to key posts in state and local government. White anti-segregationists now had to consider black voters and be careful of what they said in public.

Overall, it was a victory for both black and white moderates. Nevertheless, change came too slowly for some African-Americans. Stokely Carmichael began to rival King in the civil rights movement. Carmichael argued in favour of using violence against whites and spoke of the need to achieve "black power". The black power movement gave birth to the armed violence of the Black Panthers in California and Northern cities.

Another radical black movement of the mid-1960s, one which drew more supporters than the Black Panthers, was the Nation of Islam. Members of the Nation of Islam rejected Christianity as the religion of the slave-owners under whom their ancestors had suffered. They preached separation of blacks from whites, who were said to be evil or corrupt. With the help of Allah, it was taught, blacks would eventually rise up and conquer the whites. In the ghettos of Northern cities, the Nation of Islam provided a disciplined way of life which provided an alternative for thousands of blacks. Men had to wear white shirts and suits, give up tobacco and drugs, and avoid sex before marriage. Women had to wear long dresses and cover their heads. In its struggle against the whites, the Nation aimed to meet violence with violence and had no use for the multiracialism of the civil rights movement.

By 1963, the leader of the Nation of Islam, Elijah Muhammad, was being eclipsed by Malcolm X, who had become the Nation's most popular speaker. ("X" represented his discarded slave name.) Malcolm impressed listeners with his intelligence, eloquence and self-confidence. He rejected co-operation with whites, calling them devils. Blacks should stand on their own feet and did not need the help of liberal whites. Seeing Malcolm X on television, many African-Americans were electrified by his message. In 1964 Malcolm broke away from the Nation of Islam, visited Africa, studied Islam and returned to build his own political movement. He was assassinated in 1965 by hostile members of the Nation of Islam. Malcolm X's outstanding leadership qualities and his early death made him a figure of inspiration for later generations of African-Americans.

Extremists such as the Black Panthers and the Nation of Islam were minority movements. Most African-Americans were moderate and supported Martin Luther King's civil rights movement. By the late 1960s, Southern segregation was being systematically dismantled. In this, the civil rights movement had succeeded. Nevertheless, racial discrimination in the rest of the country had produced a concentration of poorly educated, unemployed blacks in city centres. Their anger and sense of hopelessness exploded into violence in the mid-1960s. In 1965 Los Angeles was torn apart by race rioting. King's call to end the violence was ignored. Worse still, in 1966 and 1967, a series of race riots gripped cities across the United States. State police and the National Guard frequently had to be brought in to control the violence. Although much had been achieved, the United States was still a long way from reaching King's dream of racial harmony.

President Johnson and the Great Society

When he was assassinated, Kennedy was succeeded by vice-president Lyndon Johnson. In his inaugural speech, Johnson promised to continue with the reforms which Kennedy had begun. These were the civil rights bill initiated by Kennedy and a bill to help eliminate poverty by investing more money in education and job training. Johnson declared a "war on poverty". Over 20 per cent of Americans were considered to be living below the poverty line, proportionately more among African-Americans, Mexican-Americans and one-parent families. Both bills were passed by Congress in 1964. Johnson showed great skill in getting Congress to do what he wanted. At the same time Congress was unusually favourable towards liberal reform. Most Americans at the time were determined to honour the memory of the dead president by supporting the liberal ideas he stood for. Congress reflected that mood.

In 1964 Johnson won the Democratic nomination for that year's presidential election. Governor Wallace of Alabama, a Southern Democrat, entered the race. A popular speaker, he was a demagogue who knew how to exploit the fears of working-class people, especially concerning the race issue. Wallace entered the presidential campaign as an independent candidate (not belonging to any party), hoping to take enough of the Democratic vote away from Johnson to enable the conservative Republican candidate, Barry Goldwater, to win. As a strong opponent of Big Government, Goldwater as president would put an end to the reforms.

Johnson won the 1964 presidential election with one of the biggest landslide victories of the 20th century. Only six states voted Republican; all were Southern. Their loss to the Democrats was a result of Johnson's support for the civil rights movement. The South's switch from Democrat to Republican was one of the biggest political changes of the period.

Voters' approval of Johnson's year as president led them to vote overwhelmingly for him. Goldwater lost millions of votes by telling old and poor people that he intended to cut federal spending on them. The Democrats benefited, too, from the Congressional elections, which returned significant Democratic majorities. With his great election victory and the Democrats dominating Congress, Johnson was ready to launch the "Great Society", one of the most ambitious programmes of liberal reform in the century.

In 1965, his first year as an elected president, Johnson succeeded in getting a record amount of reform legislation passed by Congress. His achievement can be compared only with Roosevelt's, when Roosevelt became president in 1933. Johnson's main reforms covered four areas: education, health, voting rights and immigration.

Education

A bill providing federal aid for schools, which Kennedy had failed to achieve, was passed by Congress. The baby boom had increased the number of school-age children, so the public school system needed expanding. Johnson got provisions for education for people on a low income included in the bill.

Health

Medicare and Medicaid ensured that old people were medically insured but stopped short of providing a full national health system. It did nothing to lower the rate of infant mortality, for example, which was higher than that of some other industrialized countries— and was especially high among low-income groups.

Voting rights

Johnson's bill giving voting rights to African-Americans in segregated Southern States was passed by Congress in 1965. The Voting Rights Act outlawed practices, such as literacy tests, that had been used to keep African-Americans from registering to vote.

Immigration

Johnson seized the opportunity to liberalize US immigration laws. Quotas (numerical limits) for individual countries were abolished. Look at the graph below to review the long-term changes to the racial origins of new US citizens.

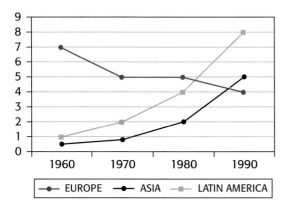

Where foreign-born Americans came from, 1960–90, in millions. In each of these years, Americans born outside the USA were asked to identify where they came from. Which trends can you see in the ethnic-racial composition of the US population? What impact do you think these trends had on American political life?

Source: Adapted from US Census Bureau. www.census.gov

Reform initiatives in the late 1960s

In 1966 Johnson got a Model Cities Act through Congress that
provided federal funds to improve housing, education, health care,
crime prevention and leisure facilities in America's decaying inner
cities. The last item of reform legislation—passed in 1968—during
Johnson's presidency was an "open housing" bill, which aimed to put
an end to racial discrimination. Discrimination in housing had
resulted in the growth of black and other ethnic ghettos in the inner
cities. Congress's willingness to pass the open housing bill, however,
was more a reaction to the shocking riots of 1966–7 than a result of
any initiative by Johnson.

Thereafter, the Vietnam War absorbed most of President Johnson's
attention. During the second half of the 1960s, Congress bcame much
less willing to pass reform legislation. Burning and looting in the riots
of 1966–7 showed a breakdown of law and order. The crime rate rose
steadily, as did the divorce rate, the number of teenage pregnancies
and families headed by single women. Conservatives worried that a
generation of children were growing up outside the framework of the
traditional family. Single-parent families, it was pointed out, were
frequently dependent on welfare money. In general, there was
resentment of the number of people who lived on welfare handouts.
The use of drugs such as marijuana and LSD increased as hippies
openly enthused about them. Hippies ridiculed traditional American
values, calling on people to "turn on" and "drop out". Working-class
and older people disliked the radicalism of the anti-war movement,
in which young people and students were the main activists. Tax
money was being wasted, they felt, on privileged students who spent
their time demonstrating not studying.

To sum up, Johnson was an effective reformer—one of the greatest in
the 20th century—in the early years of his presidency. The Great
Society programme lost momentum in the second half of the 1960s,
due to a conservative swing in public opinion and the Vietnam War.
Johnson's attention was increasingly taken up by the demands of the
war, although this was largely financed by **deficit spending**. Any
assessment of the Great Society's attempt to eliminate the effects of
poverty and disadvantage etc. should bear in mind the fact that
poorer Americans benefited from the strong economic growth which
persisted until the end of the 1960s, creating unparalleled wealth. It
is hard to say how much the rising standard of living among African-
Americans in the late 1960s, for example, was due to the boom and
how much to the Great Society's programmes.

Deficit spending occurs when a
government finances itself through
borrowing money. The Johnson
administration's deficit spending led to
a huge national debt. This undermined
confidence in the US economy, forcing
President Nixon to devalue the dollar
in 1971.

The impact of the Vietnam War on American domestic politics

You can read about the Vietnam War in chapter 9 (see pp. 471–7).
The impact of the war on American domestic politics was also
significant. Johnson feared losing Vietnam, just as Truman,
Eisenhower and Kennedy had before. The loss of South Vietnam, it
was feared, would trigger a "domino effect" in Southeast Asia, a
chain reaction of countries turning communist. America's credibility
in the world was at stake. The situation in South Vietnam was
critical, with increasing areas of the country coming under
communist control, an unpopular government and an army suffering

from low morale. Johnson decided to escalate the scope of US intervention cautiously, after the 1964 elections were over. He feared that a major war in Southeast Asia might endanger his Great Society programme. Each escalation failed to bring the hoped-for outcome, resulting in new rounds of escalation, intensifying bombing and increasing the numbers of American troops. In his determination not to lose Vietnam, Johnson made the mistake of personally taking over the conduct of the war, which absorbed most of his time and came to be closely associated with his political future.

By 1967 US troops in Vietnam numbered about half a million. Throughout 1966 and 1967, Johnson received considerable support from both Democrats and Republicans for his handling of the war. Majority public opinion was still behind him but a large anti-war movement had grown. Television played a major role in negatively influencing public opinion. Vietnam was the first war to be fully televised. People saw graphic scenes from the war on a daily basis, particularly devastating were the effects of bombing on civilians.

Black leaders, including King, had opposed the war as early as 1965. A disproportionate number of black Americans were being drafted. The draft system exempted college/university students (who came mainly from the wealthier classes). Opposition to the war at home and the horror of close combat anti-guerrilla warfare affected the morale of American troops badly. Draft-dodging (avoidance) became widespread among the young men targeted for military service. The radical left-wing Students for a Democratic Society (SDS) organization grew rapidly in 1966. It played a leading role in organizing anti-war demonstrations.

1968—a turning point
1968 was a presidential election year. The era of liberal reform which had begun with Kennedy and continued with Johnson came to an end. Political conflict, much of it violent, reached a peak. The Vietnam War dominated the country's politics. Students and young anti-war activists fought police, some of whom reacted with unreasonable brutality. The violent demonstrations and radical talk of revolution and black power caused a conservative reaction in the older generation.

In Vietnam, the communist Tet offensive of 1968 convinced US press and TV commentators that the generals were wrong; victory was not just round the corner. Public opinion among moderate Americans turned against the war. Vietnam seemed a bottomless pit, into which ever more American soldiers were disappearing. Business leaders became nervous about the country's ability to run the huge deficit needed to finance the war. Johnson accepted that escalation had not worked and announced a partial stop to the bombing and a willingness to negotiate with North Vietnam.

The anti-war movement reached a peak of intensity, with student demonstrators seizing campus buildings in some universities. Realizing that his conduct of the war had divided the nation and his own party, Johnson announced that he would not stand for re-election.

In April Martin Luther King was assassinated, resulting in a wave of violence by outraged blacks in Washington.

In the Democratic primaries, Senator Eugene McCarthy gained the support of young Democrats by opposing the war. Running against McCarthy was Senator Robert Kennedy, who enjoyed tremendous popularity both as the brother of John Kennedy and in his own right. In June, Bobby Kennedy was assassinated—at the point where he looked poised to take the Democratic Party's nomination. His assassination was profoundly discouraging for liberals in the Democratic Party and robbed the party of the only presidential candidate who could perhaps have united it.

During the Democratic Party convention in Chicago, political activists fought running battles with Mayor Daley's brutal police. In the end, the nomination went to a moderate Democrat, Senator Hubert Humphrey. But he lost the support of liberal Democrats by defending the actions of the Chicago police.

In 1968 George Wallace of Alabama stood again as a candidate for the presidency (he had founded his own party) and proved even more popular than in 1964. Again, his main support came from the South but he benefited from a conservative backlash all over the country. Many Americans agreed with Wallace that the country had been run too long by "liberals, intellectuals and long-hairs". But, unlike Wallace, most of the new conservatives were politically moderate. If anything, they were religiously motivated. Many of them were part of a revival in evangelical ("born-again") Christianity, which emphasized traditional Christian values and an appeal to patriotism.

The person who benefited most was Richard Nixon. He won the Republican nomination and ran a well-funded, professional election campaign. Nixon promised that he would be able to end the Vietnam War successfully. He benefited from voters' loss of faith in the Democrats and big programmes of social reform. Voters were ready to listen to Nixon's questioning as to whether government-led reform could achieve what it set out to do. Nixon won the election. The great age of reform was at an end. But his majority was small and Democrats kept their majority in both houses of Congress.

Another point to note about the 1968 presidential election is the increasing number of people who did not make use of their right to vote. The trend continued into the 21st century. In the light of this, it became difficult for any newly-elected president to claim that he had the support of the majority of Americans for carrying out any far-reaching reforms.

Women's rights

Although women achieved political equality in 1920 by getting the vote, they remained socially disadvantaged. In the mid-1960s women were still paid less than men and excluded from many professions. In 1966 the National Organization for Women (NOW) was founded to campaign against sex discrimination in applications for employment and in rates of pay. The women's movement of the 1960s was not confined to legal equality. Betty Friedan had a huge response among women to her best-selling book *The Feminine Mystique*, that was published in 1963. Friedan criticized traditional male–female roles in society. By the late

1960, the focus on equal rights was giving way to the broader idea of Women's Liberation. While NOW concentrated on women's legal rights, the Women's Liberation movement went further in demanding a revolution in the traditional relationship between the sexes.

In 1967 President Johnson included sex along with race, creed (religion), colour and national origin in federal laws to prevent discrimination. But a women's Equal Rights Amendment to the constitution failed to pass through Congress. Conservatives and moderates argued that such an amendment might result in women being burdened with the disadvantages of equality, such as being drafted into the army.

NOW's campaigning succeeded in increasing public awareness of women's issues. Federal government and Supreme Court action did much to end discrimination against women at work. Additionally, feminist activists won the legal battle for the right to abortion. In 1973 the Supreme Court ruled that state laws making abortion illegal were unconstitutional.

More effective than political campaigning, as a gauge for women's increasingly more influential position in society, was the steady increase in the number of women in paid employment. In 1960, 38 per cent of women over 16 years of age were in the workforce. In 1970 the figure was 43 per cent and rising. Again, Women's Liberation did less to increase women's sexual freedom than the near perfection of birth control in the form of the Pill.

Native Americans

According to official statistics, there were only 340 000 Native Americans in the United States in 1950. The 1950s were a dark decade for Native Americans. Lacking economic resources, many reservations had become islands of poverty and hopelessness. Eisenhower's administration followed a policy of Indian assimilation (integration). State law was to be extended over the reservations in order to extend "all the rights and privileges" of US citizenship. This meant terminating federal aid to the reservations. The termination policy meant that tribes were denied a legal status and the reservations abolished. Native Americans' attachment to their land was not respected. They lacked a powerful lobby in Washington to represent their interests. The federal Bureau for Indian Affairs encouraged Native Americans to relocate to the cities. By the end of the 1960s, an estimated 40 per cent of Native Americans were living in cities.

Things began to improve in the 1960s. It was increasingly recognized that the loss of land rights was a disaster for Native Americans. In their election campaigns, Kennedy spoke of the importance of obtaining Native Americans' consent to any changes on the status of the reservations, while Nixon emphasized the traditional heritage of Native Americans. Integration was dropped in favour of community development plans to improve life on the reservations through education, job training and health services. To provide jobs, companies were encouraged to set up plants in the reservations. The number of children attending school in the reservations rose and parents were given more opportunity to participate in the way the schools were run and what was taught.

By 1968 there was increasing public awareness of the great wrong which had been done to Native Americans. African-Americans' success in gaining civil rights encouraged Native Americans to improve their situation. Robert Kennedy took up the Native American cause in the election year. At the same time, President Johnson sent a message to Congress emphasizing the right of Indians to remain in their homelands, if they chose. He promised his administration's support for developing the reservations through improving education, job training and health services. Johnson urged Congress to respect "the right of the first Americans to remain Indians while exercising their rights as Americans."

TOK link
Mathematics

The number of Native Americans, together with the whole population of the United States, is counted regularly by the federal government, in what is called a "census". Those who process the census data use a branch of mathematics called "statistics".

Here are the statistics of the growth of the Native American population in the USA, derived from the census:

1940   334 000
1950   343 000
1960   509 000
1970   793 000

From these statistics, we would probably conclude that the Native American population began to revive in the 1950s and 1960s. Politicians seeking to show how well their policies were working might well cite these statistics. However, a closer look will show us that the natural increase (with no immigration) between 1950 and 1960 is nearly 50 per cent. This looks strange when compared to the tiny increase in the ten years before 1950.

Again, the increase between 1960 and 1970 shows an incredibly high rate of increase—56 per cent. If we took these figures at face value, we would have to say that there was a population explosion among Native Americans between 1950 and 1970, with their numbers more than doubling. But all the evidence—poverty and the break-up of their traditional life-style—points the other way.

In fact, the reasons for the increase in the number of Native Americans recorded in the census have nothing to do with a natural increase in their population.

See if you can deduce any of these reasons yourself. (The explanations for the increases are given on page 291.)

Google any disadvantaged group in the country in which you live. Check their increase or decrease in population over time.

 How do political parties use statistics to support their policies (either as the government in power or in opposition)?

Statistics are very much open to interpretation. This insight may be useful to you when giving a TOK presentation or writing a TOK essay.

Despite the talk, Native Americans' quality of life remained poor in comparison to the rest of the nation. Accordingly, Native Americans turned to direct action during Nixon's presidency to draw attention to their cause. The island of Alcatraz was seized and Wounded Knee in South Dakota, where the Sioux had been massacred in 1890, occupied. The Bureau of Indian Affairs in Washington was taken over, too. The Nixon administration responded favourably, settling some land claims in favour of Native Americans and recognizing tribal control over property on the reservations. An Indian Education Act was passed in 1972, providing federal funds for children's schooling. But poverty and isolation continued to affect most Native Americans, especially on the reservations.

President Nixon and the Watergate scandal

Nixon's presidency

Despite opposing Johnson's expensive programme of social reform during the election campaign, Nixon did little to dismantle Johnson's programmes. Measures to eradicate poverty, improve health and education, end sex discrimination, provide job training, and increase benefits for poor families and social security payments all continued and even grew under the influence of a Democrat-controlled Congress. With one eye on the 1972 presidential election, Nixon increased support for the elderly—a growing block of voters—and the disabled.

Instead of cutting back on government benefits to disadvantaged groups, Nixon argued that responsibility for social welfare should be transferred to state and local governments. Nixon called this "New Federalism" and later Republican presidents continued with this policy. In practice, Nixon's New Federalism was only moderately successful. His plan to re-channel federal assistance for families through state and local governments was unpopular and Congress rejected it. But Nixon's "revenue-sharing plan" did succeed in handing over billions of dollars of federal tax revenue (money) to state and local governments to spend on social welfare and local initiatives.

Despite his conservative talk, Nixon established the **affirmative action** principle which continues to be an important feature of American life today. This action went well beyond Johnson's equal opportunities measures and was carried out on Nixon's executive order, not by Congress. The action was controversial, because it restricted employers' freedom of choice. Critics claimed that Nixon was trying to capture the black vote for the Republican Party. Whether or not that is true, Nixon's affirmative action initiative helped transform the United States into a multicultural society and was adopted among democracies the world over.

By the early 1970s, an environmental movement had become active in the protection of the environment and the preservation of endangered species. Both parties in Congress supported a number of environmental bills, including one setting up an Environmental Protection Agency, and President Nixon made them into law.

TOK link
Mathematics/Statistics

The explanations for the increases in the population of Native Americans are as follows:

1 1950–60 Alaska joined the Union in 1959, bringing more Native Americans into the US total.

2 Native Americans, like African-Americans, were beginning to take more obvious pride in their ethnic/racial identity. More were now willing to identify themselves as "Indian".

3 1960–70 Disadvantaged groups now qualified for welfare. This encouraged more people of Native American descent—mixed-race people, for example—to register themselves as Native Americans.

Under **affirmative action**, places were set aside for ethnic or racial minorities–African-Americans, Mexican-Americans, Native Americans–to have access to government employment. Private companies receiving federal aid were forced to do the same; as were colleges and universities, in student admissions, and labour (trade) unions, when recruiting members. According to the policy, the number of places reserved for ethnic or racial minorities should reflect the proportion of these groups in the country or region where the organisation is located.

During the Nixon era, race relations mainly focused on the issue of "busing". The desegregation of schools was moving slowly. Following the lead of the Supreme Court in 1971, courts ordered local government authorities to provide bus transportation for disadvantaged African-American children to attend privileged schools in white neighbourhoods. Busing was very unpopular with many whites, who saw their privileges undermined. In response, Nixon deliberately appointed conservatives and Southerners opposed to busing to the Supreme Court, whenever he had the opportunity. Nixon's actions did nothing to improve race relations but they did gain him the continued support of conservative voters, whom he called "the silent majority".

The skill with which he managed to appeal to different groups—old people, Southerners, the working-class, African-Americans—within the electorate ensured that Nixon would be re-elected in 1972. The Democrats' left-wing candidate, George McGovern, appeared to be no match for Nixon. Nixon's spectacular successes in foreign policy (see below) also did much to strengthen his position.

Although Nixon was re-elected by a large majority in the presidential election of 1972, voters returned a Democratic majority to the House of Representatives and the Senate in the Congressional elections of that year. Congress remained dominated by the Democratic majority throughout Nixon's presidency. Voters, it seemed, preferred a Republican like Nixon, with a strong anti-communist background, to run the country and bring the Vietnam War to a successful conclusion. But at the same time, by voting for Democrats in Congress, they showed that they wanted to make it difficult for a conservative president to abolish the gains made during the 1960s in social equality and rights for ethnic and other minorities.

Another reason for Americans to vote Democrat at Congressional elections was the performance of the economy. In the early 1970s, economic growth slowed down, the number of jobless people grew and inflation began to rise. Although Nixon's policies had not caused the economic downturn, people associated it with his administration and expressed their dissatisfaction by "splitting" their vote (Republican for president, Democrat for Congress). The downturn was in fact a long-term trend, a result of trade competition from Japan and West Germany and, in the case of inflation, the effects of the deficit spending used to finance the Vietnam War.

Economic stagnation was deepened by the oil crisis of 1973. Arab leaders showed their resentment of US support for Israel in the Yom Kippur War by declaring an oil embargo (refusing to sell). They followed this up by steeply increasing the world price of oil. The United States had become dependent on Middle Eastern oil. The era of cheap energy, one of the foundations of the post-Second World War boom, was at an end.

TOK link

Integrating areas of knowledge—human sciences and ethics

Studying and predicting human behaviour is something we do both consciously and unconsciously every day. Students should consider the validity of the methods used by the various human sciences—such as observation, value judgments, motivation, language, statistical evidence, qualitative and quantitative tools— and may influence the conclusions reached.

Ethics involve a discussion of the way in which we live our lives and justify moral actions and attitudes. Judging people in the past can be problematic, without a full understanding of the political and social context.

By carrying out social reform, Johnson hoped to eliminate poverty in American society. The Johnson administration was engaging in what is referred to as "social engineering". A number of measures (in education, health, social security, welfare payments) were financed by the government to lift certain sectors of society out of poverty. People still argue about how effective Johnson's Great Society reforms really were.

One criticism of such attempts at social engineering is that it assumes that governments can eliminate social problems by "throwing money at them". Conservatives argue that welfare entitlements simply create a dependency problem by encouraging people to depend on government handouts. People who receive government money may spend that money on alcohol or drugs rather than on their families.

Many conservatives believe that the only way for people to stand on their own feet is for them to learn to help themselves. Some even believe that people in low-income groups are genetically predetermined to remain poor because they are less intelligent or less motivated to work hard.

There are complex reasons why it can take a lot of time and effort to overcome social disadvantage and inequality among lower socio-economic groups. A positive attitude to education and the development of higher social, professional and personal aspirations can take a long time to develop. There are also many restrictions in place that impede social advancement.

TOK exercises

1   In carrying out social reform, president Johnson's policies of social engineering and president Nixon's focus on affirmative action were based on ethical and political theories about the responsibility of a state for its citizens. What are these responsibilities? List them and discuss them with your class.

2   Consider which of the following ethical theories best fit the actions of the two presidents:

   ● ethical egoism

   ● altruism

   ● utilitarianism.

   What concepts best fit the values of the Democrats or Republicans? Is there much difference between them?

3   Is it possible to eliminate poverty through government action? Should the government provide a welfare state for its citizens and what does that mean to you?

4   How reliable are statistics provided through such methods as surveys and opinion polls in determining numbers for procedures such as Affirmative Action? Would you feel justified in protesting against a university or an employer for accepting that ethnic diversity is more important than academic achievement or skills?

5   Consider these TOK questions and write a response to each of them:

   ● When the moral codes of individuals or nations conflict, what are the justifications for taking actions against either the person or the state?

   ● To what extent do the classification systems, (social categories) adopted in surveys and research, affect the knowledge we obtain?

   ● To what extent do information and communication technologies influence the way we think about the world? ?

   ● In what ways do our values affect the way we see the world?

Activity:

Change over time

In the 20 years from 1953 to 1973, the USA underwent fundamental changes. In 1953, Americans were still making the transition from the Second World War era. In 1973, things did not look so different from today.

Use this textbook and any other sources to review the changes in politics, society and the economy between 1953 and 1973.

- In politics: programmes of political parties, the role of the media, political extremism (left-wing and right-wing), political activist groups

- In society: increased welfare entitlements, changed attitudes to racial and ethnic minorities, more rights for disadvantaged groups, an increase in crime and violence

- In the economy:
  - ▶ the standard of living: research the per capita GNP of Americans in 1953 and 1973
  - ▶ the number of people living below the poverty line (measured in annual dollar income)
  - ▶ national wealth: research the US GNP (gross national product) or GDP (gross domestic product = GNP without foreign earnings) for 1953 and 1973, and the federal government's annual budgets (total spending for the year)
  - ▶ the health of the economy: research unemployment and inflation rates.

	1953	1973
Politics		
Party programmes:		
Republicans	Cut down on "big government"	Nixon maintains and expands welfare state
Democrats		
Role of the media		
Society		
Welfare entitlements		
Attitudes to		
racial/ethnic		
minorities		
....		
....		
Economy		
Per capita GNP		
GNP/GDP		
Unemployment		
Inflation rate		

The impact of Nixon's foreign policy on US domestic policies

During the election year, Nixon visited Beijing and Moscow. A new era seemed to be dawning in American–Chinese relations; and, in Moscow, Nixon and Brezhnev, the Soviet leader, signed the first Strategic Arms Limitation Treaty (SALT 1). The visits were carefully staged for the media and won Nixon strong public approval at home. After a quarter century of Cold War, Nixon and his National Security Advisor, Henry Kissinger, had brought about a relaxation of tensions. The period of détente had begun.

Vietnam remained by far the most important foreign issue for Americans. Nixon's policy of Vietnamization, the replacement of American troops by South Vietnamese ones, appeared to be working. The number of American soldiers in South Vietnam was down to 95 000 in 1972. To make up for the troops, Nixon relied on massive bombing. The use of such methods on a defenceless civilians (people not employed in the armed forces) enraged anti-war activists and made ordinary people uneasy. The worst incident of violence in the anti-war movement came in 1970, after the US invasion of Cambodia. Protesting students were shot by National Guardsmen. Four were killed and nine wounded. But Nixon's silent majority held steady. The incident, and the student rioting which followed, did not result in any increased support for the anti-war movement.

Johnson had hesitated to bomb the North for fear of the Chinese reaction. But the rapprochement (understanding) with China made Chinese intervention in Vietnam look unlikely. The Soviets, too, appeared to be more interested in détente than in helping North Vietnam. Nixon's and Kissinger's strategy of forcing the Vietnamese to the negotiating table by the threat of merciless bombing worked sufficiently well for a "peace with honour", as Nixon called it, to be signed in 1973. The war in Vietnam had ended for the United States, although few believed that it was a genuine peace with honour. South Vietnam was overrun by the North two years later.

Despite the peace in Vietnam, Nixon and Kissinger authorized the bombing of Cambodia in the following months to prevent further communist gains there. During 1973, the USA dropped 250 000 tons of bombs on Cambodia, more than the total amount dropped on the Japanese during the Second World War. Congress finally acted to limit the president's powers to make war. It cut off funding for further bombing. It then passed a War Powers Act, forcing the president to inform Congress within 48 hours of deployment of US forces abroad. Nixon **vetoed** the Act but Congress overrode his veto.

Vietnam had deeply divided the nation. People felt misled about the way in which both Johnson and Nixon had conducted the war. Johnson had never asked Congress to declare war on North Vietnam. Each escalation in the number of troops and each bombing offensive were simply announced to Congress and the public after they had already been decided. Each escalation was justified by claiming that victory was just round the corner.

The president can **veto** a bill passed by Congress by stating his objections to it and withholding his signature. Congress can then drop the bill altogether or modify it to take in the president's objections. But if there is still sufficient support for the original bill, Congress can override the president's veto by both houses voting by two-thirds majority in favour of the bill.

The Watergate scandal and the fall of Richard Nixon

Topic 2 is about the ways in which democratic systems face both internal and external threats to the national interest. The Watergate scandal was an internal threat which exposes very clearly the working of the US Constitution. The checks and balances built into the Constitution by the Founding Fathers were designed to minimize the possibility of the misuse of federal government power. Nowhere is this intention clearer than in the structure of the federal government, which is characterized by the separation of powers—legislative (Congress), executive (the president) and judicial (the Supreme Court and other federal courts of law). The three powers are constitutionally equal—none is superior to the others. In the Watergate scandal, the executive got into conflict with the other two branches of the federal government. After a lengthy power struggle with Congress and a legal struggle involving the Supreme Court, president Nixon was forced to resign.

During the 1972 election year, members of the Republican Committee to Re-elect the President (CREEP) were authorized by one of Nixon's aides to tap (listen in on) the telephone of the Democratic National Committee chairman. They hoped to get useful information about the Democrats' campaign plans. The wiretap broke down, so CREEP sent three men, Cuban exiles, to fix it. They were caught breaking in to the office of the Democrats' national headquarters in the Watergate complex of buildings in Washington. They were arrested and CREEP were also incriminated.

Whether Nixon knew about the break-in—he always denied it—is uncertain. But at that point he could have publicly announced what had happened, denied his own involvement and dismissed the members of CREEP who ordered the break-in as well as the aides who had authorized it. Instead, he decided on a cover-up. The Cubans and their controllers in CREEP were bribed to keep them quiet. Nixon ordered the CIA to stop an FBI investigation of the break-in, which was illegal. If CREEP's illegal activities had become public in an election year, it would certainly have damaged Nixon's campaign. But Nixon put his own re-election above the law. The cover-up was characteristic of the secretive way in which he worked.

But it failed. Bit by bit, during 1973 the involvement of CREEP and other top Nixon aides was revealed. The scandal grew, dominating the media. Two journalists employed by the *Washington Post*, Bob Woodward and Carl Bernstein, became famous for their investigative reporting of the Watergate scandal. A jury had found the Cuban exiles and their two CREEP controllers guilty. The Senate set up a committee to investigate possible involvement of higher administration officials. Several of these resigned under pressure from Nixon, who did not want himself associated with them any more. Nixon even fired his two closest aides, the super-loyal "Berlin Wall", HR Haldeman and John Ehrichman (both of German descent). The wiretapping, Nixon's authorization of illegal "hush money" to keep the Watergate burglars quiet, and suspicions of his illegal use of the CIA all became public during the course of the Ervin committee's questioning (named after Senator Sam Ervin, who headed the committee). The committee's hearings were televised and followed with fascination by millions of Americans.

A member of the White House staff revealed to the committee that Nixon had all conversations in the Oval Office (the president's personal office in the White House) secretly recorded. Americans were shocked. The judge who had tried the Watergate burglars demanded that the president's tapes be handed over. The scandal now focused on the legal issue of whether or not the president could be forced to hand over the tape-recordings of his confidential discussions. Nixon claimed that he could not, citing "executive privilege". The chief executive of the federal government, so went the argument, could not be forced by the other branches (the legislature or the judiciary) to reveal information which could damage its ability to function effectively. A similar argument had been used by Eisenhower against Senator McCarthy in his investigation of the army in the early 1950s. Eisenhower was successful, but the circumstances then had been very different.

Nixon was forced by the Senate to appoint a special prosecutor to investigate White House involvement in the Watergate break-in. Despite having been appointed by Nixon, the special prosecutor had a battle to get hold of the tape-recordings. Nixon ordered the attorney general to fire the special investigator. Rather than do so, the attorney general and his deputy both resigned. The acting attorney general then appointed a new special investigator but he proved just as determined to get the tapes as the last one. Nixon then handed over some of the tapes, but they contained gaps. By now the legal battle over the tapes had escalated into a struggle between the judiciary and the executive. It was a major constitutional crisis.

While the Watergate scandal was unfolding, late in 1973, the vice-president, Spiro Agnew, was forced to resign for reasons of tax evasion (not paying taxes). Nixon appointed Gerald Ford, leader of the Republicans in the House of Representatives, as vice-president. Following that, Nixon's own financial affairs were investigated and it was found that he owed tax himself. He had to defend himself on television and promise to pay all the tax he owed.

In 1974 the struggle over the president's tapes continued. Nixon handed over some paper transcripts but these could easily have been edited. They contained many "expletive deleted" entries, indicating that Nixon frequently used bad language, an unpleasant discovery for many Americans.

Nixon appealed to the Supreme Court on the executive privilege issue. In June 1974 the Supreme Court ruled against him. He then finally handed over the tapes. But by this time the House of Representatives Judiciary Committee had voted to **impeach** Nixon for violating the constitution. Those who voted in favour of impeachment included Republicans. Meanwhile the tapes proved that Nixon had indeed ordered the CIA to stop the FBI investigation. Leading Republicans, including Henry Kissinger, advised Nixon to resign. In August it became clear that in the Senate, where Nixon's impeachment trial would be held, only a few senators continued to support him. On 8 August 1974, Nixon announced his resignation on television. He was the first president to resign. The reaction was one of relief; few were sorry. Vice-President Gerald Ford was sworn in as president.

The Constitution allows the president to be removed by **impeachment**, should he misuse the powers of his office. The impeachment process requires the House of Representatives to vote for it by a simple majority (50%+) in favour. The president is then tried in a court. The court is the Senate. After its hearings, the Senate votes on whether the president is guilty or not. It requires a two-thirds majority of the Senate to remove the president.

The presidency after Nixon

Vietnam and Watergate discredited the presidency, which had steadily grown in power and prestige since the time of Roosevelt. The Nixon era ended with the powers of the "imperial" presidency (as some journalists called it) being reduced. After the nightmare of Vietnam, Nixon's bombing of Cambodia in 1973 pushed Congress to reassert its control over the president's war-making powers. The courts' final victory over Nixon in the Watergate scandal reassured many Americans that even the president was not above the law. Congress had succeeded in removing a president who had violated the Constitution. An over-mighty executive branch had been cut back—for the time being, at any rate—by the judicial and legislative branches. The authority of the Constitution had been reaffirmed.

Activity:

Cause and consequence

An important function of historians is to explain why events happened and what the consequences were.

Taking the three events or processes listed in the table below, note down their causes and consequences.

A useful technique is to divide the issues and outcomes up into short- and long-term causes and consequences. (The long-term consequences of the Watergate scandal are not covered in the text, so you will need to look for these elsewhere.)

	Long-term causes	Short-term causes	Short-term consequences	Long-term consequences
The civil rights movement		Protest acts of individual activists in 1950s	African-Americans could vote in the South	
The Vietnam War (domestic causes and consequences)	Popularity of taking a hard line against communism			
The Watergate scandal	Increase in the power of the president (the "imperial presidency")			

South Africa, 1991–2000

This section on South Africa begins with the background to the transition to majority rule in the 1990s. South Africa was ruled by a white minority government run by the National Party. Its policy of apartheid aimed at the complete separation of Africans and whites, gave the African majority few rights and condemned most of them to poverty.

An anti-apartheid movement grew in the 1950s, led by activists like Nelson Mandela in the African National Congress (ANC). In the 1960s the white government banned the ANC and other anti-apartheid movements. By the end of the 1980s, urban riots and a declining economy made it clear to many whites that apartheid had no future. The government was negotiating secretly with Mandela, who was in prison. Frederik de Klerk became president and decided to abolish apartheid. Mandela and other ANC leaders were released.

Official negotiations on a new, multi-racial constitution began in 1991 and were led by de Klerk and Mandela. Parallel to the negotiations, a campaign of violence was secretly conducted by state security forces to destabilize the peace process. It aimed to increase ethnic mistrust between Africans. With civil war threatening, an interim (provisional) constitution was agreed upon in 1993 and the first free elections were held in 1994, giving a massive majority to the ANC.

The ANC led a coalition of all the main parties with Mandela as the first African president of the country. A Truth and Reconciliation Commission was formed. At the same time, Mandela's Government of National Unity started an ambitious programme of development. Much was achieved but progress fell short of expectations. Mandela retired in 1999 and was replaced by ANC leader Thabo Mbeki, who increased affirmative action policies on behalf of Africans. He was heavily criticized in the early years for being slow to act effectively against the AIDS epidemic.

South Africa

Background

South Africa is a large country rich in natural resources—gold, diamonds, metallic ores and coal—with fertile agricultural land. Industrially, it has for a long time been the most developed country in sub-Saharan Africa. Its ethnically varied population—including Africans, Europeans, Asians (from India) and people of mixed Asian–African descent—grew rapidly in the second half of the 20th century from 13 to 43 million. The African population grew fastest, making Africans by far the biggest ethnic group.

In the late 19th century, South Africa was a British colony. The white Afrikaners, descended from Dutch colonizers, broke away and declared their independence. After finally defeating them in two wars (referred to by the British as the Boer wars), the British allowed South Africa to run its own affairs as a self-governing Dominion in 1910. Numerous segregation laws were passed, which reduced "Natives" (Africans) to a poor underclass of labourers and servants. The "colour bar" forced Africans to live in reserves, prevented them from owning land outside the reserves and controlled their movement inside the country. In 1931 South Africa effectively became independent. In 1939 whites divided over the issue of entering the Second World War on the British side. English-speakers supported an alliance with the British but Afrikaners opposed it. While Afrikaners were defeated on the issue, they split politically from rest of the whites by forming a separate National Party. In the 1948 parliamentary election the National Party was victorious and began a period of rule which was to last until 1990 and was characterized by the policy of apartheid.

Apartheid

Apartheid (Afrikaans, meaning literally "apartness") aimed at completing the process of segregation so that eventually there would be total physical separation of the races. Apartheid had become the official policy of the South African government in 1948, when the National Party won the national elections. The National Party was dominated by white Afrikaners. Under apartheid, all positions of political, economic and military power were reserved for whites. Despite making up the vast majority of the population, Africans—referred to as "Bantus" in the language of apartheid—were forced to live in separate "Townships" or in certain areas of the countryside considered to be their original tribal "Homelands". Meanwhile, the movement of Africans inside South Africa were controlled by having to carry an identity pass at all times. Where they were needed as cheap labour to work on white farms or in their factories and mines, Africans had to remain segregated from other races as far as possible. This involved having separate railway wagons, buses, public toilets, restaurants, hotels, and camps for African industrial workers and miners. Racially mixed marriages and sexual relations were illegal.

Other races living in South Africa were classified as Asians and Coloureds (of mixed race) by the apartheid regime. Numerically smaller than the whites, they enjoyed more rights than the Africans in South Africa's racial hierarchy, but less than the whites themselves.

Despite the inefficiency of trying to run a country in such a way and the difficulty of enforcing segregation, for over 40 years the apartheid regime went to great pains and spared no cost to make the system work. Only the growing resistance of the African majority and increasing international isolation forced the leaders of the National Party in 1990 to give up apartheid.

Africans

Africans formed the largest racial group in South Africa's population. The African population grew very rapidly in the second half of the 20th century, nearly doubling from 10.9 to 20.8 million between 1960 and 1980. The Africans of South Africa were and are a very multicultural population. The Xhosa, Zulu, Swazi, Ndebele, Tsonga, Tswana, Venda and Sotho nations all have their own languages and customs. The growing African population was forced to live in rural Homelands and smaller Reserves. These lacked job opportunities and sufficient farmland. The Homelands were run by chiefs, who owed their positions of power to the government in Pretoria (the capital of South Africa') and thus had little interest in fighting for the rights of their own people. Eventually all the Homelands were supposed to become independent states. However these lands were fragmented, as they received only the land that the white farmers were willing to give up. Furthermore, they were totally dependent upon the government in Pretoria for their security and infrastructure.

Mandela burning his Pass in 1959.

The Townships were the areas where the urbanized African population lived. The apartheid regime always tried to limit the number of Africans living in the cities, seeing these people as harder to control. Despite very poor housing, schools and infrastructure (lack of running water and electricity), opportunities were better in the Townships than in the rural Homelands. Consequently, the urban African population grew fast as Africans migrated from the Homelands. By 1990 urban blacks outnumbered urban whites by nearly 5 to 1. Due to overcrowding, poverty, inadequate schools and growing unemployment, the crime rate rapidly increased. Black Township police and politicians, regarded as servants of the apartheid regime, were despised. Gangs of criminals controlled these territories. Alcoholism and drug abuse flourished and the murder rate was the highest in the world.

Other racial groups under apartheid

Under apartheid, the term "Coloureds" applied to people of mixed race, mainly those of Asian–African origin. More numerous than the Asians but fewer in number than the whites, "Coloureds" were allowed to live in cities but not in areas reserved for whites. Enjoying a relatively privileged position under apartheid, some Coloureds, especially the less well-educated ones, were content to live under the apartheid regime. In turn, the government gave Coloureds a small say in the running of the country in 1984 by granting them the right to elect representatives to parliament, although they were forced to sit in a separate "chamber" of the parliament.

Asians were the next highest group in the racial hierarchy of apartheid South Africa. Economically significant as skilled traders and business people, Asians were privileged and they also received the right to elect representatives to parliament in the 1984 constitutional reform. Like Coloureds, they, too, had their own separate chamber of parliament.

The white population of South Africa was divided mainly between the Afrikaans-speaking Afrikaner and the more liberal English-speaking whites. The Afrikaner-dominated National Party continued to hold an unchallenged position of power in South Africa until 1990. The army, the police, industry, mining and the best agricultural land were all in the hands of the whites. Although white South Africans, a total of 4.5 million people, made up no more than 16 per cent of the South African population by 1980, they controlled most of its wealth.

The opposition to apartheid

The African National Congress (ANC) was founded in 1912 by a group of Africans educated by Christian missionaries to represent African interests in the newly founded British Dominion.

In the 1940s, an ANC Youth League was founded by young African men in Johannesburg—including Nelson Mandela—who were impatient with the moderate position of the ANC.

In the 1950s, the ANC began to confront the government on a number of issues, such as the Pass law controlling the movement of Africans inside the country and the forced relocation of Africans. Black residential areas were bulldozed and inhabitants forced to relocate in Townships. The chosen method of confrontation followed the example, some 40 years earlier, of Mohandas Gandhi who used the strategy of non-violent protest against racial discrimination.

The Pan-Africanist Congress (PAC), which also played an important role in the struggle against apartheid, was led by a group of radicals who broke away from the ANC in 1959. They became impatient with the ANC's commitment to racial equality, instead preferring to put Africans first in the struggle against apartheid. Many members of both political movements, the ANC and the PAC, were secretly members of the banned South African Communist Party, which had played a leading role since the 1940s in resisting the apartheid regime and had been banned by the government. Fear of communism during the Cold War caused many Western governments to support the South African government in spite of its racist policies.

Asians had their own Congress dating from Gandhi's time in South Africa. So did the Coloureds, and there were white liberals and communists who also opposed apartheid.

When the ANC and PAC were banned in 1960, Mandela and others decided to fight the government inside the country, while Oliver Tambo left South Africa to organize international support. Mandela went into hiding, and founded a military wing of the ANC (Umkhonto we Sizwe, "Spear of the Nation", abbreviated to MK). Mandela was soon caught and was imprisoned in 1964 (see the biography on pages 304–5). Tambo eventually set up an ANC headquarters in Lusaka, Zambia, which had become independent in 1964. From there the ANC continued the armed struggle. By the 1980s, MK had thousands of guerrillas fighting the South African army in the "frontline states" (Angola, Mozambique and Zimbabwe) and carrying out acts of sabotage inside South Africa.

After the temporary crushing of the ANC and the PAC, relative calm returned to South Africa until the mid-1970s. A few years before that, a Black Consciousness movement had grown among students, centring on the charismatic figure of Steve Biko. Influenced by the 1960s' Black Power movement in the USA, Biko rejected white organizations and aimed at starting up alternative student organizations for Africans. This was seen by Biko and others as a long-term strategy which could avoid the mistake made by the PAC of head-on violent confrontations with the government. However, in 1976, students began demonstrating in the Soweto Townships. A Black Consciousness-led revolt followed, which spread to other Townships around Johannesburg and Cape Town. The government reacted with great brutality, crushing the revolt by force and imprisoning the leaders. Biko was eventually caught and beaten to death by the police. Arrested or forced into emigration, this generation of politically active Africans now came into contact with the older ANC leaders outside South Africa or in prison. After his death Biko became a world famous figure—the subject of rock songs, a best-selling book and a Hollywood movie—almost rivalling Mandela as a symbol of black South Africans' freedom struggle.

Apartheid on the defensive

In the 1980s President PW Botha worked out a strategy to strengthen support for the government by carrying out reforms designed to give the appearance of improved political status for Asians and Coloureds. A new constitution gave them limited representation in parliament. But control of political power remained securely in white hands. Botha also tried to buy off urban Africans by giving them greater self-government in the Townships. This merely increased hatred of corrupt local Township leaders. To help revive the economy, the government recognized African **trade unions**, hoping to improve the industrial skills of the black workforce. Instead it produced a generation of experienced African political negotiators, such as Cyril Ramaphosa, who later helped negotiate an end to apartheid.

Trade unions (American labor unions) are organizations set up to represent the interests of workers in different industries (for example, there is a miners' union in South Africa). In democratic countries the right of unions to represent workers (in negotiations on pay and working conditions, for example) is recognized by the government. At the national level, trade unions often co-operate to exert a strong influence on political parties, especially left-wing parties which rely on workers' votes.

Nelson Mandela (1918–)

Nelson Mandela (Rolihlahla Mandela) was born in the Transkei in present-day Eastern Cape Province in 1918, a member of the royal family of the Thembu people, a tribe belonging to the Xhosa nation. He was given the British name Nelson in school.

He was sent to boarding schools run by British Methodist missionaries. Later he attended a small elite university run by missionaries mainly for Africans at Fort Hare. Among Mandela's fellow students were several future political leaders, including Oliver Tambo, who was to be his lifelong political associate.

Mandela then went to Johannesburg, where he met another future leader of the ANC, Walter Sisulu, who helped him enrol at the University of Witwatersrand to study law. In the early 1940s in Johannesburg Mandela came increasingly into contact with political activists—black, white, Coloured and Asian. In particular, he became involved with the African National Congress.

In 1944 Mandela, Tambo, Sisulu and others founded the Youth League of the ANC, which breathed new life into the struggle for Africans' rights. In 1948 the National Party came to power and established the system of apartheid. Mandela played a leading role in the ANC's anti-apartheid campaign of 1952.

Mandela was now working in Johannesburg as one of the few African lawyers. He was an impressive figure—tall, physically fit (he was an amateur boxer) and highly cultured (he could quote Shakespeare). At the same time, he and his ANC Youth League friends were busily transforming the ANC into a mass movement aimed at winning equal rights for Africans. Mandela believed in a multi-racial approach and cooperated closely with Asians and Coloureds, who also suffered under apartheid. Whites were also welcome, among them communists such as Mandela's old friend Joe Slovo.

In 1955 Mandela played a leading role in organizing a large multiracial political meeting at which the Freedom Charter was adopted, which asserted the equality of all races in South Africa. The Freedom Charter remained the basis for the ANC's political programme throughout the anti-apartheid struggle.

In 1956 Mandela was arrested for treason along with 155 African, white, Asian and Coloured anti-apartheid activists. During the long trial Mandela was able to publicize the justice of the ANC's cause through eloquent speeches. He and others gave the ANC clenched-fist salute in the courtroom. They were finally found not guilty in 1961. Following the massacre by armed police of demonstrators, including children, at Sharpville in 1960, the government banned the ANC and other anti-apartheid political organizations, forcing Mandela to continue his struggle by going into hiding.

Up until now, Mandela and the ANC had believed in non-violent methods for achieving their aims. Gandhi had been the first to adopt such methods in South Africa in the early years of the 20th century and they were still influential. However, the government's ban removed any basis for legal political action. Decades of peaceful campaigning had achieved no results. Consequently, Mandela founded a military wing of the ANC, Umkhonto we Sizwe, in 1961 to engage in a campaign of sabotage to destabilize the government.

In 1962 Mandela was caught and put on trial. In 1964 he was found guilty of terrorist activities and, together with six others, including Sisulu and Govan Mbeki, condemned to lifelong imprisonment. In his closing statement, Mandela summed up his political beliefs:

> *During my lifetime I have dedicated myself to this struggle of the African people. I have fought against white domination, and I have fought against black domination. I have cherished the ideal of a democratic and free society in which all persons live together in harmony and with equal opportunities. It is an ideal which I hope to live for and to achieve. But if needs be, it is an ideal for which I am prepared to die.*

Mandela and fellow ANC prisoners were sent to the most isolated prison in South Africa, Robben Island in the Atlantic Ocean off Cape Town. They did hard labour breaking rocks in a quarry. Nights were spent sleeping on thin mats on the stone floor of their cells. Food consisted mainly of maize porridge, bread being reserved for non-Africans. During the 18 years he spent on Robben Island, Mandela emerged as the natural leader of the political prisoners there. Despite the daily abuse of prison warders, he held unwaveringly to his goal of a democratic, multi-racial South Africa. He kept up his morale by developing an iron self-discipline, spending an hour each morning doing physical exercises in his cell. He read widely and continued his law studies. Mandela's release became a celebrated political cause in South Africa and all over the world. "Free Mandela" was the slogan chanted at demonstrations and rock concerts, sung in pop songs, appearing on car bumper stickers, posters, placards and T-shirts.

In 1982 Mandela and other ANC leaders were moved to Pollsmoor prison near Cape Town. The government was preparing to hold unofficial talks with Mandela, who was seen as a possible partner for negotiations on reforms. Part of the government's strategy was to offer him his freedom if he would renounce ANC goals.

But Mandela always refused to compromise. In 1985 he was moved into another cell, apart from the others. He began talks with top government officials, choosing to tell no one in the ANC. Meanwhile, political violence in the African Townships raged. Government troops were unable to control a younger generation impatient for change. The South African economy was struggling under the impact of UN economic sanctions.

In 1989 Frederik de Klerk became state president and adopted a radical reform course. Mandela was released in 1990, after 27 years in prison, and the ban on the ANC and other anti-apartheid groups was lifted. In 1991 Mandela became president of the ANC and multiparty negotiations for a new constitution began. They were led by Mandela and de Klerk. The negotiations stopped and restarted several times. Both sides had violent elements among their followers who threatened to get out of control. The relationship between Mandela and de Klerk worsened as the violence increased. Civil war threatened. But the two leaders persevered and finally persuaded extremists to join in the election, the first one in which all races would have the vote. The election was held in April 1994.

The ANC won the election with a big majority. Mandela became South Africa's first African president, with de Klerk and Thabo Mbeki as vice-presidents. Mandela's Government of National Unity included representatives from all the main political parties and races and lasted until 1999, when his five-year term as president ended.

As president, Mandela saw his main task as reconciling the different ethnic groups in South Africa. He publicly forgave those who had imprisoned him. A Truth and Reconciliation Commission was set up. An ambitious Reconstruction and Development Programme was launched to create jobs and improve the standard of living for Africans. But many problems remained—a very high crime rate, corruption, massive unemployment and an AIDS epidemic.

In 1999, at the age of 80, Mandela retired from politics. All sides, particularly the Afrikaners, paid tribute to Mandela, both as a man of great virtue and as a politician who was uniquely able to transcend differences, to reach out to former enemies and to overcome old feelings of hostility.

In protest against the ineffectiveness of the reforms, a United Democratic Front (UDF) was formed. Most of the UDF's leaders had an ANC background. In many ways, the UDF represented the ANC while it was banned. It was dedicated to the ending of apartheid. The UDF was made up of a broad alliance of organizations, trade unions and religious groups. Among the latter were the well-known Anglican (Church of England) Bishop of Cape Town, Desmond Tutu, as well as white and Coloured ministers of the Dutch Reformed Church, which many Afrikaners belonged to.

UDF protests became increasingly radical, leading to violent uprisings in the Townships. In 1986 the government declared a state of emergency. Troops were sent into the Townships to crush the revolt and government security forces started assassinating political activists. In 1988 the UDF was banned. But the future remained bleak. Political violence would surely return. The outlook for the economy was gloomy. UN trade sanctions were affecting exports and nervous multinational companies were pulling out.

Meanwhile Botha's government engaged in an undeclared war against freedom fighters in Angola and Mozambique. South Africa continued to illegally occupy South West Africa (today's Namibia) in the 1980s. In 1979 white rule in Rhodesia collapsed. The country was renamed Zimbabwe, and in 1980 Robert Mugabe took over the government, adding thousands more communist-influenced guerrilla fighters to the struggle against South Africa. From Namibia, the South African army mounted campaigns to defeat pro-Soviet forces in Angola, which were fighting pro-Western forces in a civil war. Into this situation the Soviet Union quietly introduced thousands of well-trained Cuban troops, who proceeded to defeat the South Africans in 1988. This defeat, together with the Townships revolt, convinced members of the Botha government that change was unavoidable. South Africa pulled out of Angola and finally accepted Namibian independence in 1990.

These setbacks caused many among South Africa's government and business leaders to rethink their attitude to the ANC, the largest, oldest and most respected anti-apartheid organization. An unofficial delegation of influential whites met Oliver Tambo in Lusaka in 1985 and gained a surprisingly positive impression. In 1987 a large delegation of South African whites met ANC leaders including Thabo Mbeki (later South Africa's second post-apartheid president) in Dakar, Senegal for talks on a negotiated agreement. Secret talks had been going on, too, between influential Afrikaner and ANC leaders in London. In 1989 the ANC, meeting in Harare, Zimbabwe, issued a declaration stating that a negotiated peace might be possible if the white government negotiated "genuinely and seriously". However, ANC leaders in Lusaka remained deeply divided over the issue of official negotiations with the South African government.

The government also established another unofficial channel of communication with the ANC. This was with the country's most celebrated political prisoner, Nelson Mandela. Mandela knew nothing of the Lusaka ANC's contacts with the government. In the mid-1980s he decided to start his own initiative for ending the confrontation between the government and African opposition groups.

In 1982 Mandela and three other ANC leaders were moved from Robben Island to Pollsmoor prison on the mainland. The government realized that Mandela, through his intelligence and the force of his personality, had become the leader of the African political prisoners. In 1985 Mandela was moved to a separate part of Pollsmoor prison, where it was possible for contacts between him and government ministers to be kept secret. Mandela was offered freedom several times on the condition that he become moderate and reject revolutionary ideas. He spurned these offers but requested an interview with the justice minister, Kobie Coetsee, whom he met several times to discuss ways to end apartheid. In 1988 the government set up a committee of leading government officials to carry on the secret negotiations with Mandela. They were unable to persuade him to give up either the armed struggle, the ANC's alliance with the Communist Party or its commitment to majority rule. But Mandela's realism and emphasis upon reconciliation between blacks and whites impressed them. "What would stop Africans from turning on the white minority once they had control of the government?", the officials wanted to know. In reply, Mandela simply pointed to the **Freedom Charter**, still the ANC's party programme, which stated that South Africa belonged equally to all the people living in it, black and white. This is how Mandela described his reasons for approaching the National Party leaders in the mid-1980s.

> We had been fighting against white minority rule for three-quarters of a century. We had been engaged in armed struggle for more than two decades. Many people on both sides had already died. The enemy was strong and resolute. Yet even with all their bombers and tanks, they must have sensed they were on the wrong side of

The **Freedom Charter** was adopted by the ANC and a number of other anti-apartheid political groups in 1955. It proclaims equality of all races in South Africa, politically, culturally, economically and in the right to own land. The preamble states: "South Africa belongs to all who live in it, black and white".

history. We had right on our side, but not yet might. It was clear to me that a military victory was a distant if not impossible dream. It simply did not make sense for both sides to lose thousands if not millions of lives in a conflict that was unnecessary. They must have known this as well. It was time to talk. This would be extremely sensitive. Both sides regarded discussions as a sign of weakness and betrayal. Neither would come to the table without the other making significant concessions.

A decision to talk to the government was of such importance that it should only have been made in Lusaka [by the ANC party leadership in exile]. But I felt that the process needed to begin, and I had neither the time nor the means to communicate with Oliver [Tambo]. Someone from our side needed to take the first step, and my new isolation [in Pollsmoor prison] gave me both the freedom to do so and the assurance, at least for a while, of the confidentiality of my efforts.

I chose to tell no one what I was about to do. Not my colleagues upstairs [the other ANC leaders in Pollsmoor prison] nor those in Lusaka. I knew that my colleagues upstairs would condemn my proposal, and that would kill my initiative even before it was born. There are times when a leader must move out ahead of the flock, go off in a new direction, confident that he is leading his people the right way. Finally, my isolation furnished my organization with an excuse in case matters went awry: the old man was alone and completely cut off, and his actions were taken by him as an individual, not a representative of the ANC.

Mandela, N. 1994. *Long Walk to Freedom*. UK. Abacus. pp. 626–7

International pressure for Mandela's release continued to grow. The government recognized that Mandela could well become the leader of South Africa if Africans were given the vote. In December 1988, he was moved to another prison near Cape Town, where he lived in a house on his own. He was treated as an honoured guest and allowed to see visitors.

In July 1989, Mandela had a secret meeting with President Botha. The meeting was brief and nothing important was said. Botha was too old to change his ways. But Botha's days were numbered. He had already been replaced as National Party leader in February 1989 and in August he resigned the presidency. He was replaced in both roles by Frederik de Klerk, an Afrikaner, a long-standing member of the National Party and a conservative member of Botha's government.

TOK Link
Ways of knowing

How could the government know that Mandela was telling the truth when he said that he planned no acts of revenge against the white minority once the black majority was in control of the country? Even if Mandela were telling the truth, what would stop him changing his mind later on?

Which way of knowing—reason or emotion—would have provided the most reliable guidance for government ministers trying to reach a decision?

- **Emotion** Feelings of admiration and respect for a man (Mandela) who had endured so much suffering and showed no hatred.

- **Reason** What reasons were there to trust Mandela? Were they strong enough to outweigh the advantages of keeping him locked up and the ANC banned?

Advantages to be gained from freeing Mandela	Disadvantages of freeing Mandela
Advantages of keeping Mandela locked up and ANC banned	Disadvantages of Mandela locked up and ANC banned

Transition to majority rule

The end of apartheid

De Klerk quickly drew the conclusion that apartheid no longer had a future. Since apartheid began, the African population in South Africa had grown much faster than the white one. In 1948 whites made up 21 per cent of the population; in 1988 it was only 14 per cent and still dropping. Four and a half million whites could not continue indefinitely to dominate 25 million Africans (by the 1980s) if the latter refused to co-operate. During the same period of time, southern Africa had changed from being a region of European colonies to one of independent black African states. South Africa was isolated.

De Klerk considered that if change were to come, it would be better to negotiate sooner rather than later, while the National Party government was still in a position of strength. The international scene was also favourable for a fundamental change of course. International communism hardly posed a threat to South Africa any more. With Mikhail Gorbachev, the Soviet Union had renounced its revolutionary role in world affairs in favour of friendly relations with the West. By 1990 communist regimes were beginning to crumble in Europe. The following year, the Soviet Union itself disintegrated.

In January 1990, de Klerk met Mandela shortly before taking the decision to release him. The following month, de Klerk announced that the ban on the ANC, the PAC and the South African Communist Party was being lifted. Restrictions on the UDC and trade unions were also to be lifted and many political prisoners were to be released. The death penalty was to be suspended. That went a long way to meeting Mandela's conditions for entering into negotiations. A few days later, Mandela was released from jail, after being a prisoner for 27 years. Amid emotional scenes celebrating his release, Mandela went off to Lusaka to meet the ANC leadership. From there he toured the world to gain international support for the ANC. De Klerk did the same for the National Party. The courageousness of his decision to end the deadlock had gained him much popularity abroad.

All apartheid laws were repealed (cancelled) soon after. In return, the Mandela announced the end of the ANC's armed struggle. But political violence was far from over. In fact it increased. Although there were outbreaks of violence among ANC supporters, most of the political violence came from units within the South African security forces who were determined to destabilize the peace process and preserve white supremacy. Over 16 000 people were killed through political violence between 1990 and 1994.

Mandela walking out of prison, holding hands with his wife, Winnie, 11 February 1990.

Mandela suspected secret government involvement. Worse still, he believed that de Klerk knew about this murderous "Third Force". His relations with de Klerk deteriorated.

In 1990 the Zulus, under the political leadership of Chief Buthelezi, founded the Inkatha Freedom Party to lead their struggle against the ANC for control of the KwaZulu Homeland and Natal province. State security forces secretly supplied Inkatha with weapons and support. The struggle soon spread to the Johannesburg area.

The first official meeting between the ANC and the National Party government, May 1990. Mandela is speaking to reporters, while de Klerk looks on.

Negotiations begin

In 1991 Mandela was made president of the ANC after Tambo had fallen ill. Knowing there was no alternative to negotiations, he set aside his growing dislike of de Klerk. The two began a series of private meetings aimed at getting multi-party negotiations started.

In December 1991, representatives of eight political parties and ten Homelands met in a Convention for a Democratic South Africa (CODESA) to work out an interim (transitional) constitution and plans for a parliamentary election to be held on the basis of **universal suffrage**. Extremist parties on both sides, such as PAC and the Afrikaner Conservative Party, refused to participate in CODESA. Inkatha and the Bophuthatswana Homeland delegation refused to agree to CODESA's main aims.

Suffrage, also called **franchise**, is the political term for the right to vote at elections.
Universal suffrage stands for the right to vote in elections, extended to all adults—in the case of South Africa, everyone over 18 years of age.

Mandela and de Klerk at a conference in 1991. At times the appearance of unity broke down.

Chief Buthelezi refuses to shake hands with Mandela and de Klerk at the same conference in 1991.

How genuine are the emotions shown by these politicians and what kind of poltical messages does their body language convey?

Discussion point: the role of the individual in history

To what extent did the peace process depend on the leadership role of Nelson Mandela?

Nelson Mandela was approached by the white South African government as a partner in its negotiations. In spite of the violence against ANC members, he remained committed to reform through peaceful negotiation.

Use the sources on Nelson Mandela in this section—the photographs, biography and the passage from his autobiography to support your assessment of his leadership role.

How much was the successful implementation of reform leading to free elections, regime change and the end of the apartheid era, based on the Mandela's personal qualities as a leader?

Negotiations: breakdown, restart and final agreement

Under pressure from white conservatives to stop the negotiations, de Klerk held a **referendum** in March 1992 on continuing the negotiation process. The result was a strong majority (of whites—Africans could not yet vote) in favour. This strengthened de Klerk's hand, so he toughened his position. This was too much for the ANC, which also could not be seen to be giving away too much. Consequently, CODESA talks broke down in May.

This was the signal for the level of violence in the country to escalate. In June, Zulus massacred nearly 50 people in Boipatong near Johannesburg. De Klerk visited Boipatong to show his support, but outraged demonstrators threatened his police escort, which opened fire on them, killing several people. With tempers running high, Mandela had little choice but to suspend the negotiations. He suspected de Klerk was trying to weaken the ANC's position by encouraging Inkatha violence.

In September, ANC radicals led a march on the Ciskei Homeland capital aiming to take it over. Ciskei local police opened fire, leaving 28 dead. With the country sliding into civil war, both Mandela and de Klerk saw the need to get talks started again. Western governments applied pressure on both sides to return to the negotiation table. In fact, the two sides had never stopped talking. Their chief negotiators, Cyril Ramaphosa (for the ANC) and Roelf Meyer (for the government) had been continuing to meet throughout the crisis.

Setting aside their growing dislike of each other, Mandela and de Klerk met again in September. De Klerk agreed to Mandela's demands for the disarming of Inkatha members during demonstrations but was not able to get Mandela to agree in return to some form of white veto in the constitution. But Mandela understood that whites had to be reassured before they would finally agree to black majority rule. Communist leader Joe Slovo solved the problem by proposing that existing (white) government employees—including judges, police and army officers—would be allowed to keep their jobs for ten years under an ANC government. As 40 per cent of employed

In a **referendum** all voters are given the opportunity to vote on an important issue. Governments hold referendums (the plural form may also be "referenda") when they feel the need for public support on a decision of national importance. Governments can influence voters' behaviour in referendums by the wording of the referendum text. This is why referendums are no substitute for parliamentary government.

Afrikaners worked for the government, this concession—known as the "sunset clause" (the last moment in the day of white minority rule)—was crucial in persuading the Afrikaners to accept the principle of majority rule.

Negotiations went well enough between the ANC and the government for a Multiparty Forum for all political parties in April 1993. In the same month, a white extremist belonging to the racist Afrikaner Weerstand Beweging (Afrikaner Resistance Movement or AWB) shot and killed Chris Hani, the popular young Communist Party General Secretary. But Hani's assassination did not succeed in its aim of destabilizing the peace process. Mandela came on national television appealing for calm. His personal authority in the country had overtaken de Klerk's.

The rule of law

Multiparty Forum negotiations on an interim constitution proceeded with Inkatha and the Conservative Party continuing to stay out. Fighting intensified between Inkatha and ANC supporters. Nevertheless, an interim constitution was agreed upon in November 1993. De Klerk gave way on his demand for Cabinet decisions to require a two-thirds majority. It was a victory for the ANC but the sunset clause provided sufficient reassurance for

This cartoon by Kevin Kallaugher on de Klerk's referendum was published in *The Economist* on 21 March 1992. Why does de Klerk appear as a Roman general and what does "across the Rubicon" mean? Once you have found out, work out the message of the cartoon.

the government to accept it. This is how the historian Leonard Thompson described the interim constitution:

> It was ... a vindication [justification] of Mandela's vision and persistence in concentrating on the negotiation process and ignoring the cries of ANC hotheads for the continuation of an armed struggle that was unlikely to achieve victory in the foreseeable future.
>
> Thompson, L. 2000. *A History of South Africa*. New Haven, USA.
> Yale University Press. p. 257

In December, the old white-dominated parliament approved the interim constitution. The historian Robert Ross commented:

> Importantly, this meant that the transition from apartheid to democracy was achieved with constitutional continuity, something on which both Mandela and de Klerk, two lawyers of conservative temperament, always insisted. The country's laws might be changed; the supremacy of law was maintained.
>
> Ross, R. 1999. *A Concise History of South Africa*. Cambridge, UK.
> Cambridge University Press. p. 191.

Elections were set for 26–29 April 1994. They would be South Africa's first ever universal suffrage elections.

Activity:

Comparing and contrasting

The following article is from *Newsweek* in March 1993. It reports on what each side, the ANC and the National Party, aimed to achieve for itself in the negotiations on how to establish a multiracial government.

1　After you have read the article, compare each side's demands with what it actually achieved in the interim constitution of November 1993.

2　If one side gave way over one of its demands, does this mean that:

　　a　It was weaker?

　　b　It had more to gain by giving way?

　　c　It did not expect its demands to be fully accepted by the other side?

Crucial features of South Africa's interim rule are still not clear

Brutal experience has taught South Africans not to let their hopes run out of control. Nevertheless, a cautious but growing sense of optimism pervades the country. After so many false dawns and miserable letdowns, the next few months may finally produce a framework for creating a democracy to replace the present white-ruled system. Multiparty talks on drafting a new constitution, on hold since last May, are scheduled to resume this week. The two principal groups in the negotiations, President F.W. de Klerk's ruling National Party and Nelson Mandela's African National Congress, seem determined to make it work. Where they lead, the rest of the country has little choice but to follow. Nevertheless, they still have far to go. The basic snag remains the conflict between the black majority's aspirations and the white minority's fears. …

De Klerk is eager to reorganize the whole system and weaken the state president's office. By shifting as much power as possible from Pretoria to regional and local governments, a semblance of white autonomy (self-government) could be preserved in some areas. In this issue, at least, de Klerk has an ally in another player at the talks: Zulu chief Mangosuthu Buthelezi, founder and leader of the Inkatha Freedom Party, supports decentralization as a way of maintaining unchallenged sway over his stronghold in Natal. But the ANC wants no such dilution of central authority.

Even if the central government is kept strong, however, the next president won't be free to choose his own cabinet. The ANC and the National Party have each suggested formulas for making the Cabinet reflect the country's new multiracial partnership. De Klerk's negotiators have proposed limiting cabinet membership to parties that win at least 15 percent of the popular vote. That arrangement would effectively create a bipartisan [two party] government, since only de Klerk's National Party and the ANC can reasonably expect to attract such a level of support.

But the ANC want to lower the floor to 5 percent, which would probably give at least one ministry each to Inkatha and the radical Pan-Africanist Congress (PAC). "The government of national unity must be as broad as possible," says ANC negotiator Joe Slovo.

Whatever agreement the National Party and the ANC ultimately reach, they must try to sell it to the PAC, Inkatha and the white parties to the far right. All three groups have repeatedly displayed their willingness to use violence when they consider it necessary.

Source: *Newsweek*. 8 March 1993.

The interim constitution

The interim constitution was a complicated document. It was based on liberal US and Western European ideas, which were adapted to the complexities of the situation in South Africa. Its main points were as follows:

- Nine provinces were created out of the four old ones. This allowed the Homelands to be integrated into larger territorial units which better reflected the ethnic and economic realities of South Africa.
- The National Party, backed by Inkatha, wanted a federal model, with the provinces free to run themselves as far as possible. The ANC wanted a central state, which would enable a national government elected by the African majority to push through the changes needed to improve the standard of living for all Africans. The ANC gave way on this point. The federalism of Germany provided a suitable compromise model. This allowed for important aspects of government, such as education, to be carried out at the provincial level but was not as decentralized as the USA. Each province was to have its own provincial legislature, the members of which were elected by the voters.
- In a further concession to ethnic differences, no fewer than 11 languages were declared to be official South African languages. They included English, Afrikaans and nine African languages.
- The new national parliament was to be **bicameral**—one house, the National Assembly, representing the people and the other, the Senate, representing the provinces. Members of the Senate were not to be elected directly by voters as they are in the USA, but nominated by the provincial legislatures. Legislation had to be approved by a majority in both houses.
- The President of the Republic was to be elected by the National Assembly, not directly by the people. This ensured that the president would automatically be the leader of the biggest party in the National Assembly. The president was not just to be head of state. Like the American president, the South African president was also to be head of the government, with the power to appoint the members of **Cabinet**.
- Power sharing among the political parties was to be compulsory until 1999. All parties receiving over five per cent of the vote were entitled to at least one ministerial post in the Cabinet. Parties with more than 20 per cent would be able to nominate a vice-president. Thus the first democratically elected government of South Africa was to be a **coalition government**.
- Following the example of the US Supreme Court, a constitutional court would have the power to judge whether or not laws passed by the parliament were in accordance with the constitution.
- Current government employees could keep their jobs until they retired (the sunset clause).
- **Representation** in parliament was to be **proportional** to the total vote in the country received by the various political parties. This ensured that the National Party, which represented the white minority, would be fairly represented. It also gave a lot of power to the political parties, which were responsible for drawing up lists of candidates who would get seats in the National Assembly,

A **bicameral** legislature has two "chambers" or "houses". A majority in both houses is needed to get bills (new laws) passed. Both South Africa and the USA have bicameral legislatures.

Cabinet, meaning literally a "private room", consists of the head of government together with his government ministers (called "Secretaries" in the USA and Britain), who head the main government departments or ministries. The president (in Britain, the prime minister) usually discusses important political issues in the Cabinet, before coming to a decision.

Coalition governments occur quite often in parliamentary democracies. They are an alliance of political parties which have agreed to co-operate in a government. Parties go into coalitions for several reasons. Small parties join coalition governments because it gives them the chance to have some influence. On the other hand, big parties sometimes form coalitions if none of them has gained a convincing majority after an election. Another reason for big parties to form coalitions is to ensure national unity at times of crisis. This was the case in South Africa in the 1990s.

depending on how well their party did in a parliamentary election. (In the **first-past-the-post** system it is the individual candidates who people vote for by name in each electoral district who get seats in parliament.)

- The right of tribal chiefs to apply customary (traditional) law in their communities was upheld.
- Following the American **Bill of Rights**, the political rights of all citizens were guaranteed.
- Additionally, economic and social rights were proclaimed. Many of these would be very difficult to enforce, such as the right of children to basic health and nutrition.
- Among the social rights was the equality of women and men. As has been stated (see above—rights of tribal chiefs), however, provision for customary law was also asserted. This subordinated women to men, contradicting the principle of **gender** equality.

> **Gender**, as opposed to sex, is the term for political, economic and social issues in which the relationship between men and women is the main issue.

On the brink of civil war

With the election set for April 1994, parties were given the deadline of 12 February to register. However, as the deadline came and went, a number of important parties failed to register. They included the Conservative Party, Inkatha, the ruling parties in the Ciskei and Bophuthatswana Homelands, the Pan-Africanist Party (PAC) and the radical Azanian People's Organization (AZAPO). The latter two wanted to continue the armed struggle. If so many political groups refused to participate in the election, democracy would stand little chance of surviving.

While PAC and AZAPO continued to make armed attacks on whites, they had a much smaller membership than the ANC and lacked effective political leaders. The leaders of the Ciskei and Bophuthatswana Homelands were unpopular with their own people, as they were seen as collaborators with the white government. That left the real threat to democracy coming from the Conservatives and other right-wing white groups and Inkatha.

Inkatha was demanding that KwaZulu Homeland be practically independent. The majority of Zulus, who made up 22 per cent of the South African population, backed Inkatha and had been building up firearms for years, supplied secretly by the state security forces.

On the white right wing, the Conservative Party, the Afrikaner Weerstand Beweging (AWB) and others joined together into a Volksfront led by former army chief Constand Viljoen. The Volksfront had many supporters in the army, the police and security forces. It was therefore potentially very powerful. It aimed at turning South Africa into a loose **confederation** of states, including the Homelands and a "Volkstaat" (people's state') for Afrikaners. Violence between Inkatha and ANC followers reached new levels of intensity, while white right-wingers bombed the ANC offices. To make matters worse, the Volksfront formed an alliance with Inkatha and the governments of the Ciskei and Bophuthatswana Homelands.

Mandela's main aim was to win over Buthelezi and Viljoen. He and Thabo Mbeki had for months been holding secret meetings with Viljoen and other army generals, aimed at winning their confidence. On 16 February, a few days after the deadline for parties to register

> **Electoral systems**
>
> The alternative to **proportional representation** is sometimes called the **first-past-the-post** system. (The winner of the race is the first to cross the finishing line marked by posts.) Such a system produces clearer election results by favouring bigger parties at the cost of smaller ones. In each electoral district, only the candidate with the most votes gets a seat in parliament. The other candidates get nothing. Under proportional representation, however, votes for parties coming second, third, fourth, etc. in each electoral district are added up nationwide and seats reserved for them in parliament in proportion to their national total.

IB Learner Profile link

Inquirer

Find out which African nations (Zulu, for example) live in South Africa. Research their customary laws and identify potential problems (in particular, in relation to the rights of women and girls).

Open-minded

Many students in international schools come from privileged backgrounds and have a Western outlook. To what extent should people with Western values respect non-Western values when these conflict?

Critical thinker

Weigh up the advantages and disadvantages on both sides:

- forcing traditional societies to give up certain practices
- allowing abuses of human rights to go on in the name of respect for cultural difference.

 Evaluate the arguments for and against respecting customary law.

Activity:

Comparing and contrasting

The constitutions of South Africa and the USA

Compare the following aspects of the South African and US constitutions, and answer the questions:

- **The role and constitutional position of the president**
  - ⊠ a head of state who is just a figurehead, as in several European countries, or a powerful figure who heads the government
  - ⊠ directly elected by the people or not (in the case of the USA, the electoral college provides a complicated model)
  - ⊠ relationship to the legislature: separation of powers.

 Does the South African constitution separate the legislative and executive powers as in the USA?

Does the South African president have to work with a National Assembly in which another party can have a majority?

- **Electoral systems**
  South Africa uses proportional representation and the USA the first-past-the-post system in Congressional elections.

What impact can this have on election outcomes?

- **Federalism**
  The ANC wanted a more centralized national government, while the National Party and Inkatha wanted to give more power to the provinces. In the end, the ANC had to give way. Nevertheless, South African federalism does not give as much power to the provinces as the USA does to the states. Does this make the South African president more powerful than the US president?

- ⊠ In both the USA and South Africa, the relationship between the states/provinces and the central/federal government was an important political issue. President Nixon's New Federalism wanted to decrease federal power in favour of state power and de Klerk wanted to do something similar.

Does this mean that conservative and right-wing political parties in general favour decentralized political systems? Do liberal and left-wing ones prefer the opposite?

- **Political parties**
  In multi-party states, political parties are not usually cited in the constitution because they can change over time. Nevertheless, the South African constitution is designed to give considerable power to political parties. In the US constitution, no particular role is foreseen for political parties.

  In reality, it is the political parties which breathe life into the dry paragraphs of a constitution. In this respect, the difference between South Africa and the USA is significant. The ANC's huge majority has led South Africa to be called a "single-party democracy". (See chapter 6 for further discussion on this topic). The USA, on the other hand, has a two-party political system in which two big parties dominate political life. In some European countries, there are three big parties. In countries with proportional representation, smaller parties can hold the balance of power between the big parties, enabling them to force bigger parties to give them representation in the government. When this happens, it is called a "coalition" government.

Does this mean that South Africa, with only one dominant political party, is less democratic than other countries with two or more?

for the election, Mandela announced further concessions to the Afrikaners and Zulus. The possibility of peacefully setting up an Afrikaner Volkstaat after the elections was a task for the future parliament, and the KwaZulu Homeland was to be joined together with Natal province, forming a single big Zulu-dominated province. The deadline for registration was extended to 4 March. Viljoen then decided to register a political party—called the Freedom Front—for the election.

The unpopular governments of Ciskei and Bophuthatswana collapsed but Buthelezi continued to hold out. Despite the appeals of Mandela and de Klerk, Buthelezi refused to join in the election. Eventually, realizing that Inkatha would face destruction by the army of a democratic South Africa if he continued to stay out, Buthelezi agreed to participate one week before the election was to due to take place.

Majority rule

The election, 26–29 April 1994

In the election from 26 to 29 April 1994, South Africans of all skin colours voted for the parties of their choice. For Africans it was an entirely new experience. The violence stopped and international observers reported that, on the whole, the elections had been fairly held. The results were as follows:

	Percentage of the vote	Seats in the National Assembly
ANC	63	252
National Party	20	82
Inkatha	10.5	43

Viljoen's Freedom Front and the PAC did poorly, each getting under 2 per cent of the vote and thus failing to gain a representative in the Cabinet. Coloureds voted mostly for the National Party, helping it to reach the 20 per cent mark, thus qualifying to have a vice-president.

In a joyous day of celebration, Mandela was sworn in as president on 10 May 1994. Mbeki and de Klerk were his vice-presidents. Power was shared in the Cabinet between the representatives of the ANC, the National Party and Inkatha, including Buthelezi. Cabinet ministers included sixteen Africans, eight whites and six Asians and Coloureds. Mandela ensured that two of them were women.

A government of national unity

A democratic political system had been created and civil war avoided. The dignity of Africans in South Africa had been restored. In this respect, Mandela and the ANC had reached their goal. But beyond lay the even more challenging task of creating a democratic society. The Government of National Unity faced the huge problems inherited from apartheid:

- an urgent need for reconciliation between the races
- an enormous gap in wealth between white South Africans and the black African majority

A **confederation** is a loose association of states. It is looser than a federal union. The Southern states in the American civil war regarded themselves as a confederation, as did the states of Germany before German unification in 1871. (Although Switzerland today is officially known as a confederation, its national government has a federal structure similar to those of other modern federal states.)

Countdown to the election

1991 CODESA multiparty talks begin on a new constitution for South Africa

1992 de Klerk holds referendum on continuing negotiations with the ANC

CODESA talks break down

Boipatong massacre

Threat of civil war as violence increases between ANC, Inkatha and other groups

Talks between Mandela and de Klerk restart

Joe Slovo proposes "sunset clause" to protect whites under a black government

1993 Chris Hani, Communist Party General Secretary, is assassinated by white extremist

Multiparty Forum is set up for negotiations on working out an interim constitution

Multiparty Forum agrees on an interim constitution providing for democratic elections and a Government of National Unity

1994 March: General Viljoen agrees to the Afrikaner Volksfront taking part in the election

April: One week before the election, Chief Buthelezi agrees to Inkatha taking part

26–29 April: First universal suffrage parliamentary election in South Africa

- a **civil service** and army made up of two million white South Africans who would resist reforms
- a lack of experienced Africans to take up administrative posts in the new government
- an army dominated by Afrikaners trained to enforce apartheid
- a corrupt, unpopular black police force
- hopelessly inadequate health and education systems that served the majority of the population
- high unemployment, widespread crime and corruption
- a lack of housing, electricity and clean water for urban Africans
- a growing AIDS epidemic.

On the positive side, South Africa had great economic potential with rich natural resources, a well-developed infrastructure and plenty of well-trained professionals—doctors, lawyers, journalists, engineers and business people.

> A **civil service**, as opposed to the armed services, is made up of government employees who administer the services of government that provide for the population's health and education, a functioning infrastructure, law and order, etc.

Reconciliation

Mandela saw his first task as reconciling the races, especially Africans and Afrikaner whites. Africans expected justice. But putting Afrikaner policemen and security officials on trial for torturing and murdering Africans might result in a violent white backlash. Eastern Europe and Latin American countries provided recent examples of how to restore democracy after years of brutal dictatorship. Democracy can only work if everyone consents to participate in peaceful political processes. To integrate thousands of former apartheid supporters into democratic processes, forgiveness and national unity had to be placed above victims' demand for justice.

Activity:

Comparing and contrasting
Challenges to democracy

Compare and contrast the racism and political extremism of South Africa and the United States. Find similarities and differences between the two countries in comparing points 1–4.

South Africa

1. The Volksfront's demand for a separate state for whites within South Africa.
2. The AWB's racist-motivated violence.
3. The assassinations of African political leaders by security forces.
4. The role of Frederik de Klerk.

The USA

1. The resistance of white Southerners to civil rights for African-Americans.
2. The racist-motivated violence of right-wing segregationists in the South.
3. The FBI's failure to provide security for African-American political activists.
4. The role of presidents Kennedy and Johnson.

Influenced by these examples, a multi-racial Truth and Reconciliation Commission (TRC) was set up in 1995 to heal the wounds of human rights abuses under apartheid. Archbishop Desmond Tutu was appointed to head the commission. The TRC was empowered to grant **amnesties** to those who came forward and publicly gave a truthful account of their crimes. Under criticism from all sides, Tutu insisted that ANC members who had engaged in political violence should also have to give testimony. Mandela, against the protests of his own party, backed him. The TRC worked for over two years and its hearings revealed to the world for the first time the full horrors of the apartheid regime. De Klerk, Mbeki and Buthelezi all rejected the TRC's findings but there can be no doubt that its work was a valuable attempt to heal the wounds of the past.

The provinces of South Africa today

On the other side, the demands of thousands of former ANC and PAC guerrilla fighters, returning home from their bases in the frontline states, needed to be satisfied. It took all of Mandela's political skills to get them to agree to integrate into the white-dominated South African Defence Force. To bring the civil service into line with the needs of the new government, Mandela created 11 000 new government jobs which were to be filled by affirmative action.

An **amnesty** involves cancelling the punishment for someone who has broken the law. It is similar to the US president's right to pardon offenders. Amnesty is a useful political instrument in times of political tension when the punishment of offenders would deepen political divisions in a country.

The economy

Just as difficult as reconciliation were the economic problems inherited from apartheid. Mandela's government needed to create economic growth, which involved investment, training and the introduction of new technologies. This alone could provide the wealth needed to improve the standard of living for Africans. But that would take time. Meanwhile ANC voters expected the government to act immediately to eliminate poverty. Caught between these conflicting demands, the government adopted a Reconstruction and Development Plan (RDP). The RDP aimed at:

- job creation through **public works** schemes
- an ambitious house-building programme
- providing clean water, sanitation and electricity to all homes
- improved welfare services
- land redistribution to Africans.

Public works schemes are government-financed projects, such as the building of roads, schools and hospitals, to improve the national infrastructure and create employment opportunities.

The ANC's economic ideas were based on state planning following the model of the Soviet Union. But the Soviet Union had passed into history and central planning was discredited. So, once in government, the ANC adopted Western capitalist policies, opening up the country to foreign investment and trade and co-operating closely with big business. Mandela and others frequently travelled abroad to encourage foreign investment. The USA, Malaysia and European countries provided development aid but not enough to meet South Africa's needs. Meanwhile private investors held back, nervous about the coutry's instability.

By 1996 the RDP goals had clearly not been met. Economic growth remained low and 37 per cent of Africans over 15 years of age were unemployed. Consequently, the RDP was scrapped and replaced by a new policy called Growth, Employment and Redistribution (GEAR). GEAR concentrated on economic growth at the expense of trying to raise the standard of living straight away. GEAR was equally unsuccessful. The economic growth rate stagnated and South Africa went into a **recession** in the late 1990s.

> A **recession** is a time when the economic growth rate of a country becomes negative (expansion turns into contraction) for a period of six months or more, leading to recession.

Social policies

Mandela's government made substantial progress in increasing the availability of housing, although little land was returned to those who had lost it under apartheid. By 1997 much had been done to provide electricity, telephones and piped water to households. Nevertheless, 41 per cent of all South African households still lacked electricity and 12 million people were without piped water in their homes. Furthermore, 61 per cent of Africans remained below the official poverty line (353 rand or US $60 per month). But despite these statistics, a black African middle class began to develop as jobs in government, education and business opened up to educated Africans.

In healthcare, progress was made in building hospitals in rural regions previously without health services. But the standard of medical care in large hospitals in urban areas declined. The scourge of AIDS spread uncontrolled. In 1999, 3.6 million South Africans were HIV positive and by 2002 a quarter of a million were dying of AIDS each year, creating a generation of orphans who were forced into crime to survive.

Progress in improving education for the African majority was especially disappointing. Desegregation of schools progressed slowly. The standard in most schools was low and continued to drop. The government was financially unable to meet its target of providing free schooling for all South Africans. Education standards were generally low, due to a lack of qualified teachers and low salaries. The situation in the universities was no better. Academic standards fell. Qualified African professors were few in number and former black universities were incompetently run and lacking in funds. Mandela's education minister declared that the educational condition of the majority of people in the country amounted to a "national emergency".

Crime and corruption

Crime and corruption was endemic. The murder rate in South Africa was at least ten times higher than that of the USA and the incidence of rape judged to be the highest in the world. The high crime rate affected the economy negatively by discouraging foreign investors and tourists and persuading white professionals to leave the country.

Corruption occurred in the central government and, even more so, in the provincial and local governments. Billions of rand in public money disappeared. Many previously poor African officials saw their new positions of power as a source of enrichment. In Gauteng province, school examination papers were put on sale before the examination. Pensions were stolen, and police made illegal arrests, demanding money before they would release people.

Mandela steps down

Mandela had no intention of hanging on to power like many other African leaders. In 1997 he handed over the presidency of the ANC to Mbeki and delegated most of the business of running the government to him. In the 1999 parliamentary election, the ANC won again with 66 per cent of the vote. By this time the once-mighty National Party had disintegrated. De Klerk had resigned from the government over the issue of future power sharing. Thabo Mbeki became South Africa's second African president. A permanent constitution replaced the interim one and power sharing between the political parties was no longer required. With Buthelezi's Inkatha integrated into the government and the National Party no longer a force, the ANC was in a position to reduce the power of provincial governments too.

In his farewell speech to parliament, Mandela was critical of the crime and corruption which continued to hold back progress. While calling for greater efforts, he nevertheless held out hope for a brighter picture.

> We dare to hope for a brighter picture because we are prepared to work for it. The steady progress of the last few years has laid the foundation for greater achievements. But the reality is that we can do much, much better.

Thompson, L. 2000. A History of South Africa. New Haven, USA.
Yale University Press. p. 288.

Although many of his government's efforts to improve the quality of life for the majority of people had led to disappointing results, Mandela left behind a stable democratic system and a commitment to the rule of law.

Activity:

Points of view

Practise evaluating different historical interpretations by summarizing and commenting on the ways in which these three historians interpret the effectiveness of the Truth and Reconciliation Commission.

1 *The Truth and Reconciliation Commission, chaired by Archbishop Tutu … provided intangible but genuine satisfaction. The terms were that all stories could be told and amnesty would be granted to those who admitted to human rights violations … It was of real importance to the victims and their relatives that the testimony could be heard in public, and also to see some at least of the former rulers doing penance [showing that they were sorry] for their actions.*

Source: Ross, R. 1999. *A Concise History of South Africa*. Cambridge, UK. Cambridge University Press. pp. 199–200.

2 *The TRC discovered and revealed a great deal of information about the heinous [evil] behaviour of agents of the apartheid regime … The Commission also showed that some ANC operatives, too, had committed serious crimes. But the TRC did not advance the cause of racial reconciliation. Indeed, in the short run it had the opposite effect, accentuating [emphasizing] the racial divisions in South African society. Nor did the TRC bring justice to the victims of political violence. Many killers and torturers walked free for talking about their crimes, and victims received little compensation.*

Source: Thompson, L. 2000. *A History of South Africa*. Yale, USA. Yale University Press. p. 278.

3 *The report of the TRC provides a benchmark [a standard against which further developments can be measured] against which future white behaviour as well as the conduct of governments may be judged. It is a historic record of a brutal regime whose primary motive was to maintain a racial minority in power. And it is a reminder of how easily power and the desire to retain it can corrupt and destroy a people's integrity. How much this exercise in exposing truths that a majority of the whites wished only to hide or ignore will assist the new South Africa to forge a racially integrated future remains to be seen. Throughout the sittings of the TRC it was clear that new non-racial South Africa was an ideal that had yet to be created.*

Source: Arnold, G. 2005. *Africa. A Modern History*. London, UK. Atlantic Books. p. 787.

Thabo Mbeki's presidency

Mbeki's Cabinet included 25 ANC members and three Inkatha members, including Buthelezi. ANC Cabinet members included whites, Indians and Coloureds, as well as Africans. This reflected the ANC's continuing commitment to multiracialism. "The rainbow nation" became the official national slogan, which celebrated the differences as well as the interdependence of South Africa's races. Mbeki also included seven women in his Cabinet, illustrating the increasing importance which the ANC attached to equal opportunities for women. The Democratic Party replaced the National Party as the main opposition in the National Assembly.

Mbeki increasingly centralized power in his own hands. The Democratic Party accused him of wanting to be a dictator. But the ANC under Mbeki had received such a convincing majority in the 1999 election that there could be no doubt that he had the support of the vast majority of South Africans. The ANC's unchallenged position of power led some commentators to call South Africa a "one-party democracy" in the first years of the 21st century. (See chapter 6 for further discussion of the limitations of single-party rule).

Mbeki's first year as president did little to change the main trends in South Africa's economy and society. GEAR remained as the government's economic policy. Privatization was carried out slowly but economic growth continued to stagnate. With little to fear from the white minority, Mbeki increased affirmative action on behalf of Africans, thereby reducing the cultural, political and economic influence of the white minority. He was heavily criticized in the early years of his presidency for being slow to act effectively against the threat posed by the AIDS epidemic.

Summing up six years of majority rule

Although South Africa's progress during Mandela's presidency and the first year of Mbeki's was distinctly unimpressive, most of the main problems confronting the government had been inherited from the days of apartheid: poverty, crime, poor performance of the economy and a poor educational system. Political democracy had been established, but social and economic rights proclaimed in the constitution were still a long way from being achieved. The "Long Walk" (Mandela gave his autobiography the title "Long Walk to Freedom") had begun but there was still far to go. The massive social problems of a nearly a century of segregation and apartheid could not be changed overnight. Six years of democracy was a short time by comparison.

Activity:

Comparing and contrasting
Civil rights and majority rule

The civil rights movement was triumphant in the USA in the 1960s. The struggle for majority rule was triumphant in South Africa in the 1990s. As a result, African-Americans in the USA and Africans in South Africa obtained full civil rights and improved living and working conditions.

List the similarities and differences in the two movements, covering the following points:

● the rights acquired as a result of the struggles

● the role of the leaders (Martin Luther King and Nelson Mandela)

● the political philosophy of the leaders and their political movements

● the methods of political activism used by the leaders and their followers

● African-Americans in the USA and Africans in South Africa as a proportion of the total population of their countries

● the political and legal status of African-Americans in the USA and Africans in South Africa prior to the progress of the movements for social change. Did African-Americans before the 1960s have as few rights as Africans living under apartheid in South Africa?

● the economic situations of African-Americans and Africans in South Africa before and after the triumph of civil rights and majority rule.

Activity:

Comparing and contrasting
Economic and social policies

Compare and contrast the economic and social policies of the USA and South Africa with regard to the reforms of Johnson's Great Society and Mandela's Government of National Unity. Consider the following points:

● education

● health

● vocational training and job creation

● social insurance/social welfare

● housing.

Exam questions

1 Compare and contrast the electoral systems in **two** 20th-cenury democratic states.

2 Discuss gender issues, social welfare and education in **two** countries in the Americas.

3 In what ways and to what extent did the Civil Rights movement in **one** democratic state succeed in ending racial discrimination?

4 Analyse the role of Nelson Mandela in South Africa's transition to majority role.

5 In what ways and with what results did economic policies improve the standard of living in **two** democratic states, each chosen from a different region.

6 What important issues affected domestic policies in the United States between 1954 and 1974.

7 Compare and contrast democracy in Japan after 1945 and Australia between 1965 and 1975.

8 "Democratic states have allowed pressure groups to have too much influence on their policies." To what extent do you agree with this statement?

9 For what reasons and with what results did Weimar Germany fail?

10 Analyse the successes and failures of **either** President Alfonsin of Argentina (1983–1989), or President Nixon of the United States (1968–1974).

Recommended further reading

The United States

Patterson, James. 2005. *Restless Giant. The United States from Watergate to Bush v. Gore*. Oxford, UK. Oxford University Press.

Patterson, James. 1996. *Grand Expectations. The United States 1945–1974*. Oxford, UK. Oxford University Press.

Tindall, G, Shi, D and Pearcy, T. 2001. *The Essential America*. New York, USA. Norton.

Written for advanced High School students. Covers the entire history of the United States from colonial times.

South Africa

Mandela, Nelson. 1994. *Long Walk to Freedom*. London, UK. Abacus.

Mandela's autobiography is probably the best eye-witness account of the struggle against apartheid.

Ross, Robert. 1999. *A Concise History of South Africa*. Cambridge, UK. Cambridge University Press.

Sampson, Anthony. 1999. *Mandela. The Authorized Biography*. London, UK. HarperCollins.

Thompson, Leonard Monteath. 2000. *A History of South Africa*. New Haven, USA. Yale University Press.

Stokes, Gale. 1993. *The Walls Came Tumbling Down*. Oxford, UK. Oxford University Press.

6 Origins and development of authoritarian and single-party states

The single-party, totalitarian state is a phenomenon of the 20th century—a new development with a number of unique characteristics which sets it apart from previous forms of authoritarian rule. These earlier forms were almost invariably absolute monarchies which largely disappeared in the 19th century. The closest example to a modern totalitarian, single-party state prior to the 20th century was the Jacobin dictatorship established in the 1790s in revolutionary France. The impact of single-party states, their leaders and their ideologies has been monumental in every aspect of human endeavour and has caused some of the most significant destruction and dislocation in history. They continue to provide an enormous wealth of material for students of politics, mass movements and human behavior in times of crisis.

This chapter will provide a method by which to approach the study of single-party states as outlined in the *History Guide*. The major themes are: the origins and nature of authoritarian and single-party states, the establishment of single-party states and the impact of their domestic policies. The first major theme focuses on the conditions and circumstances that contribute to the rise of single-party states. The key role of the leader in the rise to power is also analysed by examining personal characteristics, ideas and strategies. The nature of the totalitarian states that are an outcome of this process is also explored. The second major theme deals with the methods by which single-party states establish and maintain their power. This involves an examination of the methods that they use to eliminate their opposition and the role of ideology and the policies implemented to consolidate their power. The third major theme revolves around an analysis of domestic polices. This theme supports an analysis of economic and political policies, but also those with broader social implications, with an emphasis on the role of education, the arts, gender policies and attitudes towards religion.

Many of the examples of single-party states are well-known: Nazi Germany, the Soviet Union, Cuba and China. In addition some source material from George Orwell's novel *1984* is included as it provides excellent descriptions of the social conditions and their impact on the lives of people subject to the excessive control and manipulation of the state. Students are encouraged to seek other fictional models and documentary material on single-party regimes to support their investigations. This chapter will provide students with guidance on how to organize their research and a focus on the major themes relevant to more detailed case studies.

By the end of the chapter, you should be able to:

● define the nature of a single-party state

● understand the reasons for the rise of single-party states, and their historical context

● understand the importance of a leader's abilities, ideology and political platform in acquiring and maintaining power

● determine the various strategies that have been used by single-party leaders to acquire and hold onto power

● identify the forms of government adopted by single-party states and the differences in their ideologies

● understand the type and extent of opposition to single-party regimes and how this opposition is controlled or eliminated

● give an overview of the domestic polices that are characteristic of totalitarian states

● comment on the role of women in single-party states

● comment on attitudes towards minority groups in single-party states

● analyse the role of the media, education, marketing and communications in single-party states.

The nature of single-party states

Single-party states are crisis states as described by Carl Friedrich and Zbigniew Brzezinski. This means that single-party states have arisen during periods of conflict, division or confusion in a society. They are the outcome of war (including the aftermath of wars), economic collapse, religious or ethnic strife, or deep social divisions and class conflicts. These stresses may lead to a sense of hopelessness or despair in the population, a fear for the future or concerns about society descending into chaos. Under such circumstances, the population may be attracted to extreme measures or ideologies which promise to restore some measure of hope, optimism or order in daily life.

These extreme measures often involve surrendering political power to one party which seeks to implement its ideology across all aspects of society. Other political parties and points of view are suppressed through legal means or physical force. Many institutions are eliminated or controlled in order that the new rulers may have complete unopposed dominance of all aspects of the state. In effect, all aspects of life—social, economic and cultural—are brought under the control of the party and must conform to their value system and viewpoints. These measures are enforced though harsh repressive techniques, propaganda to eliminate other points of view and other policies which attract support for the regime and allow it to consolidate its power.

Totalitarian dictatorship is described by Friedrich and Brzezinski as a system of rule for realizing totalist intentions under modern technical and political conditions. This makes it a novel form of autocracy. They also contend that fascist and communist totalitarian dictatorships are basically alike. This thesis is supported by their classification of the characteristics common to all totalitarian states. The thesis can be tested by examining individual totalitarian states and comparing and contrasting them in a number of key areas.

 Are right-wing and left-wing states very different in their goals, policies and structures?

Source analysis

These documents refer to the characteristics of totalitarian states.

Source A

The origins of totalitarian states.

If it is evident that the regimes came into being because a totalitarian movement achieved dominance over a society and its government, where did the movement come from? The answer to this question remains highly controversial. A great many explanations have been attempted in terms of the various ingredients of these ideologies. Not only Marx and Engels, where the case seems obvious, but Hegel, Luther, and a great many others have come in for their share of blame. Yet none of these thinkers was, of course, a totalitarian at all, and each would have rejected these regimes, if any presumption like that were to be tested in terms of his thought. They were humanists and religious men of intense spirituality of the kind the totalitarians explicitly reject. In short, all such "explanations", while interesting in illuminating particular elements of the totalitarian ideologies, are based on serious invalidating distortions of historical facts. If we leave aside such ideological explanations (and they are linked of course to the "ideological" theory of totalitarian dictatorship as criticized above), we find several other unsatisfactory genetic theories.

The debate about the causes or origins of totalitarianism has run all the way from a primitive bad-man theory to the "moral crisis of our time" kind of argument. A detailed inspection of the available evidence suggests that virtually every one of the factors which has been offered by itself as an explanation of the origin of totalitarian dictatorship has played its role. For example, in the case of Germany, Hitler's moral and personal defects, weaknesses in the German constitutional tradition, certain traits involved in the German "national character", the Versailles Treaty and its aftermath, the economic crisis and the "contradictions" of an aging capitalism, the "threat" of communism, the decline of Christianity and of such other spiritual moorings as the belief in the reason and the reasonableness of man—all have played a role in the total configuration of factors contributing to the over-all result. As in the case of other broad developments in history, only a multiple-factor analysis will yield an adequate account. But at the present time, we cannot fully explain the rise of totalitarian dictatorship. All we can do is to explain it partially by identifying some of the antecedent and concomitant conditions. To repeat: totalitarian dictatorship is a new phenomenon; there has never been anything quite like it before.

Source: Friedrich, CJ and Brzezinski, ZK. 1965. *Totalitarian Dictatorship and Autocracy*. Cambridge, USA. Harvard University Press. pp. 18–19.

Source B

Totalitarian dictatorships all possess the following:

1. *An elaborate ideology, consisting of an official body of doctrine covering all vital aspects of man's existence to which everyone living in that society is supposed to adhere, at least passively; this ideology is characteristically focused and projected toward a perfect final state of mankind–that is to say, it contains a chiliastic claim, based upon a radical rejection of the existing society with conquest of the world for the new one.*

2. *A single mass party typically led by one man, the "dictator", and consisting off a relatively small percentage of the total population (up to 10 per cent) of men and women, a hard core of them passionately and unquestioningly dedicated to the ideology and prepared to assist in every way in promoting its general acceptance, such a party being hierarchically, oligarchically organized and typically either superior to, or completely intertwined with, the governmental bureaucracy.*

3. *A system of terror, whether physical or psychic, effected through party and secret-police control, supporting but also supervising the party for its leaders, and characteristically directed not only against demonstrable "enemies" of the regime, but against more or less arbitrarily selected classes of the population; the terror whether of the secret police or of party-directed social pressure systematically exploits modern science, and more especially scientific psychology.*

4   *A technology conditioned, near-complete monopoly of control, in the hands of the party and of the government, of all means of effective mass communication, such as the press, radio, and motion pictures.*

5   *A similarly technologically conditioned, near-complete monopoly of the effective use of all weapons of armed combat.*

6   *A central control and direction of the entire economy through the bureaucratic coordination of formerly independent corporate entities, typically including most other associations and group activities.*

The enumeration of these six traits or trait clusters is not meant to suggest that there might not be others, now insufficiently recognized. It has more particularly been suggested that the administrative control of justice and the courts is a distinctive trait; but actually the evolution of totalitarianism in recent years suggests that such

administrative direction of judicial work may be greatly limited. We shall also discuss the problem of expansionism, which has been urged as a characteristic trait of totalitarianism. The traits here outlined have been generally acknowledged as the features of totalitarian dictatorship, to which the writings of students of the most varied backgrounds, including totalitarian writers, bear witness.

Source: Friedrich, CJ and Brzezinski, ZK. 1965. *Totalitarian Dictatorship and Autocracy*. Cambridge, USA. Harvard University Press. pp. 22–3.

Source-based questions

1   Why do Friedrich and Brzezinski say that they cannot explain the rise of totalitarian dictatorships?

2   Is it necessary for a crisis to exist for a single-party state to emerge?

3   What are the common traits of totalitarian states?

The rise to power

Understanding the methods, circumstances and decisions that lead to a country being taken over by a single party and a single leader are crucial to an understanding of 20th-century history. There have been many examples on all continents of individuals who have sought to achieve one-man, one-party rule. Their activities have dramatically influenced international affairs and produced various military, diplomatic, economic and social crises. An analysis of the rise to power of authoritarian regimes and their common denominators can provide insights into many aspects of the process that allowed them to obtain power, providing useful models for study.

Categories of Analysis

An analysis of the reasons for the rise to power of a single-party in a state can be organized under three major headings:

1   The leader
2   The historical context
3   The elimination of the opposition

Addressing these themes will assist students to analyse the situation in those countries where single-party states have emerged. Students will be able to compare and contrast the rise to power of various leaders and parties, of a range of ideological persuasions, from different parts of the world.

It will also allow students to identify common factors in the rise to power of single-party states which can be used to analyse other leaders or parties that may emerge in the future.

Discussion point:

What type of crisis or situation would cause individuals to sacrifice their freedom, individuality or traditional values?

The leader

The single-party state places great emphasis on the unique talent, intelligence, insight and courage of the leader. The leader is so dominant that the term single-party state is almost a misnomer as in every case the leader personifies the party to the point of being virtually synonymous with it. These are in fact single-person states—the party in essence provides the support structure through which the leader gains extraordinary personal power.

It is important to understand how much a leader contributes to the rise to power of the party or organization. When studying the rise of a single-party state, we must also consider the significant role played by the growth in status of its leader. The qualities to be considered may include but not be limited to:

- physical characteristics—size, physical appearance, personal magnetism, show of strength and power
- intelligence, spiritual depth, ability to articulate a programme of reform and advancement for the nation
- personal skills and qualities, such as public speaking (oratory), ability as a writer, personal charm, magnetism (charisma) and the ability to project an aura of confidence, determination, sincerity
- ability to recruit and gain the support of other powerful and talented individuals and maintain a large following among the general population
- personal history—evidence of heroism, courage, record of personal sacrifice and struggle against injustices real or perceived
- a necessary motivation and commitment to succeed.

Leaders may be able to use their physical and\or personal attributes to give themselves the appropriate image. They wish to appear powerful, confident and dominant as a presence in the political arena. They wish to create the idea in the minds of the public and the party that they have the power, insight and special qualities that will attract support and inspire confidence. The appeal may come from their strength of mission and purpose. In essence, the leader must find a way to inspire confidence, loyalty and a large following among the people, both to their person and the significance of their ideas.

Leaders must also recognize the need to surround themselves with able and loyal subordinates who complement their talents and bring needed skills to the organization. Good examples would be Joseph Goebbels and his creation of the Nazi propaganda machine and the organizing genius of Leon Trotsky in the Russian revolution.

It is crucial to understand that the rise to power is a political process. And, as with all political processes, it requires the support of the public at various key points. A critical part of this appeal is to create a mythology about the leader which paints him in heroic, almost superhuman terms. In conformity with the gender stereotype—the identification of essentially masculine values—the mythology may be based on examples of strength and physical courage as demonstrated in war or other conflicts. It may also be based on a record of support for particular principles and ideals such as nationalism, social justice, economic reform. The leader is portrayed as a man of unique empathy who identifies with the population and whose personal story has allowed him to appreciate their struggles. He must be seen as a man of action prepared to take risks and make personal sacrifices in the interests of the cause.

In the case of Hitler, his war record, economic struggle as a young man and his role in the Munich Putsch would all be used to expand his public image. Fidel Castro gained fame for his brave attack on the Moncada barracks which brought him national attention and a reputation as a patriot and a fearless supporter of reform.

Discussion point:

Gender

All totalitarian leaders in the 20th century have been men. Many of the stereotypical qualities of leadership summed up in the phrase "a man of action", including courage, determination, commanding physical size and strength, are strongly identified as masculine attributes.

This raises many questions about the search for potential leadership. Are men perceived as stronger or more ruthless and capable in times of crisis? Is the essentially military nature of totalitarianism automatically associated with men?

Are societies in which totalitarian leaders have come to power more rigid and traditional in their attitude to power and authority? This was the case in Nazi Germany, the Soviet Union, fascist Italy and Spain. In these societies there may have been women behind the scenes but they played no official or acknowledged role.

 Is it possible to have a female totalitarian leader? Are societies that value gender equality less likely to seek extreme solutions to their problems?

Ideology and political platform

The leader must present both an ideology—a statement of broad principles and vision of the future —as well as a political platform which translates these broad concepts and ideals into tangible, coherent policies, programmes and actions. This is also a political process and the leader must create a vision which not only indicates the direction of his party and the regime but inspires and attracts enthusiastic followers.

Ideology may present ideas that that are too vague or obscure to be grasped and supported by the broad mass of the public who are seeking specific answers to problems. The **Peace, Land and Bread statements** of Lenin prior to the October revolution were not examples of Marxist ideology but a pragmatic political platform to address the immediate issues. The translation of the ideology into practical policies is possibly the most important thing that the leader can do. In addition the successful leader must be prepared to adjust

Peace, Land and Bread This was a slogan developed by the Bolsheviks in April 1917 to attract support for the Bolshevik party in the struggle for power after the fall of the Tsar. It was intended to address the grievances of the soldiers, workers and peasants which the provisional Government had failed to satisfy. This slogan was easily remembered, often repeated and was responsible for attracting considerable support to the Bolsheviks.

or adapt the particular ideology and political platform to changing circumstances to be able to attain or retain power. Ideology which impedes the goal of gaining power will be abandoned or ignored in the quest for power. Hitler did not feel bound to the original Nazi ideology proclaimed in 1921 as he realized that many parts of it were hindering his political goals. Lenin, to retain power abandoned Marxist ideology with the **New Economic Policy**.

Crucial to the success of a single-party leader are the means of identifying and addressing the immediately important issues even if this necessitates abandoning or postponing the key parts of an ideology. Hitler understood that his first priority was job creation not expanding German borders. Mao put off his communist vision in favour of land reforms which turned millions of peasants into landowners. These leaders clearly appreciated that the important thing was to obtain power by any means. Only when power was obtained might the larger or long-term elements of their ideology be addressed.

> **New Economic Policy (NEP)** This was a policy instituted by the Bolshevik government in March 1921 as a result of financial collapse and political uprising following the First World War. It was a reversal of the Bolshevik philosophy that was so unpopular with the Russian population and that placed considerable burden on the peasantry. The NEP allowed the peasants to keep their surplus and sell it for profit. In 1928, after the USSR reached 1913 levels of production, Stalin chose to end NEP for a full command economy—the Five Year plans. The NEP is often seen as an example of Lenin's pragmatism to ensure that he remained in power.

Source analysis

Source A

Hitler's speech at his trial after the Munich Putsch

For not you, gentlemen, will deliver judgment on us; that judgment will be pronounced by the eternal court of history, which will arbitrate the charge that has been made against us. I already know what verdicts you will hand down. But that other court will not ask us: did you or did you not commit high treason? That court will judge us, will judge the Quartermaster-general of the former army, will judge his officers and soldiers, as Germans who wanted the best for their people and their Fatherland, who were willing to fight and die. May you declare us guilty a thousand times; the goddess of the eternal court will smile and gently tear in two the brief of the State Prosecutor in the verdict of the court; for she acquits us.

Source: Fest, JC. 1977. *Hitler*. London, UK. Penguin. p. 193.

Source B

Castro's speech at his 1953 trial became his political manifesto.

Castro used his 1953 trial to condemn Batista's dictatorship. In the process, Castro honoured José Martí, often called the Apostle by the Cuban people. And he promised all Cubans a better life after Batista was gone.

Castro described the attack on Moncada as an effort to keep alive the ideals and the memory of the Apostle. He asked, "Cuba, what would you have become if you had let the memory of our Apostle die?"

Castro asked not to be freed but to be sent to prison with his comrades. He ended his speech with these famous words, "¡Condenádme, no es importa! ¡La Historia me

absolvera!" or "Condemn me! It doesn't matter! History will absolve me!"

Source: Markel, Rita J. 2008. *Fidel Castro's Cuba*. Minneapolis, USA. Twenty First Century Books. p. 57.

Source C

The fact is, Hitler looks every man in the eye. His looks wander from one trooper to another as the SA marches by. We, old-time national Socialists, did not join the SA for reasons of self-interest. Our feelings led us to Hitler. There was a tremendous surge in our hearts, a something that said: "Hitler you are our man. You speak as a soldier of the front and as a man; you know the grind, you yourself have been a working man. You have lain in the mud, even as we—no big shot, but an unknown soldier. You have given your whole being, all your warm heart, to German manhood, for the well-being of Germany rather than your personal advancement or self-seeking. For your innermost heart will not let you do otherwise."

Source: Simpson, William. 1991. *Hitler and Germany*. New York, USA. Cambridge University Press. p. 37.

Source-based questions

1 What personal qualities about Hitler and Castro are revealed in Sources A and B?

2 Would these speeches be effective in attracting support?

3 How would the sentiments stated in Source C affect the public image of Hitler? Is there a possibility that this would have a negative impact?

Discussion point:

Ideology

The ideology of a leader or party may be analysed by asking the following questions:

- What ideas are proposed?
- What issues or grievances do they address?
- Do they represent a new form or structure for the society?
- Do they introduce entirely new concepts, values or goals to the society?
- Have they been inspired by a particular individual, school of thought or philosophy?
- How relevant or effective are they in attracting support within the local, regional and international community?
- Is it revolutionary, visionary or inspirational?
- Can it inspire support, cause excitement? Does it appeal to broad sectors of society? Who does it attract?
- Which groups in the society will feel challenged or threatened by the new ideas?

Policies and political platform

The key to success is how effectively a leader can design a political programme that speaks to the concerns of significant numbers of people. This platform must contain concrete statements and proposals that focus specifically on the causes of the country's problems and promise relief. These policies, often in the form of short, direct slogans or phrases, attract support and increase a leaders' popularity. They help attract followers and give a sense of momentum or inevitable triumph. The leader becomes the saviour of the nation in the minds of many and they devote themselves to the particular platform through politics, guerilla war or other forms of direct action. The ability of the leader to address the crisis with specific solutions rather than vague utopian ideology is a clear advantage. Hitler promised jobs, Mao and Castro supported land reform. These were the pressing issues of the day, and would guarantee popular support. Consider the questions below:

- What are the problems or issues that the leader must address?
- How does the ideology translate into real policies?
- What connections can be made between the political platform, slogans or statements of the leader and the ideology?
- Which sections of the ideology are omitted or ignored? Why?
- Is the platform a pragmatic document which clearly identifies and addresses the key issues?
- Does it attract a significant response from a large proportion of the population?
- Which groups are most likely to respond? Why?
- Which groups will not support the platform? Are they important and if so should the platform be changed to win them over?

Source Analysis

Source A

Extract from statements by Fidel Castro.

A revolutionary government, after making the 100,000 small farmers owners of the land for which they now pay rent, would proceed to end the land problem once and for all. This would be done first by establishing, as the Constitution orders, a limit to the amount of land a person may own for each type of agricultural undertaking, acquiring any excess by expropriation; by recovering the lands usurped from the stage; by improving the swamplands; by setting aside zones for tree nurseries and reforestation. Second, it would be done by distributing the rest of the land available among rural families, preferably to those large in the number; by promoting cooperatives of farmers for the common use of costly farm equipment, cold storage and technical-professional guidance in the cultivation of crops and the breeding of livestock. Finally, it would be done by making available all resources, equipment, protection, and know-how to farmers.

A revolutionary government would solve the problem of housing by lowering rent 50 percent, by giving tax exemption to houses inhabited by their owners; by tripling the taxes on houses built to rent; by substituting the ghastly one-root flats with modern multistory buildings; and by financing housing projects all over the island on a scale never before seen, which would be based on the criterion that if in the rural area the ideal is for each family to own its parcel of land, then in the city the ideal is for each family to own its house or apartment. There are enough bricks and more than enough manpower to build a decent house for each Cuban family. But if we continue waiting for the miracle of the golden calf, a thousand years will pass and the problem will still be the same. On the other hand, the possibility of extending electrical power to the farthest corner of the Republic is today better than ever before because today nuclear energy applied to that branch of industry, lowering production costs, is already a reality.

With these three initiatives and reforms, the problem of unemployment would disappear dramatically, and sanitation service and the struggle against disease and sickness would be a much easier task.

Finally, a revolutionary government would proceed to undertake the complete reform of the educational system, placing it at the same level as the foregoing projects, in order to prepare adequately the future generations who will live in a happier fatherland.

Source: Leonard, Thomas M. 1999. *Castro and The Cuban Revolution*. Westport, USA. Greenwood Press. p. 126.

Source B

Extract from statements by Benito Mussolini.

Our programme is simple: we wish to govern Italy. They ask us for programmes, but there are already too many. It is not programmes that are wanting for the salvation of Italy, but men and will-power. … our political class is deficient. The crisis of the Liberal State has proved it … We must have a State which will simply say: "The Stage does not represent a party, it represents the nation as a whole, it includes all, is over all, protects all."

This is the State which must arise from the Italy of Vittorio Veneto. A State which does not acknowledge that the strongest power is right; which is not like the Liberal State, which after fifty years of life, was unable to install a temporary printing press so as to issue its paper when there was a general strike of printers; a State which does not fall under the power of the Socialists … we want to remove from the State all its economic attributes. We have had enough of the State railwayman, the State postman and the State Insurance official. We have had enough of the State administration at the expense of Italian tax-payers, which had done nothing but aggravate the exhausted financial condition of the country. It still controls the police, who protect honest men from the attacks of thieves … [and] the army which must guarantee the inviolability of the country and foreign policy.

Source: Robson, Mark. 1992. *Italy: Liberalism and Fascism 1870–1945*. London, UK. Hodder and Stoughton. pp. 53–4.

Source-based questions

1 Compare the platforms of Fidel Castro and Benito Mussolini. What is the most significant difference?

2 Which one is most appealing?

3 What does Source B suggest is the main strength of Mussolini and his party's platform?

Source analysis

Source A

Excerpt from Joseph Goebbels' speech on the Tasks of the Reich Ministry for Public Enlightenment and Propaganda, 1933

> *Propaganda is not an end in itself, but a means to an end. If the means achieves the end then the means is good. … The new Ministry has no other aim than to unite the nation behind the ideal of the national revolution. …*
>
> *I consider radio to be the most modern and the most crucial instrument that exists for influencing the masses. I also believe—one should not say that out loud—that radio will, in the end, replace the press …*
>
> *First principle: At all costs avoid being boring. I put that before everything … You must help to bring forth a nationalist art and culture which is truly appropriate to the pace of modern life and to the mood of the times … You must use your imagination, an imagination which is based on sure foundations and which employs all means and methods to bring to the ears of the masses the new attitude in a way which is modern, up-to-date, interesting, and appealing; interesting, instructive but not schoolmasterish.*

Source: Laver, John. 1991. *Nazi Germany 1933–45*. London, UK. Hodder and Stoughton. p. 25.

Source B

The man who invented Castro

> *The first journalist to interview Castro in his secret mountain headquarters was New York Times writer Herbert Matthews. In his report, Matthews presented Castro as a hero and described the rebels as strong, young Cubans ready to fight for their country's future. Castro later said that Matthew's report helped him seize power.*

Source: Markel, R. 2008. *Fidel Castro's Cuba*. Minneapolis, USA. Twenty First Century Books. p. 66.

Source C

Poster by Vladimir Mayakovsky, 1921.

> *If you want something—join up.*
> a) *Do you want to overcome cold?*
> b) *Do you want to overcome hunger?*
> c) *Do you want to eat?*
> d) *Do you want to drink?*

Source: Laver, John. 1991. *Russia 1914–1941*. London, UK. Hodder and Stoughton. p. 34.

Source-based questions

1 What do these documents tell us about making propaganda effective?

2 How do they show the importance of the media as a delivery system?

Delivering the message

What is the relationship between the platform and the way that it is delivered? Should we consider that the message may be less important than the manner in which it is presented? This is an important issue about the nature of propaganda and the selling of a particular product represented by the leader and his platform.

There is no doubt that modern communications techniques, technology and advertising psychology can give an enormous lift to the platform of any political leader. Whenever one considers the quality of a political platform, it must be recognized that its appeal may lie in the delivery. The carefully staged rallies designed by Goebbels in the Nazi era gave an enormous boost to the power of Hitler's speeches—the emotions caused by these dramatic spectacles were often overwhelming and led the crowds to uncritically accept the statements of the leader.

The Nazis were among the first to use radio as the new wave of technology to reach a broader audience. Other leaders quickly understood the power of broadcast media—film, television and, today, the Internet—to distribute their message in a more effective manner. Modern advertising has spent millions studying how to convince humans to act in a certain way—i.e. buy the product. Leaders seeking power are also selling something and they capitalize on the scientific findings of the psychological community to help them in their task.

The strategies used to take power

There are a variety of techniques that single-party leaders employ to gain power. These are used in various combinations and with different degrees of emphasis depending on the country and its situation. Some of the most well-known tactics for gaining power include: civil war, political campaigns, coups d'état, mass uprising, alliances with foreign powers, intimidation of opponents, propaganda and media control.

The approaches to gaining power are numerous and the successful power seeker will choose the one that best suits the condition of their society. Hitler and Mussolini realized that they could take advantage of the existing political system and engineer an internal takeover with moderate violence and confrontation. Others such as Castro and Mao resorted to guerrilla warfare to attain power while Lenin engineered a military coup d'état.

TOK link

The medium is the message

"The medium is the message" is an influential phrase coined by Marshall McLuhan. His point was that the message of any medium or technology is the change of scale or pace or pattern that it introduces into human affairs. Such theories help us to analyse the effective employment of communication technologies and advertising techniques to mount propaganda campaigns in the 20th century.

Analyse the propaganda techniques employed by the Nazis during their rise to power. Explain how the following methods of delivery contributed to their propaganda campaign:

- short slogans and phrases
- coloured flags, uniforms and posters
- music and song, film and radio broadcast
- modern communications technologies
- mass public rallies and spectacles
- the focus on youth and young families.

The historical context

Events or occurrences can create the conditions in which a single party-state may arise. Single-party states are characterized as crisis states. Therefore it must be accepted that single-party states arise because many people are prepared to accept extreme solutions to problems that overwhelm, their social group or society as a whole. Societies with democratic and liberal traditions may be prepared to accept dictatorial or repressive governments if they feel that all other methods have failed. The prospect of economic collapse, political revolution or social anarchy are powerful inducements for radical change. Crisis environments may be accompanied by a breakdown of order in the society and many people are prepared to accept radical solutions if some sort of order and stability or predictability can be restored to their daily lives. Crisis states are induced by:

- war, including the aftermath of war
- economic crisis
- political instability
- lack of leadership
- unpopular or tyrannical governments
- fear of revolution
- new ideas introduced in politics
- nationalism, independence movements.

Single-party states do not emerge in times of peace, prosperity or optimism in society. They are the creation of violence, despair, division, anger and fear. In fact, it may be asserted that they cannot emerge in societies that do not exhibit these desperate characteristics. They are extreme solutions called forth from the political margins by extreme circumstances or events. One of the best-known examples is the extreme suffering which occurred in Russia as a result of the First World War. The defeats, famine, unemployment and political chaos brought down the tsar and provided conditions for the rise of Lenin. Similarly, Hitler's rise to power in Germany cannot be explained without the economic crisis, fear and societal chaos brought on by the Great Depression in Germany—the hardest hit of all Western countries. In China, Mao emerged following a long and bitter period in this country's history that was marked by invasion, conquest, foreign intervention and civil war.

Discussion point: Who gains power?

Why did Lenin and the Reds triumph over the Whites?

Why did the Nazis gain power in Germany and not the communists?

A successful take-over of power requires strong leadership, an appropriate ideology and political platform, good communication strategies and an organized and efficient party machine.

Source analysis

Two historian's viewpoints on the historical context for the successful take-over of power.

Source A

Even though Kornilov's attempted coup came to nothing, Kerensky had no room for comfort. Peasant conscripts were deserting the army en masse, seizing land from the nobility when they returned. The soviets were becoming more radical and by September the Bolsheviks enjoyed a majority on both the Petrograd and Moscow soviets. With the German army close to Petrograd, food shortages in the capital city became more acute than ever. Still Kerensky refused to abandon the war effort. Co-operation between the soviets and the Provisional Government was breaking down but the Mensheviks and the Social Revolutionaries were reluctant actually to take power for themselves. Only one party had its sights firmly fixed on power and that was the Bolsheviks. Their radical policies and powerful slogans of "Peace, Bread and Land" and "All Power to the Soviets" seemed increasingly to coincide with the aspirations of the soldiers, the peasants and the urban masses. After his long years in exile, Lenin was now convinced that his party could successfully carry out a coup in the capital city. First of all he had to get back from Finland and persuade his Bolshevik colleagues that the time for an uprising was ripe. At the start of October, Lenin donned a wig and returned to the capital. Having begun 1917 with its leaders in exile and a membership of around 25, 000 the Bolshevik party was now on the brink of power. Why was this party more successful in 1917 than its rivals?

Source: Traynor, J. 1991. *Challenging History: Europe 1890–1990*. Nelson Thornes. p. 205.

Source B

Until 1928 Nazism was an insignificant political force trying to win factory workers away from Marxism … It was a marginal political movement on the radical rise. But under the impact of the slump, the rise of communism and the political stalemate of parliamentary politics the movement began to attract more attention. Nazism became the authentic voice of the small townsman, the anxious officials and the small businessmen, the peasant who felt he had had a raw deal from the Republic … The Nazi party was made up and led by people like this: Nazi leaders articulated their fears and desires, and promised to end the crisis. Nazism gave expression to the latest nationalism of the conservative masses by blaming the Allies and reparations for Germany's ills. Above all, Nazism was violently anti-Marxist. It was the only party demonstrably, visibly combating the threat of communism on the streets. Although the violence alienated many respectable Germans, they hated communism more. Social disorder and disintegration seemed a reality in 1932 with eight million unemployed. In the chaos Nazism promised to restore order, to revive German fortunes, to bring about a moral renewal, to give "bread and work".

Source: Richard Overy, quoted in Traynor, J. 1991. *Challenging History: Europe 1890–1990*. Nelson Thornes. p. 191.

Source-based questions

1   How crucial was the historical context for the success of the revolutionary party in each of these examples?

2   Do you think that all revolutionary situations which produce totalitarian states require a similar context to succeed? Why?

Activity:

Rise and fall of the leader: Copy this chart and fill in the details to explain the succession to single-party rule.

Country	Leader	Origin/cause of the crisis	Failure to respond	Leader	Nature of the opposition	Elimination of the opposition	Downfall
Russia	Alexander Kerensky, prime minister, Russian Provisional Government to 1917						
Germany	Weimar government. Various leaders.	Great Depression. Germany most affected. Financial and leadership crisis.	Failure to form effective govt. Collapse of the Weimar Republic.	Adolf Hitler sworn in as chancellor 30 January 1933.	Communists	Communists outlawed/ imprisoned	Soviet invasion of Berlin. Hitler commits suicide 30 April 1945.
			President Hindenburg agrees to coalition govt with Nazis.	Enabling Act passed 15 March 1933, granting full legislative power to the chancery.	Trade unions/ democratic parties	Unions and democratic parties dissolved/ made illegal. Party members killed and/or sidelined.	Germany surrenders 8 May 1945.
Italy	Victor Emmanuel III, king of Italy and Albania, Emperor of Ethiopia			Benito Mussolini			
China	Chiang Kai-Shek, leader of the Republic of China 1928–48			Mao Zedong			
Cuba	Fulgencio Batista, president of Cuba, 1952–9			Fidel Castro			

The elimination of the opposition

The mistakes or shortcomings of opponents are crucial to the success of the new leader and the party in their attempt to seize and hold onto power. In almost every case of a single party acquiring power, it can be shown that prior to the regime change, the defeated power had failed to respond effectively to the problems in society, and/or the crises at hand, effectively opening the door to its opponents. This failure may stem from a rigidity of approach. It may be the result of a weak and indecisive leader or governing class that is unable to appreciate the size of the challenge that is being faced. The principal ways in which governments in power may be unable to withstand the challenge of a single-party movement may include:

- weak or unpopular policies
- rigid or insensitive attitudes to some sectors of the population
- lack of experience and a failure to recognize problems
- failure to embrace reform or a determination to retain traditional structures and policies
- divided leadership—no clear direction in the face of a focused and determined challenger
- underestimating the strength and popularity of the opposition.

In some cases, as in Italy after the First World War, the government was simply too feeble and lacking in any effective policies to address the collapse of the economy, widespread violence and threats of a socialist revolution. This allowed Mussolini to move into the vacuum, presenting himself as a strong force who could restore order, discipline and direction to society. In essence, power was lying on the ground waiting for an assertive person to pick it up.

The crisis of the Great Depression was not handled with great skill or imagination in many countries: governments clung to the traditional responses used for times of economic slowdown—this caused problems in these countries and, to some degree, political upheaval. In Germany the application of traditional policies had enormous consequences. Germany had the worst experience of any Western country in this period—the country could not survive a lack of effective leadership. The Weimar government paralysed by its electoral system and traditional economic policies was not able to cope with what amounted to complete societal breakdown verging on civil war.

In China, Chiang Kai-shek could not shake off his commitment to a traditional social structure in which power remained in the hands of the landowners. His failure to oppose Japan weakened support for his leadership. He failed to appreciate the strength of the opposition and the fact that his military strategy was completely unsuitable for a guerrilla war. These are, as most people realize, essentially political struggles and are often won by the side which has the better political programme. Chiang fell because he failed to develop any programme which could gain majority support.

Some governments make the mistake of continuing with traditional repressive tactics and failing to respond to the growth of new movements for change, as in the case of Fulgencio Batista in Cuba. He failed to see that there had been a political shift in Cuba, that the rebels under Castro had a popular political programme and were receiving support from the middle class who had previously supported Batista. When Batista began to use repressive tactics on the middle class, their support for him evaporated. Similarly, popular opinion in the United States was no longer in favour of the brutal measures he employed and the US government withdrew its support for him. This proved fatal to Batista's hopes to retain power.

Other groups in power have similarly failed to realize that their societies may have undergone a dramatic change in social and political attitudes, leading to the rise of a single party to power. This is clearly demonstrated in the period after the Second World War when colonial rulers had lost power and credibility in the eyes of their colonial subjects and were vulnerable to leaders proposing independence and social change. Both Ho Chi Minh in Vietnam and Sukarno in Indonesia are excellent examples of this transference of power. The former colonial governors could not recognize or were unwilling to accept that they could no longer dominate their populations with traditional values and social structures.

Source analysis
Two historian's viewpoints on the failure of the opposition.

Source A

The real problem in German history is why so few of the educated, civilized classes recognized Hitler as the embodiment of evil. University professors; army officers; businessmen and bankers–these had a background of culture, and even of respect for law. Yet virtually none of them exclaimed: "This is anti-Christ". Later, they were to make out that Hitler had deceived them and that the bestial nature of national socialism could not have been foreseen. This is not true. The real character of national socialism was exposed by many foreign, and even by some German, observers long before Hitler came to power. It could be judged from Hitler's writings and his speeches; it was displayed in every street brawl that the Nazi brownshirts organized. Hitler did not deceive the responsible classes in Germany: they deceived themselves. Their self-deception had a simple cause: they were engaged in fighting the wrong battle and in saving Germany.

Source: Taylor, AJP. 1990. *From the Boer War to the Cold War*. London, UK. Hamish Hamilton,. p. 347.

Source B

Mussolini realised that the attitude of the king was critical. As commander-in-chief he could order the army to crush Fascism if he so wished.

By the last week of October preparations were complete. On the night of the 27th, Fascist squads seized town halls, telephone exchanges and railway stations throughout northern Italy. In the early hours of 28 October the government of Luigi Facta finally found the courage to act, and persuaded the king to agree to the declaration of a siege.

Police and troops prepared to disperse the Fascist columns converging on Rome by road and rail. However, by 9 am King Victor Emmanuel had changed his mind. He now refused to authorize the declaration of martial law which would have sanctioned the use of force against the Fascists. This would prove to be a fateful decision: it was a sign that the king lacked confidence in his government and was anxious to avoid a violent showdown with Mussolini's Fascists. It is still uncertain why Victor Emmanuel made this decision—he may have over-estimated the number of Fascists marching on Rome and feared a civil war; he may have feared that his cousin, the Duke of Aosta, a known Fascist sympathizer was waiting to depose him if he acted against Mussolini. Probably more plausibly, the king had little love for the existing Liberal politicians and, believing Mussolini's protestations of loyalty, considered that Fascists should be brought into the governing coalition.

Their nationalism, their anti-socialism and their energy might breathe new life into the regime. Victor Emmanuel certainly did not realise that his decision would open the way for a Fascist dictatorship.

Source: Robson, Mark. 1992. *Italy: Liberalism and Fascism 1870–1945*. London, UK. Hodder and Stoughton. pp. 56, 57, 58.

Source-based questions

1 Identify the mistake made by the ruling group in these sources.

2 Were these people foolish or were circumstances beyond their control?

Totalitarianism—the extent to which it was achieved

The aim of totalitarianism is evident from the word itself. It is about creating a society in which all aspects of life—social, economic, religious, political—are completely controlled, directed and determined by the leader and his party. No rival ideas, organizations, value systems or views are permitted. Furthermore, this concept of totalism extends beyond mere control, to the belief that man and his nature can be reshaped by the ruling group into something ideal. This distinguished the totalitarian single-party state of the 20th century from the autocratic monarchies and oligarchies of earlier ages.

Totalitarianism is aided by the use of modern technology to monitor, record, track, film, and in every way oversee the activities of its citizens. Totalitarian states have embraced new technologies and monopolized their uses to further their power and control over their citizens. There are many variables that could influence the degree to which the state achieves the total control that it desires. Crucial to achieving this goal is the skill and dedication to the task of the leader and key government officials. Are they diligent and efficient taskmasters? Are they single-minded in their goal of achieving a totalitarian state? One can identify differences in the habits and approaches of leaders that might determine their future. Stalin was extremely focused and hard-working in pursuit of his goals. Hitler was not prepared to put in quite so much effort, and as a result oversaw a state with considerable disorganization and chaos in government.

The physical size of the country may be an aid or impediment to totalitarian control. Previously existing attitudes and cultural norms would have a strong influence on the ability to impose true totalitarianism. Germany and Italy had strong traditions of individualism, liberalism and some democratic traditions whereas the Soviet Union and China had always been autocracies with no individual rights, constitutions or traditions of individualism.

It is clear that the enthusiasm and dedication of the ruling party will assist in the imposition of a totalitarian state. The degree to which the leadership can convince the population that their measures have been successful in solving problems and improving lives, is the measure of their success. It should be recognized that if the ruling party loses this zeal and becomes corrupt and stagnant as in the USSR, then its grip will weaken. This will also occur if it consistently fails to produce the results promised to the citizens. Terror will suffice for a while but ultimately the party and/or its leader will begin to lose its grip as faith in the movement weakens, even amongst the party members. Mao's Cultural Revolution was partly an attempt to root out laziness and corruption, to restore the zeal to the party and to continue the task of totally transforming China and its people.

Establishing and maintaining power

The ability to acquire power is one thing but the real challenge is to hold on to it for a long period of time. This principle is analogous to a politician who wins an election, but must then spend his time in office working hard to win the next one. Most leaders whether from single-party states or democracies wish to maintain power over some period of time. It may in fact be more of a challenge to retain than to attain power. The crisis that brought the new party to power may well be continuing and the public will demand quick solutions. There may be extravagant expectations from many sectors of society who embraced the new movement as an answer to a host of problems and will rapidly become disillusioned if results aren't forthcoming.

A party or group which has acquitted power must move very quickly and effectively to consolidate their power by addressing the circumstances that brought them to power and eliminating possible challenges from either individuals or groups. The consolidation or establishment of power in any state is achieved by a blend of repression and attraction. That is, the leader has power because he builds a loyal following based on his policies that appeal to both his supporters and to a large proportion of the population. He also identifies and eliminates or controls all potential challenges from individuals or groups in society and within his own party.

Attracting support

This is an effective method of power consolidation in that it minimizes opposition by turning many citizens into supporters. This can be achieved by:

- carrying out promises made during electoral campaigns or the revolutionary period: e.g. job creation, economic stability, land reform, nationalization of industry, elimination of unpopular or oppressive groups
- instituting policies that will attract favourable support from key sectors that support nationalism, rearmament, industrial expansion, territorial acquisition, new welfare and social programmes.

Source analysis

Source A

Adolf Hitler: The effect of his government's policies on German unemployment figures. (The number of unemployed in millions.)

Year	January	July
1932	6.042	5.392
1933	6.014	4.464
1934	3.773	2.426
1935	2.974	1.754
1936	2.520	1.170
1937	1.853	0.563
1938	1.052	0.218
1939	0.302	0.038

Source: Gebhardt, Bruno. 1959. *Handbuch der Deutschen Geschichte*, vol. 4. Stuttgart, Germany. Union Deutsche Verlagsgesellschaft. p. 352.

Source B

Fidel Castro: The first 100 days.

Within one hundred days of his victorious march into Havana, Castro drove the Mafia out of Cuba and closed down the casinos. He cracked down on crimes related to the gambling industry, such as drug sales and prostitution.

Castro also brought down the cost of living for the poor. He raised the lowest salaries and lowered rents for impoverished people. He nationalized (imposed government control over) Cuba's utility companies, including U.S.-owned companies, such as the national telephone system. He began sending Cubans who could read to teacher those (mostly in rural areas) who could not. He moved many doctors from the cities to rural areas to treat the poor and began new medical programs to train others.

Source: Markel, R. 2008. *Fidel Castro's Cuba*. Minneapolis, USA. Twenty First Century Books. p. 85

Source-based questions

1 How would the facts revealed by these sources contribute to the regime's consolidation of power?

2 Locate and explain similar examples from other totalitarian regimes.

Other methods to attract support demonstrated a significant use of the media and other avenues for communication such as education and the arts. The objective is not only to publicize the programme of the new party but to emphasize its unique, revolutionary, progressive and overall beneficial nature. The propaganda machine needs to continually emphasize the value of the new programme and to destroy any credibility attached to the work of previous regimes. This message is not only communicated through the traditional media but is made part of the school curriculum and becomes the subject of state-supported arts.

Another aspect of this campaign is to focus on the leader as the source of these wonderful new ideas. This builds the mythology of the leader as all-knowing, visionary, inspired and uniquely qualified to address the needs of the nation. This image of the leader lays the groundwork for the cult of personality and is one of the most powerful methods by which a leader can retain power in society.

A key method of attracting support is to get public endorsement from powerful and respected individuals or groups in society. Hitler was careful to gain the support of the German military whose prestige was unequalled and whose support would give him the respect and authority he needed. Mussolini discovered that he needed to reach an accord with the Vatican if he was to avoid a serious confrontation that would lessen his support from the Italian people.

Repressing opponents

Single-party states emerge in periods of conflict and crisis—the single party often takes power from the existing government in a violent way. This means that substantial pockets of opposition may remain or will develop when the leader seeks to implement his policies.

In order for the new regime to consolidate and retain power it must be prepared to take firm steps to identify and eliminate all sources of opposition. These opponents will be found both outside and inside the new ruling party

Potential sources of opposition must first be identified and then eliminated by forceful threats and intimidation. These opponents will be found both outside and inside the leader's organization or party.

Source analysis

Source A

Following the Enabling Act, Hitler was able to pass unopposed the Law for the Restoration of the Professional Civil Service, 7 April 1933.

> DA Purge of the Civil Service:
>
> Officials who are of non-aryan descent are to be placed in retirement.
>
> Officials whose past political activity does not furnish a guarantee that they will at all times identify themselves unreservedly with the national state may be dismissed from the service.

Source-based questions

1   Which groups are most crucial to control when a totalitarian regime takes power?

2   What methods besides force could be used to control potential opponents?

Source B

Cuba: Castro controls the unions.

> *Castro also checked the power of Cuban institutions. For example, he cast a wary eye on trade unions. He knew these unions had the potential to quickly rally large numbers of workers against him, so he looked for ways to weaken them. Anti-Communist labor leaders were told to unite with Communists for the sake of the unity needed to sustain the revolution. The Communists were well practiced at infiltrating and overtaking unions once they were admitted. Castro used these tactics to make sure he had loyal followers within all of Cuba's main labor unions.*

Source: Markel, R. 2008. *Fidel Castro's Cuba*. Minneapolis, USA. Twenty First Century Books. p. 89.

Activity:

Adolf Hitler's rise to power

Make a timeline of Hitler's steps to the consolidation of power.

Include some of these dates, and explain their significance.

30 January 1933	Hitler becomes chancellor of Germany
28 February 1933	Reichstag Fire Decree
5 March 1933	Reichstag election. Communists and Social Democrats largely excluded (Nazis gain 44% of the vote)
23 March 1933	Enabling Act passed
7 April 1933	Reform of Civil Service law passed, removes Jews and dissidents from public office
2 May 1933	Weimar Republic trade unions outlawed
10 May 1933	Nazi German Labour Front founded
20 July 1933	The Roman Catholic Church signs a Concordat with the Nazi Government
29 June 1934	Night of the Long Knives.

Questions

Review the timeline for Hitler's consolidation of power

1   How much of a mandate did Hitler receive from the electorate?

2   How did his regime eliminate the sources of opposition?

3   What forms of repressive behaviour proved most effective?

Groups which may be a source of opposition

Groups outside the party structure that may become sources of opposition:

- political parties
- social classes
- trade unions
- religious groups
- media organizations
- armed forces/police
- businessmen
- local or state governments.

Opponents inside the new ruling party:

- rivals for the leadership
- dissident factions
- philosophical opponents

The new regime uses all the methods at its disposal to eliminate sources of opposition. These may take a quasi-legal form which bans other political parties or restricts civil liberties. The transformation of the police and the courts to seize and prosecute suspected dissidents is a familiar tactic in single-party states. Laws are rewritten to prohibit any behaviour which the regime opposes and to legitimize any and all forms of punishment for enemies of the state. Hitler's first concentration camps were designed for communists, trade unionists and members of rival political parties. The state makes use of any and all means of intimidation to ensure that no challenges to their power can be successfully organized.

The leader also makes use of internal party purges to maintain authority. Famous examples of this are the Night of the Long Knives in Nazi Germany, Stalin's purges and the Cultural Revolution organized by Mao.

Some of the methods are listed below and others may be added depending on the regime studied:

- arrest and detention of members of rival or dissident groups
- execution/deportation of supporters of rival groups or factions
- closing and disbandment of specific organizations
- seizure of property and financial assets of opponents
- laws prohibiting certain organizations to exist
- propaganda to destroy the credibility of political opponents.

The leader may use these methods from the outset but they are not enough on their own. It is crucial to emphasize that a significant degree of popular support or at least acquiescence is essential if a regime is to retain power for any period of time. Sometimes this requires a degree of subterfuge to obtain results that resemble a popular movement. Hitler was able to achieve single-party rule following the passing of the **Enabling Act**, officially called the "Law for Removing the Distress of the People". The "distress" had been caused by the Nazis themselves, who burnt down the Reichstag building and blamed the communists. Enlisting the support of the army, who rallied for far-reaching measures to guarantee public

Enabling Act An enabling act is legislation that authorizes a government or organization to take certain immediate actions. An Enabling Act was passed by Germany's Reichstag and signed by president Paul von Hindenburg on March 23, 1933. It was the second major step, after the Reichstag Fire Decree, through which chancellor Adolf Hitler obtained the power to enact laws by decree (i.e. without requiring an act of parliament).

safety (as enshrined in the **Reichstag Fire Decree** issued on 28 February), the new legislation effectively enabled government without parliament.

Forms of government control

The structure of governments for single-party states is similar to that found in most countries. This occurs because the single party often takes over the existing structure of government but operates it in a different fashion. The government structure in these cases becomes much less important than the party structure and hierarchy. This is because the single-party state demands that all positions of importance be held by a member of the party. Because the party is a tightly organized and disciplined hierarchical organization, its members who hold government posts always carry out the wishes of the party in their government portfolios.

Joseph Stalin could control all government decisions and policies in the USSR because he was the head of the party which exercised rigid discipline over its members who occupied all key government posts. In revolutionary situations where the new party represents a major change in ideology, as occurred in China and Russia, some changes will be made to the existing governments—adding new ministries charged with carrying out the governments polices and programmes often in the area of economic and social change, education and security

These governments are all authoritarian in nature as explained in the theoretical models proposed by Castro, Friedrich and Brzezinski (see documents on pages 323–4). In addition to normal government functions and ministries, they rely on secret police and judicial systems whose sole job is to locate and punish dissent in any form. Some are clearly more efficient in the operation of an authoritarian state than others but the basic elements are present in all of them. To promote and reinforce the desired behaviour and attitudes among the general population, authoritarian states make extensive use of propaganda by taking control of the media and all avenues of communication to drive their message home.

Ideological differences

Single-party states are often classified as right wing or left wing and this gives the impression that their policies may be very different. In fact one should examine both their policies and their governmental structures to determine what, if any, real differences exist. One will see that they are very similar in their approach to many issues. Where do they differ? Right-wing governments may have a different approach to the ownership of property by individuals and they may emphasize nationalism more than the left. Left-wing regimes may adopt a crusading tone, a missionary task to spread the philosophy to other countries in the region. In practice, left-wing countries can also be very nationalistic as in the USSR and **Socialism in One Country of Stalin**. Right-wing states may also try to convert other countries to their message or a version of it, or assist those who sympathize with them as in the case of Hitler and Mussolini who assisted Franco. It is notable that right-wing governments, eager to assert control over economic activities, do in fact place limits on private property.

Reichstag Fire Decree Improvised on the day after the Reichstag fire, the decree invoked the authority of Article 48 of the Weimar Constitution which allowed the president to take any appropriate measure to remedy dangers to public safety. The decree consisted of six articles. Article 1 suspended most of the civil liberties set forth in the Weimar Constitution—freedom of the person, freedom of expression, freedom of the press, the right of free association and public assembly, the protection of private property and the secrecy of the post and telephone. Articles 2 and 3 allowed the Reich government to assume powers normally reserved for the federal states. Articles 4 and 5 established severe penalties for certain offences, including the death penalty for arson to public buildings. Article 6 simply declared that the decree was to take immediate effect.

Socialism in One Country Stalin's 1924 policy opposed Trotsky support for revolution in the industrial countries of Europe. Stalin accepted that world revolution had not taken place and was unlikely to occur in the near future. He proposed that a socialist state be constructed in the USSR to demonstrate the superiority of socialism and act as a model for other countries. This policy appealed strongly to Russian nationalism and recognized that efforts to build socialism in the Soviet Union would require considerable resources that should not be dissipated by supporting revolutions in other countries. After the expulsion of Trotsky from the Party and the USSR this became the official Soviet policy.

The extent of opposition

The extent of the opposition is often hard to measure because it is illegal and of necessity an underground or hidden movement, subject to repression. Occasionally, opposition to single-party states is overt as in assassination attempts, mass protests or marches and the defection of prominent individuals to other countries. These examples are relatively rare as the government reaction to such events is usually draconian in nature. Individuals or groups who risk public protest will be subject to harsh reprisals as may their families, ethnic group, and anyone with whom they are associated.

The degree of opposition groups will vary and will depend on not merely the institutionalization of conformity as demonstrated in George Orwell's novel *1984* (see extract) but also on the degree of popularity of the regime. Many single-party states come into power with elaborate promises to improve conditions in a number of areas. To the extent that they are successful, they will see their opposition reduced. Hitler was extremely popular in the early years of the Nazi regime because he had cured the unemployment crisis and had successfully redeemed his promises to overthrow Versailles and return Germany to a position of importance. Mao gained great popularity by instituting land reform when he acquired power and by a host of social reforms aimed at removing the burdens on ordinary people. Castro moved quickly to promote land reform, education and health programmes and to inspire a sense of pride in many Cubans.

This popularity may diminish over time as the promised changes either do not appear or fail to satisfy expectations. Mistakes by the party which lead to mass hardship, defeat in war etc. may lay the basis for opposition to develop. External opposition or the emergence of new ideas and movements may encourage groups within the country to consider opposing the regime in some form.

The treatment of opposition in single-party states is always in some form repressive. The degree of repression will be directly proportional to the insecurity of the regime, the degree to which it feels threatened or the personal characteristics of the leader and his fear of rivals. Stalin purged many individuals and eliminated popular members of the party (such as Sergei Kirov) because he was concerned that they would try to replace him.

All single-party states have networks of secret police, surveillance and informers to identify and punish anyone suspected of opposition. As no trials are held, opponents can be condemned on suspicion alone, which deters most people from taking part in any active intervention. Citizens are further encouraged to watch each other and act as agents of the regime in reporting suspicious activity, as was the case with the Spanish Inquisition and more recent examples of mass condemnation. Single-party states rely to a large degree on this phenomenon to identify opponents or suspected opponents. This reduces the need for police and other surveillance techniques as many individuals will gladly act as informants. The reasons for this include self-preservation (to divert suspicion from oneself by pointing at others), a fanatic devotion to the regime encouraged by propaganda (brainwashing), or a desire to settle scores with others against whom you may have a grudge of a non-political nature.

Source analysis

Source A

Stalinist Russia: The rationale behind the mass terror.

The principles and aims of mass terror have nothing in common with ordinary police work or with security. The only purpose of terror is intimidation. To plunge the whole country into a state of chronic fear, the number of victims must be raised to astronomical levels, and on every floor of every building there must always be several apartments from which the tenants have suddenly been taken away. The remaining inhabitants will be model citizens for the rest of their lives–this will be true for every street and every city through which the broom has swept. The only essential thing for those who rule by terror is not to overlook the new generations growing up without faith in their elders, and to keep on repeating the process in systematic fashion. Stalin ruled for a long time and saw to it that the waves of terror recurred from time to time, always on an even greater scale than before.

Source: Mandelstam, N. 1971. *Hope Abandoned.* London, UK. Collins Harvill Press. pp. 316–17.

Source-based questions

1   How does Source A support the idea in Source B?
2   Has terror been successfully implemented in the description in Source A? What about Source B?

Source B

Extract from George Orwell's novel *1984.*

"Ah well–what I meant to say, shows the right spirit, doesn't it?–mischievous little beggars they are, both of them, but talk about keenness! All they think about is the Spies, and the war, of course. D'you know what that little girl of mine did last Saturday, when her troop was on a hike out Berkhamsted way? She got two other girls to go with her, slipped off from the hike, and spent the whole afternoon following a strange man. They kept on his tail for two hours, right through the woods, and then, when they got into Amersham, handed him over to the patrols."

"What did they do that for?" said Winston, somewhat taken aback. Parson went on triumphantly:

"My kid made sure he was some kind of enemy agent— might have been dropped by parachute, for instance. But here's the point, old boy. What do you think put her on to him in the first place? She spotted he was wearing a funny kind of shoes—said she'd never seen anyone wearing shoes like that before. So the chances were he was a foreigner. Pretty smart for a nipper of seven, eh?"

"What happened to the man?" said Winston.

"Ah, that I couldn't say, of course. But I wouldn't be altogether surprised if – –'" Parsons made the motion of aiming a rifle, and clicked his tongue for the explosion.

"Good," said Syme abstractedly, without looking up from his strip of paper.

"Of course we can't afford to take chances," agreed Winston dutifully.

Source: Orwell, George. 1949. *1984,* Bungay, UK. Penguin. p. 49

Examples of the reporting of dissidents can be found in George Orwell's novel *1984* in which children are encouraged to report on their parents for expressing anti-government sentiments. Further examples of this kind of community oversight and enforced conformity can be found in the **Street Committees** of Mao's China whose job it was to monitor and report suspicious activity as well as the Committees to Defend the Revolution of Castro's Cuba who reported any suspicious or unorthodox behaviour to the police. This is the ideal situation for suppression of opposition as the society, in essence, supervises itself and clamps down on any behaviour unacceptable to the regime.

The fear of denunciation and severe punishment creates an environment where no one can trust anyone else or is willing to express an opinion, even to family members. This makes it virtually impossible to organize any form of coherent resistance to the regime. Effective propaganda can be a key to encouraging such tactics to prevent the development of an opposition. The state repeatedly emphasizes loyalty and conformity and brands any other ideas as

Street Committees Neighbourhood organizations set up by the Chinese Communist government. Their job was to report on any suspicious (anti-government) behaviour by residents of a particular street or apartment complex. They constituted a network of informers that passed information to the government and enforced conformity on their friends and neighbours. In this way they helped the government's ability to control the population and identify dissidents. They also organized neighbourhood rallies and demonstrations in support of government policies and distributed government propaganda.

criminal and party to treason. This is particularly true in the education system and in youth groups where the regime seeks to inculcate its values and create automatic loyalty from an early age. Complete control of the media and total censorship of any and all forms of unfriendly communication means that opposition movements have very limited ways to transmit their messages.

Single-party states show little hesitation in using extremely harsh methods to dissuade or destroy opponents or suspected opponents. Opposition members may be imprisoned, tortured, exiled, executed or fined and can lose their citizenship status. A widespread way of punishing dissidents and discouraging others is to punish the family as well as the offender. This further encourages conformity. The often random nature of these punishments further instils fear in the population and encourages the utmost conformity and docility as the only way of avoiding devastating punishments.

Source analysis

Source A

With those children, he thought, that wretched woman must lead a life of terror. Another year, two years, and they would be watching her night and day for symptoms of unorthodoxy. Nearly all children nowadays were horrible. What was worst of all was that by means of such organizations as the Spies they were systematically turned into ungovernable little savages, and yet this produced in them no tendency whatever to rebel against the discipline of the Party. On the contrary, they adored the Party and everything connected with it. The songs, the processions, the banners, the hiking, the drilling with dummy rifles, the yelling of slogans, the worship of Big Brother—it was all a sort of glorious game to them. All their ferocity was turned outwards, against the enemies of the State, against foreigners, traitors, saboteurs, thought-criminals. It was almost normal for people over thirty to be frightened of their own children. And with good reason, for hardly a week passed in which The Times *did not carry a paragraph describing how some eavesdropping little sneak— "child hero" was the phrase generally used—had overheard some compromising remark and denounced its parents to the Thought Police.*

The sting of the catapult bullet had worn off. He picked up his pen half-heartedly, wondering whether he could find something more to write in the diary. Suddenly he began thinking of O'Brien again.

Source: Orwell, George. 1949. *1984*. Bungay, UK. Penguin. p. 23.

Source-based questions

1 Why have children been made agents of the state?
2 What does this demonstrate about the desire of the state to eliminate opposition?
3 Do these methods identify an actual opposition?

Structure and philosophy of government

Totalitarian states do not often have structures that differ significantly from the government of a democracy. They have all the trappings of democracies: legislatures, constitutions, elections. This may give them a somewhat benign or less repressive appearance. The differences are in the way the government organizes the various arms of government and the philosophy or values that determine government policies. In these societies, the exercise of power and decision making do not reside in the normal organs of government. Power resides entirely in the hands of the leader and the single political party. This party represents a small elite of society—probably not more than five per cent of the population. The party is a hierarchical organization with rigid military-style discipline that obeys the orders of the leader or his immediate associates. (Failure to obey or any sign of disloyalty by party members is severely punished as was seen in Germany, Russia, China, Cuba and many other totalitarian states.)

The party which has seized power simply takes over the existing government structure, evicts the previous office holders and replaces them with party members. This allows the party to use the machinery of government: police, courts, banks, tax collectors and armed forces to implement its policies. All key government officials are party members and, as such, obey directives from the leader without question Legislatures, constitutions etc. are mere window dressing in these circumstances as they can only operate according to the dictates of the party. No dissent is permitted, all opponents have been silenced and there are no competitive sources of power or influence. There is after all only one party so elections, legislatures etc. are obviously hollow structures.

All totalitarian states operate in this way—they all have similar government structures—which on the surface appear familiar to us but operate in a very different way to democratic societies. Everyone is conscious that the decision-making power lies in the party hierarchy and that government posts are of little value if one is not also a member of the party. Party members can exercise great influence over local officials and non-party civil servants as they have connections to the true sources of power. This means that in a single-party state the way to power, influence, wealth and social status lies through the party hierarchy.

Economic policies

Single-party states all seek to direct the economy of their country in an attempt to achieve or support their ideological or political goals. In a single-party state, all goals are state oriented and in some measure state directed. The development, focus and direction of the economy is crucial to fulfilling the broader objectives of the regime. These may include improvements in living standards, modernization, industrialization, or improved defence.

To support this, single-party states develop some form of planning of economic activity which is overseen by a party or government agency and has very specific goals. The obvious examples are the Five Year plans that originated in the Soviet Union and were then used in other communist states, the Four Year plan of Nazi Germany or the Great Leap Forward of Mao's China. The goals of these plans may vary but they all have a similar objective: to direct economic activity to serve the needs of the state and the political or ideological goals of the party in power.

Source analysis

An article written in 1931 by Stalin in which he justifies the pace of industrial development.

It is sometimes asked whether it is not possible to slow down the tempo a bit, to put a check on the movement. No, comrades, it is not possible! The tempo must not be reduced! On the contrary we must increase it as much as is within our powers and possibilities. This is dictated to us by our obligations to the workers and peasants of the USSR. This is dictated to us by our obligations to the working class of the whole world.

To slacken the tempo would mean falling behind. And those who fall behind get beaten. But we do not want to be beaten. No, we refuse to be beaten! One feature of the history of old Russia was the continual beatings she suffered for falling behind, for her backwardness … for military backwardness, for cultural backwardness, for political backwardness, for industrial backwardness, for agricultural backwardness. She was beaten because to do so was profitable and could be done with impunity … It is the jungle law of capitalism. You are backward, you are weak–therefore you are wrong; hence, you can be beaten and enslaved. You are mighty–therefore you are right; hence, we must be wary of you. That is why we must no longer lag behind. …

Do you want our socialist fatherland to be beaten and to lose its independence? If you do not want this you must put an end to its backwardness in the shortest possible time and develop a genuine Bolshevik tempo in building up its socialist system of economy. There is no other way. That is why Lenin said during the October Revolution: "Either perish, or overtake and outstrip the advanced capitalist countries."

We are 50 or 100 years behind the advanced countries. We must make good this distance in ten years. Either we do it, or they crush us.

Source: Laver, John. 1991. *Russia 1914–1941*. London, UK. Hodder and Stoughton. pp. 60–1.

Source-based questions

1 How does this demonstrate the role of the economy in fulfilling a number of goals of the totalitarian state?

2 Why is war metaphor used in the document?

These plans are also the method by which a regime will seek to fulfil the economic promises that it made to the population during the period when it was trying to acquire power. These may include such things as land reform, nationalization of foreign property, or the introduction of new industries or employment opportunities.

The impacts of these plans may be very extensive over time: peasant societies may be industrialized and urbanized much faster than under normal conditions; property ownership may be dramatically altered or eliminated; massive infrastructure developments may alter the country physically but also provide an entire new range of public services in education, health and housing. In other ways the standard of living of a society may suffer a decline if these plans involve the diversion of resources into government projects which do not directly serve consumers. This would include defence spending, and large capital projects.

The overall success or failure of these economic polices in reaching their goals will have a large influence on the ability of the regime to carry out its broader objectives or even to retain power. The USSR was not able to develop enough economic strength to improve the standard of living at home and maintain a vigorous defence and foreign policy. This economic failure contributed to the ultimate collapse of the regime. The failures of the economic system of Mao's China required a major change in direction if the Communist party were to continue to retain power in China. Similarly Hitler's Four Year Plan did not succeed in providing the necessary economic strength to sustain a lengthy war effort.

Social policies

All single-party states have some ideas about the nature, form and direction that their society should have. Some states may wish to maintain or impose a traditional model which looks to the past for its forms and practices.

This is the case in right-wing or conservative regimes which seek to create or recreate what they see as a previous golden age. This model usually supports traditional values in relation to the status of men and women, family life, education, moral values, occupations, class structure and hierarchy. Respect for tradition and authority, nationalism, racism and suspicion of liberal or progressive ideas are common.

Left-wing or radical states would tend to support more progressive social ideas. These might include: gender equality, elimination of social classes, looking to the future rather than back to the past for inspiration. More liberal treatment of minorities, the poor and other traditionally lower-ranked individuals is a common concern.

All single-party states, whether traditional or progressive, engage in extensive social engineering in which they seek to produce citizens whose values are consistently and automatically those of the state. They will carry out the aims of the state with minimal supervision as they have been conditioned to conform to its strictly articulated guidelines.

Source analysis

The egalitarian state

In a speech made in Berlin on 1 May 1937 Hitler claims to have broken with the old class system.

We in Germany have really broken with a world of prejudices. I leave myself out of account. I, too, am a child of the people; I do not trace my line from any castle: I come from the workshop. Neither was I a general: I was simply a soldier, as were millions of others. It is something wonderful that amongst us an unknown from the army of the millions of German people—of workers and of soldiers—could rise to be head of the Reich and of the nation. By my side stand Germans from all walks of life who today are amongst the leaders of the nation: men who once were workers on the land are now governing German states in the name of the Reich. … It is true that men who came from the bourgeoisie and former aristocrats have their place in this Movement. But to us it matters nothing whence they come if only they can work to the profit of our people. That is the decisive test. We have not broken down classes in order to set new ones in their place: we have broken down classes to make way for the German people as a whole.

Source: Baynes, N.(ed.). 1942. *The Speeches of Adolf Hitler, April 1922 – August 1939*. London, UK. Oxford University Press. pp. 620–1.

Question

What is the Nazi's social goal as expressed in this document?

Mao attempted through the Great Leap Forward and the Cultural Revolution to construct a new socialist man. This individual would act as a true socialist, always consider others first—and would always work to support the group rather than self-interest. This would take away the desire for personal profit or gain that undermined the movement towards a true Communist state. A similar experiment was undertaken in the early 1960s in Cuba, as in other left-wing states that formulated policies to modify the behaviour of their populations.

In addition to supporting psychological changes, single-party states may also seek to create a genetically ideal society based on a particular racial or ethnic group. Such examples of genetic and social engineering supported the creation of a society of racially pure and/or physically perfect specimens of humanity. This was clearly the goal of the various eugenics experiments and policies of the Nazis, whose desire for perfection led to campaigns to eliminate those who were physically or mentally deficient. The euthanasia campaign was not racially motivated but was brought on by a desire to eliminate any genetic weakness in the Aryan gene pool.

Many single-party states display elements of racism, either in an overt way as in the case of the Nazis and others who support genetic purity, or through more targeted forms of discrimination. Such extremism can lead to genocidal or other forms of racially motivated violence against distinct social groups. The various types of discrimination or social exclusion can be particularly harsh on minority groups.

TOK link

Integrating ways of knowing—emotion and reason

TOK is ideally placed to embody many of the attributes in the IB Learner Profile that promote self-awareness, reflection, critical thinking, empathy and a sense of personal responsibility.

Reason is the way in which people construct meaning and justify knowledge claims. As such, it is appropriate to consider which elements of these ways of knowing might be present in the motives and actions of the leaders of single-party states.

Mao talked about creating a "new socialist man" as did Castro in Cuba. Other single-party state leaders have been strongly motivated to change people's attitudes and outlook. None of the single-party state leaders was able to bring about the degree of change that they sought.

All totalitarian rulers have, ultimately, been unsuccessful in achieving their goals in the long term. Societies have also had to endure long and painful struggles to undo the harm that repressive regimes create as a legacy.

The perpetrators of repressive actions and policies also suffer serious consequences in later life—not least, being ostracized and exiled from the very societies they tried to influence and contain.

TOK questions

1 Are these motivations to control and influence other human beings based on reason, emotion, natural instincts or learned behaviour?

2 What specific outcomes did these leaders wish to achieve through modifying attitudes and behaviour?

3 Is it realistic to think that human behaviour can be modified in a short period of time?

4 How would you explain the difficulty in changing people's social, cultural and economic attitudes? What would be the best method to induce human beings to change?

5 How do people experience living in a totalitarian state? What advantages are there? What are the disadvantages? What happens to a society when the regime fails?

Integrating areas of knowledge—human sciences and ethics

Ethics involves a discussion of the way in which we live our lives, and justify our actions. Judging the past requires us to understand the specific historical circumstances that conditioned people's actions and responses to events.

It also gives us the opportunity to reflect upon our own attitudes towards race, gender and class (for example) as determined by our own present social circumstances. We have the benefit of hindsight, and also the privilege perhaps of looking back on events from a safe distance!

In totalitarian states the positions of minorities, both ethnic and religious, was often difficult or dangerous.

1 The focus of Nazi Germany on achieving a racially pure state did not allow for the presence of undesirable racial, cultural or genetically "inferior" elements.

   ● What policies were used to achieve such a racially pure state?
   ● What scientific knowledge informed the goal of racial purity?
   ● What ethical issues arose from these goals?
   ● Are the same issues present when the policy is applied to plants and animals?

2 Many states were aware of the Nazi racial policies towards minority groups but took no action to protect the persecuted.

● Why would other nations not take action to help the victims?
● Was this an ethical position to take?
● Have views on this issue changed in the past 50 years? What is the evidence for this?

3 Many but not all totalitarian states have engaged in a variety of campaigns to eliminate or severely control minority groups.

   ● What do you see as the motives for this behaviour?
   ● Are democratic states less likely to engage in these discriminatory practices? If so why?
   ● Has this always been the case or have we seen changes in policies in democracies during the 20th century?

Communication strategies

Education, the arts and media, are all aspects of communication by which single-party regimes seek to deliver their message and prevent the transmission of opposing views. This begins with the young in schools and continues through the control of the media and all forms of entertainment. It involves both a negative function (censorship) and an active function (propaganda) and supported through the creation of various art forms to reinforce the message.

In essence the regime allows only one legitimate source of media, curriculum development and cultural practice. All of these sources of information must be monitored by the central authority so that they can convey the appropriate messages, values and images in support of the regime and its leader.

Education policies

Public education in the Western world began in the 19th century and was soon recognized as an excellent vehicle through which to inculcate the values of the society into young people in whom the effect would be most lasting. States controlled the curricula, reading materials, discipline, organization etc. in order to create citizens who were patriotic, disciplined, docile, well-trained and supportive of the values of the state.

Single-party states are no different in their approach to education except that they may pursue the goal more openly and aggressively than democracies. They want to use education and all activities associated with youth to instill, as deeply as possible, the values, goals and ideology of the society. A loyal, disciplined, obedient citizenry is the goal—one that accepts without question the party, the leader and their objectives. Single-party states rewrite curricula, control all books and education materials, and eliminate unreliable teachers in an attempt to make students accept the mainstream point of view.

All school and youth activities are organized to support the goals and values of the regime, be it political loyalty, physical fitness, military training or acceptance of a traditional role in society for girls and young women. Devotion to the regime rather than friends and family is often made a key part of the psychological conditioning of young people—the state becomes the family and the focus of their loyalty. The process of indoctrination involves extensive efforts to rewrite school curricula and retrain or eliminate unco-operative teachers.

The constant insertion of messages, both subtle and overt, in school curricula lays the groundwork for later control. It is assumed that students instilled with these values at a young age will become obedient followers of the regime later in life. To the extent that schools have often been a vehicle for the inculcation of values and norms— single-party states seek to use the provision for public education as an even stronger mechanism for maximizing social control.

Extra-curricular education is also crucial in promoting the regime's values and programs.

Source analysis

Source A

From official instructions on the teaching of history, issued by the German Central Institute of Education, 1938.

The Teaching of History

The German nation in its essence and greatness, in its fateful struggle for internal and external identify is the subject of the teaching of history. It is based on the natural bond of the child with his nation and, by interpreting history as the fateful struggle for existence between the nations, has the particular task of educating young people to respect the great German past and to have faith in the mission and future of their own nation and to respect the right of existence of other nations.

Source B

Questions from mathematics textbooks published in the 1930s.

Some Maths Problems

The construction of the lunatic asylum costs 6 million RM. How many houses at 15,000 RM each could have been built for that amount?

A modern night bomber can carry 1,800 incendiaries. How long (in kilometres) is the path along which it can distribute these bombs if it drops a bomb every second at a speed of 250 km per hour? How far apart are the craters from one another? … How many fires are caused if 1/3 of the bombs hit their targets and of these 1/3 ignite?

Source: Laver, John. 1991. *Nazi Germany 1933–45*. London, UK. Hodder and Stoughton. p. 44.

Propaganda

Single-party states understand the value of propaganda that supports their rise to power. The techniques are not dissimilar to modern advertising methods which include the creation of simple, catchy slogans that can be repeated, chanted and learned even by the young or uneducated. Lenin's "Peace, Land and Bread" is a classic as are the messages of Hitler and others. Propaganda is used to support the regime in power both through promoting its essential messages and values and the form of its delivery. The Nazi control of the radio is a crucial example of the power of a medium and the uses which it might serve. Today it is TV, and the growing power of the Internet, that provide the instant vehicle for the mass dissemination of ideas.

Controlling these powerful devices prevents alternative, conflicting opinions from reaching the broad public. Therefore all totalitarian states move quickly to monopolize the media and limit access to broadcasting any messages other than their own It is crucial to control and mobilize all forms of culture and art in the service of the state. This means that everything from plays, movies, paintings, statues, books and writing must be censored and integrated to support the message. Artists who refuse to conform or criticize the regime will not be given opportunities to exhibit or present their work, and could be imprisoned or exiled. No one will be able to possess or display works of art that are inconsistent with the message of the state.

The ideal Aryan Family. Poster issued by the Office of Racial Politics of the NSDAP, 1938 [Kalendar der rassenpolitischen Amtes der NSDAP, 1938].

In Nazi Germany, Soviet Russia, Maoist China and other totalitarian regimes art was brought into the service of the state to reflect its essential themes and messages. This idea of the public role of art has been with us for a long time. Artistic freedom and individualism are new and far-from universal concepts. Through much of human history, artists have had to work in support of the state, religion or other ruling powers and wealthy patrons.

Status of women

All single-party states have policies that relate to the status of women. These polices are usually consistent with the general direction of their broader social polices and will reflect the intent of those policies. In conservative or right-wing states such as Nazi Germany, women's status may undergo some change and is most likely be in the direction of restoring women to the traditional role of wife, mother and housekeeper. They will be discouraged from seeking employment and will have limited access to education or influential positions in society. Not a single member of the Nazi hierarchy was a woman. This was an attempt to reverse the trend in women's emancipation that had been developing in the 19th and 20th centuries. Women had the vote and were beginning to be accepted into the professions and in political organizations.

"Work hard during harvest time and you'll be rewarded with plenty of bread." 1947 poster.

Left-wing societies, which consider themselves to be socially revolutionary, extend this concept to the status of women. They make statements and pass laws declaring the equality of women, giving them citizenship, property and voting rights and eliminating traditional practices such as arranged marriages. Prominent examples can be found in china after 1949, and Cuba in the 1960s when the status of women was altered by legislation and declarations of policy.

The impact of both right-wing and left-wing policies on women's lives is difficult to quantify. The extent to which they have been successful in their goals varies widely and is determined by a number of circumstances. The Nazi attempt to reverse a trend in Western society had very limited effect. This was partly due to the fact that they were only in power for 12 years, and that half of this term was taken up by the Second World War by which time women had proved themselves to be too indispensible to remove from the workforce. In effect the Nazi's were going against the tide of a movement that existed not only in Germany but across Western Europe and America.

Left-wing regimes have tended to provide women with more concrete rights at least in the form of legislation. Many traditional restrictions have been removed and women have gained access to education and occupations previously closed to them. In addition, they have gained control over their own lives in relation to marriage, divorce, property and inheritance. What has been more difficult to change is the attitudes of men towards women. Many women still suffer from discrimination, harassment and limited access to positions of power. This is the result of the fact that while laws have changed, social values have not or not as quickly. This is the case in all societies but may be compounded in single-party states by the lack of democracy, inhibiting opportunities to exert political pressure on governments or express alternative viewpoints.

Source analysis

Women's place in the Nazi state

In his address to women at the Nuremberg party rally on 8 September 1934, Hitler summed up the Nazi view of woman's position in society.

> *If one says that man's world is the State, his struggle, his readiness to devote his powers to the service of the community, one might be tempted to say that the world of woman is a smaller world. For her world is her husband, her family, her children and her house. But where would the greater world be if there were no one to care for the small world? … Providence has entrusted to women the cares of that world which is peculiarly her own. … Every child that a woman brings into the world is a battle, a battle waged for the existence of her people.*

Source: Baynes, N. (ed.) 1942. *The speeches of Adolf Hitler: April 1922 – August 1939*. London, UK. Oxford University Press. pp. 528-9.

The 1950 Marriage Law in Communist China

One of the first laws passed by the new government was the Marriage Law which made women the legal equals of men. It was promulgated on 1 May 1950.

> **GENERAL PRINCIPLES:**
>
> *Article 1. The arbitrary and compulsory feudal marriage system, the supremacy of man over woman, and disregard of the interests of children is abolished.*
>
> *The new democratic marriage system, which is based on the free choice of partners, on monogamy, on equal rights for both sexes, and on the protection of the lawful interests of women and children, is put into effect.*
>
> *Article 2. Bigamy, concubinage, child betrothal, interference in the marriage of widows, and the exaction of money or gifts in connection with marriages, are prohibited.*

Source: Benson, L. 2002. *China since 1949*. London, UK. Pearson. p. 93.

Source-based questions

1 What is the difference in attitudes towards women shown here?
2 What obstacles to the implementation of these ideas might be encountered?

Religious policies

Single-party states seek to either eliminate or subjugate existing religious institutions or organizations. This is fundamental to their goals as authoritarian states in a number of ways. Religions represent rival ideologies, value systems, and concepts of ethics and morality. Single-party states wish to impose their own values, ideology, philosophy and world views. They cannot and will not accept any deviation or doubt that their message is the only one and must be followed by all citizens.

Religious organizations also represent rival power groups in that they possess property, hierarchical structures, an economic base, communication skills and education systems as well as an active role as providers of services to the population. These services in support of welfare, charity, education, youth and other community groups make them rivals to a single-party state which seeks to control such activities. Their traditions, wealth and infrastructure helped religious groups to mount a challenge to the single-party state. Religious groups also have international connections and may receive support either spiritual or physical from powerful countries and individuals such as the pope. Attacks on religious groups may be condemned in other countries. This could be a disadvantage to the regime in undermining its international credibility.

The success of single-party states in eliminating or controlling previously existing religions varies widely. The USSR launched a draconian assault on the Russian Orthodox Church after the October revolution. It might be assumed that this was inspired by the Marxist condemnation of religion as the opiate of the masses. In fact, the church was a target in Russia because it was an official arm of the tsarist government and thus associated with oppression in the eyes of many. Under Stalin, the church was outlawed, priests were killed, buildings and treasures demolished and confiscated. Nevertheless the Soviet state was not able to extirpate the church entirely—ironically Stalin was forced to resurrect the church during the Second World War in a desperate attempt to gain the loyalty of Russian society when the Germans invaded. This was a clear recognition that the church still maintained a hold on many citizens, possibly because it provided the emotional solace that a brutal regime was unable to provide. The rapid reappearance of the church after the fall of the Soviet Union is a testament to its continued role in the lives of many Russians.

Mussolini was never able to control or subjugate the Roman Catholic Church as its hold in Italy was very deep and the presence of the pope in Vatican City created a powerful and outspoken opponent who could not be easily controlled. Mussolini sought a truce with the Church which helped to buttress his regime by removing internal opposition. The Church entered into the **Lateran Treaty** to preserve its position, and influence in the lives of the people while leaving politics to the state. The Church of Rome was in fact sympathetic to Mussolini's anti-communism.

Lateran Treaty This is one of the Lateran Accords made in 1929 between the Kingdom of Italy and the Holy See. It recognized the sovereignty of Vatican City, recognizing the rights of the Roman Catholic Church in Italy and made a financial payment to the Church as compensation for lost property. This treaty was important as it removed a source of opposition to Mussolini and gained him greater support from the church which was a powerful force in Italy.

The story in Nazi Germany is less clear and of course limited by the fact that the regime was only in power for 12 years. Hitler wished to suppress the Christian churches and replace them with his own religion inspired by the ancient Teutonic gods of German mythology. In order to solidify his power in the early years, he had reached a Concordat with the Catholic hurch and its political wing to help him pass the Enabling Act. Many Christian churches had supported him in the early years as he seemed to share some of their values such as anti-communism, nationalism and a return to traditional social structures. They also realized that by seeking a political accommodation in the short-term they might avoid persecution and survive what they hoped would be a temporary storm in the form of Nazism.

Many single-party states seek to establish their own version of religious worship through adoting some of the rituals, liturgies, ceremonies, images and mysteries associated with established religion. They create or reintroduce past traditions in an attempt to provide alternative spiritual models for the population. They may also assign mystical or god-like qualities to the leader. The purpose of these new creations is to satisfy the human need for psychological engagement and the emotional support provided by religious belief. Associating the regime with spiritual beliefs creates enthusiasm for the new state and its goals. An attempt to create a new religion in support of a new authoritarian society was also devised at the time of the French revolution and in the Nazi period where there was an attempt to resurrect the gods of ancient Teutonic folklore to inspire the population and give credence to the goals of the regime.

This new religious foundation may be personified through the cult of personality, through which the leader assumes the omnipotent and omniscient qualities of a deity. This was very much the case with Joseph Stalin and Mao Zedong who actively cultivated this image of themselves. This was not merely vanity but an effective method of maintaining control and preventing any viable opposition—they became irreplaceable, infallible, unapproachable and as such could not be evicted from power. Societies were conditioned to believe that like gods in the past, everything flowed from them and was dependent on them. The existence of such an individual creates a spiritual focus in the society as an object of worship and devotion to replace former religious icons.

Minorities

A discussion of policies towards minorities normally addresses ethnic or religious minorities. This is where most of the attention has been focused because of the Holocaust and the persecution of ethnic minorities in the Soviet Union, China and other states. It should be noted, however that other groups which might be classified as social minorities are also the objects or targets of single-party state policies. These would include homosexuals, mentally and emotionally challenged individuals and people with physical disabilities other than war-related injuries. The treatment of minorities will vary from state to state and will depend on the ideological nature of the regime or whether it sees minorities as a negative influence.

Regimes with a strong nationalist or racial emphasis will discriminate against and seek to eliminate minorities. This may be the result of their ideological or political beliefs or because they wish to gain favour with the majority who oppose the minority. Minorities are also subject to discrimination because they are seen by single-party states as representing alternative social or political philosophies that may conflict with the views of the regime. They may also have leaders whose appeal or charisma might be seen as a threat to the dominance of the party leader.

Minorities, by their presence, may impede the desire to create a uniform culture, language or ideal racial type in the society. The desire to create a standard, uniform culture is a common aspiration of single-party states as they do not wish to give credence to alternative societies. Tolerance for different cultures or the acceptance of a multicultural state is therefore rare. The Soviet Union imposed strict policies of Russification which banned the use of any language but Russian and forbade the celebration of any culture other than Russian. Non-Russian people were regarded as inferior, potentially disloyal or incapable of leadership.

In many single-party states where minorities continue to exist, they are often placed in inferior positions legally and socially. The regime establishes a form of racial hierarchy to indicate their lower status. This was the case in Nazi Germany and in China where non-Han Chinese such as Tibetans experience discrimination. Minorities may also be suppressed because they have links to groups or societies outside the country or seek guidance from external sources which may oppose the new regime. In extreme cases they might be regarded as saboteurs working on behalf of outside forces to undermine the new regime. During the Second World War, the USSR relocated many minority groups whom it felt might prove disloyal and ally themselves with the German invaders. These people lost their land, many died from the hardships of relocation and were forced to live in hostile conditions far from familiar places.

Activity:

Role models: Animal Farm

George Orwell's novel *Animal Farm* published in 1945 is an allegorical indictment of the Soviet Union as a single-party state. The insights may be used to analyse the rise to power and policies of a variety of authoritarian states.

Exercise

1   Draw up a table with headings to comment on techniques in support of the:

   - rise to power
   - role of ideology
   - emergence of a dominant leader
   - emergence of a party elite
   - consolidation of power
   - suppression of opponents
   - aspirations achieved.

   Fill out responses to the novel in one column, and responses to similar stages in the history of the USSR.

2   Add another column to carry out a third comparison with a single-party state of your own choosing.

3   Select one or more of the figures in the novel and compare them to an individual or individuals who played a role in a single-party state, as either the perpetrators or victims of oppression and authoritarian rule. Examine the characteristics of the fictional characters and determine how closely they resemble real individuals in terms of their actions and attitudes.

4   Stage a debate to analyse the statement that "All single-party states fail to remain true to the principles that they proclaimed when they were seeking power."

De-Stalinization, mature communism and political instability, 1953–81

Single-party states as totalitarian governments are a unique phenomenon of the 20th century. They are distinct from the monarchies and absolutist governments of earlier centuries in a number of ways. Totalitarian states, as the term implies, seek to establish total control of all aspects of their citizens lives as to both thoughts and deeds. Their ability to establish this unprecedented level of control has been made possible by modern technologies of surveillance and record-keeping which makes it impossible for individuals to escape identification. In addition, by harnessing the mass media in support of the state, totalitarian regimes were able to control or strongly influence the ideas, opinions and emotional life of its citizens. Such strategies can function as a form of subterfuge or distraction from the critical actions or inaction of governments. This phenomenon of the manipulation of public information, and the covering up and even promotion of state-sanctioned violence, distorting and altering society's core values, is vividly described in the fictional example of George Orwell's *1984*. It is true that some states have been more successful in controlling their citizens: Russia, China and Cuba are examples while others such as fascist Italy were less successful in the application of totalitarian methods.

Many single-party states have made attempts to go beyond the strict control of citizens' lives to fundamentally alter basic human psychology and behaviour patterns in an attempt to produce an entirely different form of society. This new society was supposed to fulfil a vision contained in the ideology of the single-party state or its leader. Examples of these experiments include the new socialist man proposed by Mao and Castro or the ideal Aryan society promoted by Hitler. It is typical of the degree of control and influence that these states have exerted over their populace that they think it possible to alter thousands of years of human development and behaviour patterns. It should be noted that all of these efforts ultimately failed to achieve their goals and often harmed the societies in which these experiments were tried. Thirty million Chinese died as a result of one of these experiments between 1958 and 1960 in the famine that followed the Great Leap Forward.

How did such societies emerge in the 20th century when humanity was better educated, more sophisticated and progressive in outlook? There are unique answers to this question in each totalitarian single-party state but the key fact is that they all share three key common denominators which can explain their emergence in each case. The first is the existence or emergence of some form of national crisis which creates the need or desire for a radical new form of government. These crises take various forms and may include the impact of war as in Russia, economic catastrophe as in Germany or Italy, the constraints of governments trying to hold onto traditional social structures as in China and Egypt or the collapse of a ruling power in Kenya and Indonesia. These crises and the fears and uncertainties that they promoted created opportunities for charismatic leaders equipped with new ideologies or political policies promising solutions to emerge. Whether it was the "Peace, Land and Bread" slogans of Lenin or the anti-colonial rhetoric of Kenyatta and Sukarno these new leaders had programmes that attracted wide political support. Their attempts to seize power were made easier in all cases by the ineptitude, inertia or weakness of those they challenged for power.

Once power has been obtained, it must be consolidated and made permanent. This means that all possible sources of opposition either in the form of individuals or organizations must be banned, exterminated or converted to the cause. Single-party state leaders often use the same methods to eliminate opposition: the concentration camp or gulag, persecution of minorities, secret police, informers and removal of all civil rights. In addition censorship and propaganda convert the masses as does the promulgation of popular programmes: job creation, territorial expansion, ethnic cleansing to name a few. No single-party state can permit the existence of any form of opposition if it is to achieve total control over the population.

The policies that single-party states enact when they achieve power may be thought to differ through the espousal of ideologies that are either right-wing (such as fascism) or left-wing (such as communism or revolutionary socialism). The remarkable thing, however, is that despite their apparent ideological differences, they all enact similar domestic policies. Some give the appearance of being revolutionary as in the case of left-wing states or reactionary as in the case of right-wing states, but when one examines what they are actually doing, these differences largely disappear. They are all anti-democratic, centrally planned and regulated economies that control the media, communications and education and, for the most part, vigorously oppose religion. There may be differences in the rhetoric surrounding some of these policies and there may be modest differences in their application but fundamentally their methods and aims are identical. Examining why some states and their policies fail and some succeed, gives us significant opportunity to learn from their example and to identify the prevalence of such models in the world's trouble spots today.

Minorities can be treated as scapegoats on whom the public are encouraged to vent their frustration. Hitler blamed the Jews for the defeat in the First World War as well as Germany's economic ills and the tsars regularly used pogroms to deflect the people's anger from the regime. In these cases the minority groups were targeted so that the state could increase or maintain power by transferring discontent onto others. The impact of this discrimination can be catastrophic as in the case of the Holocaust, the Rwandan genocide or the famine in the Ukraine in the 1930s.

Source analysis

The following documents are examples of the cult of personality that supported the repressive regime of Joseph Stalin.

Source A

The men of all ages will call on thy name, which is strong, beautiful, wise and marvellous. Thy name is engraven on every factory, every machine, every place on the earth, and in the hearts of all men.

Every time I have found myself in his presence I have been subjugated by his strength, his charm, his grandeur. I have experienced a great desire to sing, to cry out, to shout with joy with happiness. And now see me—me!—on the same platform where the Great Stalin stood a year ago. In what country, in what part of the world could such a thing happen?

I write books. I am an author. All thanks to thee, O great educator, Stalin. I love a young woman with a renewed love and shall perpetuate myself in my children—all thanks to thee, great educator, Stalin. I shall be eternally happy and joyous, all thanks to thee, great educator, Stalin.

Everything belongs to thee, chief of our great country. And when the woman I love presents me with a child the first word it shall utter will be: Stalin.

O great Stalin, O leader of the peoples,
Thou who broughtest man to birth.
Thou who fructifiest the earth,
Thou who restorest the centuries,
Thou who makest bloom the spring,
Thou who makest vibrate the musical chords …
Thou, splendour of my spring, O Thou,
Sun reflected by millions of hearts …

Source: *Pravda*, 1 February 1935. Quoted in Rigby, TH. 1966. *Stalin*. Englewood Cliffs, USA. Prentice-Hall. pp. 111–12.

Source B

Stalin at the Helm, a poster from 1933.

Source-based questions

1 How is the leader portrayed? Why would he want to be represented in this way?

2 Find examples of similar deification from other totalitarian states.

3 Is a cult of personality characteristic of all totalitarian states?

Activity

Complete this table

Comparative analysis: single-party states						
The Left				**The Right**		
Lenin	**Stalin**	**Castro**	**Peron**	**Mussolini**	**Hitler**	

Govt & opposition:

• Closure of Constituent Assembly Jan 1918. Assumed autocratic leadership role • Bolsheviks dominate Council of Peoples Commissars. Only Mensheviks & Left SR's tolerated • Party leaders purged from other parties after Terror following 1918 assassination attempt • Purges after Terror following 1918 assassination attempt • Set up CHEKA, state police	• Assumed leadership of the Communist Party as Gen. Sec. No clear successor nominated by Lenin. Assumed power through sidelining other senior party members • Eliminated Party rivals in leadership takeover. (Zinoviev, Kamenev and Trotsky) • Great Purge 1937–8. Post-WW2 purge. Frequent purges of dissenters, and other nationalist groups, as well as those loyal to the Party, perceived as threat to command structure • Lenin's secret police continued: OGPU=NKVD=KGB					

Domestic policies:

• Support of Trostsky as head of War ministry, in leading the civil war. Period of War Communism (1917–21) placed strict control over peasants especially. Slogan: Bread, land and peace • NEP enterprise model to support increased industrial and agricultural output after failed collectivisation policy, 1921	• 5Yr Plans initiated strict central control of industry & agriculture through collectivisation • Enlarged prison system of Gulags, work camps. • Legal system controlled through appointment of judges. Show trials • Agricultural policies resulted in systemic shortages, including famine-genocide in Ukraine 1932–3					

Foreign policies:

• Treaty of Brest-Litovsk signed in 1918 to end hostilities with Germany, independence of Finland, Estonia, Latvia, Ukraine, Lithuania • Founds Comintern (Communist International) 1919 supporting revolutionary activity across Europe • Treaty of Rapallo 1922. Germany and Russia agree on mutual recognition, cancellation of debt claims, normalization of trade relations, and secret co-operation in military development	• By the 1930s Stalin had given up on revolution in other countries, though he still supported communism abroad. Socialism in one country: favoured federated USSR • Supported the Republican Government in the Spanish Civil War • Replaced Comintern (disbanded 1943) with support for communist leaders in SSRs, and annexed border territories (Baltic States) • Following later allegiance with Western allies, against Nazi Germany, joins the war against Japan, gaining control of northern China. Used this to support pro-Soviet regimes in China and North Korea, and later Vietnam					

Press:

• 1917 Decree on Press banning all non-Bolshevik papers	• Lenin's Press control continued • Cult of personality					

Education & Youth:

• Religious schools closed	• Education strictly controlled • Education for the needs of the state • Intellectuals controlled: Lysenkoism (Creationism)					

Culture & Religion:

Role of women:

Minority groups:

Exam questions

1 Examine the conditions that led to **two** single party states.

2 Compare and contrast the rise to power of **one** right-wing, and **one** left-wing, leader of a single-party or authoritarian state.

3 Analyse the methods used by either Mao or Peron to maintain power.

4 Discuss the successes and failures of **either** Stalin **or** Sukarno.

5 In what ways, and with what results, did **one** ruler use the following: religion, propaganda, and the arts?

6 Compare and contrast the domestic policies of Kenyatta (Kenya) and Nyerere (Tanzania).

7 Analyse the social and economic policies of Hitler.

8 In what ways, and to what extent, did the status of women change in **two** single-party states, each chosen from a different region.

9 In 1924 Stalin said: "the state is an instrument in the hands of the ruling class, used to break the resistance of the enemies of that class." How did Stalin carry out this belief?

10 In 1953 Castro declared: "History will absolve me." To what extent do you agree with his claim?

Recommended further reading

Benson, Linda. 2002. *China since 1949*. London, UK. Pearson.

> A very good short history and chronology with supporting documents.

Gott, Richard. 2004. *Cuba: A New History*. New Haven, Connecticut, USA. Yale University Press.

> A recent volume with a good background history of Cuba which puts Castro into context.

Layton, Geoff. 2004. *Germany: The Third Reich*. London, UK. Hodder and Stoughton.

> An excellent overview of the rise to power of Hitler and the policies of the Third Reich. Source documents, illustrations and study materials included.

Lee, Stephen J. 1994. *The European Dictatorships 1918–45*. London, UK. Routledge.

> An excellent introduction to the inter-war period in Europe. A concise account with excellent photographic resources.

Leonard, Thomas, M. 1999. *Castro and the Cuban revolution*. Westport, Connecticut, USA. Greenwood Press.

> A good introduction to the topic with supporting documents.

Lynch, Michael. 2007. *Bolshevik and Stalinist Russia*. London, UK. Hodder, Murray.

> Very sound treatment of both the rise to power of Lenin and Stalin, also providing details on their key policies.

Mack-Smith, Denis. 1983. *Mussolini*. New York. Vintage books.

> The standard work on the subject and a good place to begin.

Overy, Richard J. 2004. *The Dictators: Hitler's Germany and Stalin's Russia*. New York, USA. WW Norton & Co.

> A well-known author who has written a number of books on this period. A well-written and well-documented volume.

Robson, Mark. 2001. *Italy: Liberalism and Fascism*. London, UK. Hodder and Stoughton.

> An excellent history of the period, providing a solid background to the fascist rise to power as well as source documents, illustrations and material for further study.

Pipes, Richard. 2001. *Communism: A History*. New York, USA. Modern Library.

> The author is a well-known authority who has written a number of books on the Russian revolution that would also be very helpful for the study of this topic.

Vansittart, Peter. 1973. *Dictators*. London,UK. Studio Vista.

> Interesting overview of this topic with references to dictators in previous centuries and a general analysis of the various aspects of the nature and character of dictators.

7 Decolonization and independence movements in Africa and Asia

This chapter concerns topic 4: nationalist and independence movements in Africa and Asia. The selected countries of Angola, Ghana, Vietnam and Zimbabwe are traced from the origins of their nationalist and independence movements, through to the achievement of independence from their colonial overlords and into the formation of new states and post-colonial governments.

The formation of these new states after the First World War led to the creation of a majority of the states that are in existence today. In 1946, there were 51 countries representing the United Nations in San Francisco; today there are 204. These states have come to exist through the break-up of empires. This chapter examines the end of the French, British and Portuguese empires, while the following chapter explores the effects on selected nation states of the dissolution of the Soviet Empire. Many of the challenges and problems that exist today are the result of the way in which these states were created.

A major problem with the study of **decolonization** is that, while certain patterns may emerge, there is diversity in how independence was achieved. Nearly all countries engaged in armed struggle, but the intensity of the engagement and its relative importance differed. Many of these countries were created with borders that crossed national or tribal boundaries, making ethnic differences a source of immediate conflict in the post-colonial era; other countries were formed through partition along national or religious lines and faced less internal conflict after independence. Furthermore, the level of cultural, economic and political/administrative influence that the colonial powers held over these countries—both during the period of political awareness and struggle for independence, through to the establishment of new regimes— varied widely. Some imperial powers sought to maintain links with their former colonies in very direct ways, while others preferred to keep their influence unofficial.

These countries faced common challenges such as developing a sense of nationhood in countries which had artificial boundaries drawn by colonial powers. Other concerns included the evolving nature of their political systems and economic problems of widespread poverty and the need for investment in development and infrastructure, doubled with the growing divide between rural and urban communities. On the whole, the newly emerging states were still in a period of peasant-based agriculture and extractive industries—there was little if any advanced industrial development in these countries.

The solutions attempted and the degree of success also varied widely. In the political sphere, Ghana, Tanzania and Vietnam became single-party states while India remained a democracy. There was prolonged civil war in Angola, Congo, Pakistan and Vietnam and military

> **Decolonization** The process by which European colonies in Africa and Asia became fully independent states. It could involve wars of liberation or gradual, peaceful constitutional change.

IB Learner Profile link

Too many IB candidates select examples of wars and single-party states from Europe, with occasional reference to China or Cuba. This topic gives you the chance to focus on the particular challenges faced by people living in newly formed independent states in Africa and Asia.

? **How important is it for us to be open to different values and systems of governance?**

Consider the particular challenges faced by people living in economically deprived and politically unstable regions of the world.

intervention in most of these states. Given the difficulty of generalizing about new states in Africa or Asia, this chapter is largely devoted to case studies of the achievement of independence for Ghana and Vietnam, with more summary coverage of the situations in Zimbabwe and Angola.

By the end of this chapter, you should be able to:

- understand the political, economic and social challenges for post-colonial governments

- evaluate the relationship between ideology and nationalism in independence movements

- account for the origin and rise of nationalist/independence movements in Africa

- describe the role of armed struggle and mass movements, leaders and political parties in the achievement of independence in Africa with particular reference to Ghana, Zimbabwe and Angola

- compare and contrast the experience since independence of Ghana, Zimbabwe and Angola

- understand the importance of the Second World War to Indochinese independence movements

- analyse the role of Ho Chi Minh in the establishment of the Vietnamese state

- compare and contrast the regimes in North Vietnam and South Vietnam

- explain why the Vietnamese communists won both Indochina Wars

- evaluate the domestic and foreign policies of the Socialist Republic of Vietnam.

Activity:

Give a presentation for or against colonial rule

Choose a colonial power and/or region to discuss specific examples of:

- French rule in Indochina and Algeria

- Portuguese rule in Angola

- Belgian rule in the Congo

- British rule in India and Ghana.

Historians are still debating how far the achievements of independence movements were due to decisions made by the European colonial powers, and how much of these outcomes were determined by Europe's own economic and political decline or can be ascribed to the efforts of nationalist leaders in Asia and Africa.

TOK link
History

Independence was achieved fairly peacefully in most African and Asian colonies but there were armed struggles in some—notably Algeria, Angola and Zimbabwe. Those fighting for independence under majority rule in Zimbabwe called themselves "freedom fighters". The white minority government called them "terrorists".

 When are citizens justified in taking up arms against the government?

It is difficult to generalize about the extent to which post-independence governments succeeded in solving their political, economic and social problems. They faced certain common challenges such as developing a sense of nationhood in countries which had artificial boundaries drawn by the colonial powers. Other concerns included the evolving nature of their political systems and the economic problems of widespread poverty and the need for investment in development and infrastructure, doubled with the growing divide between rural and urban communities. But the solutions attempted and the degree of success varied very widely. In the political sphere, Ghana and Tanzania became single-party states while India remained a multi-party democracy. There was prolonged civil war in Congo and Angola and military intervention in both Ghana and the Congo. Given the difficulty of generalizing about new states in Asia or Africa and the need for some depth of analysis, the following section will be largely devoted to a case study of the achievement of independence for the Gold Coast/ Ghana and the role of Francis Kwame Nkrumah before and after independence, followed by a more summary coverage of the situation in Zimbabwe and Angola.

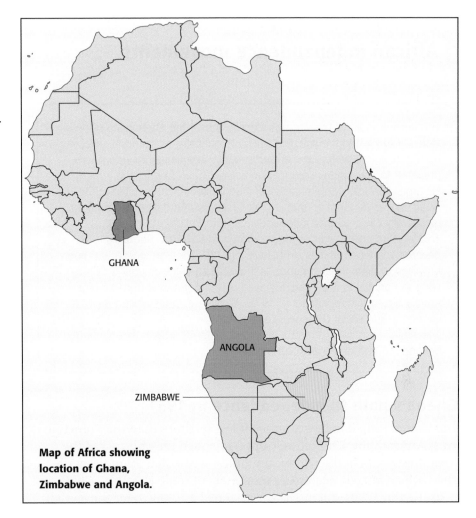

Map of Africa showing location of Ghana, Zimbabwe and Angola.

The reason for choosing Ghana is that it is more typical than the other three African countries selected as case studies: Algeria, Angola and Zimbabwe. These countries had large white settler communities and achieved independence after a prolonged, violent war of liberation. All the former Italian colonies achieved independence peacefully as did the French colonies (excluding Algeria). It was a more complicated picture for the former British colonies. Ghana is representative of many African countries where a gradual process of decolonization involved increasing African involvement in local government, in legislative councils and finally upon ministerial commission, a process that culminated in an Independence Day, on which the colonial flag was lowered and the new national flag raised in the presence of the new African leaders and representatives of the departing colonial powers.

African independence movements

> This section looks at the decline of imperial rule, the emergence of new states in Africa and the different types of nationalist movements involving both non-violent protest and armed struggle. The United Kingdom was prepared to grant independence to the Gold Coast and Francis Kwame Nkrumah became prime minister of independent Ghana in 1957. The situation was different in Southern Rhodesia, where the settler minority unilaterally declared their independence from British rule in 1965. This led to a prolonged war of liberation with Southern Rhodesia becoming independent as Zimbabwe in 1980. The Portuguese had been unwilling to grant independence to their African colonies until a military coup in Portugal in 1974 was followed by a hasty retreat from empire. Angola became independent in 1975. All three countries faced political, economic and social challenges, exemplified by the case of Angola, which was engulfed in civil war and a proxy war of the Cold War that continued beyond the end of the 20th century.

Ghana's path to independence in 1957

The United Kingdom had conquered less territory than the French in West Africa in the 19th century but had ended up with two of the wealthiest states in the region, the Gold Coast (Ghana) and Nigeria. The UK had already acquired a monopoly of trade along the Gold Coast by the 1870s and in 1874 proclaimed a colony over the coastal Fante states. They later defeated the Asante, who resorted to armed resistance in 1900, and the colony of the Gold Coast was proclaimed.

The Gold Coast had been the world's leading rubber-producing country in the 1880s but when rubber plantations were rapidly developed in Malaysia and Indonesia it turned to cocoa and by 1911 it was the world's leading producer. This was a success story for African peasant production, but the Gold Coast was also typical of colonial economic exploitation. European companies controlled the export trade and fixed low prices for the peasant producers and then resold the cocoa at a much higher profit. There was also considerable growth in the gold trade to the benefit of Europeans. The European-owned Ashanti Goldfields Corporation paid their workers less than African cocoa farmers paid theirs.

Nana Agyeman Prempeh I (1872–1931)

The reign of Prempeh I, king of Asante coincided with civil war in the 1880s and the British colonisation of Asante in 1896. Prempeh I refused to accept a British protectorate over his state. As a result, he and other member of the Asante royal family and chiefs were imprisoned and later exiled to Sierra Leone in January 1897 and the Seychelles Islands in 1900. The Asantes bitterly resented the deportation of their king, leading to ongoing civil unrest in Kumasi and surrounding towns. However, it was seen differently in some of the Brong states to the north and northwest of Kumasi who were relieved to be free of the dominance of the Asante. The British authorities released Prempeh I, and 54 other exiles on 12 September 1924, and he was permitted to return to Kumasi. After the people of Kumasi petitioned the British government, he was reinstated as king in 1926. On his death in 1931 his nephew, Prempeh II, was elected Kumasihene, and then Asantehene in 1935, when the Golden Stool, symbolic of Asante power, was returned by the British and the traditional Asante Confederacy was restored.

Nationalist movements began early in the Gold Coast for a number of reasons including the growth of the Western-educated elite, who mostly attended mission schools, Fourah Bay College in Sierra Leone and universities in the UK. Resenting their exclusion from the colonial civil service, their demands included the desire for more universities, more places in legislative councils and the civil service. They also campaigned for the interests of the peasants. The Aborigines Rights Protection Society (ARPS), founded in the Gold Coast in 1897, successfully fought attempts to declare unoccupied land Crown land and delayed from 1911 to 1927 the implementation of the Forest Bill to establish forest reserves in unoccupied land. Several of the Western-educated elite in the Gold Coast wrote books on the country's history and land issues.

Casely Hayford, who had trained as a lawyer in Cambridge and London published his influential account in 1903, *Gold Coast Native Institutions: With Thoughts Upon A Healthy Imperial Policy for the Gold Coast and Ashanti,* in which he expressed the hope of unity between the coast people and the Asante. Hayford was an early nationalist and pan-Africanist, who strongly advocated African rights against the interference of the British colonial administration. But the ARPS remained largely a Fante ethnic organisation rather than a genuinely nationalist movement. It won a few concessions but could not fundamentally alter the exploitative and unrepresentative aspects of colonial rule till the early 1950s. Casely Hayford organized the National Congress of British West Africa in 1920 but it could not overcome the difficulties caused by the lack of mass support, the physical separation of Britain's colonies and political competition between the Western-educated elites and the traditional chiefs.

In many African colonies the British adopted a policy of indirect rule. The return of the exiled Prempeh I stimulated an indirect rule policy in Asante region. In the Northern region, to which the policy was extended, there was great difficulty finding native authorities among mainly non-centralized peoples. Frederick Gordon Guggisberg, governor of the Gold Coast from 1919 to 1929, has been described as "the founder of the modern Gold Coast as surely Kwame Nkrumah was the founder of modern Ghana." He encouraged more African representation in the Legislative Council, boosted the country's economy with the construction of railways and tarred roads, and increased the number of educated people through his foundation of Achimota College in 1927.

Frederick Gordon Guggisberg (1869–1930)

Brigadier-General Sir Frederick Gordon Guggisberg was born at Galt, Ontario, Canada, and educated in England at Burney's School, near Portsmouth, and the Royal Military Academy, Woolwich. In 1902 Guggisberg was employed by the Colonial Office to survey the Gold Coast Colony and Ashanti, and later became director of surveys in Southern Nigeria. When the plan to amalgamate Southern and Northern Nigeria was approved in 1912, Guggisberg was made acting surveyor-general. After serving in the the First World War, he returned to West Africa in 1919 as governor and commander-in-chief of the Gold Coast, where he embarked on an ambitious programme of development of the railways and port facilities, the Korle Bu Hospital and the Prince of Wales College at Achimota. Rare for colonial administrators of the period, Guggisberg was committed to developing the country for the benefit of Africans rather than Europeans. In 1928 Guggisberg was appointed governor and commander-in-chief of British Guiana, but owing to failing health he returned to England, where he died in Bexhill, in 1930.

Although thousands of soldiers were recruited from the Gold Coast by the British to fight in their East Africa campaign against the Germans in the First World War, the war did not lead to an upsurge of nationalism nor weaken Britain's desire to maintain its empire, which was increased by the acquisition of German colonies and parts of the Ottoman Empire. The British Empire was weakened by but survived the Great Depression in the early 1930s. Another event in the 1930s stimulated nationalism in Africa including the Gold Coast. Kwame Nkrumah recalled:

> On the placard I read: "MUSSOLINI INVADES ETHIOPIA". That was all I needed. At that moment it was almost as if the whole of London had suddenly declared war on me personally. For the next few minutes I could do nothing but glare at each impassive face wondering if those people could possibly realize the wickedness of colonialism, and praying that the day might come when I could play my part in bringing about the downfall of such a system.

The invasion of Ethiopia in 1935 by Mussolini's Italian troops was a death blow to the credibility of the League of Nations of which Ethiopia was a member. It offered no intervention. Nkrumah and Jomo Kenyatta, future leaders of Ghana and Kenya, were students in London at the time and described later how those events increased their determination to end colonial rule.

The Second World War had a more profound effect on the British and other colonial empires. It resulted in the defeat of Italy as a colonial power and the humiliating occupation of metropolitan France and Belgium by the Nazis. Defeats in Asia as in Singapore exposed British weakness. Africans throughout the continent contributed to the Allied war effort as soldiers or by contributions to wartime production. Soldiers from many parts of Africa including the Gold Coast had fought and died to help liberate Burma from the Japanese. They had also witnessed the strength and feeling of the Asian nationalist movements, for example in India. Those who stayed at home could no longer believe in Europeans as a privileged aristocracy after seeing the activities of ordinary British and American soldiers and airmen serving in West Africa. Before the end of the war, colonial secretaries were beginning to consider self-government for African colonies though not yet independence.

The demobilized soldiers expected rewards and the fulfilment of promises made to them. Only neutral Portugal could avoid the issue of post-war reform in its colony of Angola. New promise of colonial freedom was implied in the Atlantic Charter and in the charter of the United Nations established in 1945. The Colonial Secretary approved in 1942 Governor Burns's proposal to include Africans on the executive council of the Gold Coast but significantly did so in the hope of preserving the British empire rather than hastening the independence of the Gold Coast.

The Second World War turned the UK into a debtor nation and encouraged it to make the colonies more economically efficient. Britain's African colonies came to be considered as more crucial. British officials regarded the Gold Coast as a model colony. They thought they could continue to share power with the chiefs and give a lesser role to the educated elite. Events in 1947 and 1948 would, however, force them to abandon their gradual approach. In the end the UK, like other colonial powers in Asia and Africa, would grant independence to the Gold Coast under conditions not of its own choosing.

In 1947 India and Pakistan became independent and the Gold Coast's educated elite, led by lawyer JB Danquah, established the United Gold Coast Convention (UGCC). They sought self-government in "the shortest time possible" and greater representation on the legislative council, where they already had a majority under the 1946 Burns Constitution. Kwame Nkrumah took up the post of General Secretary.

After being educated at Achimota College in Accra, Nkrumah had studied abroad, living in the USA and the UK as an impoverished student for 12 years. He was the organizing secretary of the Pan-African Congress in Manchester in 1945 attended by Jomo Kenyatta and Hastings Banda. Kwame Nkrumah soon presented the UGCC with a detailed report on how it must become a disciplined party with mass support and branches in towns and villages. He won over thousands to UGCC membership.

On 28 February 1948 riots broke out in Accra. Grievances had accumulated since 1945. Ex-servicemen were discontented by the foreign control of trade and the denial of import licences to aspiring businessmen, who were unable to use their gratuities to buy lorries. Market women saw big companies diverting supplies to their own stores. Local government reform seemed to strengthen rather than limit the power of chiefs. Farmers objected to instructions to cut down cocoa trees infected with swollen shoot. As tensions mounted, a police commander in Accra killed two protesting ex-servicemen. This led to widespread rioting and looting in four towns, the deaths of 29 people and over 200 injured. By colonial standards the disorder was relatively brief and limited and the damage to life and property inconsiderable but the colonial authorities were deeply shocked. In the same month there had been a coup in Czechoslovakia and with Cold War fears British officials briefly detained the six leading officials, thereby making them popular heroes and increasing UGCC membership.

The official enquiry into the disturbances, the Watson Commission, was sharply critical of the Gold Coast government and concluded that in the "conditions existing today in Gold Coast a substantial measure of reform is necessary to meet

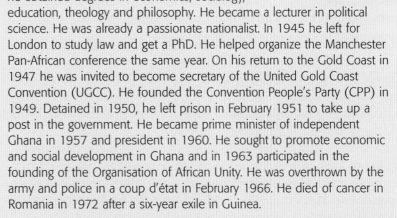

Francis Kwame Nkrumah (1909–1972)

Francis Kwame Nkrumah was born into the Akan tribe at Nkroful in Western Ghana, probably in September 1909. He was baptized a Catholic, educated in a mission school for eight years and was then trained as a teacher in Accra. An uncle helped him go to the United States in 1935 where he obtained degrees in economics, sociology, education, theology and philosophy. He became a lecturer in political science. He was already a passionate nationalist. In 1945 he left for London to study law and get a PhD. He helped organize the Manchester Pan-African conference the same year. On his return to the Gold Coast in 1947 he was invited to become secretary of the United Gold Coast Convention (UGCC). He founded the Convention People's Party (CPP) in 1949. Detained in 1950, he left prison in February 1951 to take up a post in the government. He became prime minister of independent Ghana in 1957 and president in 1960. He sought to promote economic and social development in Ghana and in 1963 participated in the founding of the Organisation of African Unity. He was overthrown by the army and police in a coup d'état in February 1966. He died of cancer in Romania in 1972 after a six-year exile in Guinea.

the legitimate aspirations of the indigenous population". It did not, however, recommend an early transfer of power. The government then appointed an all-African Committee under Justice Coussey to work out a new constitution. Danquah took part in the committee but Nkrumah broke with his colleagues, labelling them "men of property and standing". In June 1949 he launched a rival Convention People's Party (CPP).

Kwame Nkrumah and the CPP

Kwame Nkrumah was more aware than ever of the power of mass action and of the need to force the British government into setting a timetable for full independence. They had studiously avoided this till then and instead had spoken rather abstractly about self-government. Nkrumah adopted the uncompromising slogan, "Self-Government Now" and in January 1950 he began a campaign of strikes and boycotts to stimulate positive action. Nkrumah and his associates were promptly re-arrested for subversion. This and his three-year sentence transformed him into a martyr and increased popular following for him and the party. He became the most popular nationalist leader the country had ever known. In February 1951, the first elections were held under the new constitution, and it came as no surprise that the CPP easily defeated the UGCC, winning 34 out of 38 popularly elected seats.

The new British governor, Sir Charles Arden-Clarke, had a choice between repression and independence for the Gold Coast. He chose the latter and he summoned Nkrumah from prison and invited him to take up the position of leader of Government Business, charged with the duty of nominating colleagues for ministerial office. The United Kingdom wanted continued access to the Gold Coast dollar-earning resources and from 1951 to 1957 rising cocoa prices increased government revenue by over 50 per cent. Decolonization in Ghana was facilitated by the absence of white settlers. The goldmines were expected to continue under British ownership. There was a good working relationship between African and expatriate civil servants. The African farmers producing cocoa, the major source of the Gold Coast's wealth, could be expected to continue to trade with the UK. Arden-Clarke developed a close working relationship with Nkrumah. The 1951 constitution had reserved half the parliamentary seats for chiefly nominees but Nkrumah and the governor negotiated a new constitution which brought fully-elected, internal self-government to the Gold Coast in 1954.

The CPP won the new round of elections but with a reduced majority. They lost control of the North and the Northern opposition united with the Asante cocoa farmers, who resented the way Nkrumah's government maintained marketing boards which brought in large profits for the government, restricting the price paid to farmers. They formed the National Liberation Movement, which wanted to keep power regional in a federal state as they distrusted Nkrumah and the southern Fante, who dominated coastal towns and government. This ethnic rivalry could have delayed independence but Arden-Clarke continued to support Nkrumah in his determination to achieve a peaceful transition to independence in a unitary state. The CPP won elections again in 1956 and the Gold Coast became independent on 7 March 1957 as Ghana, reviving the name of an ancient West African empire to reflect pride in the country's African identity.

The course of decolonization had been conceded rather than directed by the United Kingdom. The UK was prepared to accept that Ghana was ready for independence but the speed of change was determined by the charismatic Nkrumah, his well-organized party and followers including young school-leavers, market women who were experts in the retail business, wage-earners and war-pensioners. The lawyers of the old UGCC would have preferred to slow the process, favour regional interests and retain some power in the hands of the chiefs. The CPP had successfully both tapped into popular discontent and persuaded the British that it was led by reasonable men who would safeguard their interests. The UK lost the desire to retain Ghana but without Nkrumah and other nationalists there would have been no independence for Ghana in 1957.

"No imperial power has ever granted independence to a colony unless the forces were such that no other course was possible, and there are many instances where independence was only achieved by a war of liberation, but there are many other instances when no such war occurred. The very organisation of the forces of independence within the colony was sufficient to convince the imperial power that resistance to independence would be impossible or that the political and economic consequences of a colonial war outweighed any advantage to be gained by retaining the colony."

Kwame Nkrumah

TOK link

The ethics of colonization

 Is there a moral justification for imperialism?

The 19th century European colonizers in Africa certainly thought so. Kipling wrote a poem, *The White Man's Burden*, about the duty of the European to rule other peoples in order to "civilize" them.

Cecil Rhodes said: "The more of the world the British inhabit, the better it is for the human race." Back in the 12th century, the pope authorized King Henry II of England's conquest of Ireland to reform their morals.

If imperial expansion can no longer be justified, should states which are its legacy—like the United States, the United Kingdom, China or the Democratic Republic of Congo—now break up into smaller units?

Ghana after independence under Kwame Nkrumah

Ghana after independence was one of Africa's wealthiest former colonies. Its people already enjoyed a relatively high per capita income, a good network of roads and railways, a well-developed education system, an efficient civil service and a variety of exportable natural resources that included gold, diamond, manganese, bauxite and a long tradition of successful cultivation of cocoa by peasant farmers.

During the first three years, Kwame Nkrumah acted cautiously and pragmatically. He allowed foreign companies to continue to dominate the import and export trade and the mining, insurance and manufacturing sectors. The establishment of many new industries created more employment opportunities. There was an annual growth rate of 5 per cent of GDP, reasonably stable prices and a slow rise in the cost of living. Ghana was consolidating the achievements of the first Development Plan drawn up by British officials in 1951 but taken over by the CPP. Under the plan three-quarters of spending had been allocated to infrastructure development and social services.

The Second Five Year Plan (1959–64) allocated even more to both, and was replaced in 1961 by an even more ambitious set of objectives. By this time Nkrumah had come to favour a socialist approach to development which involved state control and by 1965 the establishment of 47 state corporations. Most of these were running at a loss because of a lack of trained personnel and proper planning as well as corruption in the dispersal of funds and recruitment of unqualified staff. There were severe shortages of basic commodities, soaring inflation and acute unemployment. Nkrumah's government failed to transform Ghana into the modern industrial state he dreamt of but instead had led his country to bankruptcy and to the edge of economic collapse. On the plus side there were major improvements in the provision of public services including a doubling of the number of hospitals and health workers and students enrolled in primary and secondary school. There was a growing level of corruption and extravagance among Nkrumah's closest supporters in the CPP. Agriculture, the base of the country's economy, was neglected while vast sums were squandered on prestige projects like a new presidential palace, a motorway to Accra airport and the Volta dam. This dam was typical of the lavish spending in Ghana and other West African countries on expensive industrial and prestige projects with inadequate analysis of their suitability and viability. The huge hydro-electric project did supply plentiful electricity to the capital, Accra, though even that later proved inadequate. But it left Ghana with a crippling international debt and was of little benefit to most Ghanaians.

Nkrumah is remembered for his desire to unite Ghana with its neighbours in a federation, which proved very short-lived, and his devotion to the ideal of the political and economic unity of Africa.

Conferences were held in Accra, notably the All African Peoples' Conference in December 1958. Ghanaian troops served with the UN in the Congo early in the 1960s. Though Ghana became disillusioned with the United States and drew closer to the Soviet Union, Nkrumah avoided entanglement in the Cold War conflict.

The fall of Kwame Nkrumah

Many Ghanaians felt that Kwame Nkrumah spent too much time trying to achieve the impossible goal of African unity, which was still very far from being achieved by the end of the 20th century. But he did contribute to another objective—the total liberation of Africa from colonial rule. Like many other leaders of former colonies in Africa, Nkrumah made his country into a single-party state. He did so in 1964 and in 1965 he announced by radio the names of the 104 MPs he had chosen. As early as 1958, the government had passed the Preventive Detention Act. The veteran UGCC leader Joseph Danquah died in detention. No competitive parliamentary elections were held after 1956 (nor party elections). In effect Ghana almost became a no-party state, one in which all major decisions were taken by the President's Office and to a lesser extent by the state bureaucracy. On 24 February 1966, while Nkrumah was in Beijing, he was overthrown by the armed forces and police and replaced by a National Liberation Council. The coup was justified on the grounds of Nkrumah's political repression and silencing and imprisonment of opponents, along with the failure of his socialist centralizing economic policies.

A dam on the river Volta, 1959.

Children around a fallen statue of Kwame Nkrumah during the coup that overthrew his presidency of Ghana in 1966.

Source analysis

History as a human science

Compare these two contrasting accounts of Kwame Nkrumah's government and priorities in the early years of Ghana's independence.

Ocran's view

Kwame Nkrumah was dictatorial to the extreme. Under the guise of strengthening his party he strengthened his personal control throughout the country. Apart from him there existed no centre, no source of power.

Kwame Nkrumah became power-drunk and forgot his God. It is authoritatively reported that he still consults Kankan Nyame, the fetish, to help him back to power. There is no doubt he also became highly immoral. He had created the backbone of his personal political machine; the whip of a tyrant had been fashioned. He could and did dismiss public officers at will. He had assumed all powers, leaving not even one effective check or balance.

Over the years and by devious means including corruption, extortion and acceptance of questionable gifts, Kwame Nkrumah extracted from various sources enough private wealth to make him a millionaire.

Nkrumah's self-aggrandizement, his pleasure in subjecting honourable and respectable citizens to public degradation, ridicule and contempt was well-known. He wanted to be not only the one and the only one in Ghana but the most important personage in the whole of Black Africa. The Ghanaian was made to suffer as a result of his so-called African Unity which was in fact a means of feeding fat a few disgruntled refugees, mostly from independent African countries, who were being trained to cause confusion in their own states.

In my view Africa is not poorer for Nkrumah's overthrow. It is much safer. The Organisation of African Unity should be better off without an intriguing and selfish propagandist like Nkrumah. I think with the discoveries of the dishonesty and great immorality which the inquiries have produced, it is inconceivable that Kwame Nkrumah can still be held in honourable estimation by right thinking African rulers of Africa today.

Source: Ocran, Albert Kwesi. 1968. *A Myth is Broken*. Harlow, UK. Longman, pp. 24, 25, 92.

Segal's view

With one of the highest standards of living in Africa already, Ghana was fast industrializing, while the construction of schools—2,000 primary ones opened in 1962 alone—hospitals, roads and community centres promised the 7,000,000 Ghanaians greater social as well as economic progress than any probable alternative to Nkrumah's regime could reasonably offer. Nkrumah's place in African history is already secure. The leader of the first independent black State in Africa to struggle out of colonialism, he inspired Africans throughout the continent to believe that they were capable of emulating his example. It is difficult to exaggerate the effect, for instance, that his emergence on to the world stage had upon Africans enduring the race rule of Dr. Verwoerd. In addition, though often antagonizing by too speedy and energetic a partisanship, Kwame Nkrumah must surely rank the African leader who has done the most concretely to further the ideals of Pan-Africanism.

Kwame Nkrumah has already contributed more to the continent that he so patently loves than any of those—inside and outside of Africa—who find it so easy at the moment to belittle him.

Source: Segal, Ronald. 1962. *African Profiles*. Harmondsworth, UK. Penguin, p. 277.

Source-based questions

1 How do we reconcile such opposing viewpoints?

2 How much of the criticism is likely to have escalated with the failure of Kwame Nkrumah's economic and social policies.

3 What does study of the rise and fall of Kwame Nkrumah offer to studies of regime change in this period?

The path to independence in Rhodesia/Zimbabwe

Both Angola and Zimbabwe achieved independence late—Angola in 1975 and Rhodesia/ Zimbabwe in 1980—long after most other African countries, and both after an armed struggle. Internal and external pressures contributed to the achievement of independence for both.

The Central African Federation had been created in 1953 because the United Kingdom wanted to make a single viable colony out of the protectorates of Nyasaland, Northern Rhodesia and the self-governing colony of Southern Rhodesia. But the territories were racially and economically quite different. African nationalists denounced the Federation as a device to preserve white control and Northern Rhodesia and Nyasaland left to become the independent states of Zambia and Malawi in 1964. Southern Rhodesia, dominated by its large white population, mostly farmers but also with an urban middle and working class, had been self-governing since 1923 and now wanted independence but under white rule. The ultra-conservative Rhodesian Front had been elected in 1962 and Ian Smith became prime minister in 1964. He rightly concluded that the UK would not use military force against its own "kith and kin" and made an illegal and unilateral Declaration of Independence (UDI) in November 1965.

 What were the particular challenges faced by Angola and Zimbabwe?
Consider their route to independence and the ongoing legacy of conflict.

Robert Gabriel Mugabe (1924–)

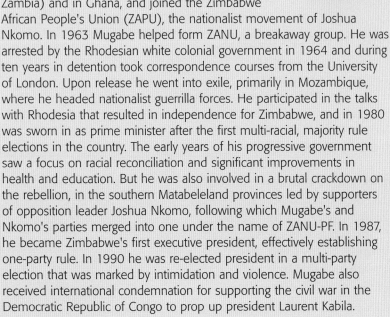

Robert Gabriel Mugabe was born in Kutama, then Southern Rhodesia. Educated by the Jesuits, he became a teacher in a mission school. He later studied at the University of Fort Hare, Alice, in South Africa. During the 1950s he taught in Southern Rhodesia and Northern Rhodesia (now Zambia) and in Ghana, and joined the Zimbabwe African People's Union (ZAPU), the nationalist movement of Joshua Nkomo. In 1963 Mugabe helped form ZANU, a breakaway group. He was arrested by the Rhodesian white colonial government in 1964 and during ten years in detention took correspondence courses from the University of London. Upon release he went into exile, primarily in Mozambique, where he headed nationalist guerrilla forces. He participated in the talks with Rhodesia that resulted in independence for Zimbabwe, and in 1980 was sworn in as prime minister after the first multi-racial, majority rule elections in the country. The early years of his progressive government saw a focus on racial reconciliation and significant improvements in health and education. But he was also involved in a brutal crackdown on the rebellion, in the southern Matabeleland provinces led by supporters of opposition leader Joshua Nkomo, following which Mugabe's and Nkomo's parties merged into one under the name of ZANU-PF. In 1987, he became Zimbabwe's first executive president, effectively establishing one-party rule. In 1990 he was re-elected president in a multi-party election that was marked by intimidation and violence. Mugabe also received international condemnation for supporting the civil war in the Democratic Republic of Congo to prop up president Laurent Kabila.

UDI and African reaction

African nationalist movements launched guerilla warfare against the Smith government. The UN applied sanctions but these were not well supported and were evaded with the help of South Africa and Portuguese-ruled Mozambique. It was difficult for the UK to negotiate with African leaders until legality was restored. A new constitution in 1970 dealt a blow to the prospects of this and the British Government broke all diplomatic relations with Rhodesia.

Guerilla war was waged by African nationalist forces, and began in earnest on a new front in the north-east border in 1972–3 from bases in Mozambique. It was this war which eventually forced concessions from the Rhodesian Front Government in 1979 after negotiations held at the Lancaster House Conference. The nature of the struggle was dramatically changed when Mozambique became independent in 1975. Ian Smith, under pressure from South Africa, released several leading nationalists from detention to allow them to attend talks in Lusaka. These included Joshua Nkomo, veteran leader of the Zimbabwe African People's Union (ZAPU), Ndabaningi Sithole, leader of the Zimbabwe African National Union (ZANU) and Robert Mugabe also of ZANU who replaced Sithole as leader at the end of 1976.

Under pressure from the United States and South Africa's prime minister John Vorster, Ian Smith announced a move to majority rule within two years. In preparation for a conference in Geneva to discuss details for this, ZANU agreed with ZAPU to form the Patriotic Front (PF). The conference ended in failure (December 1976) because the PF representatives had no confidence in Smith's promises. Guerilla war intensified with ZAPU and ZANU troops both in action under separate commands. Smith, under pressure from the war and sanctions made a deal with Bishop Muzorewa's new party, the United African National Congress (UANC). Elections were held in April 1979 but were boycotted by the PF. The war was stepped up when Muzorewa became prime minister under a constitution which allocated 28 per cent of seats to the white minority.

The end of war and achievement of independence

Finally in August 1979 the UK acted on an invitation from the independent African states involved in the war to organize a conference involving the PF. This was held at Lancaster House and led to the appointment of a British governor to Southern Rhodesia. This ended UDI and restored legality. A cease fire was signed and elections, supervised by Commonwealth observers, were held in February 1980. The elections were won by Robert Mugabe's ZANU PF with 57 of the 80 common role seats. Nkomo's PF, Mugabe's main rival, won 20 seats and Muzorewa's UANC only 3 seats. Mugabe became prime minister of independent Zimbabwe on 18 April 1980 heading a ZANU PF government with PF and white members. Mugabe initially adopted a conciliatory attitude to his rivals. His decisive election victory had partly been made possible by a campaign of intimidation waged by his supporters in Ndebele territory, the stronghold of his rival, Joshua Nkomo.

António Agostinho Neto (1922–1979)

António Agostinho Neto was born in 1922 in Kaxixane in Bengo province in Angola. He later moved to Luanda, where he finished secondary school. He completed his medical studies in Portugal from 1947 to 1958 despite several periods of imprisonment, the result of his speeches and poems denouncing Portuguese colonial rule in Angola. He returned to Angola in 1957, set up a medical practice and was a leader of MPLA. After his escape from two years in detention, he became president of the MPLA in 1962. He lived in Congo-Léopoldville, later Zaire, and in Tanzania. He travelled widely to gather support for the MPLA but the military commanders fighting a guerilla war in the Angolan bushlands were unhappy about supporting a leftish intellectual leader. Neto nevertheless managed to remain its leader and became president of Angola in 1975. Hampered in this role by ongoing civil war, he became ill and died in a Russian hospital in 1979.

Western Civilization

*Sheets of tin nailed to posts
driven in the ground
make up the house.*

*Some rags complete
the intimate landscape*

*The sun slanting through cracks
welcomes the owner*

after twelve hours of slave labour.

*Old age comes early
A mat on dark nights
Is enough when he dies
Gratefully
Of hunger.*

António Agostinho Neto

The path to independence in Angola in 1975

The Portuguese saw the future development of her colonies lying in closer union with the mainland and certainly not in devolution or independence. In 1951 Angola became an "overseas province" of Portugal. It was, however, impossible that Angola would remain immune from the unrest and growing sense of nationalism which was sweeping over Africa in the 1960s. The first serious uprising in the capital Luanda in 1961 began the liberation war, but resistance forces in Angola remained divided. The first to emerge, the Movement for the Popular Liberation of Angola (MPLA) attracted support from civil servants in Luanda. It was led by the Marxist intellectual, Agostinho Neto.

The Union for the National Independence of the Totality of Angola (UNITA) attracted support from the central and southern Ovimbundu people. It made secret overtures to the Portuguese, offering to help them destroy the left-wing MPLA in return for favoured treatment in a compromise settlement of the colonial struggle. The deal sowed the seeds for many more years of conflict in the highlands of Angola.

The liberation war had two intense phases, separated by a long period of stalemate in which the colony remained on a war footing but few casualties occurred. The first was led in February 1961 by the MPLA. Inspired by the sudden decolonization of the Belgian Congo and stirred by peasant starvation, the MPLA tried to liberate its imprisoned leaders in an attack on Luanda jail. The Portuguese retaliated with a large metropolitan army and up to 60 000 may have died trying to retain control of Angola. As the poorest European colonial power, Portugal believed that her colonies were indispensable to the growth of her economy. Many Portuguese had been encouraged to settle in Angola to alleviate unemployment back home. Unlike most other colonial powers Portugal was a dictatorship and persistently ignored the rising tide of negative public opinion—both internal and international—including criticism from the UN. Portugal was still insisting in the early 1970s that her colonies were overseas territories and an integral part of Portugal. South Africa and some Western countries which invested in South Africa regarded Angola as essential to the defence of the "white south". They were willing to offer military aid to Portugal in her struggle with the African liberation forces in Angola. The West sympathized with the Portuguese domino theory that if white power collapsed in Southern Africa, it would be replaced by black communism.

A new economic policy, including the exploitation of oil resources, brought moderate economic well-being, even to Africans, and helped postpone the second phase of active fighting till 1975. By then, the MPLA and UNITA had failed in their bid for freedom and the conflict was not about liberation itself but who would inherit the spoils in a colony that had become rich and successful. There was conflict both between and within MPLA and UNITA and they achieved no nationalist victory. Over 40 per cent of the armed forces they were fighting against were fellow Angolan Africans.

Though unable to complete their own liberation, the MPLA and UNITA helped produce conditions for the liberation of Portugal itself. The maintenance of a conscript army, more than 60 000 in Angola, placed increasing strains on Portuguese society and its economy. The Portuguese army lost the will to resist and suffered further losses before overthrowing the Portuguese dictatorship in a coup in 1974. Angola soon benefited as the new military regime gave independence "to the people of Angola as a whole" on 11 Nov 1975.

Post-colonial states in Africa

The new post-colonial governments in Africa all faced major political, economic and social challenges. Some generalizations might be valid but it must be stressed that there was considerable variation in the type and extent of challenges from country to country, and in the policies adopted to deal with them. Perhaps the most important political legacy of the colonial era were the **artificial boundaries** created by the European colonial powers at the time of the partition of Africa. At independence there was an absence of a sense of national identity or ethnic homogeneity in most African countries. Relative ethnic homogeneity could be cited as a factor helping national unity in Botswana or Lesotho or Tanzania. It did not help in Somalia where the people shared a common ethnicity, language and religion but were influenced by clan rivalry. African countries at independence inherited a system of politics and government established by the colonial power and this was generally based on a multi-party system especially in the former British colonies that encouraged competition among parties.

Some parties were truly national in appeal but others had a purely ethnic or regional focus. A multi-party system could therefore, with the encouragement of tribal and regional interests, be a major obstacle to national unity, stability and security. So multi-party systems sooner or later gave place to single-party states in most African countries. Julius Nyerere, president of Tanzania from 1964 to 1985, argued that single-party systems were compatible with democracy providing the party presented a choice of candidates in each constituency. The establishment of such systems could simply involve changing the constitution to recognize the reality of a de facto one-party state as in Tanzania. In other countries like Ghana and Kenya the main motive was to keep an ambitious leader in power. This was accompanied by oppressive measures such as detention without trial and press censorship. A few African countries like Botswana successfully kept the multi-party system inherited at independence. This was more likely to happen in countries with a greater degree of ethnic cohesion. Single-party government led all too often to abuse of power by members of the ruling party, serious mismanagement of the economy and failure to deliver promises to the people. This could often provoke, or be used as a justification for military intervention and many countries, especially in West Africa, came under military rule.

Artificial boundaries The borders of most African countries were lines drawn on maps by European officials without regard to which tribe lives where. Thus many Maasai had to learn to be Kenyan and others to be Tanzanians.

Activity:
Leadership debate
Divide into teams and select speakers to propose and oppose the motions that:

- This House believes that newly independent states should adopt socialist policies.
- This House believes that newly independent states should adopt one-party systems for the sake of national unity.

A factor which helped to promote national unity was the charismatic leadership of many of the first generation of post-independence leaders in Africa, notably Kenneth Kaunda in Zambia, Seretse Khama in Botswana, Houphouet-Boigny in Cote d'Ivoire and Jomo Kenyatta in Kenya.

Ethnic conflict and civil war

The biggest challenge to national unity was ethnic rivalry which often led to civil war. Leaders like Mugabe in Zimbabwe, Milton Obote and Idi Amin in Uganda and Juvénal Habyarimana in Rwanda fuelled ethnic tensions. Power-hungry leaders like Charles Taylor in Liberia or Jonas Savimbi in Angola also exploited such divisions. There is no one explanation for the causes of civil war in Africa even though a common factor behind most civil wars was the perception that only violent protest could accomplish change. The circumstances which led to the attempted secession of Biafra and the civil war in Nigeria, for example, were quite different from those which led Yoweri Museveni and a small band of men to attack Kabamba barracks and begin a war of insurgency in Uganda. Ethnic factors were predominant in Burundi and especially Rwanda, where they led to genocidal conflict between Hutus and Tutsis in 1994. It is, however, important to stress that each civil war—whether in Angola, Burundi, Chad, Congo/Zaire, Ethiopia, Liberia, Mozambique, Nigeria, Rwanda, Sierra Leone, Somalia, Sudan or Uganda—is related to the history of a particular country. The Congo/Zaire had two civil wars, one soon after independence, and the other more recently, with quite different causes. The Sudanese civil war was a result of the deep division between the Arab north and black African south, with ethnic as well as religious aspects to the revolt against colonization.

The impact of the Cold War

Africa soon became a focus of Cold War tension. Egypt was in the early years of Nasser's presidency when the United States withdrew offers of aid upon realizing that Nasser was doing business with the Soviet Union. The events that led to the Suez Crisis in 1956 and its outcome can be linked to the impact of the Cold War.

In the Congo Crisis, the Soviets backed Patrice Lumumba, the first prime minister of the Congo and the Americans supported and largely financed the UN peacekeeping force that restored public order and ended the secession of Katanga. The USA was suspected of complicity in the murder of Lumumba and later gave support to Mobutu, which helped maintain him in power until the end of the Cold War (see chapter 9, pages 466–8, for further discussion of the Congo Crisis).

Angola became the focus of the most active Cold War confrontation between the superpowers, and this will be discussed later in the chapter. Namibia only achieved independence after the end of the Cold War and the withdrawal of Cuban troops from Angola. The Cold War helped to prolong South African rule in the country at a time when the South African government was also paranoid about communism, presenting itself as a bastion of "Christian civilization". Ethiopia under Mengistu was also supported by the Soviet Union. Cold War rivalry was partly responsible for the outbreak of the Ogaden war in 1977. The massive military aid given by Warsaw Pact and NATO countries encouraged Ethiopia and Somalia to settle differences on the battlefield. The Cold War intensified conflict within and between countries. In Namibia it delayed independence, while the Congo conflict resulted from the developments just after independence. In the Congo the United States was on the winning side, but in Angola the reverse was true. One very damaging aspect of the impact of the Cold War on Africa, which is often given too little attention, was the indifference of Western governments to official corruption and human rights abuses in Africa as long as African governments were on the "right side".

There was a dramatic change of attitude when the Cold War ended and Western governments and financial institutions began to demand more transparency and accountability and greater respect for human rights such as freedom of expression and association and free and fair elections. This led many African countries to adopt multi-party systems of government.

Economic and social challenges

The post-colonial states in Africa faced major economic and social challenges. Some generalizations are valid for many countries. At independence, most Africans depended on subsistence farming in rural areas. African economies had been directed towards exporting cheap agricultural raw materials and unprocessed minerals to Europe. Prices for the commodities were controlled by developing countries. Cultivation of food for subsistence had been neglected. The transport system and infrastructure were generally inadequate. Agricultural marketing boards paid low fixed prices to farmers. The new African leaders saw rapid urban-centred industrialization as the means to achieve economic self-sufficiency. But many early schemes were over-ambitious or inappropriate. Most of the expertise, technology, machinery and building materials had to be imported from the West. This could lead to huge international debt which together with drought often stifled African economic development in the 1980s and 1990s. Governments had to accept structural adjustment programs imposed by the International Monetary Fund (IMF), to which they had to turn for emergency loans, to reduce state controls and employment in the public sector, maximize exports and remove price and exchange controls. Mass urbanization and population growth made it increasingly difficult to create full employment and overcome poverty.

Some governments coped well with the challenges while others aggravated the problems by pervasive official corruption which discouraged foreign investment and donor funding. The challenges were often aggravated by political instability and civil war. There was considerable variation in the type and extent of challenges from country to country and in policies adopted to deal with them. The economic policies of Kenya and Tanzania were in sharp contrast, as were those of former British and French colonies. France, as the major aid donor, exercised considerable control over the economic development of francophone countries. After the Arusha Declaration, Nyerere took Tanzanian development in an entirely new direction. Governments which had achieved independence through guerilla struggle often based their subsequent economic development on adaptations of socialist principles. Zambia had specific problems related to over-reliance on the copper industry at a time of dramatic falls in world commodity prices.

Source analysis

Socialism versus capitalism

A statement by Kwame Nkrumah on the benefits of the socialist model in a newly formed independent state.

Once freedom is gained, a greater task comes into view. All dependent territories are backward in education, in agriculture and in industry. The economic independence that should follow and maintain political independence demands every effort from the people, a total mobilisation of brain and manpower resources. What other countries have taken three hundred years or more to achieve, a once dependent territory must try to accomplish in a generation if it is to survive. Unless it is, as it were, "jet-propelled", it will lag behind and thus risk everything for which it has fought.

Capitalism is too complicated a system for a newly independent nation. Hence the need for a socialist society. But even a system based on social justice and a democratic constitution may need backing up by measures of an emergency nature in the period which follows independence. Without discipline true freedom cannot survive. In any event the basis must be a loyal, honest, hard-working and responsible civil service on which the party in power can rely. Armed forces must also be consolidated for defense.

Source: Nkrumah, K. 1965. *Neo-Colonialism: The Last Stage of Imperialism*. London, UK. Thomas Nelson and Sons.

Questions

1 How does Kwame Nkrumah's statement blend optimism and realism in his assessment of the challenges facing newly independent states?

2 Do you agree with Kwame Nkrumah's assessment of the limits to capitalism?

3 How crucial is the role of the defence forces in his model of the state?

Social problems: health and education

Social problems for emerging African states included the need to provide better health care, and from the 1980s to deal with the AIDS pandemic. Since gaining independence, African states have also made concerted efforts to extend the European model of education which was dominant in the colonial period to as large a number of people as possible. They did not, however, succeed to the same extent in modifying much of its alien character. Although progress was made in educating a significant number of people, not only for political and social consciousness but to build and operate the political, cultural, economic and industrial institutions, the efforts did not accomplish the desired goals relative to the quality and number of graduates. Millions of young people and adults received no education.

Education was not equally accessible to all segments and classes of society. Female were often under-represented. Rural areas fared worse than urban areas. For a variety of reasons some ethnic or linguistic groups were inadequately served. The curricula and methods of instruction often remained bookish and lacked relevance to the local realities and problems confronting Africa. School facilities, libraries and equipment were often inadequate. The list of problems is long and compounded by the fact that the material and human resources in most African nations were limited and already over-extended. The provision of education, especially at university level, is expensive, and most of the costs are borne by national treasuries.

The status and role of women

Most changes in the role of women can be related to the many Western influences, notably the spread of Christianity, Western education and Western technologies, which began to affect traditional African lifestyles before independence but did so much more rapidly once independence was gained. Education has provided women with career opportunities and career reasons for planning their families.

The pace of change has varied from rural to urban environments, from one social class to another, and for a broad range of cultural reasons. Women, especially those living in towns, have become less likely to be part of a polygamous relationship. Traditions died harder in rural areas where women's roles remained dominated by agricultural work, market life and providing fuel and water. Provision of clean piped water has freed women to perform other jobs.

The scope for paid employment has also increased. Women have become judges, professors, pilots, business executives, doctors, creative writers and artists and politicians. But African society still remains male dominated and progress in the political, social and economic empowerment of women has been uneven and relatively slow in some countries.

The impact of urbanization

Migration to towns, already important in the colonial period, was accelerated in the 1960s by education, population growth and employment opportunities. This involved the rapid growth of provincial centers as well as capitals. By the early 1990s, townspeople comprised 30 per cent of the population in sub-Saharan Africa. The most rapid migration was by those fleeing rural dislocation notably in Mozambique and other states with civil wars. Need has fast outpaced the provision of housing, resulting in a rapid growth in slums. Urban wages far exceeded rural earnings during the 1960s but fell over 30 per cent on average in the 1980s. Urban unemployment rose in many countries to over 20 per cent with the social consequences of rising crime rates, and problems associated with the increase of street children, prostitution and drug abuse.

Survival in decaying cities depended heavily on informal occupations, which employed some 72 per cent of Nigeria's urban labour force in 1978. The "second economy" was an important field for entrepreneurship and often relied on ethnic ties. Private schools, informal enterprises, illicit trading groups, vigilante forces and urban welfare associations all mobilized ethnic solidarities.

Capital cities were also important centers of political activity. The success of military coups depended on capturing key installations in the capital. Urban riots, often over food prices, destabilized several governments, such as those in Liberia, the Sudan and Zambia. From the end of the late 1980s insurrections that rose up against single-party regimes, weakened by economic crisis, were largely urban and encouraged by Western backers, unwilling to continue to support authoritarian regimes once the Cold War had ended. This led to a dramatic rise in multi-party states. Mass urbanization, combined with population growth and economic decay, helped to create the armed youth who terrorized Mozambique, Liberia, Somalia and Sierra Leone.

Zimbabwe since independence

The rulers of Zimbabwe and Angola also faced political, economic and social challenges. When Robert Mugabe became prime minister of independent Zimbabwe in 1980, he was cautious in honouring pledges for land redistribution and he encouraged the white commercial farmers to stay on. An impressive economic plan attracted international support but was rendered precarious by drought and political instability. Mugabe was unexpectedly moderate in his economic policies in his first two decades as a ruler, maintaining the economic system built by Ian Smith and avoiding the Kwame Nkrumah policy of attempting to radically transform his country into a socialist state.

Like Nkrumah, however, he showed dictatorial tendencies and could deal ruthlessly with opponents. There was ethnic tension between the majority Shona led by Mugabe and the minority Ndebele led by Joshua Nkomo. They had worked together in the liberation struggle but in 1980 Nkomo's ZAPU party became the de facto opposition. Nkomo was briefly a cabinet minister but was expelled from government in 1982 and accused of plotting a coup. The Ndebele became progressively more alienated and distrustful, an estranged fifth of the population. Their protests were ruthlessly suppressed by North Korean-trained soldiers of the Fifth Brigade. There were many executions, detentions without trial, rampages by army units and the diversion of food from selected areas especially Matabeleland, causing starvation. Mugabe in 1984 increased pressure to create a single-party state at ZANU's second party congress. ZANU and ZAPU merged in 1987 when a unity pact was signed and Nkomo became vice-president. Zimbabwe became a de facto single-party state but a sign of division within the party was its refusal to formalize this political objective. In the 1990s, economic problems forced Mugabe in the 1990s to adopt the structural adjustment policies recommended by the International Monetary Fund (IMF) but the problems intensified and led to major strikes and demonstrations in the capital Harare.

> The end date for the IB syllabus specifications for this course is 2000 so discussion of more controversial aspects of recent Zimbabwe history including land seizures, disputed elections and the treatment of political opponents in the Movement for Democratic Change in the multi-party era are not required.

Angola since independence

For the 25 years following independence Angola was engaged in a civil war that was also a destructive proxy war being fought by the USA and the Soviet Union. This involvement—the most active Cold War confrontation between the superpowers in Africa—did much to prolong the war and inflict incalculable suffering on the Angolan people. With its abundant supplies of oil and diamonds, Angola should have become one of the most economically and socially developed countries on the continent. War destroyed that hope.

When the Portuguese withdrew in 1975, the MPLA had secured the capital, but the National Liberation Front of Angola (FNLA) led by Holden Roberto invaded from the North, equipped by the USA and supported by the Zairean army and white mercenaries. The MPLA leader Agostinho Neto managed to expel them with the help of 13 000 hastily summoned Cuban troops equipped by the Russians. Thousands of Angolan slaves had been shipped to Cuba in the 18th and 19th centuries so there were strong historical links between the two countries. Meanwhile South Africa held on to South West Africa (Namibia) and destabilized Mozambique and Angola in order to maintain white minority rule. The South African Defence Forces (SADF) fought alongside UNITA in Southern Angola, giving them weapons and logistical support paid for by the United States and by UNITA's export of ivory and diamonds. The SADF also attacked the South West African People's Organisation (SWAPO) and ANC camps inside Angola. SWAPO was fighting for the independence of South West Africa, now Namibia.

The civil war intensified throughout the 1980s under the new Cold War begun by US president Ronald Reagan. Towards the end of 1980s, with improved relations between the superpowers under Reagan and Gorbachev, the United States was ready to restrain South Africa, and Cuba and Russia were ready to negotiate. The South African government agreed to free elections in Namibia that brought a SWAPO government to power in 1990. Cuban and Soviet support to the MPLA government was withdrawn and Cuban troops left. This paved the way for a peace process monitored by the UN elections in 1992. MPLA won a majority of seats in an election judged free and fair by the international community but Savimbi and UNITA would not accept the results and resumed fighting. Savimbi would not give up his power base or his control over diamond revenues. Only his death in combat with government troops in 2002 offered hope for lasting peace.

The impact of civil war

The civil war had a devastating economic and social impact on Angola. By the end of the 20th century there were over a million internally displaced persons, tens of thousands of street children and 70 000 amputees as a result of landmines. Agricultural production collapsed as peasant farmers fled from the war into the cities. Urban unemployment grew to over 30 per cent. Oil revenues, however, increased and provided 90 per cent of government revenue in the late 1990s. Most of the oil production was offshore and benefited from new deep-water mining technologies and was not affected by the war. Since independence, Angola had turned from being a food exporter to being heavily reliant on imports paid for by mortgaging future oil revenues. Military leaders in both MPLA and UNITA benefited from controlling the diamond mines and selling diamonds illegally. They were also enriched by foreign arms dealers in return for arms contracts. MPLA politicians benefited from selling off oil concessions. To complete the picture, during this period, two-thirds of the urban population had sunk to living below the poverty line, and

10 per cent now live in extreme poverty. Resources such oil and diamonds have fuelled conflicts in several African countries since independence and have proved to be more of a curse than a blessing to most people in Angola, Congo and Sierra Leone.

Prime minister Jawaharlal Nehru, first prime minister of India (1947–64), with Kwame Nkrumah, first prime minister of Ghana (1957–60), in 1960.

Activity:

Role-playing

Divide up into groups of four with each person assigned to play one of the following roles:

- Ruler of a newly independent state in Africa or Asia.
- Independent spokesperson: a sharp critic of the regime.
- Reporter to interview the ruler.
- Reporter to interview the independent spokesperson.

Select rulers from both Africa and Asia (some good examples include Kwame Nkrumah, Robert Mugabe to the year 2000, Jawaharlal Nehru and Ho Chi Minh).

The independence movement in Vietnam

There are two phases to Vietnam's route to independence: the attempt to eliminate the French colonial presence (1945–54); and the attempt of the North Vietnamese to eliminate further Western influence and establish a unified Vietnamese state (1959–75). In Southeast Asia, nationalism and socialism were regarded as compatible ideologies, and the independence movement that originated with Ho Chi Minh in the Second World War epitomized this. Once the Japanese and French were expelled, the Vietnamese still had to negotiate outside influences as agents in the Cold War. In the north, Ho Chi Minh established a socialist state, while in the south the Vietnam Republic was virulently anti-communist and relied on assistance from the United States. After almost 30 years of guerrilla warfare and armed struggles, the USA withdrew and the regime in the south collapsed. Although he had been dead for five years, Ho Chi Minh's dream of a unified, socialist Vietnam was realized.

The Second World War brought about a number of changes that led to decolonization in the region. While the Middle East and Indian subcontinent already had strong movements based on Western, democratic models, East Asia's models were more nationalistic and socialist, reflecting the demography of the region and the ideological influences that permeated East Asia. Most of East Asia was influenced by China, and by the middle of the 20th century, this presupposed that national self-determination went hand-in-hand with Marxism. Furthermore, the Japanese occupation of most of Southeast Asia finally eradicated the notion of Western, white superiority. The Europeans could not re-establish themselves in the region as Japanese occupation had created either collaborationist regimes or opposition groups that took over after their departure. The British, Dutch and French tried to reclaim their colonies in Burma, Indochina, Indonesia and Malaysia and failed. By 1961, the entire region was decolonized.

The Vietnamese independence movement provided the model for other countries. Under the leadership of Ho Chi Minh, the **Viet Minh** had fought against the Japanese in 1945 and occupied much of the country in the period immediately following the Second World War. However, the French did not recognize the Viet Minh as the potent political force that they were, and did not honour their promises to grant local autonomy as part of the French Union. This led to not one, but two protracted wars that ultimately resulted in the creation of a unified Vietnam as a communist state. The country remained poor and underdeveloped due to the centrally planned economy that the country had in place until the 1980s. At that point, they began to adopt a Chinese model, introducing market-oriented policies while maintaining a communist political system. As in China, this has led to internal conflict between party pragmatists and ideologues who feared that Vietnam was losing its socialist base.

The **Viet Minh** was a coalition of communists and nationalists who resisted Japanese occupation of Vietnam during the second world war. The Viet Minh later opposed France's colonial rule over Vietnam, and were ultimately successful against them. They were later absorbed into the Communist Party in North Vietnam.

The history of French colonialism

France had begun to make inroads on Vietnam even before it began military campaigns to consolidate control over Indochina. In the 17th century French Catholic missionaries went to the region to try to convert the indigenous population and had marginal success. As a result, the French established themselves there, giving the government a pretext for further action in the region. Formal French colonization began in earnest in 1859 with a series of military campaigns that ended with France establishing a protectorate over Indochina. Although the Vietnamese royal family continued to be its nominal rulers, this was largely ceremonial. The French were interested in Indochina for its strategic location, proximity to China and its rubber production. Indochina was one of the France's most prized possessions and, as was later revealed, France was willing to fight long and hard to retain this possession. Prior to the Second World War, uprisings against the French were limited and easily suppressed.

The Second World War

The Second World War proved pivotal for the establishment of an independent Vietnam. During the war, Vietnam was taken by the Japanese but as a member of the Axis powers its administration was left under the Vichy regime in France. The Vichy government's collapse in March 1945 led to its direct annexation by Japan. In the north, a military force called the Viet Minh (League for Independence of Vietnam) led by Ho Chi Minh fought against the Japanese using guerrilla tactics and gained momentum against its foreign occupiers. When Japan surrendered on 14 August 1945 the situation reached a critical juncture. On 2 September 1945 Ho Chi Minh proclaimed the creation of the Democratic People's Republic of Vietnam (North Vietnam). Hoping for further support from the USA, Ho Chi-Minh was disappointed when the change of government saw a cooling off of its prior support for the independence movement. While President Roosevelt had been very sympathetic to its nationalist cause, and General Stillwell (commander of US forces in India, Burma and China) had backed the Viet Minh, the ascendancy of Harry Truman and the onset of the Cold War left the USA with little room to support a Marxist regime despite its anti-colonial rhetoric.

The French attempted to mollify the North Vietnamese by forming the Indochinese Federation and recognizing North Vietnam an independent state within the French Union. When the French Union did not immediately materialize, the North Vietnamese maintained their independence and the Viet Minh fought against the French in what is referred to as the First Indochinese War.

The First Indochina War, 1946–54

The First Indochina War began in November 1946 with a French assault on Vietnamese civilians in the port city of Haiphong. Until 1954 the French military battled against Vietnamese forces. The Viet Minh had considerable popular support in the rural, agricultural regions of Vietnam, while the French strongholds were in the urban areas, resulting in a long bloody struggle. In the first four years of the war, there was actually very little fighting. General Võ Nguyên Giáp spent most of this time recruiting peasant support and expanding the size of the Viet Minh army. By 1954 Giáp had enlisted 117 000 to fight with him, although outnumbered by the 100 000 French and 300 000 Vietnamese soldiers on the side of the French. What restored the odds after 1949 was the military support provided by the Chinese Communists that included heavy artillery, later put to good use in the final, decisive battle. The battle of Dien Bien Phu took place in an improbable mountain area near the border with Laos. It began in late 1953 when the French occupied Dien Bien Phu to try to interrupt supply routes from Laos into North Vietnam. The Viet Minh responded by blockading all roads in and out of the area, although the French felt confident that they could supply their forces through aerial drops. Taking advantage of the situation, General Võ Nguyên Giáp mounted a surprise attack, arriving with 40 000 Viet Minh forces that soon surrounded the 13 000 French and broke their lines. On 7 May 1954, the base was taken by the Vietnamese and the French surrendered.

Geneva Accords

At this point, the French government decided that the conflict in Indochina was too costly, and negotiated a settlement in an international conference in Geneva. Discussions had already begun in Geneva on April 26, and so now the object was to negotiate an end to the war. The result was known as the Geneva Accords—a set of ten non-binding agreements that:

- established a cease-fire line in Vietnam along the 17th parallel
- gave 300 days for the withdrawal of troops on both sides
- called for Viet Minh evacuation from Cambodia and Laos
- ordered the evacuation of foreign troops—except military advisers
- prohibited the distribution of foreign arms and munitions
- called for free elections in Cambodia and Laos in 1955, and elections for the whole of Vietnam to be held by July 1956
- advised that implementation of these would be conducted by representatives from Canada, India and Pakistan.

The Accords effectively accepted the existence of a communist regime in the North and tried to bring about stability in Vietnam through the temporary division of the country. At the signing of the Accords, the Viet Minh controlled nearly three-quarters of Vietnam. Non-communist countries hoped that this would weaken their support throughout the country. Instead, it seemed to consolidate their control of the north, and gave them a boundary behind which it could retreat.

By 1954, Vietnam was free of colonial rule, but it was divided into two states: in the north, the Viet Minh under Ho Chi Minh retained control; in the south, a pro-Western regime was established with support from the United States. This division was only intended to serve until elections could be held throughout the country. However, such elections never occurred and instead, conflict in Vietnam renewed as the country engaged in a civil war involving the United States, the Soviet Union and the People's Republic of China.

Võ Nguyên Giáp (1911–)

Võ Nguyên Giáp was a Vietnamese politician but is best known for his skills as an army officer for the Viet Minh and later the North Vietnamese Army. He directed the best-known assaults of both Indochina wars—the Battle of Dien Bien Phu, the Tet Offensive and the final offensive of the war, the Ho Chi Minh Campaign. He was Minister of the Interior under Ho Chi Minh and later defence minister and commander of the Peoples Army of Vietnam after unification until 1980. He was a member of the politburo until 1982. He is retired and writes about military matters.

? **Which do you think was more important to Ho Chi Minh—socialism or self-rule for the Vietnamese people?**

IB Learner Profile link
Principled and critical thinkers

After the Second World War the administration of Vietnam south of the 16th parallel was placed under the command of the British Lord Mountbatten, who dispatched General Douglas Gracey to Indochina to restore French rule. His decision to employ Japanese soldiers to fight in South Vietnam gave the French time to send reinforcements but strained relations between the American and British military forces in Asia. By the end of 1945 the French had 5000 troops in Vietnam.

A revealing response to this expedient solution came from US General Douglas MacArthur, who said: "If there is anything that makes my blood boil it is to see our allies in Indo-china and Java deploying Japanese troops to reconquer the little people we promised to liberate."

1 This comment both supports independence movement and self-determination in Southeast Asia but also perpetuates ideas of Western superiority and racism. Discuss the implications further in your group.

2 There are numerous accounts of the harsh treatment of Allied prisoners of war at the hands of the Japanese. Why, then, would General Gracey use Japanese soldiers against Indochinese resistance? How would this have affected relations between the Allied forces?

Discussion point:

In attendance at the Geneva Conference (1954) were:

● Cambodia
● United Kingdom (UK)
● France
● United States of America (USA)
● Laos
● Union of Soviet Socialist Republics (USSR)
● People's Republic of China (PRC)
● Viet Minh (North Vietnam)
● State of Vietnam (South Vietnam)

The Accords were agreements among representatives of Cambodia, France, Laos, North Vietnam and South Vietnam. Why were American, British, Chinese and Soviet representatives present? What did they hope to achieve in the negotiations? Who do you think was most successful?

Ho Chi Minh (Nguyen Sinh Cung) (1890–1969)

Ho Chi Minh was the founder of the Indochinese Communist Party in 1930, the Viet Minh in 1941 and the first president of the Democratic People's Republic of Vietnam from 1945 until his death in 1969.

Born and raised in rural Vietnam, he became a school teacher, before taking a job, in 1911 as a cook aboard a French ship that took him to Africa, the Americas, the United Kingdom, and eventually France. It was in France that he developed both socialist and nationalist ideals. During the Paris Peace Conference, he created a 19-point petition in which he demanded that France grant equal rights to the Indochinese, but predictably received no response from the French. In December 1920, he became a founding member of the French Communist Party that split from the Socialists on the heels of the successful Bolshevik Revolution in Russia. In 1923 he went to Moscow, and became known for a eulogy he wrote upon the death of Lenin, and for criticizing the French Communist Party for not mounting significant opposition to colonialism.

At this time he began to formulate his own ideas regarding socialist solutions to independence for the Vietnamese. Notably, he emphasized the importance of mobilizing the oppressed peasants. This distinguished him from other communists who felt that the industrial workers were the foundation of revolution. He also saw successful Vietnamese communism as a mixture of socialist and nationalist ideas.

For the remainder of the 1920s and most of the 1930s Ho spent time in both the Soviet Union and China, hoping to mobilize expatriate and exiled Vietnamese. In 1930 he founded the Indochinese Communist Party in the hope of uniting socialists in the colony. This was followed by an armed insurrection of communists that was put down by the French. Ho was condemned to death in absentia and could not return to his homeland.

It was the outbreak of the Second World War that led Ho to return to Vietnam. In January 1941 he created the Viet Minh initially as a political party, but it soon became an army under the leadership of General Giáp. Hoping to gain the support of Chiang Kai-shek against the Japanese, Ho went to China to ask for assistance and was imprisoned, but was eventually freed and returned to Vietnam.

During the Japanese occupation of Vietnam, Ho found an opportunity to further the cause of Vietnamese independence. His forces conducted a guerrilla war against the Japanese, at which time Ho sought US support and began working with the US Office of Strategic Services (OSS)—the forerunner of the CIA. The Viet Minh made steady progress against the Japanese, and by August 1945, after the Japanese surrender, they quickly marched on Hanoi and took the capital. On 2 September 1945, Ho proclaimed Vietnam independent and socialist. When the French refused to accept this, Ho and his Viet Minh forces fought a 10-year war until the French were ousted. Although his forces controlled most of Vietnam, he agreed to a temporary division of the country that gave his communist government control of the north and time to consolidate power before launching a socialist war of unification in 1959.

Ho Chi Minh became an important communist diplomat, acting as an intermediary between the PRC and USSR when relations worsened, and he convinced both countries to assist him in his war against South Vietnam and the United States. The Western powers mistakenly saw him as a puppet of the major communist powers, but this was far from the truth. The developing world saw him more for the independent leader that he was, and he was regarded as a model for other leaders seeking to implement their own version of communism in newly emerging states.

Lê Duan (1907–1986)

Lê Duan was Secretary General of the Communist party of Vietnam. He was a founding member of the Indochinese Communist Party (1930) and rose through the ranks as a supporter of the Viet Minh, becoming a military commander in the south during the First Indochina War. He succeeded Ho Chi Minh as Secretary General in 1959, becoming the chief policy maker, advocating total war against the south to bring about unification. With increased US involvement, Lê Duan remained convinced that continued struggle would bring about their withdrawal, rather than triumph. After the war ended, he emphasized the need to restructure and socialize the South so that unification would be not just political, but economic and cultural. As Secretary General, he tried to stay out of party politics and was largely successful in doing so, assisting the state with achieving political stability. He died in 1986.

A divided Vietnam

Like the Vietnamese themselves, the country was divided into a northern, largely rural peasantry that supported the Marxist ideas of Ho Chi Minh, while in the south, a number of inept and corrupt leaders—beginning with the Emperor Bao Đai and Ngô Đình Diem—ruled. In 1959, Vietnam was plunged into a civil war that determined most of the policies of both Vietnams. During this period, Ho Chi Minh became more of a figurehead and less of an active political figure. His death in 1969 did not mark the end of the war, or of revolutionary struggle in the north.

North Vietnam

The Democratic Republic of Vietnam was recognized by all of the communist states. The North Vietnamese received limited assistance from China and the Soviet Union, but in the early years of its foundation, Ho Chi Minh was more focused on internal affairs in the north than the spread of revolution to the south. The main reason for this was that Ho Chi Minh was consolidating communist power. Unlike his counterpart in the south, Ho Chi Minh was incorruptible, while adhering strictly to his nationalist-Marxist ideas. His focus was on the elimination of class enemies. In 1955 and 1956, anyone branded a landlord, traitor or French sympathizer could be targeted, and many were killed by the North Vietnamese. Northern Catholics were also identified, as they were regarded as pro-French, forcing whole villages to flee south. During these years, one million Vietnamese fled to the south to escape persecution or execution.

In the north, the communists continued to implement policies of land reform that they had begun during the First Indochinese War. From 1946 on, the Viet Minh had launched a programme of agrarian reform centered on the distribution of land to the peasants. Much like their Chinese counterparts, the Viet Minh prided themselves on moving into the regions, liberating the peasantry and assisting them in their acquisition of land tenure. Landlords lost their economic and social control over the peasantry as the Viet Minh relieved peasants of their annual rents and established communities in which the peasants worked collectively.

Ho assisted southern communists through founding the **National Liberation Front** and the **Viet Cong**, and began the construction of what would become the Ho Chi Minh trail that went through Laos and Cambodia. He also began to support the communist Pathet Lao in Laos and the Khmer Rouge in Cambodia. Recognized as the father of Vietnamese independence, his death in 1969 did not mean an end to the revolutionary struggle or the drive for Vietnamese independence; indeed, many of his followers saw it as imperative to complete his mission.

National Liberation Front Founded in 1960, this was the political arm of the Viet Cong. It gave South Vietnamese communists a political party.

The **Viet Cong** were communist troops in South Vietnam after the Geneva Accords. According to the agreements, communist forces were supposed to withdraw to north of the 17th parallel but a number of operatives were from the south and remained behind after the Indochina War. Initially the Viet Cong conducted political assassinations and subversive tactics, but later became a full-blown military force. The level of direction received from Hanoi is still debated.

South Vietnam

The situation in South Vietnam was more complex as there were a number of leaders who had different plans and policies for stopping the spread of communism into the south, but all of whom had regimes that were characterized by chaos, corruption and brutality towards the perceived enemies of the state.

The French initially had a plan of restoring the Vietnamese Emporer Bao Đai to serve as a puppet leader of what they hoped would be a client state, but France had withdrawn and Bao Đai proved to be too weak. The United States, with its fears of communist expansion, assumed the position of patron of southern Vietnam. In the waning years of the First Indochina War, the USA had provided France with $3 billion to fund its war against the Viet Minh. It sought a stronger leader for its Vietnamese client state and found one in Ngo Dinh Diem, a nationalist and Catholic who had patriotic credentials stemming from his open opposition to French rule in the 1930s. Under US direction, Bao Đai recalled Diem in 1954 and made him prime minister. In 1955, Diem ousted Bao Đai and recreated the government in the south. In a referendum that was clearly rigged the South Vietnamese voted in favor of a Vietnam Republic with Diem as president. His regime became increasingly corrupt and brutal, leading eventually to the renewal of conflict in Vietnam.

One of the first issues that Diem needed to tackle was land distribution. A number of radical and moderate groups advocated land distribution so that the Vietnamese peasantry would have sufficient land. When they occupied the south, the Viet Minh had helped the peasants by redistributing roughly 600 000 hectares of land through which countless peasants had acquired land tenure, effectively abolishing rent payments since 1945. In 1955, Diem reversed this, and required peasants to resume paying rent. Further, in 1958, the peasants were expected to purchase the land they farmed in six annual installments. This was extremely costly, and it alienated a peasantry who had come to see that land as their own.

Diem's policies were in clear reaction to the communist regime to the north. He was in constant fear of opposition and, increasingly, assassination. He worked hard to eliminate any potential threats to his rule. In 1956, he refused to hold the elections stipulated in the Geneva Accords, arguing that northerners would be compelled to vote communist. He imprisoned opposition leaders and targeted Viet Minh that remained in the south. He also favored Catholics over the Buddhist majority: roughly 10 per cent of the population was Catholic, and many were northerners who had escaped to the south as refugees. This favoring of the minority interest led to further dissatisfaction with his regime, and opposition within the south itself. Beginning in 1957, South Vietnamese communists, called the Viet Cong, took advantage of peasant alienation and began to organize resistance groups in the countryside and plot political assassinations against government officials. There were an increasing number of assassinations—1200 in 1959, and 4000 in 1961. Despite these figures, and the growth of the Viet Cong and its political arm, the National Liberation Front (founded in 1960 by Ho Chi Minh), Diem maintained control over the cities of South Vietnam and much of the countryside.

To the ire of many South Vietnamese peasants, their villages were forcibly disbanded and they were placed in what where called Strategic Hamlets. While the South Vietnamese government said that these were to protect the peasantry from looting and pillaging by the Viet Cong and other bandits, the main objective was to isolate the Viet Cong from their power base and prevent them from gaining any support from the peasants. The hamlets were regularly patrolled by the Army of the Republic of Vietnam (ARVN) to prevent Viet Cong infiltration, but this policy only further alienated the peasantry, making them even less likely to assist the government in eliminating the Viet Cong.

> **Bao Đai** (1913–1997)
>
> Bao Đai was the last emperor of Vietnam. He was crowned emperor in 1925, but a regency was established until he completed his education in France in 1932. The position was largely ceremonial as a result of French colonization but Bao Đai hoped to convince the French to give more power back to the Vietnamese and grant them limited independence. Instead, war came and Bao Đai remained emperor. He cooperated with the Japanese, making him unpopular with those who resisted occupation, namely the Viet Minh. At the end of the war Ho Chi Minh demanded his abdication and he agreed. He was in exile for most of the post-war period but returned briefly to Vietnam after the Geneva Accords. He was, however, regarded as a French puppet, so he lost his support base and was overthrown in a 1955 referendum. He was then exiled to France. He remained popular among some Vietnamese and the Viet Minh even considered establishing a coalition government with him in 1972 but he declined and instead called for peace and an end to war, choosing to remain outside of Vietnam for the rest of his days.

Even the United States was becoming alarmed by reports of Diem's brutality. In particular, his widely publicized suppression of Buddhist monks left many Americans horrified that they were supporting such a leader. Thus, it should come as no surprise that a plan to overthrow Diem by members of the South Vietnamese military received the tacit support of the American government. In November 1963, Diem was assassinated and initially replaced by a military junta that had little popular support. In 1965, General Nguyễn Văn Thiệu became president, providing a veneer of stability, but his regime was just as corrupt, and his officers as inept as those under Diem. Thiệu's policies were not ideological, just based on the necessity of maintaining resistence to the incursion of the North Vietnamese and the Viet Cong and of maintaining his support base through personal favours and connections that perpetuated, rather than eradicated the corruption of Diem.

It was, however, under Thiệu that the South Vietnamese government attempted land reform. In 1954, 60 per cent of the peasantry were landless, and 20 per cent owned parcels of land of less than two acres. Furthermore, the tenant farmers had to pay approximately 74 per cent of their annual crop yield to their landlords. In the 1940s and 1950s, the Viet Minh had gained the support of much of the southern peasantry through rigorous redistribution of land. The Viet Minh had done this by going into villages, imprisoning the landlords and forcing them to cede their lands to the peasants who worked on it. The Viet Cong continued these policies and through redistributing the land owned by absentee landlords gained further allegiance from ther peasants in support of their guerrilla operation.

Diem had sided with the landlords and attempted to return the land to them. To try and undercut peasant support for the Viet Cong and distance himself from Diem, Thiệu introduced the first of his land reforms in 1968. The first programme gave 50 000 families government land. Even more sweeping was the March 1970 Land-to-the-Tiller Act which ended rent payments and granted ownership to those who worked the land. To distribute land fairly, he determined that the maximum amount of land that could be owned was 37 acres. Through this act, 1.5 million acres were distributed to 400 000 landless peasants by 1972 and by 1973, all but seven per cent of peasant farmers owned their own land.

> **Nguyễn Văn Thiệu** (1923–2001)
>
> Nguyễn Văn Thiệu was president of the Republic of Vietnam from 1967 to 1975. Upon graduating from military college, Thiệu served as an officer in the State of Vietnam under the French and then the Republic of Vietnam, after its founding in 1954. He became a general in 1962 and was a member of the military junta that overthrew Diem. From 1965–67 he was head of state—a ceremonial position with little authority, but in 1967 he ran for President in South Vietnamese elections and, with 37 per cent of the vote, won the election and remained President until just before the collapse of the government in April 1975. The Thiệu government was corrupt and marred by cronyism and brutality, yet under his leadership, massive land reforms took place in the south. He was kept in power by US support, and upon American troop withdrawal in 1973, his army faced a series of defeats that led to the end of his government. Thiệu resigned as president just before the fall of Saigon and fled to Taiwan before permanently settling in the United States.

Despite positive measure of agrarian reform, the poor treatment of the population by the ARVN and the corruption and ineptitude of the leadership continued to alienate much of the population. The combined forces of the North Vietnamese Army (NVA) and the Viet Cong, who were determined to fight until Vietnam was united and socialist, resulted in an ongoing war of attrition against the USA until American public opinion demanded withdrawal, following which the ARVN collapsed under the combined assault of regular and guerrilla warfare from the north.

A "bourgeois" landowner, executed after a trial before a committee in 1955.

The Second Indochina War, 1959–75

When the Vietnamese renewed the conflict in 1959 the situation was complex. On one side were the North Vietnamese and the Viet Cong who had the support of the Soviet Union and People's Republic of China. On the other side was South Vietnam with the support of the United States. This war was often misjudged as an episode of the Cold War, but South Vietnam faced adversaries within its own borders as well as outside of it, and the military were hampered by the persistent problem of identifying the members of the Viet Cong. Although the amount of aid received by the South vastly outpaced that received by the North, in the end North Vietnam prevailed due to their superior organization and single-minded commitment to the struggle. This was a war of attrition that the communists believed they could win. Once the Americans withdrew, the Army of the Republic of Vietnam (ARVN) could not stop the tide of North Vietnamese leading to the fall of Saigon in April 1975 and an end to the war.

Even more than the First Indochina War, this conflict wrought tremendous damage on the people of Vietnam. The statistics are horrifying: approximately one in seven, or 6.5 million Vietnamese were killed; there were countless casualties; and the country was destroyed by the massive bombing campaigns and use of Agent Orange to exfoliate the jungles and expose guerrillas.

Neither side could take the high ground in the treatment of the population. Both sides used coercion and indoctrination to engage support. While there were some who were ideologically bound to supporting one side or another, most people chose sides by necessity. Both sides augmented their forces through conscription—and there was no option to remain neutral. Whichever side arrived first in a village coerced all able men to fight. The war also limited agricultural production. The women, children and elderly who remained did the best they could to survive in the absence of adult men, but there were food shortages in many areas.

In South Vietnam, the Viet Cong led guerrilla operations and began assassinating public officials in 1957. It was often assumed that the Viet Cong were simply taking orders from North Vietnam but this was untrue. In fact, the Viet Cong were a largely

These smiling women soldiers take some time off from fighting to do a little farming. They are planting rice in a paddy somewhere in North Vietnam, 1968.

autonomous group of cells who worked independently of one another and of North Vietnam, partly in an attempt to keep their cadres from being identified by the South Vietnamese government. Their main advantage was their anonymity and their seeming ability to strike anywhere unexpectedly. While relying on military assistance from the north, most of their operations were designed by local commanders who knew the areas where they fought. Throughout the 1960s the Viet Cong became increasingly powerful and their ranks swelled, reaching a peak in 1968 just before the Tet Offensive.

Army officer peers from an exit of the famed Cu Chi Tunnels near Saigon. During the Vietnam War, Vietcong hid in the tunnels; now they are a tourist attraction.

Being a traditionally-trained army, the ARVN had great difficulties in combating the guerrilla tactics employed by the Viet Cong. Furthermore, they lacked the leadership; too many officers had their positions due to family connections and tended to be incompetent or corrupt. They were also infiltrated by Viet Cong who worked as their servants and delivered information to the communists. It was all too easy for the Viet Cong to launch a guerrilla attack, cause destruction and then melt into the jungle where the ARVN could not follow them.

In the Spring of 1959 the Viet Cong felt sufficiently strong to engage openly against their adversaries and began to confront the ARVN in direct combat, rather than maintaining their initial methods of ambush and assassination. In Hanoi, the Party leadership met to discuss the formalization of hostilities. The decision to renew the war was the result of a meeting of the Central Committee Worker's Party in July 1959. There it was agreed that to truly establish socialism in the north, unification with the south was necessary.

As the ARVN faltered, the United States sought to fill the gap by providing the South Vietnamese with supplies and eventually men. The intensification of US involvement led to further escalation of the war as North Vietnam now saw the conflict as an anti-imperial war in which their objective—along with unification—was to expel the US forces.

To support and perhaps exert some control over the Viet Cong, the North Vietnamese sent a number of their troops south using the **Ho Chi Minh trail** to transport them through Laos to avoid the border crossing. This increased the pressure on the ARVN and the government of South Vietnam that had proved unstable until the appointment of General Nguyễn Văn Thiệu in 1965. Even so, South Vietnam was in political disarray and the ARVN seemed incapable of stemming the tide of North Vietnam. This meant a further escalation in assistance from the US forces to prevent the spread of communism

Ho Chi Minh Trail was a network of paths from North Vietnam into South Vietnam, going through Cambodia and Laos to prevent detection. It was used to supply the Viet Cong during the war.

south. It was not just the US that believed in the domino theory: Australia and New Zealand sent troops to Vietnam in support of **SEATO**. They felt threatened by the idea of a communist Vietnam, linked to the Soviet Union and China. These fears highlighted the general ignorance of Ho Chi Minh's nationalist goals, and overestimation of the intentions of the major communist powers.

The Tet Offensive is generally remembered as a turning point in American public opinion, but it is also a turning point for the role of the Viet Cong and North Vietnamese army in the course and outcome of the war. The Viet Cong, with between 70 000 and 100 000 soldiers in their ranks, decided to conduct a formal attack on the urban areas of South Vietnam. The attack that took place in January 1968 in the holiday period, traditionally a period of cease-fire, was truly a shock for the South Vietnamese and Americans. The Viet Cong had the element of surprise and the determination to fight, but in the end they had to withdraw. The ARVN did not break ranks and held out until they received reinforcement from US troops.

The casualties for the Viet Cong were disastrous. It has been estimated that they suffered 40 000 to 50 000 deaths in the Offensive and never managed to regain their strength. Instead, their ranks were replaced by the North Vietnamese Army that began to assert itself in the south. As an autonomous unit, the Viet Cong contributed very little to the fighting after Tet, and henceforth most of the fighting was between the ARVN (and the US) and the North Vietnamese army.

After the Tet Offensive, the US and ARVN recovered quickly but American confidence was shaken and there was increasing pressure to negotiate for a withdrawal. American diplomats in Moscow were enlisted in secret talks to intimate the United States's willingness to withdraw. At the same time, president Nixon began a phased American withdrawal—first with an announcement that 25 000 soldiers would be coming home in 1969, with further plans for another 150 000 to return home in 1970. This mollified the public at home but contributed to the demoralization of those troops still stationed in Vietnam.

In 1968 peace talks began in Paris that lasted until 1973. The main participants in these talks were US Secretary of State Henry Kissinger and Lê Đức Thọ, representing the North Vietnamese. North Vietnam insisted on the complete withdrawal of American forces and the replacement of the South Vietnamese regime with a coalition government. Their position was strengthened by an increasing number of military defeats and the pressure that the American government was

SEATO: The Southeast Treaty Organization was established in 1954 to prevent the spread of communism in the region. The founding members were the United States, United Kingdom, France, Pakistan, New Zealand, Australia, the Philippines and Thailand. The countries of Indochina—Cambodia, Laos and the two Vietnams, were specifically forbidden from joining the organization. It had no military force of its own, and while members conducted annual joint operations, SEATO emphasized economic development and political stability as methods for preventing the spread of communism in Southeast Asia. After the fall of Saigon and the unification of Vietnam under the communists, SEATO ceased to exist and was disbanded in 1977.

Lê Duc Thọ (1910–1990)

Lê Duc Thọ was North Vietnam's primary negotiator at the Paris Peace talks, and he was largely responsible for their outcome. He was one of the founding members of the Indochina Communist Party (1930) and later joined the Viet Minh in their struggle for independence. In 1955 he became a member of the politburo and oversaw the communist uprising in the South against the Republic of Vietnam. In 1968, he insisted that the USA stop bombing North Vietnam before anything was decided. Upon Ho Chi Minh's death in 1969 he worked closely with the collective leadership that succeeded him. With Henry Kissinger, he won the Nobel Peace Prize in 1973 but refused to accept it, arguing that there was no real peace in Vietnam. In 1975 he returned to South Vietnam and from 1975 to 1986 he served on the politburo and was the Worker Party's chief theoretician. He resigned in 1986 due to the continuing economic problems in Vietnam.

under to withdraw. By 1971 the United States had openly considered withdrawal, and the North Vietnamese no longer insisted on a coalition government in the South. These two changes were compromises that allowed the talks to move forward and both sides felt confident that an agreement could be reached.

South Vietnam was not, however, party to the negotiations. When presented with what they saw as a *fait accompli*, the government in Saigon insisted on making changes to the treaty to show its input in the process. Kissinger's presentation of these changes incensed the North Vietnamese who thought they had negotiated a settlement. In return, they demanded further changes. The United States responded with an intense bombing campaign that succeeded in bringing the North Vietnamese back to the negotiation table and on 27 January 1973 the Agreement on Ending the War and Restoring Peace in Vietnam was signed by representatives of South Vietnamese Communists, North Vietnam, South Vietnam and the USA. The United States agreed to withdraw all its forces in 60 days, and a cease fire was scheduled for January 28. By March 1973 all the American troops were gone and war began again in Vietnam. The North Vietnamese already had numerous troops in South Vietnam, and they gained momentum after the withdrawal of American forces and the end of US bombing campaigns. The regime in the South was plagued with inflation, corruption and food shortages, making it even more unpopular. The situation was exacerbated by massive desertions from the ARVN.

In March 1975 the North launched their final offensive. Planning for it to take about two years, they were as surprised as anyone when it was over in two months. The government in Saigon collapsed and with it, the army. Thiệu resigned from office on April 21 and fled to Taiwan. The North Vietnamese army took city after city, culminating with Saigon on 30 April 1975.

This action is often referred to as the fall of Saigon, but in reality the North Vietnamese Army marched unopposed into the city. No army remained to fight them, and the population was resigned to their occupation. The American troops were evacuated, leaving behind hundreds of thousands of South Vietnamese civil servants and officers who would face the wrath of the North Vietnamese. However, the war was finally over and Vietnam was unified.

Indochina

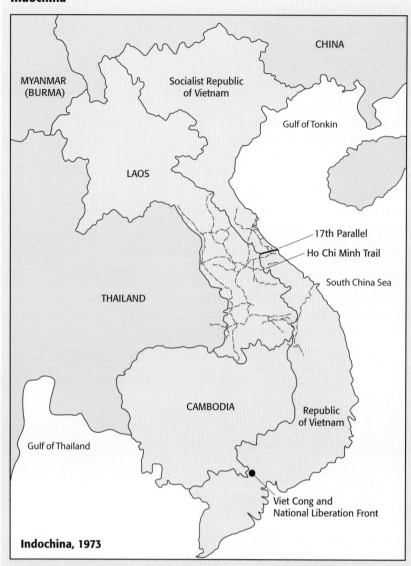

Indochina, 1973

Cambodia and Laos, the two other countries that make up Indochina as recognized in the Geneva Conference, had equally turbulent histories. Both became communist countries at the same time that the North Vietnamese consolidated their control over Vietnam and unified the country. From 1975 to 1989 all three countries were socialist and, although dominated by their neighbour Vietnam, Cambodia and Laos had quite different histories.

Cambodia

In 1954 the Cambodian monarchy was restored to the throne through the strength of Prince Norodom Sihanouk. His parents were the reigning monarchs, and he was head of state, continuing in this role upon the death of his father in 1960. The government was relatively stable in Cambodia and Cambodia tried to maintain its neutrality in the Vietnam War but this proved difficult as the North Vietnamese and Viet Cong used Cambodia as an alternative route to South Vietnam. In 1970, when Sihanouk was abroad, General Lon Nol overthrew Sihanouk, but struggled with the same predicament caused by the North Vietnamese continuing to use the Cambodian trails. As a result the US bombed Cambodia to destroy the North Vietnamese routes. At the same time, the communist Khmer Rouge emerged as a guerrilla movement fighting for the removal of the government in power. Pol Pot, its leader, advocated an extreme form of agrarian communism in which the cities would be depopulated and moved to the countryside for re-education. This movement had tremendous rural support and wore away and defeated Lon Nol's regime in April 1975.

From 1975 to 1979 Cambodia existed as Democratic Kampuchea.

The country was notorious for its so-called "killing fields". When the Khmer Rouge was in power an estimated 1–2 million people (20 per cent of the population) were killed in a class war against all but the rural peasantry; the rest were sent to the countryside for re-education. The government tightly regulated the economy, eliminating currency and banking during its tenure. The government opposed technology as Western and thus much of the infrastructure, including most of the available motor vehicles, were destroyed. All aspects of the lives of its citizens were scrutinized by the leadership, and anyone accused of opposing the regime was imprisoned, tortured and/or executed. The people faced hunger and starvation on a large scale.

Though communist, the Cambodians resented Vietnamese incursions in their country and so the government was strongly anti-Vietnamese. They periodically invaded Vietnamese villages near the frontier and the Vietnamese responded in kind. There was a period of escalation until finally in January 1979 Vietnam ousted Pol Pot and occupied Cambodia until 1989. After UN intervention and a cease-fire agreement brokered by UN Secretary General Javier Pérez de Cuéllar, the Vietnamese finally withdrew and Cambodia finally had control over its own political future. It established a constitutional monarchy in 1993 and free elections were held. Although Cambodia had a period of growth and relative stability at the end of the 20th century, political conflict has once again arisen in the country.

Laos

The Geneva Accords granted Laos its independence and elections were duly held in 1955. These elections led to a coalition government in 1957 that promptly collapsed due to extreme political differences of the coalition partners and a civil war ensued that would endure until 1975 when the communists would seize control. Pathet Lao (Land of Laos) had emerged as a communist and nationalist party during the colonial period, but it lacked the strength to take power after 1954. As a result, there were a series of governments, none of which exerted meaningful control over the country. When the Soviets endorsed and began to assist the neutralists and Pathet Lao, the United States responded by supporting the rightists in the civil war. The USA and the North Vietnamese both used Laos in this conflict; the North Vietnamese constantly violated Laotian neutrality through their use of the Ho Chi Minh trail and the US bombed the region.

After Cambodia and Vietnam established communist regimes, Laos soon followed. The Pathet Lao took control over the country, establishing a single-party state and eliminating the monarchy. To secure communist control, a centrally planned economy was implemented with nationalization of the land and the imposition of collective farming. Laos became very dependent upon Vietnam for economic and military support and signed a 25-year friendship treaty to cement relations with its neighbour.

As in other Asian communist countries, the collapse of the Soviet Union and the changes in the People's Republic of China forced Laos to look for other sources of income. As a result, Laos ended its socialist economic policies and adopted capitalist economic policies in the 1990s. Although the Communist Party retains tight political control, there has been economic liberalization since the early 1990s.

The Socialist Republic of Vietnam

With the unification of Vietnam, the north sought to impose communist policies on the entire country. This was done systematically and ruthlessly. This single-party state prohibited opposition parties and groups, imposed rule through censorship, forced collectivization and industrialization. This had negative consequences for the entire country as productivity declined resulting in widespread malnutrition. To remedy this, in the 1980s the country introduced market-oriented policies and limited its more aggressive intentions to spread revolution to neighbouring states.

The surrender of South Vietnam to the advancing North Vietnamese armies prevented the destruction of Saigon and led to the consolidation of communist control over the country. In 1976 the country was officially unified and renamed the Socialist Republic of Vietnam. The Communist Party was the only legal party in a single-party state. The country was governed by executive and legislative branches that were elected by the population, but the Communist Party determined who could run for office, and so, as in many other single-party states, the system appeared to be bottom-up democracy, but was in reality a top-down autocracy.

Unlike other recently unified and independent states, the Vietnamese political leadership had some experience and saw the unification of Vietnam as an extension of the governance they had previously held over North Vietnam. The Central Committee was composed of colleagues of Ho Chi Minh, increasingly elderly, and most of whom had been officers and active combatants in the war for unification.

The civil servants and military officers from the South Vietnamese regime were quickly identified and arrested by the North Vietnamese. Rather than being systematically executed, they were instead sent to rural re-education camps to be indoctrinated. In the now unified Vietnam, 80 per cent of the population lived in the countryside and most were poor peasants. If left to their own devices they would not have supported the northern or southern regimes that had previously existed, but they had little choice but to unconditionally accept North Vietnamese control. Once again, the rural peasantry saw its livelihood threatened as the government insisted on the imposition of socialist economic policies across the countryside.

The Economy

The economy was centrally planned, and from 1975 to 1985 the government tried to implement collectivization and the development of heavy industry. The peasants that had recently been granted land in redistribution programmes in both the north and the south were now forced onto government-owned collectives. Private businesses were seized by the state and it was illegal to transport food and goods between provinces. The entire economy was directed by the government, which had very little revenue. As a result, Vietnam joined the COMECON, hoping to take advantage of its export markets and, until Gorbachev came to power, received approximately $3 billion per year in assistance from the USSR.

In 1986, however, Vietnam changed its economic policies dramatically, with the implementation of Doi Moi, or renovation. The economy had stagnated, and there were shortages of food, fuel and consumer goods. In the early 1980s there had also been hyperinflation that led to the imposition of further austerity measures. The political leadership was divided: the reform-minded pragmatists advocated a shift towards more capitalist policies while the ideologues held onto the ideas of a socialist economy, fearing that economic liberalization would lead to the decline of socialism. The pragmatists prevailed and in a nod to the changing economic policies in the PRC and USSR, Doi Moi introduced market-oriented policies, allowing the small entrepreneurs to develop businesses that created small-scale consumer goods. This was initially successful, but seeing the political problems faced by the Soviet Union through the introduction of glasnost, the government once again clamped down on reform policies. China's ability to implement economic reform while maintaining political control gave them renewed confidence in Doi Moi, and reforms were once again encouraged. Vietnam achieved around 8 per cent annual GDP growth from 1990 to 1997 while foreign investment grew threefold and domestic savings quintupled.

Social policies

Like other single-party states, the will of the state was enforced through secret police, the *Cong An*. These security forces were responsible for maintaining order, and any form of anti-government speech, art or publication could result in public punishment, including imprisonment. To rid the country of its colonial and capitalist influences, art and literature created before 1975 was banned. All cultural production had to be government sanctioned with pro-communist, pro-nationalist messages. To this end, there was censorship of the arts and also the media. Government-sanctioned news agencies produced the news that was delivered via government-owned newspapers, radios and eventually television. Due to the proximity to Thailand it wasn't possible to keep out all foreign news, but it was significantly limited.

Over 90 per cent of the population of Vietnam are from the same ethnic group, so any actions against minorities was limited to religious, rather than ethnic or racial minorities. Religion was brought under government control: only state-controlled churches were allowed to exist and their activities were closely monitored by the Cong An. The Protestant Montagnard of the central highlands and the Hoa Hao Buddhists of the south claimed they had been persecuted and protested against the seizure of their land. Generally, however, the homogeneity of the country has meant that persecution was largely focused on class, with landowners and southern elites targeted and sent either to re-education or labour camps.

Like other communist countries, Vietnam has had to contend with the flight of refugees. In the days immediately after the fall of Saigon, hundreds of thousands of Vietnamese escaped across the frontiers to bordering countries or through the South China Sea on makeshift rafts and boats. It is estimated that one million Vietnamese fled, ending up in refugee camps in Thailand, Indonesia or Malaysia for as long as five years while they waited for asylum. These boat people have been accepted in Australia, New Zealand and the United States. Also, a number of Vietnamese in the north sought refuge in China.

Foreign policies

During the Cold War Vietnam was clearly part of the communist bloc, and at times served as a bridge between the USSR and PRC, receiving assistance from both during the Vietnam War. However, the Vietnamese had been under Chinese influence for centuries and were keen to limit its encroachment, along with the Western, colonial influences of France and the United States. Relations between Communist China and Vietnam were strained as both sought to establish their influence in Cambodia, and in 1979 there was a brief conflict between the two countries which led to a three-week invasion of Vietnam by Chinese forces. Although the Chinese withdrew and the matter was reconciled, relations remain fraught.

Vietnam enjoyed the benefits of Soviet patronage. In addition to economic assistance, the USSR provided Vietnam with military assistance in the form of training and materials. This allowed for the build-up of the Vietnamese army, which the Soviet Union encouraged to deter Western aggression in the region. The collapse of communism in Eastern Europe and the end of the USSR meant an end to Soviet assistance and markets for Vietnamese produce. This, in turn, led to a decline in the Vietnamese economy, as Vietnam struggled to find other trading partners.

Twenty years after its withdrawal, the United States extended diplomatic recognition to Vietnam, and with this opened up trade relations. The end of the Soviet regime in Russia did not exactly benefit Vietnam but it did give her access to new markets with more disposable income and purchasing power. Additionally, it opened Vietnam to tourism from the West.

Vietnam was isolated during the Cold War. Its policy of supporting communist regimes in Indochina further alienating its neighbours. In Laos, Vietnam assisted the Laotian communists in their attempt to seize power. The Khmer Rouge government under Pol Pot had Chinese backing but the Vietnamese supported a pro-Vietnamese regime, and invaded Cambodia (Kampuchea) in 1978, which led to a ten-year occupation; it was only in 1989 that Vietnam withdrew its forces. Since then, relations with their neighbors have improved as Vietnam has become less aggressively pro-communist in its outlook.

TOK link

Reasoning

While the North Vietnamese Army was fighting South Vietnam and the United States, they had been taught that the South Vietnamese people were oppressed both by the South Vietnamese regime and American elites. Much to their surprise, when they began the occupation of the South after the fall of Saigon, the North Vietnamese saw that the people in the south enjoyed a far better life: their fields were more productive and consumer goods were available.

Imagine that you are a soldier in the North Vietnamese Army. You are a dedicated socialist and have fought for years to spread communism throughout Vietnam and to liberate the south from its overlords.

For a person who believed firmly in the socialist ideals of North Vietnam, how would you rationalize this discrepancy? To what extent would you admit that you might have been misled by your government? Would this change your ideas about the government? What about socialism?

Conclusion

After nearly 60 years of hardship and upheaval, Vietnam finally seems to have a stable government that is accepted in the international community. Like its neighbour to the north, Vietnam has a capitalist economic programme while maintaining its socialist government. There have been changes in governance since the collapse of the USSR. The Communist Party is an institutionalized party, and the only path to political development. But the country has seen limited social and political reform. Despite the volatility that it suffered from 1945 to 1975 it is now one of the longest-lasting socialist regimes in the world, and is politically stable with a dynamic economy.

Exam questions

1 Analyse three factors that fostered the growth of independence movements in **either** Africa **or** Asia.

2 Examine the role and importance of leaders, in independence movements, in **either** Africa or Asia, or in Africa and/or Asia.

3 In what ways and with what results were **either** Jinnah **or** Kwame Nkrumah important in obtaining independence for his country.

4 In 1942 Ghandi said: "India will have an assembly with powers to draft a constitution after the war is over." To what extent were Ghandi's actions and the Second World War responsible for Indian independence?

5 Discuss the importance of **two** of the following challenges to new states: conflicts with neighbours; social and religious issues; separatist movements.

6 "Neo-colonialism was a term coined by Nkrumah to describe the ability of Western capitalist powers to retain economic and political control over former colonies." To what extent did neo-colonialism hinder independence and economic progress in former colonies?

7 To what extent did the Cold War affect independence movements and new states **either** in Africa and Asia, **or** in post 1945 Central and Eastern European states?

Recommended further reading

Vietnam/Indochina

Appy, Richard. 2008. *Vietnam: The Definitive Oral History*. Ebury Press.

Richard Appy interviewed 135 people and compiled their different perspectives. He has interviews from all sides of the conflict that date from initial involvement through the fall of Saigon in 1975.

Smith, Ralph Bernard, and Williams, Beryl (ed.). 2008. *Communist Indochina. Routledge Studies in the Modern History of Asia*. London, UK. Routledge Press.

Covers the history of Indochinese communism from its roots in the early 1930s through to the imposition of communist rule in Vietnam, Laos and Cambodia. The emphasis is on regional history and politics, and there is detailed examination of economic and social policies in these countries.

Duiker, William. 2002. *Ho Chi Minh: A Life*. London, UK. Hyperion

A thorough and comprehensive biography of Ho Chi Minh.

Hall, Michael. 2008. *The Vietnam War*. 2nd edn. London, UK. Longman.

Examines the impact of the Vietnam War on the USA and Vietnam. It covers the root causes of the conflict and ends with the communist victory in 1975.

Logeville, Frederick. 2001. *The Origins of the Vietnam War*. London, UK. Longman.

An examination of the root causes of the war from the French colonial period through to the escalation of US involvement in 1965.

Africa

Thorn, Gary. 2000. *End of Empires: European Decolonisation 1919–1980*. London, UK. Hodder and Stoughton.

This book in the Access to History series has excellent analysis of British, French and Portuguese decolonization. Many chapters end with study guides and exam advice. The concluding chapter is especially helpful.

The following books are concise, advanced scholarly analyses but without the features mentioned in the book above.

Betts, Raymond. 1998. *Decolonization*. London, UK; New York, USA. Routledge.

Hargreaves, John D. 1996. *Decolonization in Africa*. London, UK. Longman.

Birmingham, David. 1990. *Kwame Nkrumah*. London, UK. Cardinal.

Chamberlain, Muriel Evelyn. 1985. *Decolonization: The fall of the European Empires*. Blackwell.

Useful websites

US Perspectives on different countries (including their histories, government, economy and politics) can be found at http://countrystudies.us. There is an index for on-line versions of books previously published in hard copy by the Federal Research Division of the Library of Congress as part of the Country Studies/Area Handbook Series sponsored by the US Department of the Army between 1986 and 1998.

The United Nations and Decolonization

http://www.un.org/Depts/dpi/decolonization/main.htm

Casahistoria: Imperialism and Decolonization

http://casahistoria.net/decolonisation.htm
Website for students of modern history, with an IB curriculum focus.

Laos Mekong National Committee

http://www.lnmc.gov.la/lnmc/; includes a link to Vientiane Times, the largest newspaper in Laos.

Embassy of the Laos People's Democratic Republic

http://www.laoembassy.com/

Royal Government of Cambodia

www.cambodia.gov.kh

Socialist Republic of Vietnam, Government Web Portal

http://www.gov.vn

8 Nationalist and independence movements in post-1945 Central and Eastern European states—Poland and Czechoslovakia

This chapter looks at topic 4 from the IB *History Guide*, covering post-1945 nationalist and independence movements in Central and Eastern Europe, and concentrates on two of the countries identified for detailed study, Poland and Czechoslovakia. In addition, as required by the *History Guide*, particular attention is invested in the leadership of Lech Wałęsa in Poland and Vaclav Havel in Czechoslovakia.

From outside it is tempting to see the Soviet sphere of influence as a monolithic bloc of nations, each conforming to the demands of the Moscow leadership. Poland and Czechoslovakia certainly share a lot in common; the people of both nations are predominantly Slavs, sharing similar languages and cultural traditions. Nationalist aspirations of sustained independence in both countries would continue to be limited by their geographical position between powerful neighbours. However, this chapter also highlights the ways in which these close neighbours differed in their experience of war, Soviet control, revolution and post-communism.

Topic 4 requires the student to explore the origins and growth of movements challenging Soviet or centralized control. The role and importance of leaders, organizations and institutions should be also considered along with the methods of achieving independence. These syllabus themes should be kept in mind as you work your way through the first part of this chapter, focused on Solidarity in Poland and Civic Forum in Czechoslovakia. You will need to evaluate how significant these organizations and their leaders were, relative to the external factors which contributed to the end of the Cold War.

When considering the methods used in achieving independence, the relatively peaceful events of 1989 in Poland and Czechoslovakia need to be contrasted with the earlier street fighting of 1956 and 1968 and the civil war in Yugoslavia. Students are expected to consider how new states were established and how they dealt with the new political, economic, social and cultural challenges of becoming democratic states. Some states, including Czechoslovakia failed to survive the transition; others like Poland survived despite massive upheaval. Yugoslavia disintegrated in the bloodiest way imaginable.

When the authors of this section of your textbook were in secondary school nothing seemed more permanent than the division of Eastern and Western Europe behind the iron curtain. Now, 20 years after the destruction of the Berlin Wall, our IB Diploma students in the former socialist republic of Czechoslovakia, are amongst the first of a generation born after the Velvet Revolution of 1989. They inhabit a city in which the capitalist symbols of MacDonalds and Ikea seem as natural and inevitable as the Berlin Wall once was. Now, communism is ancient history; more than that, it has become part of the heritage industry, a curiosity to entertain. Now you can visit a museum to communism in Prague or a park of communist statues in Budapest.

In all of this, communism appears to have been an aberration, a detour, that can be examined with a degree of what the French philosopher Henri Bergson called "retrospective determinism". Taking Poland and Czechoslovakia as case studies, in the final section of this chapter, we explore the background to the eventual, and some would say inevitable, collapse of the Soviet Union.

By the end of this chapter, you should be able to:

● explain how Poland and Czechoslovakia came under Soviet control

● explain the characteristics of Communist Party control over Central and Eastern Europe

● compare and contrast the experiences of Poland and Czechoslovakia during the periods of occupation, revolution (1989) and post-communist transition

● evaluate the role and importance of leaders, organizations and institutions in challenging Soviet control and achieving independence.

How was Soviet control established?

Both Poland and Czechoslovakia achieved independence in the aftermath of the First World War, Poland as the re-creation of a state that had existed until partitioned by Russia, Austria and Prussia in the 18th century, and Czechoslovakia as a new name on the map of Europe. In the Second World War, both countries suffered Nazi occupation and then Soviet liberation. This section explains how, for Poland and Czechoslovakia, liberation was followed by absorption into the Soviet empire.

Poland

The experience of being "liberated" by the Russian Red Army at the end of the Second World War very quickly felt like occupation in Poland. The difficult relationship with its eastern neighbour would not only be a recurring theme through the following decades, but would also characterize the relationship of the Polish Communist Party with the parent party in Russia. In 1939, Poland had fought a bitter war with the Soviet Union on its eastern border. In 1940 thousands of captured Polish officers were murdered on Stalin's orders at Katyn and, in 1944, 200 000 died as the Polish underground Home Army (AK) in Warsaw was crushed in an uprising, while the Red Army appeared to hold back on the opposite bank of the Vistula River. As the Red Army progressed westwards, Soviet reparation squads dismantled Polish industrial complexes and removed them to the USSR and the leaders of Poland's war-time resistance were arrested and put on trial for treason. The experience of war, in which 18 per cent of Poland's pre-war population died, meant that when Stalin came to impose his will on the Polish people there were no means left to resist.

And then there was Yalta, the decisive meeting of Allied leaders in February 1945, at which the post-war settlement was agreed. Poland was abandoned by Roosevelt and Churchill to the Soviet sphere of influence. This "betrayal of Yalta" would take on mythical proportions in the minds of Poles. When there was so much else to be decided and other Allied aims still to be achieved, Poland was not considered enough of a priority to be saved. In the absence of a promised Allied second front in Western Europe, the Soviets were appeased with an acceptance of the new **Curzon Line** borders of Poland. She would lose 70 000 square miles (about 180 000 square kilometres) to Russia in the east and would be compensated with 40 000 square miles (about 105 square kilometres) from Germany. A Polish Committee of National Liberation was established under Soviet guidance in Lublin in July 1944. It was this organization that the Allies recognized at Yalta as Poland's provisional government, rather than the London-based group which had acted as a government in exile throughout the war.

Map of pre- and post-war Poland

To show how little home-grown support there was for a communist take-over in Poland, Stalin himself remarked that "imposing communism on Poland is like putting a saddle on a cow". Poland's pre-war Communist Party had been dissolved on Stalin's orders in 1938 and approximately 5000 of its activists murdered. As the war came to an end, there were "hardly enough native Polish communists to run a factory, let alone a country of some 30 million people", as historian Norman Davies has noted.

Hugh Seton-Watson identified three stages of a communist seizure of power: coalition, bogus coalition and dictatorship. In contrast to the democratic successes of communist parties in Czechoslovakia and Hungary, Poland went straight from "bogus coalition" to dictatorship without any genuine electoral success. During the stage of the "bogus coalition", the power to control elections required significant security and policing functions to be implemented by the Party. In Poland, they controlled the Ministry of Public Security and a militia of more than 100 000. When the first post-war election was held in January 1947, the Communists were able to rig the vote, arresting 142 candidates and thousands of opposition supporters. The Communists therefore won the election and immediately introduced a Soviet-style constitution.

Poland became a Stalinist democracy. The Party was to have dictatorship over the people; statues of Stalin appeared everywhere; newly nationalized industries focused on heavy industry and the peasants were evicted and handed over to the collective "Polish Agricultural Enterprises". However, compared to other states in Central Europe undergoing the Stalinist transformation, Poland

The **Curzon Line** was the line of demarcation used to settle Poland's eastern border in 1945. It was based on previous efforts to resolve territorial disputes in the area and was named after a British Foreign Secretary. The strength of Stalin's position in 1945 is demonstrated by his success in securing the "A" option, which awarded the Soviet Union the greater territorial gains, including the city of Lwów.

The recurring changes to Poland's borders are a source of insecurity and indicate the problems arising from Poland's lack of natural boundaries.

dragged its feet. There were no great famines, no mass purges or **show trials**, and the Church managed to remain the focus of Poland's spiritual and social life.

Czechoslovakia

Czechoslovakia emerged from the collapsed Austro-Hungarian Empire. It was an artificial creation comprising mainly of Czechs and Slovaks, plus large German and Hungarian minorities. The new state satisfied the Allies' demands for a reorganization of Central Europe and the Czech nationalists' demands for autonomy, and represented an improvement in status for the Slovaks. Thus Czechoslovakia was founded on opposition to imperial control.

As neighbouring countries succumbed to dictatorship in the 1930s, Czechoslovakia developed as a relatively prosperous democracy. Czechs and Slovaks shared this new state, as they did mutually comprehensible languages, ethnic ties and a common interest in supporting each other against powerful neighbours and non-Slavic minorities.

In 1938, abandoned by the Western powers at the Munich Conference, Czechoslovakia lost the Sudetenland to Nazi Germany. In March 1939, Germany invaded the remainder of the Czech lands and established a puppet regime in Slovakia. During the war, in London, ex-president Edvard Beneš worked hard at promoting Czechoslovakia's diplomatic interests. He established a government in exile and, by 1943, had gained recognition from Stalin even though Czechoslovak communist leaders, such as Klement Gottwald, had gathered in Moscow. Beneš, aware of his country's vulnerability to hostile neighbours, even entered negotiations with his Polish counterparts regarding a possible post-war Czecho-Slovak-Polish Federation. The most concerted attempt at self-liberation, the Slovak National Uprising of 1944, ended in tragic failure. With the Soviet forces poised on the border, both Stalin and the Western allies failed to deliver promised assistance in time.

However, it was the Red Army, eventually, which liberated most of Czechoslovakia. The Americans halted their advance at Pilsen in the west and then, in accordance with the Yalta agreement, withdrew. Some continuity with the pre-war regime was achieved when Beneš returned as president; Gottwald's Moscow Communists, under Stalin's orders, agreed to co-operate in a "National Front" coalition government. This generosity masked the fact that within the new coalition, the

> **Show trials** are trials held for propaganda reasons, in which the charges are usually false and the confessions of the accused are extracted under extreme duress, including torture. The victims were often prominent Party members, such as Rudolf Slánský and Otto Šling in Czechoslovakia. Their executions provided a terrifying reminder to others of the arbitrary cruelty of Stalinist discipline.

Czechoslovakia, 1919. What were the strengths and weaknesses of the new state?

Communists secured control of several key ministries, including control of the police and the military.

In the first post-war elections, held in 1946, the Communists emerged as the largest party, gaining 38 per cent of the vote, one of the best ever performances by any communist party in a free election. Gottwald became prime minister within a new coalition, and, pressed by Stalin, took steps to increase his party's control. Memories of "Munich" remained a factor as Czechoslovakia reorientated towards the East. At the end of a decade in which the capitalist system had struggled from crisis to crisis, the Western democracies had sacrificed Czechoslovakia in a notorious act of betrayal. Neither the Czechoslovak Communist Party nor the Soviet Union had ever accepted the Munich Agreement. Communist propagandists, airbrushing their own inconsistencies regarding the Nazi–Soviet Pact, relentlessly contrasted their record of heroic liberation with the weakness of the liberal democracies. In addition, as the Czechs sought revenge against Nazi sympathizers, Communists took a leading role in the deportation of the German minority. The Communist-run Ministry of the Interior and Ministry of Agriculture distributed the Germans' confiscated land among Czech workers, shoring up further sources of support.

Pre-war Czechoslovakia had been economically the most developed country in the region, an advantage that had increased in relative terms as neighbouring states suffered greater war damage. As Gottwald's regime fomented a class war against the rich, there was plenty of wealth to be redistributed. Gottwald uncharacteristically flirted with pursuing a foreign policy independent of the Soviet Union when he declared an interest in accepting **Marshall Aid**. Stalin forced the reversal of this policy, exposing the limits of Czechoslovak independence and underlining the Soviet intention to dominate the satellite nations within its sphere.

Within Czechoslovakia the intimidation of non-communist politicians increased, prompting several resignations. In March 1948, Jan Masaryk, the foreign minister, died after falling from a window, with the obvious suspicion of foul play. President Beneš, increasingly isolated and struggling against ill health, resigned in June and died soon after. New elections were held, this time uncontested. Gottwald became president, and the Communist coup was completed.

Discussion point: Reliability of evidence

In 1946, referenda were held on the communist programme. They were supported by significant majorities, on an impressive 85 per cent turnout of voters. However, in 1990, after the opening up of the Party archives, it was revealed that 73 per cent of votes had been cast against the communist regime. The results had quite simply been falsified.

? **What does this tell us about the reliability of statistics produced by the communist regimes?**

Marshall Aid Economic and technical aid provided by the United States to assist the recovery of European countries devastated by the war and to encourage international trade.

Activity:

The mystery of Jan Masaryk— murder or suicide?

Official investigations at the time concluded that Masaryk, by jumping from a third-floor window, had committed suicide. However, one does not have to be an obsessive collector of conspiracy theories to have doubts about the findings of the communist investigators. Although the passage of time makes it unlikely we will ever have a definitive answer, we can find evidence supporting each theory and in doing so reveal something of the nature of the communist seizure of power.

Research and prepare a presentation on the following:

- the basic facts of the case
- evidence that Masaryk committed suicide
- evidence that Masaryk was murdered.

Through Gottwald's puppet government, a style of government subservient to the policies of the Soviet Union and bearing many features of Stalinism was imposed. The Party established monopoly rule based on its single, dominating ideology. The private sector was replaced by a nationalized, centrally commanded economy. Civil society, in the form of clubs, churches, unions or charities, was brought within Party control or destroyed. State security forces were used to intimidate, imprison and kill opponents.

Membership of the Party was no guarantee of security though, and as the show trials of the early 1950s, which led to the executions of such prominent Party figures as Rudolf Slánský and Otto Šling demonstrate, it was often events outside Czechoslovakia, as well as internal personal rivalry, that determined who would fall victim. Yugoslavia's desertion of the Soviet bloc, to pursue their own path to socialism, was a particular source of paranoia. Expressions of independent thought risked accusations of Titoism. As a result, an ability to recognize, and not deviate from, Soviet orthodoxy became valued over initiative.

Josip Broz Tito (1892–1980)

Josip Broz Tito was the leader of the Socialist Federal Republic of Yugoslavia from 1945 until his death in 1980. During the Second World War Tito organized the anti-fascist Yugoslav Partisans that liberated the country from Nazi occupation. Tito's People's Front, led by the Communist Party of Yugoslavia, comfortably and legitimately won the elections of November 1945. Yugoslavia under Tito developed independent socialist economic and foreign policies which earned the wrath of Stalin and expulsion from Cominform. In response, Tito negotiated Marshall Aid from the United States and took up a leading role in the Non-Aligned Movement. The death of Stalin led to rapprochement with the USSR but socialist experiments in profit-sharing workers' councils and freedom of speech resulted in an uneasy relationship with Moscow. Tito's funeral in 1980 was attended by 128 world leaders, including Margaret Thatcher and Saddam Hussein. His greatest achievement was probably maintaining the unity of six regional republics and two autonomous provinces which made up Yugoslavia, and which disintegrated a decade after his death.

 How do the experiences of Poland and Czechoslovakia compare with those of neighbouring countries in Eastern and Central Europe that underwent Stalinization?

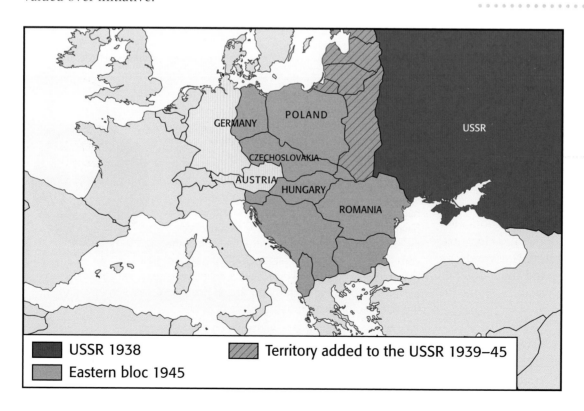

| USSR 1938 | Territory added to the USSR 1939–45 |
| Eastern bloc 1945 | |

De-Stalinization, mature communism and political instability, 1953–81

This section examines the ways in which the nature of communist rule varied markedly from country to country as local politicians sought to adapt communism to suit local circumstances. The death of Stalin in 1953 and the subsequent liberalization allowed the Polish Communist Party to establish some limits to Soviet domination. In Czechoslovakia in 1968, attempts to extend the scope of national independence met with Soviet invasion and defeat.

The death of Stalin led to the New Course policy in the Soviet Union and a break with the Stalinist past. The international context was also changing. The USSR returned to the conference table, recognized a capitalist Austria and withdrew her troops; even Tito was rehabilitated as Khrushchev recognized the possibility of "different roads to socialism". By the time Polish Communists leaked the content of Khrushchev's "secret speech" in February 1956, Poland had already begun a process of de-Stalinization.

In June 1956, however, from the point of view of the Party leadership, things went too far. Polish workers in Poznan rioted in response to wage cuts and changed working conditions. After two days of fighting with police, 53 were dead and over 300 were injured. Premier Józef Cyrankiewicz warned the demonstrators that he "who will dare raise his hand against the people's rule may be sure that … the authorities will chop off his hand."

Despite the threats, it was the Party itself that looked more likely to collapse. By July 1956, the Party leadership was divided into a pro-Soviet faction opposing change and a reformist wing advocating greater liberalization and economic reform. In August, a decision was taken to restore Władysław Gomułka's Party membership. He had been purged in 1949 and as a martyr of Stalinism he quickly became the focus of pro-reform opinion. Elevated into the Polish **politburo** without the approval of Moscow, Gomułka now became a symbol of defiance for Polish reformers. The Soviet army in Poland was made ready to move on Warsaw and a 50 000 strong army of the Polish secret police protected Gomułka and the central committee.

Politburo An abbreviation of "political bureau", the leading government committee in Soviet bloc countries.

On 19 October, Khrushchev made an unscheduled visit to Warsaw. At the same time, Soviet army units left Wroclaw, heading for the capital, and the Soviet fleet appeared off Gdańsk. The control tower at Warsaw airport initially refused landing permission and the Soviet delegation was put into a holding pattern. At the same moment, the Polish politburo proposed the re-election of Gomułka as secretary general, suspended their meeting and rushed to the airport. When finally allowed onto Polish soil, Khrushchev railed against the Poles: "We shed our blood for this country and now you want to sell out to the Americans." The tense debate which followed produced the compromise which resulted in a Polish road to socialism, in return for

Polish loyalty in the recently formed Warsaw Pact. In the words of Norman Davies, "The Polish People's Republic ceased to be a puppet state, and became instead a client state." But Khrushchev would not back down again. Within a few days, a demonstration in support of the Poles in Budapest would trigger the Hungarian Uprising.

What made Poland different to the other satellite states of Central and Eastern Europe?

First, collectivization was cancelled and peasants were allowed to own their own land. This created a significant independent private sector in a communist economy. Second, the compromise agreement with the Catholic Church created the only fully independent church in the Eastern bloc. And third, there was a much higher degree of personal freedom, freedom of speech and the arts.

Although the year 1956 would later be embroidered on the banners of the Solidarity movement in memory of the martyrs who had opposed the regime, Poznan and its consequences would have more in common with events in Czechoslovakia in 1968 than Poland in 1981. In 1956, Polish discontent was channelled through and resolved by the Party. The events of 1956 have been described by historians as a revolution that half-succeeded. It is better characterized by the Hungarian historian Ivan Berend as "less a revolution of half-successes than a successful half-revolution". It succeeded within the context of the Polish Communist Party and its relationship to Moscow, but it did not challenge the Communist Party's leading role. By the 1970s, circumstances had changed and a full revolution was on the agenda. An alternative non-Party opposition was organizing in the industrial heartlands and, quite independently of the Party, the name of the organization would become Solidarity (see page 428).

Why did the Czechoslovak regime resist de-Stalinization?

Gottwald loyally attended Stalin's funeral in Moscow but, having become ill at the event, developed pneumonia and, following his master to the end, died nine days later. Stalin's death allowed a tentative loosening of the strict Soviet-style structures and practices elsewhere in the Eastern bloc, but not in Czechoslovakia. As reforms were discussed in Poland and Hungary, and Khrushchev prepared his denunciation of Stalin, Gottwald's successor, Antonín Novotný, demonstrated his regime's continued pursuit of the old cult of personality by commissioning the world's largest statue of Stalin, a 50-metre-high colossus overlooking Prague. Czechoslovakia's relative wealth meant that popular discontent caused by social deprivation did not put pressure on the leadership to permit concessions. This underlines a particular characteristic of the Communist empire, in which the Soviet core was less economically advanced than peripheral colonies such as Czechoslovakia. When the inefficiencies of state control caused even the robust Czechoslovak economy to falter in the mid-1950s, this was used as a pretext to purge leading economists rather than to reform, further stifling initiative. The violence against leading Communists during the Hungarian Uprising further strengthened the position of those arguing against opening the door to any pluralism of ideas.

What was the Prague Spring?

By the mid-1960s, the proclamations of "actually existing socialism" could no longer mask the true scale of economic decline. Some prominent Party members, including Alexander Dubček, were prepared to acknowledge the problems and urged reform. Novotný opposed such moves but could not muster support from Party colleagues. As a Czech, his antagonistic attitude to the Slovaks meant even ideological hardliners there were unwilling to offer their backing. Leonid Brezhnev, the new Soviet leader, also declined to offer Novotný his support, commenting only that "it's your business," when asked to pass judgment on the rival Party factions.

In January 1968 Dubček replaced Novotný as Party First Secretary. His open, approachable manner and easy smile contrasted with the austere severity of previous Party bosses and made him the personification of "socialism with a human face". The reformists had gained the upper hand and in April articulated their political aims in an Action Programme. This was a key moment in what became known as the Prague Spring. The document called for increased democratization, including more open debate with representatives of other groups in society, the use of opinion polls to inform policy, a relaxation of censorship, the freedom to travel abroad and greater autonomy for Slovakia. The economy was to be guided towards a socialist market in which businesses would remain state-owned but would compete with each other and be subjected to the forces of supply and demand. This was not to be an attempt to dismantle the system but simply to improve it. The Action Programme contained the shibboleths required of loyal members of the Soviet Empire: "The basic orientation of Czechoslovak foreign policy ... revolves around alliance with the Soviet Union and the other socialist states." But from Moscow's perspective it was a serious challenge to the foundations of the Soviet empire.

Beyond the Party membership, ordinary Czechoslovaks, encouraged by these liberalizing measures, were able to speak out, no longer cowed by the threat of a late-night visit from the security forces and a long spell in a labour camp. Potential opposition parties emerged, such as K-231, which represented the demands of ex-political prisoners to be fully rehabilitated. Students

Stalin statue, also known locally as the "meat queue". What are the features of socialist realist art? How does the Stalin statue illustrate these? What do political leaders hope to achieve through public art? Can you think of any effective/ineffective examples from your own or other countries?

formed independent unions and writers tested the limits of the new freedom by criticizing the Party's past mistakes. KAN—the Committed Non-Party Members—sought to articulate the political views of non-Communists. Václav Havel, a KAN member, described the atmosphere as one where "fear vanished, taboos were swept away, social conflicts could be openly named and described ... the media began to do their job, civic self-confidence grew, the ice began to melt." However, expectations soon extended beyond the provisions of the Action Programme. Dubček's offer of Party-led democratization was not enough when genuine democracy seemed attainable.

As spring turned to summer, it seemed that events had taken on a momentum beyond Dubček's control. Neighbouring regimes, fearing a domino effect, became nervous at the prospect that their own populations might demand similar freedoms. East Germany's Walter Ulbricht and Poland's Wladislaw Gomulka urged Soviet intervention. Brezhnev took steps to bring Czechoslovakia back into line. Previously arranged Warsaw Pact military manouvres in Czechoslovakia were brought forward and extended, a not so subtle reminder of Soviet power. At a series of meetings through the summer, Dubček was warned of the dangers of deviating from the Soviet-approved version of socialism but steadfastly stuck to his principles. Finally, in August, the Prague Spring ended, as Soviet and other Warsaw Pact forces invaded Czechoslovakia.

Dubček is often criticized as being well meaning but naive. The Action Programme recognized the need for the Communist Party to strive constantly to earn the people's consent but fudged the obvious question of what happens when that consent is withdrawn. The expectation that rival groups in a multi-party system would remain content with a subordinate role also seems unrealistic. Certainly, Brezhnev viewed events as a step towards capitalism and a threat to Soviet hegemony in the region. The **Brezhnev Doctrine** made clear what should have been obvious from previous challenges, such as the Hungarian Uprising in 1956, that the Soviet Union would enforce its own interpretation of socialism whenever it felt threatened.

Dubček's reforms had been immensely popular in Czechoslovakia, but led to demands for more radical change that threatened the Party's leading role. A lifetime within the Party had denied Dubček the perspective of those on the outside. In the same way, Dubček's natural inclination towards an idealistic view of the Soviet Union made the invasion of 1968 a revelation and a crushing blow.

The Czechoslovak army, as in 1939, was ordered not to confront the invading forces, though many citizens fought back in brave but ultimately futile acts of resistance. Clandestine radio stations managed to remain on air long enough to refute the Soviet depiction of the invasion as "fraternal assistance" requested by the Czechoslovaks themselves to confront "counter-revolutionaries". A final free meeting of Party members reaffirmed the ideals of the Prague Spring even as Dubček and his colleagues were removed at gunpoint to Moscow. There, Dubček and his colleagues were threatened and bullied until they signed a document of capitulation agreeing with the Soviet version of events.

Activity:

The Brezhnev Doctrine

Speech to the Polish Workers' Congress, November 1968

Read the text of the Brezhnev Doctrine in Source A on page 183 of chapter 3.

Summarise the key points of the doctrine in no more than three sentences.

The failure of the Prague Spring demonstrates the difficulties of attempting reform from within. Dubček and his fellow reformers had risen through the Party ranks in the preceding decades and could hardly have been unaware of the crimes committed by the Party, the show trials, the executions, the dishonesty, or of the brutal cynicism of the Soviet leadership. Their own complicity in these events made them flawed standard bearers for a new era of reason and justice.

The Soviets' concern that the Prague Spring would eventually turn Czechoslovakia into a democratic state and undermine the Empire may well have been correct. As Gorbachev's later experience shows, dictatorships are at their most vulnerable when attempting reform. However, the invasion also crushed a genuine attempt by a communist party to adapt to new political and economic challenges. Was this a missed opportunity for the Soviet Empire to regenerate? Or simply another doomed attempt at divining a **Third Way**? As it was, the reimposition of rigid Soviet control established a regime that Josef Smrkovsky, Dubček's colleague, insisted that military resistance would have been futile. "Our country was occupied by a tremendous military power; to resist it in the same manner would have been absolutely hopeless and was out of the question."

The historian M Dowling reports a contrasting view expressed by many Czechoslovaks: "three times we had an excellent army and three times we were not allowed to use it, 1938, 1948, 1968."

> **Third Way** A political philosophy that seeks to combine the most successful elements of free-market capitalism and democratic socialism.

 How far do you agree with the decision not to fight?

What was "normalization"?

Gustáv Husák led Czechoslovakia through the next 20 years of "normalization". The Party was purged of reformers, censorship was restored, travel restrictions were reimposed, the maximum period of detention without trial was extended, and there was a return to centralized economic control. The state demanded at least an outward appearance of compliance. As the wayward satellite returned to disciplined loyalty, tens of thousands of its citizens left the country. The new government undemocratically imposed by Moscow, was clearly dependent on the continued Soviet military presence and therefore could not attain popular legitimacy.

In these unpromising circumstances, Husák had to consolidate his rule and achieve some form of social contract with the people. The state proved able to provide basic economic security, full employment, free universal health care and subsidized holidays, and pensions were guaranteed. Workers' wages were lower than their Western counterparts but the average Czechoslovak could

A Bratislava man confronts a Soviet tank, August 1968. This image has become the defining iconic image for Slovaks of the events of 1968. What do you suppose are the reasons for its enduring popularity? The image can now be found on T-shirts and coffee mugs—is this commoditization of history a positive development?

afford a modest supply of consumer goods and, by the late 1980s, Czechoslovakia ranked second in the world in the number of country cottages per capita; as many as 80 per cent of families had access to these second homes. In these ways, a form of consent existed and the police state retained all the apparatus of coercion (prison, loss of career) where this proved insufficient. For many, the lesson of 1968 was that rebellion was futile.

Charter 77

Charter 77 was an opposition group based on a petition calling on the government to respect its own commitment to the 1975 Helsinki Agreement on human rights. The Soviet Union, the United States and most of Europe had agreed to respect the fundamental freedoms of thought, conscience, religion and belief. Czechoslovakia clearly did not respect these freedoms but, as the agreement had been signed, Helsinki gave the dissidents a legalistic avenue of opposition. They accepted the futility of open revolt against a well-armed regime, backed by an interventionist, central Soviet authority, but believed that the system could be undermined by spreading the truth and defending human rights. The resulting persecution suffered by those brave enough to sign the Charter highlighted the reality of totalitarian rule and attracted publicity abroad.

Activity:

Verdicts on Dubček and the Prague Spring

Pluralism, democratization, market reform and the abolition of censorship in Czechoslovakia ... represented the antitheses of Soviet style rule at home; they posed a real threat to the stability of other Communist states in the region whose people would undoubtedly be encouraged to do the same. Anyone who truly acknowledged the totalitarian essence of Soviet communism would have realised this. Dubcek was wilfully blind to the system he had grown up around.

Source: Shepherd, Robin. 2000. *Czechoslovakia: The Velvet Revolution and Beyond*. Macmillan Press.

Dubcek was the first and last genuinely popular Communist leader of Czechoslovakia. The slogan "socialism with a human face" was coined for him ... his ready smile made it easy to identify him with the concept. ... Dubcek's popularity was based on the fact that he believed in his own words and policies, and accordingly people trusted him.

Source: Dowling, M. 2002. *Brief Histories: Czechoslovakia*. London, UK. Arnold Publishers. p. 107.

Scepticism about the hypothetical future of this experiment may be misplaced. ... It is possible that by allowing the full play of democratic forces within the Party itself, Dubcek might have enabled the Communists to remain both sensitive and responsive to the aspirations of the people.

Source: Shawcross, W. 1990. *Dubcek: Dubcek and Czechoslovakia 1918–1990*. London, UK. The Hogarth Press. p. 207.

Dubcekism stood for right-wing opportunism and was characterised by its double-faced policy and a contradiction between words and deeds. It was a loss of class approach in solving the vital internal and international problems, a complete failure to understand the international context of Czechoslovak development in the present world divided along class lines.

Source: *Pravda*, Bratislava, 8 October 1969.

1 Use the sources to identify the criticisms of Dubček.

2 How far are these criticisms justified?

3 What did the Prague Spring achieve?

Václav Havel (1936–)

Václav Havel was born into a prominent, wealthy family in Prague in 1936, and as a child experienced the disasters of the Nazi occupation. To the post-war communist regime, families such as Havel's were class enemies and were made to suffer the confiscation of property, exclusion from education and harassment. Despite these obstacles, Havel pursued his interests in the arts, in Czech culture and, in particular, in the theatre. He carved out a career as a playwright, using membership of officially sanctioned writers' groups to push the bounds of censorship. His plays often contained thinly veiled criticisms of the absurdities of communism and in 1971 they were banned. In 1975 Havel wrote an Open Letter to President Husák, criticizing the regime for its cynical oppression:

> *… for fear of losing his job, the schoolteacher teaches things he does not believe; fearing for his future, the pupil repeats them after him … Fear of the consequences of refusal leads people to take part in elections and to pretend that such ceremonies are genuine elections … fear that someone might inform against them prevents them from giving expression to their true opinions.*

Duberstein, John. 2006. *A Velvet Revolution, Vaclav Havel and the Fall of Communism*. Greensboro, North Carolina, USA. Morgan Reynolds Publishing. p. 95.

In 1976 the regime provided an example of how it would use this "fear" to enforce conformity when members of a rock group, The Plastic People of the Universe, were put on trial accused of deviancy, hooliganism and disturbing the peace. To Havel, this was more than the harassment of a few hippy prog-rockers—it was an attack on art, youth and freedom, "an attack by the totalitarian system on life itself"and provided the motivation to form the Charter 77 group.

Despite the risks, Havel exemplified his own moral exhortation to "live in truth" even as government propaganda strove to portray him as a self-indulgent, bourgeois dilettante, out of touch with the real concerns of the working class. He faced repeated harassment, arrest and imprisonment.

By 1989, as the regime came under increasing pressure, Havel's consistent defiance, public profile and organizational skills made him the obvious leader of the Civic Forum opposition group. Havel had begun the year with yet another spell in prison but, in December 1989, the Federal Assembly unanimously elected him president of Czechoslovakia. Unable to prevent the "Velvet Divorce" of 1993, when the country split up, he resigned but was re-elected president of the new Czech Republic. He remained in this role until his retirement in 2003.

Discussion point:

Charter 77 (abridged)

The right to freedom of expression is in our case purely illusory. Hundreds of thousands of other citizens are denied that "freedom from fear" mentioned in the covenant, being condemned to the constant risk of unemployment or other penalties if they voice their own opinions.

Countless young people are prevented from studying because of their own views or even their parents'. Innumerable citizens live in fear of their own or their children's right to education being withdrawn if they should ever speak up in accordance with their convictions.

Any exercise of the right to "seek, receive and impart information and ideas, regardless of frontiers, either orally, in writing or in print" or "in the form of art" specified in Article 19 is followed by criminal charges, as in the recent trial of young musicians.

Freedom of religious confession is curtailed by interference with the activity of churchmen, who are constantly threatened by the state.

Workers are prevented from establishing trade unions, and from freely enjoying the right to strike.

Civic rights are seriously vitiated by interference in the private life of citizens by the Ministry of the Interior, for example by bugging telephones and houses, opening mail, following personal movements, searching homes, and setting up networks of neighbourhood informers.

Charter 77 is an association of people united by the will to strive for the respecting of human rights in our country and throughout the world—rights accorded to all by the Helsinki Charter.

Prague, 1 January 1977.

? **Which violations of the Helsinki Human Rights Charter does Charter 77 identify?**

What forms of coercion could the state use against its citizens?

To what extent was Charter 77 an "anti-political movement"?

Poland—what were the origins of Solidarity?

The origins of Solidarity can be traced to events in December 1970. Just before Christmas, the Party decided to increase food prices by 36 per cent. The people responded with strikes and demonstrations, most notably in the Baltic shipbuilding port of Gdańsk. In December, Gomułka ordered a crackdown against the "counter-revolutionaries" and Polish soldiers shot at and killed Polish workers.

Why was December 1970 so important?

First, the strike, the demonstration and the shootings took place at the giant Lenin Shipyard in Gdańsk, which would later become the birthplace and organizational core of Solidarity. One important member of the strike committee in 1970 made it his career to settle the account of injustices committed. His name was Lech Wałęsa.

Second, unlike in Poznan in 1956 or in Prague in 1968, the protest was organized outside the context of the Party. The protesters appealed to international law to legitimate their independent trade union activity as a workers' organization against the workers' state.

The response of the Party in 1970 was, however, similar to 1956. Changes were promised and reforms introduced; most notable was the replacement of Gomułka by Edward Gierek. In addition, as in 1968, the workers and middle classes remained divided. In January 1971, Gierek successfully appealed to workers to return to work, claiming "I am only a worker like you", and launched an ambitious plan of "consumer socialist", economic regeneration on the basis of Western loans and imported technology.

The consequence was massive national debt, at a time when the world economy was slipping into the 1973 oil crisis. The Poles now expected more and the crisis-ridden state was increasingly unable to deliver. By 1976 something had to give. Without warning, food prices were increased by 60 per cent and again the country went on strike. There were riots and violent state retribution, but again the Party gave way and the increase in food prices was withdrawn.

Solidarity did not emerge merely as a result of economic factors. It is the social and cultural context that explains the unique character of what would become Solidarity and what sort of people became Solidarity supporters. With the highest post-war population growth, a new generation was reaching adulthood in the 1970s. One third of the industrial working class was under 25 years of age. Unlike the Party **nomenklatura** that constituted a significant portion of the older generation, they had no prospect of significant social mobility. They were better educated than those above them, had higher expectations than the previous generation, but were destined to a life of manual labour. In addition, having been inculcated with the ideas of Marxist egalitarianism, they were confronted with daily injustices that rewarded Party careerists with "front of the queue" access to social provision and hard-currency access to exclusive shops that stocked Western consumer goods.

Nomenklatura Members of an elite group within communist parties in the Soviet Union and other Eastern bloc countries, the nomenklatura held various key administrative positions in all spheres of those countries' activity: government, industry, education, etc.

This new working class was therefore susceptible to the new ideas and organizations that began to emerge in the 1970s. The most significant of these was the Workers' Defence Committee (KOR), a group of intellectuals who initially organized the legal defence of the workers who had participated in the 1976 riots. KOR managed to unite the intellectuals who had revolted in Warsaw in 1968 with the workers who had led the protests in 1970. They also produced, by an underground press, uncensored journals and newspapers, such as *Robotnik*, that would be read in secrecy and passed on and devoured by eager workers. It was through an initiative of KOR that the first independent trade unions were formed. On May Day 1978, the first free trade union was launched in Gdańsk. Among the leaders of Free Trade Unions of the Coast, was Lech Wałęsa—sacked for trade union agitation two years previously, he was now to be found selling *Robotnik* outside the Lenin Shipyard gates.

Why was there another crisis in Poland in 1980?

Perhaps the most significant moment in the pre-history of Solidarity occurred in June 1979, with the official visit to Poland of Pope John Paul II. Karol Wojtyła, Archbishop of Kraków, had been elected pope the previous year. As many as 12 million Poles attended the open-air sermons of his eight-day tour during which the organizational reality of the communist state seemed to disappear. The Pope's simple message of human rights and peace had clear implications for the communist state: "The future of Poland will depend upon how many people are mature enough to be non-conformists", said John Paul II. By the end of the 1970s, the Polish opposition was more united and better articulated than at any time in its history. The workers' unions, the intellectuals of KOR and the Church stood ready to lead a nation against Soviet control. All that was needed was a spark.

The initial causes of the 1980 unrest were again economic. Poland's international debt had risen drastically. Faced with pressures from international creditors, the Gierek regime agreed to increase food prices. The sporadic strikes that resulted were contained through judicious, localized pay rises. The turning point, however, came in mid-August and, significantly, the cause was not economic. The sacking of a popular union activist resulted in a demonstration not only for her reinstatement but also for that of Lech Wałęsa. The director of the factory followed the previously successful tactic of promising better conditions if the workers returned to their jobs. But as the crowd seemed on the verge of accepting the offer, Wałęsa climbed up behind the director, tapped him on the shoulder and said, "Remember me? I worked here for ten years … I have the confidence of the workers here." By 18 August, some 200 factories from the Gdańsk region had joined Wałęsa's strike committee, soon to be christened Solidarność (Solidarity).

Solidarity—which came first, the name or the logo?

Where did the name Solidarity come from? Since Deputy Premier Jagielski could not let the phrase "Free Trade Unions" pass his lips, we consulted the experts. This was a "solidarity" strike and our Bulletin was called Solidarity. So the name chose itself.

Source: Anna Walentynowicz, quoted in Kemp-Welch, A. 2008. *Poland under Communism*. Cambridge, UK. Cambridge University Press. p. 268.

… a young design student gave the movement a name by producing a striking logo based on the word Solidarność, the Rubicon was crossed.

Source: Stokes, G. 1993. *The Walls Came Tumbling Down*. Oxford, UK. Oxford University Press. p. 36.

… the name was suggested by one of the first dissidents, Karol Modzelewski

Source: Berend, IT. 1996. *Central and Eastern Europe, 1944–1993. Detour from the periphery to the periphery*. Cambridge, UK. Cambridge University Press. p. 258.

Krzysztof Wyszkowski … the man who may have suggested for the shipyard strike bulletin—and hence perhaps the whole movement—the name 'Solidarity'.

Source: Garton Ash, T 1990. *The Magic Lantern: The Revolution of 1989 Witnessed in Warsaw, Budapest, Berlin, and Prague*. Michigan, USA. University of Michigan/Random House. p. 365.

Lech Wałęsa (1943–)

Lech Wałęsa was born in Popowo, Poland. His father was a carpenter, who died soon after the war as a result of injuries sustained in a Nazi concentration camp. A devout Catholic and Polish patriot, Wałęsa, together with his brothers and sisters, was raised by his mother, aunt and uncle. After school he trained as an electrician and got a job at the Lenin Shipyard in Gdańsk. He was elected a member of the illegal strike committee in 1970 and was sacked for his trade union activities in 1976. In June 1978, he joined the illegal underground Free Trade Unions of the Coast. In August 1980, Wałęsa became leader of the occupational strike at the Lenin Shipyard. The spread of the strike led to the establishment of the free trade union, Solidarity, which elected Wałęsa as leader. He was arrested again on 13 December 1981 and imprisoned for nearly a year as Poland suffered under martial law. In 1983 he received the Nobel Peace Prize but, as part of the continual harassment he now suffered, he was unable to attend the prize-giving ceremony. From 1987, Wałęsa organized and led the Temporary Executive Committee of Solidarity. His brokerage of the deal that set up the 1989 round-table discussions between Solidarity and the communist government was one of the most significant personal interventions in the fall of communism. The resulting June elections marked the beginning of the end of communist rule in Poland. In 1990, increasingly isolated and without a position in the Solidarity-led government, Wałęsa was elected president. His five-year term was marked by political instability during a difficult transition from a planned to a free-market economy. He was narrowly defeated in the 1995 presidential election. Wałęsa gained a reputation for high-handedness, both in his leadership of Solidarity and, later, in his leadership of Poland. But in the face of criticisms of his style of leadership, he asked, "Can you steer a ship through a stormy sea in a wholly democratic way?"

The strike committee produced a list of 21 demands, which went beyond issues of pay and conditions and included the radical demand for the right to form independent trade unions. At the same moment, both KOR and the Catholic Church issued statements in support of this fundamental "right of workers to free associations in unions which genuinely represent them". Although the government drew up plans to crush Solidarity by force, the Polish politburo decided for a negotiated settlement. When, on 31 August 1980, a settlement was reached,

Lech Wałęsa on the campaign trail

Poland became unique in the communist bloc for allowing the paradoxical situation whereby an independent trade union could represent the workers against the workers' state. As Jacek Kuroń later put it, "I thought it was impossible, it was impossible, and I still think it was impossible."

Solidarity was allowed to exist for 469 days, during which the tensions of being in an "impossible" situation were never far from the surface. That Solidarity was allowed to exist as long as it did was due in large part to the leadership and diplomacy of Lech Wałęsa. On the one hand, Solidarity was legally anti-political and recognized the leading role of the Communist Party. On the other hand, Solidarity exercised enormous influence as the de facto representative of the Polish working class and had approximately 10 million members by mid-1981. Solidarity articulated the workers' grievances but, other than the threat of a general strike, it lacked the mechanisms to do anything about it.

What did Solidarity achieve in the 469 days?

Solidarity created a social and political pluralism in Poland that had never before been achieved in the Eastern bloc. It was an intellectual pluralism that would not be seriously challenged even after the temporary imposition of martial law in 1981. One of the most important successes of Solidarity, therefore, was to create new precedents. Solidarity gave local groups a national focus; it was capable of providing a challenge to the state but self-consciously limited the extent of that challenge. Solidarity eschewed not only violence but also antagonistic, overtly political methods. It was in this sense that Solidarity was an anti-political movement. Wałęsa even issued six commandments, including the injunction "to keep peace and order". In other words, Solidarity did not challenge the state, rather it wanted a partnership with it and the Church; in the words of Andrzej Gwiazda, it was "a moral revolution" not a political one. It negotiated and compromised, won concessions from the government but gave concessions also: it won the right of "Rural

Solidarity" to exist but not as a union, it successfully opposed the introduction of two working Saturdays but had to accept one. But all the time the leadership struggled to contain the militant rank and file, who wanted more.

The turning point came in Bydgoszcz in March 1981. A Solidarity demonstration in favour of Rural Solidarity was violently halted by the security forces. On 27 March, Solidarity called a four-hour general strike in protest; it was almost universally heeded. But with an indefinite, general stoppage imminent, Wałęsa and the leadership reached a compromise agreement with the government which satisfied no one. To have gone ahead with the general strike would have overstepped the anti-political boundary, for Wałęsa "the risk was too great". In the previous months, Soviet troops in the Ukraine and Baltic states had been on manoeuvres and, in addition, the Church was preaching restraint.

The consequence was division on both sides of the dispute. Wałęsa's authority was damaged by resignations and internal criticisms and Solidarity increasingly moved in a political direction. This culminated in Solidarity's 1981 October Program, which directly challenged the right of the Communist Party to govern Poland unopposed. For the authorities in the Party, divisions were also rife. On the one hand, reformists succeeded in introducing greater internal democracy in the Party; on the other hand, hardliners called for strong, military leadership to deal with the economic crisis, which had seen the reintroduction of rationing and an inability to pay the foreign debt. Prime minister General Wojciech Jaruzelski stepped into the breach. In the early hours of 13 December 1981, almost all of Solidarity's leaders were arrested along with thousands of activists. **Martial law** was imposed, along with full censorship and the reintroduction of the six-day week. Jaruzelski declared that Poland was on the "edge of an abyss". Protest strikes were called but, in the absence of leadership and coordination, they were easily put down. However, such an excessive response also discredited the communist government.

Polish National Opinion Poll November 1981

Percentage of respondents who expressed confidence in the following national institutions:

Solidarity	95%
Church	93%
Army	68%
Party	7%

Martial law When the military takes over control of the key functions of government, especially the justice system.

Challenges and collapse, 1981–9

This section compares the experiences of opposition and revolution in Poland and Czechoslovakia. Opposition in Poland centred on Lech Wałęsa's Solidarity trade union, and dissatisfaction with economic issues repeatedly extended into political challenges to the regime. This mass workers' movement was in stark contrast to the narrower opposition of the intelligentsia which emerged in Czechoslovakia, where people were cushioned from the worst of the economic distress felt in Poland, and where the regime was challenged on explicitly moral grounds by dissidents such as Václav Havel.

In 1989, the year of revolutions, Poland led the way. Free elections were held, in which Tadeusz Mazowiecki became the first non-communist leader in the Eastern bloc, and thereafter the neighbouring regimes tumbled like dominoes.

The difficulty facing the student seeking to explain the collapse of the communist regimes in 1989 is how to evaluate the relative importance of what historians often describe as internal and external factors. Textbooks written with an international relations Cold War focus inevitably emphasize the ending of détente, the more confrontational policies of the New Right leaders, US president Ronald Reagan and British prime minister Margaret Thatcher, and in particular the sea change that was brought about by the arrival of Mikhail Gorbachev in 1985.

There is little doubt that the changed international focus does much to explain the macro-historical features and in particular the timing of the revolution. But the external factors do not explain the micro-historical nature of the revolutions on the ground. The communist edifice was crumbling throughout the Eastern bloc; this was a result of the interplay of both external and internal factors. But the fact that in some states the crumbling edifice needed a concerted shove, while in others it was merely a question of picking a route through the rubble, can only be explained in terms of the local context.

Poland, 1981–9

Despite initial appearances to the contrary, the imposition of martial law by Jaruzelski did not bear comparison with the process of "normalization" in Czechoslovakia after the Prague Spring. Although Jaruzelski attacked Solidarity and its leadership, he at no point sought to rewind time. He accepted that Poland had been changed for good by the Solidarity days. For example, although initially the media and artists were once again controlled, as long as they distanced themselves from Solidarity they were largely left alone. The same was true of the Catholic Church, which under the leadership of Archbishop Glemp reached a satisfactory accommodation with the Jaruzelski regime.

How significant was Solidarity?

Despite the successful removal of the Solidarity leadership, a few activists did escape capture and continued the opposition underground. New leaders, inspired by Václav Havel, continued the tradition of KOR's anti-politics. This meant not choosing between revolution and compromise but rather undermining the state by ignoring it. This did not require an organized, centralized opposition but rather localized, personal resistance. Compared with the relative intellectual isolation of Czechoslovakia's Charter 77, underground Solidarity found widespread, popular support for a resistance campaign. It is significant that all this occurred before Mikhail Gorbachev introduced glasnost.

However, the decentralized, anti-political actions encouraged by Solidarity also created problems for the organization. The leadership faced difficulties in trying to organize more traditional protests and strikes. A generational divide opened up between old Solidarity and the plethora of anti-political movements that Jaruzelski's actions had encouraged and of which Solidarity was merely one representative.

The years 1983 and 1984 were difficult ones for Solidarity. Although out of prison, the leadership was continually harassed and, despite receiving the Nobel Peace Prize, Wałęsa was unable to motivate a populace that was benefiting from a slightly improved economic situation. Local elections in 1984 produced a turnout of at least 60 per cent, despite calls from Solidarity for a boycott. The state, with the collaboration of Cardinal Glemp and the Catholic Church in Poland, seemed to have Solidarity under control.

Solidarity may have been under political control but the social forces that had been released in 1981 would not go back in the bottle. Jaruzelski, to his credit, realized this. Political control was exercised alongside judicious reforms and concessions. Events surrounding the murder of Father Jerzy Popiełuszko illustrated this very well. Popiełuszko, a pro-Solidarity priest, was found dead in October 1984; remarkably, Jaruzelski put the security police responsible for the murder on public trial. This allowed Jaruzelski both to win popular support and to undermine conservative opposition in the Party. In September 1986, Jaruzelski granted an amnesty to all people who had been detained during martial law. He quickly became Gorbachev's most open supporter of glasnost and oversaw the most liberalized of Eastern bloc societies. International economic sanctions were dropped and, in September 1987, US vice-president Bush made an official visit to Poland, meeting both Jaruzelski and Wałęsa.

What would make Jaruzelski's delicate balancing act impossible to sustain was the underlying weakness of the Polish economy, which, by 1987, was once again on the verge of collapse. The shortage economy was famously summed up by Adam Michnik when he said, "Everybody's fondest dream was to be able to find a roll of toilet paper." The government proposed some radical reforms, including

The underground society

"Instead of organizing ourselves as an underground state, we should be organizing ourselves as an underground society … Such a movement should strive for a situation in which the government will control empty shops but not the market, employment but not the means to livelihood, the state press but not the flow of information, printing houses but not the publishing movement, telephones and the postal service but not communication, schools but not education".

Wiktor Kulerski, former Solidarity member and Secretary of State for education in Poland

Solidarity election poster, 1989. Why do you think Solidarity chose to use this image? There are many examples of opposition groups in the Eastern bloc using humour to make a political point. Why is this?

the creation of private firms, but also significant austerity measures which would result in major price rises. Most radical of all was how they planned to introduce the changes. In November 1987 the government conducted a national referendum asking the public for their approval of the changes. When the government unexpectedly declared itself defeated, Solidarity announced that Poland had entered "a new phase" and that the "war was over".

In early 1988, the Solidarity leadership fought to maintain discipline and control over the rank and file, as widespread strikes broke out. For the young strikers, many of whom were not members, the lack of militancy in the Solidarity leadership, was a sign of weakness. In August 1988, Wałęsa was called to a secret meeting with government ministers. If Wałęsa could get the strikes called off, the government offered to discuss the legalization of Solidarity. Despite contrary advice from many of his closest advisers, Wałęsa agreed and, after three days of cajoling, the workers went back. Jaruzelski likewise faced internal opposition to his plan of legalizing Solidarity. The central committee plenum (a government meeting) broke up without reaching a decision in December 1988 and only the threat of Jaruzelski's resignation in January 1989 forced the decision through.

The historic round-table discussions between the government, the Church, opposition political parties, intellectuals and trade unions including Solidarity began on 6 February 1989. The most significant decisions were that Solidarity would be legally recognized and would be given minority representation in the new parliament.

The elections were called for 4 June, allowing Solidarity just two months to prepare. In contrast, the Communist Party coalition candidates would have the advantages of staff, offices, money and a monopoly over the media. Despite this, Solidarity prepared well; they nominated one candidate per seat, produced striking posters featuring images of Wałęsa and the famous Solidarity logo and they relied on a national network of enthusiastic volunteers.

No one predicted the sensational results. After the second round of voting, Solidarity candidates won all the 161 seats they contested in the **Sejm** and 99 out of the 100 seats available in the **Senate**.

Solidarity proposed a coalition government, led by their prime minister, Tadeusz Mazowiecki. After a phone call from Gorbachev and an assurance from Solidarity that Polish membership of the Warsaw Pact was not threatened, Jaruzelski accepted Wałęsa's coalition proposal. On 21 August, the 21st anniversary of the Soviet invasion of Czechoslovakia, 10 000 people took to the streets of Czechoslovakia. They sang "Long Live Dubček", but they also sang "Long Live Poland". The success of Solidarity was about to influence the most extraordinary autumn in living memory.

"They must have known they would win! But they didn't. I sat with an exhausted and depressed Adam Michnik over lunch that Sunday, and he did not know. I drank with a nervously excited Jacek Kuroń late that evening, and he did not know. Nobody knew."

Historian and eyewitness,
Timothy Garton Ash

The Polish parliament consists of an upper house, the **Senate**, and a lower house, the **Sejm**.

TOK link

Eyewitness vs Historian

Timothy Garton Ash was an eyewitness to the revolutionary events he describes and he is also a historian. He acknowledges the advantages and disadvantages of the eyewitness compared to the historian.

> *The disadvantages of the witness as against the historian are those of partiality in space, time and judgement. The witness can only be in one place at one time, and tends to attach an exaggerated importance to what he personally saw or heard. The historian can gather all the witnesses' accounts and is generally unswayed by that first-hand experience. What happened afterwards changes our view of what went before. The historian usually knows more about what happened afterwards, simply because he writes later. Finally, there is partiality in judgement … Such are the grave disadvantages of a witness. But there are also advantages. The witness can, if he is lucky, see things that the historian will not find in any document. Sometimes a glance, a shrug, a chance remark, will be more revealing than a hundred speeches. In these events, even more than in most contemporary history, much of great importance was not written down at all, either because it occurred in hasty conversations with no note-takers present, or because the business was conducted on the telephone, or because the words or pictures came by television. (The importance of television can hardly be overstated. Future historians of these events will surely have to spend as much time in television archives as in libraries.) The witness can see how things that appear to have been spontaneous were actually rigged; but also how things that appear to have been carefully arranged were in fact the hapless product of sheer confusion. And perhaps the most difficult thing of all for the historian to recapture is the sense of what, at a given historical moment, people did not know about the future.*

Source: Garton Ash, Timothy. 1990. *The Magic Lantern: The Revolution of 1989 Witnessed in Warsaw, Budapest, Berlin, and Prague*. Michigan, USA. University of Michigan/Random House. p. 21–2.

What are the strengths and weaknesses of the eyewitness compared to the historian's account?

How far do you agree with Garton Ash's view on the importance of television?

Czechoslovakia, 1981–9

In 1985, Mikhail Gorbachev came to power in the Soviet Union. He acknowledged the mistakes of his predecessors and the comparative economic failure of the Soviet Union. The Eastern bloc economies were unable to match the technological advances achieved in the West or to keep up in the arms race. Soviet attempts to intervene in support of their puppet regime in Afghanistan were failing. Western leaders such as Ronald Reagan and Margaret Thatcher, perhaps sensing their opponent's weakness, had departed from the accommodating rhetoric of 1970s détente and characterized the Soviet bloc as an "Evil Empire".

Gorbachev called for economic perestroika (restructuring), a relaxation of central planning and the introduction of market forces. Hardliners within the Party opposed this as a step towards capitalism. Gorbachev sought to widen the debate through greater political glasnost (openness), and a willingness to discuss mistakes and allow the expression of alternative ideas. This liberalization proved popular among non-Party members. However, the lack of internal Party unity on the issue of economic reform denied Gorbachev the option of the Chinese model of economic reform accompanied by tight political control. The only way to pursue the necessary perestroika was to draw on the support of those outside the Party, in effect to abandon the Communist Party's long held monopoly of the truth.

A new, reform-minded leader, an attempt to save the system by a loosening of economic and political control, tolerance of alternative opinions— the parallels with the Prague Spring were obvious. Husák's regime was based on a rejection of that previous effort to achieve "socialism with a human face"; they had purged the reformers of 1968, and had clung onto power through the intervening years of normalization. The dynamic, new leadership in the Soviet Union was in stark contrast to the aging Czechoslovak **apparatchiks**. Their political careers had rested on adherence to Moscow's line, but how could they now join in criticisms of the years of stagnation without implicating themselves? The comparison was made explicit by a Soviet spokesman in 1987. When asked what the difference between perestroika and Prague Spring was, he replied, "19 years." Even more threatening to Husák's regime was Gorbachev's rejection of the Brezhnev Doctrine:

> It's time to abandon foreign policy influenced by an imperial standpoint. Neither the Soviet Union nor the USA is able to force its will on others. It is possible to suppress, compel, bribe, break or blast, but only for a certain period. ... That is why only one thing— relations of equality—remains.
>
> Gorbachev, M. 1987. Quoted in Todd, Allan. 2001. *The Modern World*. Oxford, UK. Oxford University Press. p. 236.

This was later summarized by Soviet foreign ministry spokesman Gennadi Gerasimov as the Sinatra Doctrine, each satellite free to "Do it their way". The threat of Soviet intervention had been removed. Another Charter 77 dissident, Ludvik Vaculik was pessimistic about the reform process:

> I observe all this in sceptical suspense, as a socialist, and ... as a Czech ... True, that country has needed for a long time for someone to come and shake it up, and yet it's all rather sad: by the time an idea has been grasped by the Russian bureaucrat, it is hardly new where the rest of the world is concerned. We saw this in cybernetics 40 years ago, later it was jazz, and now we are being presented with the Moscow version of the 1968 Prague Spring. Our people are understandably puzzled, asking one another what's in it for us.

Apparatchik A member of the Communist Party bureaucracy.

At the same time I watch our government reluctantly giving us information and trying to calm down expectations: don't worry, nothing as momentous as that is going to happen here. After all, every country has the right to go its own way, courageously declared [Government Minister] Biľak. There you are then—after all these years we have longed for a government that would not act as someone's arse-licker, and now we have got it! Is this not indeed a historic moment?

Vaculik, Ludvik. "Glasnost—a feuilleton in A Cup of Coffee with my Interrogator". Quoted in Spafford, Peter (ed). 1992. *Interference—The Story of Czechoslovakia in the Words of its Writers*. Cheltenham, UK. New Clarion Press. p. 131.

At the same time, the other pillar of Husák's regime, the fragile social contract with the workers, was being eroded by economic decline. The widening gap between East and West was impossible to hide in an age of improved communication, in which Western television and radio could endlessly demonstrate the material and cultural shortcomings of the Soviet bloc. As the economy stalled, even the celebrated social mobility that characterized the rapid industrialization of early state socialism and that enabled peasants and workers to access greater education and employment opportunities had ground to a halt. Ambitious, younger employees found promotional prospects blocked by long-serving political appointees. Party membership declined throughout the region and the numbers of those who genuinely believed in the parroted slogans of Leninist purity dwindled.

The Velvet Revolution, 1989

Encouraged by the fresh winds blowing from Moscow, increasing numbers of Czechs and Slovaks were prepared to voice their opposition to the regime. Some, such as the "Bratislava Aloud" group, which in 1987 published a report criticizing the government's disregard for the environment, developed from single issues. Other sources of opposition emerged from non-communist student groups. Although Czechs and Slovaks in general are less drawn to organized religion than their counterparts in Poland, the churches also grew bolder as centres of opposition; in 1988, rallies demanding religious freedom were held in Prague and Bratislava. A petition formulated by the Archbishop of Prague attracted 500 000 signatures. Václav Havel was again arrested and imprisoned following his participation in anti-government demonstrations. This heavy-handed reaction provoked yet more protests and Havel was released.

Elsewhere in the region, Soviet control was collapsing rapidly. Reform communists in Hungary and Poland attempted to reach compromises with their opponents. In May 1989, the border between Hungary and Austria was dismantled, allowing free travel. In June, Solidarity won a share of power in free elections. In October and November, mass demonstrations in East Germany culminated in the dismantling of the Berlin Wall. On 17 November, in Prague, an officially sanctioned commemoration of Jan Opletal's death at the hands of the Nazis turned into yet another anti-government protest. The riot police violently assaulted the protesters and rumours that a student had been killed led to further outraged protests. Throughout the country citizens poured onto the streets.

Havel sought to harness the strength of popular feeling, gathering like-minded opponents to form Civic Forum, an umbrella organization which articulated the people's demands. The government struggled to respond to the gathering strength of opposition and, ruthlessly purged of reformists, contained no credible alternatives to the architects of normalization. This legacy of 1968 made it difficult for them to follow the lead of the Hungarian and Polish parties. Another option, as attempted unsuccessfully in Romania the following month, was to adopt the Chinese Tiananmen Square example and order security forces to violently suppress the opposition. In retrospect, it is tempting to view the events of 1989 as inevitable, but this threat of violence was a real risk that each individual involved in a street demonstration had to weigh up. In particular, the term "Velvet Revolution" glosses over the bravery required by those who openly confronted the state. However, so rapidly was support evaporating that even the loyalty of the police and military could no longer be guaranteed. The Czechoslovak Revolution was to be peacefully "velvet".

The rebels drew encouragement from events in neighbouring countries. Emboldened by the expanding possibilities, and legitimized by the masses of people on the streets, Civic Forum and their Slovak counterparts, People Against Violence, could demand ever greater concessions from the government. On 24 November, Husák's successor as president, Miloš Jakeš, resigned. Huge crowds greeted Dubček and Havel as they appeared together in Prague. A general strike on 27 November showed that the revolution had spread beyond Prague, beyond the intellectuals and students, to encompass the workers in a national rejection of the regime. In the following days, the Party renounced its right to a leading role and plans were made for free elections. Before the end of the year that had begun with his arrest and imprisonment, Václav Havel was elected as president of Czechoslovakia.

How did Poland and Czechoslovakia deal with the challenges of post-communism?

Post-communist Central and Eastern Europe faced a number of serious barriers to the peaceful transition to democracy and market economies. We can identify four major interrelated problems.

The first of these was the lack of democratic traditions. Only Czechoslovakia among the former Eastern bloc regimes had any real democratic experience prior to the Second World War. This was as much a social and cultural issue as a political problem. The social groups that had led opposition to communism were not democratic political parties but broad groupings of a wide range of different interest groups, united by what they opposed rather what they stood for. Now that the common enemy was defeated, what did the opposition want to do and in whose name were they going to do it?

The second problem resulted from the limited, peaceful nature of the revolution. The Communist Party may have been swept aside, but the communist state with its organizational apparatus (including bloated security forces) and personnel (nomenklatura) were very much still in place. A liberal democracy requires more than periodic elections; it requires legitimate state structures attuned to the needs of constitutionality and personnel committed to upholding constitutional practices. Put simply, the problem was that building liberal democracy would have to rely upon communist builders.

The third problem was perhaps the most pressing. Had the Eastern bloc economies been able to sustain the levels of economic growth achieved in the 1950s, there would never have been revolutions in 1989. In 1990, the new leaders of post-communist states faced the problem of resolving the economic crisis that had brought them to power in the first place. The moribund command economies were to be exposed to the harsh realities of the global market and the people would no longer be protected by a state that was ideologically established to do so. Furthermore, many of the opposition groups that were now in power, most notably Solidarity, had been formed to protect their members from the very forces of marketization that they were now expected to introduce.

The final problem was socio-cultural. The communist state was much more than an economic or political system, it had attempted to intervene in all aspects of the individual's life. After the socialist utopian dream had faded, people's emotional energy had been dedicated to the movements that had opposed communism. Now that this was achieved, would people make an emotional commitment to the market? The inherent problems of economic transition to a market economy were accompanied by the loss of traditional support structures and uncertainty.

Key economic indicators, 1988–90					
	Economic growth (%)			Inflation (%)		
	1988	1989	1990	1988	1989	1990
USSR	6	3	-4	7	9	10
Poland	5	0	-12	60	241	800
Czechoslovakia	2	1	-3	0	1	14
Hungary	2	1	-5	16	17	29
Romania	0	-11	-12	1	2	20

Source: Deutsche Bank. 1991. *Rebuilding Eastern Europe.* Frankfurt, Germany.

It is not surprising that people sought solace in the attachments that communism had worked so hard to replace: religion and nationalism. Newly democratic politicians, unable to provide reasons for economic malaise, exploited the emotional power of tribal and religious affiliation with devastating consequences for the region, most notably in Yugoslavia.

The break-up of Yugoslavia

"the glue that held Yugoslavia together, the League of Yugoslav Communists" simply disintegrated. As in Poland, Yugoslavia under the leadership of Ante Markovic' underwent market-orientated, economic "shock therapy" in 1990. But, unlike in Poland, the unpopularity of the measures was successfully exploited by politicians within the regional republics for nationalist political ends.

The different Yugoslav states had distinct visions for the future of Yugoslavia. The economically powerful states of Slovenia and Croatia favoured greater autonomy for the regions within Yugoslavia, whereas the politically powerful state of Serbia under the leadership of Slobodan Milošević' favoured strengthening the power of the centre in Belgrade. In 1991, Slovenia and Croatia became the first republics to declare independence from Yugoslavia. With well-established borders and no significant ethic minority groupings, Slovenian independence presented relatively few problems. In contrast, Croatia with its significant Serbian minority and history of anti-Serbian persecution, could only declare independence at the expense of Serbian national feeling.

In contrast to the peaceful nature of most of the revolutions of 1989, events in Yugoslavia developed into the most violent seen in Europe since the end of the Second World War. Between 1991 and 2001, more than 140 000 people were killed and considerably more made homeless and/or displaced. The wars were characterized by an unusual brutality that included ethnic cleansing, systematic rape and the deliberate destruction of priceless historical and cultural artifacts. In 1993 the United Nations established the International Criminal Tribunal in The Hague for the former Yugoslavia, where more than 150 individuals have since been indicted for war crimes.

The reasons for the violence revolve around the fundamental weakness in the concept of Yugoslavism itself. The country was a federation of six republics: Slovenia, Croatia, Bosnia and Herzegovina, Macedonia, Montenegro, and Serbia. What held Yugoslavia together was not the common ethnic identity of "South Slavia" (a literal translation of "Yugoslavia") but rather Marxist ideology, relative economic prosperity and the leadership of Josip Tito.

Tito died in 1980 and by then the economy, as in other parts of the Eastern bloc, was already in decline. Events in Eastern Europe produced a crisis of legitimacy for Marxism and consequently

The Croatian War of Independence began in April 1991 when Serbian minorities in Croatia declared their independence in the form of the Republic of Serb Krajina. In 1992, war spread to Bosnia, to which both Serbian and Croatian nationalists lay claim. Bosnian Serbs, led by Radovan Karadzic and backed by Serbia, faced Bosnian Muslims (Bosniaks) and Croats backed by President Franjo Tud-man in Zagreb. The Bosnian conflict, with the sieges of Sarajevo and Srebrenica, were the bloodiest of the Yugoslav Civil War. The war ended with the signing of the Dayton Agreement in December 1995, after successful military action by Croatia had restored its 1991 borders.

Conflict continued in the region as Albanian national minorities in Kosovo sought greater autonomy from Serbia. The three-year conflict in Kosovo only ended with the NATO bombing of Serbia in 1999. Slobodan Milošević' was put on trial in The Hague in 2002 but died a few months before the verdict was due in 2006. Radovan Karadžic' was captured in Belgrade in July 2008 and like Milošević' faces war crimes charges in The Hague. The instability in the region continues with the disputed declaration of independence of the Republic of Kosovo in February 2008.

IB Learner Profile link

Inquirers and communicators

Do a presentation on the experiences of another Eastern bloc country. Include the following:

- leadership
- relations with the Soviet Union
- challenges to Soviet control
- opposition groups/leaders
- revolution
- post-communism.

Poland after communism

> When Solidarity won, Polish workers lost … with the one group that could control them [the workers], Solidarity, chiefly interested in promoting the marketization causing the emotional distress, a political crisis was inevitable.

Ost, David. 2005. *The Defeat of Solidarity: Anger and Politics in Postcommunist Europe.* Ithaca, New York, USA and London, UK. Cornell University Press.

Polish workers had been living in a state which, at least in principle, had been organized in their interest and justified on those terms. The revolutions of 1989 had been inspired by the example of their trade union, Solidarity, which was at heart a working-class organization, established to defend them. They had been led in this revolution by Lech Wałęsa, who without question was as "working class" as any of them. And yet, by sweeping aside communism in 1989 and replacing it with political freedom and democracy, they also swept aside the workers' state and replaced it with economic liberalism and the market. After the euphoria of their victory over the communist state had subsided, the workers, the vast majority of the population, would be on their own to face the vagaries of international capitalism.

On 12 September, the Sejm voted approval of prime minister Tadeusz Mazowiecki and his cabinet. For the first time in more than 40 years, Poland had a government led by non-communists. In May 1990, the first free local elections took place and Solidarity dominated. In July, the cabinet was reshuffled to remove the last remaining communists. In October 1990, the constitution was amended in order to allow the departure of President Jaruzelski. And in December Lech Wałęsa became the first Polish president elected on a popular vote. On the surface at least, the transition appears smooth and the justice of it all almost poetic. But below the surface, the country and Solidarity were being torn apart.

From January 1990, the Polish economy was subjected to market-economy "shock treatment". Price controls and trade barriers were lifted, many state subsidies were removed and the Polish złoty was made convertible with foreign currencies. Inflation was brought under control, but at massive social cost. Industrial output fell by 30 per cent, wages fell by 40 per cent and unemployment, which had been non-existent under communism, rose to over one million before the end of 1990. Within months Poland had the highest unemployment in Europe.

Not surprisingly in the face of social crisis, the Solidarity-sponsored government came under pressure. Lech Wałęsa as trade union leader had been increasingly isolated by the Solidarity intellectuals in the Mazowiecki government. Divisions opened up within the movement and factional, nascent political parties began to be formed around key personalities. The bitter presidential elections that saw Wałęsa defeat Mazowiecki exposed Solidarity's divisions. The much delayed parliamentary elections of October 1991 revealed how fragmented the Polish political scene had become. As Garton Ash has pointed out, General Jaruzelski did not succeed in dividing or destroying Solidarity, Lech Wałęsa did. What he, more than anyone, had kept together, he, more than anyone, deliberately pulled apart.

There followed a series of weak coalition governments and short-lived prime ministers. In September 1993, the former communists gained a clear majority while Solidarity received less than the 5 per cent necessary to gain representation in parliament. In the presidential elections of 1995, ex-communist Aleksander Kwaśniewski defeated Wałęsa by a narrow margin.

However, there was to be no retreat from the policies of privatization and deregulation. For all the political and economic instability in the 1990s, the policies, if not the policy makers were reliably consistent. By 2000, Poland was fully integrated within the community of European nations: her trade had successfully shifted orientation from east to west; she was now a member of NATO and she had begun the process of joining the EU—formalized on January 2004.

Solidarity, the trade union, continued to exist as one of a number of national unions, but with membership now measured in hundreds of thousands rather than millions. The old certainties had gone, along with the job security of the communist era. To be a Polish worker today is to live a life without solidarity. As the Gdańsk workers interviewed in 1999 argued, "Yes we have freedom: but what good is that if you have no money to buy the shiny goods in the shops?"As Garton Ash summed it up:

> … the irony is painful. Workers started the great changes, yet have paid the highest price. Solidarity was originally a trade union, yet the result of its triumph is that Gdańsk workers are employed by their former workmates, now turned capitalist, in private firms with no trade unions at all.
>
> Garton Ash, T. 2002. *The Polish Revolution: Solidarity*. 3rd edn. Yale, USA. Yale University Press. p. 380.

TOK link

Francis Fukuyama, in his influential essay, described the revolutions of 1989 as "the end of history". The West had won the Cold War and the world could now expect the extension of democratic, capitalist systems as the challenge of communism receded.

> *What we may be witnessing is not just the end of the Cold War or the passing of a particular period of post-war history, but the end of history as such: that is, the end point of mankind's ideological evolution and the universalization of Western liberal democracy as the final form of human government.*

Source: Fukuyama, F. 1992. *The End of History and the Last Man*. New York, USA. Free Press.

Historians have criticized Fukuyama's work as an example of "retrospective determinism"—the sense in which the revolutions of 1989 and the triumph of market capitalism seem inevitable with hindsight.

> *Meanwhile, the passage of time produces its own peculiar distortions. One thing that happened rather quickly in the early 1990s was that history was rewritten—not in the deliberate, Orwellian way of communist states, but through the much more subtle, spontaneous and potent workings of human memory. Suddenly, Western politicians 'remembered' how they had all along predicted the end of communism. And suddenly, almost everyone in the East had been some sort of a dissident. The ranks of the opposition grew miraculously after the event. Former communist leaders also produced remarkable memoirs. Thus, in conversations after German unification, both the former Soviet foreign minister Eduard Shevardnadze and Aleksander Yakovlev, a key Gorbachev adviser, told me that they had anticipated it as early as the mid-1980s. Was there a record of that? Well no, you see, they could not have said this out loud, not even to a small group of officials—because to do so might have shaken the whole fabric of Moscow's relations with Eastern Europe. (And the difficulty for the historian is that this is also true.)*

Source: Garton Ash, T. 1990. *The Magic Lantern: The Revolution of 1989 Witnessed in Warsaw, Budapest, Berlin, and Prague*. Michigan, USA. University of Michigan/ Random House. p. 160.

1 What does Garton Ash mean by history rewritten "in the Orwellian way of the communist states"?

2 What does the extract reveal about the reliability of oral history amd memoirs by the leading historical participants?

3 To what extent were the revolutions of 1989 inevitable?

4 After Marxism, are there any significant challenges left to the Western models of liberal democracy?

Czechoslovakia after communism—the Velvet Divorce

On 1 January 1993, Czechoslovakia ceased to exist. It was the third of Europe's three communist federal states to disintegrate, after the Soviet Union and Yugoslavia, though in Czechoslovakia's case the split was carried out in a peacefully "velvet" manner. Why were Czechs and Slovaks, who had supported each other against common opponents for so long, unable to sustain their shared state?

There have since been many challenges to this argument, including the interpretation of 1989 as more of a "return to history". From this perspective, nationalism in Central and Eastern Europe had been held in check by the disciplines of the Cold War. When the Cold War ended and Soviet centralism faded, history, in the form of long-held nationalist tensions, was able to resurface. For homogeneous nation states such as Poland, this was less of an obstacle than in Czechoslovakia, where Czechs and Slovaks often had different notions of the nature of their state. As we have seen, a common enemy such as the Austro-Hungarian Empire or the Soviet Union could unite Czechoslovakia, but the idea of "Czechoslovakism" failed to survive the removal of these external forces.

As the larger nation, Czechs were less likely than Slovaks to question the idea of Czechoslovakia, it was easier for them to conflate Czechoslovak and Czech identity, while for Slovaks it was clear that these were different concepts." The "hyphen war" of 1990, in which Slovaks argued that the country should be renamed "Czecho-Slovakia" was indicative of these varying perspectives. The asymmetric model, whereby Slovak institutions, based in Bratislava, existed alongside Czechoslovak counterparts, based in Prague, had failed to obscure that it was the latter who had wielded real power.

A further constitutional complication was the need for consensus to pass new laws and the relative ease with which a minority of deputies could block legislation. When parliament had only to act as a rubber stamp for communist policy, this was not a problem, but post-1989 it led to delays and splits, often along national lines.

Among the emerging political parties, most competed for seats in either the Czech lands or in Slovakia; there was no popular Czechoslovak political force. The dominant politicians, the Czech Václav Klaus and the Slovak Vladimír Mečiar, offered sharply contrasting solutions to Czechoslovakia's problems. Klaus advocated a rapid transformation to free-market economics and expressed frustration with Mečiar's arguments for a more gradual approach. Havel's efforts at mediation failed. The option of splitting the country offered both leaders a chance to pursue their policies unfettered by the other. The Czech right could pursue a more radical short, sharp-shock route to economic transformation, while Slovakia had to endure several years of Mečiar's idiosyncratic authoritarianism.

Thus, the political elite agreed the collapse of Czechoslovakia. This occurred without violence but also without any great popular demand. There was never a referendum on the issue and opinion polls from the time do not show a majority in favour of the split. This indifference meant the split could go ahead in an atmosphere of restraint, without the violence that accompanied the collapses of the Soviet Union and Yugoslavia. The external forces that had held Czechoslovakia together no longer existed. The prospect of EU and NATO membership offered new international frameworks within which both the Czech Republic and Slovakia could prosper.

The Czech Republic and Slovakia, 2009. Opinion polls show that Central and Eastern European countries are more positive about European Union membership than Western Europeans. Why do you think this is?

Coercion, persuasion and consent—why did the communist states of Central and Eastern Europe survive so long?

All states maintain control over their citizens through coercion, persuasion and by generating consent. Most accounts correctly draw attention to the way in which violence was used by Eastern bloc regimes to uphold the rule of the Communist Party, notably in 1956, 1968 and 1981. In addition, with Eastern bloc regimes we can distinguish between internal and external coercion. Jaruzelski's imposition of martial law in 1981 was a prime example of internal coercion. But the limitations of the governments of Eastern bloc states were also externally defined; as Polish dissident Bronislaw Geremek put it, "Limitation is the movement of Soviet tanks". Persuasion, through state censorship and propaganda, was also important. The state maintained various levels of censorship and propaganda, through the control of education, leisure, the arts and the media.

But it is equally important to recognize that the Eastern bloc regimes could not have survived for as long as they did, unless the states were able to maintain the consent of a significant proportion of the populace and the apolitical indifference of significantly more. As desribed by Norman Davies:

> The essence of good policing lies in prevention rather than punishment … The ordinary citizens of a communist state were so enmeshed by petty rules and regulations, that meekness and subservience towards authorities was the only way to ensure a quiet life.

Davies, N. 2001. *Heart of Europe: The Past in Poland's Present.* Oxford, UK. Oxford Paperbacks. p. 31.

Consent was generated through the system of nomenklatura—a command economy operating without the "invisible hand" of the market requires the very visible hands of millions of these state officials. These were Party members recruited from the working class and therefore the beneficiaries of significant social mobility. They had a significant stake in the maintenance of the communist system. But perhaps more significantly, beyond the nomenklatura class obedience was generated by the simple fact that the state controlled all means of social advancement and access to scarce resources. As historian Neil Harding put it:

> We need not invoke either too lofty or too base a view of human nature to explain the durability and stability of the state formations of Communist regimes. We need only accept the commonplace, that in most times men are guided by a prudent concern for their own welfare and for that of those who are close to them. It is, therefore, unremarkable that where all the prospects for advancing that welfare are in the hands of the state, and where it is clear that the condition for advancement is support for its policies, then few will rebel.
>
> Harding, Neil. 1985. *The State in Socialist Society*. Basingstoke, UK. Macmillan/St Antony's College. p. 229.

Consent began to break down in the Eastern bloc partly as a result of the political trauma of the Soviet invasion of Czechoslovakia in 1968—after which it became increasingly implausible that the communist system might reform itself internally—but also as a result of the economic failure of the command economy model, which became evident after the 1973 oil crisis. The workers' state was increasingly unable to provide the material basis of its own legitimacy.

The Soviet-style, state socialist model had proved adept at rapidly modernizing backward, agricultural economies and providing unprecedented levels of social welfare provision. Indeed, the economies of both Eastern and Western Europe were rebuilt after the Second World War in remarkably similar ways: nationalization of heavy industry and essential services, coupled with universal welfare provision were as much a feature of Britain and France as they were of Poland and Czechoslovakia. If anything, the economies of the Eastern bloc did relatively better in the post-war years.

Per capita GNP (in 1960 dollars)					
	Western Europe		Eastern Europe		Eastern Europe
Year	$	index	$	index	As % of the West
1860	384	100	214	100	56
1913	678	177	389	181	57
1938	839	218	509	238	61
1973	2 257	588	1 861	870	82

Per capita GNP as a percentage of the European average			
Country	1910	1938	1973
Europe	100	100	100
Czechoslovakia	98	82	117
Hungary	75	67	89
Poland	70	55	89
Romania	61	51	66

Source: Berend, Ivan T. 1996. *Central and Eastern Europe, 1944–1993*. Cambridge, UK. Cambridge University Press, p.187–8.

The period from 1945 to 1973 was something of a golden age for the command economy. There were not only real improvements in the standard of living, there was also the memory of pre-war depression, the common sacrifice of wartime and the shining model of Stalin's Russia, whose towering achievement had been the defeat of Nazi Germany. For many there was genuine belief in what was being achieved in the name of socialism: whether the comprehensive housing and heathcare programmes, full and secure employment, the Russian space programme or the success of East German women athletes in Olympic Games, all were sources of pride and steps on the road to a socialist utopia. So, as long as the Party provided the material goods and the social opportunities, there was little opposition.

But when capitalism in the West began to shift to a more consumer-driven, **post-industrial** economy that depended on technological innovation associated with microchips and the telecommunications revolution, the inflexible, command economy could not compete. A command economy cannot plan innovation any more than an actor can improvise the words of Shakespeare. The Eastern bloc did not and, more importantly, could not produce a Silicon Valley or an entrepreneur like Steve Jobs or Bill Gates.

> **Post-industrial** A post-industrial society is a society in which an economic transition has occurred from manufacturing to a service-based economy.

In addition, the post-war regimes would become victims of their relative economic and social success. A young family struggling to survive didn't have time to revolt. By the end of the period, they had become accustomed to economic growth, health and welfare provision that, when threatened, produced serious political grievances. The communist regimes could dig themselves out of trouble only by short-term economic measures which hastened them into long-term structural crisis. This was the vicious circle which characterized the periodic economic crises and political reform in Poland. The regimes also produced not only higher expectations from their citizenship, but also the high quality, universal education system which provided the citizenship with the means of articulating them. Communism, to borrow a phrase from Marx, had created its own gravediggers.

Activity:

Former satellite states of the USSR.

Complete the following table to provide a summary of key developments in the four former Communist states named in topic 4 of the IB syllabus. An outline for Czechoslovakia has been provided for you but will need to be expanded. Information contained in this chapter and elsewhere in the book will help you to begin to complete the table, but wider research will be necessary if it is to be successfully completed.

	Experience of World War Two.	Date and method of Communist takeover	Important groups and individuals that challenge Communist rule	Unsuccessful challenges to Communist control	Successful challenges to Communist control	Transition from Communism and current status
Czechoslovakia	Czech lands occupied by Nazi Germany, 1939. Slovakia run as a Nazi puppet state. Liberated by American and Soviet armies 1945.	1948 Soviet-backed, Communist coup.	Alexander Dubcek, Reform Communists. Vaclav Havel, Charter 77 Civic Forum (Czech) People Against Violence (Slovakia)	1968, Prague Spring	1989, Velvet Revolution	Peaceful transition followed by Velvet Divorce. The Czech Republic and Slovakia are now independent democratic states within the EU and NATO.
Poland						
Hungary						
Yugoslavia						

Questions

1 How did each state experience the Soviet takeover of Central and Eastern Europe?

- In pairs or small groups, choose one of the countries in the table. How unique was the experience of that country during the Second World War and in the take-over of the Communists after the war? As well as identifying the experience of your chosen country, remember to identify similarities that it shared with the other countries.

2 Why was Yugoslavia able to successfully challenge Soviet influence in 1948 but not Hungary in 1956 or Czechoslovakia in 1968?

3 Compare the methods used by opposition groups in these countries. Why were they unsuccessful before 1989?

4 Identify the problems experienced by these countries in the transition to independence/ capitalism/democracy.

5 Two communist federations, Czechoslovakia and Yugoslavia, both collapsed during the 1990s but their experiences were very different.

- What were the reasons for the breakup of these federations? How similar were these reasons?
- What political, economic, social and cultural problems would you expect when a state breaks up? Which of these applied to Czechoslovakia and/or Yugoslavia?
- Why was the experience of Czechoslovakia so much more peaceful than Yugoslavia?

6 As an extension to this exercise, you may wish to add to the list Romania, Bulgaria and the German Democratic Republic of East Germany.

Exam questions

1 Assess the reasons for the growth of movements challenging Soviet control in **two** Central or Eastern European states.
2 Analyse the role and success of **either** Václav Havel **or** Lech Wałęsa in freeing their countries from Soviet control.
3 For what reasons and in what ways did **either** Hungary **or** Poland challenge Soviet control.
4 To what extent did the Cold War affect independence movements and new states **either** in Africa and Asia, **or** in post-1945 Central and Eastern European states?

Recommended further reading

http://www.internationalschoolhistory.net

Includes an expanded, hypertext version of this chapter with guides for further research

Berend, Ivan T. 1996. *Central and Eastern Europe, 1944–1993. Detour from the periphery to the periphery*. Cambridge, UK. Cambridge University Press.

A most engaging overview of the Eastern bloc from a man who spent most of his life living through what he analyses

Dubček, Alexander. 1993. *Hope Dies Last*. New York, USA. Kodansha America.

The autobiography of the man at the centre of events in Czechoslovakia

Garton Ash, Timothy. 1990. *The Magic Lantern: The Revolution of 1989 Witnessed in Warsaw, Budapest, Berlin, and Prague*. Michigan, USA. University of Michigan/Random House.

An excellent account of 1989 by a journalist/historian and eyewitness—the author captures the immediacy but with his critical faculties intact.

Kemp-Welch, A. 2008. *Poland under Communism*. Cambridge, UK. Cambridge University Press. Detailed focus on Poland

Kenney, Padraic. 2002. *A Carnival of Revolution*. Princeton and Oxford, USA. Princeton University Press.

Restoring the people to the revolution

Shepherd, Robin, HE. 2000. *Czechoslovakia: The Velvet Revolution and Beyond*. Basingstoke and London, UK. Macmillan Press.

A skilfully explained account of both the revolution and the subsequent "velvet divorce"

Stokes, Gale. 1993. *The Walls Came Tumbling Down*. Oxford, UK. Oxford University Press.

An excellent comparative account of the revolutions.

9 The Cold War

This chapter is an examination of aspects of the Cold War, which lasted from the end of the Second World War until the collapse of the Soviet Union in 1991. In a general sense it was a war between two rival factions, but more specifically it was a war between the USA and the USSR. It was a conflict that was waged on many continents, and in all aspects of the lives of those affected. It was an extensive, total war, in which the main belligerents never engaged in direct conflict with each other; nor did they seem to wish to do so.

A variety of examples of material for detailed study of this topic (topic 5) are provided, and an attempt has been made to choose examples from throughout the world and throughout the course of the Cold War. Coverage includes:

- Yalta and Potsdam
- the Truman Doctrine, the Marshall Plan and Comecon
- NATO and the Warsaw Pact
- the Korean War
- the Non-Aligned Movement
- the Suez Crisis
- the Hungarian Uprising
- the Cuban Missile Crisis
- the Congo Crisis
- the Vietnam War
- China's relations with the USA and USSR
- arms control and détente
- the end of the Cold War.

All of these events mark turning points in the Cold War and show the shifts in the policies of the United States and the Soviet Union and how these shifts affected international relations.

Now that there is a certain amount of historical distance and the Russians have opened up access to a considerable proportion of the Soviet archives to historical study, it is possible and indeed necessary to look at this event from multiple perspectives. This subject provides an opportunity to look critically at official history versus declassified sources, and not just from the Soviet perspective. As anniversaries of certain key milestones in the struggle have passed, US government documents on events are also becoming available and a number of the major players in Cold War events have produced memoirs. In many cases, this means further corroboration of the facts presented by both sides, although the interpretations remain very different. The personal ideology and agenda of historians is also becoming increasingly important for students to understand and view critically.

Topic 5 explicitly addresses the ideas of knowledge and history. Much of the study of the Cold War has an ideological focus, and the selectivity of information and variety of interpretations that permeate the topic lend themselves to clear links with the theory of knowledge

(TOK) course. This is a subject that must be approached historiographically; in your study of the Cold War, it is recommended that you seek alternative views on why events progressed as they did. You need to look at the nature of the information available to you in the present day, but also to compare that with the information that was available to the general public and to policy makers during the height of the Cold War.

By the end of this chapter, you should be able to:

- explain the various reasons given for the origins of the Cold War
- evaluate the different historical interpretations for the beginning of the Cold War
- compare and contrast events of the Cold War that took place in different regions around the world
- understand the complex relationship between the USA, the USSR and the People's Republic of China (PRC)
- describe the role of culture in influencing the Cold War and vice versa
- give your views on the development of the Cold War
- determine for yourself the reasons for the end of the Cold War and the decline and fall of the Soviet Union.

Introduction to the Cold War

East–West relations, or, more specifically, US–Soviet relations until the collapse of the USSR, are referred to as the Cold War. Very simply put, from 1945 to 1991 there was conflict between the United States and the Soviet Union that never erupted into a full-blown war between the two powers. Although there were numerous **proxy wars** in which one power was directly involved, there was no direct conflict between these two powers. This was a war that remained Cold—no direct conflicts between the superpowers—largely because they tacitly agreed to avoid open conflict. This, then, is a diplomatic history that centres on an uneasy coexistence based on the fear of mutual destruction. In fact, fear was a guiding principle not just in diplomacy, but also to a large extent in popular culture. This was a far cry from the Grand Alliance that won the Second World War and defeated the Axis powers.

Proxy war A war instigated by one (or more) of the major powers who don't participate directly in the subsequent conflict.

Lend Lease An American program whereby the US government provided material assistance to the Allies even though they were initially prohibited through US neutrality laws. They bypassed these laws by asserting that they were not providing aid but were leasing—or renting—antiquated equipment to the belligerent powers. The United States spent roughly $50 billion dollars ($700 billion in 2007) provisioning allied forces between March 1941 and September 1945.

After the battle of Stalingrad in Europe and the battle of Midway in the Pacific, the Axis powers were steadily (if sometimes slowly) in retreat and victory for the Allies was certain, even though the world was unsure as to how long it would take. At the first signs of victory, the war-time alliance of the USSR, the UK and the USA became increasingly strained as the reason for the alliance began to fade. The spirit of co-operation engendered in the Declaration of the United Nations and **Lend Lease** gave way to competing interests, especially in Eastern Europe. In meetings at Teheran, Yalta and Potsdam, the

Big Three (as they were called) met and tried to jockey for post-war position while ensuring continued co-operation in the war effort.

There were a number of complicating factors that further increased tensions between the USA and the USSR in particular. First and foremost among these was the successful explosion of an atom bomb in the United States in July 1945. This was to have long-term implications for the rivalry between the two main victors of the Second World War. Until 1949, the United States held a monopoly on this form of military technology, giving it a distinct advantage over the Soviet Union. However, the USSR continued to pursue nuclear technology itself, finally achieving parity and eliminating the gap in technology. Rather than allay (calm) any potential problems between these powers, however, this served only to raise tensions.

Another issue that heightened US–Soviet tensions was the end of the Great Power status of the previously dominant European powers. Germany, of course, was vanquished and would not be allowed to rise again as it had in 1939. But France and the United kingdom had also lost their status as major powers. Their colonial power was waning and they had lost the military and political advantages they previously held. Instead, there were two superpowers that remained: the Soviet Union and the United States. It was their charge to provide the post-war mandate by necessity, not by design. These were the only countries which had sufficient power to exert their will over others, and their visions were rarely complementary. This set up a bipolar world, in which countries seemed to fall into one or the other's sphere of interest.

The world was a very different place in 1945; the United States could no longer retreat back to the western hemisphere and ignore the events in Europe. It was now necessary for the USA to remain a constant actor in international affairs. And it may have wished to have a dominant role in Asian affairs, too, but as the war-time co-operation between rival factions in China deteriorated, the spectre of communism in east Asia was an increasing possibility.

The situation, then, was far from simplistic or Eurocentric. There were numerous nascent socialist and communist movements in the colonies that were battling imperialist domination over their countries. Decolonization was to bring with it not just an end of European political dominion but a challenge to democracy from independence movements. The Soviets, for their part, battled fiercely in an attempt to support these regimes just as the United States battled for non-communist, capitalist regimes in the hopes of building democracy and market economies in these same countries. In the middle were the colonial powers themselves, losing their grip yet trying to maintain some links and control over the areas, especially where there were substantial emigrants from the mother country or vast material wealth.

The world in 1950 was rather different to the world prior to 1939. The Cold War was in full swing, as was decolonization. These two concurrent trends changed not only the nature of global politics but also the daily lives of people all over the world.

Origins of the Cold War

This section provides some context for the origins of the Cold War, examining the goals and objectives of the main peacemakers at the end of the Second World War through the consolidation of the two blocs—one led by the USA and one by the USSR. The period 1943–9 is full of actions and counteractions by the Allied forces as they sought to forge a post-war world that upheld their expectations. To explain the initial perspectives of the victor powers, the war-time conferences (Yalta and Potsdam) are covered, as is the foundation of the United Nations.

To show the roots of the US policy of containment, there is discussion of the Truman Doctrine, the Marshall Plan and the formation of NATO. The section ends with the victory of the Chinese Communist Party following a period of civil war and the potential implications of this victory.

The timing for the end of the Cold War is somewhat debatable—the end of communism in Eastern Europe, the collapse of the Berlin Wall and the break-up of the Soviet Union point to an end to this conflict that influenced global policies from the close of the Second World War until 1991. However, the beginning of the Cold War is harder to determine as it involved the collapse of a war-time alliance that did not seem as tenuous as it appears in retrospect. Rather than looking at the irreconcilable ideologies, students of history should perhaps focus on the pragmatism that engendered this Grand Alliance. In the 19th century, the most democratic state in Europe (France) formed an alliance with the most autocratic one (Russia) due to mutual interests and fears. Similarly, the UK, the USA and the USSR had a mutual interest in defeating Germany and Japan in the middle of the 20th century, and it was this that made them strong allies, committed to pushing their opponents to unconditional surrender.

There was a bit of a paradox in their alliance, and this could be seen very clearly in the war-time conferences that occurred from 1943 to 1945. On the one hand, they show the willingness of the countries to work together; but on the other, their differing ideas as to how decisions should be made and what the post-war world should look like were exposed. And these were not simply differences between the Communist USSR and the Western democracies: the pragmatism of British prime minister Winston Churchill—as seen most clearly in the **Percentages Agreement**—was contrary to the idealism of US president Franklin D Roosevelt.

There were numerous conferences even before the USA and the USSR entered into the Cold War: the **Atlantic Charter** and the US decision to provide Lend Lease assistance to the UK and later the USSR are examples of this. These meetings involved those that President Roosevelt would call the Four Policemen: the USA, the UK, the USSR and the PRC. According to Roosevelt's post-war view, these four countries were the principal world powers that supported the Allies and that would shape post-war policy, thereby preventing a

The **Percentages Agreement** was the result of a meeting between Stalin and Churchill in October 1944 in which they divided eastern and southeastern Europe into spheres of influence. According to the meeting, the USSR would have 90 per cent influence in Romania and 75 per cent influence in Bulgaria, the UK should have 90 per cent influence in Greece, and Hungary and Yugoslavia should be split 50–50.

Atlantic Charter A joint declaration of the USA and the UK, made in August 1941, in which the two countries committed to pursuing a post-war world that was free from totalitarianism.

political vacuum after the defeat of Germany and Japan. The USA and the UK were represented at all of these meetings; China participated at Cairo and the USSR in Tehran. The meetings laid the foundation for what were the two most important conferences in terms of establishing a template for the post-war world: Yalta and Potsdam (see below).

Three men were instrumental in hammering out the post-war vision: Churchill, Roosevelt and Soviet leader Joseph Stalin. These men worked together, each jockeying to preserve their positions of power and further the agendas of their countries. Their positions were not dictated simply by ideology, but also by domestic concerns and their contributions to the war effort. The United Kingdom was clearly the declining power of the group, but through Churchill's manoeuverings, and the UK's longstanding battles against the Axis powers, it held a strong position. Churchill sought a restoration of the balance of power insofar as it would be possible after war, and sought to preserve the British empire, though this proved impossible. Although not attacked until well after the UK had stood up alone against Germany, the USSR insisted that, due to the substantial losses it had sustained, it deserved compensation in Eastern Europe. American involvement was delayed and its losses were substantially smaller than those of the other two Great Powers. The USA felt vulnerable after the **Pearl Harbor** attack but the population, while mobilized for war, was fairly insulated from the war by geography. What the USA wanted was focused much more on the situation in Asia, where it had been providing support to the Chinese even before Pearl Harbor and where it feared it would be enmeshed in a long and costly war. Thus, many of the agreements that Roosevelt (and later Truman) made were based on keeping the UK and the USSR in the war against the Axis even after the defeat of Germany.

Pearl Harbor The US naval base in Hawaii that was unexpectedly attacked by Japan on 7 December 1941. The attack took place on a Sunday morning when most of the sailors were asleep and caused considerable damage to the American Pacific Fleet. This attack was the reason for the US entrance into the war. On 8 December the US Congress voted to declare war on Japan; Germany and Italy subsequently declared war on the United States.

Yalta, February 1945

When the Yalta conference was convened, the Allied powers were assured of victory in Europe and the question was when, not whether, the Germans would be defeated. As the negotiations were taking place, the Western Allies were advancing through France and Belgium, approaching the Rhineland, and the Soviets were in Poland, heading to Berlin. All three parties agreed that it was imperative to draw up a plan of action for the occupation of a defeated German state. It had already been decided that only unconditional surrender would be accepted, so the war reached a period of attrition in which the Allies were trying to wear the Germans down until they were so weakened that they would surrender.

The terms were informed by the Red Army's occupation of Eastern Europe. It was agreed that Germany would be divided into four zones, one for each of the main Allied powers. There would be joint inter-Allied co-operation but each country would be responsible for distinct sectors of Germany, Berlin, Austria and Vienna. Additionally, the German leadership was to be put on trial for war crimes. Non-German territories in Central Europe were to be restored as independent countries and were to hold free elections. Poland was to lose territory in the east and gain territory in the west, from Germany. They were also to form a coalition government before they would then determine their political future.

Outside of Europe, the USSR agreed to join the United Nations and also agreed that it would participate in the war against Japan two or three months after the German surrender. In exchange, it would regain part of Sakhalin Island and the Kurile islands and would reassert control over Port Arthur and the Manchurian Railway.

Potsdam, August 1945

The situation was rather different when the members of the Grand Alliance met in Germany. In April 1945, Roosevelt died, leaving his largely left-out-of-the-loop vice-president as Chief of State. Harry Truman came to Potsdam without much knowledge of American foreign policy or the pursuit of the war. Indeed, the new president had no foreknowledge of the **Manhattan Project**, and the successful detonation of the atom bomb in the New Mexico desert was more of a surprise to him than to Stalin, who had spies relaying information to him. This weapon had been developed for use against the Nazis, but they had been defeated. If, how and when it would be used were uncertain, but that was not necessarily important as this weapon gave the USA a distinct technological advantage.

In May 1945, after the suicide of Adolf Hitler, the Germans surrendered to the Allies unconditionally. Germany and Austria (and Berlin and Vienna) were divided into four occupation zones and were under the martial law of the USA, the UK, France and the USSR. The main enemy of the UK and the USSR had been defeated and their major theaters of operation were now closed. It was the United States that was most insistent on the continued prosecution of war against Japan. The United Kingdom was equally interested in Asia as it desired the liberation of its colonies, but it lacked the firepower necessary to be a decisive factor. Long the leading naval power in the world, the UK had not developed its aircraft carriers as extensively as the USA and Japan and thus faced a distinct disadvantage in the Asian theatre. Aircraft carrier battles and island hopping were the primary types of engagement, and it was largely US and Japanese forces that did battle. The USSR had very limited interest in engagement in Asia but was encouraged by the possibility of regaining the territory it lost in 1905 in the Russo-Japanese War.

Lastly, the UK held elections, and Churchill was replaced by Clement Atlee in the middle of the conference. The US transition in leadership kept the same political party in power, but the UK saw a shift in parliamentary leadership from Conservative to Labour. Atlee's agenda was that of a Labour government, and while there was foreign policy congruence, from Atlee's point of view, the war was essentially over and the UK needed to focus on domestic affairs. This was complicated by the determination to keep the USA involved in Europe, as the UK feared that another bout of US isolationism could leave the European continent vulnerable to Soviet encroachment. Despite British attempts to hold onto their empire, it had become very clear that India was slipping away and the UK was preparing for the loss of its most valued colony.

Manhattan Project An American programme to build atomic weapons that was initiated on the USA's entrance into the Second World War. The program was conducted in secret in a variety of places throughout the United States, with people working in isolation, unsure of what they were working on. The project came together in Los Alamos, New Mexico (USA) where a number of scientists, many of whom were refugees from Hitler's Europe, gathered to create the atom bomb. Successful detonation occurred in July 1945 at Trinity Site, New Mexico. The atom bomb was used to end the war against Japan when bombs were dropped on the cities of Hiroshima and Nagasaki in August 1945.

At Potsdam, Stalin was the only person who had participated in the previous meetings and he used this to his advantage. He also downplayed the importance of the atom bomb, even though it was reported that he was truly shaken by the destruction that was relayed to him. The USSR had suffered tremendous casualties and Stalin used this to gain concessions. Furthermore, he managed to portray the Soviet army as strong and, despite vast losses, capable of force against Japan.

The conference in Potsdam did not do much beyond expanding and clarifying the policies agreed upon at Yalta. However, it was significant in that it showed the strain of the war-time alliance. The USA and the UK were trying to extract guarantees from Stalin that Poland would be granted free elections, and that self-determination would be the rule in Eastern Europe, but they found themselves in an impossible position. The Soviet army occupied the Baltic countries and most of eastern and southern Europe. Greece was mired in civil war and Yugoslavia had liberated itself from the Germans, but the rest of the region owed its liberation to the USSR. As much as the UK and the USA wanted to insist on Soviet withdrawal, they could not eject the USSR from the region. Thus, they were caught in a moral dilemma: the UK had gone to war to protect the territorial integrity and independence of Poland and yet their ally sought to impose its rule over Poland just as the Nazis had. The Polish government in exile in London was being challenged by a new faction called the Lublin Poles, who took orders from Moscow. Bulgaria, Romania, Yugoslavia and Hungary were firmly in communist hands. Only Czechoslovakia resisted communism and established a multi-party state. The United States was more inclined to accept Soviet domination in Eastern Europe as it felt that it needed Soviet assistance in defeating the Japanese, and any attempts at preventing the USSR from establishing control would mean a delay in the demobilization of US troops. Thus, compromises were reached, decisions were delayed and the war against Japan continued for a short time.

The establishment of the United Nations

There is a tendency to highlight the conflicts and competing interests of the three powers; what is often forgotten is that these conferences were a concerted attempt by all three countries to continue the war-time alliance in an effort to stabilize not just Europe, but the world. The USSR, the UK and the USA all desired post-war stability, and wanted to pursue common, mutually agreed policies. The United Nations was the most concrete example of this. Its charter and the decision of all the powers to participate and encourage other countries to join showed that there was a common goal of post-war co-operation and a desire to replace the balance-of-power model with a new model of peacekeeping. Like its predecessor, the UN did not have an independent military force, but the authorization of force under the aegis of the UN seemed more likely with the collaboration of the main powers.

Unofficial Delegate

What does this cartoon say about the decision-making at Potsdam in July 1945?

The idea of governance by unanimity or consensus was, however, deemed irrational, if not impossible. The paternalistic attitude of the Great Powers towards other countries may be criticized but it was understandable; having seen the impotence of the League of Nations and the constant paralysis due to the virtual veto power that all council members held, made the main powers hesitant to grant the same privileges to all countries. Instead, in an amalgam of Roosevelt's Four Policemen and the League, it was decided that in matters of security the most powerful countries should have the right to prevent action, so the five Permanent Members were given veto powers.

Although the UK and, to a lesser extent, France were still considered Great Powers, it was clear that a new reality had emerged out of war. There were two powers capable of asserting their will globally: the USA and the USSR. They became superpowers due to the power vacuum that existed after the two world wars, and it was their role to create a new international order. However, these two countries had very different objectives and conceptions of the post-war world. Once Germany and Japan were defeated, their sometimes competing interests were exposed and the situation changed from one of war-time collaboration to a post-war rivalry. This was seen most clearly in Germany but it occurred elsewhere, too.

The articulation of two blocs

The rivalry was most clearly stated by Winston Churchill in what came to be known as the Iron Curtain Speech. In this speech, Churchill attacked the Soviet Union for exerting its will over the countries of Eastern Europe and said that Europe was now divided into totalitarian and free Europe and that it was the duty of free countries to prevent the further spread of communism into West Europe. This proved to be the opening salvo in the Cold War.

Shortly thereafter, Stalin replied, making counterclaims against Churchill's allegations. In an interview in *Pravda*, Stalin likened the UK's position of dominance in the English-speaking world to Nazism and accused the British (and, by extension, the Americans) of having similar desires for world domination. Both Stalin and Churchill ignored their collaboration in determining a post-war world as they had done with the Percentages Agreement, in which Churchill had conceded much of Eastern Europe to the Soviets. Also, the USA and the UK had conspicuously chosen to ignore the Soviet annexation of the Baltic countries, even though this was a result of the Nazi–Soviet Pact. Although the United States never recognized the Baltic States—Estonia, Latvia and Lithuania—as part of the USSR, their incorporation was never challenged.

Just as Churchill had recognized Eastern Europe as being in the Soviet sphere, Stalin agreed that Greece would fall into the British sphere of influence. After the Second World War, the British assisted the Greek government—a constitutional monarchy—in its attempts to re-establish control over the country. Greece was in the midst of a civil war, in which Greek communists were battling against the royalist regime. The USSR remained outside of the conflict, but Yugoslavia, under communist leadership, was providing assistance to

Greek communists. As this war dragged into its second year, the economically wrecked British government informed the USA that it would not be able to continue its support of the royalist government and that it would be withdrawing all aid.

The Truman Doctrine and the policy of containment

Greece was seen as different to other countries, as it had not been occupied by Soviet forces. Additionally, Turkey was seen as vulnerable to Soviet expansion—this would give the USSR its coveted access to the Mediterranean and the increasingly important Middle East. This forced the USA to confront communism and determine its stance towards expansion of the ideology. There were practical and ideological results: the Truman Doctrine and the **policy of containment**, respectively. The Truman Doctrine (March 1947) stated that the USA would provide economic and military assistance to Greece and Turkey to prevent the spread of communism. In his speech to the US Congress, Truman outlined the policy of containment that had originated with **George Kennan** in his Long Telegram of 1946 and that had been further refined as US–Soviet relations deteriorated. The US policy from this point forward would be to avoid conflict with the USSR over countries already under communist or Soviet domination but to prevent the further spread of communism. This policy would remain in force throughout the Cold War, although its application was a little uneven.

The Marshall Plan and the ERP

The US Secretary of State, George Marshall, proposed providing economic assistance to European countries to help them rebuild after the devastation of the Second World War. The **Marshall Plan** (June 1947) and the subsequent European Recovery Program (ERP) was offered to all countries in Europe, including the Soviet Union. Participating countries would receive grants and loans from the USA to help rebuild. The Soviets refused and pressured the other Eastern European countries to do the same. The lone holdout was Czechoslovakia; it was also the only coalition government in the Soviet sphere. In February 1948, the communists removed all other political groups from power, essentially executing a coup. This signalled the USSR's unwillingness to tolerate dissent. Prior to the Soviet refusal, there had been considerable speculation that the US Congress might not accept the ERP, but Soviet actions solidified the American commitment to remain in Europe.

The Berlin airlift, NATO and the political division of Germany

Just as these policies signified a bipolar world, so did the situation in Germany. Divided into four zones, the American, French and British zones were increasingly co-operating with one another and combining to form a unified German government. At the same time, the Soviets were exerting control over East Germany, which was made somewhat difficult by the division of Berlin: in the Soviet enclave there were occupation forces from the other three occupying powers. In the midst of this struggle, the British, French and

Policy of containment US foreign policy articulated by President Truman in 1947 in which the USA stated that it would do what it could to prevent the spread of communism beyond its 1947 reaches.

George Kennan An American diplomat and foreign policy expert. Kennan was stationed in Moscow at the beginning of the Cold War and was asked to explain Soviet objectives and foreign policy to the American executive. The result was his famous "Long Telegram'", an 8000-word summary of historical Russian objectives and the designs of the Soviet leadership. His ideas formed the basis for the containment policy articulated in the Truman Doctrine in 1947.

Discussion point:

the Marshall Plan and the Soviet response

The Marshall Plan and the Soviet response are readily available on the Internet. To look at this subject in greater detail, download copies of both of these. In his speech, General Marshall said that his plan was not directed against any specific country or ideology. Soviet deputy Foreign Minister Vishinsky criticized the Truman Doctrine and the Marshall Plan as aggressively anti-Soviet.

 Choose the one that you disagree with the most and then defend that position.

Americans announced that they were establishing a new currency that they would implement in West Berlin in June 1948. This in turn led to the Berlin blockade, as Stalin attempted to push the other Allied forces out of Berlin by refusing to allow railroad transport into West Berlin, thereby preventing the supply of food and fuel from entering the city. The US response was swift: British and American forces would begin an airlift of necessary supplies to the citizens of West Berlin. The decision for an airlift (as opposed to forcibly breaking the blockade as US military officials suggested) was a deliberate attempt on the part of France, the USA and the UK to assert their occupation without using military force. The Soviets were equally unwilling to use force. Ultimately, the stance of the Western countries prevailed and, through negotiation, the Berlin blockade was lifted on 12 May 1949.

Further developments in 1949

This coincided with further developments in 1949 in relation to Germany and East–West relations:

The formation of NATO

In April the United States signed the treaty creating the **North Atlantic Treaty Organization (NATO)**. This was a military alliance of 12 North American and European countries that was based on the principles of collective security. The Soviets argued that it was an aggressive alliance directed against the USSR and Eastern Europe and that it violated the principles of the United Nations. Truman's response was that it was a defensive alliance that was consistent with the UN covenant as it was designed to prevent aggression. Through NATO, the USA remained a presence on the European continent.

The creation of the FRG and the GDR

Equally important to the development of the Cold War was the creation of the Federal Republic of Germany in September 1949. The Soviets issued a formal protest that the creation of a separate state violated the Potsdam agreements. Their main form of counteraction was the creation of the German Democratic Republic. In the middle of this nascent state was West Berlin, which would prove to be a problem for the communists until the end of the Cold War.

Atomic weapons

On 29 August, the Soviets successfully detonated an atom bomb, giving them technological parity with the United States. Now that the USA no longer held a nuclear monopoly, the relations between the USA and the USSR, and the question of the use of atomic weaponry, had to be reconsidered. Prior to this, US policy was based on the knowledge that they had superiority in weaponry but inferior manpower. The USA would retain its advantage in terms of the number of atomic weapons it possessed, but this was beside the point. The USA no longer had an absolute advantage in any military aspect against the Soviet Red Army.

Activity:

Debate

Your teacher will assign to each student a country in the United Nations. It is November 1949 and the Chinese Communists have defeated the Nationalists. Organize a debate in which the USSR proposes that the PRC be recognized as the legitimate government and the USA opposes it. Then, after the debate, explain how each country would vote and why. Note: The results of the debate don't necessarily have to mirror the actual outcome.

Victory of the Chinese Communist Party

Finally, in October 1949, after a protracted war of starts and stops, the Chinese Communists, led by Mao Zedong, defeated the pro-US Nationalists and forced them to leave mainland China. The Nationalists fled to Taiwan, where they established their government. Despite victory on the mainland, the United States and other Western powers refused to recognize the People's Republic of China (PRC) and denied it a place in the United Nations. Instead, Taiwan, or the Republic of China, was recognized as the legitimate government and retained its position on the Security Council; the PRC was recognized by only a handful of countries, most of whom were Soviet satellites. To protest against this action, the Soviet Union reacted by boycotting the UN, an action that ultimately led to the sole authorization of force by the UN during the Cold War.

Activity:

Essay writing—the introduction

One of the most critical components of an essay is the introduction. Here, the tone is set and a template provided so that the reader can understand what will be argued.

To ensure that the introduction is laid out clearly, try using the **RIOT** method. Simply stated, there are four sentences that develop the essay.

R: Related idea, or putting the essay into its historical context

I: Issue, or explaining what the argument is

O: Opposing viewpoint

T: Thesis

Write introductions using the RIOT method, as started below.

1 At what point, and why, were the USA and the USSR engaged in the Cold War?

Component	Sentence
Related idea	In September 1945, the Second World War ended when Japanese Emperor Hirohito surrendered to US General Douglas MacArthur.
Issue	
Opposing viewpoint	
Thesis	

2 How significant was the development of the atom bomb to the development of the Cold War?

Component	Sentence
Related idea	Some have argued that the Cold War was well underway before the USA successfully detonated an atom bomb in July 1945.
Issue	
Opposing viewpoint	
Thesis	

Development and impact of the Cold War: its global spread

This section on the Cold War is the largest and most extensive, yet it only touches upon events from 1950 to 1985. In this period, the Cold War ceased to be regarded as a transatlantic US–European affair, and instead was recognized for what it was: a struggle between two ideologies that had an impact on the rest of the world.

The UN began to take shape as an organization that could take military action based on the consensus of the Security Council. As decolonization created new states, they chose which path to follow both in the UN and outside of it. These states had three options: Western, Communist or the newly emerging Non-Aligned Movement.

It was also in this time that China began to re-emerge as a major power, leading to further possible alliances and agreements. It was not that the Cold War had become global; it was more that globalization was foisted upon foreign relations. Countries could not be isolated, as all but the most determined states were integrated into the global community.

The Korean War, 1950–3

In the 1940s, the geographical focus of the Cold War was Europe and the military focus was on nuclear weapons and technology. Both of these were to change in 1950, as the world focused on Asia and the resumption of limited, conventional warfare with the onset of the Korean War.

Korea had been annexed by the Japanese in 1910 and so the issue that arose with Japan's surrender was how to administer this once-independent country. In the immediate aftermath of the war, the USA and the USSR agreed to divide Korea at the 38th parallel and occupy the country until it was ready for political independence.

Once the occupation period began, the country found itself with two distinct governments: in the north, the communist leader Kim Il-sung emerged under Soviet tutelage; in the south, the USA supported Syngman Rhee, the American-educated president of the Korean government in exile from 1919.

In 1948 the USSR declared the Democratic People's Republic of Korea (DPRK) in the north and the United States responded by the creation of the Republic of Korea in the south. With these actions, it became clear that unification of the country

Kim Il-sung (1912–94)

The first premier of North Korea from 1948. He was born into a farm family and migrated to Manchuria with his family in 1926. While there he joined the nascent Korean Communist Party in 1931 and gained notice by fighting against the Japanese in the Second World War. After the war Kim returned to Korea and established control in the northern area, which was in the Soviet sphere. He sought to extend control and waged the Korean War in an attempt to establish a fully Communist Korea. After three years of stalemate, North Korea signed an armistice that the South refused. North Korea remained largely isolationist during Kim's leadership, and the enforcement of a cult of personality. In the late 1980s, he began to entrust his son with leadership of the Communist Party but he kept control over the government. He died in 1994, and the country had a three-year period of mourning. After his death, his son Kim Jong-il emerged as the leader of North Korea.

through UN-overseen elections would be impossible and the USA began to evacuate its troops, leaving South Korea's defence to its own military.

Kim was encouraged by this move and began to press Stalin to agree to an invasion of the south. Kim argued that the south would welcome his rule and would willingly become part of the DPRK. Statements made by Secretary of State, Dean Acheson, made it clear that the USA did not feel that Korea was in its sphere of influence and Stalin came to believe that the USA would not intervene if Kim were indeed to attempt to unify the country by force. Thus, in 1950, he authorized Kim's plan to invade and, on 25 June 1950, North Korean forces invaded the south, taking the South Korean government and army by surprise. By the end of the week, the North Korean army controlled most of the peninsula, including the southern capital of Seoul.

The United States was surprised and shaken by this attack, and immediately referred the matter to the United Nations. In a series of swift and decisive resolutions, the UN agreed to take military action against the invading North Korean forces. This was made possible only because the USSR had been boycotting the UN. Fifteen countries agreed to send troops to defend South Korea, though the majority of foreign troops were American.

The UN forces were led by US general Douglas MacArthur, who developed a risky but ultimately successful plan. Rather than simply battling the North Koreans in the toehold that the South held in Pusan, the UN armies would also launch an amphibious attack at the port of Inchon, near Seoul. The North Koreans were surprised by this tactic, and quickly lost ground to the UN army. Not only did they lose their control over the south, but by October 1950 the UN army had chased the North Korean armies as far as the Yalu River, the Korean border with China.

The moment the UN forces crossed the 38th parallel, the issue of the nature of the war was hotly debated. Those who were strict adherents to the policy of containment argued that UN forces should not have gone beyond the South Korean border. Furthermore, General MacArthur was contemplating an attack on the Chinese army as a pre-emptive measure and in an attempt to undermine the newly-established communist regime there. Truman and Acheson both argued against this and stated clearly that it was not the objective of the United States to attack mainland China.

In the midst of this debate, and during a period in which the USA was congratulating itself on a rapid victory, Chinese volunteers crossed the Yalu River and launched a counter-attack against the American forces. This surprise attack was effective and once again the UN forces were driven south, out of DPRK territory and back to the South. However, in January 1951 the UN forces recovered their technological advantage and the Chinese army was forced to retreat.

Although the UN forces had technological superiority, the North Korean and Chinese forces were larger in number. In an attempt to prove their strength and assure a privileged position in the communist world, Chinese leader Mao Zedong provided unlimited numbers of "volunteers" to defeat the UN forces. MacArthur went so far as to suggest the use of nuclear weapons against the Chinese, something that Truman was adamantly against. The fear of the use of these weapons was that the Soviet Union would retaliate using its own supply, most likely in Europe. Due to the public nature of this disagreement, MacArthur was relieved of his command in April 1951 and was replaced by General Matthew Ridgway.

Meantime, the battle lines had stabilized near the 38th parallel, not far from the borders of North and South Korea. The United States and the UN decided that they would not advance into North Korean territory again, and there was discussion of an armistice. However, the main result was stalemate. From 1951 to 1953, the two sides were engaged in sporadic battle while cease fires were declared, terms for armistice discussed and talks broke down. The main conflict was over the repatriation of prisoners of war. While the US and UN forces argued for voluntary returns, the Chinese would agree only if a majority of North Korean and Chinese forces would return voluntarily and this did not happen.

Behind the scenes, and conspicuously absent from all discussions and official participation, was the USSR. Although it is now known that Soviet pilots did engage US aircraft in battle, this was kept secret by both sides, and the official position of the USSR was one of neutrality. It seemed fairly clear, however, that Stalin was unwilling to accept a communist defeat in Korea and this further complicated the armistice talks. Thus, the death of Stalin in March 1953 was of critical importance to the end of the Korean War.

With Stalin's death, a power struggle ensued in the Soviet leadership, and Korea was no longer regarded as crucial to Soviet power and influence. The United States was governed by a new president, Dwight Eisenhower, whose election was partially based on withdrawal from Korea. In 1953, the two main powers were therefore governed by men who did not see Korea as vital to their interest. On 27 July 1953, the UN, North Korean and Chinese forces signed a cease fire and agreed to the division of Korea near its pre-war borders; only South Korea refused to sign.

Korea was the first major war in the Cold War and its significance for all sides is great. Of paramount importance is the decision made by the nuclear powers to limit wars, and not directly engage against one another in any official, legal capacity. The United States questioned but ultimately stood by its policy of containment. The Soviets remained officially neutral to prevent direct conflict.

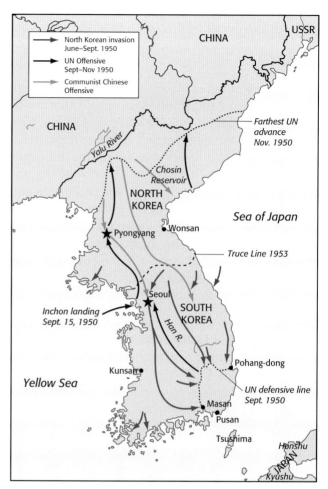

The Korean War, 1950–3, showing troop movements of the North Koreans, the UN and the Republic of Korea, and Communist China

The Non-Aligned Movement

As in the Korean War, events of 1956 show very clearly that Europe no longer took precedence in international affairs. As revolutions threatened the Soviet regimes in Eastern Europe, other countries, while not unsympathetic, did nothing to assist them in their attempts at liberalization. Instead, the world was focused on the crisis in the Middle East that began in the summer of 1956. The Suez Crisis showed the importance of that region and, more generally, of the emerging Non-Aligned Movement.

Nasser, Tito and Nehru in 1956 at a meeting of 25 neutral countries in Brijuni (Croatia)

In the face of the formation of NATO and the Warsaw Pact, there were also countries, most of which were in Africa and Asia, who were trying to resist being drawn into the bipolar paradigm that had existed since the end of the Second World War. Twenty-nine countries participated in the Asian–African conference in Bandung, Indonesia in April 1955. Through the Bandung Conference and subsequent Belgrade Conference (1961), they created the Non-Aligned Movement, through which they agreed to resist colonialism and imperialism in all forms and promote Afro-Asian co-operation. This movement was critical to UN voting patterns that would provide a solution to the situation in the Middle East and decry the colonialism of Western democracies, while it left Hungary's pleas for acceptance as a neutral state unanswered and remained silent on the issue of Soviet imperialism in Eastern Europe.

 Why did these three men become the leaders of the Non-Aligned movement? What similarities and differences were there in their policies?

One of the primary leaders of the Non-Aligned Movement was Gamal Abdul Nasser, who became the leader of Egypt in 1954. Pursuing a strongly anti-colonial policy, he sought to remove Western influence not just from Egypt but from all of the Middle East and North Africa. He was seen as the father of Arab nationalism, a secular, transnational idea in which all Arab countries would be united to some degree by a common language and heritage. **Pan-Arabism** put Nasser in conflict with France, due to Egyptian support of Algerian independence movements; with the UK, due to the desire to eject the British from the Suez Canal and their traditional position of privilege in Egypt; and with the USA, due to his willingness to accept Soviet assistance, his refusal to recognize the state of Israel and his support of Palestinian organizations (see chapter 2).

Pan-Arabism A movement for unification of the peoples and countries in the Arab world that was initiated by Egyptian president Nasser and reached its apex with the creation of the United Arab Republic, a merger of Egypt and Syria, that lasted from 1958 to 1961. The ideas of pan-Arabism were later used by the Ba'ath Party that currently has power in Syria and had power in Iraq under Saddam Hussein.

The Suez Crisis

Nasser would be the main player and architect in a series of actions that were to have a significant impact on the further decline of France and the UK and on the evolution of the United Nations. The Suez Crisis was the result of a number of factors that started with the US decision to stop funding the Aswan High Dam project, that Nasser considered to be critical for the development of Egypt as an economic power. In response, on 26 July 1956 the Egyptian army nationalized the Suez Canal and blocked the Straits of Tiran, Israel's only route to the Red Sea.

Activity:

1956 Suez Crisis

Examine the map below and explain the importance of:

- the Egyptian blockade
- the reason for Israeli troop movements towards the Canal
- the deployment of British and French paratroopers.

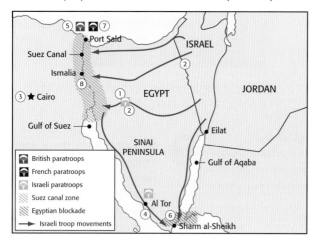

Troop movements, October–December, 1956	
① 29 October	Israeli paratroops dropped east of town of Suez
② 30 October	More paratroops dropped to the east of Mitla Pass. Troops begin crossing the border at Qussaima
③ 31 October	British bombs dropped on Cairo and Cairo international airport
④ 2 November	Israeli paratroops land near Al Tor, west of Sinai
⑤ 5 November	British paratroops land west of Port Said. French paratroops land south of Port Said
⑥ 5 November	Israelis capture Sharm al-Sheikh to lift blockade of Gulf of Aqaba
⑦ 6 November	Anglo-French invasion force bombardment and landings
⑧ 7 November	Anglo-French forces claim to have occupied most of the Suez Canal zone as far as Ismailia, when UN orders a halt to fighting
21 November	First UN troops land at Port Said
23 November	British and French forces begin withdrawal from Egypt
22 December	Withdrawal completed at midnight

The British and French, whose citizens were the main shareholders of the canal, were outraged and demanded a return of the canal to its ownership, but Nasser refused. The British and French still wanted a return of what they still regarded as their territory but knew that they could not act openly. Thus, they collaborated with the Israelis, persuading them to take action against the Egyptians and, on 29 October, the Israeli army invaded the Sinai Peninsula and occupied the territory. The plan—denied by all three governments at that time—was that the Israelis would secure the canal and then British and French navies would come in to restore peace and reoccupy it.

The matter was almost immediately referred to the UN, who issued a proposal for the withdrawal of Israeli troops. The problem in the UN at the time was that the ambassadors were also trying to come to an agreement regarding the revolution in Hungary and Nagy's appeals for assistance. The Suez Crisis, however, was seen as more immediately important to a greater number of countries as so much of the world's oil was transported through the Suez Canal.

The United States had clearly stated it opposed any military action being taken in the region and had counselled France and the UK against this after the nationalization of the Suez Canal. On 4 November 1956, the UN resolved to send an emergency force to the Middle East to stabilize the situation until Israeli and Egyptian troops would withdraw. This action created the Blue Helmets, or UN forces that are dispatched to conflict areas to help keep the peace. The role these forces were to play was not clear; they were not to be active belligerents as UN forces had been in the Korean War, and they were to march under the flag of the UN, rather than those of individual countries.

Another outcome of the Suez Crisis was what came to be called the **Eisenhower Doctrine**. According to this plan, the USA would provide assistance to Middle Eastern countries to prevent the spread of communism and Soviet influence in the area. To some extent, this was done because the UK and France had lost their influence in the region, and were no longer seen as the dominant world powers they once had been. The Suez Crisis had accelerated decolonization, especially in Africa, and while the UK and France still had considerable economic influence in their former colonies, they had little political influence.

Most importantly for the Non-Aligned Movement, Nasser was the hero of the Suez Crisis. He was able to use and manipulate the tension between the USA and the USSR to achieve success for Egypt. By establishing closer ties with the Soviet Union to complete the Aswan High Dam project and arm Egypt, he left the United States in a difficult position, now willing to engage in diplomacy to attempt to woo him back, just as they had done with Tito in Yugoslavia. Unfortunately for the Hungarians, whose attempts to break free from the grip of the Soviet Union were not seen as nearly so essential to security, their story was rather different.

> **Eisenhower Doctrine** The idea that the USA would use force to stop imminent or actual aggression against the USA. This doctrine gave war-making powers to the US president, in a deviation from the historical decision that only Congress had the right to declare war. It targeted Middle Eastern countries and was created to counter Nasser's popularity in the region.

The death of Stalin, 1953

Stalin had dominated all aspects of communist life, and did his best to oust those who did not follow his line. As a result, the "renegade" Yugoslavian leader Tito had been ousted from the Soviet sphere in 1948, yet the Chinese, whose brand of communism was somewhat different from the Soviet style, were embraced and accepted. Without Stalin's iron fist, the situation after his death was bound to change, and indeed it did. By 1956, Khrushchev and other leaders of the Communist Party of the Soviet Union (CPSU) sought to show that both foreign and domestic policies were changing.

In February 1956, in an attempt to distance himself from his predecessor, Khrushchev gave his famous secret speech entitled "On the personality cult and its consequences", referred to as his de-Stalinization speech. In it, Khrushchev condemned Stalin's actions against the people of the Soviet Union, carefully avoiding condemnation of events that would have implicated him and his peers. Even so, the speech had a mixed reception. Mao Zedong, himself subject to a personality cult, was highly critical of the speech and accused Khrushchev of **revisionism**. Other leaders who relied on their own charisma or individual base of support to keep the communists in power did the same: notably Enver Hoxha in Albania and Kim Il-sung in North Korea. However, other leaders in the communist sphere were encouraged by the speech and by subsequent actions that they saw in the USSR after its delivery.

> **Revisionism** In the context of the Soviet sphere this term means a deviation from Marxist–Leninist policy and an adoption of new, more capitalist views of economic and political development. To be called revisionist was a criticism, especially in Communist China under Mao Zedong.

At this time, the Soviet Union loosened some of the government controls over the private lives of its citizenry. This was seen as encouraging to Western leaders and dissenters within the communist world, but communist leaders outside of the USSR, many of whom owed their position of power to that country and the Communist Party power structure, were highly critical of this shift in policy.

Most notably, Mao was very critical of Khrushchev's attacks on Stalin's regime, as this could also be interpreted as an attack on his form of leadership in China. This began a strain in Sino-Soviet relations that would worsen throughout the 1950s.

The Hungarian Uprising

In the satellite states, many were encouraged by Khrushchev's attitude and began to challenge the authority of their own government and party leaders. In 1955 there was reconciliation with Tito and an acceptance of his position as a confirmed communist who remained outside the Warsaw Pact. In Poland, workers protested against government policies with mixed results; but the strongest challenge to the communist system came in Hungary. Having seen the Poles successfully challenge the established system and effect changes for their country, the Hungarians were emboldened to act themselves. (For more on Poland, see chapter 8.) The result proved to be disastrous as, much to their disappointment, the US policy of containment did not mean direct US support for the revolutionaries in Hungary.

On 23 October 1956, Hungarian students began the revolution with demonstrations. After seeing the reforms that Poles had managed to gain, the students provided their own list of demands that went much further. In addition to freedoms and civil rights, they demanded the departure from Hungary of Soviet troops that had been stationed there since 1945, and the return of the leadership of Imre Nagy, a reform communist who had been expelled from the Party and later rehabilitated. The demonstrations almost immediately turned into a full-blown revolution; on the very next day, Soviet tanks stationed in Budapest were set alight and government buildings were seized. Nagy was named prime minister.

The Poles modified their brand of communism, and it seemed as if the Hungarians were about to do likewise. The Soviets seemed to be accepting the idea of a nationalist communism for Hungary and withdrew their tanks from Budapest. Rather than mollify the situation, this acceptance served only to incite the Hungarians, who increased their demands. Hungary, they argued, was a sovereign state that should be allowed to determine its own political future and, as such, it should be allowed to be a multi-party state, withdraw from the Warsaw Pact, and eject all foreign forces from its soil.

The American reaction was difficult to read; on the one hand, officials in the US government remained silent—after all, it was highly unlikely that the United States would send troops in to support the nascent democratic state and threaten Soviet security. On the other hand, the spirit of democracy was heartily supported in the exhortations of the Hungarians' most consistent access to the USA: Radio Free Europe. RFE was (and remains) an independent radio station funded by the US government but not directed by the government. This gave the Hungarians the illusion that American assistance would be forthcoming, and that the world supported their attempt to break free from the Soviet sphere.

Hungarian prime minister Imre Nagy began the revolution as a communist seeking reform, but he was quickly caught up in the spirit of the movement and, by the end of the revolution, he was advocating democracy and neutrality. This proved to be fatal both for him and for the revolution. On 30 October he abolished the one-party state, and on 1 November he announced that Hungary would be neutral and appealed to the UN to recognize its neutrality, but never received a reply.

On the same day that the UN voted to send emergency forces to end the Suez Crisis, the issue of Hungary was also raised. The UN voted that the Soviet Union should remove its troops from Hungarian soil, but it was a resolution without teeth: there was no mechanism to enforce this decision. Unlike the Suez Crisis, it did not have universal support—the Warsaw Pact countries voted against the measure and a number of Non-Aligned countries (including all Middle Eastern countries) abstained.

On the same day, Warsaw Pact troops moved in and crushed the revolution. The Communist Party was reinstalled as the only legal party in Hungary and János Kádár was made the head of the government. Nagy, who had sought refuge in the Yugoslav embassy, was later captured and deported. He was put on trial and executed for his actions against the Communist government. As the tide turned, it is estimated that 200 000 Hungarians fled the repression of the returning Soviet forces and Hungarian Communists; in a population of nine million, this is a very significant number. Many went to Austria, where the borders were quickly closing.

The revolution was a bloody affair that cost the Soviets as well as the Hungarians, but it confirmed Soviet dominance over their satellite states. The United States was complicit in this by doing nothing; the Americans made it clear that they would not use force to assist independence from the Soviet sphere, but would encourage peaceful evolution. Responding to objections, US Secretary of State, John Foster Dulles, said that there was no basis for assistance and that the USA had no commitment to the communist states—a bleak statement that led to much criticism both in and outside of the United States.

 What does this photo tell you about the reasons for the Hungarian Uprising?

Hungarians in front of the National Theatre in the Blaha Lujza square, Budapest in 1956. Demonstrators pulled the statue of Stalin to the ground at Dozsa Gyorgy on October 23 and hauled it by tractor to Blaha Lujza where it was later smashed to pieces.

The Congo Crisis, 1960–4

The Korean War illustrates the problems that faced newly independent states in their struggle for a new government. The Suez Crisis showed how the USA, the USSR and the UN intervened in a matter concerning an established independent country that was seeking to oust foreign economic influence. The Congo Crisis is an amalgam of these two events: a newly independent country that lacked a unified government, battling to remove a foreign influence, and attempting to achieve some degreee of stability.

The Congo was given independence from Belgium in June 1960. Initially, a government was established under the leadership of prime minister Patrice Lumumba (see chapter 7) and President Joseph Kasavubu—but this government lasted barely two weeks. In early July, the army mutinied and committed acts of violence against the remaining Belgian and European residents, undermining the authority of the government.

In response, the Belgian government sent paratroopers who were charged with protecting the roughly 100 000 European residents located in and around the capital, Leopoldville. This was clearly an illegal act, as the Congo Republic was an independent country, and the Belgians were seen as suspect. Although it had been granted independence, the southern region of Katanga was incredibly rich in resources and a rival force under Moise Tshombe had established power there. Katanga's resources were particularly important to the superpowers—60 per cent of the world's uranium and 80 per cent of its industrial diamonds came from this region. Due to the region's wealth, Tshombe had the support and assistance of European investors and industrialists.

In an attempt to attract outside assistance within a legal, international framework, Lumumba appealed to the UN. In accordance with Resolution 143, the UN sent troops but would not take sides; they were instructed that they could fire on belligerents only if they themselves were fired upon. This was not what Lumumba had hoped for: he wanted UN assistance in defeating Tshombe's competing leadership in the south, arguing that the Congo would never be truly stabilized until this region was under the control of the central government. When UN Secretary Dag Hammarskjöld refused, Lumumba accused the UN of siding with the Europeans and appealed to the USSR for help.

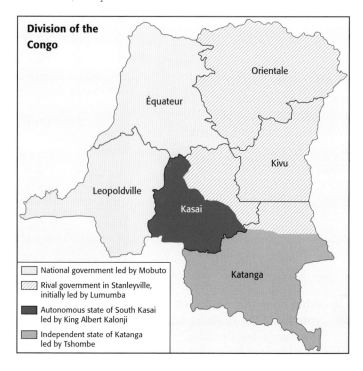

Division of the Congo

Orientale

Équateur

Kivu

Leopoldville

Kasai

Katanga

☐ National government led by Mobuto

▨ Rival government in Stanleyville, initially led by Lumumba

■ Autonomous state of South Kasai led by King Albert Kalonji

▨ Independent state of Katanga led by Tshombe

The Soviets agreed to provide military assistance and Lumumba launched an attack on Katanga that proved unsuccessful. As a result, President Kasavubu removed him as prime minister. Lumumba, however, continued to have popular support, especially in the eastern provinces. In fact, the parliament reinstated him as prime minister but to no avail. At this point, Lumumba established another government—this one in Stanleyville—again requesting Soviet assistance. The USSR provided him with weapons and it appeared that he would be able to defend his position. In November 1960 he was arrested by Mobutu's forces but, even when detained, Mobutu considered him a threat to his own control and feared that as long as Lumumba lived he would have a support base that would be powerful enough to stage a coup against the Congolese government. On 17 January 1961, Lumumba was arrested, publicly beaten and forced to eat copies of his own speeches; after this he disappeared from public view and it was later confirmed that he had been murdered on the same day. His government in Stanleyville still existed and in 1961 four different groups claimed a certain degree of control or autonomy in the Congo. (The fourth was a break-away republic led by the self-appointed King Albert Kalonji.)

At this point it looked as if the Congo was heading towards civil war, in which the many different sides and allegiances were unclear. To prevent civil war, the Security Council gave the UN forces the right to use force. Perhaps alarmed by this potential for invasion, three of the four competing groups convened to agree upon a government. All but Tshombe's faction met and agreed to accept a government under Cyrille Adoula, who appealed to the UN to assist the reunited government in defeating the Katanga government. Surprisingly, the UN agreed and, in August 1961, 5000 troops launched an attack on Katanga that reunited it with the rest of the country by 1963.

The situation in the Congo had two important ramifications for the UN. First, it showed that the UN could use force in a civil disturbance if asked to do so by the legitimate government of that country. Many criticized the UN for what was perceived as taking sides, yet others saw this as critical in preventing the outbreak of civil war and keeping the Congo together as a viable country. It also helped define the role of the Secretary General. Hammarskjöld was not simply a bureaucrat or public face; he was instrumental in making policies and pushing through the Security Council resolutions that allowed the use of force. His untimely death in a plane crash in the region led to the appointment of the Burmese diplomat U Thant, who continued to support Hammarskjöld's policies and played an equally active role in UN decision making. Furthermore, the UN's humanitarian aid was seen as critical to preventing the spread of disease and famine through food and medical relief programmes.

In the aftermath of the Congo Crisis, a number of countries protested against the UN's actions by not providing their agreed-upon allocation to pay for the intervention in the Congo. This amounted to $400 million and nearly bankrupted the UN. In particular, the USSR and Belgium refused, but this was seen as self-interest on their parts. The Congo Crisis saw the intervention of both of the superpowers, as a further development of the Cold War. The Eisenhower administration had supported the Belgian intervention due to its fear that Lumumba might put into place a pro-Soviet government, while the Soviets clearly denounced it. When Lumumba appealed to the UN in 1960, the USA agreed to support UN forces in the area to replace Belgian troops. Furthermore, it has been argued that the CIA was active in trying to assassinate Lumumba, even going so far as to transport viruses to use in covert attempts. What is a bit clearer is that CIA chief Allen Dulles ordered Lumumba's assassination and the agency made contact with Congolese willing to carry this out.

When he seized power from Kasavubu in 1965 with the assistance of the CIA, Mobutu continued to have the support of the West, who saw him as anti-communist and pro-Western. His regime lasted as long as the Cold War itself, but once the USSR collapsed in 1991, Western powers no longer saw his brutal, dictatorial regime as desirable, and his international support base eroded. In 1996, the opposition leader Laurent Kabila launched an assault on the Mobutu regime and ousted it, placing himself in power. Mobutu died one year later in exile in Morocco.

Mobutu Sese Seko born Joseph Désiré Mobutu (1930–1997)

Mobutu in his trademark leopard-skin hat.

Mobutu ruled in Zaire from 1965 to 1996. His authoritarian regime was one of the longest-lasting and most corrupt governments in post-colonial African history. Although Zaire had vast natural resources, Mobutu's excesses and embezzlement of funds (a reported $5 billion US) left the country very poor. He managed to remain in power because he retained the support of the United States, which saw him as a bulwark against communist expansion in the region.

In 1967 when the Popular Movement of Revolution was founded, Zaire became a single-party state and compelled all its citizens to join the party. Its slogans included "revolution, nationalism and authenticity", and "neither left nor right." The policy of authenticity was about replacing the colonial legacy with African culture, as demonstrated in the use of African names for people and places in Zaire. The policy of nationalism involved the expropriation of most foreign-owned industries and government control over labour through one labour union.

When the Cold War ended, Mobutu saw most of his Western support evaporate, and allegations of corruption and human rights abuses were levelled against his regime. The United States, France and Belgium—all supporters of his regime in previous decades—withdrew their support and the economy of Zaire plummeted. In the face of economic crisis, local opposition to Mobutu intensified, and the rebel leader Laurent Kabila began a military campaign to oust him in October 1996. Mobutu attempted to battle Kabila's forces, but his government collapsed, and he fled the country in May 1997 first to Togo and then to Morocco where he died in September 1997.

From brinksmanship to peaceful coexistence: Kennedy, Khrushchev, Castro and the missiles in Cuba

Around the same time of the Congo Crisis, the USA and the USSR were in more direct conflicts over Berlin and Cuba, two of the most contentious sites of the Cold War. Soviet conventional wisdom held that the Western democracies would eventually grow tired of supporting the Western enclave in the Soviet sphere and that West Berlin would eventually be absorbed into Berlin proper, but instead it remained a Western outpost in the communist world, and a thorn in the side of Soviet leaders. West Berlin was easily accessed and created an interesting paradox: until 1961, any Berliner could cross into the western sector and so the United States used this as a showpiece for the benefits of Western, capitalist democracy, enticing Easterners by displaying the latest in Western consumer goods. More directly, it was

Brinksmanship A strategy in which a power pushes a situation to the point of disaster in an attempt to force the other side to back down. This was used most notably by both the USA and the USSR in the Cuban Missile Crisis of 1962.

a gateway to the West; by crossing into West Berlin, Easterners could then cross into West Germany, leaving the communist sphere behind.

Fidel Castro came to power in Cuba, in 1959, to launch an initially, undefined social revolution. It was evident that Castro was seeking to change the rampant corruption of the Cuban government and economic dependence on the USA, but beyond that he was deliberately vague as to his exact ideological programme. Like Nasser, Castro sought to exploit the East–West rivalry and to advance his cause domestically by railing against US imperialism.

The Berlin Crisis

Trying to bring an end to the paradox of Berlin, in early 1958 Khrushchev unilaterally demanded an end to the four-power occupation of the city. More specifically, he threatened to withdraw and turn East Berlin over to the East German government, no longer treating it as its own separate political entity. In doing so, he thought this might put further pressure on the Western states, who would then withdraw their own forces and leave Berlin to the communist East Germans. When the other powers refused to accept this, Khrushchev was left with few options. He considered the use of nuclear weapons, but the questions that arose included who would be targeted and whether or not Berlin was worth nuclear war. In the end, he decided that it was not, and this threat was disposed of, but the idea of a conventional military conflict between the powers in Berlin was not abandoned. In fact, at one point, there was a stand-off right on the border, between American and Soviet tanks, but this was solved diplomatically. Ultimately, Khrushchev took another view in 1961 and decided to wait out Western occupation.

The Berlin Wall in Chausseestrasse is completed under the watch of East German soldiers, 4 December 1961.

However, they still needed to do something to stop the flow of people from east to west. By 1961, 2.7 million East Germans had left and in July 1961 alone it was estimated that 30 000 moved from East Berlin. East German leader Walter Ulbricht had previously suggested erecting a wall as a deterrent, but the idea had been vetoed by the Soviet leadership, who saw this as soul-destroying for the communists. However, given the economic distress that this stream of emigration was causing, Khrushchev reversed his previous decision and, on the evening of 12–13 August 1961, the East Germans constructed a wall, first with barbed-wire and later fortified with concrete, and ordered guards to shoot to kill anyone who tried to cross from east to west. Although this was not the ideal solution to the issue of Berlin, it prevented any future conflicts between the two superpowers, and even Kennedy admitted that the wall was preferable to war.

This crisis was, in some respects, a prelude of things to come, an event in which two powers nearly came to blows over ideological spheres and in which Khrushchev pulled back, avoiding direct confrontation. The Cuban Missile Crisis remains the closest that superpowers ever came, as far as we are currently aware, to nuclear war; and yet, through the determination of the political leadership, conflict was avoided.

The Cuban Missile Crisis

President Eisenhower was infuriated by the success of Castro and his decision to nationalize American industries. Castro came to power with two clear promises to his people: to improve the social welfare of the population and to rid Cuba of the neo-imperial dominance of the USA. Initially, he tried to stay away from American interests but his social and economic programs were quickly depleting the Cuban government's coffers and he needed money. Thus, the decision was made to accept Soviet oil at below-market prices. The United States responded by refusing to refine the oil, so the Cuban response was to nationalize all American-owned refineries. Nationalization of other foreign-owned entities quickly followed.

Eisenhower authorized the training of anti-Castro exiles to attempt to overthrow the Cuban regime and Kennedy inherited this plan. Although he was skeptical, Kennedy agreed to support the plan and, in April 1961 the Bay of Pigs invasion took place. Fifteen hundred exiles landed on a beach head and attempted to dig in. The plan was that, once they had established a beach head, the USA would provide support for a government that asked for assistance. The plan was dependent on popular support, however, and this was sorely lacking. Those who remained in Cuba supported the revolutionaries who had overthrown a brutal regime and were in no hurry to see the return of the elites. Also problematic was Kennedy's last-minute decision not to provide air support for the counter-revolutionaries. The plan was a disaster from start to finish, but it convinced Castro and the Soviets that the USA was determined to oust Castro. This in turn led to the decision to install nuclear weapons in Cuba.

The Soviets had long been vulnerable to potential medium-range nuclear attacks as the USA had weapons deployed in the UK and Italy and, most notably, had Jupiter missiles that had been placed in Turkey in the 1950s. In addition, the Soviets wanted to help extend the revolution that had begun in Cuba into the rest of Latin America and the Caribbean, and wanted to ensure the continuation of Castro's regime. Thus, in the summer 1962, the installation of medium-range nuclear weapons in Cuba began. Throughout the summer, American intelligence operatives in Cuba reported increased Soviet activity there, but they were largely ignored by Washington. However, in October, an American U2 spy plane flying over Cuba photographed sites that were easily identified as ballistic missile sites and the president was notified.

US and Soviet leadership spent the next 13 days trying to prevent the outbreak of war, while achieving their own objectives. The United States wanted the weapons dismantled;

Aerial view of a Cuban missile launch site, 24 October 1962.

the Soviets wanted the protection of Cuba from further invasions and a withdrawal of US nuclear weapons from Europe. The USA blockaded Cuba but, not wanting to violate international law, called it a quarantine. At the same time, a Soviet ship was heading to Cuba, and the question was whether the ship would break the quarantine and provoke war. US and Soviet forces were put on alert and the American people were notified via a televised address that president Kennedy gave to the country, apprising them of the situation. After much negotiation and near-constant communication between Kennedy and Khrushchev, the Soviet ship turned around and headed back home. The Soviets agreed to withdraw the weapons and the United States agreed publicly that it would no longer threaten Castro's regime, while privately it agreed to withdraw its Jupiter missiles from Turkey. Both sides generally achieved what they wanted, and nuclear war was averted.

On the one hand, the Cuban Missile Crisis reflects the implementation of the policy of brinksmanship. On the other hand, it reflects the determination of Kennedy and Khrushchev to avoid nuclear confrontation. In both of these crises, the notion of peaceful coexistence trumped brinksmanship, and war was averted. The superpowers, with the concept of **mutual assured destruction** firmly entrenched, found that nuclear **deterrence** was far stronger than the idea of nuclear war. Conventional warfare and proxy wars remained the methods by which the Cold War was fought.

Mutual assured destruction (MAD)
The theory that if either side of the Cold War conflict engaged in nuclear war, the retaliation from the other side would lead to the destruction of both powers.

Deterrence The military strategy by which a power accrues as many weapons as they possibly can—and perhaps recruits such a large army—that no power would risk going to war against it. It is the strategy generally used to justify the continued production and stockpiling of nuclear weapons.

Vietnam

On the tail of both the Berlin and Cuban Missile Crises, the United States found itself escalating its involvement in the Vietnam War. The USA had been involved since the end of the Second World War, but the defeat of the French and their subsequent expulsion left the USA as the uncomfortable supporters of a non-communist regime in South Vietnam in an attempt to prevent the further spread of communism into Southeast Asia.

Indochina's situation was very similar to those other colonies that had been occupied in the Second World War. The French colony of Indochina was reluctant to find itself back under colonial control and the communist resistance leader Ho Chi Minh shifted his fight against the Japanese to counter French reassertion. At the end of the war, Ho announced the creation of the Democratic Republic of Vietnam, a communist country with as yet undefined borders.

The result was a bloody, costly war that ended in 1954 with a French defeat in the battle of Dien Bien Phu. Under the mediation of the Chinese communists, the USSR, the UK and the USA, Indochina was divided into four de facto states. Cambodia and Laos reverted to a prior status as independent kingdoms, but Vietnam was more problematic. Ultimately, the Geneva Accords settled on a division of Vietnam at the 17th parallel—the north under the communist leadership of Ho, the south under non-communist leadership with the Vietnamese emperor Bao Đai as the figurehead for the regime.

In 1955, the USA endorsed the rule of Ngô Đình Diem, a Catholic Vietnamese politician who was opposed to the French colonial regime. Diem challenged Bao Đai and won in what was clearly a rigged election, and Bao Đai went into exile in France. Like Rhee Syngman in Korea, Diem pursued authoritarian tactics that made his regime increasingly unpopular among the Vietnamese, even though most were predisposed to accept a non-communist regime over the communism of the north. Even so, approximately one million Vietnamese fled to the south to escape the regime of Ho, while it is estimated that 90 000 South Vietnamese went north in support of Ho.

The USA was involved almost immediately in supporting Diem's regime by offering to train the new South Vietnamese army. Not surprisingly, Ho went to Moscow and in July 1955 accepted Soviet aid to preserve his newly established communist regime. In a nod to the status quo, the Soviet Union proposed a two-country solution in which North and South Vietnam would be recognized as two separate, independent countries by the UN and the world community. However, this proposal was rejected by the United States, who still hoped to regain control over the entire peninsula.

The USA saw unification of the entire country as key to its own security. According to the **Domino Theory**, if North Vietnam were allowed to remain communist then it would assert its authority and use its military strength (and that of the USSR and the PRC) to extend its influence over the rest of Indochina and would, from there, threaten the rest of Southeast Asia and potentially the Indian subcontinent. In response to this threat, the United States had formed the Southeast Asia Treaty Organization (SEATO) in 1954 as a collective security organization, meant to prevent the spread of communism beyond North Vietnam.

The **Domino Theory** was created to justify US actions in Southeast Asia after France's losses in Indochina. It stated that if one power were to fall to communism then surrounding countries would also be susceptible. According to this theory, China and North Korea had already fallen, and Vietnam was about to fall. From there, Laos, Cambodia, Malaysia, Indonesia, Burma, India and perhaps even Australia would be poised to fall to communist aggression.

Ngô Đình Diem (1901–63)

First president of South Vietnam, 1955–63. Diem came from a Catholic, well-connected family that had relationships with upper-class Vietnamese and the French. In 1933 he was appointed minister of the interior by Emperor Bao Đai. He later broke from the emperor due to the French domination of the country and withdrew from the government. In 1945 the North Vietnamese leader Ho Chi Minh offered Diem a place in his government, but he refused, seeing communism as irreconcilable with his Catholicism. Instead, in 1950 he went into self-imposed exile. While he was in the USA, the Eisenhower government began to feel that he would make a good political leader in Southeast Asia and started to position him as such. After the signing of the Geneva Accords, Diem returned to South Vietnam as prime minister at the behest of the USA. He violated the Geneva Accords by holding elections only in the south (fearing Communist victory if the north were included). As a result of these elections, the Republic of Vietnam was established in the south with Diem as president. His regime was seen as repressive and violent as he favored Catholics over the majority Buddhist population. He installed friends and family members in positions of power, including making his own brother, Ngô Đình Diem , minister of interior and head of the secret police. As opposition to his rule grew, there were large public demonstrations, which provided stark visuals of Buddhist monks self-immolating in protest and of the deaths of protesters. The USA was increasingly uncomfortable with their support of Diem, so when a group of officers approached the US ambassador with the suggestion of a coup, they were told that the USA would not object. On 2 November 1963, Diem and his brother were assassinated, leading to a subsequent period of instability in Vietnamese leadership.

It was the North Vietnamese who initially escalated the tension in March 1959 by announcing a People's War to unite Vietnam under the leadership of Ho. This led to the decision to begin to construct a route from north to south that would cross into neutral Laos and Cambodia so that those travelling could do so undetected. This trail was instrumental to the movement of people and weapons from north to south and became a target of bombing campaigns. Shortly after this, the National Liberation Front (NLF) was established in South Vietnam, giving the military wing of the communists, the Viet Cong, a voice in South Vietnamese politics.

The policies of Kennedy and Johnson

When Kennedy succeeded Eisenhower in 1961, he continued the US policy of assisting South Vietnam, but the Americans were increasingly uncomfortable with the brutality of Diem's regime. The USA counselled Diem to remove his brother from power but Diem did not do so. US discomfort escalated as Diem imposed martial law while attempting to control Buddhist riots and demonstrations against the regime. Even his own support began to erode, and in November 1963 the regime crumbled and Diem was arrested and assassinated by a group of South Vietnamese colonels. There was no clear leader to succeed Diem and the South Vietnamese faced a succession of political leadership kept in power by the South Vietnamese army with US assistance.

Meantime, the USA had undergone its own regime change with the assassination of Kennedy. Newly sworn-in President Johnson promised that the United States would not lose Vietnam. Although the USA had been assisting the South Vietnamese, Johnson spearheaded a substantial escalation in American assistance after the summer of 1964. In late July, an American ship, the USS *Maddox*, was attacked by North Vietnamese patrol boats 10 miles (16 km) off the coast of Vietnam. As a Democrat, Johnson did not want to seem soft on communism, so this provided him with a convenient rationale to escalate US participation in the war. The result was the Gulf of Tonkin resolution of August 1964, in which both houses of the US Congress agreed to support the president to take "all necessary measures to repel any armed attack against the forces of the USA and to prevent further aggression."

This resolution gave the US president far-reaching powers in Indochina, including the power to send troops and to determine when assistance to South Vietnam should cease. The importance of Vietnam escalated somewhat when Khrushchev was ousted in October 1964 and was succeeded by Leonid Brezhnev. The USA was hoping to take advantage of this regime change to defeat the North Vietnamese and in 1964 a poll showed that 85 per cent of Americans supported US efforts in Vietnam. However, the Viet Cong controlled approximately 50 per cent of the rural population of South Vietnam, making victory a difficult proposition at best.

This shifted US involvement from that of military advisors (23 000 of whom were already in Vietnam) to full military intervention. After his landslide victory in the 1964 elections, Johnson further escalated the campaigns against North Vietnam and the Viet Cong. In 1965, Operation Rolling Thunder began—a massive aerial bombing campaign that targeted the Ho Chi Minh Trail, Viet Cong areas in the south and industrial and military areas in the north. Meant to last eight weeks, Rolling Thunder dragged on for over three years. In this campaign, pilots made three million sorties, dropped eight million tons of bombs and created approximately three million civilian refugees in South Vietnam. It was ultimately cancelled in November 1968 when it was decided that it did not fulfil its objectives of raising South Vietnamese morale and convincing Ho Chi Minh to halt his conquest of South Vietnam.

In 1965 Johnson also requested (and received) $1.7 billion, authorized the use of napalm and sent the first combat troops to Vietnam. By the end of the year, the United States had sent 184 300 troops, but this did little to ameliorate the situation. The South Vietnamese army had 90 000 desertions, and 50 per cent of the countryside remained under the control of the Viet Cong.

The Tet Offensive

The Tet Offensive of 1968 is often seen as the turning point of American public opinion regarding the war in Vietnam. Until this battle, Americans clearly supported US actions in Indochina. And it seems that the American forces were making headway in Vietnam, controlling the major cities and increasing their support from South Vietnamese peasants. Thus, the North Vietnamese decided to launch an all-out military assault on US and South Vietnamese troops throughout the south on the Vietnamese holiday of Tet, which had previously been a day of ceasefire for the whole country. The North Vietnamese army and Viet Cong simultaneously attacked the five major cities of South Vietnam and the provincial capitals throughout the country. In Saigon, they attacked the airport, presidential palace, and, most notably, fought their way onto the grounds of the US embassy. In a battle that was televised to the American people, it took US forces nearly a week to subdue the Viet Cong. Although the battle resulted in victory for the USA, the announcement by American General Westmoreland that the United States would need to send an additional 200 000 troops to Vietnam eroded much of the public support for the war.

Vietnam had become a quagmire for both American troops and the USA, and this was very difficult for the American population to understand. Although the overwhelming majority of the population supported US involvement in the Vietnam War, there was an anti-war movement among university students as early as 1964 that began to gain momentum as casualties and costs mounted. Private citizens and government officials were increasingly dividing themselves into the categories of **hawks** and **doves**, depending on their stance regarding Vietnam. Although many still supported the USA, there was a feeling that there needed to be a change in US policies and tactics regarding Vietnam.

One of the reasons that the USA could not be successful was clearly articulated by General Võ Nguyên Giáp of the North Vietnamese army. Since the North Vietnamese were willing to fight until victory,

Hawks and **doves** The slang terms used in American politics and journalism to describe a person's outlook regarding war. "Hawks" are those people who believe in an aggressive foreign policy, a strong military and the use of force. "Doves" reject the use of force to achieve foreign policy objectives. In the context of the Vietnam War, hawks advocated continued military support for South Vietnam while doves advocated withdrawal.

they would always find those who supported their cause and the war would continue. Another reason was that, in enlisting the support of local populations against the USA, the North Vietnamese and Viet Cong had a tremendous advantage. The USA had to take complete control of a region or city to eliminate the guerrilla element from the fight. So long as they were willing to fight and sustain heavy casualties, the communists would persevere. It was highly unlikely that the USA would have the stomach for such a long war.

On 2 September 1969, Ho died, naming Lê Duan as his successor. In his final testament, Ho charged the North Vietnamese to continue fighting until the Americans left Vietnam. This was indeed the North Vietnamese policy as implemented by Lê Duan, the political leader; Giáp, the military leader; and Lê Đuc Thọ, the diplomat.

Nixon and US withdrawal from Vietnam

In the face of such an increasingly divisive issue, Johnson decided he would not run for re-election. The 1968 elections in the United States were fraught with problems for the Democratic Party, especially after the assassination of Robert Kennedy, so it came as little surprise that the Republican candidate Robert Nixon was elected in November 1968. He inherited a situation just as problematic as the one Johnson had faced in 1963, with 500 000 US troops in Vietnam, an average of 1200 US deaths per month and continued anti-war protests. Increasingly, Nixon relied on national security advisor Henry Kissinger to develop his foreign policy.

Kissinger's ideas were focused on rapprochement with China and solving the problem that Vietnam had become. There were three options available to the USA: escalation, status quo and withdrawal. Each of these options had their own advantages and disadvantages. In the end, US policy was developed along the lines of two main ideas: Vietnamization and traditional diplomacy.

Vietnamization meant that the South Vietnamese would increasingly take a leadership role in the war against North Vietnam and that the USA would withdraw gradually, while training South Vietnamese troops and preparing them to take complete political and military control over South Vietnam. This policy needed time for implementation and the American public was increasingly unwilling to allow this time to elapse. Nonetheless, this policy was implemented and it took the United States until November 1973 to withdraw all troops from Vietnam.

At the same time, Kissinger engaged in diplomacy with the North Vietnamese. Initially kept secret from the US population, the peace talks between the United States and the North Vietnamese took place sporadically from 1969 to 1973. Initially, the USA proposed the simultaneous withdrawal of American and North Vietnamese troops from South Vietnam, but this was rejected by the North Vietnamese. Kissinger and Thọ then brokered the agreement that became the Paris Peace Accord of January 1973. According to this agreement, the USA would end its military involvement in Vietnam and the North and South would agree to a ceasefire and would hold their positions. Additionally, the South Vietnamese would be given the opportunity to decide their political future through free elections and any unification of Vietnam would occur peacefully.

Although the United States promised to retaliate against the North if they took any action against the South, US domestic issues soon took over, and South Vietnam was left to its own devices. The North Vietnamese continued their attempted overthrow of the South's government, finally driving South Vietnamese president Thieu into exile and leaving the South with a political vacuum. Shortly thereafter, the North Vietnamese launched an offensive against the South that led to the fall of Saigon in June 1975 and a unification of the country under the northern communists. The USA had evacuated the last Americans from its embassy on 30 May 1975.

Communist support for North Vietnam

Soviet and Chinese involvement was neither sustained nor consistent. US policy until 1969 maintained that the communist world—unless there had been a decided rift, as with Yugoslavia—had a monolithic foreign policy dictated from Moscow. Instead, the North Vietnamese found themselves in a position to use the Sino-Soviet split to their own ends, getting support from both countries. Khrushchev had made some nods to a US plan to refer the conflict to the UN Security Council but this was quashed when Brezhnev came to power in October 1964. The Soviets publicly stated that they would support communist North Vietnam against a US attack in an attempt to keep North Vietnam in their sphere. The material support the Soviets provided was transported by the PRC in a unique show of unity against the Americans. The USSR never felt it could control the leadership in Hanoi, which used its independence from both major communist powers to suit their own needs.

China's relations with North Vietnam were even more complicated. Spurred by fear of a US attack on North Vietnam, the Chinese pledged to assist the North Vietnamese as the Soviets had done. However, Chinese policy was ambivalent at best, as the domestic upheaval of the **Cultural Revolution** led to fissures in the Party itself. On the one hand, some leaders feared the costly involvement of the Korean conflict; on the other, the idea of revolutionary enthusiasm was put forth as a reason to assist the North Vietnamese. To show their support, the Chinese stationed troops near their border with North Vietnam. They also provided anti-aircraft defence systems to counter Operation Rolling Thunder and sent technicians (engineering corps, mostly) to the North so that the North Vietnamese army could be free to engage in military operations. This seemed to work well initially, but as the relationship between Moscow and Hanoi improved and the Soviets provided the North Vietnamese with more aid, relations between Hanoi and Beijing deteriorated. In addition, North Vietnamese incursions in Laos and Cambodia had a negative effect, as North Vietnam was taking over where China had traditionally dominated. By July 1970, all Chinese troops had been withdrawn from North Vietnam, although material support did continue. China ultimately fought a brief "Third Indochinese War" against Vietnam in 1979 in retaliation for the Vietnamese invasion of Cambodia in 1978 that toppled the Khmer

Rouge regime. Although the Chinese army advanced into Vietnam and withdrew, declaring victory, they found the Vietnamese a formidable force and suffered numerous casualties.

The legacy of the Vietnam War went beyond the Cold War and the position of the belligerents. Cambodia and Laos were both dragged into the conflict by their proximity to Vietnam and the North's use of their countries in the construction and operation of the Ho Chi Minh Trail. Cambodia faced a series of coups that culminated in the rule of the Khmer Rouge under Pol Pot. His regime promoted a radical, agrarian socialist program that led to the deaths of two million Cambodians due to executions and starvation, in addition to approximately 100 000 casualties from US bombing campaigns that lasted from 1969 to 1973. Though not as extreme, the war destabilized Laos and led to a long civil war, in which the communists finally emerged victorious in 1975. However, the regime was beholden to the Vietnamese communists and thus had to bow to pressure from that government, even severing ties with the People's Republic of China, leaving the country isolated except for trade relations with Vietnam.

The USA was dealt a serious blow, as this was the longest war fought in its history and one they lost. The war had begun when there were fissures in the American social fabric, and these were ripped open by the war. It led to a serious re-evaluation of US foreign policies. Most clearly, the Nixon Doctrine epitomized it, stating that the United States would still support non-communist movements abroad with economic and military aid, but it would not commit US forces to fight on foreign soil. Its main Cold War rival, the Soviet Union, was satisfied by the US defeat; but it would repeat the mistakes of Vietnam in its own patch—Afghanistan.

IB Learner Profile link

The American public increasingly gained information about the Vietnam War from television reports. On CBS news, there was an especially venerated newsman, Walter Cronkite. On 27 February 1968, he said the following:

> *It seems now more certain than ever that the bloody experience of Vietnam is to end in stalemate. This summer's almost certain standoff will either end in real give-and-take negotiation or terrible escalation; and for every means we have to escalate, the enemy can match us.*

Source: Kissinger, H. 1995. *Diplomacy*. New York, USA. Anchor Books. p. 671.

Critical thinkers

Newsreader or news maker?

Principled

Is the statement above appropriate for someone mandated to report the news? Why or why not?

Reflective

How important is the media in reflecting and directing public opinion for or against the government?

China's military supply to Vietnam, 1964–75											
	1964	**1965**	**1966**	**1967**	**1968**	**1969**	**1970**	**1971**	**1972**	**1973**	**1974**	**1975**
Guns	80 500	220 767	141 531	146 600	219 899	139 900	101 800	143 100	189 000	233 500	164 500	141 800
Artillery	1 205	4 439	3 362	3 984	7 087	3 906	2 212	7 898	9 238	9 912	6 406	4 880
Bullets (1000s)	25 240	114 010	178 120	147 000	247 920	119 170	29 010	57 190	40 000	40 000	30 000	20 060
Artillery shells (1000s)	335	1 800	1 066	1 363	2 082	1 357	397	1 899	2 210	2 210	1 390	965
Radio transmitters	426	2 779	1 568	2 464	1 854	2 210	950	2 464	4 370	4 335	5 148	2 240
Telephones	2 941	9 502	2 235	2 289	3 313	3 453	1 600	2 424	5 905	6 447	4 633	2 150
Tanks	16	-	-	26	18	-	-	80	220	120	80	-
Naval vessels	-	7	14	25	-	-	-	24	71	5	6	-
Planes	18	2	-	70	-	-	-	4	14	36	-	20
Automobiles	25	114	96	435	454	162	-	4 011	8 758	1 210	506	-
Uniforms (1000 sets)	-	-	400	800	1 000	1 200	1 200	1 400	1 400	1 400	1 400	-

Arms race, proliferation and limitation: the role of détente in the Cold War

The nuclear arms race was at its height during the Cuban Missile Crisis at the point in which the superpowers showed the world that they were unwilling to use nuclear armaments against one another for fear of massive retaliation. In theory, and in military strategies planned by generals and admirals, nuclear weapons were seen as an instrument to be used in war. But Truman decided early on that the use of nuclear weapons should be a political decision, not a military one. His very public conflict with MacArthur sprang from precisely this change; never before had political leaders made what could be seen as military decisions. It was up to the politicians to make decisions about war and peace, and then it was up to the military leaders to decide how to implement the decisions made.

Truman was followed by Eisenhower, a military man who in some respects reversed Truman's approach. He saw the use of nuclear weapons as an instrument of both policy and war, and encouraged his Joint Chiefs of Staff to integrate their use into military strategy. Despite the fact that Eisenhower's Joint Chiefs of Staff planned extensively for total war, including the use of nuclear weapons, his tenure (1953–60) saw the longest period of stability.

The United States had an atomic monopoly for only a very brief period; this ended in 1949 with the Soviet development of nuclear technology, followed by that of the UK, France and China in 1964. The proliferation of weapons was not simply the stockpiles of weapons but also the expansion of the number of countries that counted as nuclear powers. This proliferation led to necessary negotiations about the spread—and limitations—of these weapons. The USA and the USSR found themselves on the same side in this particular endeavor: neither sought to increase the number of countries that had nuclear weapons; both wanted to keep the technology up to the discretion of the main powers that could be trusted to be rational actors. Even in the midst of conflicts in Vietnam, the Congo and Latin America the USA, the UK and the USSR brokered and signed the Non-Proliferation Treaty (NPT) in July 1968. This was an amendment to the 1963 Test Ban Treaty, in which the USA and the USSR agreed to cease underwater, space and atmospheric testing of nuclear weapons.

Although Brezhnev proved to be a hardliner, he was also a realist, and in 1967 accepted President Johnson's invitation to begin bilateral talks regarding arms limitations. They were hindered somewhat by US domestic politics but eventually evolved into the Strategic Arms Limitations Talks (SALT). Formal negotiations took place, beginning in 1969 under President Nixon and Brezhnev. SALT I, as it was later called, was implemented in 1972. According to the terms of the treaties signed, the USA and the USSR agreed to freeze the number of ballistic (flying) missile launchers and would only allow the use of new submarine ballistic missile launchers as these and older intercontinental ballistic missile (ICBM) launchers were removed from use. They also signed the Anti-Ballistic Missile Treaty, which limited the number of ABM systems that would defend areas from nuclear attack.

This was followed by SALT II, brokered through a series of talks that took place between 1972 and 1979. The main difference is that SALT II involved negotiations to reduce the number of nuclear warheads possessed by each side to 2250 and banned new weapons programs from coming into existence. The treaty was never ratified by the US Senate, arguably due to Soviet actions in Cuba and in Afghanistan, but both sides honoured the terms of the agreement until 1986, when US president Reagan accused the Soviets of violating the pact and withdrew from the agreement. In 1983 he had announced the decision of his administration to pursue the Strategic Defensive Initiative (SDI) or Star Wars programme, which it was hoped would put a shield over the USA against nuclear attack.

At the same time, the USA was engaged in another set of talks, the Strategic Arms Limitations Talks, or SALT. Initiated in Geneva in 1982, these sought to put into place yet another set of limits on nuclear weapons. A limit would be placed not on weapons but on the number of warheads, which would be capped at 5000 plus 2500 on ICBMs. Since both sides had been placing more than one warhead on each ICBM, it was also proposed to limit the number of ICBMs to 850. This proposal was weighted heavily in favor of the United States, as it appeared to be an attempt at parity when really the USA had tremendous superiority, especially with ICBMs. As the talks dragged on through the 1980s, both sides continued to develop and produce more nuclear weapons, rather than less. In the end, the Treaty that was signed in 1991 allowed for both sides to possess over 10 000 warheads, while limiting the number of fighter planes, attack helicopters, tanks and artillery pieces. Its implementation, however, was hindered by the collapse of the Soviet Union six month later. Subsequently, the United States had to sign separate treaties with Russia and other former Soviet states that possessed nuclear weapons. The USA signed treaties with Russia (which remains a nuclear power), Belarus, Kazakhstan and Ukraine, all of whom voluntarily dismantled their nuclear weapons and sent them to Russia for disposal.

The nuclear arms agreements were the most high-profile areas of **détente**, but there were other treaties that signalled a willingness to change entrenched Cold War policies on both sides. In 1970, the Federal Republic of Germany (FRG) signed a treaty with the USSR recognizing the borders of Germany, including the Oder–Neisse line that delineated the border of Poland and the German Democratic Republic (GDR). Shortly thereafter, a quadripartite agreement was signed in which it was decided that Berlin would be represented by the FRG in international matters but it would not become part of the FRG. Lastly with regard to Germany, 1972 saw the normalization of relations between the two German states, including the establishment of permanent missions and the admission of both states into the UN. This complemented the West German policy of **Ostpolitik**, a distinct shift toward Eastern Europe in an attempt to improve relations with the GDR that, it hoped, would eventually lead to reunification.

The most wide-ranging aspect of détente was finalized in Helsinki in 1975 with the Conference on Security and Cooperation in Europe (CSCE). The Final Act contained three "baskets": security in Europe, in which post-war frontiers were accepted; co-operation in science, technology and environmental concerns; and human rights. The improvement of relations between East and West seemed to be at its high point, yet five years later, Soviet actions in Poland and Afghanistan renewed Cold War tensions.

TOK link

Natural sciences and areas of knowledge: ethics and psychology

One of the main reasons for the disarmament talks was the fear of mutual assured destruction (MAD).

MAD is the military strategy whereby the development of nuclear weapons gives all nuclear powers the capability to destroy their opponents. Once there were enough weapons on both sides, it was thought that there would be enough firepower to destroy the world.

In 1967, the US Secretary of Defense, Robert McNamara, wrote:

> *It is important to understand that assured destruction is the very essence of the whole deterrence concept. We must possess an actual assured-destruction capability, and that capability also must be credible. The point is that a potential aggressor must believe that our assured-destruction capability is in fact actual, and that our will to use it in retaliation to an attack is in fact unwavering. The conclusion, then, is clear: if the United States is to deter a nuclear attack in itself or its allies, it must possess an actual and a credible assured-destruction capability.*

Source: McNamara, R. "Mutual Deterrence" speech. 18 September 1967. http://www.atomicarchive.com/Docs/Deterrence/Deterrence.shtml

The concept of MAD remains a theory, as it has not been tested. There have been two "tests" of the atom bomb in Hiroshima and Nagasaki, and the effects of nuclear contamination have been demonstrated in accidents such as the Chernobyl disaster. But, for obvious reasons, there has never been an attempt to prove the hypothesis underlying MAD.

How, then, do we know that MAD is a valid theory?

Would MAD pass the coherence or correspondence tests? Why or why not?

Does the validity of the theory really matter if people believe in it?

Détente The easing of tensions between the USA and the USSR in the 1970s.

Ostpolitik (Eastern politics, German) A policy that sought to improve relations with West and East Germany through collaboration and assistance to bring about eventual reunification. Willy Brandt, the West German chancellor, championed this policy that was maintained until the collapse of communism in Eastern Europe in 1989.

China and the superpowers

The relations between the USSR and the People's Republic of China are complex, to say the least. The problem for the Western world was that for too long it had seen the communist world as monolithic, and under the stern leadership of Stalin there was some truth to this. However, there were very real differences among communists, especially among those leaders who achieved their positions of power independently. Initially, Mao deferred to Stalin as leader of the communist world, and respected his position as head of the most successful Marxist–Leninist state to date. But with the death of Stalin and Khrushchev's de-Stalinization policies, the situation changed.

It may be surprising in today's world to think of China as a client state, rather than as itself a superpower itself, but this was the case for much of the Cold War, especially from the point of view of the Western world. Seeing all Marxists as equal and linked, the prevailing view among Western policy makers was that the Chinese followed the same line as the Soviets, and took their orders from Moscow. The idea that these two countries were acting in concert was supported by international actions and statements of the Soviet and Chinese governments. However, this was far from the case: the Russians and Chinese had a long and troubled history that was informed as much by nationalism and conflict as it was by ideology and co-operation.

US policy was a hindrance to developing an in-depth understanding of the intricacies of communist relations. In 1950, when the Chinese Nationalists were expelled from mainland China and fled to Taiwan, the United States refused to recognize the communist government as the legitimate government and blocked its recognition by the UN. As a result, the USA had no diplomatic relations with Communist China and thus very little insight into its distinct nature and approaches to domestic and foreign policy. When Stalin was still alive, this was perhaps understandable. Mao Zedong looked to Stalin as the leader of the communist world, head of the country that had begun the Marxist–Leninist revolutionary process. Accepting leadership from Moscow meant having a reliable ally and a powerful, industrialized country that could help China to develop in the same way. It was, after all, Stalin who had taken a largely agricultural, peasant-based system and transformed it into the industrial society and nuclear power that it was by the time Mao and the Communist Party of China (CPC) came to power. He therefore provided a template for implementing the Marxist–Leninist ideals. Additionally, Stalin's cult of personality appealed to Mao, who sought to establish something similar, if not better, for himself.

In 1950 the Soviet Union was China's closest ally. They signed a Treaty of Friendship, agreeing to a 30-year military alliance and the Soviets agreed to provide low-interest loans to China amounting to US$300 million. The USSR also sent experts, machinery and the newest technology to assist China in a much needed push for industrialization. However, the amount of Soviet assistance actually provided was not as much as China had expected. Even in the Korean War, when Chinese troops received air support from Soviet MiGs, the level of support was seen as inadequate.

The Sino-Soviet split was a gradual process that began in the late 1950s and continued through the 1960s. Once again, Khrushchev's condemnation of Stalin and Stalinism was a catalyst for a change in the nature of relations within the communist world. As indigenous Marxist movements spread, there was increased competition between the Chinese and Soviets as to which type of communism the revolutionary parties would adopt. Often, those decisions were based on where the aid came from; in some cases, countries would have two Marxist parties, one following a Chinese line and one following the Soviet line. In attempting to gain support, the Chinese referred to Khrushchev's policies as deviationist; the Soviets considered Mao something of a maverick.

Khrushchev's calls for peaceful coexistence were anathema to Mao, who felt that the communist world had an obligation to engender revolutions elsewhere, and that co-operation was the same thing as embracing capitalism. The Soviets began to withdraw their specialists and stopped any assistance they had given China in its pursuit of nuclear weapons. In 1962 Mao criticized Khrushchev for backing down in the Cuban Missile Crisis. The Soviets had also provided assistance to India in its war with China. When Khrushchev was ousted in October 1964, his successors followed a similar policy, which the Chinese saw as hostile, and the tension between the two dominant communist powers escalated.

When the conflicts and tensions between the USSR and China are so desribed the break seems obvious, but this was not the case for US policy analysts. The few China experts who saw the fissures in the communist world were largely ignored by both the State Department and intelligence communities. However, the actions of 1969 dramatically changed this.

Although the Americans periodically found themselves engaged in negotiations in which China was also a contributing member (such as those in regard to Vietnam in Geneva), from 1949 to 1969 the USA refused to recognize the PRC and instead remained loyal to the Nationalist government on Taiwan, called the Republic of China (RoC). At times this meant some involvement in affairs regarding the PRC; one such being the conflicts in the 1950s between Taiwan and the PRC over the islands in the Taiwan Straits which the Nationalists held. These islands were right off the coast of mainland China and the Nationalists had fortified them to use as a point for reconquest of the mainland. When the PRC challenged these actions through shelling the islands, the United States responded in support of Nationalist forces, even going so far as to threaten use of nuclear attack. The USA later provided the Nationalists with air-to-air missiles to prevent PRC aerial aggression against the islands. Interestingly, one of the reasons for the PRC's second assault on the islands was to show Chinese autonomy from Moscow. The US support of the Nationalists was a foregone conclusion.

The border between the PRC and the USSR was one that had been negotiated by the Nationalists at the end of the Second World War and stemmed from the unequal relationship between Imperial China and Tsarist Russia. Even though they were ostensibly allies, both countries had amassed a large number of troops along their border. By 1968 the Soviets had 25 divisions and 120 medium-range missiles along the border, double what had been stationed there in 1961. Then, in March 1969, there was a border clash at the Ussuri River, initiated by the Chinese, followed by a subsequent attack in August in the western area of Xinjiang. According to Russian statistics, the Chinese suffered 800 casualties and the USSR 60, but these figures are contested by the Chinese, who argue that they suffered far fewer casualties. By the end of 1969, there were 500 000 troops on the border. Through negotiations, a solution was reached and the fighting stopped, even though there was no official agreement or terms. In the midst of this conflict, Soviet diplomats hinted to Americans of the possibility of a nuclear strike on China's nuclear weapons.

The most significant effect of this conflict was that the USA finally saw the split in the communist world and opted to use it to its own ends. Fearing the USSR's growing nuclear strength, the USA saw an advantage in engaging the PRC in diplomatic talks. In addition to non-recognition, the USA had placed an embargo on the PRC due largely to Chinese assistance to the Vietnamese. At the height of its involvement in 1967, the Chinese had 170 000 troops stationed in North Vietnam, providing support so that the Vietnamese could fight in the south. The border clash showed that the PRC and the USA had a similar interest: to counterbalance Soviet strength.

US–Chinese rapprochement

As often happens, the trigger for political change was not a particular diplomatic or military action. That trigger in the reopening of relations between these two powers came through a sporting event. In April 1971, at the world championships in Japan, a young American ping-pong player boarded the bus transporting the Chinese national team and was engaged in conversation by a Chinese player. Much to the surprise of American officials, the US team subsequently received an invitation to play in Beijing, and were granted visas to travel to China. This simple opening led to Henry Kissinger's secret trip to China, where he approached the leadership to begin opening relations. President Nixon was subsequently invited to China and in February 1972 he had his fateful meeting with Mao Zedong. The countries issued a joint statement, the Shanghai Communiqué, in which both countries pledged to do their best to normalize relations, and the USA stated a one-China policy. (According to this policy, which most Chinese both in Taiwan and the PRC subscribe to, there is one China and Taiwan is part of China.) After this, the United States established the Liaison Office, which gave the two countries a method with which they could negotiate. By the end of 1978, economic relations had resumed and negotiations concluded.

On 1 January 1979, the United States officially recognized the PRC as the legitimate government of China and full diplomatic relations were established. Even before these diplomatic overtures had taken place, other countries in the Western sphere felt comfortable embracing the PRC and recognition of the PRC increased. In 1971, the UN voted to replace Nationalist China with the PRC on the UN

Nationalist China and Taiwan

Currently there are 23 countries that recognize Nationalist China. In the past more did, but the issue of recognition is usually based on which countries require assistance, and in recent years the PRC has outbid the Nationalists in the developing world. The USA passed the Taiwan Relations Act in 1979, giving them a venue at which they can engage the Nationalists without formally recognizing the government. In sports, Taiwan is called Chinese Taipei and uses a different flag.

Security Council. The issue of Taiwan remains difficult to resolve both for the USA and for the international community.

This did nothing to assuage (calm) Soviet fears and indeed further alienated the Chinese and the Soviets. Although there was no official break, in 1979 the Treaty of Friendship lapsed, and neither side approached the other to re-establish such an alliance. Just as the Soviets had assisted the Indians in 1962, the Chinese assisted the Islamists in Afghanistan against the Soviets, and supplied the Contras in Nicaragua against the Soviet-backed Sandinistas, showing that national interest trumped ideology.

When Gorbachev came to power in 1985, he tried to normalize relations and reduced the number of Soviet troops on the border. Under Gorbachev—and Deng—the situation steadily improved, so that in May 1989 Gorbachev made a much publicized visit to Beijing. Due to this visit, there were numerous foreign reporters in China, which led to the widespread coverage of the democracy movement, or June 4th movement as it is called, that culminated in the Tiananmen Square massacre.

Meanwhile, the change in Chinese domestic policies, especially with regard to economic policies and allowing foreign visits, increased relations between the USA and China—trade relations in particular but also cultural exchanges and similar endeavours. Despite popular support for the democracy movement among the American public, relations between the two countries were not significantly strained by the repression of the movement seen at Tiananmen Square in 1989. At present, the PRC is the main trading partner for the USA; it has a favorable balance of trade and has considerable investments in the United States. Despite problems with pollution and infrastructure, the 2008 Beijing Olympics attracted numerous tourists from the West. This relationship between the USA and the PRC seems to be as defining today as the Cold War relationship between the USSR and the USA was previously.

End of the Cold War

> The death of Leonid Brezhnev led to a fundamental shift in Soviet policies. A long period of political and economic stagnation ended, leading to fundamental changes in Soviet policies towards its client states, and the Soviet Socialist Republics (SSRs) within its own state. By 1991, the system had collapsed and the USSR was gone.

When Brezhnev died, the Soviet Union faced a struggle for succession that mirrored what had occurred in China in the previous decade. At that point, the old guard in the politburo was aged and infirm, and the question was who would replace him: another member of the old regime or someone new. Initially, two successors—Yuri Andropov and Konstantin Chernenko—were Brezhnev's contemporaries, but they too met their demise before 1985. A new generation of politicians took the lead in the USSR in 1985, when Mikhail Gorbachev became the head of the government.

It is a mistake to view Gorbachev as anything other than a Communist committed to preserving the regime. In some respects he faced a situation similar to that of Lenin: to preserve the communist regime, he needed to make some changes that seemed to reverse the course of socialism. Thus, the policies of perestroika and glasnost should be compared to Lenin's New Economic Policy (NEP); Lenin's call for "one step backwards, two steps forwards" is just as apt for Gorbachev's economic reforms.

Gorbachev had to deal with signifiant economic and social problems. In particular, the citizens of non-Russian Soviet Satellite states made an increasingly volatile issue out of their nationalist claims. As the Warsaw Pact countries were winning autonomy, they began to agitate for recognition. The Baltic countries, with connections and borders with the West, were demanding first autonomy and then independence. Unlike the other SSRs, these countries had been incorporated into the USSR through agreements made with Nazi Germany. Although their integration into the USSR was not challenged by the West, neither were they ever recognized as members. Thus, their political agitations for independence were supported not just by anti-communists but also by those who were reacting against a Nazi action that had been accepted by the international community.

In foreign policy, initially Gorbachev's route did not deviate much from that of his predecessors. In 1985 he renewed the Warsaw Pact and he supported leftist revolutions, particularly that of the Sandinistas in Nicaragua. Unlike Brezhnev, however, he sought an end to the costly war in Afghanistan, and began to announce troop reductions, negotiating an agreement with the Afghans in 1988 that led to Soviet withdrawal by 1989.

That same year, 1989, also proved to be the decisive year for Eastern Europe. By January 1990, only the isolationist Albania remained communist. Gorbachev's statement that its allies should be able to pursue socialism in ways compatible with their histories and cultures had led to the collapse of communism. In June 1990, the Warsaw Pact countries agreed to its dissolution, signalling to a large extent the end of the Cold War.

The United States is often seen as the victor in the Cold War and one issue under discussion is how much US foreign policy, and particularly the policies of presidents Reagan and Bush, is responsible for the end of the Cold War. Reagan took a very strong stance that often reflected his background as an actor. In 1983 he referred to the Soviet Union as the "Evil Empire" and his SDI program was nicknamed "Star Wars". While such pop-culture references may seem comical today, they were very potent in engaging an American public that had been stung by Vietnam and that viewed any form of aggressive US foreign policy with trepidation. The nuclear threat was further heightened by the much publicized accidents at Three Mile Island in the United States and Chernobyl in the Soviet Union. The Cold War's influence in American culture was once again renewed, as was fear of a nuclear threat.

The Cold War ended quickly and abruptly, but the end was the result of long-term causes. The weaknesses of the Soviet dominion had been clear as early as 1948, when Czechoslovakia tried to remain outside the Eastern bloc and failed, and when Yugoslavia was expelled and then had economic success beyond that of other communist countries due, to a large extent, to the receipt of American aid. Uprisings in East Germany, Poland and Hungary in the 1950s showed the tensions within the Warsaw Pact, as did the Prague Spring of 1968. Rather than a show of strength, the **Brezhnev Doctrine** in some respects was an articulation of Soviet weakness, as force was required to prevent countries from leaving their sphere.

The Cold War did not end communism, nor did it end ideological conflicts. However, it signalled the end of the bipolar world that had existed since 1945 and left a power vacuum. It has seen the Balkanization of Central and Eastern Europe and an increase in sectarian violence. This is not to say that the Cold War was a desired state of affairs, but it was a conflict between two rational actors that had parity of power and were guided by ideological differences. The world today is not so simple.

Discussion point:

Are there winners and losers in the Cold War?

Consider the aftermath of the Cold War, also in terms of subsequent conflicts and the long-term economic and human costs for both the Western world and the Eastern bloc, and their allies.

Brezhnev Doctrine The policy whereby the Soviet Union asserted its right to intervene in the domestic politics of any communist country to perpetuate its status as socialist. It was developed in light of the Prague Spring of 1968 and subsequently used to justify Soviet intervention in communist countries.

Activity:

Leadership timeline

When studying the Cold War, one of the main problems is remembering who is in power when, and where. It is a good idea to establish a table of the relevant countries and personalities involved so that at any given point in time, you know who was in power.

Here is a table for you to copy and complete.

	Leader (USSR)	President (USA)	Party (USA)	Prime minster (UK)	Your country's government
1945–50	Stalin				
1951–5	Stalin (to 1953) Khrushchev				
1956–60	Khrushchev				
1961–5	Khrushchev (to 1964) Brezhnev				
1966–70	Brezhnev				
1971–5	Brezhenv				
1976–80	Brezhnev				
1981–5	Brezhnev (to 1982) Andropov (1982–4) Chernenko (1984–5)				
1986–91	Gorbachev				

Social, cultural and economic impact of the Cold War

> The Cold War was being fought in proxy wars and in the realm of popular culture. The nature of the struggle permeated all aspects of society, but perhaps the most lasting effect was the fear of nuclear war as expressed in the media during the course of the Cold War. Books, film and music all addressed the issue in speculative ways, asking the ultimate "what if" question. Additionally, areas as diverse as language and sport were affected. The end of the Cold War can be seen as a triumph of one political system over the other, but it can also be seen as a cultural shift.

The social, cultural and economic effects of the Cold War are inextricably linked to the politics of the era. In the 20th century, popular culture was far more widespread than in previous eras, when cultural trends had tended to be limited to a particular class or geographical region. Through the new technology that had been adopted in the arts and media—radio, television, film—everyone could have access to cultural developments, regardless of where they came from; language and distance were not deterrents to its spread.

This meant, to a large extent, a homogenization of society. While a certain amount of this had previously been seen as desirable (in 19th-century Germany and Italy, for example, one official language may have pre-empted dialects but it helped standardize official documents and education), there was now some questioning of this homogenization, as artists in particular feared the loss of local identity and the idea of cultural imperialism echoed the tsarist policies of **Russification**. This position was especially strong in the Baltic countries, which had escaped Soviet domination until the Second World War. Once again, the use of local language could be seen as an act of rebellion against a monolithic empire—even one that purported to represent the interests of all within its borders.

The Soviets had been successful in removing religion from the mainstream but they had by no means eliminated it. In the European and Caucasian parts of the Soviet Union, the Orthodox Church continued to exist, even if repression took place and the numbers of people (mostly old women and young children) attending religious services declined. In central Asia, Islam maintained a foothold and was a potential source for counter-revolution; the concern over Afghanistan and the determination of the Soviet state to intervene and prevent the establishment of an Islamist regime there was in part predicated by a fear of the rise of radical Islam within the USSR, especially on the heels of the Iranian revolution.

Cultural homogenization was also seen in the Western world, and American culture was increasingly seen more generally as Western culture. This was both embraced and resented by other Western states. Regardless of the language of a population, English was quickly becoming the common tongue—the one that students were most likely to learn after their own. In the face of US political dominance, it was perceived as the most logical and useful language to learn. But there were also those who were determined to reverse this trend. In France, the strongest reaction occurred—the Académie Française established rigorous rules to prevent English from encroaching on the French language.

There were other movements against this linguistic imperialism. Created in the 1890s, the invented Esperanto language saw a resurgence. In smaller states that were being eclipsed by larger language groups, learning Esperanto was seen as a way to embrace internationalism that did not represent cultural imperialism. However, this was a quixotic (idealistic) endeavor and most pragmatists chose to learn English or Russian.

The United States, which was created on foundations of religious freedom and tolerance, saw a backlash in the 1960s at the same time that the civil rights movement was in full force. Although religious freedom was a core tenet of the US constitution, the country was still overwhelmingly Protestant and suspicious of those who were not. When the Catholic John Kennedy was elected president in 1960, he had to impress upon Americans that he would not be

Russification A policy dating back to tsarist Russia whereby all national minorities were suppressed and the primacy of Russian language, culture and religion was put forth as the only recognized forms of expression. In an attempt to create a universal communist system, the Communist Party pursued similar policies of repression, adopting the Russian language as a standard and marginalizing the languages and cultures of the other SSRs.

Esperanto poster against international fascism, 1936–9.

following the will of the pope or consulting with him in his decision-making process. Although he was heralded as an American hero later in his career, he won the election with the narrowest margin in history to date, and this was partly due to his Catholicism.

The Cold War ushered in the television era and its effect on the general knowledge of the population and the policies made by governments was particularly strong in the West. While those under authoritarian regimes had limited avenues for obtaining information, the Western world saw a significant reduction in censorship. The Cold War represented the golden age of autonomy for journalists in particular and the media more broadly. It was in this era that the dogged determination of two journalists was able to bring about the resignation of a US president (Nixon) through the Watergate scandal (see chapter 5, pages 296–7).

In previous decades, culture had been used by governing bodies to perpetuate their point of view and this did not abate with the onset of the Cold War. The Western world used the media for its own propaganda purposes; Radio Free Europe and Voice of America are two examples of how the United States used media to spread its own ideology in the hopes of toppling Soviet regimes. While the USA may have been unwilling to support revolutionaries in an open and direct manner, they would certainly encourage them from the sidelines.

Film and television were the main media for advocating the particular position of the writer, director or producer. The Vietnam War provides many examples of how films were used to influence mainstream America, and how public opinion shifted throughout the course and aftermath of the war. Three films immediately come to mind: *Green Berets; The Deer Hunter*; and *Platoon*. Filmed in 1968 with John Wayne as the lead, *Green Berets* was an unapologetic endorsement of the Vietnam War, characterizing the Americans who fought there as heroic, while the North Vietnamese were portrayed as absolute villains. The film was produced and released before the Tet Offensive had been broadcast on American televisions and was bolstered by the support that the US public had for the war at that time. In contrast, *The Deer Hunter*, was released in 1978, after the US disaffection with the Vietnam War. In this film, the director explores not just the war itself but the ruined lives of the men who enlisted. Lastly, *Platoon* (1986) is Oliver Stone's attempt to explore both sides of the American military intervention using two platoon leaders as archetypes: one a grizzled, battle-worn pragmatist and the other an idealist trying to keep his men on the right path. In the latter two films there is a certain amount of moral ambivalence and the war itself is not seen as an indictment of US government actions—but its treatment of the volunteer soldiers certainly is.

The use of films to portray the risks inherent in the Cold War dates back to its onset, as do the movies that exploited the irrational US fear of communism within its own borders. In *On the Beach*, the northern hemisphere has been destroyed by nuclear war and survivors have to come to terms with the fact that the human race is facing extinction. The movies of the era did not necessarily assign blame; as mutual assured destruction became the prevailing theory of the era, neither side was seen as completely guilty or innocent. Instead the themes tended to focus on the intertwining of technology and warfare—with technology both welcomed and suspect. The ideas put forth in *1984* and *Brave New World* were further developed after viewing the destruction wrought on Hiroshima and Nagasaki. As might be expected, Western popular culture was much more self-critical, as writers and film makers in places with free speech could show their own governments as culpable.

These cultural reflections led to an omnipresent sense of disaster on both sides of the Cold War. With the fear of mutual assured destruction, there was always a sense that the other side was not rational and might attempt to win the unwinnable war. In *War Games*, it was a teenage computer geek who put the world on a path of destruction by unknowingly breaking into a US Department of Defense computer that may or may not have the capability to override human decisions; it was only the determination of the military to avoid war that de-escalated the situation. This film was, in effect, a replay of the Cuban Missile Crisis, where one side had to trust the other to bring about the end of the crisis.

At the centre of this was the youth culture of the era that prevailed on both sides of the Cold War. After the Second World War, there was an increase in the birth rate. The "baby boomers", as they were called, were the children born in the aftermath of the Second World War, and their large numbers meant that culture and consumerism targeted this generation. In the United States, the baby boomers were children of an affluent society that had disposable income and a substantial amount of leisure time. In Europe and the USSR, this generation still felt the effects of the war; for example, it is often forgotten that the British did not have rationing until after the war, and that it continued until 1954.

In the USA, this meant a change in direction, especially in the latest music and film. There were radical shifts as American youth embraced rock 'n' roll. This began in the 1950s, but the metamorphosis of music continued well into the 1960s as bands and singers acceptable to parents were increasingly eclipsed by those that symbolized rebellion. In the 1950s, this shift was exemplified by Elvis Presley, who represented an American music movement that incorporated jazz and blues into popular music. In the 1960s, the British provided further deviation as the Who, the Rolling Stones and, most importantly, the Beatles became the most popular bands of the age. All of this music was seen as a rejection of parental, and by extension, societal values. Even within this narrow time frame, there is a strong cultural shift; Presley voluntarily joined the army and showed himself to be a patriotic American; the 1960s bands and musicians protested against the military actions of their governments.

As this generation went to college, their ideas were further supported by liberal university professors. Away from their parents for the first time and experimenting with different ideologies, Western youth began to question and criticize their parents' unquestioning hatred of communism and socialism, especially as countries such as Sweden were providing positive models of how a socialist system could work.

This gave rise to radical organizations throughout the West, including the Weather Underground in the USA and the Baader-Meinhof group in Germany. Such groups advocated the violent overthrow of their governments in an attempt to establish a more equitable society. They often engaged in political violence, resulting in the deaths of politicians and innocent bystanders. While they represented the radical factions of young society, such groups show that the young in the 1960s were fully in favour of changing the balance of power in their countries away from the establishment (written with a capital "E"). Though their political clout was limited at best, this showed a change in attitudes.

All of these ideas converged and were exemplified in the Woodstock concert of 1969. Perhaps in a foreshadowing nod to the baby boomers, the concert was initially meant to be a profit-making venture in which people would attend a three-day concert with 32 musical groups taking the stage. Approximately 186 000 tickets were sold, but the event quickly became free as the fences to the farm where the concert took place were cut. The event soon took on a life of its own as it represented the rejection of the Establishment: roughly 500 000 people participated in an anti-war, pro-drug, free-love party that in some respects became a mini-nation unto itself for four days. A US film company was there to document the concert and thus Woodstock entered into the US national consciousness as emblematic of the hippie culture of the 1960s and early 1970s.

While this reaction against the government is keenly remembered, particularly in the United States, there was also the part of the Cold War that supported conservative American politics. After Johnson chose not to run for re-election, the USA was governed by Nixon and Ford—two Republicans—and then after the presidency of Jimmy Carter, by Reagan and Bush. All but six years in a 24-year period were dominated by a conservative executive and this was reflected in the culture, too. After the innovations of the 1950s and 1960s (and when the baby boomers reached adulthood), the 1970s and 1980s were a time in which culture was once again mainstreamed. The counterculture (seen in movements such as punk, rap, hip hop and grunge) was once again under the radar, seen only in independent movies and heard only on college radio stations.

Another area where the Cold War was fought was on the athletics field. After the Second World War, the Olympics in particular, but all world sporting events, took on mythic proportions as every event was seen as an apologia or indictment of Cold War politics. For most of the Cold War, the communist countries poured immense sums of money into their sports programmes so that they could prove their superiority in the sports arenas, and they were very successful. In communist Eastern Europe, children were targeted as talented and began training in special schools and camps at a very young age. They became master practitioners in their given sports, to which the majority of their time and energy was devoted. This was focused on particular sports in particular countries: East Germany was well-known for its women swimmers (and was accused of using steroids to bring about such successful results); Romania became known as a centre for gymnastic excellence—Nadia Comăneci and Béla Károlyi became international stars after the 1976 Olympics in Montreal, Canada. The communist countries faced increasing international scrutiny, as such sporting events were supposed to be between amateur players, not professionals.

The most dramatic Cold War events centred on two ice hockey competitions, largely due to this issue of amateur status. The Soviets were seen as recruiting a team of players that may not have been officially professionals but in essence were. On the other hand, in Canada and the USA, which both had professional hockey leagues, international competitions were largely the domain of college students. However, in 1972, the Summit Series was a seven-game competition between Team Canada—the best of their professional hockey players—and the USSR. The series had to be extended to eight games because each team had won three, and one game was a tie. In the eighth game, the Canadians scored a winning goal with 34 seconds remaining, giving the series to the Canadians.

Even more dramatic than this event, perhaps, was the so-called "Miracle on Ice" that occurred in the 1980 Winter Olympics in Lake Placid, New York (USA). This game was all the more important because at the time President Carter was considering boycotting the summer 1980 Olympics due to the Soviet invasion of Afghanistan. The US team consisted mostly of college students and several graduate amateurs and the Soviets were the dominant team; everyone fully expected the USSR to win the gold medal. The USA made it through to the medal round, where it was expected that they would be eliminated by the Soviets and play either Sweden or Finland for the bronze medal. Instead, in a stunning turn, the US team defeated the Soviets and went on to defeat Finland for the gold medal. This was used in the United States to show the moral superiority of American sportsmanship in a David vs Goliath fight. In the USSR, *Pravda* did not even publish the results of the game and the Soviet silver medal (won after defeating Sweden in their final match) was downplayed.

Misha the bear, mascot of the 1980 Moscow Olympics, in a view from the opening ceremony.

The USA was going through dramatic social and economic changes in the 1970s and 1980s but the situation in the USSR remained stagnant. The planned economy still focused on the production of heavy industry and weapons at the expense of consumer goods. Vast sums of money were spent on what was considered to be traditional culture in the Soviet sphere: classical music, ballet and Olympic sports benefited from the Cold War. Meanwhile, Eastern European popular culture lagged behind the West, and much of the success of Radio Free Europe and Voice of America came from their ability to broadcast Western music. Similarly, the black market was full of Western goods—Levi's jeans were sold at premium prices, and hard currency was purchased at well above the official value.

Western Europe recovered remarkably after the war, and the Marshall Plan must be credited for a large chunk of this recovery. The $13 billion that went to European countries helped them to build the new infrastructure that made them competitive with other states. In turn, and in time, they too had the disposable income necessary to purchase consumer goods, and engage in trade with the USA and other markets. This created a prosperity in the West that did not exist in the East; it further led to feelings of discontent in Eastern Europe and dissent grew. Unlike the Stalinist era of the early 1950s, the political leadership found it increasingly difficult to suppress dissenters and opposition to the regimes grew. It is not an exaggeration to say that the demise of communist Eastern Europe was due not just to political oppression but also to a sense of economic and social disparity. The average Eastern European wanted the right to cultural self-determination and economic prosperity, and this is what they saw in the West.

Nature of the Cold War

There are a number of views on the reasons for the Cold War, and its duration. These can be seen as a clash of ideologies between a communist USSR and the capitalist, democratic USA, or as a balance-of-power struggle between the world's two biggest countries. The superpowers formed alliances to try to improve their power vis-à-vis their opponent but often found the relations with their allies and client states very troublesome, often bringing them close to conflict with one another rather than stabilizing the situation. Diplomacy was rarely simply due to the number of allies—often these allies embroiled the superpowers in unwinnable wars such as Vietnam and Afghanistan.

Ideological differences

When examining the nature of the Cold War, two main schools of thought tend to emerge regarding the reasons for the conflict between the United States and the Soviet Union. On the one hand, there are those who believe very firmly that it was national self-interest that perpetuated the conflict until the collapse of the Soviet Union. The other group of scholars, sometimes referred to as ideologists, see the Cold War as the inevitable result of two inherently incompatible ideologies.

It can be argued that the USSR and the USA were truly in ideological opposition in terms of economic and political systems. At the base of this difference was the role that these governments felt that they played in the lives of their citizenry. The United States believed very firmly in the rights of the individual; this meant that individuals have the right to choose their government and that individuals should oversee the economic life of a country. In contrast, the Soviet Union believed that the individuals in its society were subordinate to the goals of the state. In order to benefit the most people possible, it was up to the state to determine the form of government and to govern the economic life of the country. On the one hand, then, there was democracy and capitalism; on the other, communism.

Marxism–Leninism openly advocates overthrowing capitalist regimes, thereby making the Soviet Union the aggressor in the Cold War. This argument was used repeatedly by the USA throughout the Cold War to explain its policy of containment and its intervention in a number of civil conflicts. On the other hand, capitalism is seen as inherently expansionist, as new markets need to be created. The Soviets exploited this aspect of Western society to show the USA in an aggressive light, with the government in the role of lackey to capitalists and members of the **bourgeoisie**.

The **bourgeoisie** were the upper middle class and those, according to Marx, who opposed the proletarians in achieving a classless society.

Returning to the idea of self-interest is equally important. That idea can be expressed in expansionist terms or defensive terms. For the former, one can point to the necessity of the USA to find more markets for its goods and how it thus sought to expand its influence far beyond its borders, and to the American concept of **Manifest Destiny**. For the latter, one can look again at historical Russian policies and see a desire for security as a reason for Soviet expansion, especially in Eastern Europe and central Asia. Also supporting self-interest was the desire of both superpowers to secure a foothold in the Middle East due to oil. This is further linked to military supremacy, as petroleum was increasingly necessary for an army to be effective. Even in the face of nuclear weapons, conventional armies were of paramount importance.

In the United States, both schools of thought can find their roots in George Kennan's Long Telegram. While Kennan ultimately came down on the side of the ideologists, he also felt that Soviet policies were driven by historic Russian aspirations and fears. When the end of the Cold War and the collapse of communism are viewed, the ideologists seem to prevail. According to them, the Soviet Union began its collapse when Gorbachev introduced reforms that deviated significantly from communist ideology. By allowing satellite states to pursue their own paths, the USSR also found itself opening up through policies of perestroika, glasnost and democracy. However, those who support self-interest can also argue that communism no longer served Russian self-interest.

Superpowers and spheres of influence

As the superpowers divided it up, the world's power structure was largely bipolar: communism vs the West. In the early stages of the Cold War, it seemed necessary for countries to be under the protection of one of the two superpowers. By the end of the 1950s, this was not necessarily the prevailing belief; decolonization had made newly emerging nations suspect the USA and its allies of trying to dominate them, and the communist model was not necessarily any better. After Yugoslavia's expulsion from the communist camp in 1948, the Czechoslovak coup and the crushing of the Hungarian Uprising, the Soviets were viewed just as warily. Thus, the Non-Aligned Movement arose in response. Nonetheless, the dominant political and military paradigm was between the two superpowers.

Comecon

Soviet actions, particularly in Europe, can be seen as reactions to US policies there. In 1949, the Soviets formed the Comecon or Council for Mutual Economic Assistance, arguably in response to the ERP (see page 455). Having refused to allow its satellites to participate in the Marshall Plan, the USSR instead offered this programme of trade to its allies. It was eventually extended beyond the borders of Europe and included Mongolia, Vietnam and Cuba as full members. There were also countries that were considered to be co-operating non-communist countries, such as Finland, and observers from communist countries as varied as China, Ethiopia and Afghanistan. Rather than dictating policies, the idea behind the Comecon was to co-ordinate economic development to benefit all member states. Prices were kept relatively stable as communist countries were not subject to currency fluctuations in the same way that market

Manifest Destiny An idea developed in the 19th century which stated that it was the fate of the USA to expand from the Atlantic to the Pacific oceans. Attached to the idea is the notion that the USA has a moral obligation to incorporate other peoples into its institutions and government because they are the most desirable. In the 19th century there was a missionary quality to the idea; that God determined that it was the US destiny to spread.

economies were, and this allowed for longer-term central planning. Since the state held the monopoly on foreign trade, it quickly became an instrument of political policy. For example, as oil and natural gas became increasingly scarce, the Soviet Union would provide these resources to other Comecon countries at below-market prices. Additionally, to bolster the Cuban economy after the 1959 revolution, other Comecon countries purchased sugar at above-market prices.

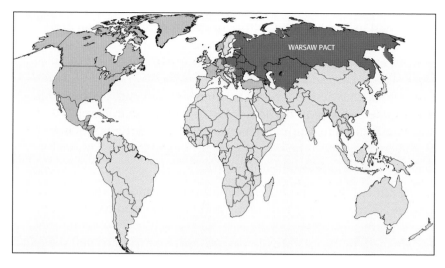

The Cold War alliances: NATO and the Warsaw Pact.

NATO and the Warsaw Pact

In 1955, West Germany joined NATO, furthering Soviet fears of US dominance of the European continent. In response, the USSR complained that allowing West Germany to enter NATO would lead to German rearmament, and that this would make reunification impossible. But more decisively and significantly, it led to formation of the Warsaw Pact. The signatories to the Warsaw treaty agreed to assist any co-signatory that was the victim of aggression. Although not specifically stated as such, it was clearly an anti-NATO pact, just as NATO had been an anti-Soviet agreement.

Both countries also sought to expand their spheres of influence outside of Europe. The USA had a historic relationship of dominance in the Western hemisphere that it sought to preserve. Dating back to the 1820s and the **Monroe Doctrine**, the USA had stated that it would protect nascent independent states from European domination by supporting their governments. By the onset of the Cold War, US predominance was clearly established but their benevolence was questionable at best. Not surprisingly, political leaders in Latin America and the Caribbean were emerging who desired the removal of US interests in their countries, which often predisposed them to socialist or communist ideologies.

In Asia, the victory of the Chinese Communists against the Nationalists bolstered socialists in the region, as did Soviet support in installing Kim Il-sung in North Korea. In Vietnam, the Communist Ho Chi Minh had won considerable support for forming the backbone of the resistance movement against the Japanese, and the French were incapable of ousting him. This made the USA determined to keep in place regimes that strayed far from the democratic ideals it espoused: South Korea, the Republic of China (Taiwan) and South Vietnam were all led by authoritarian rulers who could be as brutal as their communist counterparts, yet the USA supported them and kept them in its sphere.

 What does the map reveal about Cold War alliances? If countries are not shaded, does that mean they are neutral or non-aligned? Explain.

Monroe Doctrine (1823) A statement issued by US president Monroe after most of South America declared itself independent from Spain and Portugal, to the effect that European powers could no longer intervene in affairs in the Western hemisphere (Americas). If any European country tried to intervene, the USA would see it as an act of aggression and take military action to defend the hemisphere. In 1904 it was expanded through the Roosevelt Corollary, which stated that the USA had the right to intervene in the economic affairs of smaller powers in the Americas if they could not repay their debts. President Theodore Roosevelt said that this was to bring stability and peace to the region.

But perhaps the most important area where both struggled to establish themselves was in the Middle East. The USA had oil interests in the region, but also had been instrumental in the establishment of the state of Israel and felt it was their duty to help preserve this state that had been created under the aegis of the UN and in response to the Holocaust. At the same time, the Soviets were seeking to expand their influence in the region, notably in Iran and Afghanistan, where they had historic ties, and in Egypt, where they were hoping to exploit anti-imperialist fervor among the elite. This competition for influence in the region was perhaps the most dangerous, and had the least to do with ideology.

Alliances and diplomacy

The idea that Cold War allies and subordinates were completely dominated by their superpower counterparts is simplistic and ignores how smaller states used the Cold War to preserve their own regimes. This could be seen very clearly on the Korean peninsula, where the Americans uncomfortably supported an increasingly authoritarian South Korean president Syngman Rhee while the Soviets fostered a similar relationship with Kim Il-sung. Just as Khrushchev was denouncing Stalin's cult of personality, Kim was consolidating his own, and isolating his people as much as possible from both the capitalist and the communist world. Khrushchev proposed reforms for North Korea, which Kim rejected, arguing that any deviation from the Stalinist form of government that he pursued would destabilize his regime and give a Cold War victory to the Americans.

Rhee made similar threats to the Americans. Any suggestion of the USA that encouraged Rhee to make further inroads towards democracy was thwarted by Rhee, who argued that authoritarianism was necessary to stem the flow of communism from the north to the south. Thus, the USA signed a bilateral treaty with South Korea and American troops remained in Korea, protecting it from the north.

The USA and the USSR alike had problems with their respective Chinese allies too. After fleeing the mainland to Taiwan, the Nationalists managed to retain several islands including Quemoy and Matsu. When Mao began to shell the islands in 1954, Chiang Kai-shek (Jiang Jieshi) appealed to the USA, arguing that the loss of these islands could lead to political destabilization in Taiwan and perhaps its collapse. To support Chiang (Jiang), the United States negotiated a mutual defence treaty with Taiwan in the hopes of deterring the Chinese Communists from further action. When Mao ignored this and continued to assault the islands, even occupying one, the USA responded that, if necessary, it would resort to using nuclear weapons to prevent Communist occupation of Quemoy or Matsu. Although Mao backed down at this point, he learnt a lesson about manipulation of the superpowers similar to that of Kim and his rival.

Several years later, the situation resumed. In 1958, Mao once again began shelling the islands and the United States threatened nuclear force against Communist action. The Soviets were alarmed by this development, especially as Mao had not consulted them. However, Khrushchev felt compelled to react in kind, threatening the use of nuclear weapons if any action were taken against the Chinese Communists. The situation was defused but it showed that the superpowers weren't always the driving factor in alliances.

One last example of this can be seen with France. France had been a member of NATO, had benefited from ERP and was an initial signatory to the Treaty of Rome. It also felt its loss of Great Power status even more than the UK, particularly due to its struggles in Indochina and Algeria. Thus, under the leadership of Charles de Gaulle, the French began to develop their own independent military defense plan. By 1959 France had withdrawn its navy from NATO's Mediterranean fleet and forbidden nuclear weapons on French soil and by 1966 was outside of NATO, opting to collaborate with NATO operations at times (such as the Cuban Missile Crisis) or not. Once France became a nuclear power in 1960, the USA had very little recourse against the country and attempted collaboration without formal alliance.

On the other hand, some countries were seen as too important to US and Soviet policies, and thus the superpowers took aggressive actions to keep them in their spheres of influence. In the 1970s, the United States took numerous actions in Latin America to preserve its hegemony there, most notably in Chile and Nicaragua. In 1973, the CIA assisted the Chilean military in enacting a coup d'état that overthrew Salvador Allende's government—a democratically elected socialist government that tried to redistribute wealth and remove the dominance of foreign interests in the Chilean economy. In Nicaragua in the 1980s, the USA supported a conservative group called the Contras in their attempts to overthrow the revolutionary Sandinistas that had seized power in 1979. Although the 1984 elections were determined to be free and fair by the UN, and the rule of the Sandinistas was confirmed, the USA challenged their right to rule Nicaragua and even tried to use covert means to oust them but ultimately had to accept their rule as legitimate.

In a similar manner, the Brezhnev Doctrine (see page 183) articulated the Soviet determination to keep certain countries within their sphere of influence—especially those in Eastern Europe. Although it predated this doctrine, the crushing of the Hungarian revolution in 1956 was an example of this, as was the dispatch of Warsaw Pact tanks to Czechoslovakia in 1968 and the intervention in Afghanistan that began in 1979. Countries were given a certain latitude to act but only insofar as they did not threaten Soviet security interests.

Ultimately, the Soviet Union found it too costly to uphold the Brezhnev Doctrine and support its allies. The crumbling economy in the USSR was responsible for the shift in attitudes towards its satellite states and allies. However, US policies still provide support for loyal allies—to this day Egypt and Israel are among the largest recipients of foreign aid from the USA.

Discussion point:

Is ideology important to history?

Discuss the role of ideology in 20th-century conflicts.

Activity:

Comparing and contrasting

The constitutions of the USA and the USSR

In groups of four to six, examine the US and Soviet constitutions. Outline the main points, paying attention to their similarities and differences.

Then discuss how consistent their Cold War policies were with their constitutions.

Exam questions

1 How important was mutual suspicion and fear in the origin of the Cold War?

2 "Ideology played a small part in the origin of the Cold War." To what extent do you agree with this assertion?

3 Assess the importance of **two** of the following Soviet policies in the origin and development of the Cold War: Sovietization of Eastern and Central Europe; Comecon; Warsaw Pact.

4 Compare and contrast the parts played by Korea and Vietnam in the Cold War.

5 In what ways and to what extent did containment affect the development of the Cold War up to 1970?

6 Analyse the part played by **either** Kennedy **or** Reagan in the Cold War.

7 "The non-aligned movement had little impact on Cold War policies and development." To what extent do you agree with this assertion?

8 Discuss the impact of the United Nations on the Cold War.

9 Evaluate the impact of the arms race on East–West relations.

10 Explain the role and importance of
   a internal problems, and
   b external pressures,
   in causing the break-up of the Soviet Union.

Further reading and resources

Billington, James H, Director, The Soviet Archives Exhibit, Library of Congress. http://www.ibiblio.org/expo/soviet.exhibit/repress.html.

A virtual exhibit that was created by the US Library of Congress and is divided into two "floors" or divisions. The first floor is specific to the internal workings of the USSR and the second floor relates directly to Soviet–US relations. As the website states, it "shows how Soviet–American relations were conducted between governments, between the publics of the two countries, and between the Communist parties of the USSR and the USA." In particular, it provides primary Soviet sources regarding the course of the Cold War.

Wilson Center. Cold War International History Project. http://wilsoncenter.org.

Provides a variety of primary sources that give differing historical viewpoints and sources on a number of Cold War topics, including the Korean War, the crisis in Poland (1981), Soviet intervention in Afghanistan and the end of the Cold War.

Dobbs, Michael. 2008. *One Minute to Midnight: Kennedy, Khrushchev and Castro on the Brink of Nuclear War*. New York, USA. Knopf.

Published in 2008, in English, this text on the Cuban Missile Crisis focuses on the military conduct and actions of the USA, the USSR and Cuba, providing a new view on the conflict.

Gaddis, John Lewis. 2005. *The Cold War: A New History*. New York, USA. Penguin Books.

An analysis of the Cold War that follows a very conservative perspective but provides different examples that highlight the relations between countries in both blocs. Rather than focusing on the omnipotence of the USA and the USSR, Gaddis looks at their weaknesses and insecurities.

Chen Jian. 2000. *Mao's China and the Cold War*. Carolina, USA. University of North Carolina Press.

An insight into the Chinese attitudes and policies regarding the Cold War.

Judt, Tony. 2005. *Post War: A History of Europe since 1945*. New York, USA. Penguin Books.

A comprehensive text that covers all aspects of European politics and society from 1945 to the present. The sections on the collapse of communism in Eastern Europe are particularly enlightening.

Kissinger, Henry. 1995. *Diplomacy*. New York, USA. Anchor Books.

Covers the subject of diplomacy from Cardinal Richelieu through to Gorbachev and George W Bush. Although Kissinger was active in American foreign policy from the 1950s, the book provides a balanced view and well-researched evidence on the course of the Cold War.

Westad, Odd Arne (ed.). 2000. *Reviewing the Cold War: Approaches, Interpretations, Theory*. London, UK. Frank Cass Publishing.

A collection of texts showing how the release of new information from the Soviet and Eastern European archives after the collapse of communism have affected interpretations of the course and end of the Cold War. The contributors seek to show the limitations of prior knowledge and the importance of the more recently released information.

Zubok, Vladislav and Pleshakov, Constantine. 1996. *Inside the Kremlin's Cold War: From Stalin to Khrushchev*. Cambridge, MA, USA. Harvard University Press.

One of the first texts published by Russians using previously unreleased information from the Soviet archives, this provided a new interpretation on Soviet motivations and actions during the Cold War. In particular, it shows Soviet involvement—or lack thereof—in conflicts in Korea and Cuba.

10 Index